# Old Southern Apples

# Old Southern Apples

*A Comprehensive History and Description of Varieties for Collectors, Growers, and Fruit Enthusiasts*

CREIGHTON LEE CALHOUN, JR.

REVISED AND EXPANDED EDITION

Chelsea Green Publishing
White River Junction, Vermont

The first edition was published and copyrighted in 1995
by The McDonald & Woodward Publishing Company, Blacksburg, Virginia.

Color illustrations used courtesy of US Department of Agriculture Pomological Watercolor Collection. Special Collections, National Agricultural Library, Beltsville, MD 20705

Use of the images in the US Department of Agriculture Pomological Watercolor Collection is not restricted, but a statement of attribution is required. Please use the following attribution statement: "US Department of Agriculture Pomological Watercolor Collection. Special Collections, National Agricultural Library, Beltsville, MD 20705."

Project Manager: Patricia Stone
Developmental Editor: Benjamin Watson
Copy Editor: Cannon Labrie
Proofreader: Helen Walden
Indexer: Lee Lawton
Designer: Peter Holm, Sterling Hill Productions

Printed in the United States of America
First printing, December, 2010
10 9 8 7 6 5 4 3 2 15 16 17 18 19

**Our Commitment to Green Publishing**
Chelsea Green sees publishing as a tool for cultural change and ecological stewardship. We strive to align our book manufacturing practices with our editorial mission and to reduce the impact of our business enterprise in the environment. We print our books and catalogs on chlorine-free recycled paper, using vegetable-based inks whenever possible. This book may cost slightly more because we use recycled paper, and we hope you'll agree that it's worth it. Chelsea Green is a member of the Green Press Initiative (www.greenpressinitiative.org), a nonprofit coalition of publishers, manufacturers, and authors working to protect the world's endangered forests and conserve natural resources. *Old Southern Apples* was printed on Rolland Opaque Natural, a 30-percent postconsumer recycled paper supplied by RR Donnelley.

**Library of Congress Cataloging-in-Publication Data**
Calhoun, Creighton Lee, 1934–
Old southern apples : a comprehensive history and description of varieties for collectors, growers, and fruit enthusiasts / Creighton Lee Calhoun, Jr. — 2nd ed.
p. cm.
Includes bibliographical references and index.
ISBN 978-1-60358-294-0
1. Apples—Southern States. 2. Apples—Varieties—Southern States. I. Title.

SB363.2.U6C35 2011
634'.110975—dc22

2010035485

Chelsea Green Publishing
85 North Main Street, Suite 120
White River Junction, VT 05001
(802) 295-6300
www.chelseagreen.com

FOR EDITH

*My wife, sweetheart, best friend, helpmate*

# CONTENTS

# Color Section Illustrations

*Note:* Variety name given first corresponds to illustration title in names in this book. Variety names in brackets indicate the spelling used in the color plates, if different.

# ACKNOWLEDGMENTS

Looking back, I am amazed at the work that has gone into this book: six years of research and two years of writing for the first edition; fifteen years of collecting additional information and a year of writing for this second edition. None of this was possible without the constant help and encouragement of my wife.

For the first edition, Edith worked with me to search the libraries of southern universities for apple information. She was beside me for the weeks we worked in the National Agricultural Library in Beltsville, Maryland. There, grimy from searching dusty boxes holding a hundred thousand old nursery and seed catalogs, Edith trudged up and down stairs to reproduce each valued southern nursery catalog.

I wrote in longhand for two years on the first edition, and Edith typed all my words into her computer. Together we went through six revisions. More recently I worked a year rewriting *Old Southern Apples,* and Edith again typed my writing into her computer and helped with revisions. I trust it is obvious that this book would never have seen the light of day without my wife.

Publication of the first edition of *Old Southern Apples* had one unforeseen consequence: it assembled a cadre of men and women to join me in the hunt for missing old southern apple varieties. Never more than a dozen people, and now fewer as death thins our ranks, these dedicated apple hunters searched for old trees, questioned elderly people, and followed every lead. I have tried in this second edition to credit these apple hunters by name, all of whom I consider my friends. I value each one, but I give special credit and thanks to Tom Brown, who has been totally dedicated to the hunt for over ten years and whose apple adventures and discoveries deserve and would fill another book.

Every rediscovered old apple needs to be "vetted" to prove it is what it is supposed to be. This is a painstaking task of document research and field observation, taking up to ten years for some varieties. Dave Masters of South Carolina is doing this arduous task, growing close to a thousand new and old apple varieties in his orchard, and comparing flowers, fruit, and disease susceptibilities to confirm identity. Working carefully, he has resolved much of two centuries of confusion.

John Frederick of Columbus, Ohio, has researched the early nurseries of Ohio for many years. When he uncovers facts about old southern apples, he shares them with me. I thank him for his generosity and have used his information throughout this second edition.

Joni Praded, Editorial Director, Patricia Stone, Project Manager, and the staff of Chelsea Green Publishing have been understanding and helpful. I especially thank Ben Watson of Chelsea Green for jump-starting this edition and guiding it along the path to publication.

LEE CALHOUN
1 August 2010

# INTRODUCTION

The modern, fast-paced, urbanized South has moved so far from its agrarian past that large parts of its heritage have been virtually forgotten. Southerners delight in restoring old houses and urban neighborhoods, and many city dwellers buy old farms and restore the buildings for a weekend retreat. But our unique southern heritage is more than Victorian houses and heart-pine floors, mahogany furniture and Coin silver; it is also Bloody Butcher corn, Red Ripper peas, Ledmon watermelons, Greensboro peaches, upland cotton, Gold Dollar tobacco, and James grapes. These are living threads that lead directly back to three hundred years of the southern agrarian past.

This book is about apples—southern apples—a fruit cherished below the Mason-Dixon Line since soon after Jamestown was settled in 1607. The importance of apples in the South surprises many people—and why not? In the supermarkets are apples from Washington, Michigan, New York, New Zealand, and Chile, but almost never any southern-grown apples. We have forgotten that apples were grown on farms in every part of the South for centuries and that the South developed hundreds of unique apple varieties.

To reclaim some knowledge about southern apples, you need only to talk to elderly southerners who grew up on a farm. Their eyes light up as they speak of almost-forgotten apples: Red June, Buckingham, Yates, Nickajack, Fallawater, Magnum Bonum, Blacktwig, Horse Apple, Hunge, Smith's Seedling, Sally Gray, Summer Orange, Edwards' Winter, and on and on. They will tell you of apples fried for breakfast in the drippings from sausage or side meat. They remember storing boxes of apples through the winter in unheated rooms of the farmhouse and how those apples perfumed the whole house. They recall drying apple slices on a tin roof, and they can tell you how to make cider and vinegar. But most of all they remember the incomparable taste of a freshly picked southern apple, dense and high in soluble solids, baked right on the tree by those long, hot southern summers.

A letter to me from a man in Arkansas clearly illustrates the many uses of apples in days gone by:

> I can recall my grandmother telling me often, when I was a child, about the part apples played on her family's small Arkansas farm in the late 1800s. She spoke of a room off their kitchen that had shelves on which they stored apples for the winter. On winter evenings, she said, the family would sit around the fireplace cracking nuts and eating apples, sometimes with popcorn popped in the fireplace. My grandmother used to lament the narrowing of varieties of apples available in stores as she aged, and would tell me the names of the many varieties available when she was a child, and how each apple was grown for a different reason.
>
> Apples continued to be a large part of her family's life into the twentieth century. My great-uncle made cider and cider vinegar, and my mother and her sisters tell me that their mother would slice them and dry them under cheesecloth on the hot roof in the summer. Dried apples would be stored in cloth bags until used for fried pies (called "tarts" in this area of the state). Apples were also fried for breakfast and were made into pies all year round. My mother's first cousin, who lived near the old homeplace in Grant County, was renowned for a green apple pie she made each June for the family homecoming.

We are living in the last days of the southern apple. When these elderly southerners are gone, so will be the lore of southern apples. Indeed, most of the unique southern apple varieties have already passed over into history; perhaps 80 percent of them are extinct.

Thirty years ago, not long after I retired from the

Army, an elderly friend challenged me to find the Magnum Bonum apple, a cherished memory from his youth. My two-year search for that apple was an education. I found that rural southerners remembered the old apples, but no one grew them anymore. Finally I found a few old Magnum Bonum trees in Virginia. Shortly thereafter I discovered a tree of the Summer Orange apple here in my own county and then an old tree of Bevan's Favorite in a neighboring county. These discoveries were proof enough that at least a few of the old southern apples were still out there, surviving as gnarled old snags in remote places. The search goes on, and I am no longer alone in the quest to save old southern apple varieties. Friends have been recruited to expand the search net, and we have joined with others who also have long sought old southern apples.

My hunt for old apple varieties led to a concurrent search for historical information about these apples. Libraries and used bookstores yielded a number of nineteenth-century books describing American fruit, but, with one minor exception, these books were written by northerners who gave short shrift to southern apples. Nowhere in the old pomological texts was there a good compilation of information about southern apples. The South had its great pomologists in the 1800s, but none of them ever wrote a definitive text. Bits and pieces of information were scattered everywhere: in old books and horticultural magazines, in old nursery catalogs, agricultural bulletins, and newspapers, in the minutes of state horticultural societies, in letters buried in almost forgotten USDA files, and in the memories of elderly southerners still alive.

About 1988 I became determined to fill this void by writing the history and description of every old southern apple. My initial estimate was that perhaps 300 or 400 different apples had been grown in the South, but research has proved this estimate to be absurdly low—over 1,800 apple varieties are described in this book.

Let us consider for a moment just how and why so many different apple varieties arose in the South. To start at the beginning, there must be a little understanding of apple biology. In the South apple trees bloom in April each year. Flowers on apple trees contain both male and female sex parts, the male part being the stamen with its pollen (the male sex cell) and the female part being the pistil with ovules (the female sex cell) in a swelling at the base of the flower. Most apple varieties are not receptive to their own pollen (or pollen from other trees of the same variety) but must be "cross-pollinated" with pollen from a different apple variety. Apple pollen is too heavy to be carried by wind, so cross-pollination is performed by bees and other small flying insects, which carry pollen grains on their bodies from tree to tree, depositing the pollen on the pistils as they crawl over the flower.

When a pollen grain is deposited on a pistil, the male chromosomes in the pollen grain unite with the female chromosomes in an ovule at the base of the pistil to form a fertilized egg with its full complement of chromosomes. This fertilized egg develops into an apple seed. (Each of the several seeds inside an apple is pollinated separately, and each may, in fact, receive pollen from different apple varieties.) The fleshy swelling at the base of the flower that surrounds the ovules develops into the flesh of the apple. This fleshy swelling is tissue from the mother tree and is not involved in the fertilization of the ovules inside. Thus, a Red June apple tree will always bear Red June apples because the skin and flesh of the apples come entirely from the mother tree. Only the seeds inside the apple have been cross-pollinated.

Apple seeds contain genetic material from both the mother tree that carries the apple and the father tree from which the pollen originated. This fact, plus the random sorting of genetic material in the formation of pollen and ovules, means that each apple seed is genetically different from all other apple seeds and will, if planted, produce a tree and fruit different from all other apple trees and fruit. In this respect apples resemble humans because every human is genetically unique and different from all others.

To follow this analogy further, consider the human population as a whole. Most of us are born, live, and die as ordinary people, with little to distinguish us from the millions around us. Only very occasionally does a human rise above the crowd by mental genius or exceptional ability. No one can predict when a random sorting of genetic material will produce an Einstein, a Leonardo da Vinci, or an Alexander the Great. This analogy holds true for apples; every apple

## The Southern Heritage Apple Orchard at Horne Creek Farm

The sudden death of Henry Morton in Gatlinburg, Tennessee, in the 1990s was a double tragedy. His family and friends suffered a loss, and those of us who search for old apple varieties lost much of his unique collection of Appalachian mountain apples, which Henry had found over many years of searching mountain coves and hollows. This loss made obvious the temporary nature of the several private collections of antique southern apple varieties. What was needed was a permanent site for southern apples.

The state of North Carolina owns and operates twenty-seven historic sites including Horne Creek Living Historical Farm twenty miles north of Winston-Salem. The state purchased the old Hauser farm and restored it to demonstrate farm life in piedmont North Carolina around 1900. The centerpiece of Horne Creek Farm is the modest 1875 farmhouse that Thomas and Charlotte Hauser built and where they raised their twelve children. Over 35,000 people visit Horne Creek Farm each year to walk through the house, gardens, and outbuildings of the farm and to see the farm animals.

In 1997 the site manager of Horne Creek Farm agreed to make available a seven-acre parcel for an orchard to preserve antique southern apple varieties. With a $50,000 grant from the state, the Southern Heritage Apple Orchard was born.

The Heritage Orchard is fronted on the north side by a paved road. The site is a long ridgeline sloping from north to south with excellent air drainage. The soil is fertile clay loam.

The orchard site has been enclosed in an eight-foot-high, all-steel anti-deer fence and laid out to contain four hundred antique southern apple varieties, two trees of each. One tree of each variety is freestanding on semidwarf rootstock. These trees are spaced twelve feet apart in rows eighteen feet apart. The second tree is on dwarf rootstock, espaliered on wires, and spaced two to eight feet apart in rows twelve feet apart. Having two trees of each variety gives a source of scions for grafting a replacement for a dead tree. Most of the trees are bearing fruit now.

The four hundred small trees are espaliered on wires using five classic espalier shapes. Three hundred small trees are in the oblique cordon shape. The remaining hundred dwarf trees are espaliered in the Belgian Fence, vertical cordon, horizontal cordon, or double-U palmate shapes to demonstrate the beautiful possibilities of espalier and its suitability for urban lots.

The Heritage Orchard is visitor-friendly and open to the public (closed Sundays and Mondays). It is kept mowed, and a gravel road bisects the orchard to a gravel parking lot. Shade trees have been planted and, when they are larger, picnic tables will be placed under them. A full-time, state-employed horticulturist takes care of the orchard. If you plan to visit the Heritage Orchard, call ahead, (336) 325-2298.

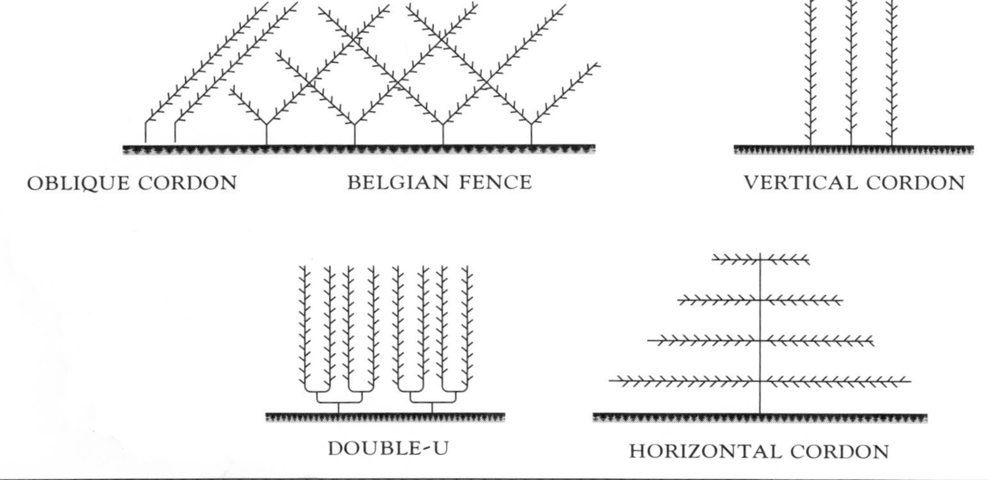

seed will grow into a unique tree, but almost always this new tree and its fruit will be quite ordinary. Only once in a long while, and unpredictably, will a seedling apple tree rise above the rest, distinguished by the health and vigor of the tree or the outstanding quality of the fruit. It has been estimated that modern plant breeders get only one in ten thousand apple seeds to grow into a tree with fruit worthy of further consideration.

When a seedling tree bearing good apples is discovered, it cannot be reproduced by the seeds of its apples that, of course, have been cross-pollinated. In the old days good seedling trees could be duplicated by digging up root sprouts that sometimes grow up around apple trees, a very slow method of propagation. A faster way of duplicating trees is by grafting, a process whereby a twig is cut from a good apple tree and inserted into the pencil-diameter, severed trunk of a young apple tree. The twig and trunk fuse together and grow into a tree identical to the tree from which the twig was taken. By grafting, hundreds of apple trees can be propagated each year by cutting twigs from a single tree, and each new tree will bear fruit identical to the original tree.

Every one of the 1,800 apple varieties described in this book originated when an apple seed grew into a tree bearing exceptional fruit. Some of these seedling trees were "chance seedlings." Fallen apples might roll downhill or be carried away by heavy rains, and perhaps a seed would grow into a seedling tree in a fencerow or ditch. Seeds of apples squeezed for cider were discarded in fields and along woodlines, and some of the seeds would take root. Apples were fed to hogs and other farm animals, and chance seedlings grew in the corners of feedlots and pastures.

Although chance seedlings were the original source of many unique southern apples, most old apple varieties originated when rural southerners deliberately planted apple seeds in order to have an orchard. Seedling orchards were common in the South from the early 1600s until the mid-1800s. This was a time of great movement of people and the opening of enormous new lands. Apple seeds were durable and portable, and they cost nothing in a time when money was scarce and grafting was a rare skill. The men and women who planted apple seeds had no illusions about what they would get from seedling trees. They knew some trees would bear poor fruit that could be fed to the hogs, and other trees would have apples best used for cider and vinegar. But these rural southerners expected a number of their seedling trees would bear apples good enough for cooking and fresh eating and for keeping through the winter.

Millions of apple seeds were planted in the South between the early 1600s and the mid-1800s to grow seedling orchards. Out of this great number of seedling trees, some were found to be exceptional. It was these exceptional apple varieties that southerners cherished, shared root sprouts with neighbors, and which were eventually grafted and sold by southern nurseries.

The yardstick that past generations of rural southerners used to measure the quality of apples is different from ours today. Certainly over 80 percent of apples sold in today's supermarkets and farmers' markets are eaten fresh. Just the reverse was true on southern farms for hundreds of years; most apples were used for cooking, drying, cider and vinegar, and only a small percentage was eaten fresh. After all, even large rural families could hardly snack their way through all the apples from a farm orchard that might have forty large trees. Apples good for cooking or drying or cider have different qualities from those used for fresh eating. It is a waste of time to bite into an old apple variety and then disparage its taste or texture. Likely this particular apple was prized in bygone days because it quickly cooked to pieces when stewed or because it stayed white when dried or perhaps it would keep through the winter without refrigeration.

For sixteen years my wife and I sold trees of old southern apples through our small nursery, mostly to rural southerners who wanted the kinds of apples that their parents or grandparents once grew on the farm. We also sold to an increasing number of people who wanted to grow some of their food and who were willing to make the effort to have a garden and small orchard. We always urged purchasers to extend the use of apples beyond fresh eating. It is somehow satisfying to stew apples for supper and fry them for breakfast, to make a batch of applesauce or apple butter, and to store some apples in plastic bags in the bottom of the refrigerator for winter eating. The only way to appreciate the full palate of old apples is to make the effort to use them in the varied ways they were intended originally.

Growing old southern apples is not just an exercise in nostalgia; a look at the latest USDA Plant Hardiness Zone Map shows why this is true. Virtually all of the great commercial apple-growing regions in the United States are in zones 5 and 6, with average minimum winter temperatures of 0°F to minus 20°F. (Roughly, zones 5 and 6 fall north of a line stretching from northern Virginia westward through Kentucky and on through northern Arkansas, plus a long finger running down the spine of the Appalachian Mountains.) Most of the apple-breeding work being done in the United States today is to develop apples for commercial production in zones 5 and 6. But the great majority of southerners live in warmer areas, zones 7, 8, and 9, and no one in the United States—not agricultural colleges, agricultural experiment stations, or the USDA—is targeting apple-breeding work for these zones. Rarely do new apple varieties bred for cooler regions do well in zones 7, 8, and 9; usually they do not and exhibit heat intolerance by the fruit dropping before ripening, rotting on the tree, or developing a soft texture. Southerners can look to the old southern apples and find many that were originally selected because the trees grew well and produced good apples in warmer areas. In the old varieties, too, will be found apples especially suitable for cider, drying, cooking, and winter storage for those southerners who wish to expand their apple horizons.

## You Are Enlisted in the Search

Of the roughly 1,800 apple varieties that were once grown in the South, some 500 are known to still exist. There are others out there, undiscovered, and you are asked to help in locating them. Ask your elderly neighbors or grandparents if they know of any old apple trees that can still be identified with a name. If you find anything even remotely resembling in name or synonym an apple listed in this book as extinct, please write or telephone us giving as much information as possible. By doing so, you may be instrumental in saving a small part of the southern heritage. We are: Lee and Edith Calhoun, 295 Blacktwig Road, Pittsboro, North Carolina 27312; (919) 542-4480.

# PART ONE

# Background

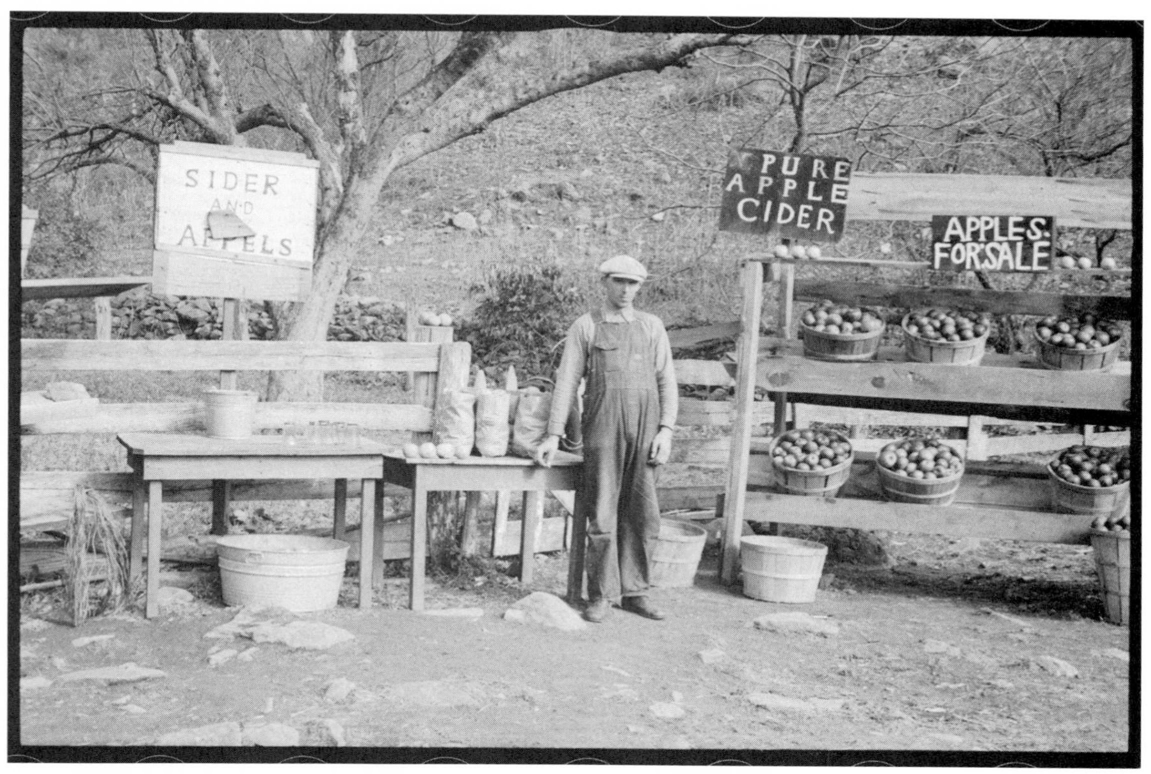

# "The Planting of the Apple-Tree"

*William Cullen Bryant*

What plant we in this apple-tree?
Buds, which the breath of summer days
Shall lengthen into leafy sprays;
Boughs, where the thrush, with crimson breast
Shall haunt, and sing, and hide her nest.
We plant upon the sunny lea,
A shadow for the noontide hour,
A shelter from the summer shower,
When we plant the apple-tree.

What plant we in this apple-tree?
Fruits that shall swell in sunny June,
And redden in the August noon,
And drop when gentle airs come by,
That fan the blue September sky;
While children wild with noisy glee,
Shall scent their fragrance as they pass,
And search for them the tufted grass
At the foot of the apple-tree.

The children of some distant day,
Thus to some aged man shall say,
"Who planted this old apple-tree?"

ONE

# History of Apples in the South

When the first English settlers in the South explored their surroundings, they found a profusion of wild fruits—grapes, persimmons, plums, berries of all sorts—but no apples. Except for several kinds of insignificant crabapples, there were no native apples in the South, or anywhere else in the New World.

In England apples were grown everywhere and had been there so long that Englishmen considered them as native to their island. We now know that the apple originated in central Asia, in what is now Kazakhstan, and that apple seeds made their way to Europe perhaps as early as 1000 B.C. The Greeks grew apples, as did the Etruscans, and the Roman writer Pliny the Elder described twenty-nine apple varieties in the first century A.D. Romans carried their superior apple varieties to northern Europe, including Britain, and the apple thrived there.

Finding no apples in America, early settlers quickly remedied the situation by planting apple seeds brought from England. In 1634 Lord Baltimore instructed the first settlers in Maryland to carry "kernalls [seeds] of pears and apples, especially of Pipins, Pearmains, and Deesons, for making thereafter of Cider and Perry." A 1666 English settlement on North Carolina's Cape Fear River was described as growing "apples, pears and other English fruits . . . out of planted kernals." Growing in virgin soils and leaving behind many disease and insect pests, it is hardly surprising that apples flourished in these first orchards. Visitors to the South in the mid-1600s remarked on the many fruit orchards, which far exceeded in yield and quality those in England. Given the suitability of the apple for subsistence farming and the English taste for cider, most southern farms of the colonial period had extensive orchards. A recent survey of old records concerning farms sold in Maryland in 1728 and 1744 shows that over 90 percent had orchards.

From the earliest days there was a class system in southern agriculture. At the top were large landowners, often owning thousands or tens of thousands of acres. These families, well-to-do or even rich by standards of the day, were educated, well-traveled, and had considerable leisure time. Virtually all were slave owners.

A much larger class, small farmers, spent their lives clearing land and tilling the soil, living in cabins and depending on their own gardens, fields, and orchards for food. Until the Revolutionary War, many small farmers did not actually own the land they cleared and planted; they leased it from one of the great landowners. It was common for the terms of the lease to require the farmer to plant an orchard and fence it in, thus increasing the value of the land for the landowner. When George Washington leased out some land in Berkley County, Virginia, in 1774, he required the tenant to plant two hundred apple and peach trees forty feet apart, fence the orchard to protect the trees from cattle, and keep the orchard well pruned.

The great landowners had extensive orchards of hundreds or thousands of fruit trees. For example, Colonel William Fitzhugh of Westmoreland County, Virginia, had twenty-five hundred apple trees on his estate in 1686, "mostly grafted and well-fenced in a locust fence." Even ordinary farmers usually had apple orchards of fifty to two hundred trees, using most of the apples for cider. A rough rule of thumb for southern farm families was six apple trees per person. This made for large orchards as rural families often had several generations living together.

The question must be asked: What kinds of apples did colonial southerners grow? We know that both grafted and seedling apple trees were grown during this period. People with money could buy grafted apple trees brought from England. An Irish physician named John Brickell described a number of European apple varieties he observed growing in eastern North Carolina in 1731. These included the (English) Golden Russet, "Red-strak'd" (Redstreak), Summer and Winter

## Evolution and Migration of the Edible Apple

Wild crabapples occur from Siberia to Europe to North America, but these crabapples are not ancestors of the modern apple. Recent DNA analysis and gene sequencing have shown conclusively that the modern apple originated in central Asia, largely on the north slopes of the Tien Shan mountains, which form the border between China and Kazakhstan.

In these mountains, slowly, over millions of years, apples evolved, starting with an ancient fruit smaller than a cherry. The Asian brown bear would eat these apple ancestors, but preferred the occasional tree bearing slightly larger, sweeter fruits. By eating more of these tastier fruits and spreading more of their seeds, brown bears ever so slowly nudged wild apples toward becoming larger and sweeter.

Wild apples still grow in Kazakhstan in the remnant forests there. Some of these wild apples are as large and as edible as apples grown in the United States today.

The edible apple remained in central Asia until wild horses were first tamed there about five thousand years ago. Horses also eat apples and can travel long distances in a single day. Westward migration by successive waves of mounted Asian nomads moved the apple toward Europe by small steps over several thousand years, through what is now southern Russia, Armenia, and Turkey. It is likely the edible apple reached Europe about three thousand years ago.

Pearmains, Winter Queen, Harvey-apple, Coddling, Jenneting, Long-stalk, and Lady-finger. A Maryland newspaper advertised apple trees imported from England in 1776, and English trees were still being imported into the South as late as 1793. Eventually it must have become obvious to everyone that most European apple varieties are poorly adapted to southern growing conditions, especially the blistering summer heat.

Whether European apple varieties thrived or not in the South was of little importance to the small farmer. He could not afford such luxuries, and, as the frontier moved inland, he was beyond reach of coastal towns where imported trees were available. The alternative was simple and cheap—plant apple seeds and take a chance with seedling apple trees. Many of the seedling trees would bear rather decent apples, but others would have nondescript fruit useful mainly for cider. Considering the popularity of cider in the colonial South, the gamble was worthwhile. Seedling trees do have one very useful trait used by rural southerners continuously since early colonial times—any sprouts that grow up from the roots of these trees are true to the mother tree. This was a way for southerners to swap root sprouts from the best seedling trees and eventually acquire a good apple orchard. It also made it possible to dig up root sprouts from the best trees to accompany the family if it moved into new lands.

Instead of importing nursery stock from Europe or planting apple seeds, why didn't colonial southerners themselves just graft apple trees? After all, grafting is a sure and quick method of exactly replicating those apple trees bearing the best fruit. In looking for the answer to this question, it becomes obvious that grafting was a rare skill in the South before the mid-1700s. Although grafting is a relatively simple technique known since Roman times, there is little evidence that it was much used to propagate southern fruit trees in the colonial period. Writing a history of Virginia in 1705, Robert Beverley said he had never heard of anyone grafting fruit trees in Virginia before that date. Twenty years later a professor at William and Mary College in Virginia wrote "the Apple trees are raised from the seed . . . which kind of Kernal Fruit needs no grafting and is diversify'd into numerous Sorts. . . ."

Beginning about 1750 grafting became more widespread, perhaps because of more settled conditions in the South with some people able to afford grafted trees. A few commercial nurseries were operating in Virginia in the 1750s, such as the nursery operated by William Smith in Surry County, which listed twenty-two apple varieties in 1755. In 1771 another nursery in Surry County, Virginia, had "14,000 grafted fruit trees" for sale. An early and important nursery, owned by John Watson, opened in Charleston, South Carolina, about

## Piece-Root Versus Whole-Root Grafting

Nurserymen and their customers today are faced with a bewildering array of apple rootstocks, over seventy different kinds at last count. It is the rootstock that determines the ultimate size of the tree, and the great majority of today's rootstocks are dwarfing rootstocks, used to make apple trees that will be between six and eighteen feet tall at maturity. For example, an apple variety grafted on M7A rootstock will result in a mature tree about twelve feet tall, but grafting on MM111 rootstock will make a tree about eighteen feet tall. The reason for the many dwarfing rootstocks lies in the nature of modern commercial apple orchards, where many small trees (often over five hundred an acre) are grown close together. Small apple trees are easier to train, prune, spray, and pick. They begin bearing sooner than bigger trees, have higher yields per acre, and bear high-quality apples. The use of dwarf trees in commercial orchards is a rather recent development. Before World War II, orchards consisted of "standard" or full-size trees close to thirty feet tall. These trees were planted thirty or more feet apart and required ladders for pruning and picking. At thirty feet apart, only forty-eight trees can be planted per acre. Except for two dwarfing rootstocks developed in France in the seventeenth century and used mainly in formal gardens, all of the dwarfing rootstocks now available have been bred since 1920.

Until well into the twentieth century, southern nurseries sold nursery stock that would mature into "standard" or full-size apple trees, although the larger nurseries sold a few apple varieties on dwarfing French rootstocks. Rootstocks for "standard" trees were obtained by planting apple seeds, then cutting off and discarding the tops of the one- or two-year-old seedling trees and using the bottoms as rootstocks. (Modern dwarfing rootstocks are not grown from seed but are produced vegetatively by a procedure known as "stooling.") Seedling rootstocks make trees with mature heights varying from twenty feet to over thirty feet, depending on genetic variations in each rootstock and the vigor of the apple variety grafted on the rootstock. These full-size trees were preferred by rural southerners who had room for the big trees on their farms and liked their ruggedness and longevity.

The universal practice today is to utilize a single small apple tree for rootstock for each graft, making the graft on the rootstock trunk several inches above the highest root. This procedure is known as whole-root grafting. Before the twentieth century, however, both whole roots and pieces of roots were used for grafting. In piece-root grafting the apple rootstock was dug up and the larger roots were cut into three- or four-inch pieces (pencil-diameter roots of mature trees could also be dug up and cut into pieces). Grafts were then made on the upper end of each root piece, and the newly grafted tree was planted so that the graft union was several inches below soil level.

Between 1880 and 1910 a lively debate arose among nurserymen and orchardists as to which was the better grafting procedure—whole-root or piece-root. Both had their proponents. One man wrote in *The American Gardener* magazine in 1891: "Oh, the misery that a 1,000 whole-root grafted orchard gave me in comparison with the very same apple varieties which were piece-root grafted! The trees blew over, leaned, suckered at the collar, got sunburnt, out grew the stocks, got full of borers owing to their roughness near the ground and returned to me about one-fourth the value in fruit as the piece-root grafted trees did, planted the following year."

The great American pomologist, L. H. Bailey of Cornell University, entered the debate, reaching these conclusions concerning piece-root rootstocks: "The roots are comparatively weak the first year or two and the trees make less growth than those on whole-roots. The root system on piece-root trees is apt to be one-sided and shallow."

Several large nurseries, particularly Stark Bro's Nursery, made a major point of advertising that they used only whole roots for grafting. Probably this advertising campaign had an effect because, by 1920, piece-root grafting had been largely abandoned.

1750. This nursery was destroyed in the Revolutionary War but was rebuilt and continued until the early 1800s. A 1776 Charleston newspaper advertisement says: "the subscriber . . . has for sale at his nursery a great variety of Apples, Pears, Plumbs, Cherries, Nectarines, Apricots, and Peach Trees, all grafted and inoxulated from the best sorts England and America afford."

The earliest documented nurseries in North Carolina were operated by the Friends (or Quakers). In 1790 a Quaker minister named Ann Jessup left her home in New Garden, Guilford County, North Carolina, and went to England as a minister and speaker. When she returned in 1792, she brought with her many European fruit cuttings, including apple scions. These apple cuttings were grafted onto seedling rootstocks by Abijah Pinson, also a member of the Quaker community in Guilford County, and Mrs. Jessup's orchard soon became famous for its quality fruits.

In 1806 Abijah Pinson moved to Westfield in Surry County, North Carolina, and started a nursery using scions from some of Ann Jessup's trees. Pinson also grafted trees of the best American apples, and the list of apple varieties sold by his nursery consists mostly of American apples: Father Abraham, Red Pippin, Jannette, Striped Pippin, Red Romanite, Yellow Summer Pippin, English Russet or Leathercoat, Limbertwig, White Winter Pippin, Striped Horse, Speckled Pearmain, White Winter Pearmain, Vandiver, Pearwarden, French Pippin, Red Winter Pearmain, and Golden Russet. Quakers spread Abijah Pinson's apple trees all over North Carolina, and his varieties were used to start nurseries as far away as Lynchburg, Virginia, and Red Lion, Pennsylvania. The great migration of North Carolinians into the Northwest Territories from 1820 to 1826 carried Pinson's apples into Ohio, Illinois, Indiana, and even into Missouri. Before leaving this colorful piece of history, I must acknowledge the late Ruth Minick, a local historian of Surry County, North Carolina, for bringing it to my attention. Miss Minick, in turn, credited Fred Hughes, a friend who did extensive research in old Quaker records. (Ruth Minick was my sixth-grade teacher where I grew up in Mount Airy.)

Many large southern landowners purchased fruit trees from the famous Prince Nursery on Long Island, New York. This nursery was established in 1730 by the Prince family, who were French Huguenots, and was initially stocked with fruit varieties brought from France. A 1771 advertisement of the Prince Nursery lists over one hundred fifty kinds of fruit trees. The twenty-four apple varieties on the list include eight European apples, but the other sixteen varieties are apples that originated in this country as seedlings. Thus, even as early as 1771, the best American seedling apples were being recognized and propagated.

The first southern nursery west of the Appalachians was started in 1790 by the Virginian Edward Darnaby (d. 1821), in "the Great Bend of the Kentucky River" in Mercer County, Kentucky. The apple varieties he sold included Striped June, Curtis, Milam, Queen, Pryor's Red, Cannon Pearmain, Limbertwig, Rall's Janet, Father Abram, and Hewe's Crab.

In the South the practice of planting apple seeds to obtain orchards was prevalent from the early 1600s to the mid-1800s, a period of almost three hundred years. Millions of apple trees were grown from seed. This means that the South was like a vast agricultural experiment station, crudely screening seedling apple varieties, rejecting most but keeping the best. The rare seedling apple tree bearing fruit of high quality found favor with its owner, was given a name, and its root sprouts were sought by neighbors. Eventually a small nursery would be established nearby, grafting and selling the best of these local trees. In time the cream of the crop of the seedling apples was sold all over the South by big nurseries. Of the millions of southern seedling apple trees, only a handful became widespread southern favorites—Horse Apple, Shockley, Hall, Yates, Carter's Blue, Limbertwig, Ben Davis, Blacktwig, Red June, Magnum Bonum, and perhaps twenty others.

The Revolutionary War ended the colonial period and found southerners pressing against the Appalachian Mountains, waiting only for the defeat of the British to flood into Tennessee, Kentucky, Alabama, and Mississippi, and then into Texas and Arkansas. Once again settlers of new lands outran nurseries, and once again seedling orchards were planted everywhere.

Most of the South from the Appalachians to the Mississippi River was occupied by the Five Civilized Tribes of Native Americans: Choctaws, Chickasaws,

## Johnny Appleseed

Johnny Appleseed (called John Appleseed during his lifetime) was a real person. John Chapman was born in 1774 in Leominster, Massachusetts, and died near Fort Wayne, Indiana, in 1845. He established at least twenty seedling apple-tree nurseries in Ohio (plus a few in Pennsylvania and Indiana) and sold or bartered his trees.

When Johnny first entered Ohio about 1800, it was a wild place where Indians and the few white settlers were often in conflict. He established his first nurseries on tributaries of the Ohio River, often traveling by canoe and planting apple seeds he obtained from cider mills near his sister's home. (For most of his life, Johnny spent the winters with his sister and her family, first in Pennsylvania, and, after 1808, in Ohio.) At first Johnny did not bother to obtain title to his nursery plots, just picking out a likely spot on a trail or path and girdling the trees to open it up for planting apple seeds. Later he became a better businessman and homesteaded, purchased, or leased land, being careful to register deeds, leases, and land sales in nearby county courthouses. There are records of almost thirty land transactions by John Chapman ranging from ½ acre to 160 acres. It is quite possible that he made more money from homesteading, buying, and selling land than from his seedling apple nurseries.

By establishing new nurseries ever northward and westward as Ohio and Indiana were settled, Johnny stayed largely on the fringe of civilization, where his seedling apple trees were most appreciated. Nurseries selling high-quality grafted fruit trees quickly filled in behind him as settlers improved their orchards with grafted nursery stock.

The seedling apple trees Johnny grew in his nurseries were useful to early settlers, bearing apples several years sooner than if they had started their own seedling orchards. Johnny traveled by foot between the many widely separated nurseries on land he owned or leased, trying to visit each nursery at least once a year. Later in life he hired his brother-in-law to care for several nurseries. During his travels he often spent the night in pioneer cabins, sleeping on the floor and distributing religious tracts about his Swedenborgian religious beliefs.

Eccentricities made Johnny Appleseed conspicuous even on the frontier and fueled many of the myths about him. He was usually barefoot and wore cast-off clothing, little more than rags. (He did not wear a cooking pot on his head like a helmet. This story, like several others, was fabricated years after his death.) He was said to revere all living things and would detour to avoid stepping on an ant or earthworm. Johnny considered grafting to be unnatural and hurtful to fruit trees and so he grew only seedlings. Of the many thousands of seedling trees Johnny originated, none ever became commercially important. None of his trees are alive today.

Except for a brief visit to Wellsburg, West Virginia (then part of Virginia), Johnny did not come south of the Ohio River and was never in the South.

Johnny Appleseed's largely mythical reputation began with a mix of fact and fancy concocted by writer W. D. Haley for an article in an 1871 issue of *Harper's New Monthly Magazine*.

The best and most factual description of Johnny Appleseed's life is *Johnny Appleseed: Man and Myth* by Robert Price, published in 1954 and reprinted most recently in 2006. Copies may be ordered from Urbana University, 579 College Way, Urbana, OH 43708.

Creeks, Seminoles, and Cherokees. Their defense against the tide of settlers collapsed in the early 1800s, and in the 1830s the tribes were forcibly expelled to Oklahoma. All of these tribes had been agricultural with fields of corn, vegetables, and fruit trees surrounding their permanent towns and in scattered clearings throughout the region. In 1801 President Thomas Jefferson had directed government Indian agents to distribute fruit-tree seeds to the southern tribes to encourage them to become more agricultural and less warlike. Upon the expulsion of the Five Civilized Tribes, settlers took over their lands and found seedling apple

## "In Praise of Johnny Appleseed"

Vachel Lindsay

"Johnny Appleseed, Johnny Appleseed,"
Chief of the fastness, dappled and vast,
In a pack on his back,
In a deer-hide sack,
The beautiful orchards of the past,
. . . .
Johnny Appleseed swept on,
Every shackle gone,
Loving every sloshy brake,
Loving every skunk and snake,
Loving every leathery weed,
Johnny Appleseed, Johnny Appleseed.
. . . .
He swept on, winged and wonder-crested,
Bare-armed, barefooted, and bare-breasted.
The maples, shedding their spinning
seeds,
Called to his appleseeds in the ground,
Vast chestnut-trees, with their butterfly
nations
Called to his seeds without a sound.
. . . .
Long, long after,
When settlers put up beam and rafter,
They asked of the birds: "Who gave this fruit?
Who watched this fence till the seeds took root?
Who gave these boughs?" They asked the sky,
And there was no reply. . .

trees by the thousands, particularly in North Carolina, Georgia, Alabama, and Tennessee.

The period from 1840 to 1900 could be called the golden age of the apple in the South. During these years there was a serious crusade to make the South a major commercial apple-growing area using apple varieties adapted to southern soils and climate. The earliest proponent of a southern apple industry was Jarvis Van Buren (1801–85), who moved from New York to Clarksville in north Georgia in 1838 where he managed the Stroop Iron Works and worked as a railroad engineer. Van Buren soon left the iron works and purchased ten acres of land in Habersham County, where he was a housebuilder and nurseryman. The Cherokee Indians had just been forced from the South, and Van Buren roamed their seedling orchards where he noticed the superior flavor and keeping qualities of the fruit borne by some of the trees. The best of the southern seedling apples, Van Buren believed, could form the basis of commercial apple orchards in the southern hill country, if a way could be found to transport the fruit to markets. Van Buren established an orchard and nursery (Gloaming Nursery) of the best southern apples, helped to organize a pomological society, and by 1860 had straightened out some of the confusing nomenclature for southern apples. He wrote about southern apples in many northern and southern publications and carried apples to fruit fairs in Pennsylvania, where they garnered much praise. Van Buren was truly breaking the trail for southern apples, which, until this time, had been ignored by northern pomologists. For example, in 1845, when A. J. Downing wrote the first edition of his monumental *Fruits and Fruit Trees of America*, he listed only 1 southern apple. Another influential American pomological text, published in the North in 1851, listed only 4 southern apples out of a total of 133 varieties.

Second only to Van Buren as a southern pomologist was Silas McDowell (1795–1879). McDowell was a poor but educated South Carolinian and a botanist of some renown who worked most of his life as a tailor and as clerk of the state superior court. In 1830 McDowell moved to a farm in Macon County, in the mountains of western North Carolina, and began grafting himself an orchard from the best local apple trees. By 1850 he had an orchard of over six hundred apple trees and sold apples, apple trees, and rhododendrons. McDowell was known for his grafting skills and grafted apple trees as far away as Asheville, North Carolina. Among his apple finds were Cullasaga, Great Unknown, Nickajack, Ellijay, Chestooah, Elarkee, and others. Like Van Buren, McDowell found many of his best varieties in old Cherokee seedling orchards.

Besides being an early and important southern pomologist, Silas McDowell was the first man to write about the phenomenon of temperature inversion and its relationship to topography, usually called a "thermal belt." Briefly, a thermal belt is a horizontal zone on a mountainside or hillside where frost or freezing is less likely to occur than at higher and lower elevations on the same mountainside. This has obvious importance to fruit growers, as even a few degrees warmer temperature when fruit trees are in bloom can mean the difference between severe frost damage to blossoms and no damage at all. This concept of the thermal belt is still being used to site commercial apple orchards in the southern Appalachians.

In the 1850s the torch of southern pomology was passed to three remarkable southern nurserymen whose influence reached every part of the South. These three men—Joshua Lindley, P. J. Berckmans, and Franklin Davis—founded large nurseries and actively collected the best southern fruits. All three fervently believed in the promise of the South as a major fruit-producing area and promoted this idea through their catalogs and articles in gardening periodicals.

Joshua Lindley was from Chatham County, North Carolina, where his family is known to have operated a small nursery in 1824, but perhaps as early as the late 1700s. About 1830 he moved to Morgan County, Indiana, where he established and operated a nursery for ten years. Returning to the South in 1840, Lindley opened a nursery in 1853 in New Garden, North Carolina (at that time five miles west of Greensboro), offering 169 different apple varieties in his first catalog. In the 1850s Lindley was vice president of the American Pomological Society. Joshua's son, J. Van Lindley, began his own nursery (Pomona Hill Nurseries) in 1874 in Pomona, North Carolina, a suburb of Greensboro. J. Van Lindley quickly built his nursery into one of the largest nurseries in the South. Consider this description of J. Van Lindley's nursery in 1895: "There are now 625,000 apple trees of various ages, five acres of apple seedlings for grafting, 400,000 peaches will be budded the summer of 1896, and there are 100,000 plum stocks for grafting, besides many thousands of apricots, nectarines, cherries, mulberries, grapes, pecans, English walnuts, Japanese chestnuts. . . . " Known far and wide, Pomona Hill Nurseries (later named J. Van Lindley Nurseries) continued to search out the best southern apples and list them in its catalogs until the 1940s, when the nursery ceased operation.

Franklin Davis first established a nursery in Rockbridge County, Virginia, but by 1858 he had moved the nursery to Staunton and listed over 300 apple varieties in his catalog. Sometime before 1869 he moved his nursery again, this time to Richmond, and later opened a second nursery in Baltimore. By 1900 Franklin Davis's nurseries were shipping fruit trees all over the South and still listed 269 apple varieties in its catalogs. In some years this nursery sold over half a million fruit trees.

Prosper Jules (P. J.) Berckmans was born in 1830 in Belgium, the son of the famous horticulturist Louis E. Berckmans. The 1848 revolution in France convinced the Berckmans family to emigrate to New Jersey. In 1858 the family moved again, this time to Augusta, Georgia, where they purchased the small Fruitlands Nursery. With characteristic vigor P. J. Berckmans quickly built Fruitlands Nursery into one of the South's largest, and its 1861 catalog listed over 200 apple varieties, most of southern origin. Fruitlands Nursery survived the Civil War and was soon prospering again. It imported plants from all over the world and introduced many fruits and ornamentals to the United States. In 1886 Fruitlands Nursery mailed out over twenty-five thousand catalogs, filling orders from all over the United States and from foreign countries as far away as Japan and New Zealand. P. J. Berckmans helped organize the Georgia State Horticultural Society and was its president continuously until just before his death in 1911. Fruitlands Nursery was still in business in 1928 but apparently closed down during the Great Depression.

Just below these three very important southern nurseries were perhaps twenty nurseries of slightly lesser rank. One of these was Southern Nurseries of Washington, Mississippi, established in 1842 by the Scottish horticulturist Thomas Affleck. This nursery had three hundred apple varieties in 1849 and sold nursery stock throughout the cotton-growing states. It apparently did not survive the Civil War. Another nursery in the second tier of importance was the Forest Nursery operated by J. S. Downer and his sons near Fairfax in Todd County, Kentucky. The 1870 catalog of this nursery listed 373 apple varieties.

William Summer (1815–78) owned and operated Pomaria Nurseries of Pomaria, Newberry County, South Carolina, and was the equal of any southerner as a horticulturist and pomologist. In 1860, a visitor to Pomaria Nurseries made the following comments: "The Nurseries contains about 35 acres—all are brimfull with trees and plants. In search of fruit-trees, we found what we wanted: good, strong, young specimens, well cut bark, budded or grafted low on sound stocks. . . . Among his 500 propagated varieties of apples are at least 300 kinds of Southern seedlings."

William Summer operated Pomaria Nurseries from 1852 until his death from pneumonia in 1878, except for the years 1865 to 1872 when the nursery was rebuilt after being destroyed by Sherman's army. His home (still standing) was set on fire by Union soldiers, but the fire was extinguished by family and servants. He was an educated and sophisticated man who wrote widely as the horticultural and pomological editor of the southern periodical *The Farmer and Planter*.

It is a wonder that any southern nurseries survived the Civil War and its aftermath. Owners were killed in the war, and nurseries were destroyed in the warfare or by Sherman's torch. For several years after the war, most southerners lived by barter. Consider this 1867 advertisement by the Westbrook Nursery in Greensboro, North Carolina: "Under the existing unsettled state of affairs, we are under the necessity of selling for cash or produce, exclusively. If any kind of merchantable produce be brought to our Nursery in Greensboro, we will exchange our Nursery productions for it."

While it is tempting to concentrate attention on the large and influential southern nurseries, there were hundreds of local nurseries that served perhaps one or two counties. Many small nurseries printed no catalogs, relying upon simple price lists or advertisements in local newspapers. These nurseries depended on walk-in customers or hired part-time traveling salesmen who were often local farmers with some free time. The great service these small nurseries performed was finding and propagating promising local apple varieties. The owner of a small nursery would hear of someone having a seedling apple tree bearing good fruit. This variety would be added to the inventory of the nursery and, by this modest advancement, might be noticed and then sold by a large and important nursery. Through this process the best southern apple varieties were brought to a wider audience.

After the Civil War it became common for southern nurseries, large and small, to use traveling salesmen to sell their nursery stock. For example, in 1896 the mid-sized Greensboro Nursery in North Carolina employed "thirty to forty men as traveling agents." In the early days these men traveled on horseback, visiting even remote farms and carrying small trees in saddlebags or on pack animals. As roads improved they used wagons or carriages and, later, automobiles. Salesmen representing southern nurseries provided a great service by carrying grafted fruit trees to farmers and by dispensing advice on fruit-tree cultivation. Unfortunately, a few unscrupulous salesmen, usually labeled "tree peddlers," largely spoiled the reputation of all by misrepresenting and mislabeling their stocks. The following tirade is taken from the 1877 catalog of the Fruitlands Nursery, Augusta, Georgia:

> There is a class of persons who annually travel throughout the South with highly-colored fruit pictures, fruits preserved in glass jars, and other devices, which they represent as being correct copies or specimens of the fruits, trees of which they offer for sale. These pictures are printed and colored in Northern cities, the fruits are likewise put up in alcohol expressly for the use of tree peddlers, and can be had by any person who is willing to pay the advertised prices. By these means, enormous quantities of trees are annually sold in the South by parties who have no reputation to make or lose, and whose abode can no more be found than the names of the trees they purport to have in their Nursery. Not satisfied with selling by wilful misrepresentations and exorbitant prices, certain parties have falsely represented themselves as agents of ours or other southern Nurseries, using our catalogues and reputation in securing orders for trees which they purchase from some irresponsible or

> unknown Northern grower, and flooding the South with unacclimated trees and worthless varieties. These parties are injuring Southern Fruit Growers and fruit growing, and annually pocket hard cash from the farmers of the South in exchange for worthless goods.

A more comic description of the tree peddler was presented to the 1903 meeting of the Alabama State Horticultural Society under the topic of fruit tree plagues and parasites:

> Dendrovendor grandeloquans or vulgarly called the windy fruit tree peddler. He is easily recognized by his polite address, never failing to administer an anaesthetic by introducing his generally rotund personality by a very high sounding name preparatory to a deluge of outrageous lies in regard to his stock, the nursery he represents, etc. In most instances, he buys a few specimens of fruit and exhibits such with the information that they came from a two-year-old tree in his nursery. He belongs to the genus of sucking beetles commonly known as humbugs. He is gregarious, generally appearing about corn or cotton planting time, and causes considerable loss by hindering people from farm work.

Throughout the nineteenth century, southern nurseries sold apple trees for twenty to twenty-five cents each, less if purchased in large lots. About 1900 the price began edging upward, and by 1928 apple trees were selling for seventy-five cents to a dollar each.

Beginning in the early 1800s, Virginia developed a small but lucrative enterprise growing Albemarle Pippin apples for export to Europe. After the Civil War there was a great increase in the acreage in Virginia devoted to the "Pippin" apple, most of it in the western piedmont along the slopes of the Appalachians. Albemarle Pippin continued as the predominant Virginia apple variety until about 1900 when it was eclipsed by red apples such as Ben Davis, Winesap, and York Imperial. The ascendancy of these red apples reflected massive new plantings of apples in Virginia, mostly in the Shenandoah Valley. (See also the discussion of the Albemarle Pippin industry under the listing of the Newtown Pippin apple.)

As early as 1850 a commercial apple industry developed in Maryland and Virginia around the Chesapeake Bay. Here, with easy access to navigable waters, farmers planted orchards with early-ripening apples such as Early Harvest, Early Ripe, Summer Queen, Red Astrachan, and Maiden's Blush. These early apples were shipped quickly by boat to northern cities and found a ready market. Commercial orcharding in eastern Virginia and Maryland was gradually abandoned after 1880.

After the Civil War the South endured military occupation and Reconstruction. For the rest of America this was a heady time of massive industrialization and burgeoning population. Throughout this period and up until the end of World War I, the price of apples was very high, and there was money to be made in commercial orcharding. When railroads finally penetrated into the southern hill country, the stage was set for a thirty-year boom in commercial apple orchards in the South.

One apple, far more than any other, fueled the southern apple boom; this apple was the Ben Davis. The Ben Davis and the apple boom were made for each other. Here was a large and lovely red apple that grew on a healthy tree. Here was an apple widely adapted to southern growing conditions. Here was an apple that would keep like a cobblestone and survive the primitive marketing conditions of the day. So what if the Ben Davis had tough texture and second-rate flavor! People were clamoring for apples, and the Ben Davis was what they got.

Arkansas may seem like a strange place for an apple boom, but more than any other southern state, Arkansas experienced the boom and bust of the southern "apple mania." The Ozark region of northern Arkansas is excellent for apple growing. Railroads reached this area in the 1880s, and the boom was on. Ben Davis and Black Ben Davis were kings. By 1890 Arkansas had 2 million bearing apple trees, and this increased to over 7 million by 1910! Benton County, alone, had over 2 million apple trees in 1910, more than any other county in the United States. Collapsing apple prices after 1920 and increasing competition from the Pacific Northwest destroyed the Arkansas apple industry. The entire state had only 120,000 apple trees in 1960.

From 1890 to 1920 Maryland and Virginia were the scene of a huge speculative expansion of commercial apple orchards. A "delirium of apple planting" in both states saw millions of apple trees set into the ground. As usually happens, this frenzy attracted a class of people that smells easy money. Both Maryland and Virginia saw the rise of stock-company orchards with investors lured by vague promises of 50 percent annual dividends.

These get-rich schemes were promoted by speculators from northern cities. Large blocks of cheap land, usually not suitable for fruit growing, were planted in apple trees and divided into tracts of five to ten acres. Tracts were sold for $300 to $500 an acre to widows, clerks, stenographers, and others who could not tell a York apple tree from a Kieffer pear.

In Maryland new apple orchards were set out across the northern tier of counties until, by 1895, there were large orchards as far west as Hagerstown. From then until 1920, most new orchards were planted in the three western counties. Maryland produced 3 million bushels of apples in 1920, with much of the crop being exported to Great Britain and South America. After this date low prices for apples squeezed out marginal orchards, and apple production dropped to less than 2 million bushels by 1960.

Virginia, with much unbridled speculation in commercial apple orchards, saw many ill-conceived orchards planted between 1890 and 1920. World War I helped to prop up apple prices, but the bottom fell out after 1920. For Virginia the number of apple trees fell from 9 million in 1906 to 4 million in 1937 to less than 1 million in 1972.

H. R. Staight of Cornelia, Georgia, planted north Georgia's first commercial apple orchard in 1895. He was soon joined by Colonel J. P. Fort of Rabun County, Georgia, and by others. By 1910 there were over 2 million apple trees growing in Georgia, but this number had declined by half in 1937.

North Carolina did not escape the apple boom and bust. It is estimated that North Carolina produced nearly 10 million bushels of apples in the early 1900s, but this dropped steadily after 1920 to a low of 1 million bushels in 1950.

Tennessee had developed two commercial apple-producing areas by 1900. In the middle of the state, near Spring Hill and Nashville, orchards concentrated on early apples such as Early Harvest, Duchess of Oldenburg, and Red June. At higher elevations in the Appalachian Mountains, especially on Signal Mountain near Chattanooga, fall and winter apples were grown. Tennessee apple production peaked in the 1930s, then dropped quickly to a level of 200,000 bushels by 1970.

There was a small commercial apple industry in Texas from 1910 to 1930 in Franklin and Camp counties. Excellent apples were grown there, mainly Yellow Transparent, Wilson's Red June, Golden Delicious, and Lowry, but depressed prices and heavy insect and disease pressures forced the commercial orchards to be abandoned.

Even though there was a painful contraction of commercial apple orcharding in the South after 1920, this was largely due to the elimination of speculative and marginal orchards. Astute and hard-working southern orchardists scrambled to ride out the bust years. The many beautiful commercial orchards in the South today are testimonials to the skills of southern orchardists. But the Ben Davis apple is long gone as an important commercial variety, entirely replaced by the early 1900s in southern orchards by Red Delicious, Golden Delicious, Rome Beauty, and Stayman.

Railroads were essential for commercial orcharding in the South, but their coming marked the death knell for farm orchards. Across the South, as the railroad network expanded, urbanization followed. Towns with good railroad service expanded into cities as factories were built and workers moved in. The lure of steady wages and the attractions of the city eroded the agrarian life of the South. Sons and daughters moved away from the farm, never to return. Subsistence farming gradually died out, and with it went the need to grow fruit for family use. Apples, shipped cheaply by railroad from as far away as Maine and Michigan (and after 1900 increasingly from the West Coast), could be bought year-round in southern towns and cities.

Southern nurseries, which had nurtured southern apples, hit hard times. Demand for local apple varieties dwindled while, at the same time, competition increased from large nurseries outside the South. Railroads allowed big nurseries, such as Stark Bro's Nursery in Missouri, to ship thousands of young apple trees into the South to be sold by traveling agents. It was unprofitable for large and distant nurseries to grow local southern apple varieties, which would have small sales even in the best of times. Stark Bro's Nursery salesmen blanketed the South, using remarkable color-lithographed sales books to sell their apple trees. The salesmen sold what their nursery grew—at first Ben Davis, Champion, Apple of Commerce, Stayman, and Black Ben Davis; then Red Delicious, Golden Delicious, and Rome Beauty.

## TWO

# Apple Cultivation Practices

Apple cultivation practices in the old South must be understood within the context of southern agriculture in general. Before the Civil War southern agriculture was a primitive and grueling occupation based to a great degree upon slash and burn cultivation methods. Until 1845, when the German chemist Justus von Liebig published his *Mineral Theory of Plant Nutrition*, there was no scientific understanding of soil fertility and what plants needed in terms of essential nutrients and minerals from the soil. Another basic scientific principle, the fact that microorganisms cause diseases in both plants and animals, was not understood until the 1860s when Louis Pasteur published his germ theory.

Of course, by trial and error, farmers had found over the centuries that certain substances enhanced plant growth and sustained soil fertility. Barnyard manure and wood ashes were standard fertilizers, but were needed in huge amounts on southern soils, most of which were acidic and had little natural fertility. One old agricultural text recommended the application of two tons of wood ashes per acre every three or four years. Southern farmers never had more than a fraction of this amount of ashes available, and had virtually no manure at all because it was standard practice to allow cattle and hogs to roam unfenced and semi-wild in forests and abandoned fields.

It was easier for southern farmers in the 1600s, 1700s, and early 1800s to clear new ground rather than try to fertilize old fields. They cut down the trees and burned them, often leaving stumps in the fields for years. The ashes from these fires, plus the thin layer of forest litter and topsoil, insured good crops for about three years. This was followed by falling crop yields until the land was completely abandoned or allowed to "lie out" and "rest" for many years. Some southern farmers tried desperately to renew soil fertility, experimenting with such things as blood, bones, burnt clay, coal tar, chalk, charcoal, cotton seed, feathers, fish, gypsum, hair, hay, horn, leaves, malt dust, marl, muck, peat ashes, rags, salt, sawdust, soot, and seaweed. In the final analysis the only thing that kept southern agriculture afloat was the availability of new ground to replace worn-out fields. In those days virgin lands must have seemed endless. In Georgia alone, between 1802 and 1840, thirty million acres of land were given away free through state-run land lotteries.

Improvements in agriculture were agonizingly slow. For example, animal bones (a good fertilizer containing calcium and phosphorus) were first used in American agriculture about 1790, but the bones were not pulverized until 1830 and were not treated with acid (to increase the solubility and availability of the phosphorus) until 1851.

In 1826 a Virginian, Edmund Ruffin, published *An Essay on Calcareous Manure* advocating the use of marl, a lime material made up of fine seashells, to neutralize acidic southern soils. (It also provided calcium for plant growth.) Following this publication, liming became more common in the South.

The first great breakthrough for sustainable agriculture in the South was the discovery of deep deposits of dried bird droppings on desert islands off the coasts of Chile and Peru. This high-quality fertilizer, called guano, was imported into the South in huge amounts in the years between 1840 and 1880, raising yields and allowing fields to be cropped year after year. About this same time it was discovered that southern field peas (a nitrogen-fixing legume), if grown on depleted land and plowed under, increased crop yields the following year. Rock phosphate deposits were found in South Carolina in 1867, and other deposits were subsequently discovered in Florida and Tennessee. Rock phosphate, treated with acid, makes superphosphate fertilizer, which quickly became essential to a sustainable southern agriculture. In Georgia for example, the number of superphosphate factories rose from a single factory in

1868 to over one hundred in 1900, but these factories could provide only half of Georgia's demand for superphosphate fertilizer.

Beginning about 1835, a number of horticultural and agricultural magazines began publication in the North with some readership in the South. Chief among these were *The Magazine of Horticulture* and *The American Agriculturist*. About this same time the periodical *The Southern Agriculturist, Horticulturist and Register of Rural Affairs* was started in Charleston, South Carolina, soon followed by *The Southern Cultivator*, published monthly in Augusta, Georgia. The net result of these scientific discoveries and publications was a gradual improvement in southern agriculture in the twenty years before the Civil War.

The Civil War and the years that followed it were a setback to southern agriculture and left most farmers in abject poverty. During this time, many scientific discoveries placed a solid footing under American agriculture in general and orchard practices in particular, but southern farmers, locked in poverty and conservatism, proved difficult to convince. In 1882 *The Southern Cultivator* lamented the southern farmer's "unbounded faith in poor land poorly cultivated, with little faith in land improvement."

Important steps were taken to get agricultural science from scholars to farmers. Two of these occurred simultaneously in the decade before 1900—the founding of agricultural colleges and the establishment of agricultural experiment stations. Agricultural experiment stations were the result of the Hatch Act, passed by Congress in 1887 and largely funded by federal money ($15,000 per year to each state). Agricultural colleges and experiment stations were almost always located together and planted orchards to test fruit varieties, fertilization practices, and chemical controls for pests. Working together, colleges and experiment stations began the long haul toward improving southern agricultural practices, including orchard management.

## Orchard Preparation and Cultivation

By the time the South was settled, apples had been grown in Europe for more than a thousand years, and much knowledge had accumulated concerning how best to grow and care for them. Southerners often ignored this accumulated knowledge and persisted in certain practices that were useless or even counterproductive. The reasons for this remain elusive, but perhaps it had to do with the single-minded concentration by southern farmers on growing tobacco or cotton. Whatever the cause, too many farm orchards were neglected, unkempt and unproductive, useful more as pastures for cattle and hogs. By the mid-1800s there were horticultural books and periodicals with clear and useful information on apple culture. Southern commercial orchardists and large landowners used some of this information, but little of it trickled down to rural families with small orchards.

All authorities stressed proper land preparation before planting an orchard. For the South this meant deep plowing, especially clay soils. Deep plowing was done in the early fall by using two strong mules or horses to pull a turning plow. Behind this team came another two-mule team pulling a subsoil or chisel plow in the same furrow, breaking the soil to a depth of about sixteen inches. Once the soil was deep-plowed and smoothed, shallow furrows were made thirty to forty feet apart in a cross-hatch pattern. At the intersection of crossing furrows, apple trees were planted. This wide spacing was necessary because apple trees in those days grew to a large size—often up to thirty feet tall.

The general practice in the South was to grow crops between the fruit trees until the trees were about ten years old. This intercropping had some benefits for apple trees, keeping down competing grass and weeds and letting the trees benefit from any fertilization the crops might receive. To avoid damaging tree roots, crops not requiring deep cultivation were grown in the orchard. These included potatoes, beans, peas, and perhaps corn. Cotton, tobacco, and small grains were not supposed to be intercropped with fruit trees, but often were.

Of course when crops were grown in orchards, the crops had to be tilled and worked with horses or mules. This presented certain hazards that were addressed in a newspaper article in 1884 by N. W. Craft, owner of a nursery in Yadkin County, North Carolina: "Many young trees are killed by allowing the single-tree and traces to drag over them when plowing. A single-tree, trace-chain, or harrow should never be allowed to even touch the fruit trees. Horses and mules are often allowed to bite off the tops or side branches of trees while plowing, causing very ill-shaped trees for years. A good muzzle on stock is a sure preventive while cultivating young orchards, even in the winter."

If the orchard could be spared from intercropping, farmers were told to enrich the soil by planting southern field peas in midsummer and plowing them under the following spring. Commercial orchardists often interplanted additional apple trees of varieties that would begin bearing the second or third year. This gave some return on the land until the main trees began bearing (often after eight to ten years), at which time the interplanted trees were removed.

When the fruit trees grew large, most orchards were allowed to go to grass. The recommendation was to mow the grass in orchards but not remove it, thus building up soil fertility and tilth. Against this recommendation most southern farmers pastured animals in orchards, damaging the trees and impoverishing the soil. (When grazing animals are removed from an orchard and slaughtered or sold, they take with them in their flesh and bones hundreds of pounds of calcium, potassium, phosphorus, nitrogen, and other minerals and nutrients from the orchard soil. This fact was not obvious to farmers in those days.) Hogs, in particular, were penned in orchards to eat fallen fruit. Large hogs rooted up and ate tree roots and were even known to climb up in trees after fruit. They did, however, have the beneficial effect of eliminating insect larvae often present in fallen apples. In 1884 a southern nurseryman discouraged putting large hogs in apple orchards but recommended small pigs that "root up every particle of grass in fall and winter, hunting insects and roots, but will not root deep enough to injure the roots of trees." Chickens, turkeys, geese, or guinea fowl were sometimes kept in orchards to eat insects, particularly the curculio, which is so damaging to southern fruit.

Southern pomologists and agriculturists recognized the low natural fertility of most southern soils and the need to fertilize fruit trees. Writing in the southern periodical *The Farmer and Planter* in 1858, the South Carolina nurseryman, William Summer, described good fertilizers for fruit trees:

> 1st. Wood-ashes, containing as they do all the elements necessary to growth (except carbon, which is supplied from the air), is a congenial element for all fruit trees and woody growth.
>
> 2d. Lime, whether in the form of marl, shells, plaster or stone-lime, is a specific for apple trees, and apples are largest and fairest when grown in a calcareous soil.
>
> 3d. Phosphates, in the form of bones (which are composed principally of phosphate of lime) or prepared super-phosphates, are specific for pears and grapes and congenial to all fruit trees.
>
> 4th. Ammoniacal manures such as guano, dung, and urine are specifics for the peach and give flavor and spirit to other fruits.

Exhortations to fertilize fruit trees were universal by all authorities, but there is little evidence that southern orchards ever received much fertilizer. Surveying tattered and neglected southern orchards in 1898, a North Carolina agricultural experiment station bulletin pulled no punches: "The main reason for failure of the apple tree is starvation and neglect. Our people spend millions of dollars annually for fertilizers to put on cotton and grain crops, but seem to think that because the trees in the forest take care of themselves, that orchard trees can do the same. . . . Soil exhaustion is the cause of more failures of fruit trees than all other causes combined."

Nurseries and farm journals always recommended that one-year-old trees be planted in the late fall of the year. This advice was widely ignored by southerners who insisted on purchasing two- or even three-year-old trees and planting them in the spring. Another recommendation was that newly planted apple trees be headed or topped low, which causes the lowest branches to develop about three feet above the ground. (Low branches shade the trunk, which helps to prevent sunscald, and a low-branched tree is easier to pick and less likely to blow over.) In the face of this good advice, most farmers pruned off all low branches so that livestock and machinery could get under the trees. Many old apple trees still can be seen with the lowest branches fully eight feet off the ground.

Until about 1900 few southern orchards, even commercial orchards, were sprayed to control insects and disease. This leads some people to believe that old apple varieties must be more disease and insect resistant than newer apples, which are sprayed in commercial orchards today with an array of chemicals. There is a degree of disease resistance in some of the old apple varieties, but some new apples have disease resistance also. Looked at as a whole, old apple varieties are no more resistant to diseases and insects than newer varieties. This means that southern farm families harvested mostly blemished apples; no one expected perfect fruit. Apples with skin defects and an occasional worm were completely normal. Housewives cut out blemishes and worms without a second thought when preparing apples in the kitchen. Men and boys kept their pocketknives sharp to do the same. The American public today demands unblemished apples, which requires orchardists to spray often with chemicals to reduce insects and disease. It is not fair or correct to blame modern apple varieties or the growers for the heavy spraying they receive—blame the customer instead.

### Diseases and Insect Control

Until the late 1800s diseases and insects were less prevalent in southern orchards than they are today. Southern families and communities tended to be scattered and isolated, especially as new areas were being opened up, and orchards had enough isolation to give them a degree of protection. As the population grew and more fruit trees were planted, pathways were established for the spread of diseases and insects.

Some fruit-tree diseases, most notably apple scab, were introduced from overseas and took many years to spread across the United States. Several insects that now prey on apple trees were originally natural pests of native American plants and did not begin attacking apples for years. The apple maggot, a very serious insect pest today, was originally the hawthorn fly, preying upon wild hawthorns. After 1820 hawthorn flies slowly adapted to feed upon apples, and by 1890 had become a major insect pest in the eastern United States.

The curculio (a small snout-nosed beetle) was first a pest of plums and peaches. In the 1800s it also began attacking apples and is now another serious apple pest.

Fire blight was a very damaging disease of apple trees in the 1800s and remains so today. Most diseases of apple trees are caused by fungi, but fire blight is a highly contagious bacterial disease spread in early spring by bees and other insects that carry the bacteria to blossoms and tender shoots. The bacteria multiply rapidly, killing the blossom clusters and new shoots, causing them to blacken as if hit by a blow torch—hence the name fire blight. Sometimes the bacteria travel downward in the sap inside the tree and kill big limbs or the entire tree.

Faced with the puzzling and discouraging damage to apple trees from fire blight (it attacks many varieties of pear trees also, even more seriously), rural southerners devised some unusual theories for explaining this dread disease. Some even suspected that the trees had been hit by lightning!

In 1844 a major epidemic of fire blight erupted from Maryland and Virginia through Kentucky, Tennessee, and states north of the Ohio River. That year the Reverend H. W. Beecher wrote to *The Magazine of Horticulture*: "The blight has prevailed to such an extent as to spread dismay among orchardists, destroying entire collections and taking half the trees in large orchards—affecting both young and old trees, whether grafted or seedlings, in soils of every kind. Many have seen the labor and fond hope of years cut off, in one season, by an invisible destroyer against which none could guard. In conflicting opinions, no one was certain whether the disease was atmospheric, insect or chemical."

Rev. Beecher then listed the prevalent theories concerning the cause of fire blight:

> 1. The rays of the sun, passing through vapors which arise about the trees, concentrates upon the branches and destroys them by the literal energy of fire.
>
> 2. The soil contains deleterious substances or is wanting in properties necessary to the health of the tree.

3. Violent and sudden changes of temperature in the air or of moisture in the earth.

4. Over stimulation by high manuring or constant tillage.

5. The effect of age, the disease beginning on old varieties and then is propagated upon new varieties by contagion.

6. The cause to be an insect.

Remedies concocted by farmers and orchardists to combat fire blight and other diseases may seem quaint or even laughable today, but these were efforts by desperate men to combat something beyond their understanding. One practice around 1840 was to bore holes in the trunks of infected trees and fill the holes with sulfur. (One contemporary critic of this method described it as "about as remedial as whistling to the moon.") Another recommendation: "Wind straw ropes round the trunk and mulch the surface of the ground over the roots." Some orchardists even attributed fire-blight to "apoplexy caused by a surcharge of electric fluid" and tried to control it by hanging old horseshoes and pieces of wire on tree limbs to conduct electricity away from the trees. Still another remedy involved peeling the bark from infected branches and applying a "weak alkaline wash."

By 1896, largely due to scientific investigations by Professor Burrill of the University of Illinois and M. B. Waite of the USDA, the causes of fire blight and the methods of its transmission were finally understood. The remedy recommended at that time was heavy spraying with copper sulfate solutions before and after the trees bloomed, followed by removal and burning of all infected limbs and twigs. Even today control of fire blight on apple and pear trees is difficult. Streptomycin sprays can be used, but are expensive and only partly effective. The old procedure of constant vigilance to detect the disease in its early stages, followed by prompt cutting out of infected twigs and branches to halt disease spread, is still a good procedure for most home orchardists.

Another disease of apple trees in the South is the fungal disease called cedar-apple rust. For many years this disease was called "apple leaf fungus" because no one realized that the eastern red cedar tree is a host for the disease, infecting nearby apple trees. After 1880 when the disease relationship between cedar trees and apple trees was established, the best control measure for cedar-apple rust was found to be the removal of cedar trees growing near orchards and liberal spraying with Bordeaux mix early in the growing season.

Fruit growers of earlier times had to contend with what was called the plant louse, known today as the aphid. A useful remedy was found to be a "tobacco infusion" made by soaking tobacco stems in hot water and spraying the resultant nicotine tea over infected plants.

One rather peculiar and widely used practice in the 1800s was the treatment of the bark on the trunk and main limbs of apple trees. There was a widespread belief that diseases and insects resided in the crevices of bark, so the rough outer bark was scraped off and the trunk scrubbed with a concoction made up mostly of lye or lye soap. (One 1859 recipe called for a wash made of one pound of caustic soda or lye dissolved in a gallon of water.) The result was a very smooth tree trunk, sometimes bright green in color!

About 1866 a copper arsenic compound called Paris green was invented in France as an effective (although highly toxic) insecticide. It was first used in an American orchard in 1878, and its use subsequently became common in the United States, particularly on fruit trees. In 1885 Professor Millardet in Bordeaux, France, first concocted Bordeaux mix. This mixture of copper sulfate and lime in water proved to be the first effective chemical to combat fungal diseases of plants (including apple scab and cedar-apple rust), and its use on fruits and vegetables was strongly recommended by the USDA and agricultural experiment stations. Southern commercial orchardists used these chemicals to boost production and satisfy the increasing demand for blemish-free apples. Because apple trees in those days were quite large, commercial orchardists used powerful and large spray equipment, usually horsedrawn and requiring two or three men to operate. The size and cost of this spray equipment prevented small farmers from spraying home orchards. Besides, blemished fruit was acceptable to farm families as even the worst of it was useful for cider, vinegar, and animal feed.

## THREE

# Uses of Apples

On talking with elderly southerners about apples, I hear variations of this statement over and over again: "When I was growing up, not a day went by that we didn't have apples in some shape or form on the table to eat." For the farm family living on its own resources, nothing could replace the apple for nutrition, variety, keeping ability and tastiness. Crocks of apple butter and apple preserves sat in the pantry beside the cider vinegar barrel. Bags of dried apple slices hung from the pantry ceiling. Mounds of fresh apples waited through the winter in the cellar or in boxes upstairs. Best of all, for six months a year, trees in the farm orchard drooped with fresh fruit. Some farm women kept a map of their orchard in the kitchen to direct their children to a specific tree for apples for a pie or to another tree for apples to be stewed for supper.

Food has always been an important part of southern hospitality, and rural families would often offer guests fresh apples. Usually men would visit on the porch, taking pride in peeling an apple in a single thin spiral of peel. Women visitors might sit at the kitchen table with a dishpan of apples, peeling and eating them while catching up on gossip.

Apples were cooked in so many different ways that the recipes would fill a book. In fact there are a large number of cookbooks devoted exclusively to apple cookery.

The subject of apple cookery requires at least the mention of that great southern delicacy—the fried pie! Made with a filling of seasoned and sweetened dried apples encased in a half-moon of pie crust, the fried pie was a special treat. Like so much else, the fried pie is

### Cooking Apples

"Cooking apples" fall roughly into two categories—those that cook to a pulp (as in applesauce) and those that hold their shape when cooked (as in apple pie). The inherent texture of each variety of apple determines which category it falls into. Texture, in turn, depends on the construction of the walls of the fruit cells and the acidity of the apple.

The flesh of an apple consists of thousands of individual cells with rigid cell walls surrounding a semi-liquid containing mostly fruit sugar and starch. Cell walls are largely cellulose, and some apple varieties have thicker walls with more cellulose. Apples with more cellulose tend to hold their shape and remain firmer when cooked.

Pectin is also found in cell walls and helps hold the cell walls together. When an apple is cooked, heat melts the pectin. Acid in the flesh firms up pectin and keeps it from melting so fast during cooking. Thus, acidic apples are more likely to hold their shape when cooked.

When Edith sends me out to pick apples for a pie, I select firm apples with slightly dry flesh and with acidity and flavor. I know these apple slices will hold their shape in a pie and will not flood the pie with juice. The apple flavor will shine through the spices in the pie filling. Slightly underripe apples may be used in a pinch.

For stewing apples or applesauce, I select juicy apples of softer, somewhat grainy texture and lower acidity. Slightly overripe but flavorful apples are fine for stewing and sauce. These apples will cook to a pulp when cooked down in a little apple juice or cider. A potato masher or a food processor makes smooth, lump-free applesauce for canning or freezing.

Cooking with apples is becoming a lost art. A recent survey of people purchasing apples at a farmer's market indicated that only 15 percent of the apples would be used for cooking.

a forgotten art, but its memory still lingers for anyone who grew up in a warm kitchen with a woodstove.

Besides being used daily for cooking and fresh eating, apples had a multitude of other uses. The following sections touch upon the most important ways apples were used by southern farm families.

### Storing Apples in the Winter

Of all the fruit grown on farms in the South, only apples could be kept through the winter to provide a taste of freshness. Think of what it meant to rural families, in the days before canning and refrigeration, to have fresh apples during long winter months of eating salted, dried, and pickled foods. Even an apple as ordinary as the Ben Davis was appreciated for its keeping ability and was eaten with gusto. (There is the story about a city "feller" who, late one winter, asked a farmer how he could eat a Ben Davis apple with such obvious enjoyment. The farmer replied: "Well, I'll tell ya. It shore beats eatin' snowballs!")

Southerners living in the mountains and in the northern tier of states had little trouble with winter storage; apples ripened late enough and winters were cold enough to keep the fruit in good condition for months. But it was a different story in warmer areas of the South where most so-called winter apples ripened in the early fall when the weather was warm and fruit spoiled quickly. These areas also had relatively warm winters, making long-term storage questionable. Is it any wonder that southerners prized their few really fine winter keepers: Hall, Yates, Mattamuskeet, Winesap, Terry Winter, Blacktwig, and not many others?

A variety of techniques were used to keep fresh apples through the winter. Many farm families did not heat the whole house in cold weather. Unheated rooms were useful for apple storage. I remember talking to one elderly man about his childhood in the North Carolina mountains. He said his family stored apples in boxes under his bed in an upstairs room. I replied that surely his bedroom was too warm for apple storage. Hearing this he laughed, saying that his room was so cold he had an inch of snow many mornings on his bed, the snow having sifted through cracks in the walls.

Root cellars were often used by southerners in mountainous areas, usually built partly underground into the side of a hill. Here apples were stored in barrels or even in open bins or boxes until the following spring. Root cellars were rather rare on farms in the piedmont and coastal plains. In place of a root cellar, farmers stored apples in shallow pits, a method called "pitting" or "banking." This description is from an 1899 issue of *The American Gardener* magazine:

> The old-fashion method of pitting is indeed preferable to the cellar, whether the fruit is in bulk or in barrels. The pit calls for three requisites: First, that it have perfect drainage; second, that provision be made for sufficient covering; and lastly, that ventilation, if it be no more than an erect sheaf of straw, be provided in proportion as the cover is thicker. The method of constructing a pit is usually this: A slight excavation is made in a well-drained spot into which the fruit is deposited. If they are stored in bulk it is best to have them in a conical shaped heap, about five feet broad at the base and of any desired length. Over the pile is placed a coat of straw one foot thick and outside of this a layer of soil of the same thickness. In some cases, shutters of rough boards, about four by six or seven feet in size are placed on the straw and the soil on top of these. Before the coldest weather arrives, cover the heap with another layer of straw, kept in place by soil. From such a pit, fruit is sure to come out in the best possible shape.

Rather than using straw, many southerners lined and covered the fruit-storage pit with dry cornstalks or tree leaves. James Anding of Summit, Mississippi, remembers an ingenious variation of the pitting technique using sweet potato vines. Some years ago he wrote this description in *Pomona* magazine:

> As a kid I helped grandpa "bank" apples. Similar to the "Clamp" of the British.

> When he dug his sweet potatoes, he would line the fresh plowed furrow with potato vines, usually about two inches thick. On these we would put the Roxbury Apples and pile them up as steep as we could. When all the apples were piled up, a layer of vines was put on the sides and top and earth was banked on the vines. It looked like one giant heap when finished. He started digging them out Christmas week and dug on until the apples were gone. But he always buried the sweet potato vines as he dug out the apples. In the spring, he cut the buried vines in foot long pieces and planted them by pushing them down in fresh plowed ground with a stick. A couple of inches were left above ground, which soon sprouted and started another crop of sweet potatoes.

Log tobacco barns were also used for winter storage of apples. The fruit was piled on the dirt floor of the tobacco barn and covered with leaves. I have talked with many elderly southerners who remember apples keeping this way until March or April.

Apples destined for winter storage were accorded special handling, as shown by this excerpt from *The Southern Apple and Peach Culturist* (1872):

> All apples to be kept through the Winter should be gathered by hand . . . as bruised apples will not keep. The gathering of Winter fruit should be delayed as long as possible to secure fine flavor, but fruit will keep longer and better if gathered before quite ripe. In the climate of Virginia, from the middle of October to the middle or even the last of November, on mountain sides and high mountain valleys, is the proper time.
>
> Winter apples should be picked in cool, dry weather, the gathering delayed as long as possible, avoiding severe frost. The fruit should be handled with care to prevent bruising and should not be allowed to lie in heaps exposed to the sun, or even stand in barrels exposed to the sun as such course is injurious to the life and keeping qualities of apple.

Southerners generally adhered to the belief that apples destined for winter storage should be picked when the moon was waning, usually expressed as "the down side of the moon." A farmers' almanac, an important source of information for rural families, could be consulted for a good time to pick and store apples.

## Dried Apples

Many southern farm families had fresh apples surplus to their needs. Too often it was difficult or impossible to move these apples to markets because of their perishability and bulk and because rural roads were often atrocious. A solution to this problem was to dry the apples. Dried apples are lighter (fifty pounds of fresh apples will dry to about seven pounds), more compact, and far less perishable. Important too, especially in the desperate years after the Civil War, dried apples were a source of hard cash for southern farm families. Certain local merchants would buy dried apples in small lots from rural families, for cash or credit. When enough dried apples were thus accumulated, the merchants would send them by wagons to railheads for shipment to larger cities. The USDA noted in 1872 that $300,000 to $400,000 worth of dried apples were shipped that year from High Point, North Carolina, alone. In 1877 a total of four million pounds of dried fruit, mostly apples, were received in Baltimore from Virginia, North Carolina, Tennessee, and Georgia. In those days dried apples netted farm families about four and one-half cents a pound, but this price rose to about eight cents a pound by 1900.

Although by the late 1800s there were a few large factories in the South to dry apples, most commercial dried apples continued to come from rural families. In 1872 a reporter for *The American Agriculturist* magazine had this to say about southern dried apples: "As enormous as the (dried apple) business is in the aggregate, no one person carries it on to any great extent. Every family has its orchard and dry house. In my travels through the (North Carolina) countryside, I did not see a house that did not have fruit of some kind curing in the yard."

An observer traveling through northwest Arkansas in the early 1900s made these comments: "I visited many local orchards where the owner and his family dried most of the fruit grown in the orchard, sacked it and sold it on the market as dried fruit. As some of these orchards were 30 miles from a railroad station, the savings in hauling the crop was considerable."

Apples that dried white, such as Maiden's Blush, were prized. To make the highest-quality dried apples, fresh apples were peeled, cored, and sliced horizontally into thin round rings, which brought a premium price in the United States. Apples for export were peeled, cored, and sliced vertically into six to eight pieces. Color was unimportant in the dried apple export trade, which went mainly to Great Britain and Germany. The amount of dried apples exported by the United States is astonishing. In 1879, 7,379,836 pounds of dried apples were exported, and this amount increased steadily to over 45 million pounds in 1907. One shipper in Baltimore sent 2 million pounds of dried fruit to Germany in 1876.

Any apple can be dried, but southerners preferred tart apples, which ripened when days were hot enough to facilitate the drying process. Tart apples become sweeter when dried and are better for cooking, the final use of dried apples. Most apples were sun-dried, which takes about two sunny days. Fresh slices were placed on clean cloths (often bleached feed sacks) or brown paper on the ground or, preferably, on the shed roof of a woodshed or porch. Sometimes the slices were covered with cheesecloth to ward off insects. Slices were usually gathered up and brought in at night or when the weather threatened, a task often assigned to children. Drying fruit could also be left in place and covered at night with a piece of canvas.

A better solution to drying apples and other fruit was the dry house. Many elderly southerners still remember the dry house on their farm when they were young, a small building of logs or rough boards with a woodstove in the center. Earlier versions had a fireplace on the outside with a flue running through the dry house to provide heat. The loose construction of the dry house was intentional, allowing moisture to escape from the drying fruit. Sliced fruit was placed on trays or shelves around the stove from floor to roof and dried in about twelve hours.

Mabel Brinkley remembered quite well the dry house that stood on her family farm near Elk Creek, Virginia, when she was a child. She said it contained wooden racks (made, she thought, from poplar laths) stacked horizontally very close together. These racks measured about two feet by four feet and were called "hurds," a name derived from the old English word "hurdle," meaning a movable frame. The dry house itself was made of vertical boards with a shed roof, and it had a stove in the center. Mrs. Brinkley's parents dried Horse Apples and Ben Davis apples (which stayed white when dried). Her favorite dried apple was the Rose Sweet (probably Sweet Winesap) dried with the peel on and which she carried in her pockets and ate like candy.

Lacking a dry house, families could escape bad weather by drying apple slices in the house in front of a fireplace or near a stove, threading the fresh slices on strings or placing them on trays or boards. Apple rings were strung on horizontal poles over the stove. The slices or rings were properly dried when they were rubbery, and they were then stored in bags in a cool place. Another way to test dryness was to press together firmly into a ball a handful of slices. If the slices were springy enough to separate when released, they were dry.

Another way southerners preserved apples was by bleaching (also called smoking), a procedure that seems to have been used mostly in the mountains. Some southerners considered bleached fruit to be inferior to air-dried fruit, perhaps because of its slight sulfur flavor.

To bleach apples, hot coals (or a piece of red-hot iron, such as an old axe head) were placed on a layer of sand in the bottom of a barrel or wooden box. About a half cup of pure sulfur was sprinkled onto the hot coals. Once the sulfur began fuming, racks or open baskets of pared, cored, and sliced apples were hung over the sulfur and the barrel was tightly covered with cloth or paper. The barrel was sometimes opened after thirty minutes for additional sulfur to be added and the apple slices stirred. This process resulted in fruit bleached white and preserved by the sulfur fumes. The bleached fruit was packed into boxes or crocks and used through the winter.

### Apple Cider

There is sweet cider and there is hard cider. Sweet cider is unfermented apple juice, usually fresh-pressed. Within a day or two after pressing, the sugars in sweet cider begin to be fermented by wild yeasts that are always present in fresh-pressed apple juice, and this fermentation process results in a slightly alcoholic beverage called hard cider. Most hard ciders range from 5 to 7 percent alcohol, which is considerably lower than the alcohol content of wines made from grapes. When one reads in old books and references about cider or "cyder," it is invariably hard cider that is being referred to.

Northerners took the making of cider quite seriously, and it was made in considerable quantities in every town and village in New England. In the 1800s, cider was a major industry around Newark, New Jersey, where there were large cider mills fed by vast surrounding orchards of Harrison and Campfield apples grown solely for cider and apple brandy. In 1810 Essex County, New Jersey, produced 198,000 barrels of cider and 307,310 gallons of apple brandy. Besides being a popular American (and southern) beverage, New Jersey cider was exported to the West Indies and to Europe. To a great degree the art and business of cider making in the North was a casualty of the temperance movement of the nineteenth century and was almost finished off by Prohibition in the twentieth century.

Southerners made cider from a very early date. In 1647 "twenty butts of cyder" were recorded as having been made in Virginia, and by the mid-1700s both cider and cider vinegar were being exported from Virginia to the West Indies. In spite of this early start, there is little evidence that southerners took cider making as seriously as their northern neighbors. Southerners certainly fermented the juice of apples and drank it with relish, but the art of cider making was often lacking in the South. We do know that both George Washington and Thomas Jefferson carefully made and blended their own cider, extolling the virtue of certain apples for this use, especially Hewe's Crab. The serious cider making that did exist in the South was dealt an almost fatal blow by the great religious upheaval that slowly penetrated southern settlements after the Revolutionary War. This fervor, also known as the Second Great Awakening (which saw the rapid rise of both Baptist and Methodist denominations), was accompanied by the rejection of alcohol, including cider. Some statistics tell the tale: In 1776 about one in six Americans belonged to a church, but this rose to one in three by 1850. During this same time period, American consumption of the alcohol in alcoholic beverages dropped from more than 7 gallons per year per adult to less than 2 gallons per year (roughly what it is today). By 1850 cider was no longer an important beverage in the South.

That the art of cider making did not entirely die out in the South is shown by these instructions written by Nicholas Nall of Moore County, North Carolina, about 1872:

> All apples fit to be eaten will make good cider. The grand secret is in cleansing them from filth and dregs as early as possible. Each sort of apple is to be crushed and pressed by themselves. Often two kinds of juice, both good, would, if mixed, make bad cider. Throw out all imperfect, sorry, and sunburnt apples, as well as dirt and trash. Crush your apples before much mellowed, as they lose their strength, soundness, and spirit if too mellow. Let them stand a half a day after being crushed, before putting into the press; then press them slowly; discontinue as soon as the juice appears thin and watery. The advantage of slow pressure is in making the liquor run pure.
>
> Let your casks, previously well cleansed, be filled quite full, to permit the froth and pomace to discharge itself at the bung. When the fermentation abates, cover the bung closely with something that may be lifted by the fixed air that escapes during the future fermentation.

> In a week, rack off [siphon off] the cider carefully, ceasing the moment you observe it to run muddy; now stop the [newly filled] cask more firmly. In ten days, rack it off a second time, and in fifteen days a third time. In every instance, the [newly filled] cask is to be clean and perfectly filled; and when filled for the last time, to be bunged close in a deep, dry cellar, never to be moved, until drawn for use.
>
> Late cider need not be racked until March, and then one racking, or at the most two, will be sufficient.
>
> Be very careful that no water, not even the little that will adhere after rinsing the cask, is mixed with the cider. The smallest quantity of rain water will render the cider unfit to keep. The addition of any quantity of distilled spirits is not only useless but injurious.

Most of the apple juice (or sweet cider) sold in stores today is undistinguished at best, usually made from cull sweet apples such as Red Delicious and Golden Delicious. Processes to clarify, standardize, and preserve the juice further subtract from its flavor. Serious cider makers have long understood that the best cider usually comes from the juice of sweet apples mixed with the juice of apples having a more tart and tannic flavor. The ratio varies, but sweet apples should make up no more than 50 percent of cider blends. In the old days farm families found their favorite cider blends by experimentation. Mabel Brinkley of Wytheville, Virginia, remembered her father used "a few sweet apples but mostly sour (tart) apples. The Cain apple was used because it was so juicy and the Fallawater was used also."

*The Southern Apple and Peach Culturist* (1872) has this to say about cider apples: "Some connoisseurs of this liquor are of the opinion that the juice of the more delicate table fruit is generally more cordial and pleasant than that of the harsher kinds; though others assert the latter to be in many respects preferable. In Virginia, very fine cider is made late in the fall with common seedling apples of various qualities, from those most sour and harsh to those that are sweet and tender. Good cider is also made during the summer from early seedling varieties."

The Harrison and Campfield apples, used in large measure during the 1800s in the New Jersey cider industry, were selected not so much for their flavor as because they resulted in cider of high alcoholic content, perhaps as high as 10 to 12 percent. On the other hand the Hewe's Crab, prized by southerners, made a cider described in 1860 as "slightly astringent, light colored, keeps well and holds it carbonic acid (carbonation) in the bottles better than any other cider, seldom or ever becoming turbid." Crab cider did not have a high alcoholic content, usually being around 6 percent, and many southerners considered well-made crab cider to be fully the equal of the best European champagne.

People making cider before refrigeration was available often found out to their dismay that hard cider will eventually turn into cider vinegar unless steps are taken to prevent it. Because the vinegar-making bacteria in cider require air, barrels of cider that had finished fermentation were carefully topped off and kept completely full of cider to exclude all air from the barrels. Another preservation method was recounted by Mrs. Brinkley, who remembered that her family in Virginia would heat the cider they intended to keep, thus killing the vinegar bacteria in it. Heating cider does alter its flavor, however.

More and more people are beginning to make apple cider again. Old cider presses are quickly bought at farm auctions, and new ones are being purchased and put to use. Little will be said here to guide today's novice cider maker as there are several good books on the subject. Modern refrigeration makes it possible to keep sweet cider (or apple juice) without worrying about its alcoholic fermentation, but it must be pasteurized or frozen for long-term storage.

As for making hard cider, fresh-pressed sweet cider at room temperature will naturally ferment to hard cider from the wild yeasts present in the juice. These yeasts grow in the cider and change its sugars to alcohol, releasing large amounts of carbon dioxide in the process. Yeasts grow best if air is excluded from the container during fermentation. A loose bung in a wooden barrel sufficed in the old days to release the carbon dioxide and exclude some air. Today the maker of small batches of hard cider can purchase plastic or glass fermentation containers as well as airlocks that allow carbon dioxide to escape while keeping air out. The best sources for these supplies are mail-order companies or local stores that sell beer- and winemaking supplies. If using purchased apple juice to make hard cider, be sure it does not contain any sulfur dioxide, which will inhibit the growth of yeasts. Pasteurized apple juice can be used, but it must be inoculated with yeast, preferably a wine yeast from stores selling winemaking supplies.

By pressing only one variety of apple at a time in a cider press and keeping the juices separate, one can experiment with custom blends of cider. For those willing to explore further, the juice of pears, grapes, blackberries, raspberries, or strawberries can be mixed with apple cider to tempt jaded taste buds. Anyone desiring to resurrect the southern cider-making tradition should plant some southern cider apples such as Hewe's Crab, Winesap, and Yates and should purchase a good book on cider making; recommended are *Cider, Hard and Sweet* by Ben Watson (Countryman Press, 2nd edition, 2008) and *Cider: Making, Using & Enjoying Sweet & Hard Cider* by Annie Proulx and Lew Nichols (Storey Publishing, 3rd edition, 2003).

## Apple Brandy

Scotch-Irish immigrants brought to the South their knowledge of the distillation of alcohol. The same copper stills used to make corn whiskey were used to make apple brandy. The process was simple: Apples were crushed (usually by pounding them in a barrel using a wooden club or pestle) and allowed to fully ferment, using the rule of thumb that 4½ bushels of apples would make a gallon of brandy. The fermented juice was pressed out or allowed to drip out and then run through the still to produce apple brandy. New brandy was water-clear and sold for a higher price than corn whiskey. Brandy improved if it was aged and was sometimes aged in a cask, charred on the inside, to smooth the brandy and give a little color to it.

One of the first acts of the new United States was to place a tax on distilled liquors. To avoid this federal tax, southerners became adept at hiding their stills and "blockading" or "moonshining" their brandies and whiskeys. While most brandy was made in illegal stills, there were also some distilleries making legal apple brandy. The following is an 1879 advertisement from the *Raleigh Observer* newspaper, placed by R. A. Bynum of Pitt County, North Carolina: "The popularity which my Old Apple Brandy has obtained induced me to bring it more generally to notice. You may be sure of its mild, stimulating, invigorating qualities from a medicinal point of view. It is receiving the unqualified endorsement of men eminent in the medical profession. . . . I am now prepared to ship it in bottles running six to the gallon at $1.25 per bottle." The reference to the medicinal value of brandy is not totally facetious. In the nineteenth century brandy was used extensively in both professional and home medicine for heart problems, circulation disorders, and rheumatism.

## Cider Vinegar

If you can make cider—hard cider, that is—you can make cider vinegar, and thousands of rural southerners did so. They needed vinegar, lots of it, to pickle foods because pickling was an important food preservation method before the advent of canning and refrigeration. And besides, southerners had to have a splash of pepper vinegar on their collards and turnip greens! Frances Hinton, who was raised in eastern North Carolina in the 1920s and 1930s, remembers homemade vinegar: "I can remember six or seven barrels of it," she recently wrote me. The grandfather of my friend, Annie Boles, had a 2,300-tree orchard in Stokes County, North Carolina, at the turn of the century. He made large quantities of vinegar, selling it to merchants in nearby towns. Mrs. Boles helped me rediscover the Smith Seedling apple, which originated in her family and which was grown in her grandfather's orchard.

Perhaps a few words are in order about the science of vinegar. Vinegar contains acetic acid and is made when a certain kind of bacteria, called acetobacter, lives and grows in an alcoholic liquid and changes the alcohol to acetic acid. Store-bought cider vinegar has 5 percent acetic acid in it. It is important to note that the acetobacter bacteria use alcohol, not sugar, to make acetic acid. That is why hard cider is required for vinegar making; hard cider has over 5 percent alcohol in it, whereas sweet cider has none. In addition to alcohol, acetobacter needs one other essential ingredient to make vinegar—air. Unlike yeasts, which work best without air, acetobacter must have oxygen, and the more air it has, the faster it changes alcohol to acetic acid. Commercial cider vinegar is made by pouring hard cider into the top of a large and tall steel column filled with something to provide a lot of surface area, such as wood chips. Air is pumped into the bottom of the column and bubbles up through it. Acetobacter live on the surface of the wood chips and feast on the hard cider trickling down the column, greatly aided by the air bubbling up the column. In a matter of hours, large quantities of vinegar can begin to be drawn off the bottom of the column in a continuous process.

Rural southerners did not use columns to make vinegar; they used wooden barrels. A barrel would be one-third to one-half filled with hard cider and turned on its side (to increase the surface area of the cider inside). The bung would be removed and the bung hole covered with a cloth. Acetobacter naturally present in the cider would slowly begin growing on the surface of the cider and eventually would form a thick mat on the surface. Within three to nine months, depending on the temperature, all of the alcohol would be converted to acetic acid. Because of the preservative properties of vinegar, a barrel could be kept for years by rural families as the vinegar was slowly used up.

The Horse Apple, which ripens in midsummer, was a great southern favorite for both cider and vinegar. Perhaps this is explained by the following discourse on southern vinegar making from *American Pomology* (1867).

> In the South, where the summers are long and hot, it [cider vinegar] is made by fermenting new cider in a warm room or shed fronting the south or exposed to the sun with the bung loose in the open air; under ordinary circumstances, without any other aid, it will become good vinegar in the course of a few weeks, especially if it be made in the early part of the Summer.
>
> The apples best adapted to this use are the early seedlings or any early ripening apples that are not so good for other purposes. The cider for vinegar should be made from ripe, sound apples as early in Summer as the maturity of the fruit will allow—and it may be put in sour barrels. It is not proper to rack it off at all, nor does it need any foreign ingredients to add to its strength or body. . . . By Fall it may be good vinegar, but it will not attain perfection until the next Summer.

Mabel Brinkley was a great source to me of apple lore as practiced on her family farm in Virginia early in the 1900s. Her recall was sharp with precise details. Her family made cider vinegar using a "pummy-hopper." The pummy-hopper may have been unique to the area near Elk Creek, Virginia, as it is not mentioned in any old pomological references. Mrs. Brinkley asked her octogenarian cousin John Green, who lived near Elk Creek, to make me a scale model of a pummy-hopper!

The pummy-hopper was a wooden trough on legs, about three feet long or longer and standing waist-high. The trough was placed so one end was slightly lower than the other, and a crock was put under the lip of the lower end. The wooden vee of the trough was lined with clean straw standing upright along the sloping sides. Pomace (the pulp left over from cider making) and apple peelings were used to fill the trough, which was then covered with a piece of tin. Within a day or two, vinegar would begin dripping out the bottom end, where it was strained through a cloth over the crock. Mrs. Brinkley remembered the vinegar as being of very high quality. The name "pummy-hopper" refers, of course, to the use of pomace in it. It was a quick way to make cider vinegar because the surface of the straw provided a large surface for the acetobacter to colonize, and the hollow cores of the straw provided air to the bacteria.

Homemade cider vinegar is tasty and easy to make in small batches in the modern kitchen. Fresh-squeezed sweet cider or a gallon of purchased apple juice can be used, but be sure it has had no sulfur dioxide added as a preservative. Stores selling organic foods are good sources of unadulterated apple cider. If you are using pasteurized apple juice or cider, you will also need "vinegar mother," which is a starter batch of acetobacter. This can be bought from stores selling winemaking supplies or obtained from friends who make vinegar. Cider made from your own apples will always have acetobacter in it from the skins of the apples.

The first step to vinegar is to make hard cider as previously described. This process takes about a week in the kitchen at room temperature. If working with a small batch of cider, use a glass gallon jug filled almost full and capped loosely (or use an airlock). After a week, filter the gallon of fermented cider (now hard cider) through cheesecloth or a coffee filter and divide the liquid between two glass gallon jugs, each about half full. Add vinegar mother to each jug, if needed, and tie a piece of cloth over the necks. Return the jugs to a warm place and allow them to sit undisturbed for at least three months. A thick, leathery mat of acetobacter will slowly form on the surface of the hard cider as the bacteria multiply. Remember that these bacteria must have air, so never tightly close up the vinegar jugs. After three months taste the vinegar and, if you think it ready, filter it again (to remove gross sediment; it will not become completely clear) and bottle it. Bottles of homemade vinegar should have plastic caps or cork stoppers, never metal. Fill the bottles completely full and be prepared for a little film of acetobacter to form on the top of some bottles (completely harmless and proof of your labors). Alternatively, the filtered vinegar can be heated to 165°F for five minutes to kill the acetobacter. Incidentally, you can also use red and white wines to make your own vinegar, treating the wines like hard cider and adding vinegar mother and about one part water to three parts wine at the beginning of the process.

### Apple Butter

The making of apple butter by rural families was common in every apple-growing area of this country, most certainly including the South. Often it was made in large quantities, which served as an occasion to gather together family and friends. Many willing hands made easier the necessary task of continuously stirring apple butter as it cooked down to prevent it from sticking or scorching in the pot.

Some southern families were lucky enough to own a copper or brass kettle, esteemed for the high-quality fruit butters it made. Others used an iron pot out of doors over an open fire. Different recipes were used, but most called first for boiling down apple cider to half its original volume. This cooked-down cider added apple flavor and aroma to apple butter and acted as a sweetener in the days when store-bought sugar was an expensive luxury.

Certain apples, preferably those that were rather pulpy and aromatic, were favored for apple butter. Wolf River and Buff apples are both mentioned in old publications as being good for this purpose, and Winesaps were often used. The apples were cored, pared and quartered, and added to the boiling cider. Long wooden paddles, usually made of hickory and having holes cut through the blade, were used to stir the boiling liquid. Sometimes copper or silver coins were added to the kettle to be agitated by the paddle and help prevent sticking. It was not unusual for a large pot of apple butter to require twelve hours of continuous stirring, a task that became more strenuous as the liquid thickened. The stirrer might repeat this old rhyme: "Twice around the rim and once through the middle. That's the way to stir the apple butter kettle."

Near the end of the cooking process, spices were added plus sugar or sorghum syrup if needed for sweetening. Ground cinnamon (or cinnamon sticks) was the usual spice used, but ground cloves were often added also. (A letter to me from Virginia says oil of cinnamon and oil of cloves from a drugstore make a smoother and purer-tasting apple butter.) The apple butter was done when a spoonful would stick to an inverted plate or when no watery juice oozed from a spoonful placed on a plate or dish.

Before the early 1900s when canning became a common practice, apple butter was preserved in crocks covered with thick paper and stored in a cool, dry place. Spread on a hot biscuit, apple butter was—and still is—the ultimate apple treat for southerners.

Let me urge those who grow apples to try their hand at making apple butter. The ubiquitous crockpot, often available at yard and garage sales for a few dollars, has removed the need for tedious stirring. Apple butter simmered uncovered on the high setting in a crockpot will not scorch and needs stirring only about once an hour (because it tends to dry out on top). It can even be cooked overnight on the low setting. Any apples will do, and some of the best apple butter I have ever eaten was made from a mixture of many kinds of apples.

PART TWO

# Old Southern Apples

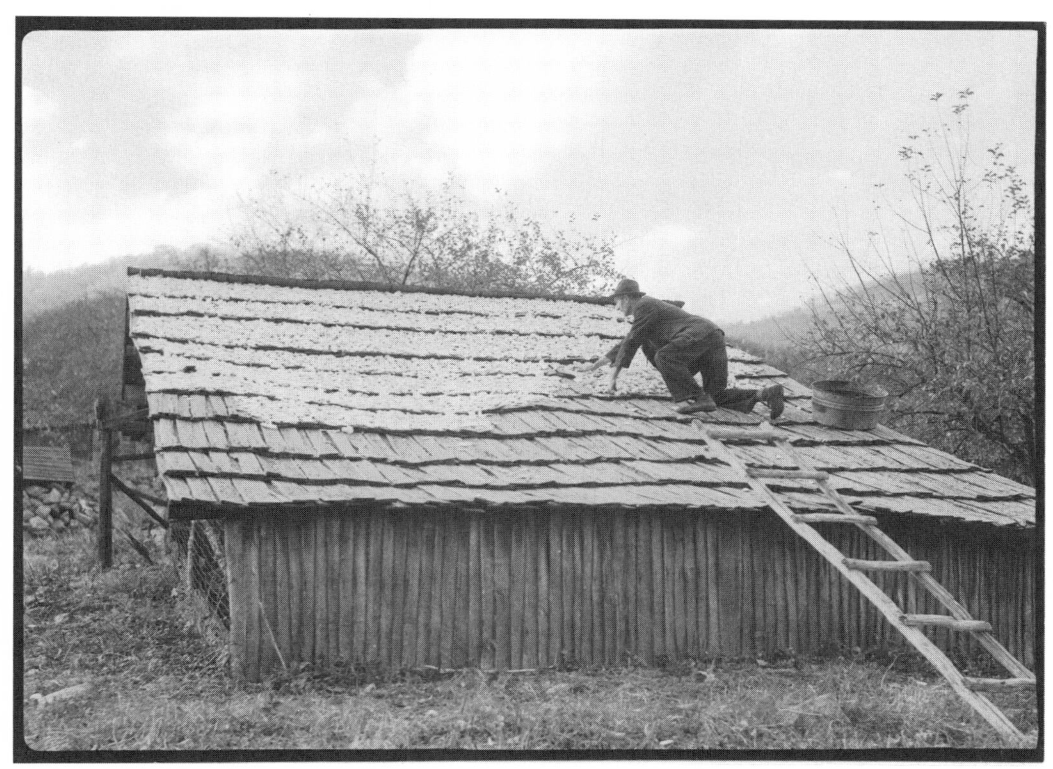

# "The Crossed Apple"

*Louise Bogan*

I've come to give you fruit from out my orchard,
Of wide report.
I have trees there that bear me many apples.
Of every sort:

Clear, streaked; red and russet; green and golden;
Sour and sweet.
This apple's from a tree yet unbeholden,
Where two kinds meet, . . .

Eat it; and you will taste more than the fruit:
The blossom, too,
The sun, the air, the darkness at the root,
The rain, the dew, . . .

FOUR

# Descriptions of Old Southern Apples

This part of *Old Southern Apples* describes about 1,800 varieties of southern apples, of which some 1,600 originated in the South. The others were sold by southern nurseries but originated in Europe or in the North. The descriptions that follow are divided into two chapters. The first, chapter 5, describes varieties of apples that are still available, and the second, chapter 6, describes those that are presumed extinct.

Perhaps 400 hundred southern apple varieties are available from the nurseries listed in the back of this book. Most can be purchased as young trees. A few are available only as scionwood to be used for grafting. Availability, however, is tenuous and changes as nurseries open, close, or change their inventories.

Roughly 1,200 named southern apple varieties are considered to be extinct because they are not listed by current nurseries, and efforts to find living trees have failed. An apple listed as extinct can be rediscovered. Since the first edition of this book was published in 1995, about 50 southern apple varieties listed as extinct have been found, and the search for others continues. We may mourn for the extinct southern apples, but let us also count our blessings; many fine apple varieties are ours for the growing.

## What Is an "Old" Southern Apple?

In 1988, when I began compiling information on southern apples, preliminary to writing the first edition of this book, I had to decide where to draw the line between old apple varieties and new ones. My decision was to go back sixty years to 1928. Although this is an arbitrary date, it is a reasonable one. By 1928 subsistence farming in the South was gone except for pockets mostly in the Appalachians. Southern farms were being consolidated and mechanized, and farm orchards were removed as unneeded or as impediments to machinery. Few southerners remained interested in finding and propagating promising chance seedlings, and seedling orchards had not been planted for over fifty years. After 1928 the introduction of new southern apple varieties fell to almost zero except for some commercial apple-breeding work done at the Virginia Polytechnic Institute, the University of Arkansas, and the USDA Research Laboratory at Byron, Georgia. A handful of southern apples introduced since 1928 are included in this book if they have qualities that recommend them to southern apple growers.

## Confusion in Apple Names

The nomenclature of southern apples was confused a hundred years ago, and it remains confused today. Back then it was usually possible to compare apples in the flesh, so to speak, to see if they were identical. Today, when close to 80 percent of southern apples are extinct, a side-by-side comparison is often no longer possible.

Problems with apple names arose because for hundreds of years southern rural families were isolated by both distance and poor roads. Named apple trees were acquired from neighbors or salesmen, but the original names were soon garbled or forgotten. The varieties were then renamed using the new owner's name, a garbled version of the original name, or a characteristic of the apple such as color, size, or time of ripening. As the frontier moved westward, southerners took young apple trees with them in their wagons, and old varieties acquired new names in new places.

Other processes of confusion were also at work. Some nurseries changed the names of apple varieties to make them more salable. Tree peddlers, faced with a request for an apple variety they did not have with them, may have relabeled a tree to avoid losing a sale.

To make matters worse, different apples often

acquired the same name. It seems that any southern apple variety with a russet skin would eventually be renamed Rusty Coat. Likewise, there was an almost irresistible urge to apply the name Striped June to all striped apples ripening in June.

For some of the more popular and widely grown southern apples, names piled upon names over the years. The Nickajack apple is the winner in name confusion, having forty-two synonyms. Just behind Nickajack is the McAfee apple with thirty-three synonyms.

The American Pomological Society was founded in 1848 and met every two years to evaluate new fruit varieties and to encourage the fruit industry in America. This organization adopted rules to try to bring order out of fruit nomenclature chaos, and these rules were later followed by the USDA. One of these rules reads: "Under no ordinary circumstances should more than a single name be employed." Thus, officially, the Magnum Bonum apple became Bonum, and the Edwards' Winter apple became Edwards. The American Pomological Society could pass its rules about single names for apples, but southerners held on to their longer and more descriptive names. Even today, in the twilight of the southern apple, rural southerners speak of the *Magnum* Bonum and the Edwards' *Winter* and use all the other longer, lovelier, more descriptive apple names.

The Division of Pomology, established in the USDA in 1886, did all it could to clear up the confusion in apple nomenclature. In 1888 the division noted that it had received 10,000 specimens of fruit for identification. "The experience of this office proves beyond question that there is, even in the oldest settled parts of the country, a considerable degree of ignorance of the names of standard varieties of fruit. It is through such ignorance that local names are given to old varieties, thus multiplying synonyms and creating confusion." In 1904 the Division of Pomology published USDA Bulletin No. 56, *Nomenclature of the Apple*, largely prepared by W. H. Ragan of that office. This monumental work, twelve years in preparation, lists over 14,000 names and synonyms of American apples and crabapples and is still an indispensable reference for anyone interested in old apple varieties.

## Family Apples, Local Apples, Historical Apples

In the many years Edith and I searched for and studied old southern apples, we devised a classification system based on the origin and subsequent history of each apple.

*Family Apple*: A unique apple passed down within a single family like a family heirloom. Almost always, root sprouts have been the means of propagation, starting with a seedling tree grown by a family ancestor in the 1800s or early 1900s. The Shumacher/Shoemaker apple, passed down in two branches of the Fairey family of South Carolina for perhaps 200 years, is a good example of a family apple.

*Local Apple*: For almost three hundred years, most southern farm orchards were started as seedling orchards. It was common for farm families to swap root sprouts of the best seedling trees and eventually acquire a good orchard. The distribution of these desirable root sprouts could be as small as a few families in a rural community or as large as several counties.

Like family apples, local apples were never recorded or described in a written historical record. Sometimes the story of the origin of local and family apples has been passed down orally; sometimes it has been lost. Lacy and Aunt Rachel are just two of the many local apples described in this book.

*Historical Apple*: If there is a written record of an old apple, no matter how obscure this record may be, the apple is classified as a historical apple. This one qualification separates historical apples from family and local apples, which have no written record that Edith and I have been able to find.

Records about old southern apples have not been easy to ferret out. Years have been spent by Edith and me in library stacks and corresponding with elderly southerners. Every little piece of information has been saved. For example, Edith typed every apple listed in almost three hundred old southern nursery catalogs into a database, eventually compiling over 10,000 entries.

## Using This Book to Identify Old Apple Varieties

Often in our search for old southern apples, Edith and I find trees at abandoned homesteads, the trees still bearing fruit. Often, too, we receive boxes of apples through the mail accompanied by a letter asking "what kind of apple is this?" Unless an unknown apple is easily recognizable, trying to identify it can be tedious and frustrating. For several reasons this book will be of limited help in identifying unknown apples.

Most importantly, most of the thousands of unidentified old apple trees in the South are chance seedlings. As we know, each seedling apple tree is genetically unique, unlike any other apple tree, and unidentified seedlings have no name. You cannot identify and find the history of an unnamed seedling apple tree from this book because it has no history or identity.

Second, there are so many historical old varieties that the sheer number of possibilities is overwhelming. Third, there are incomplete or nonexistent descriptions of many of the historical old varieties. And finally, there are only minor differences between many apple varieties. (There must be two hundred different red- or red-striped apples that ripen in September and October.)

What the descriptions in this book can do, and do well, is to confirm the identity of a historical apple variety for which a name or a synonym is still known. Some years ago a friend in Tennessee discovered an old apple being grown there under the name Ozark Pippin. A quick look in the index to this book shows that Ozark Pippin is a synonym of a Tennessee apple named Deaderick, long thought to be extinct. Is the newfound Ozark Pippin the Deaderick? A careful comparison of the actual fruit to the written description of the Deaderick apple confirms that the Ozark Pippin is indeed the Deaderick! Apple names or synonyms, however incomplete or garbled, are vitally important in identifying old varieties. Using these as a starting point and applying common sense, some sleuthing through this book can often clear up the identity of an old apple.

## Synonyms Listed for Each Apple Variety

Synonyms are listed in parentheses after the official or most important name of each apple variety. The synonyms are in no particular order, and no attempt has been made to include all the variations in spelling. Rules for spelling were very relaxed in the 1800s, and all labels and correspondence were handwritten. (Few of our ancestors wrote in a beautiful Spencerian script; an illegible scrawl was more typical.) Thus, spelling variations piled up. I also have not included most foreign names for southern apples.

## Variations in Apples of the Same Variety

Written descriptions of apple varieties must be used with common sense and caution. There is great variation among apples of the same variety, even among apples growing on the same tree! The age of the tree (apples on old trees are often smaller and atypical) and the position of the apple on the tree (apples growing in sunlight are more highly colored than shaded apples) affect fruit characteristics. Soil and climate affect apple color, shape, and ripening date. For example, a study in 1910 showed that northern-grown Ben Davis apples are far more elongated than Ben Davis apples grown in the South. See also Pryor's Red. What I am saying is that none of the written fruit characteristics are set in concrete. If you are using a fruit description in this book to help identify an apple variety, always select several well-colored apples from different parts of the tree, and remember that a mismatch in one or two characteristics does not invalidate an identity.

## Explanation of the Technical Descriptions

When viewed from the side, the primary apple shapes are *roundish*, *oblate*, and *oblong* as shown in the drawings below. If an apple tapers noticeably toward the basin, it is said to be *conical*. Thus an oblong apple that tapers is described as oblong conical, and a roundish apple that tapers is roundish conical, etc. Many apple varieties have fruit that is noticeably segmented from

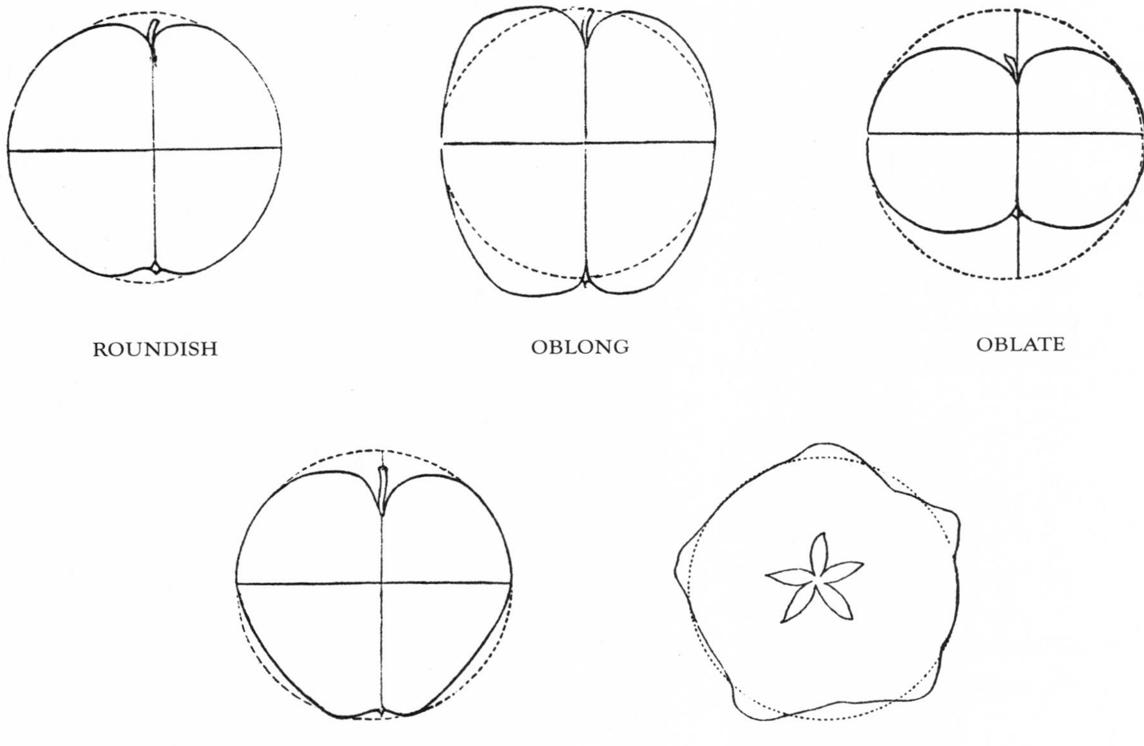


top to bottom; in written descriptions this is described as "ribbed" or "lobed."

The *cavity* is the depression that holds the stem, and the *basin* is the depression on the other end that contains the frilly calyx, the blossom remnant. Sometimes the shape of the cavity or the basin is described as "acute" or "gradually sloped." These are opposite terms; *acute* means that the slope of the depression is abrupt and steep, whereas *gradually sloped* means that the cavity or basin widens gradually, without abruptness.

The ripening times for available apple varieties is the time the apples ripen in orchards in central North Carolina and north central South Carolina (both Zone 7B).

For the extinct varieties, ripening times are taken from old references. Thus one will often see statements such as: "Ripe October–February." This means that apples picked in late autumn, when firm ripe, will keep in edible condition until about February, if properly stored. In the old days, proper storage usually meant a well-constructed root cellar or pit. Occasionally an apple will be described as "ripe January–March" or something similar. This does not mean that the apples are picked in January! It does mean that fruit picked firm ripe in late fall and properly stored will mellow and improve in flavor, with the best eating quality from January through March.

The authors of old pomological texts always rated the quality of apples, using words such as *poor, good, excellent*, and so on. I firmly believe that taste, like beauty, lies in the eyes (or taste buds) of the beholder. I do not presume to be an arbiter of apple quality, and I certainly would not quote a long-dead (and usually northern) pomologist concerning the quality of southern apples. There are other problems: How, for example, does one rate the quality of Hewe's Crab? This apple is not for eating but makes the best cider of any American apple. How, also, would one rate Maiden's Blush, which is too tart for most palates but is, perhaps, the finest American apple for drying? Apple quality, therefore, is complicated and personal. I will let the apples speak for themselves.

## The National Apple Collection

The largest collection of apples in the world is right here in the United States. This collection is maintained by the Plant Genetic Resources Unit (PGRU), a part of the USDA, located on the grounds of Cornell University's New York State Agricultural Experiment Station in Geneva, New York.

A total of about 7,000 apple varieties are maintained by the PGRU, with some 2,510 of these being field-grown in duplicate. (The numbers cited herein change frequently.) The remaining apple varieties are kept by the PGRU as seeds, buds, or pollen in cold storage or cryogenic storage (liquid nitrogen).

About 1,700 of the field-grown apples are named varieties, and some of these are antique or heirloom American apples. Of the 436 apple varieties currently in the Southern Heritage Apple Orchard at Horne Creek Farm, 48 were grafted using scions from the PGRU collection in Geneva. A list of these can be found below.

It must be understood that the PGRU collects and maintains apples for their *germplasm*, unique genetic traits that can be used by plant breeders to develop new apples and apple rootstocks. The PGRU makes no attempt to collect all American heirloom and modern apples, keeping only samples that show the diversity of American apples or that contain traits useful to plant breeders.

It has become obvious that modern American and European apple varieties share a narrow gene pool. The apple seeds that reached Europe perhaps three thousand years ago contained only a fraction of the genetic material developed by the wild apples of Asia over millions of years of evolution. The genes left behind in Kazakhstan, China, and elsewhere control traits that will be useful in developing new apples and rootstocks with disease and insect resistance, late blooming time (to avoid frost), and other desirable qualities.

From 1989 to 1996, the USDA sent seven expeditions to Europe and Asia to collect additional apple genetic material in wild apples. These trips more than doubled the genetic diversity in apples available to plant breeders.

Most wild apple genes were brought back as seeds by the USDA expeditions, but a few scions were also collected. About 950 seed-lots of different central Asian wild apples are kept in cold storage by the PGRU, with 310 of these seed-lots being grown as multiple trees for evaluation.

Many of the wild seedlings show significant resistance to apple scab, a serious apple disease, and a high percentage of seedlings from Kazakhstan, Armenia, Turkey, and China have resistance to the devastating disease of fire blight. Other useful traits will undoubtedly be found as more of the wild apples are field-grown for evaluation. Apple breeders are already at work incorporating these traits into new and better apple varieties and rootstocks.

**Apple Scions Obtained by the Southern Heritage Apple Orchard from the Plant Genetic Resources Unit**

Arkansas (Blacktwig)
Arkansas Black
Ben Davis
Black Ben Davis
Blairmont
Chesapeake
Collins June
Crimson Beauty
Early Harvest
Fallawater
Gloria Mundi
Grimes Golden
Hawkeye (Delicious)
Holly
Hoover
Ingram
King David
Lady
Liveland Raspberry
Maiden's Blush
Mother
Northern Spy (Oberle)
Oliver
Paragon
Potomac
Red Astrachan
Red Bietigheimer
Red Limbertwig
Roman Stem
Roxbury Russet
Salome
San Jacinto
Shenandoah
Smokehouse
Spencer Seedless
Starr
Stayman
Sweet Winesap
Turley Winesap
Twenty Ounce
Vandevere
White Winter Pearmain
Winesap
Wolf River
Wrixparent
Yellow Newtown Pippin
Yellow Transparent
York

# FIVE

# Available Southern Apples

**ABRAM** (Father Abram, Father Abraham, Red Abram, Abraham, Abram's Pippin): The origin of Abram is unknown. Early references say it originated in either Virginia or South Carolina, and it was listed in 1755 in a Virginia newspaper by nurseryman William Smith of Surry County, Virginia. Abram was grown extensively at one time in North Carolina, Virginia, Kentucky, and even Illinois where the fruit was prized as an excellent winter keeper and was useful for cider. Abram has been described as "not fit to eat before January," which means it mellows and improves in quality during storage. The tree is a regular bearer and holds its apples well.

Fruit small to medium, oblate to roundish oblate, ribbed; skin waxy (or greasy after long storage), greenish yellow, shaded and splashed with dull or brownish red and often rather grayish in appearance; dots inconspicuous, numerous, light-colored; stem long in a deep, bronze russet cavity; calyx closed; basin shallow, wide, wavy; flesh yellowish white, dense, fine-grained, subacid. Ripe October/November. Catalog listings: MD, VA, NC, GA, AL, KY (1844–1904). ❖ **Plate 1.**

**ACCORDIAN**: Brought to my attention by Clinton D. Vernon of Rockingham County, North Carolina, and a perfect example of what I call a "family apple." A family apple is a variety that originated as a seedling with a rural family and that has been passed down in that family, usually by root sprouts, like a family heirloom. The Accordian apple has been esteemed by the Vernon family and propagated by root sprouts for members of the family for over a hundred years. It likely gets its name from the lobes or ribs that run from top to bottom of the apples, giving the fruit a somewhat pleated appearance.

Fruit medium or above, slightly oblate conical, lobed; skin light yellowish green with a pinkish red blush mostly on the top of the apple; dots numerous, whitish and russet, sometimes with a red areole; stem short in a deep, russeted cavity; calyx usually closed; basin medium depth, corrugated; flesh slightly yellowish, fine-grained, juicy, crisp, subacid. Ripe August. No catalog listings.

**ALEXANDER** (Emperor Alexander, Aport, Russian Emperor, Russian Monarch?): A Russian apple, it is one of perhaps four hundred Russian apple varieties brought to the United States during the nineteenth century in the search for cold-hardy apple trees. The exact date Alexander first reached this country is unknown, but it was before 1830.

Alexander was sold extensively by southern nurseries because it is large and showy and a good cooking apple. After 1900, Alexander was largely replaced in nursery catalogs by its equally large and showy seedling progeny Wolf River. Alexander is particularly striking at blossom time because of its large blossoms. The tree bears when quite young, but it is not very productive and is susceptible to fire blight. The fruit often drops before ripe.

Fruit large to very large, roundish to slightly oblate, conical, symmetrical; skin rather thick, tough, smooth, often entirely overspread with red or striped and splashed with carmine; dots small and scattered; stem medium to short and rather thick in an acute, deep, broad, russeted cavity, occasionally lipped; calyx usually open; basin rather small, deep, medium width, symmetrical; flesh nearly white, firm, coarse, moderately crisp, tender, juicy, subacid. Ripe August/September and does not keep well. Catalog listings: MD, VA, NC, SC, LA, TN, KY, TX, AR (1836–1928).

**ALEXANDER'S ICE CREAM** (Ice Cream?): Sold by North Carolina nurseries from 1893 to 1915. From the 1895 catalog of the J. Van Lindley Nursery: "Introduced by W. E. Alexander of Mecklenburg County, North Carolina, and described by him as being of good size, striped with red. A real beauty. Ripens from 20th of June to 1st of September. An annual bearer. Has not missed a crop in fifteen years. Tree an extra fine grower, ornamental as well as useful. Sells readily at $1 per bushel while other apples only bring 25 cents."

A tree called "Ice Cream" by its owner, Hazel Williams, was found by the late Dr. L. R. Littleton in 1996 near Eli Whitney, North Carolina. This tree was purchased in 1946 from the Jerome Lindley Nursery near Graham, North Carolina, and was removed in 1997.

Fruit medium, roundish to oblong, very conical and pear-shaped, often irregular and oblique; skin pale greenish, dotted and striped with pale red, some apples mostly reddish; dots whitish, small to large; stem medium in a shallow, sometimes lipped and russeted cavity; calyx greenish, closed; basin small and shallow, often irregular; flesh pale yellow, moderately crisp, juicy, mildly sweet. Ripe July.

Warder (1867) describes a different apple named Ice Cream, of Kentucky origin, which is extinct. Fruit medium to large, oblate; skin yellow; flesh subacid. Ripe September. No catalog listings.

❦ **ALLUM** (Hallum, Rockingham Red, Alum): First mentioned as having been planted in a North Carolina orchard in 1843 where the fruit was valued for its keeping qualities. An 1874 letter from Joshua Lindley, the prominent North Carolina nurseryman, states that Hallum was the original name, being the name of the originator in Rockingham County, North Carolina. A few old trees still exist in Rockingham County, where this apple now is called Rockingham Red.

Fruit medium or below, roundish, irregular and often lopsided; skin rough, greenish, mostly covered with a purplish-red blush and scarf skin, often with a grayish bloom; dots numerous, tan; stem usually short in a deep, narrow, russeted cavity; calyx open, greenish; basin acute, deep, often cracked; flesh greenish, fine-grained, moderately juicy, crisp, subacid. Ripe September/October. Catalog listings: VA, NC (1859–67).

❦ **AMERICAN BEAUTY** (Sterling, Beauty of America): Originated in Sterling, Massachusetts, probably early in the 1800s. Tom Brown found a tree in McGrady, North Carolina, belonging to Freeman Royal.

Fruit large, round, obscurely ribbed; skin yellow mostly covered with red, darker red on the sunny side; dots numerous, tan and whitish; stem short to medium length in a deep, russeted cavity with rays of russet over the top of the apple; calyx closed; basin fairly deep and uneven; flesh yellowish, tender, juicy, mild subacid, aromatic. Ripe September. No catalog listings. ❖ **Plate 2.**

❦ **AMERICAN GOLDEN RUSSET** (Bullock Pippin, Golden Russet, Sheepnose, Fox Apple, Long Tom, Sheep's Snout, Crouch Apple?): Why is it that so many apple varieties that were popular in the South actually originated in New Jersey? A guess would be that New Jersey, with its extensive coastline, has a climate similar to the upper South. Whatever the reason, the fact remains that Winesap, Bevans' Favorite, American Summer Pearmain, Yellow Bellflower, and several other apples, all southern favorites, came from New Jersey. So did American Golden Russet, which originated in Burlington County before 1800.

This apple has had two lives under two different names. From 1836 to about 1870 it was listed in southern nursery catalogs as Bullock Pippin. From 1870 it was listed mostly as American Golden Russet with Bullock Pippin as a synonym.

Writing from his home in Ohio in 1876, the noted pomologist Dr. John Warder could hardly contain his enthusiasm for this apple: "This delicious table apple is a universal favorite with all who can appreciate delicacy of flavor and fineness of flesh in an apple. . . . The best I have seen were from the South and from sandstone soils."

There are several apples called Golden Russet, so one must be careful identifying apples with this name. Likewise there are different apples called Sheepnose, one of the synonyms of American Golden Russet. American Golden Russet was popular for making cider at one time because the high sugar content of this apple converts during fermentation to about 7 percent alcohol. The fruit is excellent also for fresh eating and drying. The tree is healthy but susceptible to cedar-apple rust and is often a biennial bearer.

Fruit below medium size, roundish, conical, symmetrical; skin completely overspread with "old gold" russet; dots numerous, small, obscure, russet; stem long and slender in an acute, rather deep and narrow cavity; calyx closed; basin small, shallow, wrinkled, often oblique; flesh tinged yellow, firm, fine-grained, crisp, tender, juicy, aromatic, subacid. Ripe September/October. Catalog listings: MD, VA, NC, SC, GA, KY (1836–1927).

❦ **AMERICAN SUMMER PEARMAIN** (Summer Pearmain, Early Summer Pearmain, Watkin's Early, American Pearmain, Pearmain): Described by Coxe (1817) and probably of New Jersey origin. The word *best* is the highest accolade bestowed upon an apple by pomologists, and it has been used often to describe the quality of American Summer Pearmain. Warder (1867) calls this apple "deliciously refreshing."

American Summer Pearmain was grown throughout the South on a variety of soils and was sold by southern nurseries well into the 1900s. Many southeners know this apple simply as "Pearmain." The tree is slow-growing but productive and ripens fruit gradually over a month or more. The fruit is excellent for both fresh eating and applesauce. The tree is susceptible to fire blight, and the fruit often cracks open on the tree or drops before ripe.

Fruit medium size or larger, variable in shape but usually rather oblong and slightly conical; skin mostly covered with obscure, dull purplish red stripes; dots numerous, minute, russet; stem short to medium in a deep, acute, russeted cavity; basin almost deep, quite abrupt, wrinkled; flesh yellow, very tender (fruit often bursts when it falls), juicy, crisp, aromatic, mild subacid. Ripe July/August in most of the South. Catalog listings: MD, VA, NC, GA, AL, MS, TN, KY, TX (1845–1928).

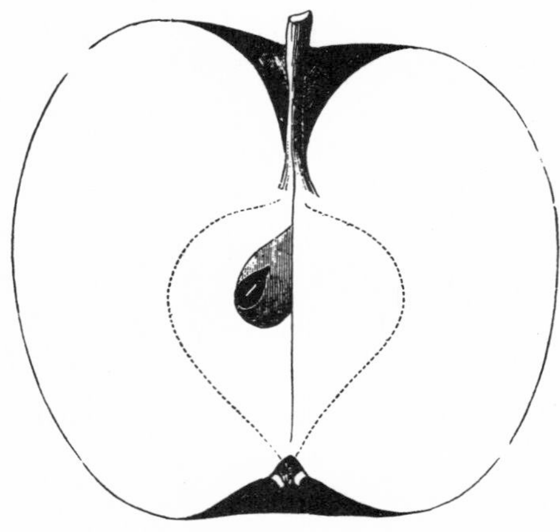

AMERICAN SUMMER PEARMAIN

❦ **AMY:** An old Stokes County, North Carolina, apple found by Fred Small of Greensboro, North Carolina.

Fruit below medium size; skin bright red, sometimes obscurely striped; dots numerous, white; stem short to medium length in a russeted cavity. Ripe late July. No catalog listings.

❦ **ANDY REED:** Grown in Cherokee County, North Carolina, for many years. The tree is reported to be very productive and disease-resistant. Scions were brought to me in 1995 by Gary Smith.

Fruit large, roundish to somewhat oblate, irregular in shape; skin almost entirely red; dots whitish, large, scattered; stem short in a russeted cavity. Ripe August. No catalog listings.

❦ **ARKANSAS BLACK:** The original tree, probably a Winesap seedling, grew in the orchard of a Mr. Brattwait, one mile northwest of Bentonville, Arkansas, and bore its first fruit about 1870.

Arkansas Black is a beautiful apple, a good keeper, and the fruit may have some resistance to the codling moth. Apples are rock-hard when first picked but soften and improve in flavor with storage. The tree is quite disease-resistant except to apple scab. A spur-type tree, which bears more heavily, is sold by several modern nurseries.

Fruit medium size, nearly perfectly round; skin covered with deep red, almost black; dots numerous, small, white; stem short to almost medium length in an acute, rather small, partly russeted, often lipped cavity; calyx closed; basin small, very shallow, slightly furrowed; flesh very firm (hard when picked), yellow, rather fine-grained, crisp, moderately juicy, sprightly subacid. Ripe October. Catalog listings: MD, VA, NC, SC, GA, TN, KY, LA, TX, AR (1890–1928).

**ARKANSAS SWEET:** Brought to notice when apples were sent to the USDA in 1905 by Henry Grabin of Scott County, Arkansas. In 1993 Ron Joyner discovered an apple of this name listed by Seed Savers Exchange and being grown by John Kenyon of Lacon, Illinois. Mr. Kenyon describes Arkansas Sweet as very sweet and crunchy and quite popular with his orchard customers. It ripens in late October in Illinois and is only a fair winter keeper.

Fruit medium, roundish; skin mostly covered with dark red with indistinct darker stripes; dots scattered, large, whitish, and small, gray; stem short to medium length ending in a knob in a medium size, shallow, fully russeted cavity; calyx open or closed; basin wide, gradually sloped; flesh whitish, moderately crisp, not very sweet. Ripe late September/October. No catalog listings. ❖ **Plate 3.**

**ARTHUR:** The origin of the Arthur apple was told to me by the late Roscoe and Ruth Oliver, who lived in Ashe County, North Carolina, and who had a tree growing beside their home. About 1870 preacher Elihu Tucker's son, Arthur, pulled a switch from a wild apple tree to use as a riding crop. At the end of the day he stuck the switch into the ground where it rooted. This tree became known locally as the Arthur apple. Danny Harvey of Ashe County, North Carolina, still grows this apple. This variety is different from the Arthur apple of Iowa origin described by Ragan (1905) and Beach (1905). No description. No catalog listings.

**ASTERUS:** Found by Tom Brown near Roan Mountain State Park in western North Carolina where the local people highly prize it. This may be the old English cooking apple D'Asterus, which predates the 1830s, and which is described by Downing (1872) as "large, roundish, conic, yellow striped with red, sweet, dry." The apple found by Tom Brown does not much fit Downing's description.

Fruit medium, roundish to somewhat oblate; skin bright red with faint, darker red stripes; cavity greenish russeted; calyx closed. Ripe late July/August. No catalog listings.

**ATHA:** Joyce Neighbors, a friend in Gadsden, Alabama, found this apple and the story behind it.

Sometime before 1900 Russell L. Baker moved from California to Baileyton, Alabama, to develop seedless grapes, but he also experimented with peaches and apples. He crossed northern and southern apple varieties and planted 2,275 seedlings in his experimental orchard from which he chose 42 trees to be listed in the catalog of his Empire Nursery.

Atha is supposed to be a cross of Yellow Transparent × Red Astrachan. It is said that Atha Warnick (d. 1906), the wife of one of Mr. Baker's employees, made the cross. One publication says: "Fruit firmer, ripens six weeks later and less tendency to biennial bearing than Yellow Transparent." As grown here, it very closely resembles Yellow Transparent. *See also* July Delicious.

Fruit very large, roundish conical to almost oblong conical, irregular, lobed; skin pale yellow, darker yellow on the sunny side; dots numerous, submerged; stem short in a compressed, greenish or russeted, very irregular cavity; calyx slightly open, greenish; basin abrupt and deep. Ripe late June/early July.

**AUNT CORA'S YARD APPLE/AUNT CORA'S FIELD APPLE:** Aunt Cora Gibson (b. 1878) died at age ninety-seven after a lifetime as a well-known black midwife in Bath County, Virginia. Her father grew these trees from seeds while a slave to a cruel master in Bath County. (One story is that when the former slave owner died after the Civil War, he was so hated by blacks and whites alike that no one came to his funeral. In final revenge for his cruelty, his former slaves buried him in an unmarked grave in the slave cemetery.) Dr. L. R. Littleton found these trees in Mountain Grove, Virginia, and traced their history. Of the two varieties, Aunt Cora's Field Apple (described below) is much higher in quality than the larger, yellow (with a blush) Yard Apple and the tree bears heavily.

Fruit below medium to almost small, roundish to slightly oblate, flattened on the ends; skin smooth, greenish yellow at the calyx end but otherwise almost completely covered with red with faint darker red stripes and some irregular russet splotches; dots grayish and some are russet; stem medium length in an acute, rather deep, pale russet cavity with russet rays over the top of the apple; calyx closed or slightly open; basin wide; flesh whitish, moderately juicy, not very crisp, fine-grained, nutty flavor, subacid to almost sweet. Ripe October and a good keeper. No catalog listings.

❦ **AUNT RACHEL/RACHEL:** Very early in my searches for old southern apples, I visited Roy Kellam in my county (Chatham County, North Carolina) on Piney Grove Church Road. He gave me scions from a tree he called Aunt Rachel, which I later found growing at other places in my county under the name Rachel. It is a true Chatham County apple not grown elsewhere, but the story of its origin has apparently faded away. I still wonder about the identity of "Rachel." This is an excellent early apple that ripens over several weeks in July.

Fruit medium, oblate, lopsided; skin pale yellow mostly covered with many broken, thin red stripes; dots scattered, whitish; stem almost short to medium length in a narrow, occasionally russeted cavity; calyx usually closed; basin medium in width and depth; flesh pale greenish, juicy, subacid. Ripe July. No catalog listings.

❦ **AUNT SALLY** (Aunt Sallie's Everbearing?, Potts?): Sold by the Cedar Cove Nursery in Yadkin County, North Carolina, from 1875 to 1902, and an apple named Aunt Sallie's Everbearing was sold at about the same time by another North Carolina nursery. In 1992 Frank Smith of Raleigh, North Carolina, brought me scions from an old Aunt Sally apple tree growing in Mecklenburg County. One story is that Sally Caroline Ridings brought this apple from Virginia to Alleghany County, North Carolina, in 1824 when she married Abraham Philips. Her female descendants were given root sprouts to start their own trees.

Fruit medium to large; skin mostly red but heavily splotched with golden russet, which can cover most of the apple; dots numerous, russet, areole; stem medium length in a grayish tan, russeted, deep cavity with russet extending outside the cavity; flesh tender, subacid. Ripe late September/October.

❦ **AUTUMN STRAWBERRY** (Late Strawberry, Fall Strawberry, Strawberry, English Strawberry, Forsyth's Seedling): Although of New York origin before 1848, this apple was sold by ten southern nurseries stretching over a sixty-year period. The 1893 catalog of the J. Van Lindley Nursery, Greensboro, North Carolina, states that it "was shown at our state fair in 1882 and was the finest looking apple on exhibition. Everyone who saw it was amazed at its beauty." In the North this is an autumn apple; in the South it ripens in late summer.

Fruit medium or larger, roundish to slightly oblong, conical, slightly ribbed; skin almost entirely striped and splashed with light and dark red; dots small, light-colored, inconspicuous; stem slender and about an inch long in a deep, usually broad, furrowed, sometimes russeted cavity; calyx open or partly open; basin deep, corrugated; flesh yellowish, fine-grained, crisp, tender, juicy, subacid. Ripe August in North Carolina, September in western Virginia. Catalog listings: MD, VA, NC, SC, GA, AL, KY, AR (1856–1917).

❦ **BALD MOUNTAIN** (Black Mountain?): The 1903 meeting of the Georgia State Horticultural Society discussed promising apples for the state. A Colonel Wade said, "I would like to add to the list the Bald Mountain apple. It originated in North Carolina and they have been bringing them down through Rabun and Habersham counties for the last eight years. It ripens late and is a good keeper."

This brief and obscure discussion is the only written record of the Bald Mountain apple. In March 1989 I received a letter from Charles W. Nolen of Franklin, North Carolina, telling me that he had Bald Mountain as well as several other rare old apples in his orchard. Mr. Nolen said that Bald Mountain originated as a seedling on Wayah Bald Mountain in Macon County about a hundred years ago. George Crawford, one of the first settlers in that area, found the tree already growing there. This is a very late-ripening apple that keeps well.

Fruit medium or above, roundish, flattened on the ends, slightly conical; skin mostly covered with bright red and a few faint, broken stripes; dots large, scattered, irregular, white and russet; stem medium length in a deep, narrow, russeted cavity; calyx greenish, open; basin very wide, gradually sloped; flesh greenish or yellowish white, fine-grained, juicy, mild subacid. Ripe October/November. No catalog listings.

❦ **BALDWIN** (Woodpecker, Pecker, Butters, Red Baldwin, Felch, Steele's Red Winter): In 1904 S. A. Beach could write in his landmark two-volume work, *The Apples of New York*, "The Baldwin is preeminently the leading variety in the commercial orchards of New York, New England, certain regions in southern Canada, in the southern peninsula of Michigan and on the clay soils of northern Ohio." At this time Baldwin had held its premier commercial position in the Northeast for over fifty years and would continue to do so until after World War I. Beginning in 1918 several terrible winters killed millions of Baldwin trees, and these were replaced with more cold-hardy varieties, especially McIntosh in New England and New York. Another important factor in the commercial decline of the Baldwin is its tendency to be a biennial bearer (a heavy crop one year followed by a light crop the next). McIntosh bears full crops each year. Baldwin is a triploid, having an extra set of chromosomes, and thus has sterile pollen. It is very resistant to cedar-apple rust.

In the South, except in the mountains above 1,500 feet, Baldwin is a disappointment. The fruit ripens as early as August, which greatly diminishes its keeping ability, and it never obtains the sprightly quality of northern-grown Baldwins. In addition it has the reputation of rotting and dropping prematurely from the tree when grown in warmer areas. Baldwin was sold by many southern nurseries, some of them cautioning in their catalogs that it succeeds only in the mountains. *See* Carolina Baldwin.

Baldwin originated about 1740 as a chance seedling on the farm of John Ball near Lowell, Massachusetts. In 1784 it was recognized as an exceptional variety by a Colonel Baldwin who introduced it widely in eastern Massachusetts. It grew steadily in popularity, becoming the most important apple in New England by 1850. Its size and color, resistance to bruising, good taste, crisp texture, and excellent keeping qualities all combined to make Baldwin the most important commercial apple for the Northeast. It also was very valuable in the export trade to Europe.

Fruit above medium to large, roundish conical, symmetrical; skin tough, yellow, nearly covered with red and striped with crimson; dots minute, gray or russet, more numerous near the basin; stem usually three-fourths of an inch long in an acute, rather deep, often russeted cavity; calyx usually closed; basin rather narrow, often furrowed; flesh yellowish white, firm, moderately coarse, crisp, rather tender, juicy, subacid. Ripe October. Catalog listings: MD, VA, NC, SC, GA, AL, LA, TN, KY, AR (1853–1928).

❦ **BALL'S CHOICE** (Harwell, Harwell's Mammoth): In 1893, Jason E. Abernathy of Buford, Giles County, Tennessee, wrote to the USDA: "This is an apple there has been a good deal of discussion about. The party propagating it claims it as a seedling of Giles County. Others say it is the old Rhode Island Greening; by some said to be Newtown Pippin. Mr. Ball of this county is propagating it. He calls it Ball's Choice." A subsequent note in the USDA files says, "This specimen received at the Division of Pomology suggests Catlin or Winter Grixon of Delaware, though not thought to be that, nor is it recognized."

Ball's Choice was sold from 1910 to 1923 by Tennessee nurseries, one saying in its catalog: "said to have originated in Giles County, Tennessee, before 1860. The original tree was of immense size and a heavy annual bearer of long keeping fruit." An 1896 Tennessee agricultural experiment station bulletin credits S. A. R. Swan of Pulaski, Giles County, Tennessee, as the originator. Don Stocker of Palmer, Tennessee, sent me scions of an old apple that his family has grown since 1906 under the name Ball's Choice.

Fruit medium, roundish to slightly oblate, irregular, sides often unequal; skin partly to mostly covered with pale red and dull red stripes; dots mostly large but variable in size, numerous, gray; stem three-fourths of an inch long in a deep, narrow, russeted cavity; calyx closed; basin greenish, slightly furrowed and cracked; flesh greenish yellow, fine-grained, juicy, crisp, subacid. Ripe September/October. ❖ **Plate 4.**

❦ **BALSAM:** A single old tree was found in 1999 in Ashe County, North Carolina, by Dan Moncol.

Fruit medium size, round; skin smooth, almost covered with dark, plum red with broken darker stripes. A heavy white bloom is present; dots numerous, rather large, whitish, russet, and gray; stem usually long in a heavily russeted, deep cavity; calyx open; basin very shallow, gradually sloped, wide; flesh pale greenish, crisp, moderately juicy, mild subacid. Ripe September/October. No catalog listings.

❦ **BALTIMORE MONSTROUS PIPPIN** (Baltimore, McHenry Pippin, Gloria Mundi?): Thatcher (1822) has this to say: "In the transactions of the horticultural society of London, published in 1817, it is stated that a large American apple, raised in the garden of Mr. Smith near the city of Baltimore, was exhibited; it had been recently imported by Captain George Hobson, of Baltimore, who sent it to Sir Joseph Banks, by whom it was presented to the society. This apple weighed one pound seven and a half ounces; it measured in circumference one foot two inches and three quarters and in height as it stood, was four inches. It proved very good, though overripe; it was very close at the core and, if a good bearer, will deserve general cultivation." Kendrick (1841) describes this same variety as "a remarkably large apple raised by Mr. Smith near Baltimore, flat in form, skin a pale citron with a faint blush next the sun; flesh well-flavored and close at the core." The 1836 catalog of Clairmont Nurseries in Baltimore lists a Baltimore Monstrous Pippin described only as ripe November/December and weighing thirty ounces. Hopewell Nurseries of Fredericksburg, Virginia, listed Baltimore Monstrous Pippin as a fall apple in its 1859 catalog.

Taking into consideration everything we know about Baltimore Monstrous Pippin, I believe that it is identical to Gloria Mundi. Charles Downing, in 1877, stated to the American Pomological Society that he had facts indicating that Baltimore Monstrous Pippin and Gloria Mundi were the same apple. His facts were that this apple was first grown soon after the Revolutionary War by Ramsey McHenry in the city of Baltimore. It was first called McHenry Pippin, later Monstrous Pippin, Gloria Mundi, etc. *See* Gloria Mundi.

❦ **BART** (Old Bart?): An old variety from the War Woman area of Rabun County, Georgia, found by Tom Brown. An apple called "Old Bart" is grown near Jamestown, Tennessee, on older farms where it is used for drying and cooking.

Fruit small, roundish; skin mostly covered with a medium red and some red stripes; dots numerous, whitish; stem medium length in a russeted cavity. Ripe August. No catalog listings.

❦ **BEACH** (Apple of Commerce, Lady Pippin, Richardson's Red, Talcum Powder Apple?): About 1870 an Arkansas nurseryman named Oliver Young was using scions of a new apple for grafting. This is the first information on the origin of Beach. In 1895 Mr. C. M. Stark of Stark Bro's Nursery found and bought twenty-nine trees growing in the orchard of Mr. A. Darnell in Arkansas. Mr. Darnell had grafted his trees from a neighbor, S. Cowan, who, in turn, had grafted his trees from another neighbor, S. W. Richardson. Mr. Richardson found eight trees of this new variety on his farm when he bought it about 1880. Subsequently these eight trees were traced back to Oliver Young, but there the trail ends.

Stark Bro's Nursery renamed this apple the "Apple of Commerce" and touted it very highly: "The Apple of Commerce, as its name implies, can rightly be called a world apple, and seems destined in the future . . . to rule in the orchards and markets of the earth." Needless to say the Apple of Commerce did not live up to this praise and was never an important commercial apple in the United States. Although a good keeper, the fruit is only of fair eating quality and often is irregular in shape. The tree is a reliable bearer. Because Stark Bro's Nursery trademarked this apple, it was listed only by one southern nursery prior to 1928.

Fruit medium to large, usually roundish oblate; skin thick, tough, smooth, yellow mottled with red and striped with darker red; dots inconspicuous, gray or white; stem slender and medium length in an acute, deep, symmetrical, russeted cavity; basin rather shallow, furrowed, often with protuberances; flesh tinged yellow, firm, moderately coarse, not very juicy, subacid. Ripe late and an excellent keeper.

**BEAUTY OF THE WORLD** (Morganton): A seedling tree found by John Mace of Morganton, North Carolina, in an old field at the foot of South Mountain. Sold by a North Carolina nursery from 1900 to 1910. Tree vigorous, bearing moderate crops annually.

Fruit medium to large, oblate (also described as roundish oblong); skin almost covered with pale red, thickly striped and mottled with crimson, purplish crimson on the sunny side; dots few, yellowish; stem short in a small or medium-size, russeted cavity; calyx closed; basin rather large and broad; flesh white, almost fine-grained, firm, subacid. Ripe November and keeps well.

**BECKHAM'S SEEDLING:** In the 1930s a seedling tree grew up beside a road on the farm of Paul Beckham in Warren County, North Carolina. This is a beautiful apple.

Fruit large, oblate, somewhat irregular in shape; skin almost covered in dark purplish red without stripes and with a heavy bloom; dots large, scattered, tannish russet; stem short in a large, greenish cavity; calyx open; basin large, abrupt; flesh cream colored, crisp, juicy, slightly tough, subacid. Ripe August/September. No catalog listings.

**BEECHER** (Beacher): An old apple variety still grown in Macon, Jackson, and Cherokee counties in North Carolina, and one of nine or ten rare old apple varieties that Charles W. Nolen preserved in his orchard near Franklin.

Fruit almost large, very oblate; skin thick, tough, smooth, almost entirely covered with dark red or mahogany; dots numerous, conspicuous, white or gray, often with a red areole; stem medium length to almost long in a deep, wide, russeted cavity; calyx closed; basin wide, gradually sloped; flesh greenish, crisp, moderately juicy, subacid. Ripe late July/August. No catalog listings.

**BELCHER MOUNTAIN:** Originated near Woolwine, Virginia.

Fruit medium, slightly oblate conical; skin mostly covered with medium red with darker red stripes; dots numerous, grayish; stem medium length. Ripe October. No catalog listings.

**BELMONT** (Gate Apple, Mamma Beam, Mamma Beamer, White Apple, Kelley White, Waxen of Coxe?): Described by Coxe (1817) under the name Waxen. Its origin is possibly Virginia but more likely Pennsylvania. Downing (1878) described Belmont as best adapted to "high, warm, or limestone soils," and "grown South, its delicacy, fine grain, and flavor are lost." The fruit bruises very easily. *See also* White.

Fruit medium to large, irregular shaped, usually round but sometimes rather oblong; skin thin, smooth, glossy or oily, light yellow with a reddish cheek when grown in the North, southern-grown apples often have brown specks and a slight russet marbling; stem slender, short to medium length in a large cavity; basin shallow to rather deep, always furrowed; flesh yellowish white, fine-grained, very tender, rather juicy, sprightly subacid. Ripe late. Catalog listings: MD, VA, NC, KY (1855–1904).

**BEN DAVIS** (New York Pippin, Kentucky Red Streak, Kentucky Streak, Kentucky Pippin, Victoria Pippin, Victoria Red, Baltimore Red Streak, Carolina Red Streak, Funkhouser, Virginia Pippin, Hutchinson Pippin, Joe Allen, Red Pippin, Illinois Red, Thornton [of southern Alabama], Robinson's Streak, Carolina, Battle Ax, Funk Apple, Tenan Red, Red Streak): If Red Delicious is the apple success story of the twentieth century, then Ben Davis is the apple success story of the nineteenth century. In 1860 a New York apple expert, Patrick Barry, described Ben Davis as "a little known fruit." Only forty-five years later, the equally eminent New York apple expert, S. A. Beach, would call Ben Davis "the most important variety known in the apple districts of the vast territory which stretches from the Atlantic to the Pacific between parallels 32 and 42."

The Red Delicious apple has its detractors who decry the unripe and insipid apples sold in supermarkets. Rightfully so, but a southern-grown, tree-ripened Red Delicious—crisp, juicy, and aromatic—can be a delight. Few people (except in a salesman's pitch) have ever said a nice word about the eating quality of Ben Davis. "Second-rate" is the phrase most often used. "Rather coarse and tough, not overly juicy, with an almost total absence of flavor" is how one man described Ben Davis in 1923. In 1911, a man said of it: "Very popular with hotel keepers. Few patrons have the hardihood to bite into one. Occasionally a greenhorn will bite into a Ben Davis."

Given the low eating quality of Ben Davis, how can one explain the tidal wave of commercial Ben Davis orchards—literally tens of millions of trees planted in the period from 1865 to 1900? The answer is twofold: First, Ben Davis was a grower's and shipper's dream apple; and second, it was a great keeping apple in a day when refrigeration was either unknown or a rarity.

Ben Davis was largely an apple of the middle latitudes, preeminently successful in the southern states of Virginia, Kentucky, Tennessee, and Arkansas as well as further north in Illinois, Indiana, Missouri, Kansas, West Virginia, and portions of adjoining states. It was grown commercially as far north as Michigan and Maine. In northern states the fruit often did not fully mature, resulting in hard, unripe apples of low eating quality (which damned all Ben Davis apples), which, however, were known for their keeping ability. Northern-grown Ben Davis apples were sometimes shoveled into freight cars with coal shovels. The railroad cars were then sent south, parked on sidings near small towns, and the apples were shoveled out into baskets or buckets brought by housewives. Even with this sorry treatment, those northern-grown Ben Davis apples often kept until May. Even Ben Davis apples grown in the South kept until January or February.

In the nursery new Ben Davis trees were noted for their rapid growth—"the joy of the nurseryman." In the orchard, over a vast range of soils and climates, the Ben Davis tree was hardy, healthy, productive, and usually an annual bearer. It even bloomed late—when the weather was better for pollinating insects.

For the shipper and marketman, Ben Davis offered large, attractive apples that could not be bruised easily. Writing in 1870 of the Ben Davis apple, an orchardist in Illinois said: "The Ben Davis will outsell the Bellflower and almost any other apple in our great markets. This is chiefly owing to its fine appearance. The millions will choose the handsomest first, and take quality on trust." Eventually, though, the poor eating quality of Ben Davis caught up with it. By 1915, the bloom was definitely off Ben Davis, and it was quickly dethroned by higher-quality apples such as Red Delicious, Jonathan, and Winesap. In 1923 at an Indiana Horticultural Society meeting it was said, "at present the consumer will not buy Ben Davis, if they know what it is, until better apples are off the market." So thoroughly were Ben Davis trees eradicated, that it is a very rare variety today in the South. People remember Ben Davis, often with fondness, but old trees are hard to find.

Because of the sudden and overwhelming commercial success of Ben Davis, belated attempts were made to trace its history and origins. By the time this occurred the apple was growing everywhere and everyone believed it had originated with his neighbor or his granddaddy. The most widely accepted history of Ben Davis is this: In 1799, William Davis and John D. Hill moved from Virginia to settle at Berry's Lick in what is now Butler County, Kentucky, near Captain Ben Davis, the brother of William Davis and the brother-in-law of John D. Hill. A few years later Hill went back to Virginia (or perhaps to North Carolina) on business. When he returned to Kentucky, he brought back some young apple trees, either apple seedlings or root sprouts. Captain Ben Davis ended up with an apple tree from what Hill brought back and soon planted a small orchard from root sprouts from this original tree. Later Captain Ben Davis moved on and was heard from no more, but the apple trees he left behind attracted attention. For twenty-five years root sprouts were used to spread this apple (now called Ben Davis) throughout Kentucky and Tennessee. Members of the Hill family moved to Illinois and took some Ben Davis trees with them where they became popular. By the end of the Civil War the commercial promise of Ben Davis was recognized, and it was off and running all over the United States.

The most common synonym of Ben Davis is New York Pippin. The story is that a man named Dick

Anderson had a nursery on the Ohio River near Brandenburg, Kentucky, before the Civil War. He peddled trees up and down the Ohio by boat. He called his Ben Davis trees New York Pippin because he thought that name would sell more trees than the rather ordinary name of Ben Davis.

Fruit above medium, roundish to slightly oblong, conical, sometimes somewhat elliptical or irregular; skin tough, waxy, bright, smooth, clear yellow, mostly mottled and washed with bright red and striped with a darker red; dots minute, few, usually gray; stem slender and medium to long in a deep, regular, acute, russeted cavity; basin medium in width and depth, sometimes furrowed, sometimes oblique; flesh white, firm, moderately coarse, not very crisp, juicy, mild subacid. Ripe October and a good keeper with flavor improving in storage. Catalog listings: MD, VA, NC, SC, GA, AL, MS, LA, TN, KY, TX, AR, FL (1857–1928). ❖ **Plate 5.**

I wish to add a personal postscript about the Ben Davis apple. I have grown it in my North Carolina orchard and eaten it for over fifteen years. While it is not my favorite apple, it does not qualify for the wide condemnation seen in old apple books and references. At worst, Ben Davis is average in fresh eating quality and is useful in cooking, especially as a baking apple. I believe most of the bad reviews of Ben Davis resulted from apples grown too far north to ripen properly. These unripe apples—starchy, hard, gummy, and flavorless—condemned all Ben Davis apples. A 1910 USDA observation bears this out. Southern-grown Ben Davis apples were found to be "generally more juicy and of notably better quality" than Ben Davis apples grown in the North.

**BENHAM** (Claiborne, Benum, Brown, Yearry, Nat Ewing): Sold by Virginia nurseries from 1887 to 1904 and grown at the turn of the century in Virginia, West Virginia, Kentucky, and Tennessee where the apples were used for fresh eating, cooking, and drying. Ragan (1905) guesses that it originated in Tennessee, and it is still fairly common there in Claiborne County. Benham was grown extensively at one time in Lee County, Virginia, and Knox County, Kentucky. *The American Gardener* magazine of September 1891 describes a different Benham apple said to have originated with F. M. Benham of Petosky, Michigan. This apple, supposedly a seedling of Baldwin, is a late- ripening apple.

John Creech, a nurseryman in Kentucky, rated Benham as the finest apple ripening in its season: "Truly an apple for the connoisseur, sugar and acid being perfectly balanced." He remembers the delicious stack cakes his grandmother made from dried Benham apples and served at Thanksgiving, Christmas, and other special occasions. The cut fruit is slow to turn brown and so is excellent for drying, canning, and freezing. Slightly immature Benhams make fine applesauce and can be dried. The tree ripens its fruit over several weeks and the "drops" provide apples for daily use.

Fruit medium or above, roundish to slightly oblate, conical, often ribbed; skin smooth, very thin, greenish yellow, sometimes with a slight blush on the sunny side, rarely striped with red; dots small, russet, often surrounded with green; stem thick and very short with a fleshy protuberance in a deep, wide, uneven, greenish russeted cavity; calyx closed or slightly open; basin abrupt, deep, corrugated; flesh slightly yellowish, juicy, fine-textured, subacid to almost sweet, nutty flavored. Ripe July/August. ❖ **Plate 6.**

**BENONI** (Fail-Me-Never): Originated before 1832 in Dedham, Massachusetts, and sold by many southern nurseries as a high-quality summer apple. The tree is small, productive, and an early bearer but often biennial in bearing. Susceptible to cedar-apple rust.

Fruit medium or below, roundish to slightly oblate, conical; skin rough, yellow, nearly covered with bright red with darker red on the sunny side; dots large, white, numerous; stem short or very short in an acute, rather narrow, deep, greenish cavity; calyx open; basin medium to deep, abrupt; flesh yellow, juicy, crisp, fine-grained, subacid. Ripe July. Catalog listings: MD, VA, NC, AL, MS, LA, KY, TX, AR (1853–1920).

**BENTLEY'S SWEET:** All the old apple reference books suppose the origin of Bentley's Sweet to be Virginia, but the exact circumstances of its origin were not known even a hundred years ago. All we know with certainty is that Ebenezer Zane had Bentley's Sweet on "Wheeling Island," in what is now West Virginia, before 1813. (Before the Civil War, West Virginia was part of Virginia.) It apparently was named for Major Solomon Bentley (1785–1865) of Belmont County, Ohio. Bentley's Sweet usually is described as a good, sweet apple and an incredible keeper. Several old references say it will keep through the winter to the following September, but others give May as the last usable date. The fruit is very susceptible to bitter rot.

Fruit variable in size but usually medium, roundish, somewhat flattened on the ends, sides sometimes unequal; skin smooth, mostly covered with blotches and stripes of pale red or dull red; dots minute (Beach says conspicuous and dark brown), moderate in number; stem medium in a deep, wide, often furrowed cavity; calyx large, closed or partly open; basin medium size, abrupt, often corrugated; flesh yellowish white, fine-grained, firm, tender, moderately juicy, crisp, sweet. Ripe October. Catalog listings: MD, VA, TX (1845–1914).

❦ **BETSY DEATON:** Grown at one time in Yancey County, North Carolina, and listed as extinct in the previous edition of this book. A tree was found by Danny Harvey in 1996 in Ashe County, North Carolina.

Fruit medium, roundish conical; skin smooth, almost covered with medium to dark red; dots scattered, medium size, often areole, gray; stem very long in a wide, slightly russeted cavity; calyx open or closed; basin wide, lumpy, often greenish; flesh pale greenish, often stained red under the skin, moderately juicy and crisp, subacid. Ripe September/October. No catalog listings.

❦ **BEVAN'S FAVORITE** (Early Bevan, Striped June, Bivins)/**IMPROVED BEVANS:** Originated before 1842 in Salem, New Jersey, and listed in the catalogs of three North Carolina and South Carolina nurseries from 1855 to 1895. Lindley's Nursery of North Carolina continued to sell Bevan's Favorite (they called it Early Bevan) through their traveling salesmen or agents until as late as 1930. In 1985 I found a single, old tree of Bevan's Favorite on the farm of E. Lloyd Curl in Alamance County, North Carolina. Four months after scions were taken from this tree, it blew down in a thunderstorm. Bevan's Favorite was reported to grow well in Mississippi in 1877.

Like most early summer apples, Bevan's Favorite does not hold its quality for long. The apples should be picked just as the background color is turning from light green to yellow. If left on the tree only a few days past its prime, the fruit becomes less juicy and soft.

Fruit small, roundish oblate to oblate, slightly conical; skin greenish yellow with broad, broken, red stripes mostly on the sunny side; dots whitish or gray, inconspicuous, submerged; stem long and thick in a shallow, green cavity; calyx closed, protruding; basin rather shallow, abrupt, corrugated; flesh white, moderately crisp, moderately juicy, fine-grained, subacid. Ripe early July.

Lindley's Nursery also sold a variety called Improved Bevans. A single tree of this variety has been found in Chatham County, North Carolina. It closely resembles Bevan's Favorite but is larger and ripens perhaps two weeks later.

Fruit medium or above, roundish oblate to oblate, slightly conical; skin light greenish yellow with bright red, broken stripes on the sunny side; dots few, whitish or russet, often areolar; stem short in a narrow, greenish cavity; calyx closed or open; basin deep, corrugated; flesh yellowish, juicy, crisp, fine-grained, subacid. Ripe late July.

❦ **BIG RED** (Pottinger, Large Winter Red?): A large cooking and drying apple described by Warder (1867) as "chiefly found in regions settled by immigrants from the South."

In 2000 the peerless apple hunter, Tom Brown, found one old tree called Big Red growing near Clyde, North Carolina, belonging to Edith Plemmons. The fruit fits the old description of Big Red below except it ripens earlier (probably a result of geography) and is medium in size.

Fruit large, oblate conical; skin light yellow, splashed and striped with light and dark red; dots small, prominent, rough; stem medium to short in a wide, greenish cavity; calyx closed; basin wide; flesh white (Warder says yellow), tender, juicy, sprightly, pleasant, subacid. Ripe October/November. No catalog listings.

**BIG STEM:** The apple hunter, the late Dr. L. R. Littleton, found this apple in Pocahontas County, West Virginia, being grown by Loy Nottingham.

Fruit above medium, roundish; skin yellow with tan russet spreading over the top of the apple; dots large, often irregular, tan russet; stem very thick and short in a heavily russeted cavity. Ripe late July. No catalog listings.

**BILLY BROWN:** This local apple was once popular in Union County and perhaps Hancock County, Tennessee. Jake Haynes of Carryton, Tennessee, says his grandfather grew this apple, which he thought had been lost. His cousin found a single old tree in the woods in Union County.

Fruit below medium, sometimes small, roundish conical; skin yellow usually with a rosy blush where the sun has hit the skin; stem short and thick ending in a knob in a russeted cavity; calyx closed; basin bumpy. Ripe July/August. No catalog listings.

**BISHOP** (Hollow Apple): A family apple sent to me by Margaret Douglas of Ashe County, North Carolina. She says the original tree was brought from England by an ancestor named Bishop before 1900 and was planted in a "hollow" near her grandfather's house in the Nathan Creek community. Some of Ms. Douglas' relatives call it the Hollow Apple. Other trees were grafted from the original tree, but all are dead except one.

Fruit medium or below, roundish, slightly conical; skin light yellow; dots green, submerged; stem short to medium in a wide, smooth, slightly russeted cavity; calyx closed; basin slightly corrugated; flesh yellowish, fine-grained, juicy, crisp, subacid. Ripe August. No catalog listings.

**BISMARCK** (Prince Bismarck): Probably originated in New Zealand (but also said to have originated in Tasmania), and was introduced from there into Germany in the late 1800s. From Germany it was brought to the United States with great fanfare. A 1910 Tennessee catalog states: "Promises to take the place of almost every other apple grown in this country," and a 1910 Texas catalog says: "It is creating a sensation as it bears at two years old and regular crops thereafter. It seems to stand any kind of climate. We have sent quantities of Bismarck trees to Cuba and some have borne apples 14 inches in circumference." Needless to say, Bismarck did not live up to its hype and was never an important apple variety in the United States.

The tree is dwarfish, and several southern nurseries advertised Bismarck as suitable for growing in pots for decorative purposes.

Fruit large to very large, oblate, ribbed; skin golden yellow splashed and striped with red with some russet and a thin bloom; flesh white, crisp, juicy, mild acid. Ripe August. Catalog listings: MD, VA, NC, GA, AL, TN, TX, AR (1898–1928).

**BLACK AMISH:** An all-purpose apple, perhaps of Pennsylvania origin, not mentioned in any old catalogs or pomological literature. The apples hang well on the tree, which is a heavy, annual bearer. We can thank John Creech of Kentucky for saving this apple.

Fruit above medium to large, roundish oblate, conical, sometimes slightly lobed; skin tough, light yellow, mostly overlaid with light red with darker red stripes, much darker red on the sunny side; dots rather numerous, large, light-colored, some with a russet center; stem three-fourths of an inch long in a deep, abrupt, heavily russeted cavity with the russet extending out over the top of the apple; basin medium to rather wide; flesh yellowish, fine-grained, firm, crisp, moderately juicy, sprightly subacid. Ripe September in central North Carolina, October in Kentucky and keeps for two months under refrigeration. No catalog listings.

**BLACK APPLE** (Small Black, Jersey Black, Black American, Dodge's Black)/**CHERRYVILLE BLACK:** The name Black or Black Apple has been used as a synonym for several different varieties, usually apples very dark red in color. Coxe (1817) describes a Black Apple of New Jersey origin, later known as Jersey Black, which was sold by southern nurseries under the name Black or Black Apple.

Fruit medium, roundish oblate; skin deep red with a purplish bloom; flesh white (also described as yellow) sometimes stained pink. Ripe late September/October. Catalog listings: VA, NC, SC, KY, TX (1845–1904).

In 1987, I collected a Black Apple from Ernest S. Sellers, a ninety-three-year-old man in Cherryville, North Carolina, which had been in his family for many years. This is not the Jersey Black described above, but probably was named for Elszy Black, the grandfather of Mr. Sellers. This apple, which I call Cherryville Black, is one of my favorite late July apples.

Fruit below medium, roundish to slightly oblate; skin light green about half covered with dull, slightly purplish red with indistinct red stripes; dots numerous, large, irregular shaped, tan; stem knobbed and short in a greenish tan, russeted cavity; calyx wide open; basin deep, abrupt, often greenish or reddish, leather-cracked; flesh almost white, very juicy, crisp, subacid. Ripe late July/August. No catalog listings.

❦ **BLACK GILLIFLOWER** (Red Gilliflower, Gilliflower, Black Spitz, Long Gilliflower, Black Sheepnose, Sheepnose, Red Ladyfinger?, Ladyfinger?, Black Annie, Crow's Egg, Winter Pear): Southern nurseries listed this apple in their catalogs as Black Gilliflower or Red Gilliflower. It is a very old variety known in Connecticut in the early 1700s. Perhaps its most distinctive feature is the shape of the fruit, being very oblong and tapering down to a narrow point at the blossom end. Black Gilliflower so closely resembles an old southern apple called Crow's Egg that they must be identical. (*See* Crow's Egg.) The flesh quickly becomes dry in overripe fruit and the tree is very susceptible to fire blight.

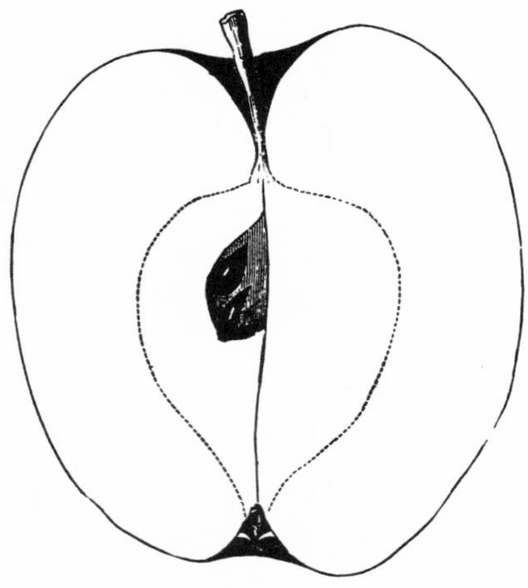

BLACK GILLIFLOWER

There has been speculation over the years that Black Gilliflower is one parent of the Delicious (Red Delicious) apple crossed with Yellow Bellflower. *See* Delicious.

Fruit medium to large, very oblong and very conical; skin dark, dull red, obscurely striped, often with scarf skin; dots numerous, gray, inconspicuous; stem medium to long, moderately thick in a rather deep, red russeted cavity; basin usually shallow and wrinkled; flesh greenish white, firm, rather coarse, moderately juicy becoming dry, aromatic, almost sweet. Ripe September/October. Catalog listings: MD, VA, NC, SC (1845–1904).

❦ **BLACK JACK:** Found by Tom Brown near Roan Mountain, Tennessee. This name is a synonym of the Greyhouse apple, now considered extinct, but Black Jack in some ways matches the abbreviated descriptions of Greyhouse and may be identical to it. *See* Greyhouse.

Fruit medium size, roundish conical to slightly oblong, but irregular-shaped and often oblique; skin greenish usually with a pale red-blushed cheek; dots large, russet with an areole, slightly protruding; stem short to medium length in a wide, deep, russeted cavity with russet over the top of the apple; calyx closed; basin greenish; flesh whitish, moderately crisp and juicy, fine-grained, subacid. Ripe October. No catalog listings.

❦ **BLACKTWIG** (Mammoth Blacktwig, Arkansas, Paragon, Arkansaw, Big Blacktwig, Thorpe's Blacktwig, Pamplin's Eclipse, Big Winesap): In March 1896 there was an article in *The American Gardener* magazine entitled "The Paragon Apple Muddle." This article was just another voice in the uproar over Paragon versus Mammoth Blacktwig. In gardening magazines, newspapers, and nursery catalogs, a battle of words was fought over these burning questions: Are these the same apple and, if not, which came first?

As a preamble you must keep in mind the uses of the name Blacktwig. Up until about 1900 Blacktwig was an old and well-known synonym of Winesap. It was so used in both Tennessee and Arkansas where the controversy was centered. After 1900 the name Blacktwig came to be used as a catch-all name for either Paragon or Mammoth Blacktwig, and it was dropped as a synonym of Winesap. In the following paragraphs I will put the name Winesap in parentheses where Blacktwig is being used as its synonym.

The controversy started in 1884 when some apples were exhibited in the Arkansas pavilion at the New Orleans World Exposition. One eye-catching variety was called Arkansas (sometimes spelled Arkansaw) or Mammoth Blacktwig and was claimed to be a seedling variety from Arkansas. Upon later examination, however, several pomologists and Tennessee apple growers declared this Arkansas apple to be identical to a Tennessee apple called Paragon. The battle lines were drawn, Arkansas vs. Tennessee, with the pomologists caught in the crossfire. People began looking back to find the origins of these two apples to see if those origins somehow converged onto a single "mother tree," a common progenitor of these two apples that were so remarkably alike.

The story of Paragon starts in 1820 when a man named John Thorpe got some apple scions from Stokes Nursery in Halifax County, Virginia. Thorpe moved to Lincoln County, Tennessee, by cart and used the scions to start a small nursery. About 1845 a local farmer named Rankin Toole purchased trees from John Thorpe's nursery, including several Blacktwigs (Winesaps), and planted himself an orchard.

In 1870 another local nurseryman, P. L. Twitty, cut scions of Blacktwig (Winesap) from the bearing-size trees in Rankin Toole's orchard. He sold most of the scions to a nursery in Alabama but grafted some for himself. When his Blacktwig (Winesap) trees began bearing, there were four trees that bore larger and redder fruit than the other Blacktwig (Winesap) trees. In 1885 he showed these larger apples to Dr. W. L. Moores of Cyruston, Tennessee, who recognized them as a new and outstanding variety. Dr. Moores went back to Rankin Toole's orchard and there found one tree, called "Big Blacktwig" by the Toole family, which had the same large apples as Mr. Twitty's four trees. Dr. Moores concluded that this single tree was a Blacktwig (Winesap) seedling, perhaps a rootstock on which the scion had died, which had somehow been planted in the Toole orchard. Scions from "Big Blacktwig" had been unknowingly mixed into Blacktwig (Winesap) scions cut in 1870 by Mr. Twitty. Dr. Moores suggested the new variety be named Twitty's Paragon, which was soon shortened to Paragon. Meanwhile this apple was spreading out in Tennessee, by root sprouts and home grafting, under the names Blacktwig, Big Blacktwig, and Thorpe's Blacktwig, and soon began being sold by nurseries under the name Paragon.

We will leave Paragon and track the origins of the apple called Arkansas or Mammoth Blacktwig, using mainly information presented to the 1895 meeting of the American Pomological Society by Colonel E. F. Babcock.

In 1842 a man named John Crawford moved into Arkansas and settled in Washington County. With him he brought seeds of Limbertwig and Blacktwig (Winesap) apples that he planted and started a seedling orchard. One of the seeds, believed by Mr. Crawford to be a Blacktwig (Winesap) seed, produced a tree bearing large, excellent apples. About 1875 William Crawford, John's brother who lived nearby, grafted some trees for his own orchard using scions from this special tree. The Crawfords called this apple Mammoth Blacktwig because it was similar to Blacktwig (Winesap) but with larger and redder fruit. Apples from William Crawford's trees were selected to be used in the Arkansas exhibit at the New Orleans World Exposition in 1884 by Colonel E. F. Babcock, who was in charge of the fruit exhibit, and it was Colonel Babcock who renamed it Arkansas when it was placed in the exhibit. Colonel Babcock became its most ardent defender when Mammoth Blacktwig was declared to be identical to Paragon.

Sorting through these two tales, there is no common origin for Paragon and Mammoth Blacktwig. They are both apparently seedlings of Winesap, but that is not a common origin as every seedling is genetically unique. The close resemblance of the fruit of Paragon and Mammoth

Blacktwig fooled even the experts. It also resulted in nurseries so mixing up these two varieties that no one today can be absolutely sure which apple is which. Many southern nurseries listed one or the other variety as "Mammoth Blacktwig (Paragon)" or often "Blacktwig (Arkansaw, Paragon)."

To be honest, there remains a tiny tickle of doubt. What about those scions cut in 1870 by Mr. Twitty and sold to a nursery in Alabama? Paragon scions were mixed in with Blacktwig (Winesap) scions. That Alabama nursery is known to have sold trees in Arkansas, some unwittingly grafted with Paragon scions. Could several Paragon trees have found their way into William Crawford's orchard which he planted "about 1875?" Probably not; the Crawford brothers were very sure their original Mammoth Blacktwig originated as a seedling.

Faced with the above information, USDA pomologists declared these two apples to be separate varieties. The controversy died down, but Tennessee apple growers still mumbled about those scions cut by Mr. Twitty in 1870.

Whatever the origins of these apples, southern nurseries touted in big print and loving detail the virtues of Paragon/Blacktwig/Arkansas/Mammoth Blacktwig. After all, southerners loved the Winesap apple and here was a new apple with Winesap taste and keeping ability but larger and redder fruit and a more vigorous tree. Only later would it be noticed that the new variety was not very productive, which limited its commercial exploitation in the South. Through the 1920s, Stark Bro's Nursery sold both Mammoth Blacktwig (Arkansas) and Paragon. They touted Paragon more highly because of its higher yields.

The fruit of Blacktwig tends to be rather tart when picked but mellows to a luscious mild subacid when stored for a couple of months. The tree is resistant to several common apple diseases including fire blight and cedar-apple rust. A statement made about Blacktwig at the 1900 meeting of the Maryland Horticultural Society was that "poorer soils bring the most apples." This trait comes from its Winesap parent, which is known for doing well on poor soils.

Writing of the differences between Mammoth Blacktwig (Arkansas) and Paragon, an observer in 1911 said: "The tree of the Paragon is a little more spreading, the fruit is a little flatter, more solid brownish red at the base, and the flesh is rather more of a greenish yellow tint. The Mammoth Blacktwig tree is slightly more upright, the fruit is a little more inclined to conical, and the flesh is more yellow."

The following descriptions are taken from old publications and are provided to let the reader compare Mammoth Blacktwig (Arkansas) and Paragon.

*Mammoth Blacktwig* (Arkansas): Fruit large, roundish oblate, conical; skin almost entirely covered with red; dots distinct, numerous, whitish; cavity regular, russeted; calyx closed; basin shallow, nearly smooth; flesh yellow with yellow veinings, firm, juicy, mild subacid. Ripe October.

*Paragon*: Fruit medium or above, roundish or sometimes somewhat oblate, slightly conical; sides often a little unequal; skin largely covered with dull, deep red with indistinct darker stripes; dots small, gray or white, sometimes rather conspicuous (Downing says thickly sprinkled with yellowish and brown dots); stem short and rather stout; cavity medium in width and moderately shallow to sometimes rather wide and deep, usually russeted; calyx closed; basin medium or shallow, often furrowed and wrinkled; flesh pale yellow (Beach says greenish or tinged with yellow), firm, juicy, mild subacid. Ripe October.

Catalog listings (under all names and synonyms): MD, VA, NC, GA, AL, TN, KY, TX, AR (1885–1928).

**BLAIRMONT:** A modern apple, one of very few developed in the South in the past fifty years. It was bred at the USDA Experiment Station in Byron, Georgia, and released in 1982. It has not become popular, commercially or in the backyard, for several reasons. It tends to be a biennial bearer and ripens late July/August when it quickly becomes mealy. It is said to have good frost tolerance at blossom time.

Fruit above medium, roundish, slightly oblique; skin covered with medium to dark red; dots tiny, whitish, scattered; stem long in a greenish cavity; calyx closed; basin rather small, medium depth, sometimes corrugated; flesh pale greenish, fine-grained, melting, juicy, subacid. Ripe August. No catalog listings.

❦ **BLOOMLESS, SEEDLESS, CORELESS** (Spencer Seedless?, No-core, Hillars Grande, No-blo?, Never Bloom, Bloomless, and Coreless): In 1890 G. W. Robinette of Flag Pond, Virginia, wrote to L. H. Bailey, the great pomologist at Cornell University. He reported finding a bloomless tree bearing seedless apples, and Mr. Robinette subsequently sent Mr. Bailey both flowers and fruit from the tree. Mr. Robinette said he and his brother planted some wild seedlings in an orchard about 1868, and one tree began to produce its strange fruit without blooming. Mr. Bailey published this correspondence in *The American Gardener* magazine with drawings of the imperfect blossoms, which had no petals or stamens but up to fifteen pistils. Letters to *The American Gardener* magazine, prompted by Mr. Bailey's article, proved that bloomless apples had occurred before Mr. Robinette's find. In 1867 a bloomless and seedless apple was found in West Virginia. Another bloomless tree was reported in Connecticut before 1840 and yet another was growing in Westboro, Massachusetts, in 1829.

Some of the Virginia apples did have seeds, but they were located near the skin at the blossom end. Beneath the calyx there was a large cavity that extended at least half way through the fruit toward the stem. This cavity accounted for the no-core appearance of the fruit, but remnants of a core could be discerned within the apple.

About 1900 a nursery was formed in Grand Junction, Colorado, called the Spencer Seedless Apple Company. It sold an apple advertised as "the world's greatest discovery in horticulture." Detective work by Charles Waters of Bingen, Washington, proved that this wonder apple was none other than the "Bloomless, Seedless, and Coreless" apple of Virginia origin, an apple worthless for commercial production.

Southern nurseries sold trees of this strange apple for a few years under several names such as "Bloomless," "Seedless and Coreless" and "Bloomless, Seedless, and Coreless."

The Virginia Bloomless Apple: Fruit small to sometimes medium, roundish oblate, oblique; skin greenish yellow with dull splashes of red and some russet; dots small, numerous, russet; cavity rather narrow, deep, russeted; calyx very large, fleshy, open, covering a very deep and wide basin with prominent protuberances; flesh yellowish, firm, juicy, sprightly subacid. Ripe late and a good keeper. Catalog listings: VA, NC (1895–1901). Apples called No-Blo and Spencer Seedless are available. *See also* Van Hoy No-Core *and* Farthing's No-Bloom.

❦ **BLUE RIDGE KING:** The late Maurice Marshall, a nurseryman in Pinnacle, North Carolina, found this apple somewhere in Virginia in the mid-1990s. It is strikingly beautiful and a delicious eating apple.

Fruit above medium to almost large, roundish, flattened on the ends; skin almost covered with very dark red with many broken darker red stripes; dots scattered, rather large, whitish; stem short to medium in a tannish, russeted cavity with russet rays extending over the top of the apple; calyx closed; basin greenish. Ripe August/September. No catalog listings.

❦ **BOGER:** This old apple, once used for drying and pies, was widely grown near Concord, North Carolina, where several trees still exist. Jack Rankin of Concord provided me with scions in 1997. A Boger apple is grown around Columbia, Tennessee, but appears to be a different apple.

Fruit medium size, usually oblate; skin rough, pale greenish, partly covered with dull red and often lightly to heavily overlaid with russet; dots rather large, scattered, whitish; stem short in a heavily russeted cavity; calyx closed; flesh pale yellow, moderately juicy, almost sweet. Ripe September/October. No catalog listings.

❦ **BOWER'S NONPAREIL** (Big Green, Big Sweet): Originated near Harrisonburg, Virginia. Listed under the name Big Green and described as a new variety in the 1870 catalog of the Forest Nursery, Fairview, Kentucky. Downing (1900) says the tree bears annually but has larger crops on alternate years. Rediscovered by Elwood Fisher of Harrisonburg.

Fruit large, slightly oblate, flattened on the ends; skin mostly covered in mottled pale red with some faint striping; dots numerous, gray, large; stem short to medium length in a deep, wide, tan, russeted cavity; calyx prominent, greenish, open; basin large, wide; flesh tender, juicy, mild subacid. Ripe August.

❦ **BRANCH** (Pickett): This is a local apple from Brunswick County, North Carolina, which is on the coast near the South Carolina line. Doris Redwine of Ocean Isle Beach, North Carolina, found this old variety for me which she enjoyed in her childhood. (*See also* Branch *in chapter* 5.)

Fruit medium size, round; skin greenish mottled with darker green and sometimes with russet mottlings and a pale reddish blush on the sunny side; stem short in a russeted cavity. Ripe August. No catalog listings.

❦ **BRICHEL SWEET** (Brickle Sweet): A local apple from western North Carolina. The tree is dwarfish. Fruit small, oblate; skin greenish to yellow. Ripe late and a good keeper. No catalog listings.

❦ **BROGAN:** The late Henry Morton's nursery catalog of 1986 describes Brogan: "A large, firm, juicy apple with unusual flavor. Favors the old Red Delicious in color and shape. One of the best for fresh eating. Originated in the backyard of D'Von Brogan, Knox County, Tennessee. The seed came from an apple from his father's old orchard in Virginia. We believe this apple will become one of the leading varieties in our collection. It has the juicy, rich flavor and taste of Blacktwig and the old Red Delicious."

❦ **BROGDEN:** Joyce Neighbors of Gadsden, Alabama, reports that the original tree grew up about 1945 as a seedling beside a road in southern Alabama near the Wiregrass Agricultural Experiment Station (near the Florida line), where a road crew noted the quality of the fruit. It is named for the late Clarence Brogden, a supervisor at the experiment station. A tree was eventually grafted into the Agricultural Extension Service orchard at Auburn, Alabama, by Joe Norton. Apparently, Brogden is a low-chill apple as an Alabama agricultural circular recommends it for southern Alabama, and it has been successfully grown in Houston, Texas.

Fruit usually above medium, roundish; skin greenish, often mostly covered with medium red with faint stripes; stem medium length in a narrow, irregular cavity; calyx closed; basin shallow, greenish; flesh whitish, not very crisp or juicy, sweet. Ripe late July to early August. No catalog listings.

❦ **BROOKS:** Found by Tom Brown near Statesville, North Carolina, where it has been grown for many years. It may be identical to Brooke Pippin but appears to be a redder apple that ripens earlier. Described as large, greenish yellow mostly blushed with red; flesh juicy, mild subacid. Ripe July/August. No catalog listings. *See* Brooke Pippin.

❦ **BRYSON'S SEEDLING:** Listed as extinct in the previous edition of this book, but found by Tom Brown in 2002 in Jackson County, North Carolina. From the 1904 catalog of the Maryland Nursery Company, Baltimore, Maryland: "Very fine, large, red, winter apple; one of the best growers and keepers, especially for the South. Originated in Jackson County, North Carolina. Samples of fruit received in February were sound and in fine condition."

❦ **BUCKEYE BEAUTY:** Listed but not described in the 1928 catalog of the Ideal Nursery and Orchard, Smithville, Tennessee. Considered extinct in the first edition of this book, but a single old tree has been found by Tom Brown at the home of Hershel Green in Watauga County, North Carolina.

Fruit medium size or above, roundish conical; skin bright yellow occasionally blushed with red; stem medium to long in a dark brown, narrow, deep, russeted cavity; calyx closed; basin small, corrugated; flesh pale yellow, crisp, juicy, mild subacid. Ripe October and keeps well.

❦ **BUCKINGHAM** (Queen, Fall Queen, Winter Queen, Red Winter Queen, Kentucky Queen, Lexington Queen, Frankfort Queen, Ladies Favorite [in Tennessee], Equinetelee, Byers, Byers Red, Ox-eye [in Kentucky], Merit, Blackburn, Henshaw, Late Queen, Sol Carter, Ne Plus Ultra, King, Red Horse, Red Gloria Mundi, Favorite, Batchelor, Iola, Fall Cheese, Gregg?, Salem, Winter Cheese, Garvis Seedling, Large Summer Pearmain, Neverfail [in Tennessee], Jackson's Red): Buckingham is the quintessential southern apple. It was grown for two hundred years all over the South where it was valued for the large size and high flavor of the fruit and the vigorous productiveness of the tree. The fruit was attractive enough and kept well enough to be useful for marketing as well as for eating, cooking, drying, and cider. To most rural southerners, Buckingham was a familiar household word. In 1871 a southerner wrote about Buckingham: "We have almost as close an acquaintance with the fruit and tree as with our own family."

In its love affair with the South, Buckingham even made it easy for southerners to propagate. The roots of the tree grow very near the surface and frequently send out root sprouts. These sprouts were dug up and planted elsewhere to make new Buckingham trees without grafting. In 1844 it was said, "from the disposition of the tree to sprout at the root, it offers inducement to many to plant its suckers and thereby obtain orchards."

As with many very old apples, the origin of Buckingham is unclear. Its early years coincided with rapid migrations of Americans into new lands west of the Appalachians, south into the southern mountains and further on into Alabama and Mississippi. Buckingham went with these settlers and acquired new names as its original name was forgotten. The account of its origins must necessarily be accepted with caution.

In 1777 Colonel John Byers was growing an apple he called Queen in his garden in Louisa County, Virginia. It was locally called Byer's Apple or Byer's Red. There is good reason to believe this apple was the Buckingham. Probably it made its way west by settlers who called it Buckingham because they had acquired it in Buckingham County, Virginia. In 1790 a settler named Edward Darnaby moved from Virginia to Mercer County, Kentucky, and started a nursery there. He is believed to have introduced Buckingham west of the Appalachians under the name Queen. It spread from Kentucky into Missouri and Indiana as Queen or Kentucky Queen, while simultaneously it spread from North Carolina into Tennessee and thence into Illinois under the name Buckingham.

At about this same time, an apple much resembling Buckingham was being grown in Georgia under the Cherokee Indian name Equinetelee. Georgians believed this apple originated as a seedling with the Cherokees, and it was listed for many years by Georgia nurseries as a separate variety. In 1856 the Georgia pomologist, Jarvis Van Buren, wrote to a friend: "Enclosed I send you two dollars for a bundle of scions of Sol Carter or Equinally. I would like enough to graft two hundred trees, and I do not intend to sell one of them for less than fifty cents. If I cannot get that, I shall set them out in my orchard, but I have no fears about it." Whether Equinetelee was actually Buckingham under a synonym, or a separate variety but a Buckingham look-alike, is unknown. By 1890 Equinetelee was being shown by most southern nurseries as a synonym of Buckingham.

The many synonyms of Buckingham and its divergent routes of introduction into new-settled lands confused even the experts. Warder, in his book *American Pomology* (1867), describes Queen, Buckingham, and Equinetelee as separate varieties. He also believed Fall Queen was distinct from Buckingham. In the 1860 meeting of the American Pomological Society, Buckingham was badly confused with Buncombe.

In most of the South, Buckingham is not a winter apple but ripens in the early fall, usually September and October. For an apple ripening this early, Buckingham keeps rather well. Fruit grown in warmer areas keeps about six weeks, while that grown in Kentucky or in the mountains often keeps until January or February. Buckingham is quite susceptible to cedar-apple rust.

Fruit usually large but varies in size even on the same tree, roundish, but often somewhat oblate, slightly conical, often oblique; skin smooth, thick, mostly covered with dull red stripes and marbling, darker red on the sunny side; dots numerous, small, light brown or white; stem short and fleshy in a broad, deep, russeted cavity; calyx closed; basin large, deep, corrugated; flesh yellowish, tender, juicy, sprightly subacid. Ripe autumn in the mountains, late summer in warmer areas. Catalog listings: MD, VA, NC, SC, GA, AL, MS, LA, TN, KY, TX, AR (1852–1928).

❦ **BUD WOLF:** Daniel Dixon, Jr., of Lowgap, North Carolina, has the only known tree. He says it originated long ago as a seedling in Harford County, Maryland, near Bud Wolf's barn. Mr. Dixon describes the fruit as "a real good cooking apple and also good to eat raw." As grown here, Bud Wolf closely resembles and may be identical to Wolf River.

Fruit large, roundish, irregular; skin pale yellow, washed and striped on the sunny side with red; stem medium length ending in a swelling in a deep, irregular, slightly to much-russeted cavity; calyx closed; basin very deep; flesh moderately crisp and juicy, pale yellow, fine-grained, mild subacid to almost sweet. Ripe September/October. No catalog listings.

❦ **BUFF** (Granny Buff, Pound, Mountain Sprout, Big Buff): In the May 1853 *Western Horticultural Review* magazine, the following history of Buff is given: "A well known apple which originated in Haywood County, North Carolina. The original tree was found growing on the farm of a German by the name of Buff. It was a seedling tree raised by the Cherokee Indians. Many fine varieties have been grown by them as they know of no other way of propagating fruit than from the seeds."

Buff has long been esteemed in western North Carolina for cooking, drying, and making apple butter. The quality of Buff has been described as very good under favorable conditions and when well ripened but otherwise "indifferent." The tree is very susceptible to cedar-apple rust. I obtained scions from Charles Nolen of Franklin, North Carolina.

Fruit of the largest size, irregular, roundish oblate, somewhat ribbed, sides unequal; skin thick, whitish yellow overspread with broad, broken splashes and stripes of dark crimson or dull red, very dark on the sunny side; dots few, greenish russet; stem three-fourths of an inch long and slender in a medium to large, deep, heavily russeted cavity; calyx open or partially closed; basin large, deep, slightly corrugated; flesh yellowish or greenish white, tender, somewhat coarse, moderately juicy, subacid, mealy when fully ripe. Ripe September/October. Catalog listings: VA, GA, SC, TN, KY (1849–89).

❦ **BUNCOMBE** (Red Winter Pearmain, Batchelor, Bunkum, Buncombe Pippin, Red Fall Pippin, Meigs, Powers, Tinson's Red, Southern Fall Pippin, Red Vandevere, Jackson's Red, Robertson's Pearmain, Red Lady Finger, Red Gilliflower, Kirby's Red, Lady Finger Pippin, Watery?): When an apple has as many synonyms as Buncombe, you can be sure it is an old variety once grown over a wide area. In 1867 Warder called it "a favorite southern apple, widely diffused through the South. . . ." There is a Buncombe County in North Carolina named for a nineteenth-century congressman, and it is assumed that Buncombe originated in North Carolina.

Tennessee's best apple hunter, Don Stocker, believed that Buncombe (or "Bunkum") is actually the Glenloch apple described in an 1897 Tennessee Experiment Station bulletin. According to this bulletin, the Glenloch originated on the farm of H. M. McCroskey, Glenloch, Monroe County, Tennessee, as a seedling of either Winesap or Red Limbertwig. In any case, Buncombe is a large and tasty apple but not very pretty. *See* Glenloch.

I have grafted Buncombe scions from two different sources in Tennessee that produced identical fruit. The fruit does not in any way resemble the descriptions in old apple references. The description below is for the fruit as currently being grown.

Fruit large, somewhat segmented, roundish to slightly oblate, conical; skin nearly covered in pale red with numerous darker red, broken stripes; dots small and large, tan or russet, often areolar; stem medium length in a deep, greenish cavity; calyx open; basin large, gradually sloped, sometimes leather-cracked; flesh whitish, juicy, moderately crisp, fine-grained, subacid. Ripe July/August. Catalog listings: MD, VA, NC, SC, GA, AL, MS, TN, KY, TX, AR (1857–1906). ❖ **Plate 7.**

❦ **BURL** (Cager): A local apple collected by Herbert Childress for his extensive preservation orchard in Dunnville, Kentucky. He describes it as follows: "A late summer yellow apple, tart, spicy flavored, aromatic. A good all-around apple." Ripe August. No catalog listings.

❦ **BURNING GREEN** (Burling Green, Burner Green?): An old apple grown in Mitchell County,

North Carolina. Danny Harvey sent me scions in 1996. It is probably the same as Burner Green, mentioned in 1868 by the Illinois Horticultural Society. A letter to me says "Burling Green" is a good keeper.

Fruit medium size or below, round; skin pale yellow; stem short. Ripe August or later. No catalog listings.

❦ **CALVIN:** Said to have been carried from Virginia to Kentucky over a hundred years ago where it was mainly used as a brandy apple, but I find it is an excellent apple for fresh eating. Jim Lawson sold it for years from his nursery in Georgia.

Fruit medium to almost large, roundish to slightly oblong, conical; skin smooth, yellow, darker yellow on the sunny side; dots numerous, small and large, russet, some submerged; stem long with a knob in an abrupt, narrow, slightly russeted cavity; calyx closed; basin small and shallow, corrugated; flesh yellowish, not very crisp, somewhat juicy, mild subacid. Ripe late July/August.

❦ **CAMACK'S SWEET** (Camak's Sweet, Cammack's Sweet, Grape Vine, Camack's Winter Sweet, Spitzburgen in western North Carolina): Originated in Macon County, North Carolina, and rather widely grown in the South before 1900. In 1997 George Barker of Climax, North Carolina, brought me some unknown sweet apples that he had found in the McMillan orchard near Cana, Virginia. These apples were a match for the picture and written descriptions of Camack's Sweet, which was listed as extinct in the first edition of this book. Mrs. McMillan says these sweet apples have been grown at her old homeplace for many years.

Fruit medium or above, nearly round, slightly conical; skin smooth, dull, yellow, usually with a blush cheek, mottled with green russet and scarfed skin; stem medium length and slender in a deep, pale greenish russeted cavity; calyx open; basin broad and shallow; flesh yellowish, fine-textured, firm, juicy, aromatic, scarcely sweet. Ripe late September/October. Catalog listings: VA, NC, GA, KY (1858–1902).

❦ **CANNON PEARMAIN** (Alpian, Red Cannon, Green Cannon, Anderson, Cannon): On October 6, 1804, Samuel Bailey listed his nursery stock for sale in a Virginia newspaper. On this list is Cannon Pearmain, making it one of a few southern apples that can be traced back over two hundred years without confusion. When Cannon Pearmain was discussed by the American Pomological Society in 1860, it was praised by delegates from Ohio and Indiana as well those from Virginia. By 1908 it was commercially concentrated in Bedford County, Virginia, where it was still an important market variety being grown mostly in older orchards. Trees seventy-five to one hundred years old were in good bearing condition. Growers there claimed there were two varieties, Red Cannon and Green Cannon, but varying growing conditions could explain minor color variations.

Elwood Fisher, professor emeritus of James Madison University, Harrisonburg, Virginia, has gone into the mountains and coves of the Appalachians seeking old apple trees still surviving in their lonely places. After years of searching he found a surviving tree of Cannon Pearmain on Headformes Mountain in Virginia's Bedford County. He was led to the tree by Bobby Parks, a dairy farmer who grew up near the mountain and who remembered that old Cannon Pearmain tree.

Cannon Pearmain is not of highest dessert quality but is an excellent general-purpose apple for cooking, drying, cider, and fresh eating. Its outstanding keeping quality and ability to withstand rough treatment made it a popular commercial apple in some southern markets. In 1860, the great pomologist Dr. John A. Warder of Ohio called Cannon Pearmain "better than anything I have seen from Boston to Virginia in the spring of the year." As is true of many winter apples, Cannon Pearmain improves in storage, being at its best after Christmas. The trees bear heavy crops of apples in alternate years and have tough limbs that seldom break.

Like Newtown Pippin, Cannon Pearmain is very sensitive to growing conditions, doing best at higher elevations on good soils. In the lower piedmont the fruit has been described as smaller, rotting and dropping badly, and inferior in appearance and flavor to mountain-grown apples. Red clay soils were believed by growers a hundred years ago to cause Cannon Pearmain to have tough flesh.

Fruit medium, roundish conical; skin smooth, greenish with a faint rusty pink blush; dots large, numerous, yellow or gray; stem long in a narrow, compressed, russeted, often lipped cavity; calyx closed; basin large, deep; flesh yellow, firm, crisp, aromatic, brisk subacid. Ripe October/November and keeps well. Catalog listings: MD, VA, SC, GA, MS, KY (1856–1904).

**CAPTAIN DAVIS:** Captain Davis of the Confederate Army was discharged at Greensboro, North Carolina, on April 26, 1865. Walking home to Mississippi, he ate some apples "somewhere in the Carolinas" and pocketed the seeds. A tree from one of the seeds grew up on Captain Davis's farm eight miles north of Kosciusko, Mississippi, and his descendents kept the apple by planting root sprouts. Mississippi apple hunter Jack Herring found a tree at the old Davis homeplace in 2003, and four other trees are growing nearby.

Steve Kelly, a friend and Virginia nurseryman, says: "This is the most fragrant apple I have ever seen. You would think you were in an apple packing house when you get near these apples."

Fruit medium or above, roundish to slightly oblate; skin greenish with a red-blushed cheek covering up to half the apple; dots whitish, numerous; stem short to three-quarters of an inch long in a russeted cavity; calyx open; basin greenish, shallow, ribbed; flesh white, fine-grained, moderately crisp and juicy, aromatic, subacid. Ripe late July/August. No catalog listings.

**CAROLINA BALDWIN** (North Carolina Baldwin?, Royal Limbertwig?, Caroline?): In 1858, S. W. Westbrook, a prominent North Carolina nurseryman, submitted specimens of an apple called North Carolina Baldwin to the American Pomological Society. In 1867 the Ohio pomologist, Dr. John Warder, described this same apple, which he said he received from S. W. Westbrook, under the name Carolina Baldwin.

Between the years 1860 and 1877 Carolina Baldwin was sold by several North Carolina nurseries, but a 1900 catalog lists it as a synonym of Royal Limbertwig, which it certainly very closely resembles. In 1879 North Carolina nurseryman Joshua Lindley said: "I am satisfied that the Royal Limbertwig and the Carolina Baldwin are distinct varieties." In 1880 another North Carolina nurseryman, C. W. Westbrook, contradicted Joshua Lindley: "Carolina Baldwin is Royal Limbertwig."

Downing (1878) describes an apple named Caroline (note the spelling), with the synonym of Carolina Baldwin, which originated before 1833 in Hanover, New Jersey, by A. G. Baldwin. This apple is a reasonably close fit to the Carolina Baldwin described by Warder but seems to have more red on the skin. My best guess is that this New Jersey apple is different from the southern Carolina Baldwin, and the southern Carolina Baldwin is identical to Royal Limbertwig. *See* Royal Limbertwig.

**CAROLINA PIPPIN:** Said to be a North Carolina apple in 1860. An old tree in Ashe County, North Carolina, at least a hundred years old and lying flat on the ground, was found in 1995 by the late North Carolina nurseryman Maurice Marshall. It is now obvious that Carolina Pippin and Fall Pippin are identical. *See* Fall Pippin.

**CAROLINA RED JUNE** (Red June, Red Juneating, June, Blush June, Georgia June, Knight's Red June, Summer Red, Jones June, Improved Red June, Red Harvest, Carolina Red, Jones Early Harvest, Sheepnose Crab, Everbearing Red June): Subsistence farming (where people grow what they eat) was common in the South until well into the twentieth century. A good early apple was prized by subsistence farmers to replace exhausted supplies of winter apples. For almost two centuries Carolina Red June was the early apple of choice for most southerners. A few varieties ripened earlier but were mainly cooking apples. Carolina Red June has enough quality to be eaten out of hand.

Like other early apple varieties, Carolina Red June simply does not have enough time to develop the exquisite sugar-acid balance of many fall and winter apples. Even so, its mildly brisk flavor is pleasurable to many and has kept it a southern favorite. It also makes a good early cider and exceptional apple pies.

Early listings of southern apples, in 1798 and 1804

Virginia newspapers, both include a "June Apple." We cannot be sure that this is Carolina Red June. W. H. Ragan, author of the USDA publication *Nomenclature of the Apple* (1905), left a handwritten "personal recollection" in the USDA files concerning Carolina Red June. He wrote that about 1827 a Tennessean named Lewis Shell settled near Mr. Ragan's father in Indiana and brought with him scions of Carolina Red June. This is the earliest reliable report of Carolina Red June and means that this variety certainly originated before 1800.

In 1868 William Summer, the owner of Pomaria Nurseries in South Carolina and a noted pomologist, had this to say about the origin of Carolina Red June: "The variety now so generally disseminated was produced within a few miles of Pomaria, South Carolina, by Henry Sieber. Persons came a day or two's ride to get scions for grafting." In the absence of any other definitive information about the origin of Carolina Red June, Mr. Summer's recollections should be accepted as correct. It is indeed unfortunate that he did not date the origin of this apple.

Several things worked together to make Carolina Red June one of the most important southern apples well into the twentieth century. The fruit begins ripening very early, continues ripening over a month or so, and has good taste and texture for an early apple. It is bright red, keeps for several weeks, and thus can be marketed commercially. The tree tends to bloom late, is very productive, and is adaptable to a broad range of soils and climates (although susceptible to apple scab and cedar-apple rust). Taken together these qualities were responsible for the success and rapid spread of Carolina Red June throughout the South and even into Illinois, Indiana, Ohio, Iowa, and other states.

Between 1845 and 1865 in the states of Indiana and Illinois, Carolina Red June became thoroughly mixed up with a very similar apple, Striped June. As a result, Carolina Red June was called Blush June by many nurseries and growers in those states, while Striped June was usually called Red June or Carolina June. This confusion did not reach into the South, where the name Red June has always meant Carolina Red June.

One peculiarity of Carolina Red June has been noted by several writers; often it blooms twice in the same year and bears a second, light crop of apples in the fall.

Several southern nurseries sold apple varieties advertised as improvements on Carolina Red June. In 1857 Fruitland Nursery in Augusta, Georgia, listed a Jones June. Clingman Nursery of Homer, Louisiana, listed an Improved Red June from 1898 to 1925: "Large red June apple, seedling of Red June, good for both table and market, keeps well. Ripe first of July." Two southern nurseries carried an Everbearing Red June. It is possible that all three of these are actually the same apple, a Georgia seedling of Carolina Red June, having larger fruit that ripens several weeks later. *See also* Mammoth June *and* Suzy Clark.

Fruit small to medium, roundish oblong to quite oblong, inclining to conical; skin smooth, almost entirely covered with red, which is darker on the sunny side; dots minute and obscure; stem variable in length in an acute, narrow cavity with a trace of russet; calyx closed; basin small, narrow, often slightly corrugated; flesh white, sometimes stained red on the sunny side, fine-grained, tender, moderately juicy, brisk subacid. Ripe June/July in most of the South. Catalog listings: MD, VA, NC, SC, GA, AL, MS, LA, TN, KY, TX, AR, FL (1836–1928).

❦ **CARTER'S BLUE** (Lady Fitzpatrick, Patton, Alabama Pearmain?): Colonel Carter of Mount Meigs Depot, near Montgomery, Alabama, originated this apple in the 1840s. Carter's Blue was grown widely in the South as a high-flavored apple borne on a vigorous, productive tree. The fruit has a purplish or bluish color due to its heavy, bluish bloom over dark red, and the foliage of the tree also has a dusty blue-green hue. The tree is susceptible to cedar-apple rust.

For many years this fine southern apple was extinct in the United States. Thanks to information from Theodore See of Corvallis, Oregon, a tree of Carter's Blue was located in the National Fruit Trust in Kent, England. The British added it to their extensive collection of apple varieties (over two thousand) in 1947 by receiving scions from an old collection of apple trees in Rhone, France. These French trees were purchased from Fruitland Nursery in Augusta, Georgia, about 1860. Scions of Carter's Blue and two other southern apples were imported from England to this country, and trees are now available.

Fruit above medium to large, sometimes very large, roundish to slightly oblate; skin green or greenish yellow washed with dull red with prominent darker red or purplish broken stripes, covered with a heavy bluish bloom; dots numerous, prominent, white; stem short and usually stout in a wide, shallow cavity; calyx closed; basin broad, fairly deep, lobed; flesh yellow or yellowish white, crisp, juicy, aromatic, mild subacid. Ripe late September. Catalog listings: VA, NC, GA, AL, MS, LA, TN, TX, AR (1858–1925).

❦ **CATAWBA:** Said to be a North Carolina apple in an 1860 South Carolina nursery catalog. Described as large, oblate conical; skin light yellow and green with patches of russet; flesh fine-grained, tender, white, aromatic, subacid to almost sweet. Ripe winter.

An apple called Catawba and generally fitting the above description has been found by Tom Brown in Troutdale, Virginia, but it ripens in August. Catalog listings: SC, GA (1860–61).

❦ **CATHEAD** (Catshead, Cathead Greening, Large Summer Russet, Round Cathead, Virginia Cathead?): Possibly the same as an English cooking apple described in England as early as 1688. Cathead was sold by a Georgia nursery in 1851 and Virginia nurseries from 1859 to 1904. In this country Cathead was first described by Coxe (1817): "This is a very large, round apple, flattened at the ends and deeply hollowed; the stalk is short and thick and so deeply sunk as to be almost imperceptible; the color a greenish yellow; the flesh white; a good apple for cooking and drying but apt to drop from the tree from its great weight; deficient in point of richness and flavour." Ripe September. This apple is different from Red Cathead. I received scions of Cathead in 1993 from Jean Miller of Laurel Springs, North Carolina, who wrote: "A large green-skin apple good for eating and drying and applesauce."

❦ **CAULEY** (Cally, Colley): A tree, fully grown, was found in 1919 in the yard of John Cauley near Grenada, Mississippi. Three young trees were grafted from Mr. Cauley's tree by J. W. Willis, who planted them at the Delta Branch Agricultural Experiment Station in Stoneville, Mississippi, where one tree survived the famous 1927 Mississippi River flood. This surviving tree averaged over a ton of apples each year during the 1930s.

Crawford Nurseries of Concord, Georgia, listed an apple called Cally in 1924, which can only be the Cauley under a different spelling: "Origin Mississippi over 50 years ago. Tree seems to be free of fire blight. Fruit green with some stripes on the sunny side; subacid. Apples gathered from the orchard of Warm Springs Fruit Company in 1922 weighed 22 ounces. This apple seems to do well in the southern part of middle Georgia. Ripens September 1st."

Although resurrected, so to speak, in 1919, Cauley is a very old apple variety. The Mississippi delegate to the 1860 meeting of the American Pomological Society mentioned, but did not describe, a large apple called Colley.

Cauley is susceptible to fire blight when young but quite resistant to this disease, as well as scab and bitter rot, when older. Its fruit is of rather high quality and can be used for cooking in mid-July. The apples ship well and are suitable for drying. The tree blooms late, has many fruit spurs, and the limbs bend but do not break under the weight of fruit. My friends and apple enthusiasts Jesse and Bonnie Thompson of Meridian, Mississippi, have a Cauley apple tree in their orchard and sent me scions of this apple.

Fruit large to very large, some apples weighing over a pound, roundish; skin light green or yellowish with a red blush and some obscure red stripes, but some apples are almost entirely red; dots scattered, whitish or russet, often areolar; stem medium length, in a deep, brownish cavity; calyx open; basin abrupt, wide, moderately deep; flesh slightly yellow, crisp, mild subacid. Ripe August/September.

❦ **CHATHAM SWEET:** Grown since the early 1900s in the western part of Alexander County, North Carolina. One tree, found by Tom Brown, belongs to Lynn St. Clair of Taylorsville, North Carolina.

Fruit medium size, roundish, flattened on the ends; skin pale greenish yellow, sometimes with a very faint blush on the sunny side; stem medium length in a russeted cavity. Ripe August/September. No catalog listings.

❦ **CHENANGO STRAWBERRY** (Sherwood's Favorite, Frank, Buckley, Early Sugar Loaf, Jackson Apple, Smyrna, Strawberry): Originated in New York or Connecticut before 1850. This beautiful apple, excellent for fresh eating and cooking, ripens in autumn in the North but is a summer apple in the South. The apples ripen over several weeks, a desirable trait for fruit trees in home orchards but a disaster for commercial orchardists. Some years ago Elwood Fisher, my friend in Harrisonburg, Virginia, recorded Chenango Strawberry apples as ripening from July 20 to September 17. He says this was his mother's favorite dessert apple and makes outstanding applesauce. For best eating quality the fruit should be picked when the skin begins to develop a milky appearance. The tree is susceptible to root rot and fire blight.

Fruit medium or larger, oblong conical; skin smooth, almost covered with crimson stripes; dots few, inconspicuous, white, small, often submerged; stem short to medium length and rather thick in an acute, deep, narrow, often furrowed cavity; basin medium to almost shallow in depth, wide, slightly furrowed; flesh white, tender, juicy, slightly aromatic, subacid. Ripe July/September. Catalog listings: MD, VA, NC, GA, AL, TN, KY, AR (1887–1920). ❖ **Plate 8.**

❦ **CHESAPEAKE:** In 1958 Frank Browning of Wallingford, Kentucky, grew this apple from a seed of Red Rome, and it was sold for several years by Bountiful Ridge Nurseries of Maryland, beginning in 1967. One evaluation is: "high dessert quality, storage qualities good, tree hardy and productive."

Fruit medium to large, shaped like Rome; skin smooth and mostly red; flesh white, juicy. Ripe September.

❦ **CHIMNEY APPLE:** Callie Ruth Price of Stuart, Virginia, wrote me in 1989: "My grandfather, W. Crawford Carter (1858–1945), had an old apple orchard in which his Chimney Apple thrived. He found the original seedling about 1875 growing beside the chimney of an abandoned cabin, hence the name. His son, J. Eldrin Carter, of Patrick Springs, Virginia, has some of these trees today, and the fruit is a very popular one in our area." When I visited Mr. Carter to get scions of Chimney Apple, he told me that this variety has been grown only in the Patrick Springs area. Before World War II, Mr. Carter loaded a railroad car with barrels of Chimney Apples each August for shipment to market. In the late 1920s and early 1930s he would fill an old school bus with Chimney Apples and peddle them on the streets of Danville, Virginia, and Durham and Burlington, North Carolina, where they sold well. The fruit is excellent for drying and fresh eating.

Fruit medium, roundish, slightly conical, flattened on the ends; skin lumpy, light green, about half covered with a brick-red blush, some apples almost entirely red; dots numerous, some tiny and white, interspersed with larger, rough, protruding whitish dots; stem short to medium length in a deep, narrow, russeted cavity; calyx closed; basin abrupt, usually greenish, cracked; flesh slightly yellow, fine-grained, juicy, moderately crisp, subacid. Ripe August. No catalog listings.

❦ **CLAPPER FLAT** (Flat Apple): Downing (1869) says this apple originated in Bethlehem, New York. Dr. Littleton found Clapper Flat near Petersburg, West Virginia.

Fruit above medium, oblate, slightly conical; skin mostly covered with stripes and splashes of red; dots whitish, large; stem medium length in a narrow, deep cavity; calyx closed; basin wide, shallow; flesh yellowish, moderately juicy, tender, mild subacid. Ripe September. No catalog listings.

❦ **CLARKE'S PEARMAIN** (Golden Pearmain, Clark's Pearmain, Yellow Pearmain, Gloucester Pearmain, Columbian Russet?): Thomas Jefferson's gardens and orchards at Monticello have been meticulously restored. Every attempt is made to find and grow the same fruits and vegetables that he grew and recorded in his journals. Mr. Jefferson had

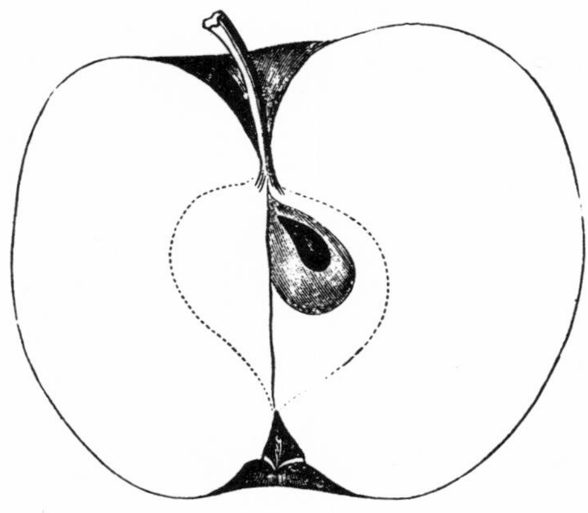

CLARKE'S PEARMAIN

an apple he called Golden Pearmain, and, as you can see above, Golden Pearmain is a synonym of Clarke's Pearmain. Clarke's Pearmain is a very old apple. A "Clark's Pearmain" was listed by Thomas Sorsby's Virginia nursery in 1755 and 1763.

An 1853 North Carolina nursery catalog listed Golden Pearmain with "Clark's Pearmain" as a synonym, so both names were still being used as primary names in the mid-1800s. In 1993 I received a letter from Dewitt Souther of Wilkes County, North Carolina, telling me of his Clarke's Pearmain tree, which he grafted from an old tree of that name planted by his father. The fruit of Mr. Souther's Clarke's Pearmain fits old descriptions of Clarke's Pearmain, and I believe this apple is identical to Mr. Jefferson's Golden Pearmain.

Fruit medium, roundish conical; skin mostly yellow or orangish, greenish yellow in the shade but much marbled and striped with dull red in the sun, some bronze on the skin; dots numerous, russet or whitish russet; stem long in a small, deep, slightly russeted cavity; calyx closed or open; basin small; flesh greenish yellow or yellow, fine-grained, juicy, firm, crisp, subacid. Ripe September/October. *See also* Columbian Russet *and* Ruckman. Catalog listings: MD, VA, NC, SC, GA, AL, MS, LA, KY (1755–1910).

❦ **CLARK'S ORANGE** (Clark): The 1877 meeting of the American Pomological Society briefly discussed this apple. It probably originated in Ohio and is one of many apples rediscovered by Dr. L. R. Littleton in Virginia and West Virginia. The only known tree of Clark's Orange belonged to Jearl Kisamore of Seneca Rocks, West Virginia. Mr. Kisamore said a ripe apple "feels like it has honey on its peeling." When Mr. Kisamore and Dr. Littleton visited the old tree, they found a bear had been there first. Mr. Kisamore wrote me: "I picked enough apples for eighteen quarts of apple sauce. The bear got the rest."

Fruit medium to large, roundish to slightly oblong; skin yellowish or orange, sometimes obscurely striped; flesh white, juicy, subacid. Ripe August/September. No catalog listings.

❦ **COBLE'S WILDER:** From the 1923 catalog of the North State Nursery Company, Julian, North Carolina: "Originated on our nursery farm. A vigorous tree. Fruit medium size, red on yellow, crisp, highly flavored. Grows in clusters. Very prolific. August." Coble's Wilder was considered extinct in the first edition of this book, but an old tree bearing this name has been found recently by my friend Jimmy Hargrove.

Fruit medium, roundish to oblong, conical; skin yellow with very faint, pale pink stripes on the sunny side; dots small, pink and russet; stem very long in a narrow, sometimes lipped cavity; calyx closed or partly open in a small, bumpy basin; flesh pale yellow, juicy, not very crisp, subacid. Ripe July.

❦ **COE:** In 1901 and again in 1910 a Coe apple was listed by Greensboro Nurseries, Greensboro, North Carolina. Briefly described as "large, roundish ovate, slightly oblique; skin smooth, red stripes on yellow; flesh tender, subacid. Ripe September/October." This apple probably originated with W. A. Coe of Vandalia, North Carolina.

In 2006 Jimmy Hargrove found a Coe apple still being grown by John Coble near Julian, North Carolina. This apple is medium, roundish, often lopsided; skin virtually covered with medium red with a few embedded darker stripes; dots numerous, large, pale gray with russet centers; stem medium length ending in a knob in a greenish, rather large cavity; calyx closed; basin lumpy; flesh pale greenish, crisp, juicy, subacid. Ripe late August.

❦ **COFFELT BEAUTY** (Coffelt, Cawfelt, Improved

Limbertwig, Wandering Spy): Originated before 1887 with Wyatt Coffelt of Benton County, Arkansas, who considered it to be a cross of Ben Davis and Red Limbertwig. Said to resemble the Red Limbertwig but larger, and superior to the Ben Davis in flavor and keeping ability. Tree healthy and a regular bearer. Fruit hangs well on the tree. As grown in Maryland in 1900 the fruit had brown warty projections on the skin that prevented it from being grown commercially there, but Coffelt Beauty was grown commercially in north Georgia until the 1940s. Beach (1905) describes an Arkansas apple called Wandering Spy that "originated in the Ozarks with Wyatt Coffelt." Its description matches Coffelt Beauty almost exactly.

An apple called Limbertwig Improved has been recently found that fits the description below of Coffelt Beauty, and is almost certainly identical to it. Coffelt Beauty was listed as extinct in the first edition of this book.

Fruit medium or above, roundish oblate, uniform in size and shape; skin almost smooth, yellow mostly covered with red and thin stripes of darker red; dots variable, often russet; cavity medium to deep, slightly furrowed, usually russeted; basin somewhat shallow to deep, medium width, often furrowed; flesh whitish, firm, rather fine-grained, somewhat tender, moderately juicy, subacid, improving in color and flavor in storage. Ripe October. Catalog listings: MD, GA, TN, KY, AR (1890–1928). ❖ **Plate 9.**

❦ **COFFEY SEEDLING** (Coffee Seedling?): The best information for this apple is in an 1890 catalog of the Catawba County Nursery, Newton, North Carolina: "Supposed to be a seedling of the Red Limbertwig, only much larger. Very large specimens weigh as high as 24 ounces. Tree vigorous. Flavor mild subacid, rich, juicy. Ripens in October." Another old nursery catalog says "originated on the farm of Levi Coffey in Caldwell County, North Carolina."

An apple I found years ago called Coffey Seedling turned out to be identical to Dula's Beauty. Tom Brown recently found a "Coffee Seedling" that has not yet fruited so cannot be identified further.

❦ **COLLINS** (Champion, Collins Red, Coss' Champion, Coss' Red, Winter Champion, Champion Red): Originated about 1865 on the old Merriman farm in the Cove Hill area of Washington County, Arkansas, and named for the nurseryman George Collins who first brought it to notice in 1886. Sold for years by Stark Bro's Nursery under the name Champion. Around the turn of the century, Champion was widely planted in Arkansas and adjoining states as a commercial variety to take the place of Ben Davis. Its good qualities include annual productiveness, holding its fruit well on the tree, and the excellent keeping ability of the apples. Unfortunately, the eating quality of Champion is no better than Ben Davis, and the apples are often smaller. The tree has a somewhat drooping growth habit. Some years ago I saw a ninety-year-old Champion tree in Virginia, unsprayed for many years, but still healthy and absolutely loaded down with a crop of perfect, if rather small, apples.

Fruit medium to large, round or slightly oblate; skin thick, tough, waxy, usually a bright dark red with indistinct darker stripes, but shaded apples have more green or yellow; dots numerous, inconspicuous, small, russet or gray; stem medium to long in a rather broad, sometimes russeted cavity; basin round, abrupt, moderately deep, somewhat furrowed; flesh nearly white, very firm, rather coarse, moderately juicy, sprightly subacid. Ripe late. Catalog listings: MD, LA, TX, AR (1899–1920).

❦ **COLLINS JUNE:** The Collins family of Tifton, Georgia, grew this early apple for years as a good cooking apple, and Lawson's Nursery of Ball Ground, Georgia, sold trees from 1975 to 1979. Tree said to be unproductive.

Fruit large, round to oblate; skin greenish yellow to yellow; flesh cream-colored, soft, subacid. Ripe June/July.

❦ **CONRAD** (Conrad's Eating?, Eating?): An apple of this name has been sold recently by Lawson's Nursery in Georgia. It may be the same apple as Conrad's Eating, briefly described by Warder (1867) as being oblate and subacid. Sold by Virginia nurseries from 1858 to 1904.

❦ **COTHREN:** Wilkes County, North Carolina, a

mountain county, has been a gold mine of old apple varieties. Tom Brown, the best apple hunter I know, has spent years tracking down the old apples of Wilkes County. Cothren is one of his many discoveries. A ninety-seven-year-old woman there remembers Cothren apples from early in her life, and at least three old trees were found by Tom Brown in 2000.

Fruit large, oblate; skin yellow, partly covered with red stripes; stem short; flesh firm, juicy, subacid. Ripe August/September. No catalog listings.

**COTTON** (Large White Sweet, Cotton Bole, Welsh)**/COTTON SWEET:** In 1888 D. J. McMillan of Washington, North Carolina, wrote in a letter: "The Welsh apple, or Cotton apple as it is called here, was brought by Welsh colonists who settled between Rockfish and Burgaw Creeks on the northeast rim of the Cape Fear. I find it nowhere else." Mr. McMillan did not describe this Cotton apple, but it is probably identical to the Cotton apple introduced to the American Pomological Society in 1858 by Mr. Westbrook, a North Carolina nurseryman, and that was sold by several North Carolina nurseries from 1856 to 1867.

An apple named White Sweet or Cotton Sweet has been found in Virginia and western North Carolina, but it is not this apple.

Fruit large, roundish oblate; skin white or pale yellow; flesh very tender. Ripe August.

**CRACK:** At the old homeplace of Kelly Bowman's mother near Taylorsville, North Carolina, Tom Brown found this tree and two others nearby.

Fruit small, oblate; skin rough with a light bloom, covered in medium to dark red with obscure stripes; dots large, protruding; stem short to medium in a wide, pale russet cavity; calyx open; basin wide, greenish; flesh moderately crisp and juicy, almost sweet. Ripe October. No catalog listings.

**CRITT:** Another old variety from the Roan Mountain State Park area of western North Carolina, described by Tom Brown as a "sour apple good for jelly and vinegar. This is a very late apple. They say they are not good to eat until after Christmas. Properly grown apples might get up to two inches in diameter." No catalog listings.

**CROW'S EGG** (Raven's Egg, Black Annie)**/CROW EGG:** Crow's Egg is a strangely shaped apple that I have found in several places in the mountains of Virginia and North Carolina. It receives high praise for its eating qualities from those who still grow it. Having now grown Crow's Egg for several years, it appears identical to Black Gilliflower. *See* Black Gilliflower.

The Worcester County (Massachusetts) Horticultural Society sells scionwood of an apple they call Crow Egg. This medium-size, oblate, red-blushed apple is completely different from the southern Crow's Egg apple and is an outstanding eating apple that hangs well on the tree when ripe in late August to September in central North Carolina.

**CULLASAGA** (Winter Horse, Cullasaja, Callasaga): Nancy Bryson (b. 1804, m. Jehodia Hunnicutt) grew Cullasaga from a seed of the Horse Apple circa 1830 at her parent's home near Salem Methodist Church in Macon County, North Carolina. It was introduced about 1850 by the great North Carolina pomologist Silas McDowell who named it for the nearby Cullasaja River and gorge. In 1894 the original tree was still standing with a trunk almost ten feet in circumference.

All old pomological references and catalogs give the name as Cullasaga, but the current name of the river in Macon County is Cullasaja. Old postal guides and Rand McNally maps show that this word has been spelled variously as Cullasaga, Cullasagee or Cullasaja over the past hundred years.

Cullasaga was grown widely in the South before 1900 but was considered extinct in 1989. In March of that year I received a letter from Bob Padgett, now deceased, who lived near Highlands in Macon County: "My neighbors have a Cullasaja apple tree. It is a very tall tree and beginning to fall apart, but it still bears apples. It is reported to be over a hundred years old." My wife and I were guided by Mr. Padgett to this wonderful old tree, which still had two strong limbs. Thanks to the owners, the Edwards and the Melvins, we obtained grafting scions. The tree, the only one ever found of Cullasaga, is now dead.

Fruit medium or above to large, roundish; skin

smooth, tough, mostly covered with brick red with a few darker stripes; dots numerous, irregular, whitish; stem fleshy, medium length in a deep, greenish russeted cavity; basin deep and corrugated; flesh yellow, compact, tender, juicy, aromatic, mild subacid to almost sweet. Ripe October. Catalog listings: MD, VA, NC, SC, GA, AL, TN, KY, TX (1859–1902). ❖ **Plate 10.**

**DAVIDSON SWEETING:** In 1994 Dr. L. R. Littleton found a single old tree in the Berrier Orchard in Cana, Virginia. Renee Berrier says the original grafts were brought from Davidson County, North Carolina, in the mid-1800s, and the apples have long been prized by the Berriers for apple preserves.

Fruit medium or above, roundish or slightly oblate; skin yellow with faint, broken red stripes on the sunny side; dots scattered, russet; stem very short in a narrow, deep, russeted cavity; calyx open; flesh fine-grained, juicy, rather soft, sweet. Ripe late July/August. No catalog listings.

**DEADERICK** (Ben Ford, Ozark Pippin): Originated about 1850 with Benjamin Ford of Washington County, Tennessee, where it was called Ozark Pippin. An 1896 Tennessee agricultural experiment station bulletin describes it under the name Deaderick, a name change probably necessary because another apple was named Ozark. In 1992 Richard Moyer found apple trees being grown in Tennessee called Ozark Pippin, and examination of the fruit proves that this apple is Deaderick. The tree seems to be rather resistant to fire blight.

Fruit large, roundish conical, sides sometimes unequal; skin tough, smooth, lemon yellow, often with a pinkish blush and having a few large, reddish, areolar spots; dots black and brown, many with pink or green bases; stem short and stout ending in a knob in a large, deep, sometimes furrowed, russeted cavity; calyx closed or partially open; basin small, very shallow, furrowed; flesh yellowish, fine-grained, breaking, juicy, mild subacid. Ripe late September/October. No catalog listings.

**DELICIOUS** (Hawkeye, Red Delicious): It hardly seems necessary to point out how this variety has replaced almost all the older apple varieties in southern orchards and gardens. The unripe, starchy Red Delicious apples found in supermarkets (and usually grown on the West Coast) bear little resemblance to a southern-grown, properly ripened Delicious, an apple of high flavor and aroma (but smaller and less colorful than those West Coast apples).

This apple first grew in the orchard of Jesse Hiatt of Peru, Madison County, Iowa. There are two slightly differing stories concerning the beginnings of Delicious. The 1907 *USDA Yearbook* says that the original tree was a sprout from the rootstock of a Yellow Bellflower tree, the top of which had been destroyed about 1875. It fruited for the first time in 1881, the fruit attracted Mr. Hiatt's attention, and he began grafting it for his own use. An old Stark Bro's Nursery catalog quotes a letter from Mr. Hiatt: "Delicious is a sprout which came up under a Yellow Bellflower and was about six years from the ground when it fruited. Was so fine a fruit I at once set some grafts and upturned sod around the tree and it soon began making strong, thrifty growths. Now about 15 years old and is 13 inches in diameter at the ground."

Another—probably greatly embellished—story is that the Delicious first grew as a seedling in Mr. Hiatt's orchard about 1870, near an old Yellow Bellflower tree. Mr. Hiatt cut the seedling down twice because it was not in his orchard rows. When it persisted in living, Mr. Hiatt began pruning it, curious as to the fruit it would bear. After tasting and being delighted with the new apple, which the Hiatt family named Hawkeye, Mr. Hiatt tried to persuade a nurseryman in nearby Winterset, Iowa, to sell the trees but was refused. In 1893 Mr. Hiatt sent some apples to a fruit show in Louisiana, Missouri, sponsored by Stark Bro's Nursery. Mr. Hiatt's apples won first prize (and greatly impressed C. M. Stark, president of the nursery) but Mr. Hiatt's name and address had been lost from his tray of fruit. He reentered the fruit in the show in 1894, and Mr. Stark personally traveled to see Mr. Hiatt and to purchase the rights to propagate and sell this apple as well as the right to rename it. Stark Bro's Nursery introduced it in 1895 as the Delicious apple, and by 1922 had sold eight million trees. The hardiness and productiveness of the tree, the beauty and eating quality of the fruit, and the ability of the variety to withstand commercial marketing saw Delicious rapidly replace most other commercial varieties throughout apple-growing regions of the United States.

Jesse Hiatt did not live to see his apple at its zenith. The old Quaker died in 1898 before Delicious really began its climb to fame and fortune. The original Delicious tree lived on until 1940 when an ice storm broke it off. A sprout grew up from the stump and still thrives in Madison County, Iowa.

The very large, completely red, "Red Delicious" apples sold today in supermarkets are sports or limb mutations of the original Delicious, having been selected and propagated for their size, shape, and color. Three hundred mutations have been found over the years, and several have completely replaced the original Delicious in commercial orchards. The eating quality of these red sports is inferior to the original or "Hawkeye Delicious" described below.

Fruit medium to large, roundish to somewhat oblong, quite conical, knobbed at the base; skin thick, smooth, glossy, taking a high polish when rubbed, clear yellow, washed over most of the surface with red and striped with indistinct darker red; dots numerous, small, whitish; stem medium in a wide, deep, greenish cavity; calyx closed; basin medium size, greenish, slightly furrowed; flesh yellowish, moderately fine-grained, breaking, juicy, mild subacid to sweet with the distinctive "Delicious" taste. Ripe September/October. Catalog listings: MD, VA, NC, GA, AL, MS, LA, TN, KY, TX, AR (1902–28).

❦ **DEVINE:** Joyce Neighbors, my good friend and a nurserywoman in Gadsden, Alabama, found this apple being grown by Mrs. J. B. Devine. Family lore is that a "sprout" of the apple was carried from South Carolina to Alabama in 1895.

Fruit medium to almost large, roundish conical; skin mostly covered with bright red with faint red stripes more obvious at the basin end; dots scattered, tannish, rather large but smaller near the basin; stem medium length in a wide, irregular, slightly to heavily russeted cavity; flesh greenish, fine-grained, subacid. Ripe July/August. No catalog listings.

❦ **DISHAROON:** An old Georgia apple, thought to be an Indian seedling, found in Habersham County, Georgia, "by a man named Disharoon." Jim Lawson of Lawson's Nursery grafted several Disharoon trees in the 1970s for nearby family members of that name. I found Disharoon apple trees in north Georgia on an old family farm owned by Juanita Davis, who gave me scions in 1998.

Fruit medium, roundish, flattened on the ends; skin green with a yellowish or golden hue on the sunny side; dots numerous, obscure, greenish with russet centers, submerged; stem medium length in an abrupt, deep, russeted cavity; calyx open or closed; basin round, deep, often corrugated; flesh pale yellow, moderately juicy and crisp, sweet. Ripe September/October. No catalog listings. ❖ **Plate 11.**

❦ **DOCTOR** (Red Doctor, DeWitt, Newby, Coon, Doctor Dewit, American Nonpareil): An old Pennsylvania apple sold by several Maryland and Virginia nurseries. First described in 1804 and even then an old variety. In 1874 it was being grown in Indiana but had lost its original name. Mr. Thomas Newby, of Carthage, Indiana, championed this old but unknown variety, and in 1894 it was renamed Newby by the Indiana Horticultural Society. Newby apples were displayed in the American fruit exhibit at the Paris Exposition in France in 1900 and attracted much attention because of their symmetrical shape and beautiful color. In that same year, apples from an old Ohio tree, known to be Doctor, were sent to the USDA. Upon comparison to Newby, the USDA realized that Newby was, in fact, the Doctor apple.

Fruit large, oblate or roundish oblate, sometimes oblique; skin thick, smooth, glossy when ripe, becoming oily in storage, rich yellow washed with red and indistinctly striped with crimson; dots scattered, russet, occasionally areolar; stem short and rather stout in a large, deep, somewhat russeted cavity; calyx usually open; basin large, deep, furrowed, downy; flesh yellowish, moderately fine-grained, breaking, juicy, subacid. Ripe September/October. Catalog listings: MD, VA, DC (1824–1904).

**DOCTOR MATTHEWS:** First grown by Dr. W. F. Matthews of Brazil, Tennessee, and listed in 1895 by Planters Nurseries of Humboldt, Tennessee. Here is a very interesting letter from Joe A. Burton, Mitchell, Indiana, dated 1917.

"The Dr. Matthews is a tree planted in the Indiana Experimental Orchard in 1900. Two trees were planted, but only one grew. We planted 160 varieties, two each. The Dr. Matthews trees were obtained from C. W. Hobbs & Sons, Bridgeport, Ind. When the apple was found to be of superior quality, I made inquiry about it but the nursery had no remembrance of it. In Ragan's *Nomenclature of the Apple*, I found Dr. Matthews was introduced in Tennessee in 1895. I wrote that nurseryman, but he had no remembrance of it. I sent him specimens but he did not recognize them. He gave me the address of Dr. Matthews, and I sent him specimens. He claimed to recognize them, but in the many things he said I concluded he did not know the apple. He had lost out on it and no trees were known to exist. That the originator, introducer, and the general public should lose sight of and totally forget an apple of such quality in 25 years is unthinkable to me.

"As to quality it is not as high flavored as Grimes Golden. It is the texture that wins. It has no fiber but seems to be just organized cider and melts in the mouth like candy. Nine tenths of those who eat it call it the best apple they ever tasted."

Fruit above medium, roundish conical, flattened on the ends, often oblique; skin tough, yellow with pale red and some stripes on the sunny side, often mostly red in the sun; dots numerous, light-colored, many with russet centers; stem medium length in a medium depth, russeted cavity; basin rather wide and deep; flesh cream-colored, fine-grained, crisp, juicy, aromatic, almost sweet. Ripe September. **❖ Plate 12.**

**DOMINE** (Dominie, American Nonpareil, English Rambo, English Red Streak, English Beauty, Wells, Cheat, Cling Tight, Striped Rhode Island Greening, Hogan, Williamson, Winter Rambo, Red Streak): Domine, widely grown in the South before 1900, is listed most often in old southern nursery catalogs under the name Dominie. The tree had the reputation of being a very rapid grower and a prodigious bearer, with branches bending down and sometimes breaking under clusters of fruit. Domine apples very much resemble fruit of the Rambo, as several of its synonyms indicate, but it is a better winter keeper. The tree has a straggling growth habit and bears biennially unless the fruit is thinned. The stems often pull out when the apples are picked.

In spite of such synonyms as English Beauty and English Red Streak, Domine is probably of American origin before 1800. Elliot (1858) says it may have originated in Maryland, but Domine was first mentioned by name in an 1805 Virginia nursery catalog.

Fruit medium, oblate, sometimes oblique; skin thick, smooth, striped and splashed with red and russet streaks in the sun, some bloom; dots rather large, scattered, irregular, yellowish gray with russet centers; stem medium to long and slender in a wide, deep, furrowed, usually russeted cavity; basin hairy, moderately deep, wide, usually furrowed; flesh white or tinged yellow, very firm, breaking, almost coarse, juicy, mild subacid, somewhat aromatic. Ripe October. Catalog listings: MD, VA, NC, GA, KY, MS, TX (1855–1914).

**DONCE:** Bobby Johnson of Traphill, North Carolina, has the only known tree. He told Tom Brown that the apple originated with Donce Johnson, one of the earliest settlers in Wilkes County. Described as large, roundish conical; skin light green splashed and striped with red; flesh firm, crisp, juicy, subacid. Ripe August. No catalog listings.

**DUCHESS OF OLDENBURG** (Duchess, Dutchess, Oldenburg, Borovinka, Borovitsky, Charlamowsky, Smith's Beauty): This Russian apple is the "King of the Ironclads," the Ironclads being those apple varieties that survive the severe winters of Minnesota, Maine, Wisconsin, and nearby states. In these states the trees of standard northern varieties such as Baldwin, Northern Spy, and Rhode Island Greening may be damaged or killed by the cold. Duchess, almost alone in the 1850s and 1860s, came through the winters "hardy as an oak." Because Duchess was known to be of Russian origin, its winter hardiness prompted the USDA to import hundreds of other Russian apple varieties in the 1870s and 1880s in a search for additional cold-hardy apples.

Duchess was grown in the South as a superior cooking and drying apple on an abundant tree that bears quickly; often fruit is borne on two- or three-year-old trees. On the negative side Duchess is susceptible to fire blight, often drops its fruit before ripe, and the fruit quickly becomes mealy when overripe.

Duchess originated before 1700 near Tula, Russia, about 100 miles south of Moscow. Its Russian name was Borovitsky. In 1815 the Horticultural Society of London brought the Duchess apple to England where the name "Duchess of Oldenburg" was acquired, how we do not know. It was imported to the United States by the Massachusetts Horticultural Society in 1835.

Fruit medium or above, roundish oblate; skin thin, dull, waxen yellow, washed and heavily streaked with dark red, almost completely red where fully exposed to the sun; dots numerous, small, whitish; stem short in an acute, deep, greenish cavity; calyx closed; basin deep, broad, acute; flesh whitish, tender, fairly crisp, juicy, subacid. Ripe July in most of the South. Catalog listings: MD, VA, NC, SC GA, LA, TN, KY, TX, AR (1858–1928).

❦ **DULA'S BEAUTY** (Dula): Originated in the late 1800s in Lenoir, Caldwell County, North Carolina, from Limbertwig seeds that Mr. J. A. Dula planted to grow rootstocks for grafting. The tree is vigorous, a prolific bearer, and is said to grow well on either bottomland or hillsides. The fruit has good dessert quality and keeps fairly well. Dula's Beauty was recommended in 1908 by the North Carolina Department of Agriculture for growing in the piedmont. One very old tree was found in 1990 in an old orchard in Watauga County, North Carolina, belonging to Inadene Hampton and her two sisters, all octogenarians. Nancy Moretz also grows Dula's Beauty near Boone, North Carolina.

Fruit large, or very large, roundish or slightly oblate, conical, irregular, and often oblique; skin rough, almost entirely covered with dark red with obscure darker stripes; dots medium size, scattered, grayish; stem medium length in a very deep, greenish russeted cavity; calyx greenish, open; basin often shallow, ribbed; flesh yellowish white, tender, crisp, juicy, mild subacid. Ripe September. No catalogs listings. *See* Coffey Seedling. ❖ **Plate 13.**

❦ **DURHAM:** Velma Johnson of Traphill, North Carolina, owns the sole surviving tree, but Tom Brown says there were many trees of the Durham apple around that area thirty years ago. Described as small, oblate, slightly conical; skin covered with brownish yellow rough russet; flesh firm, crisp, acid. Ripe August/September. No catalog listings.

❦ **EARLY HARVEST** (Yellow June, Yellow Harvest, Harvest, Prince's Harvest, Yellow Juneating, Early Juneating, July Pippin, Large White Juneating, Bracken, Early French Reinette, Glass Apple, Sinclair's Yellow, Maralandica): Early Harvest is one of those apple varieties that does well in most apple-growing areas. It has been praised from New England to Texas and points beyond, both for cooking and fresh eating. An 1859 Virginia nursery catalog says: "Taking all its qualities into consideration, it has no superior among early apples." I well remember asking an aged North Carolina farmer about an old apple tree standing in his field. "That's a Harvest apple," he said. "It's the second best apple there is. The best apple is the Magnum Bonum."

Like many early apples, Early Harvest tends to ripen on the tree over an extended period of time, often two or three weeks. Its season starts the first week of June in central Georgia but August in the higher mountains. In spite of early ripening and high quality, Early Harvest apples were not much grown for commercial purposes in the South. The thin, yellow skin shows bruises easily, and the fruit has a short keeping period. Early Harvest was largely an apple for the home orchard, grown near almost every farmhouse and prized for eating and cooking.

Early Harvest needs good soil and proper care to produce quality fruit. It is important to pick the apples at the right time; if picked too early or left too long on the tree, fruit quality is inferior. The fruit should remain on the tree just until it acquires a bright yellow color. Early Harvest trees usually bear heavily on alternate years and are very susceptible to apple scab.

Coxe (1817) first described Early Harvest under the names Prince's Harvest and Early French Reinette. It may have originated before 1800 in the famous William Prince Nursery on Long Island, New York. Warder (1867) notes this characteristic about Early Harvest: "The pale olive twigs are remarkable for their peculiar mode of production in twos and threes from a common origin." Many old trees called Early Harvest are actually Yellow Transparent, an early yellow apple that ripens a week or so before Early Harvest.

Fruit medium or above, uniform in size and shape, nearly round to somewhat oblate, skin thin, smooth, clear pale yellow to straw yellow; dots few, minute, white and green; stem medium length, slender or stout in a wide, russeted cavity; calyx usually closed; basin narrow, shallow, sometimes furrowed; flesh very white, tender, juicy, crisp, subacid or somewhat acid. Ripe late June/July in most of the South. Catalog listings: MD, VA, NC, SC, GA, AL, MS, LA, TN, KY, TX, AR, FL (1845–1928). *See also* Bracken Early. ❖ **Plate 14.**

❦ **EARLY JOE:** About 1800 Heman Chapin of Ontario County, New York, planted some apple seeds he obtained from Connecticut. From Chapin's seedling orchard came three fine apple varieties—Early Joe, Northern Spy, and Melon. Early Joe was brought to the attention of the public in 1843 by being exhibited at a fair in Rochester. Its reputation spread quickly because it was listed in southern nursery catalogs as early as 1853. The fruit is not as early ripening as Carolina Red June and Early Harvest, but its rich flavor makes it well worth growing in the South. The apples hang well on the tree, which is susceptible to scab and usually a biennial bearer.

In 1994 I found two old Early Joe apple trees, still bearing heavily, belonging to Mrs. Pearl Pickard of Pleasant Hill Church, Alamance County, North Carolina. These are the only trees of Early Joe I have ever found in the South, although apparently it was popular here a hundred years ago. Early Joe apples are small but excellent in taste and texture for an early apple.

Fruit small to medium, roundish to oblate, slightly conical; skin smooth, thin, pale greenish yellow, irregularly striped and splashed with dark red; dots russet and greenish to nearly white; stem medium to long in a large, slightly russeted cavity; basin small to medium, shallow, sometimes wrinkled; flesh yellowish white, tender, juicy, mild subacid. Ripe mid-July. Catalog listings: VA, NC, SC, GA, TN, KY, TX (1853–1910).

❦ **EARLY RED BIRD** (Crimson Beauty, Red Bird): Named and trademarked by Stark Bro's Nursery, which sold it from about 1915 to the 1930s. They advertised it as the earliest of all apples, seven to ten days ahead of Yellow Transparent. Early Red Bird originated about 1880 with Francis P. Sharp (1823–1903) of New Brunswick, Canada, who called it Crimson Beauty and first exhibited it in 1895. In 1897 Mr. Sharp had 250,000 apple trees in his orchard in New Brunswick, some of which survive to this day. He was the first person in Canada to carefully breed apple varieties, which he sold through his huge nursery.

In 1989 I received a letter from Byrd H. Bryan who lives in Pearisburg, Virginia: "The Early Red Bird I grew up with ripened here in the mountains of Virginia in July. The apples did not keep well and bruised easily. They were medium to small apples, mostly red, with white, mealy, mushy flesh, and absolutely no good to eat. *But,* if left to ripen fully on the tree, they had red veins running through the flesh. When left unpeeled, but cut and cored, they made a naturally red, magnificent applesauce with a taste unlike any other. It was not only our family favorite but the only applesauce we made. Originally, of course, we canned the applesauce, but when freezers came along we found freezing was far superior for this applesauce." Early Red Bird is also a good apple to fry with bacon or sausage for breakfast. The tree blooms very early.

Fruit medium or below, roundish to oblate, lobed; skin mostly blushed and striped red and crimson, some bloom; dots numerous, whitish, some areole; stem long in a greenish cavity; basin small and shallow; flesh white, fine-grained, not very juicy, rather soft, subacid to acid, often stained red on the sunny side. Ripe June.

❧ **EARLY RED MARGARET** (Striped June, Striped Juneating, Southern Striped June, Early Margaret, Red Striped June, Early June, Duverson's June, Early Red, Early Red Juneating, Herr's June?, Margaret, Red June [incorrectly], Eve Apple): An ancient apple of English origin, sold throughout the South with many southern nursery catalogs listing Striped June or Southern Striped June as synonyms. This is unfortunate as there has been continuous confusion concerning apples bearing the name Striped June. Striped June is a catch-all term that, sooner or later, was given to almost any striped apple ripening in June or early July. As early as 1874 the southern pomologist William Summer said, "There are three or four varieties of Striped June which have been grown for 75 years and which are distinct from the Early Red Margaret." Many old trees called Striped June continue to grow and bear in southern rural areas, and at least some of these are Early Red Margaret.

Fruit small to medium, oblong, slightly conical; skin striped with red with heavier striping at the stem end; stem short and stout in a medium, greenish cavity; calyx prominent; basin very shallow, lobed; flesh white, fine-grained, juicy, crisp, brisk subacid, rapidly becoming soft. Ripe June/July. *See also* Carolina Red June, Virginia June, Striped June, *and* Striped July. Catalog listings: VA, NC, SC, GA, AL, MS, LA, TX, TN, KY, AR (1845–1925).

❧ **EARLY RIPE** (Weidner): The best information is that Early Ripe originated about 1800 on the farm of George Delap (or Dunlap) in Adams County, Pennsylvania. The fruit ripens about ten days after Early Harvest and is of similar or slightly better quality. Many southern nurseries recommended Early Ripe for early marketing because the tree is much more resistant to scab than Early Harvest, and the fruit does not bruise as easily.

Fruit medium or above, roundish oblate, slightly conical, broadly lobed; skin dull, pale yellow or greenish yellow; dots small, indented, gray or russet; stem medium to short in an acute, shallow, greenish, rather broad, often russeted cavity; calyx closed; basin small and very shallow, wrinkled; flesh white, tender, moderately coarse, crisp, juicy, brisk subacid to subacid when fully ripe. Ripe late June. Catalog listings: MD, VA, NC, GA, AL, TN, KY (1858–1928).

❧ **EARLY STRAWBERRY** (Red Strawberry, Red Juneating, American Red Juneating, Tennessee Early Red, Duverson's June, Streaked June?): Thought to have originated in New York before 1838. The name Strawberry is a synonym for at least six apple varieties, so be careful in identifying any apple of this name. Because both share the synonym Red Juneating, Early Strawberry can be confused with Early Red Margaret, but Early Strawberry is usually more highly colored and has a longer stem than Early Red Margaret. Early Strawberry is a rather tart apple, and I prefer it to all other apples for applesauce. The apples ripen over a period of several weeks and quickly become mealy when overripe.

Fruit medium or smaller, roundish, flattened on the ends, slightly conical, often oblique and irregular, sides may be unequal; skin smooth, mostly to completely covered with fine stripes and stains of bright red to dark red; dots numerous, small, grayish, some with a red areole; stem medium to occasionally long in a deep, broad cavity, often faintly greenish; calyx closed or open, greenish; basin abrupt, rather deep, often irregular, corrugated; flesh almost white often stained red, soft, moder-

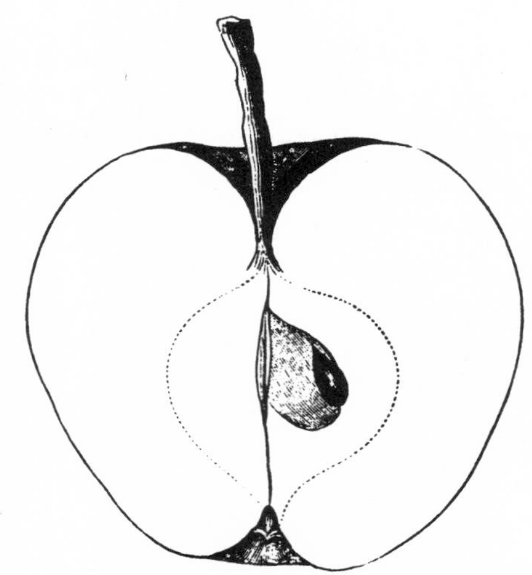

EARLY STRAWBERRY

ately juicy, aromatic, sprightly subacid. Ripe late June/July. Catalog listings: MD, VA, NC, SC, GA, AL, TN, KY (1853–1928). ❖ **Plate 15.**

❧ **EDWARDS' WINTER** (Edwards, David's Winter?, Edwards' Favorite): The original tree grew before 1869 in the orchard of Sampson Edwards of Chatham County, North Carolina, and was thought to be a seedling of Hall × Ralls Janet. An 1898 North Carolina agricultural experiment station bulletin says: "This is a seedling of the Hall, twice as large as that variety and fully as good and as good a keeper." The fruit is borne in clusters of five to seven apples. An apple variety called David's Winter was sold by Cedar Cove Nurseries of Yadkin County, North Carolina, from 1875 to 1902, but its description is almost identical to Edwards' Winter.

I searched for years for Edwards' Winter but finally gave up, believing it extinct. In early 1992 I was taken to two gnarled old trees, the remnants of a sixty-tree farm orchard planted about 1916 near Crutchfield Crossroads in Chatham County. My guide, Paul Johnson, told me the farm had been in his family for over two hundred years. One surviving tree was the Mother Apple. I was dumbfounded and delighted when Mr. Johnson named the other tree as Edwards' Winter. Mr. Johnson told me that Sampson Edwards lived on an adjacent farm and is buried in a nearby Quaker cemetery. It is likely that this surviving old tree was grafted or was a root sprout from the original tree in Sampson Edwards' orchard.

Only a few weeks later I found that a tree of Edwards' Winter was growing in the National Fruit Trust's apple collection in Kent, England, and I imported scionwood. The fruit from the Chatham County tree and from the tree grafted with the English scions is identical. (*See* Carter's Blue.)

Fruit medium, roundish oblate; skin greenish yellow or yellow, lightly striped and blushed with red or brownish red; dots numerous, gray; stem very long in a somewhat deep, slightly russeted cavity; basin round, even, medium size, corrugated; flesh yellow, fine-grained, tender, juicy, subacid. Ripe late September/October. Catalog listings: VA, NC, GA (1872–1915).

❧ **EMERGING BLAZE:** Three trees of this old West Virginia apple were found by Dr. L. R. Littleton in Grant County, West Virginia. He described the fruit as greenish yellow, partly to mostly covered with a reddish blush. Ripe September. No catalog listings.

❧ **ENOS:** A single tree was found in the 1990s on the old Hartman farm just south of Upper Tract, West Virginia, by Dr. L. R. Littleton.

Fruit medium size or above, roundish, regular, flattened on the ends; skin tough, bumpy, light yellow, occasionally blushed; dots irregular, russet or greenish and sunken; stem medium length and rather slender in a deep, partially russeted cavity; calyx closed or open; basin medium size, corrugated; flesh whitish, juicy, crisp, almost sweet. Ripe July. No catalog listings.

❧ **ESOPUS SPITZENBURG** (Spitzenburgh, True Spitzenburg): It has been said so many times that it must be true: this was Thomas Jefferson's favorite apple. My first taste of an Esopus Spitzenburg was an apple I sneaked from a tree in Jefferson's restored orchard at Monticello. I found this purloined apple to be delicious, but I now know that Esopus Spitzenburg reaches its peak of flavor when I store the apples for a couple of months in plastic bags in my refrigerator.

Esopus Spitzenburg originated before 1800 in Esopus, New York, and most old references say that it does poorly in warm areas. I find, however, that the tree in my orchard in central North Carolina bears a light crop of delectable apples that ripen in late September. The fruit is subject to a condition called Jonathan Spot that specks the skin, especially if the apples remain too long on the tree before being picked. The tree is quite susceptible to apple scab, collar rot, and fire blight and needs adequate water for quality fruit.

Fruit medium or above, roundish to slightly oblong, conical; skin tough, deep yellow, usually mostly covered with bright red with inconspicuous darker stripes, almost purple in the sun; dots large, distinct, yellow and russet, sometimes elongated near the stem end; stem medium to long in an acute, deep, wide, russeted cavity; calyx closed;

basin furrowed and rather small; flesh yellow, crisp, juicy, rather tender, aromatic, sprightly subacid. Ripe September/October. Catalog listings: MD, VA, DC, NC, SC, KY (1824–1928).

**FAIRGROVE:** My friend Harold Punch found a young seedling tree in the 1980s growing beside a "green box" (a garbage container) behind the Fairgrove Methodist Church near Hickory, North Carolina. The original tree is now gone. I keep Fairgrove in my orchard, even though it is not an old variety, because it is a good apple that keeps for months in refrigeration, and it reminds me of my old friend.

Fruit medium, roundish conical, obscurely lobed; skin mostly pale red with some faint darker stripes; dots inconspicuous, gray and russet; stem almost long, ending in a knob, in a small russeted cavity; calyx closed; basin deep with several large protuberances; flesh fine-grained, moderately crisp and juicy, scarcely sweet. Ripe September. No catalog listings.

**FALL ORANGE** (Holden, Hogpen, Glass, Orange, Summer Orange, Speckled, Red Cheek, Jones Pippin, Westbrook, White Graft, White Newell, New York Bellflower, Long Island Graft): I have spoken with several elderly southerners who remember this apple, and an old tree has been found in Chatham County, North Carolina, belonging to Inez Mann. Fall Orange seems to have been grown to a limited extent in Virginia and North Carolina for home use, both fresh eating and cooking. The original tree grew up before 1770 near the hog pen of Deacon Allen in Holden, Massachusetts, and was called Hogpen or Holden. It was taken to western New York about 1825 where it acquired the name Fall Orange.

An apple named Summer Orange was sold by a Julian, North Carolina, nursery from 1920 to 1928 (and probably for years later). Old Summer Orange trees are still alive in Chatham County, where the fruit is prized for pies and other uses. Summer Orange is identical to Fall Orange. *See* Summer Orange *and* Glass Apple.

Fruit large, roundish conical; skin pale yellow, sometimes with a pinkish or brownish blush or some russet splotches; dots conspicuous, numerous, large and small, russet or reddish, areolar; stem medium to short in a deep, medium-width, often russeted cavity; basin uneven, rather deep, abrupt, furrowed; flesh white, moderately fine-grained, crisp, tender, juicy, aromatic, subacid. Ripe late August/September. Catalog listings: VA, NC, KY (1867–1904).

**FALL PIPPIN** (Autumn Pippin, Yellow Mammoth, Carolina Pippin, Episcopal, Cobbetts' Fall, Large Fall Pippin, Philadelphia Pippin, Pound Pippin, Pound Royal, York Pippin, Golden Pippin, Prince's Large Pippin, Summer Pippin, Pond Apple): Widely sold in the South and quite popular at one time in the Shenandoah Valley as an early winter apple. *The Southern Apple and Peach Culturist* (1872) calls Fall Pippin "first among Autumn apples in Maryland and Virginia." *Gardening for the South* (1885) says it is "a splendid apple here," and it was praised by the Mississippi delegate to the 1883 American Pomological Society meeting. A few old references indicate that Fall Pippin is best suited to higher elevations and rich soils, rotting badly on the tree in warmer areas. The tree is a biennial bearer, subject to apple scab, and only moderately productive. Fruit ripens on the tree over a period of a month or longer and is excellent for cooking or fresh eating, making an outstanding applesauce.

Fall Pippin is a very old variety predating 1800 and popular in the nineteenth century in most apple-growing areas of the United States. Its origin is unknown, but it is thought to be an American

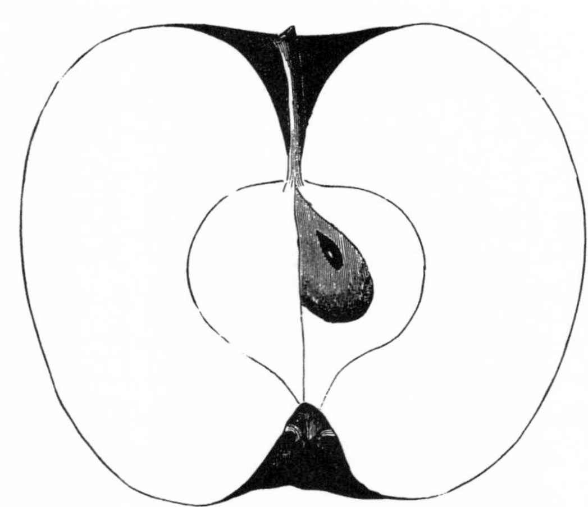

FALL PIPPIN

apple. My scions came from Wade Caudill of Alleghany County, North Carolina. *See* Carolina Pippin.

Fruit large or occasionally very large, irregular, roundish to roundish oblate but sometimes slightly oblong conical; skin thin, smooth, becoming clear yellow when ripe, sometimes faintly blushed; dots numerous, small, pale gray and russet, some greenish and submerged; stem usually about three-fourths of an inch long in a moderately deep, medium-width, russeted cavity; calyx open; basin deep, very abrupt, wavy, often cracked; flesh white or tinged with yellow, almost fine-grained, tender, juicy, aromatic, subacid. Ripe late August/September. Catalog listings: MD, VA, NC, GA, AL, LA, TN, KY, TX, AR (1836–1928). ❖ **Plate 16.**

**FALL PREMIUM:** Several old trees have been found by Tom Brown near Newland, Spruce Pine, and Plumtree, North Carolina. Doug Hundley, county agricultural agent in Avery County, North Carolina, says the Hughes community in his county still prizes this apple.

Fruit medium or above, roundish to oblate, slightly conical; skin yellowish with a pale pinkish blush and faint, broken pink stripes; dots large, gray, often with a pink areole; stem medium to long in a russeted cavity; flesh firm, crisp, juicy, subacid. Ripe September/October. No catalog listings.

**FALLAWATER** (Mountain Pippin, Green Mountain Pippin, Kelly, Fornwalder, Tulpehocken, Molly Whopper, Falder, Pound, Pim's Beauty of the West, Walldower, Waldour, Pharawalder, Fallenwalder, Brubacker, Winter Blush, Brubaker, Benjamite, Baltimore Pippin, Pfarver, Mountain Green): I find old trees of Fallawater everywhere in the mountains of West Virginia, Virginia, and North Carolina, often known by one of its many synonyms. Beyond these states, Fallawater was grown in Pennsylvania, New York, Kentucky, Ohio, Indiana, and even Kansas and Missouri. In the South it does best at elevations above 1,500 feet. Fruit grown in cooler areas ripens in late fall and is a good keeper. For these reasons, plus its resistance to bruising, Fallawater was once used for marketing and drying.

Fallawater trees tend to bear heavily on alternate years and become quite large when grafted on seedling rootstocks. A 1993 letter from Mrs. Vincent Shurtleff of Aikens, West Virginia, describes a "Waldour" tree 12 feet 4 inches in circumference. If the Fallawater tree is well cared for, the fruit can be very large. The flavor of the fruit is mild and has been described as "deficient in flavor," but the apples in my orchard have excellent texture and flavor and keep in the refrigerator until February. A letter to me from a man in West Virginia says Fallawater apples "taste best after a couple of frosts."

The exact origin of Fallawater and the meaning of its strange name are not known, but theories abound. We know for a fact that it is a Pennsylvania apple, from Bucks County, said to have grown up near Tulpehocken Creek before 1842. One theory concerning its name is quoted from Elliot (1858): "It grew up in the woods and was left standing after the other trees were cut down; hence the name Fallenwalder or apple of the cut-down or fallen woods." *The Gardener's Monthly* magazine, February 1870, has this to say: "The original name was Farawalder or Pharawalder, which signifies the Parish Minister; the tree having been found on the grounds of a German clergyman." A 1911 Pennsylvania agricultural experiment station bulletin says: "The tree was found growing on Tulpenhocken Creek. The first apple was picked up from the creek and called Fall-in-Water."

The tree is very vigorous, bears early, but is susceptible to cedar-apple rust. The fruit and leaves are large, meaning that Fallawater probably is a triploid with an extra set of chromosomes. Several old references say the tree is often attacked by root borers and tends to be short-lived, but there are many trees approaching a hundred years old scattered from North Carolina to West Virginia. (*See* Flat Fallawater.) Incidentally, I have never seen a Fallawater apple as colorful as the fruit in the watercolor illustration in this book; most are rather drab.

Fruit large, round, sometimes slightly oblate, usually symmetrical, uniform in size and shape; skin tough, usually dull or dirty green shaded with dull red or red stripes or bronze on the sunny side; dots conspicuous, whitish, often large, some areolar with russet centers; stem short in a deep, brown cavity, often furrowed; basin shallow to moderately deep, sometimes furrowed or wrinkled; flesh greenish white, tender, somewhat coarse, juicy, mild subacid. Ripe October at higher elevations, but September in warmer areas. Catalog listings: MD, VA, NC, GA, TN, KY (1858–1928). ❖ **Plate 17.**

❧ **FAMEUSE** (Chimney Apple, Snow, Pomme de Neige, Sanguineus, Red American, Royal Snow): Possibly an old French variety brought to North America around 1700 by the French. More likely it grew from seeds brought from France. Tom Burford in Virginia says that an orchard of Fameuse trees was planted by Hessian prisoners interned near Winchester, Virginia, during the Revolutionary War. Some of the trees lived on until the 1930s.

Although it is a high-quality dessert, cooking, and cider apple when northern-grown, Fameuse seems to have been less important in the South where old trees are rare. Southerners generally called it Snow Apple. The tree is susceptible to apple scab and bears heavy and light crops in alternate years. Fruit spurs are often very short. Fameuse is certainly one parent of the McIntosh apple.

Fruit medium, roundish oblate; skin smooth, pale greenish yellow with faint red streaks in the shade but a deep red blush in the sun; stem quite slender and rather short in a narrow cavity; basin narrow, shallow; flesh very white, sometimes streaked red, very tender, juicy, aromatic, subacid. Ripe September and a good keeper. Catalog listings: VA, NC, SC, AL, LA, TN, KY, TX, AR (1853–1928).

❧ **FANNY:** A Pennsylvania apple that originated in Lancaster County before 1869. Its size, crimson color, and good eating quality made Fanny a useful market apple in much of the South. The tree is vigorous, productive, and an annual bearer. Scions were obtained from Joyce Neighbors who got her tree from the Alabama Agricultural Extension Service, Auburn, Alabama.

Fruit medium, roundish to slightly oblate but sometimes varying to oblong, slightly ribbed; skin thin, smooth, mostly covered with crimson and indistinct darker red stripes; dots few, small, whitish; stem long and slender in a medium to deep cavity, sometimes russeted; basin shallow to medium in depth, usually furrowed; flesh whitish or tinged yellow, a little stained red next to the skin, tender, juicy, fine-grained, mild subacid. Ripe September. Catalog listings: MD, VA, GA, AL, TN, TX (1885–1928). ❖ **Plate 18.**

❧ **FARTHING'S NO BLOOM** (No Bloom?): Originated with H. H. Farthing of Hattie, North Carolina, and sold by the J. Van Lindley Nursery of Greensboro from 1899 to 1902. "A novelty in the fruit line. A medium-size, striped apple of good quality from Watauga County, North Carolina. Produces its fruit without showing a blossom, hence its name. An annual bearer and never gets killed by frost."

In 2000 Tom Brown found a "No Bloom" tree near Wilkesboro, North Carolina, which produces flowers without petals, thus appearing to be without blossoms. The "No Bloom" is entirely different from the Spencer Seedless discussed under the name Bloomless, Seedless, Coreless, and I believe it is Farthing's No Bloom. The tree that Tom Brown found was grafted about 1970 from a very old No Bloom tree in Ashe County, North Carolina, and is described here.

Fruit medium, very irregular in shape, lobed and sometimes barrel-shaped or pinched in around the middle of the apple; skin tough, smooth, bright yellow with a faint red blush, sometimes with russet spilling out of the cavity over the top of the apple; dots few, large, prominent, dark russet, some submerged; stem almost short in an irregular, deep cavity; basin missing and replaced with a deep hole surrounded by small round knobs and penetrating most of the way through the center of the apple; flesh pale yellow, dry, fine-grained, sweet. Ripe September. *See* Bloomless, Seedless, Coreless.

❧ **FIRED SWEET:** This old, local apple is grown around Marshall in western North Carolina.

Fruit medium or below, roundish; skin greenish with a pink blush on the sunny side; dots russet, often areole; stem medium to long in a narrow, deep, russeted cavity with russet over the top of the apple; calyx closed. Ripe July. No catalog listings.

❧ **FLAT FALL CHEESE:** The state of Virginia

established a heritage orchard on the historic farm of Cyrus McCormick (inventor of the reaper) near Steele's Tavern. This orchard was poorly maintained and was removed in the 1990s, but I managed to rescue Flat Fall Cheese before the tree was cut down.

Fruit medium size, oblate; skin tough, light yellow with a rosy blush and faint stripes on the sunny side, often almost entirely red, sometimes with a slight bloom; dots whitish, large; stem medium length in a wide, brown or greenish cavity; calyx open; basin round, almost deep, greenish; flesh yellowish, moderately crisp, juicy, almost sweet. Ripe September. No catalog listings.

❦ **FLAT FALLAWATER** (Flat Head Fallawater): I heard of this apple for several years before Danny Harvey of Ashe County, North Carolina, brought me three fine apples. Externally it somewhat resembles Fallawater, but it has a taste and texture all its own. Flat Fallawater is a local apple grown only in Ashe and adjoining counties in the mountains of North Carolina.

Fruit above medium to almost large, roundish conical, flattened on top, often lopsided; skin tough, smooth, somewhat waxy, light green, sometimes blushed brownish red on the sunny side; dots numerous, whitish and russet, often areolar; stem medium length in a narrow, acute, russeted, leather-cracked cavity; calyx open; basin quite shallow and even; flesh slightly greenish, tender, juicy, rather crisp, mild subacid. Ripe September and a good keeper. No catalog listings.

❦ **FLEMING:** Bryant Lowe of Moravian Falls, North Carolina, has a tree in his orchard found by Tom Brown. He can date this variety back to 1942, but it is much older.

Fruit medium to large, roundish conical; skin light yellow with a few pale red stripes; flesh juicy, almost sweet. Ripe August/September. No catalog listings. *See* Perkins of North Carolina.

❦ **FLOYD RICHMOND:** Coy Watkins, near Carthage, Mississippi, has this old apple that was found by Mississippi apple hunter Jack Herring.

Fruit medium, roundish to slightly oblate, often oblique; skin blushed and striped with red on more than half the apple; dots numerous, large, whitish and tan; stem medium length in a slightly russeted cavity; calyx closed; flesh yellowish, subacid. Ripe July/August. No catalog listings.

❦ **FOOT AROUND:** Montgomery County, North Carolina, is the home of this early summer apple, especially in the Liberty Hill area. Nettie Key says her parents purchased her tree in 1912, and the apples "cook real quick, make the best applesauce, so pretty and bright." This is probably the same apple as "Foot Round" listed without description by a Georgia nursery in 1851. Fruit light green, medium size. *See also* Twelve Inches.

❦ **FOUST** (Faust, Faust's Winter): Originated with the Foust family of Guilford County, North Carolina, and introduced by Squire Kinney (who also introduced Magnum Bonum). It was described in one old catalog as "much admired by many for its peculiar, aromatic flavor." A single limb grafted years ago onto an apple tree in Watauga County, North Carolina, has been identified as Faust's Winter by its owner, and fruit from this limb matches the description of Foust.

Fruit medium or larger, round or roundish oblate; skin smooth, bright yellow, overspread with a thick white bloom, sometimes shaded red in the sun; dots few, light-colored, usually submerged; stem short and stout in a wide, green cavity; calyx closed; basin shallow and wrinkled; flesh yellow, tender, not very juicy, aromatic, subacid. Ripe October. Catalog listings: NC, SC, GA (1855–1902).

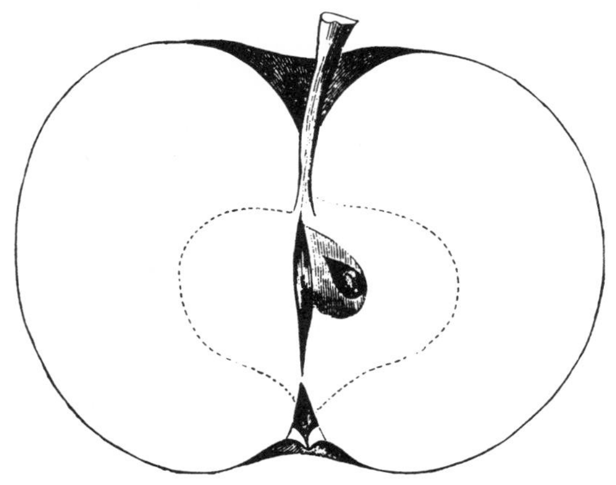

FOUST

**FUGATE:** Originated in the Fugate community on the French Broad River in Cooke County, Tennessee. It is a high-quality apple for fresh eating or cooking and was sold for years by the late Henry Morton's nursery in Gatlinburg, Tennessee.

Fruit above medium, roundish or slightly oblate; skin light yellowish green with a rosy blush on the sunny side, some apples are completely red; dots few, inconspicuous, whitish and green, often with a red areole; stem slender, medium to long in a deep, narrow, irregular, russeted cavity; calyx closed; basin medium depth, abrupt, corrugated; flesh white or yellowish, fine-grained, crisp, juicy, subacid. Ripe July. No catalog listings.

**FYAN:** Over the years of my apple searches, several southerners remembered an apple pronounced "Finn" that is actually the variety named Fyan. Fyan originated at the Missouri State Fruit Experiment Station from a cross of Ben Davis × Jonathan made in 1901 and was released to the public in 1935. Some trees made their way into the South where a few still exist. Charles Gunther of Ridgeway, Virginia, sent me scions in 2003 with this note: "I tried my dangdest to find new growth on a very old tree. My Fyan apple tree, called 'Finn' in these parts, is 75–80 years old and nearly dead."

Fruit medium, oblong to round, conical, often oblique; skin rough, tough, partly to almost completely covered in dark red with a light blue bloom; dots numerous, small, pale gray; stem medium to long in a grayish or tan russet cavity; calyx open or closed; basin acute, corrugated; flesh greenish, crisp, juicy, mild subacid. Ripe September/October. No catalog listings. ❖ **Plate 19.**

**GABLE:** Grown for over a hundred years in Randolph County, North Carolina. Allie Nelson of Franklinville gave me scions from her old tree.

Fruit medium size, somewhat oblate; skin mostly covered in light red with some scarf skin; dots numerous with russet centers. Ripe September/October. No catalog listings.

**GANO/BLACK BEN DAVIS** (Etris?, Payton, Red Ben Davis, Jacks' Red, Reagan's Red, Peyton, Chesney, Mesa Red, Ozark): The Paragon–Mammoth Blacktwig controversy had barely cooled down when, in 1903, another uproar ensued. This time it involved apples named Gano and Black Ben Davis, and once again Arkansas was in the middle of the controversy. When it involved their apples, Arkansawyers were a testy lot.

Apples were helping Arkansas out of the deep economic hole that was a southern legacy of the Civil War. A visitor in 1904 wrote, "I was surprised after entering the state at the immense planting of fruit trees. There were trees everywhere where the forests were cleared off. Every spot of upland seemed covered with fruit trees, apples principally." Arkansas (and Missouri also) was riding the crest of the massive Ben Davis wave. Fortunes were being made in apples, and growers took their business seriously. You can bet, too, that there was bad blood still around from the Civil War. Arkansas, you see, was staunchly southern and part of the Confederacy, whereas Missouri, while a slave state, refused to join the Confederacy. Nasty raids and ambushes occurred across their borders during the war. Some Arkansawyers still referred to Missouri as "Puke Territory."

By the turn of the century, apple trees named Gano and Black Ben Davis were being sold by nurseries and were being planted in new orchards in Arkansas and Missouri. Both were accepted as seedlings of Ben Davis, and both were considered to be improvements of Ben Davis because of the redder color of the fruit. Side by side, apples of Gano and Black Ben Davis look identical. As the importance of these two varieties grew, the question of their origins raised its ugly head. Stark Bro's Nursery in Louisiana, Missouri, listed them as two separate varieties, trademarked Black Ben Davis, and pushed it hard in catalogs. This suited Arkansawyers just fine because they claimed Black Ben Davis as an Arkansas seedling. Others, particularly Missourians, thought Gano and Black Ben Davis were the same apple (under two different names) that had originated in Missouri and was rightfully called Gano.

To make matters worse, there was barely concealed antagonism between Stark Bro's Nursery and L. A. Goodman, secretary of the Missouri Horticultural

Society and a prime mover in the controversy. The root of this antagonism is not known today, but it colored the proceedings of the Missouri Horticultural Society during the controversy.

In 1903 the Missouri Horticultural Society established a three-man committee that seems to have done a reasonable job of investigating the origins of Gano and Black Ben Davis. They examined specimens of fruit and leaves, visited the supposed site of the original Black Ben Davis tree in Arkansas and interviewed people. In its report the committee concluded that Gano and Black Ben Davis were "one and the same variety."

Stark Bro's Nursery was dismayed by this report. E. W. Stark stated, "As far as the personnel of the committee for the investigation is concerned, Mr. Goodman is at the bottom of the whole and responsible for it. . . . Mr. Goodman is the instigator, he never lost an opportunity to say the apples were the same, never said a word in favor, never recommended a customer to Stark Bro's Nursery."

If Stark Bro's Nursery was dismayed at the report of the Missouri Horticultural Society, Arkansawyers were enraged. At the 1904 meeting of the Arkansas Horticultural Society, one member declared, "I am not in favor of letting Missouri name our apples (applause). This is not a question of patriotism; it is a question of right, truth and justice." (Presumably to great applause and some rebel yells!) The Arkansas Horticultural Society thereupon also appointed a three-man committee. This committee apparently never looked at any fruit or other plant material of either variety. They interviewed witnesses, Arkansawyers all, who testified that Black Ben Davis and Gano were different apples and Black Ben Davis was the superior of the two. The committee's report was adopted with this exhortation by one of its members: "but what I ask you here today is to render unto Arkansas the things that belong to Arkansas" (tremendous applause). Even the president of the University of Arkansas got in a few licks, saying: "Missouri, not being content with grafting everything at home, came down to Arkansas and is now attempting to graft our seedlings."

After 1904 the Gano–Black Ben Davis controversy died down; both sides had fired their salvos. Nothing was finally resolved and still is not to this day. The available evidence seems to show that these two varieties had distinct and separate origins. Even so, side by side, the fruit is identical, even to pomologists. H. E. Van Deman, the United States Pomologist at the USDA at the time of the controversy, investigated the origins of both apples. What he found may be instructive to the interested reader.

The following account of the origin of Gano was written by H. E. Van Deman and published in the May 1900 issue of *Western Fruit Grower* magazine:

> The statement having lately been made in this publication by my friend Holsinger, that the Gano apple originated in the Parks orchard in Platte County, Mo., which orchard is now owned by Mr. W. G. Gano, I wish to give the history of the variety as I got it from Col. J. C. Evans, whom we know to be good authority for anything he says concerning fruits. This is in substance what he stated to me in the fall of 1897.
>
> The apple now called Gano, that has come prominently before the public lately, is an old variety of uncertain origin, perhaps first called Jacks' Red apple fully sixty years ago. A man named Ely Jacks emigrated from Kentucky to Howard County, Missouri, which is in the eastern part of the state, at least that long ago (1840), and with him brought scions of this variety, which he propagated in a little local nursery, so his neighbors told Col. Evans a few years ago when he visited that locality. Mr. Jacks distributed the variety more or less in the immediate neighborhood. Col. Evans found trees in old orchards there, where the variety was known as Jacks' Red.
>
> From Howard County, Mr. Jacks moved to the Platte Purchase, of which Platte County, Missouri, is now a part, and settled

on land four miles north of Parkville. Here he planted an orchard of which a part was Ben Davis and at least one tree of the kind called Jacks' Red, for there was one tree that finally became the progenitor of that notable race. This orchard afterwards passed into the possession of Col. Parks.

About 1877, Blair Brothers of Lee's Summit, Missouri, wrote to W. G. Gano, of Parkville, to cut and send them a lot of good scions of Ben Davis. Mr. Gano went to the old Jacks orchard, then belonging to Col. Parks, to cut them. After a few years, when these scions had become bearing trees in the orchards of the customers of Blair Brothers, they found a different variety among their Ben Davis trees. In 1884, some specimens of the fruit were sent to L. A. Goodman, secretary of the Missouri Horticultural Society, and to Col. Evans for examination, calling it a new Ben Davis, because the trees looked like those of that variety and the fruit likewise, except that it was redder. With the help of Mr. Gano the variety was traced back to the Col. Parks' orchard where Mr. Gano had cut the scions. Further investigation proved that the scions from one tree there were the origin of the young trees in question; and that that one tree was a sprout from the stump where the top had broken down many years before. This latter fact led them to believe it to be a sprout from a seedling, which it evidently was not. However, the Missouri Horticultural Society, believing this conjecture to be a truth, and that the variety seemed to be valuable, named it Gano in honor of the gentleman just mentioned. Thus the Jacks' Red, under a new name, was started into popular distribution.

"Therefore we are not certain where this variety originated, but probably in Kentucky somewhere. It may have been brought there from some other region. Whether or not other trees were left in Kentucky and used to propagate from we do not know; but there has been nothing of the kind brought to our notice so far. The old name Jacks' Red has become practically obsolete because it has not been carried away from the orchards of Howard County, Missouri, as far as we know. The rule of priority should not be applied to the nomenclature of this variety. Gano it is, and Gano it will be forever. Moreover, Gano is the first name published, which entitles it to become the correct one.

In 1902 Van Deman went to Arkansas to investigate the origins of Black Ben Davis. His findings were published in the October 1902 issue of *Western Fruit Grower* magazine:

As I have before said publicly about the Black Ben Davis–Gano contention, the truth is what we should know. Therefore, I made a long-contemplated trip to Washington County, Arkansas, within the last ten days to see for myself the trees in bearing in connection with another matter which took me to that state. I had long been uncertain as to the true identity of the apple which has been pushed by Stark Bro's Nursery, and had promised myself and them to critically investigate this apple on the ground where it was said to exist and learn the facts for myself. It is possible that some one may suppose that I have been hired to do so, but I affirm on the honor of a man that the Starks have not even hinted any such thing, nor would I have gone a step if they had suggested it. However, Mr. C. M. Stark kindly took me to the places where I could see what I was looking for, thereby saving me much time and trouble.

I first went to the place where the original tree was said to have stood. I had doubted whether there was such a place, but it was

> found, if we are to believe the word of honest-minded country people. The spot was shown to me at the rear of a log cabin by two old people, Mr. and Mrs. Thomas, who live there. They told me the tree died in 1889 because the chickens had roosted on it so much as to injure the branches for several years; and that the largest branch had leaned over the back part of the low roof and was cut off. The tree had borne very heavily from the time they had bought the farm. They both spoke of the apples in very approving terms, as being better tasting than Ben Davis and keeping later. The place where the tree had stood is not in line with the orchard trees that stand nearby and which are the oldest ones on the farm.

Van Deman visited several neighbors who remembered the tree, two of whom had taken grafts from the original Black Ben Davis. He also visited nearby orchards and collected both Gano and Black Ben Davis apples. Van Deman ends his lengthy article by saying: "What I have seen and heard of this matter is evidence, in my opinion, that there are differences between Gano and the apple named Black Ben Davis."

The earliest years of Black Ben Davis are confusing. The original tree was apparently first planted or grown by a man named Parson Black who homesteaded the Arkansas farm in 1869. How or where he got the original tree was unknown, even in 1900, but his name was attached to the new variety known as Black Ben Davis. Parson Black subsequently sold his farm to a family named Reagan who was there when the tree first fruited around 1880 or so. Mrs. Reagan said she asked her husband to cut the tree down as it was a seedling, but her husband decided to let it grow for the shade it would give. The Reagans sold the farm to Mr. and Mrs. Thomas and, as we have seen, the original tree died about 1889, still a rather young tree. Before its demise, it acquired a local reputation and was grafted from extensively. The stump of the original tree was found about 1903 by investigators.

The investigations into the origins of Gano and Black Ben Davis failed to "close the loop" and to find a common ancestor tree. Even so, there may have been a common ancestor. The early years of both Gano and Black Ben Davis are shrouded in mystery. Perhaps Parson Black got his tree from Mr. Jacks' early nursery in eastern Missouri where Gano probably came from, or perhaps both Mr. Jacks' tree and Parson Black's tree came from a common ancestor tree in Kentucky. We will never know now; what we do know is that there is not a penny's worth of difference between Gano and Black Ben Davis.

Fruit medium to large, roundish to slightly oblong, slightly conical; skin smooth, mostly covered with dark solid crimson; dots numerous (also said to be few), small, yellow or gray; stem medium length and slender in a wide, deep, acute, russeted cavity; calyx slightly open; basin abrupt, narrow, rather deep, sometimes furrowed; flesh white, firm, moderately juicy, mild subacid. Ripe September/October. Catalog listing: MD, VA, NC, GA, AL, LA, TN, KY, TX, AR (1890–1928).

❦ **GEORGE MACK:** Joe Harvey McClanahan of Springfield, Tennessee, brought this apple to my attention in 1998. He says the tree originated with a black man, George Mack, who bought land adjacent to the McClanahan farm many years ago for 100 gold dollars. "He lost an arm from a train accident and was known as One-armed George Mack. He could beat most men digging a ditch. I think he was a veteran of the Spanish-American War. We'll call the apple George Mack."

Fruit medium or below, roundish conical, often irregular; skin pale yellow, sometimes with bronzing or pale red and darker stripes on the sunny side; dots numerous, whitish and russet; stem short to medium length in a deep, abrupt, russeted cavity; calyx open or closed; basin wide, gradually sloped; flesh pale yellow, fine-grained, soft, sweet. Ripe September/October. No catalog listings.

❦ **GILMORE'S SPECIAL WINESAP/GILMORE'S SWEETENING:** Gilmore's Nursery in Julian, North Carolina, is still in business although it stopped selling fruit trees decades ago. In the

1940s it was owned by Glenn G. Gilmore but still retained its original name of North State Nursery. Mr. Gilmore introduced several fruit varieties in the 1940s including Gilmore's Sweetening Apple, Gilmore's Special Winesap, Gilmore's Everbearing Apple (possibly extinct), and Gilmore's Special Pear.

Bill and Nancy Staley of Liberty, North Carolina, found Gilmore's Special Winesap and Gilmore's Sweetening and cut scions for me. Gilmore's Special Winesap appears identical to Blacktwig and ripens at the same time. Gilmore's Sweetening is medium size, roundish conical; skin smooth, pale yellow, heavily striped and splotched with red; stem short in a wide, slightly russeted cavity; flesh "mild and sweet." Ripe July.

❦ **GILPIN** (Carthouse, Small Romanite, Little Red Romanite, Gray Romanite, Roman Knight, Romanite of the West, Dollars and Cents, Red Romanite, Romanite, Small Red Long Keeper): In the nineteenth century, Gilpin was used as a yardstick to measure the keeping qualities of other apples. Reading old apple literature, one sees again and again statements such as "as good a keeper as the Gilpin." Warder (1867) may have given the reason for its fabled keeping qualities when he said of it: "Bruises do not rot as in other apples." Most descriptions say Gilpin keeps until May or June and is not fit to eat until stored for several months.

Gilpin is not a high-quality eating apple but gets good marks for cooking and cider. Downing (1878) calls it a cider apple, and Warder (1867) remarks on the richness of its juice. The fruit hangs a long time on the tree, until a heavy frost finally knocks it off. The tree itself is vigorous with a spreading growth habit and has curled and somewhat sparse foliage. It is very productive on alternate years, tends to bloom late, and bears when young.

Gilpin was found by Coxe (1817) growing in Delaware, where it had been brought from Virginia. It became popular in apple-growing areas all over the United States. In the South, Gilpin was more often listed in catalogs by its synonym, Carthouse, and was often confused with Romanite. (*See* Romanite.)

Fruit medium, roundish or slightly oblong, quite truncated at the ends making it look cylindrical, sometimes oblique; skin tough, smooth, often polished looking, yellow with red stripes or sometimes almost entirely red; stem very short in a deep, rather broad, sometimes lipped, partly russeted cavity; basin often oblique, deep, furrowed (but sometimes rather shallow); flesh yellowish, very firm, somewhat coarse, becoming crisp and tender in storage, moderately juicy, nearly sweet. Ripe September. Catalog listings: MD, VA, NC, GA, KY, TX (1824–1904).

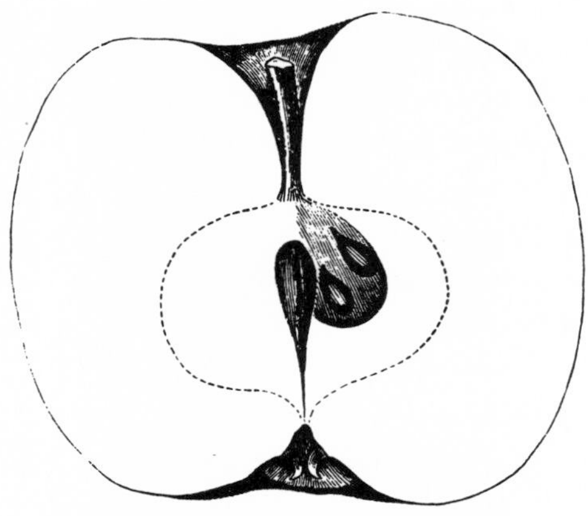

GILPIN

❦ **GLASS APPLE:** Forest Covington, Jr. of Orange County, North Carolina, contacted me in 1990 about this apple that has been grown by his family for at least a hundred years. Family lore ascribes its origin to a great-grandfather named Glass, who died in 1910, but the apples are identical to Fall Orange. Mr. Covington bottles a delicious apple wine made from Glass Apples. *See* Fall Orange.

❦ **GLOBE:** Taron Jones of Polkton, North Carolina, says his father grafted his trees in Buncombe County over fifty years ago. We do not know anything more except that this is a fine apple, well worth preserving. This is probably the Globe Giant apple discussed in chapter 5.

Fruit round; skin mostly covered with medium red; dots numerous, large and small, some areolar, whitish; stem short in a pale russeted cavity. Ripe September. No catalog listings.

❦ **GLORIA MUNDI** (Monstrous Pippin, American Mammoth, Ox Apple, Baltimore, Bull's Head,

Bullet, Knotley Pea?, White Bausel, World's Wonder, New York Gloria Mundi, Copp's Mammoth, Josephine, McHenry Pippin, Melon, Mississippi, Mountain Flora, Tennessee Mammoth, Mammoth, Titus Pippin, Spanish Pippin, Pound Pippin, Mountain Belle, Vandyne): This certainly is the largest apple ever grown in the United States. An article and full-size engraving in the December 1860 *The American Agriculturist* magazine describes a Gloria Mundi apple eighteen inches in circumference and weighing a mind-boggling *three and a half pounds*. Apples weighing a pound to a pound and a half are quite common with this variety. An 1886 North Carolina nursery catalog brags: "We have grown specimens which weighed twenty-one ounces and sold for fifty cents each." Another reference says, "owing to its great weight it blows from the tree. It would be best to grow it in protected places." An old magazine warns (tongue in cheek) of the dangers of walking in an orchard of Gloria Mundi apples: "A blow from the falling of such a meteor would cause no light casualty!"

It would be too much to hope such a behemoth also would have good fresh eating quality. It is mostly a cooking apple and prized for apple butter. The tree also has problems, usually being described as unproductive and requiring rich soils to produce the biggest fruit.

The original tree may have grown before 1800 on the farm of Mr. Crooks near Red Hook, New York, but its origin has also been credited to Long Island, New York. Its origin is further clouded by the fact that Gloria Mundi is probably the same apple as Baltimore Monstrous Pippin, which originated about 1780 in Baltimore, Maryland. (*See* Baltimore Monstrous Pippin *and* Hyatt's Wonderful.) In the South, the Gloria Mundi was sold mostly by North Carolina and Virginia nurseries that warned in their catalogs "not profitable for general culture" and "cultivated only on account of its very large size." Recent study and comparison of large green apples grown in the South under various names shows that many, perhaps most, are Gloria Mundi. These include White Bausel, Notley P No. 1, World's Wonder, and North Carolina Greening.

Fruit large to very large, shape variable but usually roundish with flattened ends, sides often unequal; skin greenish yellow sometimes with a faint bronze blush; dots small to medium, light-colored and submerged or areolar with russet centers; stem short in a large, deep, broad, furrowed, russeted cavity; basin large, deep, rather wide, furrowed and wrinkled; flesh greenish yellow, coarse, moderately crisp, somewhat acid becoming subacid when fully ripe. Ripe September. Catalog listings: VA, DC, NC, TN, KY (1845–1915). ❖ **Plate 20.**

❦ **GOLDEN DELICIOUS:** Golden Delicious was not listed by any southern nurseries before 1928 as it was trademarked and sold exclusively by Stark Bro's Nursery. *See* Golden Reinette.

❦ **GOLDEN HARVEY** (Brandy Apple): This is probably the old English apple that originated in Herefordshire in the 1600s. It seems to match the description of that apple given below. When I have tastings of apples at my orchard, Golden Harvey, when perfectly ripe, beats out all other apples. It can be truly delicious. The only southern nursery listing for this apple was in 1836 by a nursery in Baltimore, Maryland.

Fruit below medium, roundish, flattened on the ends; skin yellow occasionally with a faint blush and partly to mostly covered with a rough, brown russet in blotches and large irregular dots; calyx partly open in a brownish basin; flesh yellow, crisp, juicy, mildly sweet. Ripe August/September.

❦ **GOLDEN PIPPIN:** There are many apples with this name or synonym, including the old English dessert apple called English Golden Pippin. Green Cheese, of southern origin and widely grown at one time, has the synonym Southern Golden Pippin, and I suspect many of the apples called Golden Pippin are actually Green Cheese.

Downing (1900) describes the following apple called Golden Pippin that originated with Moses Cason of Kempsville, Virginia, and that is probably extinct.

Fruit small, oblate, slightly conical, a little oblique; skin golden yellow, sprinkled with gray dots; stem short in a rather large, deep, slightly russeted cavity; calyx closed; basin large, deep, corrugated; flesh pale yellow, tender, juicy, sprightly subacid, slightly aromatic. Ripe October. No catalog listing.

American Golden Pippin (or Pittsdown Pippin) probably originated in New England in the early 1800s and is a superior apple in the North.

Fruit medium to large, oblate to roundish oblate; skin golden yellow sometimes with a faint blush, sometimes with a faint russet netting; flesh yellowish, coarse, tender, juicy, aromatic, subacid. Ripe late fall or winter.

From 1884 to 1896 several nurseries in North Carolina and Georgia listed an apple called Golden Pippin or Southern Golden Pippin that does not fit any of the above apples and that may be a distinct variety.

Fruit very large, roundish oblong; skin golden; ripe September/October but perhaps as early as August. This apple is probably extinct.

**GOLDEN REINETTE** (Golden Rennet, English Golden Reinette, English Pippin, Kirke's Golden Reinette, Reinette Golden, Yellow German Reinette): An old English apple, originally from Herefordshire, sold by North Carolina nurseries from 1855 to 1860. It is thought to be the pollen parent of Golden Delicious.

The father of Anderson H. Mullins, who originated Golden Delicious in Clay County, West Virginia, bought some Golden Reinette trees from a fruit tree peddler in the 1880s. It is believed that bees carried pollen from its flowers to a nearby Grimes Golden tree, and this natural cross resulted in a chance seedling tree that grew up in a fence row. This seedling tree was purchased from Mr. Mullins by Stark Bro's Nursery in 1914 for $5,000 and named Golden Delicious. Golden Delicious, when southern-grown and properly ripened, is an outstanding eating and cooking apple but very susceptible to cedar-apple rust. The skin tends to have russet spots when the apples are grown in the humid conditions prevalent in much of the South.

An apple friend in Maryland highly praises Golden Reinette, which he says is of higher eating quality when grown on dry, stony land. He recommends peeling the apples to get their full flavor. Thatcher (1822) says Golden Reinette has the flavor of pineapple. Beach (1905), always stingy with his praise, rates it "excellent." The mature tree is smaller than most apple trees, and the apples are susceptible to bitter rot and cedar-apple rust. There is some confusion concerning apples named Golden Reinette as several different European varieties have this name or variations of it.

Fruit small or above, uniform in size and shape, roundish to slightly oblate; skin rough, yellow on the shady side, golden yellow in the sun, sometimes with a faint, dull red blush; dots scattered, gray and russet; stem medium length and rather thick in a deep cavity; calyx open; basin broad, shallow; flesh yellow, crisp, juicy, subacid. Ripe September. *See also* English Pippin.

**GOLDEN SWEET** (Golden Sweeting, Orange Sweeting, Early Golden Sweet, Golden Rind, Sawyer Sweet, Summer Sweet, Sweeting, Trenton Early, Lalle?): This kind of apple is rarely seen today—the very sweet apple. If you have never eaten a very sweet apple, the first bite can be a shock. It is like eating sugar or honey—sweet with no hint of acid to cut the sweetness. There were many very sweet apple varieties in the 1800s, so one must assume they were preferred by some people. Old references say that very sweet apples were considered medicinal and easy to digest, and could be eaten by those suffering from stomach or intestinal disorders. Sweet apples were usually mixed with other apples to make apple butter and cider. They were recommended also for the feeding of farm animals, especially hogs, cattle, and horses. The following is taken from an 1850 issue of *The Horticulturist* magazine: "The Golden Sweeting might be profitable for advancing the condition of the farmer's stock of swine before his crop of corn has matured, and at a season when his supplies of feed are limited. This apple and clover pasture promote swine growth as well as grain and at a much cheaper rate."

Of the very sweet apples, Golden Sweet, which is of Connecticut origin, seems to have been sold more widely by southern nurseries than any other. The tree is productive annually but rather susceptible to fire blight. My scions came from my friend Tim Strickler, at one time a nurseryman near Fries, Virginia.

Fruit medium to nearly large, roundish to roundish oblate; skin thin, smooth, waxy, yellowish green becoming pale yellow when fully ripe; dots scattered, indented, green; stem about an inch long in an acute, medium-size, partly russeted cavity; calyx closed; basin moderately deep and furrowed; flesh yellowish white, firm, fine-grained, tender, juicy, aromatic, very sweet. Ripe late June/July. Catalog listings: MD, VA, SC, GA, AL, LA, TN, KY, AR (1851–1925).

❦ **GRAGG** (Red Gragg, Winter Queen): In 1899 Thomas Coffey of Kelsey, Watauga County, North Carolina, wrote to the USDA about the Gragg: "Originated about 40 years ago on James Gragg's farm in Caldwell County, North Carolina, and is now grown by many farmers. Stands at the top of the market. It is a good cooker. The tree is thrifty, smooth, needs but little pruning, and a good bearer. The apples keep till spring." Gragg was listed in 1902 by the Startown Nursery, Newton, North Carolina.

This rare variety is listed among the apples grown about 1900 on the Moses Cone estate near Blowing Rock, North Carolina. Moses Cone was a millionaire who made his money manufacturing denim in North Carolina textile mills in the late 1800s. He built a magnificent house on top of a mountain and planted extensive apple orchards because he liked the vista of orderly rows of trees stretching down the mountainside. The house, now open to the public, belongs to the National Park Service as it sits beside the Blue Ridge Parkway. Except for a few old trees, the orchards have not survived. In 1992 I encountered several old trees of Gragg being grown commercially in the Coffey Orchard in Watauga County, North Carolina, under the name Winter Queen.

Fruit medium, roundish to oblate, conical, lobed; skin smooth, tough, waxy, with bright red on the sunny side overlaid with indistinct darker red stripes, some apples almost entirely red; dots conspicuous, large, tan; stem one-half inch long in a slightly russeted, deep cavity; calyx almost closed; basin medium in size and depth, abrupt, corrugated; flesh slightly greenish, juicy, subacid. Ripe September/October and a good keeper.

❦ **GRANDADDY:** An old Kentucky apple sent to me by Herbert Childress of Dunnville, Kentucky.

Fruit medium, roundish, conical; skin mostly red with russet dots and blotches; stem medium length in a russeted cavity. Ripe August/September. No catalog listings.

❦ **GRANDMOTHER CHEESE:** Tom Brown found three trees of this apple near Canton, North Carolina. One tree, well over eighty years old, belongs to Jasper Burnette.

Fruit medium or above, roundish to slightly oblate, sides often uneven; skin dull, pale greenish, mottled and striped with light red over about half the surface; dots russet and greenish, medium in size and number, often submerged; stem medium length to long in a tan russeted cavity; calyx wide open; basin irregular, large; flesh rather soft, juicy, almost sweet. Ripe September. No catalog listings.

❦ **GRANNY CHRISTIAN:** A 1989 letter from Eva Gibson of Roanoke, Virginia, tells all we know of this apple: "We bought our property 41 years ago and have an apple the neighbors call Granny Christian. It is great to fry and good to eat."

Fruit medium size, mostly red. Ripe September. No catalog listings.

❦ **GRANNY MACK:** The late Maurice Marshall found this old apple in Cana, Virginia. It originated in Cana circa 1930 and is named for a Mrs. McMillian. Unusual in both shape and color, Granny Mack is instantly recognizable.

Fruit medium or below, roundish, oblique, but often misshapen with bulges, protrusions and bumps; skin very rough, tough, partly to completely covered in rough golden russet with the underlying red showing through; dots numerous, large, russet; stem medium to long in an irregular, wide, greenish russeted cavity; calyx greenish, open; basin small, shallow; flesh light yellow, breaking, crisp, juicy, sweet. Ripe September/October. No catalog listings.

❦ **GRANNY NEIGHBORS:** In her self-published book *Apples: Collecting Old Southern Varieties*, nurserywoman Joyce Neighbors of Gadsden, Alabama, writes: "A seedling apple variety found on my dad's farm in Clay County about 1975 . . . and was growing in a trash dump about 50 feet from a Hackworth (apple) tree. . . . My dad named the tree after my mother." This apple variety has grown well in Illinois where it "was one of the hits of this year's tasting."

Fruit medium size, roundish conical; skin pale yellow splotched with red and some faint stripes; stem almost long in a wide, russeted cavity; dots scattered, large and small, gray; calyx greenish, open; basin corrugated, moderately shallow; flesh yellowish, subacid. Ripe August. No catalog listings.

**GRAVENSTEIN** (Banks Red Gravenstein, Early Congress): This foreign apple variety is listed in no less than seventy-nine old southern nursery catalogs and was reported in 1877 as growing well as far south as Mississippi. Gravenstein was introduced into the United States by several different people beginning perhaps about 1790. I cannot resist quoting a very interesting account of one early introduction, contained in a letter from Captain John DeWolfe of Dorchester, Massachusetts, which was published in an 1857 issue of the *Magazine of Horticulture*:

> Dear Sir, As there appears to be some discrepancy in the account of the origin, name and time of introduction of the Gravenstein apple into this country, I beg leave respectfully to hand you this statement. . . . I do not make any pretensions to be a connoisseur of fruits, but this I can say without fear of contradiction; in my early youth I had a natural instinct which enabled me to find the best apple tree in neighboring orchards on the darkest night there ever was. With this same instinct in my riper years, I could find my way, both day or night, blindfolded, to the maintop-bowline.
>
> Being at Copenhagen in the fall of 1825, I noticed at the wharves a number of small craft from Holstein with fruit, principally apples; I bought some which were recommended as the Gravenstein, a very superior apple, highly flavored as to taste and smell. I was much delighted with this fruit, never having heard of it before. Being desirous of cultivating it in my little garden in Boston, I requested my friends, Messrs. Good Raynolds & Company, to purchase for me, at the Danish nursery, two trees of that kind of fruit, and to be sure that they were the genuine Gravenstein, which they did. On my arrival in Boston, in May following, the trees being nearly seven months out of the ground, I had some doubts as to my being able to make them live. Knowing Gen. Dearborn to be an amateur in these matters, I presented him with what I thought to be the best tree, and planted the other myself; they both lived and grew vigorously. About a year after, I moved to Bristol, R. I., and took my tree with me and planted it there. When I left that place several years subsequently, it was in a bearing state.
>
> "I was desirous to know the origin of its name, and place, and was informed that it originated in a nobleman's garden in Holstein, near to a family gravestone,—hence the name Gravenstein.

Gravenstein actually got its name from being grown in the Duke of Augustinberg's garden at Gravenstein, or Graasten, in Holstein (off and on a part of Germany but now part of Denmark). One story is that it originated from seeds or scions brought from Italy about 1669. Gravenstein continues to be grown throughout Europe.

The apple is an all-purpose fruit that is good for fresh eating, cider, drying, and especially for cooking. One old reference says, "We find all other apples rejected from the kitchen as soon as the Gravenstein is introduced." The Adams House hotel in Boston was famous in its day for pies made from Gravenstein apples. Gravenstein is a triploid with sterile pollen and is susceptible to cedar-apple rust, fire blight, and root rot. The fruit tends to ripen over several weeks and to drop when ripe, necessitating daily retrieval of "drops." It is not a good keeper.

There are several redder sports or mutations of Gravenstein available, such as Red Gravenstein and Rosebrook Gravenstein, all of which seem to retain the good qualities of the original apple. In the 1920s Stark Bro's Nursery sold a Gravenstein sport called Banks Red Gravenstein that ripens ten days earlier than the original Gravenstein.

Fruit large, usually roundish oblate but sometimes oblong, conical, often lopsided; skin thin, slightly rough, greenish yellow overlaid with broken stripes and splashes of light and dark red and orange; dots few, small, gray; stem short and thick in a deep, russeted cavity; basin medium to deep, wrinkled; flesh yellow with yellow veinings, tender, crisp, juicy, aromatic, sprightly subacid. Ripe July. Catalog listings: MD, VA, NC, SC, GA, AL, MS, LA, TN, KY, TX, AR (1836–1928).

❦ **GREEN CHEESE** (Green Skin, Green Crank, Yellow Crank, Southern Golden Pippin, Winter Cheese, Winter Greening, Southern Greening, Carolina Greening, Greening, Turner's Cheese, Crank, Southern Pippin, Green): Green Cheese is one of those old apples—like Buckingham, Horse, and Limbertwig—that was swept along as southerners pulled up stakes and moved into new territories west of the Appalachians. The origin of Green Cheese is lost, but it was mentioned as early as 1763. Old references mostly cite North Carolina as its original home. It has the selflessness of some apple trees to readily send up root sprouts, which can be dug up and replanted to make new orchards. This, added to its good eating quality, keeping ability, and late blooming, made it popular and widely planted in the South until early in the 1900s. The tree is susceptible to apple scab and is a biennial bearer. Scions were obtained from Elwood Fisher who found an old tree in western North Carolina.

Fruit medium or above, roundish oblate to oblate, sometimes oblique; skin deep green when picked, turning to pale yellow when fully ripe with a slight bronze blush in the sun; dots numerous, white or brown; stem short in a large, deep, russeted cavity; calyx closed; basin broad and deep; flesh whitish or yellowish, tender, crisp, juicy, subacid. Ripe September/October. Catalog listings: MD, VA, NC, SC, GA, AL, MS, LA, KY, TX (1824–1924).

❦ **GREEN PIPPIN:** Warder (1867) says this apple originated in Indiana, but it has been grown in the southern Appalachians for many years. In 1989 Mrs. George Wood of Meadows of Dan, Virginia, gave me scions from her ancient Green Pippin tree.

Fruit medium or above, round; skin green becoming yellowish when ripe, sometimes with a pale blush on the sunny side; stem short in a russeted cavity; flesh whitish, juicy, aromatic, subacid. Ripe September and a good keeper. No catalog listings.

❦ **GREEN RIVER:** One of many old apples found by Herbert Childress around Dunnville, Kentucky. An outstanding eating apple for late August.

Fruit medium or above, roundish or slightly oblate, flattened on the ends: skin tough, smooth, pale green, partly to mostly covered with red with darker red stripes; dots rather numerous, often submerged, whitish; stem medium length to long in a greenish or tan cavity; calyx closed; basin shallow; flesh whitish, tender, juicy, mild subacid. Ripe August. No catalog listings.

❦ **GRIMES GOLDEN** (Grimes Golden Pippin, Bellflower [in Arkansas]): Out on West Virginia Route 27, two and a half miles east of Wellsburg, there is a granite monument in a small park beside the road. Carved upon the granite is the name "Grimes Golden." The monument is appropriate; Grimes Golden is one of the greatest American apples in its own right. It is also one parent of Golden Delicious, which is grown all over the world.

The best information is that the pioneer settler, Edward Cranford, planted apple seeds for an orchard about 1790 on his farm in what is now Brooks County, West Virginia (but then part of Virginia). This information (from the son of Thomas P. Grimes) means that Grimes Golden could not have originated with Johnny Appleseed who visited the Wellsburg area briefly about 1796. In 1802 Edward Cranford sold his farm to Thomas P. Grimes, who found one of the seedling trees producing fruit of a golden color, fine quality, and good keeping ability. Mr. Grimes sold the fruit from this tree and other trees in his orchard to traders who took flatboats down the Ohio and Mississippi rivers to New Orleans. Thomas Grimes and a

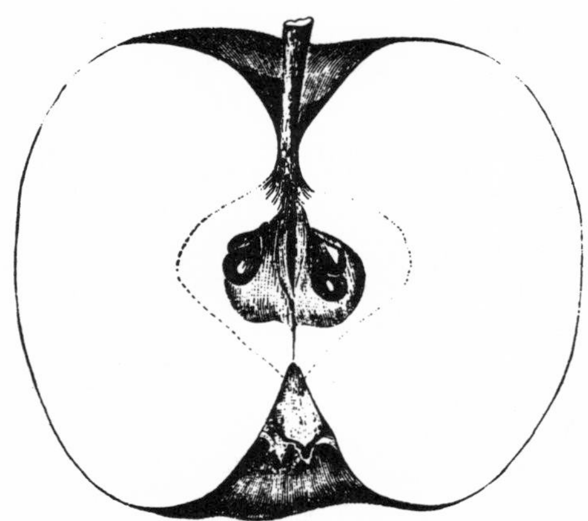

GRIMES GOLDEN

neighbor, James Lawhead, grafted from the single Grimes Golden tree, and eventually Mr. Grimes acquired an entire orchard of the delicious and beautiful golden apples.

Despite its excellence, for half a century Grimes Golden was little known outside of its local area. It was shown at the 1855 meeting of the Ohio Pomological Society by an Ohio nurseryman but failed to attract much public attention. It was not until it was highly praised in *The American Agriculturist* magazine in 1866 that Grimes Golden became widely popular.

In 1869 the son of Thomas Grimes wrote in *The Horticulturist* magazine: "From my earliest recollection this tree has never been known to fail of producing a good crop, excepting in 1834, when a partial failure was occasioned by a severe late frost in spring. Our belief is that it has not failed to produce fruit each year for the past three quarters of a century." The original tree bore fruit for over a hundred years, and there are photographs of the old tree taken in 1895. It finally blew down in 1905, carrying nearly ripe apples as it met its end. Gavels were made from the wood of the old tree and given to prominent men in the area.

The praise of Grimes Golden is universal in old pomological texts and catalogs. It is listed in virtually every southern nursery catalog from 1870 on. There are, however, some drawbacks to Grimes Golden. The tree is very susceptible to collar rot, a fungal disease that enters the trunk at ground level and eventually kills the tree. (This can be corrected by grafting Grimes Golden high up on collar-rot-resistant rootstocks.) The tree overbears and the fruit needs thinning to be sizeable. Also, Grimes Golden ripens in the early fall in warmer areas of the South, which greatly decreases its keeping ability. These faults aside, Grimes Golden is suitable for most southern locations. The fruit makes outstanding applesauce, and it is excellent for cider, which ferments to 9 percent alcohol. The tree tends to bloom late (which may account for its reliability) and is resistant to apple scab and cedar-apple rust.

Fruit medium or above, usually roundish or slightly oblong, often flattened on the ends, sides often unequal; skin yellow, tough, rather rough with russet patches; dots moderate in number, small or medium size, russet; stem short in a broad, deep, often russeted cavity; calyx closed or open; basin very abrupt, deep, sometimes furrowed; flesh yellow or slightly orange, firm, tender, crisp, juicy, aromatic, sprightly subacid. Ripe apples often have a faint anise or licorice flavor. Ripe September/October. Catalog listings: MD, VA, NC, SC, GA, AL, LA, TN, KY, TX, AR (1870–1928).

❦ **GRINDSTONE** (American Pippin, Flat Vandevere, Green Everlasting, Stone): A very old apple of unknown origin. At one time the fruit was valued for cider and its remarkable keeping ability, "but otherwise it is scarcely eatable."

Fruit medium, oblate; skin dull green with dull red patches and stripes; flesh white, firm, juicy, briskly acid. Ripe winter and has been kept a year. Catalog listings: MD, VA, NC, DC (1824–1904).

❦ **GRISSOM:** Grown for many years in the Cumberland Mountains of Tennessee.

Fruit medium size, roundish to slightly oblong, conical; skin rough, pale green with pale pinkish, obscure stripes and blotches; dots russet, small, submerged and large, protruding; stem medium to long in an irregular, russeted cavity with russet often over the top of the apple; calyx open; basin round, abrupt, sometimes leather-cracked; flesh cream-colored, juicy, not crisp, subacid. Ripe August. No catalog listings.

❦ **GUYANDOTTE** (Guyan Pippin): James R. Hall of Logan, West Virginia, wrote me about this apple: "A local seedling found 200 yards from the Guyandotte River, which bears small to medium size, all-red, somewhat elongated apples. We call it the Guyandotte or Guyan Pippin. The tree ripens a very decent crop without spraying. The flesh is yellow-gold color with a tangy sweetness that reminds me of the better russet apples I've eaten."

Fruit medium or above, roundish to oblong, conical; skin almost covered with dull red with obscure darker stripes and much scarf skin; stem long in a narrow, deep, russeted cavity with russet over the top of the apple; dots numerous, large and small, grayish; calyx closed; basin greenish, rather deep, corrugated; flesh yellowish, juicy, moderately crisp, chewy, subacid. Ripe September. No catalog listings.

❦ **HAAS** (Gros Pommier, Maryland Queen, Hoss, Fall Queen, Ludwig): Haas has been confused by some with the Horse Apple, but they are completely different varieties. Horse is a green or yellow apple (sometimes with a small blush) ripening in late July or early August in most of the South. Haas has much red on its surface and ripens in September or even later.

Gabriel Cerré originated Haas in the early 1800s in St. Louis, and it was mostly grown west of the Mississippi River and north of the Ohio River. Its synonym of Fall Queen is confusing as this is also a synonym of Buckingham.

Fruit medium to large, oblate, slightly conical, somewhat ribbed; skin smooth, pale greenish yellow, shaded and striped with light and dark red; dots few, light-colored; stem short in a medium-size, greenish cavity; calyx closed; basin small or medium size, slightly corrugated; flesh fine-grained, white, often stained red near the skin, tender, very juicy, brisk subacid. Ripe September. Catalog listings: MD, VA, GA, AL, TN (1890–1904).

❦ **HACKWORTH** (All Summer, Frederick?): Hackworth almost certainly originated with Dr. Nichodemus Hackworth (1816–93) of Morgan County, Alabama. He was a dentist and a nurseryman, but little else is known about him. The information about Dr. Hackworth fills in a gap about the origin of the Hackworth apple, and I thank Katherine Cochrane, a collateral descendent of Dr. Hackworth.

A 1907 letter to the USDA from T. W. Dermington of Lavonia, Georgia, says the Hackworth apple originated as a chance seedling in Lavonia from seed washed down from an old orchard about 100 yards up a small stream. The tree grew up in a pasture and was eaten down by cattle for several years before being allowed to grow up. It is quite possible that Dr. Hackworth got his start of the Hackworth apple from this tree.

Hackworth apples were very popular in Alabama until World War II for use in pies, sauce, and fresh eating. An old Alabama nursery catalog says, "The real all summer apple, bears fruit every day in August."

Fruit above medium, roundish conical; skin yellow with a pale reddish tint and faint stripes mostly on the sunny side; dots numerous, gray; stem medium length to almost long in a russeted cavity; basin very shallow; flesh yellowish, granular, aromatic. Ripe August/September. Catalog listings: GA, AL, TX (1912-1928). ❖ **Plate 21.**

There is another apple, Yellow Hackworth or Golden Hackworth (probably extinct), discovered about 1900 in or near Morgan County, Alabama. Identical to Hackworth except skin completely yellow and the flavor milder.

❦ **HALL:** (Hall Apple, Hall's Red, Hall's Seedling, Jenny Seedling, Small Hall, Thomas Late?): "I write about this apple with a pang of regret. For years it has been at the top of my Ten Most Wanted List of missing southern apples. I have sought the Hall apple everywhere, but it is not to be found. I believe it is truly extinct in spite of its undisputed high quality and wide dissemination in the South before 1900. It is a comment on the changes in the southern way of life that we have let such a fine apple die out completely."

The above lament is from the section on extinct apples in the first edition of this book. In 2002, Tom Brown found an apple "in the upper flat-land area of Alexander County, North Carolina" that he believes is the Hall. He says:

> It fits the description in *Old Southern Apples* exactly with the exception that the dots are not large and numerous. . . . The tree was an unknown one to its owners. I found three people who identified the apple. Henry Tevepaugh remembers his father having two Hall trees near where he currently grows apples in the Vashti section of Alexander County. A lady I met at the Stony Point Senior Center also remembers the Hall apple from her former home near Pores Knob on the Wilkes-Alexander County line. At a Waynesville restaurant, I met Paul Leatherwood who remembered Hall apples north of Hartford, Tennessee, on Raben Branch. He said that many neighbors previously had Hall apple trees. Mr. Leatherwood was positive that the apple was a Hall. He also mentioned that the trees were smaller than normal, a fact mentioned in *Old Southern Apples* that I never told him.

I have seen and tasted Tom Brown's "Hall" and can attest to its excellent flavor and texture as well as its near fit to written descriptions of the Hall. I accept this apple as the Hall unless a better candidate comes along.

The Hall originated on the farm of a Mr. Hall in Franklin County, North Carolina. It was called an old variety in 1863. The Magnum Bonum was said to have been grown from a seed of the Hall in 1828, which means the Hall probably originated before 1800. Early nursery catalogs called it Small Hall, probably to differentiate it from another apple known as Large Hall.

The Hall combines two factors seldom found in the same southern apple—outstanding eating quality and good keeping ability. Its flavor has been described by such adjectives as saccharine, rich, excellent, luscious, vinous, the best. Most old references describe the Hall as keeping until April or May. Add to these qualities a dwarfish, very productive tree, and you have one of the finest apples that ever originated in the South. Warder (1867) writes: "This variety is so great a favorite in the South as to be called their best dessert apple."

In looking for reasons for the decline of the Hall, one must focus on its small size. Small apples have long been considered as commercially worthless. Even a hundred years ago, conventional wisdom was that big apples would sell best in the marketplace. As transportation in this country improved, large mail-order nurseries slowly destroyed local nurseries. The large nurseries concentrated on growing and selling varieties suitable for commercial orchards and eliminated from their catalogs such apples as the Hall that had little commercial appeal.

Fruit small, roundish oblate to oblate, slightly conical; skin smooth, thick, mostly covered with clear or dull red; dots numerous, large, white or yellow; stem medium to long, slender, curved, in a round, wide, medium to deep, russeted cavity; calyx closed; basin rather shallow, wavy; flesh yellow, tender, juicy, fine-grained, aromatic, subacid. Ripe October/November. Catalog listings: VA, NC, SC, GA, AL, MS, LA, TN, KY (1853–1902).

❦ **HAMMOND:** Originated in Spartanburg, South Carolina, and first mentioned in 1858 as "equal to the best Newtown Pippin." Probably named for James H. Hammond, governor of South Carolina in the 1840s and a noted agricultural reformer. Described here and probably extinct.

Fruit medium, roundish or sometimes slightly oblate; skin pale green partly covered with an orange to pale red blush; dots large, numerous, white; stem pale orange and long. Ripe September. Catalog listings: NC, SC, GA (1860–72).

Jim Lawson, Georgia nurseryman, grafted an old apple called Hammond when a customer brought in scions. This apple, however, is fully russeted over a pale green skin and is probably a different apple.

❦ **HARRIS** (Ben Harris, Harris Seedling, Harris Greening): Originated with Marston Harris of Rockingham County, North Carolina, and popular in that area around 1860 as the tree is vigorous and productive. In early 1993 I received a telephone call from Jim Umstead of Orange County, North Carolina, who has three trees. He told me that the Harris apple owes its continued existence to the efforts

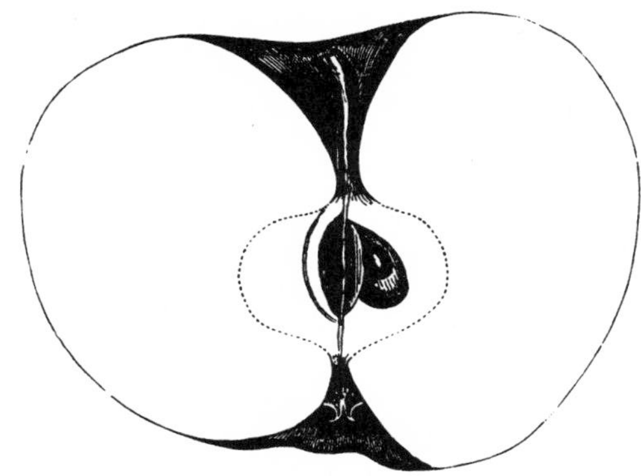

HARRIS

many years ago of his father-in-law, Edgar Y. Jones. Mr. Jones dug up and replanted root sprouts from an old and dying Harris tree, the last one known to exist at that time. At about this same time, David Vernon, a nurseryman of the area, found two other old Harris trees within fifteen miles of his nursery.

Fruit medium or above, roundish, often lobed and five-sided; skin smooth, yellow, sometimes with a faint blush; dots few, russet or pale whitish; stem short to medium in a deep, wavy, unrusseted cavity; basin large, deep, abrupt; flesh white or light yellow, crisp, juicy, acid to subacid. Ripe mid-August. Catalog listings: VA, NC, SC, GA, AL, KY (1853–90).

❦ **HARRISON** (Harrison Cider, Long Stem, Harrison's Newark): An old cider apple from Essex County, New Jersey. At one time, New Jersey was the most important cider-making area in this country, and the Harrison was much used for making "a high colored cider of great body." The fruit is said to be very free from rot and to fall from the tree about the first of November in New Jersey.

Long considered extinct, a Harrison tree was rediscovered growing in Livingston, New Jersey, in 1976 and propagated the following year in Vermont and New Hampshire. In 1989 Virginia nurseryman and apple historian Tom Burford obtained scionwood and began promoting and disseminating the apple more widely to growers and cidermakers.

Fruit medium to small, roundish oblong; skin yellow with rough, distinct, black specks; stem one inch long or longer, knobby, slanted like an accent mark; flesh yellow, rich and sweet, though rather dry and tough. Ripe early October in Virginia and keeps well. Catalog listings: MD, VA, NC, SC (1824–1904).

❦ **HAYES GREEN:** Rediscovered by Tom Brown near Robbinsville, North Carolina. Described as medium size or above, roundish conical; skin pale green. Ripe August/September. No catalog listings.

❦ **HAYWOOD JUNE:** A mountain apple once grown from Haywood County, North Carolina, south to Rabun County, Georgia. It is certainly the same apple as Haywood's June listed in 1877 without description by Pomona Hills Nursery of Guilford County, North Carolina. Jim Freel, owner of several trees, told Tom Brown his trees were grafted thirty years ago from extremely old trees. These apples make a bright pink applesauce or jelly if cooked without being peeled. Described as medium size, roundish oblate; skin very dark red with prominent whitish dots. Ripe early July in the mountains. No catalog listings.

❦ **HEGE:** A local apple long grown around Whitsett, North Carolina. Scions were given to me by Henry Foust. No description. No catalog listings.

❦ **HENRY CLAY:** The accepted history of this apple is that W. H. Knight of Hopkins County, Kentucky, originated Henry Clay before 1890. It was trademarked and introduced by Stark Bro's Nursery about 1910 and was advertised by them as the earliest-ripening yellow apple, earlier and of better quality than Yellow Transparent.

A letter to me in 1999 from Pansy McChesney Watson of Hopkinsville, Kentucky, gives another version of the origin of the Henry Clay apple. "My father, Byrd T. McChesney, was born in 1882 in Caldwell County, Kentucky. When he and a brother were very young, they were playing in the woods on the family farm and found an apple tree. They brought the tree to the homeplace and planted it in their orchard. When the tree produced fruit it was different from any the people in the area had ever seen, so they named it Henry Clay for an old neighbor, Henry Clay Hunter. Later a representative from Starks' Nursery came to my father and wanted to take cuttings for grafting, to which my father consented. I understand the tree was on the market for some time."

Fruit above to below medium, oblate to roundish, conical, often lopsided and ribbed; skin green or pale yellow, sometimes with a pinkish orange blush on the sunny side and often having spots and patches of russet; dots numerous, pale gray, submerged; stem very long in a rather wide cavity; calyx closed; basin small, wrinkled; flesh greenish white, soft, slightly acid. Ripe June/July. ❖ **Plate 22.**

**HEWE'S CRAB** (Hughes' Crab, Virginia Crab, Hugh's Virginia, Red Hughes, Cider Crab): This is the most celebrated cider apple ever grown in the South, making a dry cider unsurpassed in flavor and keeping ability. Trees nearly a hundred years old were found in Virginia by Coxe in 1817 when he wrote:

> A small fruit of light green color striped with red, and of a harsh unpleasant taste. Originated in Virginia and is highly valued as a cider fruit. Its must (juice) is less disposed, from its great acidity, to rise too high in fermentation than that of any other apple; and it has, besides, almost every other property of a cider apple. The trees bear abundantly, the fruit ripens late and is free of rot of any kind. The fruit is small and hard and, therefore, bears the fall from the tree without bruising. It grinds small and the pulp is remarkably tough, yet parts with its juice readily, and the must runs from the press very fine and clear.

A "Hughes Crab" is briefly mentioned being grown in 1741 in James City County, Virginia. An advertisement in a 1761 Williamsburg, Virginia, newspaper lists a tract of land for sale having "a very good bearing orchard and another of 150 Hughes' crabs beginning to bear."

A North Carolina nursery catalog extolled Hewe's Crab in 1879: "The cider we use comes principally from the North. It is not equal to crab cider. Cider should be made at home. All that is desired for this purpose is found in the Hewe's Crab.

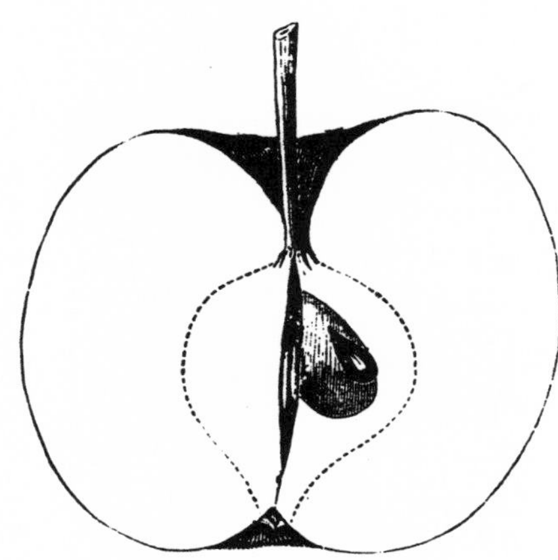

HEWE'S CRAB

This is the best winter cider crab in existence. It is hardy, productive, and makes the finest cider. The cider keeps perfectly sweet all winter and is clear and sparkling."

George Washington preferred "crab cider" to any other and arranged to get it during the Revolutionary War. Downing (1878) says Hewe's Crab is "often mixed with rich pulpy apples, to which it imparts a good deal of its fine quality." Thomas Jefferson grew Hewe's Crab in his north orchard at Monticello, which was reserved for cider apples. He called this apple "Red Hughes" and blended its juice with the juice of Golden Wilding to make a superior cider.

In most of the South Hewe's Crab is a fall or winter apple, but in the Deep South it matures as early as mid-August. Yates is probably a better winter cider apple than Hewe's Crab in the Deep South.

Fruit very small, about one and one-half inches in diameter, round; skin green, usually nearly covered with dull or purplish red; dots numerous, large, whitish; stem long, slender, and red in a yellowish cavity; calyx closed; basin shallow and small; flesh firm, fibrous, acid, astringent. Ripe September/October. Catalog listings: MD, VA, NC, GA, LA, MS, AL, TN, KY, TX (1761–1925).

An apple called Red Hewe's or Red Hughes Crab, a larger apple than Hewe's Crab, was grown before 1869 from a seed of Hewe's Crab by a Colonel Blackburn of Paris, Illinois. This apple was not sold in the South. Beeler's Crab, very similar to Hewe's Crab but a better-growing tree, was grown in

Kentucky in the mid-nineteenth century. Beeler's Crab is extinct. (*See* Kentucky Red.)

An entirely different apple named Hughes, a large eating apple, originated in Pennsylvania before 1897 but was not sold in the South.

**HICKMAN:** Hickman is a seedling of Shockley first grown by D. W. Dickinson of Hickman, Kentucky. It was sold in 1916 by the J. Van Lindley Nursery of Greensboro, North Carolina: "Valuable for the Cotton Belt; color yellow covered with light red; flesh yellow and of good quality. A good keeper." An old tree of this name has been found in Chatham County, North Carolina, belonging to Paul Johnson.

Fruit medium, roundish oblate, somewhat oblique; skin mostly pale green striped and splashed with brick red under some scarf skin; dots small and large, irregular, gray and russet; stem long in a round, even, greenish russeted cavity; calyx closed; basin rather deep, abrupt, slightly corrugated; flesh whitish, juicy, tender, crisp, mild subacid. Ripe October.

**HIGHTOP SWEET** (Sweet June, Summer Sweet, Early Sweet, Spence's Early, Yellow Sweet June, Tall Top?, Earle?): Listed as Sweet June or Yellow Sweet June in most southern nursery catalogs and sold all over the South. It is a very sweet apple used most often for baking and drying. Hightop Sweet is one of the oldest American apples, having originated in Plymouth Colony in Massachusetts in the mid 1600s. Its name reflects the tendency of the tree to have a long trunk between the lowest limbs and the ground. The tree is vigorous and productive.

Fruit medium or below, roundish; skin very smooth, light yellow or greenish yellow sometimes with a faint bronze blush; dots numerous, small, green; stem medium length in a deep, narrow, russeted cavity; calyx closed; basin shallow and slightly furrowed; flesh yellowish, tender, not very juicy, very sweet. Ripe early August. Catalog listings: MD, VA, NC, GA, LA, KY (1853–1925).

**HILLSIDE:** There are reports that this mountain apple was once grown in Wilkes, Ashe, and Graham Counties in North Carolina. Tom Brown found a single tree near Hays in 2002. Described as large, oblate, sometimes oblique; skin rough, green with a red blush and some russet; flesh very firm, juicy, almost acid. Ripe October and a good keeper. No catalog listings.

**HOG ISLAND SWEET** (Hog Apple, Sweet Pippin, Hog Sweeting, Van Kleck's Sweet): A very sweet apple that originated on Hog Island (now called Syosset Island) adjoining Long Island, New York. The tree is very productive. One old catalog says: "A very fine apple for the table and for fattening stock."

Fruit medium or above, roundish to oblate, conical; skin thick, yellow striped with red, roughened with patches of russet and having a red cheek; stem rather short in a deep, abrupt, russeted cavity; calyx usually closed; basin shallow to medium depth, furrowed; flesh yellow, juicy, rather coarse, crisp, tender, slightly aromatic, very sweet. Ripe September/October. Catalog listings: MD, VA, GA (1836–1904).

**HOG SWEET:** Although close to Hog Island Sweet in name, this is a different apple. Jim Lawson, Georgia nurseryman, believes Hog Sweet is an old apple from the mountains of north Georgia.

Fruit medium size, round; skin smooth, yellowish green with a russeted cavity; flesh intensely sweet. Ripe late July. No catalog listings.

**HOLLAND PIPPIN** (Pie Apple, French Pippin, Summer Pippin, Belvidere Pippin): Closely resembles Fall Pippin and has been confused with it. Generally considered a cooking apple "of the highest merit" and suitable for cooking while the skin is still quite green, in the early summer in the South. The tree bears continuously for several months. Little is known of its origin, and at least two different apples have been grown under this name.

Fruit large or very large, roundish or slightly oblong, slightly conical; skin pale green or yellow with a brownish red blush; dots numerous, large and small, greenish; stem medium to short in an acute, usually deep cavity; calyx closed or partially open; basin varies in width and depth, wrinkled; flesh nearly white, slightly coarse, moderately crisp, very juicy, brisk subacid to acid. Ripe July/September. Catalog listings: MD, VA, NC, GA, LA, KY (1824–1913).

❦ **HOLLOW LOG:** Several trees of this apple were found by my good friend and fellow apple enthusiast Harold Punch, who lives in Hickory, North Carolina. These trees were remnants of the Sipes Orchard in Conover, North Carolina, which grew Hollow Log apples in the 1920s and 1930s. Strangely enough, I have two reports that Hollow Log was also grown in Canada in the 1920s.

Hollow Log was listed from 1924 to 1928 by Valdesian Nurseries of Bostic, North Carolina: "Originated in Rutherford County, North Carolina, being a seedling found near a hollow log. This is a valuable variety and a strong grower. Owing to the lateness of bloom, seldom fails to produce annually an abundant crop. Begins to ripen the last of June and continues through July and into August. Large fruit, deep yellow in color, tender, crisp, very juicy, and with a most delicious, aromatic, spicy flavor. It has no superior as an eating and cooking apple. Wherever known, it is said to be the best apple in cultivation. We have sold these trees to many different sections of the country and have never had a complaint."

❦ **HOLLY:** In the chapter on extinct apples in this book, there is an old Georgia apple named Holly. Thus, when I noted a Holly apple being grown in the USDA Apple Germplasm Repository in Geneva, New York, I obtained a scion and grafted it. The Holly apple from the repository is not the old Georgia variety, it turns out, but originated as a cross of Jonathan × Delicious made in 1952 at the Ohio Agricultural Experiment Station. It is a lovely and tasty apple, seemingly well adapted to the South, so I have kept it in my orchard.

Fruit medium or above, roundish to oblong, very conical; skin completely covered in bright red in well-colored apples, without any stripes, but having a light bloom; dots numerous, medium size, whitish; stem rather short in a deep, narrow, russeted cavity; calyx usually open; basin wide, shallow, lumpy, often cracked; flesh whitish, moderately juicy, chewy, mild subacid to almost sweet. Ripe August/September. No catalog listings.

❦ **HONEY SWEET** (Honey Cider): Ragan (1905) lists six apples called Honey or having Honey in their names and three other synonyms with this name. None of these originated in the South or was widely grown here. Downing (1869) describes an apple called Honey Sweet (with the synonym of Honey Cider) as a good dessert and cider apple. An apple named Honey Sweet was rediscovered by Elwood Fisher in the early 1960s in the Shenandoah Valley. This medium-size apple has yellow skin often striped pinkish and ripens August/September. No catalog listings. *See also* Honey.

❦ **HOOVER** (Wattauga, Black Coal, Baltimore Red, Welcome, Black Hoover, Thunderbolt, Watauga): Hoover is thoroughly mixed up with apples called Black Coal, Baltimore, and Baltimore Red, and descriptions of all of them are quite similar. Black Coal was often listed as a synonym of Hoover, and Baltimore Red is listed as a synonym of Baltimore, Hoover, and Black Coal. For the sake of this description, I will discuss Hoover as if it were a separate variety, but all of these apples may be identical.

Hoover is first mentioned in the 1856 catalog of Pomaria Nurseries of Pomaria, South Carolina, where it is said to be a seedling from Edisto, South Carolina. An 1857 issue of the *Magazine of Horticulture* contains this description of Hoover:

> This singularly marked apple hails from Edisto, South Carolina, and was raised by Mr. Hoover of that place. It is rather flat in shape, narrowing towards the eye, size large; color a fine red, sometimes dark, singularly spotted with round spots about one-eighth of an inch in diameter; these spots are simply an absence of the red color and are not caused by russet; flesh white, hard, firm, and juicy; flavor a fine brisk acid; stem three-quarters of an inch long and slender; cavity wide and green within; calyx stiff, open and green; basin rather small and a little ribbed. Ripens in November and keeps until March. Quality very good.

In addition to its good eating quality, Hoover is a very showy apple, being large and dark red. In

1908 the USDA said of it: "In passing through the mountain sections of North Carolina, one sees this variety very commonly. During the fall, it is the one most often brought to the stations for sale to passengers on the trains."

Several early descriptions of Hoover remark that it leafs out very late in the spring and retains its foliage until quite late in winter. Its leaves seem to be larger than most other apple varieties, and it may be a triploid. The tree is said to be distinctively "short-jointed and resistant to fire blight." When grown at higher altitudes on good soil, Hoover apples are glossy and almost black. At lower altitudes, the color is a duller red. Hoover Pippin is not the same as Hoover but is a large, green apple from Pennsylvania. A letter to me from a seventy-seven-year-old woman in Tennessee says her family used Hoover to make apple butter. Jim Lawson sold Hoover for years from his Georgia nursery.

Fruit large, roundish oblate, slightly conical; skin mostly splashed and striped with two shades of dark red, sometimes almost black, with a light bloom; dots large, numerous, conspicuous, light colored, interspersed with patches of russet; stem rather long in a large and thinly russeted cavity with the russet spilling over the top of the apple; calyx open or closed; basin slightly furrowed; flesh yellowish, firm, tender, moderately juicy, sprightly subacid. Ripe September/October and a good keeper. Catalog listings: VA, NC, SC, GA, KY (1856–1917). *See also* Black Coal and Baltimore.

❦ **HORSE** (Summer Horse, Yellow Horse, Green Horse, Old Fashion Horse, Oldfield Horse, Mammoth Horse, Carolina Horse, McBath, Improved Horse, Trippes Horse, Hoss, and Haas [incorrectly], Yellow Hoss): In my searches for old southern apples, I find more old trees of the Horse Apple than any other variety. This was certainly the most popular apple grown for home use in the South before 1930. Warder (1867) describes it as "another southern favorite, especially as a useful family apple."

In flavor, Horse Apples may not please those people seduced by the sweetness of almost all modern apples. Horse Apples are decidedly tart until fully ripe, at which point their tartness is subdued and the fruit develops a flavor unlike any other apple. Many old catalogs extol its suitability for cooking, drying, cider, and vinegar, and these uses undoubtedly contributed to its popularity in the rural South. I believe, however, that the wide dissemination of Horse is also due to the tree's renowned health and productivity. It usually has immense crops of large apples that ripen in the heat of summer, making the fruit particularly suitable for drying. Horse seems to do well all over the South, even in the warmer areas. The tree blooms late, grows rapidly, and bears early.

A letter to me from Angela Levi, Columbus, North Carolina, gives another use of the Horse apple: "My father had a wonderful Horse apple tree. It was exceptionally hardy, enduring much in the way of weather and neglect. The apples it produced were not much for eating out of hand, but they produced jelly that was pure heaven! It required no commercial pectin and was deep amber, fragrant and luscious with flavor. One day we kids returned from school ravenous with hunger to find hot biscuits and a run of eight glasses of this jelly cooling on the shelf. In fifteen minutes there was nothing but crumbs, sticky glasses, satisfied smiles and one furious mother!"

Horse is a very old variety, and its origin is not known with certainty. Its origin was attributed to Nash County, North Carolina, by a USDA report written in 1869, but this is suspect as it was a very old apple even then. "Horse Apples" were listed in a November 4, 1763, advertisement in the *Virginia Gazette* newspaper published in Williamsburg, Virginia. A note in the USDA files, written in 1902 by W. H. Ragan, says the Horse Apple was introduced into Indiana from Tennessee about 1830. Mammoth Horse, Trippe's Horse, and Improved Horse are listed in one or two southern nursery catalogs and may be seedlings of Horse. (*See* Trippe's Horse.) Haas or Hoss is a different apple. (*See* Haas.)

Fruit medium to almost large, roundish, often lopsided and oblique, ribbed; skin thick, green becoming yellow when ripe, sometimes with a slight reddish tinge or blush on the sunny side, with irregular russet blotches or freckles all over the apple; dots small, sunken, greenish, often areole; stem short to almost medium, in a deep, acute, russeted cavity; calyx closed; basin medium size, corrugated; flesh yellow, firm, rather juicy, briskly subacid until fully ripe. Ripe late July/August. Catalog listings: MD, VA, NC, SC, GA, AL, MS, LA, TN, KY, TX, AR (1853–1928).

❧ **HUBBARDSTON NONSUCH** (John May, Old Town Pippin, Nonsuch, Nonesuch, American Blush, Van Fleet, Hubbardson's Nonsuch, Farmer's Profit, Red Winter Nonsuch): Originated in Hubbardston, Massachusetts, before 1800 and sold by a moderate number of southern nurseries, usually being listed without any description. This apple receives high praise from Beach (1905) for its eating quality and commercial possibilities in New York, but in the South the fruit often drops prematurely. Tom Burford, the Virginia apple guru, says: "Soil and climate affect the tree and fruit characteristics remarkably. This variability often makes identification difficult."

Fruit above medium to large, roundish oblong, tapering toward the calyx end; skin smooth, blushed and mottled with red, which is usually dull brownish but may be bright, overlaid with irregular deeper red stripes, usually roughened with dots and flecks of russet; stem short in a deep and russeted cavity; calyx open; basin narrow to rather wide, shallow to moderately deep, distinctly furrowed, flecked with russet; flesh yellowish, juicy, rather fine-grained, aromatic, tender, subacid to almost sweet. Ripe September. Catalog listings: MD, VA, NC, GA, KY, TX (1853–1928).

❧ **HUFFMAN RED:** I collected this unknown but lovely, good-tasting apple in 1992 from a Mr. Huffman of Kimesville, North Carolina, and named it for him.

Fruit medium or above, slightly oblate; skin mostly covered with red and some stripes; dots scattered, rather large, whitish; stem medium to long in a russeted cavity; calyx open or closed; flesh whitish, crisp, juicy, subacid. Ripe August/September. No catalog listings.

❧ **HUNGE:** In 1940 a seedling apple tree volunteered in the ditch in front of Gertrude Morris's house near Newton Grove, North Carolina. Remembering the Hunge tree in her father's old orchard in Wayne County, Mrs. Morris moved the seedling to a field near her house, cut it off near the ground and grafted it with a twig from her father's Hunge tree. When she wrote me in late August 1987, her tree was the only Hunge apple tree still in existence. She wrote: "The Hunge is my favorite apple. I never pick them, just let them fall." Southerners owe the late Mrs. Morris a debt of gratitude for saving this very old and exceptionally good apple.

Hunge originated in the 1700s as a "Hunge's" apple was listed by a Norfolk, Virginia, nursery in 1805.It was described at the 1858 American Pomological Society meeting as "an old North Carolina variety." Although many old references cite Hunge as valuable for cooking, drying, and brandy, I find it to be an excellent apple for fresh eating. I like its winey flavor. It appears to be well adapted to growing in the coastal plains of the South, where Mrs. Morris lived, which is an environment not hospitable to most apple varieties.

Fruit large, sometimes very large, roundish oblate; skin mostly covered with red without stripes if exposed to the sun, a brown russet netting (heavy in some years) overlays the skin and roughens it; dots numerous, large, russet; stem half an inch long in an abrupt, deep, narrow cavity; calyx open; basin rather wide and shallow, sometimes leather-cracked;

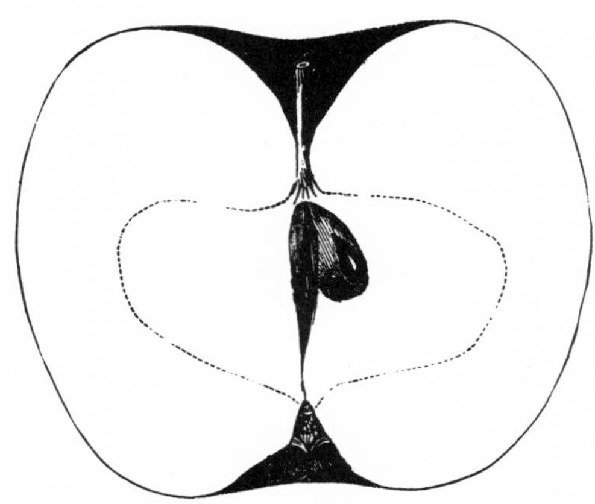

HUNGE

flesh white tinged yellowish, crisp, juicy, vinous, aromatic, almost sweet. Ripe August/September. Catalog listings: NC, VA, GA (1853–1904).

❦ **HUNTSMAN'S FAVORITE** (Huntsman): Originated about 1850 on the farm of John Huntsman of Fayette, Missouri, and widely grown before 1900 in Missouri and Kansas where it was prized for its eating quality and the productiveness of the tree. Several southern nurseries sold Huntsman's Favorite, but it was never an important apple in the South. The tree is susceptible to apple scab and bitter rot.

Fruit large, roundish oblate to oblate, sides usually unequal; skin smooth, deep yellow or greenish, rarely with a faint orangish red blush; dots large, distinct, dark; stem short and rather thick in a wide, deep, sometimes russeted cavity; basin abrupt, rather deep, furrowed; flesh yellow, firm, juicy, aromatic, subacid. Ripe September and usually a good keeper, but one old Maryland catalog says the apples lose quality "if kept late." Catalog listings: MD, VA, NC, GA, TN, AR, KY (1870–1917). ❖ **Plate 23.**

❦ **IMPROVED VARIETIES:** Many southern nurseries sold improved versions of the more popular varieties. Probably most so-called improved apples were seedlings, but some may have been limb sports or mutations having more color than the original apple. In this book, improved varieties are discussed under the name of the original variety. Among the improved varieties listed in old catalogs are: Improved Ben Davis, Improved Bevans, Improved Horse, Improved Limbertwig, Improved Red June, Improved Shockley, and Improved Winesap.

❦ **INGRAM** (Ingraham, Ingram's Seedling): A flavorful, late-ripening eating apple, one of my favorites, and an outstanding winter keeper. It originated before 1855 with Martin Ingram near Springfield, Missouri, and was thought to be a seedling of Rall's Janet, "same size but higher color." The tree is a prolific biennial or annual bearer and a very late bloomer like Rall's Janet. Beach (1905) ranks the fruit in quality with York Imperial, and it has been described as "clear of rot." The tree needs thinning to prevent limb breakage and to produce sizeable apples, and the fruit is excellent for cider and fresh eating.

Fruit medium or above, roundish but occasionally oblong, conical; skin thick, smooth, almost completely covered with dark red; dots numerous, whitish or russet, sometimes areolar; stem long in a medium to wide, deep, partly russeted cavity; calyx open; basin moderately deep, medium to narrow in width; flesh tinged yellow, firm, crisp, juicy, aromatic, mild subacid. Ripe October and keeps until February or later. Catalog listings: MD, NC, AL, KY, TX, AR (1902–26). ❖ **Plate 24.**

❦ **ISAM:** A family apple prized and nurtured by the Misenheimer family of North Carolina for over a hundred years. During all this time it has been propagated by root sprouts. Isam originated with Isam Misenheimer (1818–97) who lived and farmed at Misenheimer Springs, Stanley County, near Richfield, North Carolina. This old apple was brought to my attention in 1993 by Mrs. Walter Misenheimer and her son Larry. Mrs. Misenheimer wrote me: "I will be glad to share some cuttings with you of the Isam apple. It is fast becoming extinct."

Fruit small to below medium, roundish; skin pale yellow, lightly mottled and striped with pinkish red on the sunny side; dots large, conspicuous, russet; stem long in a narrow, deep, abrupt, greenish russeted cavity; calyx closed; basin rather shallow, corrugated; flesh tinged yellow, juicy, moderately crisp, subacid. Ripe August/September. No catalog listings.

❦ **JAKE'S SEEDLING:** I received this apple from my Kentucky friend Herbert Childress. He said it originated in Russell County, Kentucky, on the farm of J. B. (Jake) Garner and won "Best Apple" at the county fair for many years. Jake's Seedling is a beautiful and good-tasting apple.

Fruit medium, roundish, slightly conical, flattened on the ends, often oblique; skin smooth, yellowish with a dark red or purplish red blush on the sunny side, many apples almost entirely red, with a white bloom; dots small, numerous, conspicuous, indented, white and dark green; stem medium length in a round, deep, greenish or golden russeted cavity; calyx open or closed; basin large, wide, slightly corrugated; flesh white tinged greenish, crisp, juicy, fine-grained, subacid. Ripe late July/August. No catalog listings.

❧ **JARRETT:** A local apple grown for many years in Watauga County, North Carolina. Inadene Hampton of Watauga County had an old tree in her orchard and gave me scions. Fruit medium size, red-striped, flesh yellow. Ripe late September. No catalog listings.

❧ **JEFFERIS** (Everbearing, Grantham, Illinois Imperial?, Jefferis Red): Although not of southern origin, Jefferis is a high-quality apple well adapted to the mountains and piedmont of the South. It is a fall apple in the North but a late summer apple in the South, with the fruit ripening over a period of several weeks. The tree is not very productive but has some scab resistance.

Jefferis originated on the farm of Isaac Jefferis in Chester County, Pennsylvania, and was first exhibited by him in 1848. In the 1920s Stark Bro's Nursery sold a red sport of Jefferis, Jefferis Red, which originated in Montana.

Fruit medium or below, roundish; skin thin, clear waxen yellow, shaded and splashed with reddish orange, which is deeper on the sunny side; dots numerous, large, white; stem half an inch long in a deep, acute, slightly russeted cavity; calyx closed; basin wide, medium in depth, smooth, abrupt; flesh yellowish white, very juicy, tender, crisp, subacid. Ripe August. Catalog listings: MD, VA, SC, KY, TX, AR (1856–1920).

❧ **JIM DAY** (Day Apple): This apple, under the name "Day Apple," was listed as extinct in the first edition of this book. Jack Herring of Brandon, Mississippi, found a single tree of Jim Day in 2004 at the Jim Ramsey homestead north of Kosciusko, Mississippi, and sent me scions.

Originated with J. W. Day of Crystal Springs, Simpson County, Mississippi, and listed in a 1915 Alabama nursery catalog. Said to be adapted to the Gulf coast, south Georgia, and north Florida. Received a bronze medal at the 1904 St. Louis Exposition. Probably the same as Reagan described in the chapter on extinct varieties.

Fruit medium to large; skin yellow with red stripes on the sunny side; flesh juicy, crisp, mild subacid to almost sweet. Ripe late June to August.

❧ **JIMBO** (Jumbo): Grown before 1900 in Carter County, Tennessee, and Alleghany, Mitchell, and Avery counties, North Carolina. Jimbo is still grown in Avery County, in the Mountain community, especially for making apple butter.

In October 2008, Doug Hundley, the county agricultural agent for Avery County, sent me several Jimbo apples from Dee Moore's orchard. Impressive in size and color, I found the apples to closely resemble Notley P. No. 1 (which, in turn, may be Gloria Mundi). Doug has also found a Notley P. apple tree in his county and hopes to make a side-by-side comparison of Jimbo and Notley P. this autumn.

Fruit above medium to large, roundish or slightly oblate, lobed; skin yellow, often with a faint blush; dots large, whitish and russet; stem short in a russeted cavity, sometimes with russet over the top of the apple. Ripe September/October. No catalog listings.

❧ **JOE LITTLE:** That great apple hunter, Dr. L. R. Littleton, found Joe Little in 1995 near Maysville, West Virginia, in an orchard of antique apples belonging to Harry Sulser.

Fruit small to medium, roundish or slightly oblate; skin partly to almost completely covered with splashes and stripes of bright red; dots scattered, small, white; stem almost long in a yellowish cavity; calyx open; basin wide, smooth, almost deep; flesh white tinged yellow, fine-grained, rather soft, juicy, brisk subacid. Ripe July/August. No catalog listings.

❧ **JOHN APPLE:** A local apple from the Lowgap area between Mount Airy, North Carolina, and Galax, Virginia. A letter to me from Joyce Cooke of Moneta, Virginia, said that her father was eighty-four years old, and John Apple had been on the farm as long as he could remember. Another letter, from Veronica Springer of Mount Airy, says she found only one worm in a peck of unsprayed John Apples, and the slices hold their shape when cooked. Mrs. Springer acted as my guide in tracking down a tree of the John Apple that belonged to Mr. and Mrs. Carrico of Lowgap.

Fruit medium, roundish oblate, lobed; skin yellow with a pinkish blush or reddish blotches and stripes on the sunny side; dots few, dark russet and whitish; basin wide; calyx closed; flesh firm, moderately juicy, mild subacid. Ripe August/September. No catalog listings.

❦ **JOHN CONNER:** Named for a man who lived in the late 1800s in the Pore's Knob community of Wilkes County, North Carolina, where Tom Brown found one surviving tree.

Fruit medium or slightly below, roundish and quite conical; skin smooth, mostly covered in a bright red blush with a few obscure stripes; dots submerged, pale greenish or white; stem long; calyx closed in a corrugated basin; flesh whitish, fine-grained, almost acid. Ripe August/September. No catalog listings.

❦ **JOHNNY NO CORE:** An old Ashe County, North Carolina, apple. Tom Brown says the apple has very small cavity and basin indentations and a small seed bed, thus making almost the entire apple edible. Maybe identical to Vanhoy.

Fruit medium or above, round to slightly oblong, conical; skin mostly covered in red with some dark red stripes; stem long; flesh mild subacid. Ripe September. No catalog listings.

❦ **JOHNSON KEEPER:** Yet another old Wilkes County, North Carolina, apple found by Tom Brown.

Fruit medium or above, roundish, sometimes oblique; skin covered with dark red; dots few, medium size, whitish; stem almost short in a russeted cavity; flesh crisp, juicy, subacid. Ripe October. No catalog listings.

❦ **JONALICIOUS:** A chance seedling found in 1933 by Anna Morris Daniels near Abilene, Texas. Stark Bro's Nursery patented and named Jonalicious in 1958 and introduced it in their catalog in 1960. In spite of its name, it probably has no Jonathan in its parentage.

Fruit medium, round, often lobed; skin thick, tough, with a bright red, grainy blush covering most of the apple; dots scattered, whitish and russet; stem short to medium in a deep, slightly russeted cavity; calyx barely open in a lobed, corrugated basin; flesh yellowish, crisp, juicy, fine-grained, aromatic, subacid. Ripe September.

❦ **JONATHAN** (King Philip, Philip Rick, Ulster Seedling): An important commercial apple in the United States, but Jonathan territory lies north and west of the Mason-Dixon line. The major commercial Jonathan-growing states are Michigan, Washington, Illinois, Ohio, Colorado, and Pennsylvania, but there are a few commercial orchards of Jonathan in Virginia. Today, Jonathan apples represent about 4 percent of the U.S. apple crop. In 1908, a USDA observer traveling in the South noted that Jonathan "occurs only rarely" in the region, and the best southern Jonathans were from orchards at the highest elevations.

Jonathan has a legion of admirers who put its sprightly, vinous flavor and tender, juicy texture against any other apple. It seldom reaches these heights in the warmer regions of the South where the tree is very susceptible to fire blight, bitter rot, powdery mildew, and cedar-apple rust. Wherever it is grown, Jonathan requires soils in good tilth and fertility to produce acceptable fruit and tends to be a biennial bearer. Its foliage has a gray hue.

Jonathan originated as a seedling of Esopus Spitzenberg on the farm of Philip Rick of Woodstock, New York, and was first described in 1826. It was named for Jonathan Hasbrouck, who first noticed its quality. The superior quality of Jonathan has been recognized worldwide and many countries, from Romania to the Netherlands to Japan, have used Jonathan in apple-breeding programs. Over ninety cultivars have been bred with Jonathan as a parent including Akane, Holly, Idared, King David, Mutsu, Fyan, and Jonagold.

Fruit medium, roundish conical; skin smooth, thin, tough, almost completely covered with red, often dark red in the sun; dots small and inconspicuous; stem slender, medium to long in a deep, wide cavity; calyx closed; basin deep and abrupt; flesh white, crisp, tender, juicy, sprightly, vinous, subacid. Ripe September/October. Catalog listings: MD, VA, NC, GA, AL, LA, TN, KY, TX, AR (1853–1928).

❦ **JUICY FRUIT:** An old apple from the Roan Mountain, Tennessee, area and excellent for fresh eating. Mr. C. M. Putman has the only surviving tree, which was found by Tom Brown.

Fruit medium size, roundish to oblong, conical; skin greenish to pale yellow with bronzing on the sunny side and heavy scarf skin over the apple; dots scattered, russet; stem medium to almost long, often thick and ending in a knob, in a shallow, russeted cavity; calyx open or closed; flesh cream-colored, crisp, moderately juicy, sweet. Ripe October. No catalog listings.

❦ **JULY DELICIOUS:** Russell Baker bred this apple in the 1930s in his nursery in Baileyton, Cullman County, Alabama. He described it in one of his catalogs: "From Hackworth × Delicious. Shape and size of Delicious, but better color. The tree never has any blight and is the most self-shaping of all trees. In fact, it will make good without any pruning at all. Ripens 60 days before Delicious." Joyce Neighbors found a tree of July Delicious belonging to Doyle Baker of Fayette County, Alabama. *See also* Atha.

Fruit medium or below, roundish conical; skin pale yellow, splashed with bright red on the sunny side with some darker red stripes; dots few, russet; stem almost long and thickened at the base in a shallow, bronzed cavity; calyx closed; flesh pale greenish, very tender, juicy, fine-grained, almost sweet. Ripe July/August.

❦ **JULY-AUGUST GO-NO-FURTHER:** An old West Virginia apple found in 1994 by the late Dr. L. R. Littleton, who died in 2004. Dr. Littleton was a radiologist working in hospitals in Virginia and West Virginia. He would query his patients to find clues about old apple varieties. In winter he and I would track down the old trees and cut scions. Dr. Littleton's old four-wheel-drive Jeep was essential for these winter forays into remote mountain areas often covered in ice and snow.

Fruit above medium to large, round or somewhat oblong, conical, often oblique and irregular; skin yellowish, partly to almost completely covered with purplish red; dots numerous, whitish; stem short to medium length in a narrow, abrupt, russeted cavity; calyx closed; basin very corrugated. Ripe late August/September. No catalog listings.

❦ **JUNALUSKA:** About 2001 apple hunter Tom Brown was led to an unidentified apple tree in Macon County, North Carolina, about eight miles from Silas McDowell's original orchard of the 1840s and 1850s. The apples on the tree resemble the long-lost Junaluskee apple that Silas McDowell grew in his orchard in the mid 1800s, and Tom Brown believes he has found the true Junaluskee. I give here a description of Tom Brown's Junaluska, which can be compared to the description of Silas McDowell's Junaluskee in the chapter on extinct varieties.

Fruit medium, roundish to slightly oblate; skin greenish with some orangish red blotches, but the apple is mostly covered with tan russet with patches of green and red showing through the russet; dots irregular, russet; stem quite thick, short to medium length in a wide, russeted cavity; calyx closed; basin rather small; flesh dense, fine-grained, not very juicy, subacid. Ripe October.

❦ **JUNE SWEETING:** All over the South there are apples called June Sweet, June Sweeting, June Sweetener, Red June Sweet, and other variations on this theme. These are often not the same apple but share the characteristics of sweetness and ripening in June. I describe below an apple called June Sweeting that I got in 1988 from Ruby Jefferson of Bath, North Carolina.

Fruit below medium size, roundish to slightly oblate, conical; skin smooth, light green with a reddish blush (sometimes dark red) mostly covering the apple; dots small, numerous, white; stem greenish and rather thick, short to medium length in an abrupt, deep cavity; calyx usually open; basin smooth, red, abrupt, deep; flesh soft, pale greenish, fine-grained, sweet. Ripe July. Catalog listings: VA, NC (1904).

❦ **KANE** (Cain, Cane): Although this apple originated in Kent County, Delaware, it was sold only by North Carolina and Virginia nurseries from 1853 to 1888. I have spoken to several elderly people in both of these states who remember this apple and praise its quality. In February 1995 I received a letter from Thad Wiseman of Yadkin County, North Carolina, with the news that he had a tree of the "Cane" apple. After visiting with him and hearing his description of the fruit, I was convinced it is the Kane and obtained scions.

Fruit small to medium, roundish oblate, slightly

conical, often ribbed; skin smooth, waxy, whitish yellow mostly blushed with red without any stripes, especially on the sunny side; dots inconspicuous, gray, areole; stem short or medium length in a russeted cavity; calyx usually open; basin shallow to medium depth; flesh whitish, juicy, crisp, subacid. Ripe August/September. ❖ **Plate 25.**

❦ **KEENER SEEDLING** (Rusty Coat): Listed in the 1890 catalog of the Catawba County Nursery of Newton, North Carolina: "Originated in Lincoln County, North Carolina, about four miles from our place. We know this apple from first to last and find it one of the finest keeping apples for the South. It is known by the name Rusty Coat. Color greenish russet; somewhat flat; flesh white with good flavor; fine for cooking, canning, and jellies, besides being one of the best table and keeping varieties. Stays on the tree till the leaves come off and keeps until late spring."

In 1992 I received a fact-filled letter from Bertha Kiser Goodson of Lincoln County, North Carolina. She said that a Mr. Keener had a land grant along Leeper Creek in Lincoln County and first grew the Keener Seedling. About 1880 a mining engineer from Missouri, who came to work with the iron ore mines in Lincoln County, married the daughter of Mr. Keener and bought sixty-six acres of the Keener land. This man grafted fruit trees and distributed Keener Seedling trees throughout Lincoln County. Mrs. Goodson further writes: "The trees are large, some 30 or 35 feet in height. They are early bloomers and the fruit ripens in late fall. The fruit is round with a rosy, rusty-brown coloring—a good keeper. The apples will keep all winter. We wrapped ours in newspaper and packed them in barrels. The apples would sometimes hang on the tree all winter or could be found on the ground in the leaves. The meat is very white and juicy—good to eat raw—and the best apple anywhere for pies and sauce. Also dries good!"

Fruit medium or below, round, flattened on the ends; skin completely covered with brown russet with faint red stripes barely visible beneath the russet; dots inconspicuous, faint, tan; stem medium to long in an abrupt, deep, leather-cracked cavity; calyx green, open; basin wide, greenish, corrugated; flesh crisp, juicy, fine-grained, subacid. Ripe late October and a good keeper.

❦ **KENNEDY:** A Georgia apple first mentioned and briefly described in 1858: "Fruit large, round; skin striped with red; flesh subacid. Ripe November or probably earlier." A Kennedy apple was recently found by Jimmy Hargrove and is described here, but it is probably not the Georgia apple.

Fruit medium or above, round to slightly oblong; skin mostly covered in bright red or purplish red with some scarf skin, some apples may have considerable russeting; dots few to many, large, whitish; stem short to medium length in a narrow, often constricted, russeted cavity with russet over the top and often down the sides of the apple; calyx closed; flesh pale greenish, juicy, crisp, somewhat chewy, subacid. Ripe mid-July. No catalog listings.

❦ **KIMROME:** This is not an antique apple, but its size and quality keep it in my orchard. A seedling tree was found in the 1970s by Kimsey Waddell in his commercial orchard of Rome Beauty apple trees in north Georgia near Ellijay. One apple is reported to have weighed three pounds. Jerry Hensley, who now operates Waddell Orchard, says: "People drive all the way up here from Florida just to get Kimrome apples."

Fruit large to very large, round, often slightly oblique; skin pale yellow, partly to mostly covered with pinkish red to medium red with faint, darker red stripes; dots large, scattered, gray; stem short in a wide, greenish cavity. Ripe September. No catalog listings.

❦ **KING DAVID:** Thought to be a cross of Jonathan × Winesap or perhaps Jonathan × Arkansas Black. The original tree was found in 1893 growing in a fencerow on the farm of Ben Frost near Durham in Washington County, Arkansas. It was trademarked and introduced by Stark Bro's Nursery in 1902 and sold by them until the 1930s as a replacement for Jonathan in commercial orchards. Stark Bro's advertised King David as being redder in color, hanging longer on the tree, and storing better than Jonathan. The apples are good for fresh eating, cider, and cooking. The tree is a late bloomer, an annual bearer, and resistant to fire blight, scab, and cedar-apple rust.

Fruit medium, round, often ribbed at the stem end; skin greasy, pale green overlaid with deep red and some darker stripes, often almost solid red; dots numerous, small, whitish; stem almost long in a deep, narrow, occasionally russeted cavity; calyx closed; basin medium size, rather shallow, corrugated; flesh yellow, firm, crisp, juicy, subacid. Ripe August/September or later. Catalog listings: MD, GA, TN, KY, AR (1909–28).

❦ **KING LUSCIOUS:** Although this apple is not quite an "old" apple, I include it here because it is a fine southern apple still grown commercially in several small orchards in western North Carolina. King Luscious was found in 1935 growing as a chance seedling near Hendersonville, North Carolina, and was introduced by the Will Dalton Nursery. Bountiful Ridge Nursery of Maryland patented and sold King Luscious from 1960 to 1977. The tree is naturally rather small, bears heavily annually, and is tolerant to apple scab but very susceptible to fire blight. It blooms late, a week later than Rome Beauty.

Fruit medium to large, roundish to oblate, conical, often oblique; skin rather thick, tough, glossy, mostly covered with red overlaid with stripes of darker red, with a gray bloom; dots numerous, irregular, tan russet; stem short and thick, often pushed to one side in a large, deep, wide, greenish russeted cavity; calyx usually open; basin rather small and shallow, corrugated; flesh yellowish white, fine-grained, crisp, juicy, mild subacid. Ripe September/October and a good keeper.

❦ **KING SOLOMON** (Solomon): King Solomon is a Georgia apple that originated before the Civil War and was sold in 1870 by the Forest Nursery of Fairview, Kentucky. The tree is not an early bearer but is vigorous and productive on alternate years.

Fruit medium or above, oblate or roundish oblate, slightly angular; skin orange yellow with scattered stripes and splashes of light red; dots moderate in number, brown; stem short in a medium-size cavity; calyx open; basin rather large; flesh yellow, slightly coarse, moderately juicy, mild subacid. Ripe August/September.

❦ **KING TOM:** In a telephone conversation in early 1995, Troy Coggins, a county agricultural agent for Randolph County, North Carolina, delighted me by saying that his uncle had two trees of the King Tom apple. It is incredible that this old apple still exists, as it was last listed in a southern nursery catalog over one hundred and thirty years ago.

King Tom may be of North Carolina origin, but two old catalogs credit South Carolina. It was first described in an 1853 issue of *Western Horticultural Review* magazine:

> This is a very beautiful apple as well as a singular looking tree. The apple resembles an orange in form and color, is of a spicy subacid flavor, flesh yellow and rather tough and hardly first rate. Ripens about the 15th of August and keeps for some six or eight weeks. The tree forms a low head with long, thick, blunt limbs which entwine through each other like snakes, and uniformly bend down towards the ground, giving it a very singular appearance, being entirely different from any other tree. The fruit grows upon the ends of the limbs. The tree is a regular bearer and bears pretty fair crops; fruit medium size or somewhat larger with a long, stout stem. Introduced from North Carolina.

Fruit medium, roundish to oblate; skin almost covered with medium to dark red and with some scarf skin and russet blotches; dots rather large, scattered, russet; stem medium length in a wide, deep, bumpy, greenish cavity; calyx open or closed; basin wide and shallow. Ripe August. Catalog listings: VA, SC, GA, MS (1859–78.)

❦ **KINNAIRD'S CHOICE** (Kinnaird, Red Winter Cluster, Kinnaird's Favorite, Kennard, Kinnard, Black Winesap): Kinnaird's Choice fruits well in much of the South. In 1896 a prominent Tennessee orchardist and nurseryman called it "the finest apple grown in Middle Tennessee." It was highly praised in a 1908 USDA bulletin as observed in orchards in both Virginia and north Georgia: "There appears to be no reason why Kinnaird has not been more generally planted (in the South). Its good size, attractive dark red color, and pleasing dessert quality are all factors in its favor, and the tree appears to be productive." The tree blooms rather late, thus escaping some late frosts.

The first mention of Kinnaird's Choice is a discussion and description by Charles Downing in an 1870 issue of *The Gardener's Monthly* magazine. He says the apple originated about 1855 on the farm of Michael Kinnaird of Franklin, Tennessee, and was thought to be a cross of Winesap × Limbertwig. An old letter to the USDA credits its origin to Dick Kennard of Maury County, Tennessee. Yet another letter in USDA files says that the original tree was brought to Maury County in 1843 by R. O. Kinnard from Williamson County. (Presumably this is a Richard Kinnard and the same man as Dick Kennard.)

Fruit medium, roundish to slightly oblate, slightly conical, sometimes oblique; skin thick, tough, almost covered with dark red when exposed to the sun; dots numerous, small to large, light-colored; stem medium length, sometimes by a lip, in a wide, deep, russeted cavity with the russet usually extending out over the top of the apple; calyx closed; basin large, deep, furrowed; flesh yellowish, moderately fine-grained, crisp, tender, juicy, somewhat aromatic, mild subacid. Ripe September/October in central North Carolina and an excellent keeper. Catalog listings: MD, VA, NC, GA, AL, MS, TN, KY, TX, AR (1870–1928). ❖ **Plate 26.**

❦ **LACY:** A Lacy apple was listed without description by two Virginia nurseries in 1858 and 1869. In 1986 I was contacted by Tim Vaughn of Monroe, North Carolina, who told me that his grandparents had a Lacy apple tree. This variety has been grown in Union County, North Carolina, for many years because Tim's grandparents remember their grandparents growing Lacy apples. Lacy has been grown only in Union County as far as I can tell. Tim Vaughn's grandmother rooted me a Lacy tree from her old tree by bending a branch down to the ground, scarifying the bark, and rooting the branch! Tim describes Lacy apples as good for fresh eating, canning, cooking, and drying.

Fruit medium, roundish to slightly oblong, quite conical, often oblique; skin blushed and obscurely striped with light red; dots numerous, small, whitish and russet, often indented; stem usually very long and fleshy, ending in a knob, in a deep, regular, russeted cavity; calyx closed; basin very lobed; flesh crisp, juicy, fine-grained, almost sweet. Ripe late August/September.

❦ **LADY** (Lady Apple, Api, Pomme d'Api, Wax Apple, Lady's Finger, Christmas Apple): This little apple is an obvious exception to the rule that European apples do not do well in warmer areas of the South. In 1872 *The Southern Apple and Peach Culturist* said: "It is well adapted to the upland parts of Maryland and red land counties of Virginia and North Carolina. All farmers who cultivate apples for market should give special attention to this beautiful and profitable variety." Another quote, from Warder (1867): "This beautiful little French apple has been fully naturalized in our country and has received the enthusiastic admiration of the American people." After the Civil War, Lady apples were exported from Virginia to England where barrels of these Virginia apples commanded the phenomenal price of ten to thirty dollars per barrel. A New York shipper wrote to a Virginia grower in 1870: "The Ladies apple is now grown in your section better than any other."

Its diminutive size, beauty, and quality made Lady apples useful both for eating and for decorations, especially at Christmas when it was used in garlands and wreaths. Perfect fruit was demanded by both domestic and overseas markets for which the very highest prices were paid. Because the tree is susceptible to apple scab, as well as sooty blotch and fly speck, heavy spraying was usually necessary to obtain fancy fruit. Picking, too, was performed carefully to avoid any bruises or blemishes. Unlike other commercial apples where large size is desirable, Lady apples destined for distant markets were selected for their small size and red color.

Lady is an ancient French variety, dating back at least four hundred years. It has been grown in the American South for centuries, being listed in the earliest southern nursery catalogs. In addition to its beauty, the fruit is a good keeper, easily keeping until Christmas if stored in a refrigerator or a cool fruit cellar.

The tree is small and not precocious; Elliot (1858) says trees often require ten years before bearing good crops (but when grafted onto dwarfing rootstocks, the trees bear much sooner). The fruit is borne in clusters, usually biennially, and much of the flavor is in the skin of the apple.

Fruit small to very small, usually oblate but sometimes roundish; skin smooth, glossy, bright red on the sunny side and yellowish on the other side or where shaded by a leaf; dots minute, whitish or with russet points; stem short to medium length, slender, in an acute, usually rather deep cavity; calyx closed; basin rather wide, ridged and wrinkled; flesh white, firm, fine-grained, crisp, juicy, aromatic, mild subacid to nearly sweet. Ripe late August/September in most of the South but later at higher elevations and latitudes. Catalog listings: MD, VA, NC, GA, LA, TN, KY (1824–1928).

❦ **LADY SKIN:** Trees of this apple were found by Tom Brown in both Canton and Clyde, North Carolina. Described as medium size, roundish oblate; skin yellow with a pink blush on the sunny side; flesh crisp, juicy, mildly acid. Ripe late September. No catalog listings.

❦ **LADY SWEET** (Ladies Sweeting, Pommeroy, Roa Yon): This sweet apple originated before 1845 near Newburgh, New York. It was sold by a few southern nurseries that described it as a beautiful and delicious apple that keeps well. Beach (1905) says it is somewhat susceptible to apple scab and is usually a biennial bearer. The tree requires thinning to increase fruit size.

Fruit medium to large, roundish conical, often ribbed; skin thin, tough, smooth, striped red in the shade but nearly entirely red in the sun, often with a thin bloom; dots conspicuous, pale, areolar with a russet speck, some submerged; stem short in an acute, deep, furrowed, often russeted cavity; calyx closed; basin small, narrow, abrupt, furrowed; flesh whitish, rather firm, crisp, tender, juicy, aromatic, quite sweet. Ripe August/September. Catalog listings: VA, NC, KY (1869–1910). ❖ **Plate 27.**

❦ **LADYFINGER:** Ragan (1905) lists four apples named Ladyfinger or Lady Finger, and it is the synonym of three additional apples. I believe that most, perhaps all, old southern nursery catalogs that list Ladyfinger are using it as a synonym of Black Gilliflower.

❦ **LANGDON** (Morgan, Ledbetter, White Apple): Originated before 1896 in Greene County, Tennessee, where it was known as Morgan. In 1997 Roberta Anderson of Rogersville, Tennessee, sent me scions from an old tree.

Fruit medium or above, roundish to slightly oblate, usually ribbed; skin dull light green with occasionally a faint bronze blush on the sunny side; dots numerous, russet, usually areolar, among scattered russet streaks and blotches; stem medium length in a deep, russeted, and furrowed cavity; calyx closed; basin small, russeted, and corrugated; flesh fine-grained, moderately juicy, mild subacid. Ripe September but can be used for cooking and drying in July and August. No catalog listings.

❦ **LAWSON'S SEEDLING:** Moses Lawson (d. 1934) grew this apple variety from a seed near Lawsonville in Stokes County, North Carolina, where the late Maurice Marshall found a single tree in 1995.

Fruit medium size or above, roundish; skin covered in dull, dark red; dots few, large, whitish; stem short in a greenish tan, russeted cavity with much russet over the top of the apple; calyx open; basin large, deep, lumpy; flesh whitish, fine-grained, moderately crisp and juicy, sweet. Ripe late September/October. No catalog listings.

❦ **LAWVER** (Delaware Red Winter, Black Spy, Delaware Winter, Lawyer, Delaware Red): The origin of Lawver has been variously assigned to Illinois, Missouri, or Kansas. Downing (1878) says, "found in an old Indian orchard in Kansas." An article in the 1869 *American Horticulture Annual* has this to say: "This apple originated on the farm of Henry Burichter, two miles east of Parkville, Missouri." An 1865 issue of *Prairie Farmer* magazine says: "Mr. George S. Park of Parkville, Missouri, is the originator of this fine apple which was grown from seed planted by a stump near his house, where the tree bore in five years." The one thing we are sure of is that it was named for A. M. Lawver, a southern Illinois pomologist.

About 1887 Lawver was being sold in Delaware by a nurseryman named William P. Corsa, who renamed it Delaware Winter. It was sold by several southern nurseries under this name, but most southern nurseries listed it as Lawver.

Lawver has been described as a lovely red apple that keeps and ships well. Its fresh eating quality is only fair, and it is better for cooking than fresh eating. The 1891 Stark Bro's Nursery catalog says it is late to begin bearing, prone to apple scab, and does best in sunny locations on clay soils. Southern catalogs often recommended it for mountain areas. In 1994, after years of searching, I found this apple being grown in Canada.

Fruit medium to large, roundish or sometimes slightly oblate; skin rough, much covered with scarf skin, usually completely red, which may deepen to purple at the stem end; dots small and large, more numerous near the basin, whitish or russet; stem usually medium to long in an acute, deep, often furrowed and russeted cavity; calyx closed; basin rather wide, almost shallow, furrowed; flesh tinged yellowish or greenish, fine-grained, firm, crisp, juicy, subacid, somewhat aromatic. Ripe September/October and an excellent keeper. Catalog listings: MD, VA, NC, GA, AL, TN, KY, TX, AR (1869–1915). ❖ **Plate 28.**

❧ **LEATHER COAT:** It is possible that this apple is identical to Royal Russet (listed as extinct), but it is not a good fit. More likely it is an old Wilkes County, North Carolina, apple grown only around the McGrady community, where it was found by Tom Brown.

Fruit medium size, roundish oblate; skin covered with a rough, brownish red russet; flesh greenish white, crisp, mildly acid. Ripe September/October. No catalog listings. *See* Royal Russet.

❧ **LEWIS GREEN:** Lewis Green was mentioned briefly at the 1877 meeting of the American Pomological Society, and in 1904 it was said to have originated in Watauga County, North Carolina. It is still grown near Mars Hill in Madison County, North Carolina. Danny Harvey of Lansing, North Carolina, sent me scions.

Fruit almost large, oblate; skin greenish yellow, sometimes with a blush; dots numerous, dark and russet; stem long in a rather narrow and deep cavity; calyx closed; basin wide and even; flesh greenish white, tender, juicy, subacid. Ripe August/September or later. No catalog listings. ❖ **Plate 29.**

❧ **LIMBERTWIG:** This is not a single apple variety but rather a very large family of apples. It is difficult to say what exactly holds this family together—what trait the various kinds of Limbertwigs have in common. One might suppose that a drooping growth habit would be present in all Limbertwigs and, in fact, most kinds of Limbertwigs do have drooping branches as was pointed out in this comment at the 1899 meeting of the Georgia Horticultural Society: "I will say if you were to advertise for Limbertwig apples you would get as many different apples as there are letters in the name; almost any farmer who has a small orchard has Limbertwigs. Any variety with pendant branches will fill the bill." As with most rules there are exceptions, and there are some Limbertwig varieties that do not have drooping branches.

The late, much lamented Henry Morton had his own idea of what holds together the Limbertwig family, and he did more than anyone else to save old Limbertwig varieties. Mr. Morton was a Baptist preacher and a part-time nurseryman living near Gatlinburg, Tennessee. This was important Limbertwig country at one time when there were commercial orchards around Gatlinburg and in the adjacent Smoky Mountains. When the Great Smoky Mountain National Park was established in the 1920s and 1930s, many large and small orchards of Limbertwigs within the park were abandoned. It was in the scattered remnants of these orchards, and in other old mountain orchards, that Mr. Morton and others such as R. J. Howard tracked down the old Limbertwig varieties. Mr. Morton said, "Limbertwigs vary in size, shape, color, quality and tree habit, but they all have one distinguishing characteristic and that is their distinct Limbertwig flavor. No other apple that I have ever tasted has this particular flavor of Limbertwig. Once a person has tasted a Black Limbertwig or a Royal Limbertwig, one can then be able to determine if a variety is a Limbertwig."

If you search for the beginnings of the Limbertwig family, you search in vain. It is lost in the late 1700s when seedling orchards were common. Working backward from the present, one finds that all the different kinds of Limbertwigs have disappeared from southern nursery catalogs by 1860 and only one kind is listed—usually simply called Limbertwig, occasionally with the synonym James River. (The synonym James River was often erroneously applied to Limbertwig. It is, more properly, a synonym of Willow Twig, an entirely different apple.) This Limbertwig apple, presumably the progenitor of all the various kinds of Limbertwigs, can be traced back even further. It is briefly described by Kendrick (1841). A Limbertwig of Virginia origin is described in an 1829 issue of *The New England Farmer* magazine. A Limbertwig is listed in the 1824 catalog of a Washington, D.C., nursery. A letter in the USDA files says that Limbertwig was introduced into Ohio about 1812 by Robert Eness, a pioneer from Virginia. In fact, one of the oldest nursery listings of southern apples, an advertisement in a 1798 Virginia newspaper, says: "Limbertwig; James River Limbertwig, branches drooping or pendant; the fruit is of a greenish color with a blush next the sun; the flesh very juicy and pleasant at maturity. Winter. It keeps a long time." Here the tracks of this great southern apple are lost.

Is this original old Limbertwig variety still with us? I think it is—under the name Red Limbertwig. Many old nursery catalogs and other references listed Red Limbertwig as a synonym of the original Limbertwig, and the descriptions of the original Limbertwig and Red Limbertwig coincide almost exactly. This old Limbertwig was widely grown in the South for its keeping qualities, usually keeping until March or April in root cellars, pits, or caves.

Old pomological literature brings home the fact that Limbertwig (alias Red Limbertwig) was grown not only in the South but also in the states just north of the Ohio River and in Kansas and Missouri. Wherever southerners migrated, they refused to part with this apple. Consider this comment about Limbertwig made by a delegate from Illinois to the 1857 meeting of the American Pomological Society: "One of my neighbors recommends the Limbertwig and wants half of his orchard of it. He says he knows of six trees of Limbertwig that have not missed bearing in eight or nine years. A few years ago he rented the farm and made from those six Limbertwig trees half enough to pay the rent of the entire farm at one dollar a bushel—over one hundred twenty dollars—and the best late spring apple he knows. He kept some Limbertwigs in a granary where they froze and thawed through the winter. They were not much injured and could be used for cooking."

The USDA reported in 1908 that Limbertwig was widely planted in the piedmont and mountains of the South. "In some localities, especially in North Carolina, it is the only variety grown in any considerable extent. It generally does well on clay loam soils of the piedmont region in North and South Carolina and northeast Georgia. It is considered a standard winter variety in these regions."

The following descriptions of Limbertwig varieties are quoted from a past catalog of Henry Morton's nursery:

> *Appalachian Limbertwig*: Red to deep dark red with pips, round, not conical or flat. Spicy, aromatic, juicy, firm yellow flesh of excellent quality. A very heavy cropper. Medium sized, a good keeper that is excellent for eating fresh, cooking, apple butter, and cider. Apple butter of this variety is very aromatic. Can bear good beautiful apples without any spraying. Tree is hardy and long lived, a non-weeping type. Ripens mid-September to October.
>
> *Brushy Mountain Limbertwig*: A dull red with lemon yellow in color. Round and a little bit pointed but not conical. Very juicy with a most unusual aromatic flavor. Yellow flesh, will keep until June. An excellent commercial variety that is still grown

commercially in the Brushy Mountains of Alexander County, North Carolina. Ripens October. A weeping type.

*Cane Creek Limbertwig*: Another large and excellent strain of Red Limbertwig.

*Limbertwig Victoria* (Sweet Limbertwig): An apple of striking beauty with its purple color and white dots. Very juicy and of excellent quality. Very rich flavor, rated tops for fresh eating. Keeps all winter. Weeping type. [*See* Sweet Limbertwig, *below*.]

*Ben Lomand Limbertwig*: A large apple, round but not flat. Good unusual color of red and green. This is a good all purpose variety. Juicy, firm, aromatic. Good for eating fresh. This variety was grown here in the Smoky Mountains but was called another name. Rediscovered by R. J. Howard on the Ben Lomand Mountain in Middle Tennessee.

*Myers' Royal Limbertwig*: A very large apple. Color is a dull red to crimson on yellow. Has excellent quality. Juicy, firm, and very aromatic. Herbert Myers who gave us scions of this variety says it makes the best cider he has ever tasted. Semi-weeping.

*Old Fashioned Limbertwig*: One of the oldest Limbertwig varieties. A good keeper that is good for eating fresh, pies, and cider. Somewhat rough skinned. A greenish yellow with red blush.

*Swiss Limbertwig*: The most unusual colored apple that I have ever seen. Maroon color with white pips. A real beauty. Grown by early Swiss settlers of the Cumberland Mountains. Excellent commercial variety.

In addition, Mr. Morton also sold these Limbertwigs: Royal Red, Rocky River, Sequatchie, Smoky Mountain Red, Sour, Striped, Tate, Virginia Red, White, and perhaps forty others.

Most Limbertwig varieties originated in remote areas of the southern Appalachians and were never listed in nursery catalogs or other references. Several, however, do have a history:

*American Limbertwig*: In 1910, the Sparger Orchard Company of Mount Airy, North Carolina, won first prize (a power sprayer) at the National Horticultural Congress in Council Bluffs, Iowa. Their fruit display consisted of ten apple varieties including American Limbertwig. No description, but still available. Possibly identical to Red Limbertwig.

*Black Limbertwig*: This apple was exhibited at the 1914 meeting of the Georgia Horticultural Society where the tree was described as being very resistant to fungus diseases. The apples were prized for cider and apple butter.

Fruit medium, roundish; skin mostly covered with bright red; dots scattered, whitish or russet; stem short to medium length in a wide, deep, russeted cavity; calyx closed; basin medium size, corrugated; flesh yellowish, juicy, crisp, subacid. Ripe September/October. No catalog listings.

*Red Limbertwig*: (James River, Limbertwig, Green Limbertwig, Mountain Limbertwig, Brushy Mountain Limbertwig, Common Limbertwig, American Limbertwig, Red Jewel): This all-purpose winter apple is almost certainly the oldest Limbertwig, and the fruit is an excellent winter keeper. Not of high flavor, but improves in storage.

Fruit medium, roundish, slightly conical; skin rather rough, greenish yellow with a dull red blush on the sunny side, stripes indistinct if present at all; dots medium size, numerous, light brown; stem medium length to long in a broad, deep, acute cavity that is thinly russeted with green; calyx closed; basin small, shallow, uneven; flesh whitish, firm, juicy, slightly acid or briskly subacid. Ripe October and a good keeper. Catalog listings as Red Limbertwig: VA, NC, GA, AL, LA, TN, KY, AR (1875–1928).

*Royal Limbertwig*: (Imperial Limbertwig?, Carolina Baldwin?, Goosepen?): Royal Limbertwig was widely sold by southern nurseries. The fruit does not keep as well as Red Limbertwig, but Royal Limbertwig seems to be better adapted to warmer areas of the South. As grown at the University of Illinois Agricultural Experiment Station in 1896, Royal Limbertwig was found to be of high quality and was recommended for orchards in Illinois. The apples make delicious and aromatic apple butter. *See also* Carolina Baldwin.

Fruit above medium to large, roundish, somewhat conical, often oblique; skin greenish yellow partly to mostly covered with light or dull red, sometimes with some indistinct red stripes; dots large, russet or white; stem short to medium in an acute, deep cavity with grayish or greenish russet; calyx open or closed; basin broad, often shallow, irregular; flesh yellowish, rather fine-grained, juicy, tender, mild subacid. Ripe early October. Catalog listings: MD, VA, NC, GA, AL, TN, KY (1860–1924). ❖ **Plate 30.**

*Improved Limbertwig*: Synonym of Coffelt.

*Levering Limbertwig*: A rare tetraploid apple, mainly a curiosity but a decent eating apple. Originated in Ararat, Virginia, by S. R. Levering. No description. No catalog listings.

*Morrison Limbertwig*: Joseph L. Morrison originated this apple about 1870 near Chattanooga, Tennessee. The fruit is said to resemble Red Limbertwig but the tree is more hardy. No catalog listings. Extinct.

*Rose Limbertwig*: At the 1881 meeting of the American Pomological Society, Rose Limbertwig was described as a seedling of the "common Red Limbertwig." The tree is a heavy bearer and the fruit is a good keeper. No description. No catalog listings. Extinct.

*Summer Limbertwig*: (Weeping Limbertwig): Summer Limbertwig originated near Greensboro, North Carolina, and was listed by a North Carolina nursery from 1855 to 1860. Fruit medium, oblate to roundish; skin pale yellow overlaid with mixed pink and darker red stripes; flesh white, tender, fine-grained, juicy, aromatic, subacid. Ripe August/September.

*Sweet Limbertwig*: (Harpole): This apple originated before 1860 in either Grundy or Warren County, Tennessee, and was brought to attention by M. M. Harpole of Coffey County, Tennessee. It was sold by Tennessee, Alabama, and Georgia nurseries from 1890 to 1917, and probably is the same apple as Limbertwig Victoria. "The finest winter sweet apple for Tennessee."

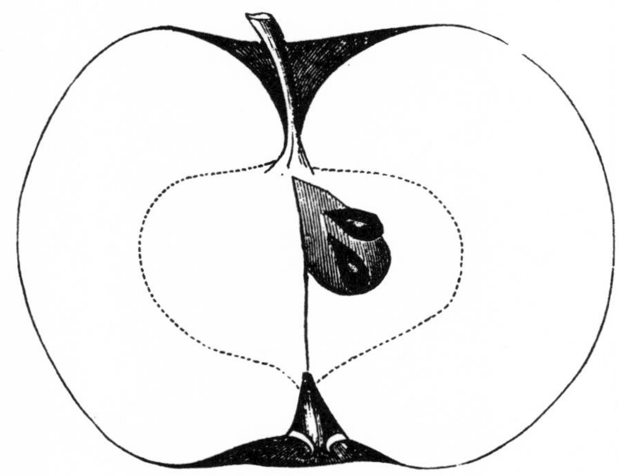

SUMMER LIMBERTWIG

Fruit medium to large, oblate conical; skin thick, tough, rough, yellow, mostly covered with crimson with dark red stripes, often with a gray bloom; dots conspicuous, yellow, some indented; stem medium length and slender in a large, wide, deep, heavily russeted cavity; calyx open; basin medium size, gradually sloped, russet netted; flesh greenish yellow, fine-grained, tender, juicy, sweet. Ripe September/October. Limbertwig Victoria is available.

*Red Royal Limbertwig*: This is one of my favorite eating apples. Origin unknown but sold by Henry Morton. Fruit medium or above, roundish conical, often lopsided; skin mostly covered with dull red; dots small, numerous, white; stem long in a shallow, lumpy cavity; basin shallow, greenish; flesh pale yellow, crisp, moderately juicy, rather coarse, almost sweet. Ripe September/October.

*Rocky River Limbertwig*: Carey Wilson of Anderson, South Carolina, sent me scions from a tree he got from Henry Morton in 1986. He says the tree is not very productive but the apples are tasty. No description.

In addition to the Limbertwig varieties discussed above, these Limbertwig varieties also have been found: Alberta, Fall, Improved, Kentucky, Ramsey, Ruby, Virginia, White, and Yellow.

❧ **LITTLE BENNY:** In 1995 Bertie Hall of Grantsboro, North Carolina, wrote me: "Little Benny is a local apple used to be found in a 50 to 75 mile radius, which is about as far distant as anyone ever went back then. The Little Benny is mostly dark red on green and a medium to small apple. It ripens early July and August. It is tart at first but then gets good to eat and is a splendid cooking apple; cooks very smooth with no lumps. Insects and worms don't bother it much."

Grantsboro is in extreme eastern North Carolina, so obviously Little Benny is well adapted to the coastal plains of the South. The tree is compact and heavily loaded with apples.

Fruit small, oblate, conical, often oblique; skin smooth, mostly covered with plum red; dots few, large, whitish; stem short to medium length in a deep, pale russeted cavity; calyx usually open; flesh whitish, moderately juicy and crisp, subacid. Ripe August. No catalog listing.

❦ **LIVELAND RASPBERRY** (Livland Raspberry, Lowland Raspberry, Red Cheek): A Russian apple brought to the United States about 1883. It gets its name from the Russian province of Lievland (Livonia, now Lithuania), which borders the Baltic Sea. The flesh is snow white and the most tender I have ever eaten—almost like eating foam. The skin is very thin and bruises easily, and the seeds are unusually small. The tree is resistant to fire blight.

Fruit medium to large, roundish conical, flattened on both ends; skin thin, smooth, polished, clear pale yellow overlaid with stripes of bright red that are heavier on the sunny side; dots small and greenish; stem rather stout and medium length in a deep, abrupt, greenish brown russeted cavity; calyx closed; basin rather shallow and wide; flesh white tinged red, fine-grained, very tender, juicy, sprightly subacid. Ripe July. Catalog listings: MD, VA, NC, TN, KY, TX, AR (1910–28).

❦ **LONGFIELD** (English Pippin): Like Liveland Raspberry, Longfield is a Russian apple imported into this country about 1883. Almost alone among the hundreds of Russian apple varieties brought to this country, most of which ripen in early summer, Longfield is a late summer or autumn apple. It was sold by several southern nurseries, but there is no information concerning its performance in the South.

Fruit medium, roundish conical, somewhat lobed, sides often unequal; skin smooth, polished, clear waxen yellow sometimes with a red blush or faint stripes on the sunny side; dots inconspicuous, whitish; stem short in a deep, narrow, russeted cavity; basin abrupt, narrow, wrinkled; flesh very white, very tender, juicy, brisk subacid. Ripe August/September. Catalog listings: MD, VA, AL, AR (1898–1920).

❦ **LONG STEM** (Late Harvest?): Ragan (1905) lists five apples with this name and three others with the synonym of Longstem. One of these may be of Virginia or Kentucky origin and is briefly described by Warder (1867) as medium size, roundish oblate; skin greenish with red stripes; flesh greenish white, mild subacid. Ripe winter.

The circa-1900 catalog of Faught Branch Nurseries of Rockingham County, Virginia, lists a Long Stem: "Above medium size; greenish yellow; oblong; flesh tender and juicy with an extraordinary rich and buttery flavor something like a pear. We regard this as the best flavored apple that we are acquainted with. Ripe July." This is probably the same apple as Late Harvest, which has the synonym of Long Stem.

About 1990 I received a Long Stem from Elwood Fisher of Harrisonburg, Virginia, which is probably the same Long Stem as the one in the Faught Branch Nurseries catalog.

Fruit medium, roundish, somewhat lobed; skin clear yellow; dots numerous, medium size, whitish; stem medium to long in a russeted cavity. Ripe July.

❦ **LONNIE'S SUMMER GIANT:** Herbert Childress of Dunnville, Kentucky, sent me scions in 1996 with a note saying "I don't know the real name as I got the wood from an old tree on a homestead that once belonged to Lonnie Luttrell. A huge summer apple with pale pink stripes. Flavor so-so." This apple closely resembles Summer Champion and is probably identical to it.

Fruit large, roundish to somewhat oblong, conical; skin pale green mostly covered with light red and obscure darker stripes; dots numerous, gray and greenish; stem medium to long in a deep, lightly russeted cavity; calyx closed; basin narrow, abrupt, deep, corrugated; flesh rather soft, moderately juicy, mild subacid. Ripe July/August. No catalog listings.

❦ **LOWELL** (Greasy Pippin, Lowell Pippin, Orange, Queen Anne, Rissley, Tallow Pippin, Golden Pippin, Michigan Golden): A very old American apple grown mostly in the North but sold by a few southern nurseries. The apples ripen on the tree over a period of a month or longer and are useful for both cooking and fresh eating. The fruit tends to drop prematurely.

Fruit large, variable in shape but usually roundish oblong, somewhat conical; skin thin, smooth, waxy, green becoming a rich yellow; dots numerous, small, inconspicuous, brown or russet; stem medium to long in an acute, often lightly russeted cavity; basin abrupt, medium in width, often furrowed; flesh tinged yellow, rather firm, crisp, tender, very juicy, sprightly subacid. Ripe August/October. Catalog listings: MD, VA, GA, KY (1858–1902).

❦ **LOWRY** (Dixie, Mosby's Best, Red Winter): John Lowry of Afton, Virginia, originated this apple on his farm about 1850 and sent several of his apples to the USDA in 1897. Lowry was sold from 1913 to 1928 by Virginia nurseries and was first described in a 1913 catalog: "A beautiful dark red apple of high quality, slightly sweet, and tinged with acid; keeps well and bears early. It is one of the very promising new apples and well worthy of trial."

A Lowry apple was advertised in an 1804 Virginia newspaper nursery list, but I believe that this apple was the Lowre (or Lowre Queen), a completely different apple. I received scions from Ken McDonald, Martinsburg, West Virginia.

Fruit medium, roundish, slightly conical, flattened on the ends; skin dark mahogany red with numerous and conspicuous whitish specks or dots; stem rather long and stout in a medium size, russeted cavity; calyx open; basin medium size, corrugated; flesh yellowish, crisp, juicy, mild subacid. Ripe September/October and a rather good keeper in refrigeration.

❦ **LUGAR RED:** A local apple grown for many years in the Sinking Creek area of Craig County, Virginia, and one of the old apple varieties collected and preserved by the late Holland Caldwell in his orchard in Sinking Creek. My friend Jerry Carper took me around Craig County several times searching for old apples and introduced me to Mr. Caldwell.

Fruit medium or above, roundish or sometimes slightly oblong, conical; skin mostly covered with dark red with indistinct darker red stripes; dots numerous, minute, white or tan; stem medium to long in a russeted cavity, often with a protuberance; calyx closed; basin almost shallow, corrugated; flesh yellowish, juicy, fine-grained, crisp, subacid. Ripe September. No catalog listings.

❦ **MAGNUM BONUM** (Bonum, Maggie Bowman, Bona, Magna Bonum, Red Bonum): Magnum Bonum would be on everyone's list of the ten greatest southern apples. It is a lovely apple of fine flavor, and the tree is hardy and productive. Southern nurseries long ago recognized its value, calling it "the standard fall apple" and "the king of all fall apples." By ripening in September, it fills the niche for a high-quality apple before the winter apples. Magnum Bonum was grown in Virginia, North Carolina, and Georgia, from the mountains to the sea. It seems to have been particularly popular as a commercial apple in the 1920s in Rappahannock County, Virginia, where it was marketed at high prices from the first of September to the middle of October. Magnum Bonum responds well to high calcium in the soil, or even a calcium spray, which improves the quality of the fruit. It should be emphasized that Magnum Bonum is an early fall apple, not a winter apple, and loses its quality rapidly if left on the tree too long. It can often be picked in August in warmer areas of the South. The tree is susceptible to cedar-apple rust.

An 1856 North Carolina nursery catalog gives the most information about the origin of Magnum Bonum: "Raised by Mr. John Kinny from a seed of the Hall apple, in Davidson County, North Carolina, in 1828. Named by Dr. Wm. R. Holt of Davidson College." (Mr. Kinny is referred to in another catalog as Squire Kinney.) The original name of Magnum Bonum was officially shortened to Bonum by the American Pomological Society in its zeal for single names for apples. Most southern nurseries continued to list it as Magnum Bonum, however, and this is the name universally used by southerners.

Fruit medium or below, roundish or roundish oblate; skin mostly covered with light red with indistinct darker red stripes; dots large, numerous, white or russet, many with a darker center; stem medium to long and slender in a wide, abrupt, deep, greenish russeted cavity; calyx closed; basin wide, abrupt, corrugated; flesh white, sometimes stained red near the skin, tender, juicy, fine-grained, aromatic, mild subacid. Ripe September in most of the South. Catalog listings: MD, VA, NC, SC, GA, MS, KY, AR (1853–1928). ❖ **Plate 31.**

❦ **MAIDEN'S BLUSH** (Maiden Blush, Vestal, Lady Blush, Red Cheek, Summer Maiden's Blush, Uchella): Maiden's Blush has been popular in the South from the early years of the nineteenth century to the present time. Old trees are often encountered, especially in mountain areas. Maiden's Blush apples were grown in some areas of the South for the early-apple market because of the lovely appearance of the fruit and the heavy crops produced by the trees. The tree is resistant to cedar-apple rust but susceptible to fire blight and scab and often a biennial bearer.

According to Coxe (1817), Maiden's Blush originated in Burlington, New Jersey, and was named by Samuel Allison, who first brought it to public notice.

Because of its rather sharp flavor, most early pomologists described Maiden's Blush as a cooking apple. When stewed, it rapidly cooks into a lump-free pulp of light color. It was extolled for drying as the flesh remains quite white when dried, "much admired by dealers." If the fruit is fully ripe, the acid in Maiden's Blush is less prominent and many people like it for fresh eating.

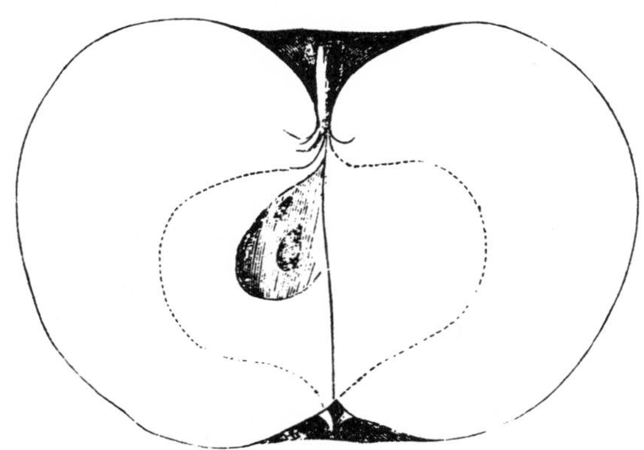

MAIDEN'S BLUSH

Fruit medium, roundish to slightly oblate; skin thin, tough, smooth, pale greenish with a light red or crimson blush, and faint darker red stripes; dots scattered, whitish and russet; stem medium in a deep, often russeted cavity; calyx closed; basin rather shallow, wide, smooth or slightly furrowed; flesh white, fine-grained, moderately juicy, tender, sprightly subacid. Ripe July/August in most of the South. Catalog listings: MD, VA, NC, GA, AL, LA, TN, KY, TX, AR (1824–1928).

❦ **MANN** (Diltz): In the late 1800s there was a concerted search for cold-hardy apple varieties that would survive in Iowa, Minnesota, and Michigan. Several varieties, especially some of the Russian imports, seemed adapted to the severe climate and were labeled "Ironclad" varieties. Mann was also one of the Ironclads but was sold by southern nurseries because the apple is an excellent keeper borne on a productive tree. The fruit has been described as "valuable for cooking and a fair table fruit."

Mann originated about 1850 as a chance seedling in the orchard of a Mr. Mann in Granby, New York. The first year the tree had fruit, the apples were all stolen by a hired helper named Diltz. With tongue in cheek, Mr. Mann named the new apple Diltz, but it was later renamed by the Western Horticultural Society.

Fruit medium to large, roundish oblate; skin deep yellow when ripe, often shaded brownish red in the sun, sometimes slightly russeted; dots numerous, light, and gray; stem short in a medium to large cavity, sometimes slightly russeted; calyx usually closed; basin rather large and slightly corrugated; flesh yellowish, juicy, mild subacid. Ripe late and a good keeper. Catalog listings: MD, VA, NC, AL, TN (1884–1928).

❦ **MARY MCKINNEY:** Grown by the late Swansie Shepherd near Lansing, North Carolina. The original tree was found in southern Virginia near the grave of a woman named Mary McKinney. The fruit is red striped and good for cooking or fresh eating. No catalog listings.

❦ **MARY REID:** A local apple from Caswell County, North Carolina. My good friend and outstanding nurseryman David Vernon, who gave me grafting scions in 1993, says it was in an orchard set out by his great-grandfather, George D. Rice (1870–1919). Mr. Vernon has two trees that are third- or fourth-generation root sprouts from the original tree. "It is our favorite type of apple."

Fruit medium or above, oblate, oblique, and often irregular in shape; skin partly to mostly covered with a light red blush; dots large, irregular, russet, often aerole, with a few larger russet blotches; stem short to medium in a wide, deep, russeted cavity; calyx usually closed; basin wide, deep, lobed, greenish; flesh whitish, crisp, juicy, briskly subacid. Ripe August. No catalog listings.

❦ **MATTAMUSKEET** (Matamuskeet, Matimuskite, Malamuskeet, Skeet): The coastal plains area of the South is inhospitable to apple trees. Summers are very hot and winters are relatively warm. The long, hot summers stress the trees and ripen apples too early for them to keep well in winter storage. Thus, to rural southerners of the coastal plains who needed a good-keeping apple, Mattamuskeet must have seemed like a gift from a benevolent deity. Of all the old apples, this variety was considered the best winter apple for the Low Country.

Mattamuskeet probably originated as a seedling near Lake Mattamuskeet in Hyde County in extreme eastern North Carolina, a county that averages ten feet above sea level. An old legend says the apple seed was taken from the gizzard of a wild goose by Mattamuskeet Indians.

The keeping qualities of Mattamuskeet are legendary. Residents of the coastal plains often stored them outdoors with little protection where they kept until May or June. An article in an 1888 North Carolina newspaper says that a woman kept a Mattamuskeet apple "perfectly sound, though not juicy, for three years." Like many other good keepers, Mattamuskeet improves in texture and flavor after several months of storage, and one old source says, "Late in the spring it has a delightful flavor."

The tree is vigorous and productive but susceptible to cedar-apple rust. One old catalog says, "The tree succeeds well if planted in rich or highly improved loamy soil, and in such soil the fruit is often of larger size and more luscious in flavor than in ordinary soil." The fruit hangs well on the tree and often can be picked in November.

I found a tree of Mattamuskeet in 1986 that belonged to Mr. and Mrs. Harold Jefferson of Beaufort County, North Carolina. They got their tree many years ago as a root sprout from a tree belonging to a friend. Since then I have encountered several Mattamuskeet trees in eastern North Carolina, where the apple is often called Skeet. Roger and Betty Swindell of Hyde County have spent years trying to save and propagate the remaining old Mattamuskeet trees in their county. They make an outstanding apple butter from the apples.

Fruit medium or below, roundish to oblate, slightly conical, somewhat irregular; skin tough, mostly covered with a dull purplish or rusty red; dots large, white or russet; stem medium to long in a deep, greenish cavity; calyx open; basin rather wide, shallow, corrugated; flesh pale yellow, firm when picked, moderately juicy, slightly acid when picked but improving in storage. Ripe September/October or later. Catalog listings: MD, VA, NC, GA, AL, MS, KY (1853–1910). ❖ **Plate 32.**

❦ **MAY** (May Apple, Yellow May, May Yellow, Early May, White Juneating, White May, Juneating, Yellow June, Mae?, Early Jennetting, Gennetting, May Pippin, Owen's Golden Beauty, Virginia May?, Joaneting): Downing (1857), Warder (1867), Ragan (1905), and Beach (1905) all describe this apple under the name White Juneating, but it is listed in eighty-one southern nursery catalogs as May or May Apple and in only three catalogs as White Juneating. To southerners this was *the* May apple. Most old catalogs say this apple is "valued mainly for its early ripening" and "affords apples for cooking far in advance of all others." For many years it was the earliest-ripening apple, but the introduction of Yellow Transparent about 1880 robbed the May apple of this distinction. Because the May apple was the first to ripen, southern children often ate too many, with inevitable stomachaches.

Most pomologists consider this to be an ancient European apple probably dating back to the early Middle Ages. Beach (1905) quotes an interesting study by the English pomologist Hogg (1884) of the origin of the name Juneating. Hogg believed that the apple was named in the Middle Ages for Saint John (called Joannis or Joannet in Latin and Jean in French) because it ripened in Europe on Saint John's Day, June 24. Thus, the original name was Joanneting, which became distorted over the years to Juneating.

Fruit small, nearly round or sometimes somewhat oblate; skin pale green turning to light yellow when fully ripe, sometimes with a brownish red cheek; stem short (Downing says rather long) in a shallow, slightly russeted cavity; calyx closed; basin very shallow; flesh white, tender, juicy, mildly acid, becoming dry and mealy quickly. Ripe end of May through June. Catalog listings: MD, VA, NC, SC, GA, AL, MS, LA, TN, KY, TX (1853–1928).

❦ **McINTOSH** (McIntosh Red): For the past sixty years or so, this has been the most important commercial apple grown in New England, southern Canada, and parts of New York. McIntosh makes up about 6 percent of America's commercial apple production. It thrives in the northern climate where the apples can be kept for six months in ordinary cold storage. Southern grown, except at high elevations, it is a disappointment and was sold by few southern nurseries. In warmer climates McIntosh is softer, poorer in color, and often drops from the tree before maturity. The tree is very susceptible to scab.

In 1796 nineteen-year-old John McIntosh had a disagreement with his parents over a love affair and emigrated from New York state to Dundas County, Ontario, Canada. He exchanged his Canadian farm in 1811 for a nearby farm owned by his brother-in-law. Finding some seedling apple trees on overgrown land, Mr. McIntosh moved them near his house. By 1820 one of these was bearing excellent apples, and Mr. McIntosh sold seedlings of this tree to other settlers. Someone taught Mr. McIntosh how to graft about 1835, and he then began selling grafted trees of this favorite apple, locally known as McIntosh Red. John McIntosh's son, Allan, continued to sell apple trees after his father's death, but it was not until 1900 or so that McIntosh became popular in the northern United States. The original tree near the McIntosh house was badly damaged when the house burned in 1894 and it finally broke off in 1910.

McIntosh has been used frequently in apple breeding, and some of its offspring may be better adapted to southern growing conditions. Cortland, Empire, and Jerseymac have been recommended for growing in Zone 7, which covers much of the southern piedmont. *See also* Baldwin.

Fruit above medium, uniform in shape, roundish to somewhat oblate; skin thin, smooth, whitish yellow or greenish, deeply blushed with red with some darker stripes, the red is obliterated where a leaf has shaded the skin; stem short and stout in a large, acute, wide, broadly furrowed cavity, often partly russeted; basin rather small, narrow, abrupt; flesh white, sometimes veined with red, firm, crisp, very juicy, aromatic, sprightly subacid. Ripe September. Catalog listings: MD, VA, TN, AR (1887–1928).

❦ **McLEAN:** Grown and prized for many years by the Templeton family of Iredell County, North Carolina. It is different from the Canadian apple of the same name. Scions obtained from Mrs. Linwood Sparrow.

Fruit medium or above, roundish to oblate, oblique, and often irregular; skin partly to mostly covered with a light red blush and some scarf skin; dots large, irregular, russet with a few larger russet blotches; stem short to medium in a wide, deep, russeted cavity; calyx usually closed; basin wide, deep, greenish; flesh whitish, crisp, juicy, briskly subacid. Ripe August/September or even later. No catalog listing.

❦ **MEANS SEEDLING:** Herbert Childress of Dunnville, Kentucky, began grafting and saving good apple varieties in his area over fifty years ago. Of Means Seedling he wrote me: "James Means had an apple tree in his barnyard which impressed me with its quality even though it was untended and unsprayed. I grafted a few trees from it and a storm destroyed the original tree the same year. A flavorful, excellent keeper."

Fruit medium, roundish, very conical, often oblique; skin almost covered with red and a few broken stripes; dots small, numerous, white; stem medium length in an abrupt, deep, greenish cavity; calyx closed; basin small, almost shallow; flesh yellowish, crisp, juicy, subacid. Ripe September/October. No catalog listings.

❦ **MELUNGEON GOLD:** This apple carries the name of the Melungeons, a mysterious group of people once concentrated along the Virginia-Tennessee line, but now mostly in and around Hancock County, Tennessee. Some believe the Melungeons lived in this area before the first white settlers moved in, and may be of mixed blood including remnants of Native Americans of the area. Other more colorful theories of the origin of the Melungeons include Spanish explorers, shipwrecked Portuguese sailors, even survivors of the "Lost Colony" of Roanoke Island, North Carolina.

Melungeon Gold was found by Tom Brown in 2006 in northeast Tennessee. No description. No catalog listings.

❦ **MILAM** (Harrigan, Blair, Thomas, Milum, Red Milam?, Red Winter Pearmain, Haragan)**/RUSTICOAT MILAM** (Russet Milam): Called "a little southern favorite" by Warder (1867) and once widely grown in West Virginia, Virginia, and Kentucky. The tree readily sends up root sprouts, which could be transplanted by settlers who knew nothing of grafting. W. H. Ragan, in a personal recollection written in 1902, says Milam was introduced into Illinois before 1850 by the pioneer nurseryman Joseph Curtis, who called it Red Winter Pearmain. The first full description in print of Milam is in an 1846 issue of *The Magazine of Horticulture* that says, in part: "Probably a native of Virginia or Kentucky where it is extensively cultivated and prized." An advertisement of nursery stock in a 1798 Virginia newspaper includes "Mylum's Pearmain," which certainly is Milam.

Thomas Milam or Milum (d. 1785) lived in Madison County, Virginia, at the foot of the Blue Ridge Mountains, where nearby Milam's Gap is named for him. His 203 acres were a land grant from Lord Fairfax in 1749. A seedling tree grew up in his yard and people came from far and near to graft from "Milam's" tree. (Another local history credits the Milam apple to Joseph Milam of Madison County.) The Milam even achieved some fame in classic American literature. This quotation is taken from *The Adventures of Tom Sawyer* by Mark Twain: "Here's a big Milum apple I've been saving for you, Tom, if you was ever found again—now go 'long to school."

A letter to me from apple hunter Greg Lam of Elkton, Virginia, says, "Around here Milams were grown in large quantities years back. Practically every homestead had at least one Milam tree, and when you mention apples to old timers, the name Milam is sure to come up."

Greg Lam sent me photos of two surviving Milam trees planted by Greg's great-great-grandfather Mathew Lamb (1825–1903), who fought for the South at Gettysburg. Originally there were seventy Milam trees in the orchard, and Mathew Lamb's grandson, Seldon Lam, "would press the Milams into cider and then run pure brandy from it. He was a notorious moonshiner."

John Creech, who owned the Turkey Hollow Nursery in Kentucky, had this to say about Milam: "At its best around Christmas; my grandmother kept Milams in her cellar until April every year. Heavy annual bearer that should be thinned for good fruit size. Seems to be more tolerant to spring frosts than most."

Fruit small to medium, roundish or slightly oblate, conical; skin smooth, dull greenish yellow, mostly covered with light red, overlaid with indistinct stripes, well-colored apples are almost crimson in the sun; dots small to large, numerous, prominent, gray, often areolar with a russet point; stem medium to long in an acute, deep, brown or green russeted cavity; calyx usually closed; basin rather small, shallow, furrowed; flesh greenish white, tender, crisp, juicy, slightly coarse, subacid. Ripe September/October and keeps well. Catalog listings: MD, VA, TN, KY (1858–1925). ❖ **Plate 33.**

Warder (1867) briefly describes an apple called Rusticoat Milam that resembles Milam except for considerable russeting of the skin. Downing (1878) lists Rusticoat Milam as a synonym of Milam. An apple found in Virginia in 1997 by Greg Lam is the Rusticoat Milam and different from Milam. No catalog listings. *See also* White Milam.

**MILES STADLER:** A family or local apple found by David Vernon and grown in Stokes County, North Carolina, for over a hundred years.

Fruit medium, roundish conical; skin red; dots medium size, numerous, whitish; stem almost long in a shallow, russeted cavity; calyx closed; basin greenish, corrugated; flesh firm, sweet. Ripe September. No catalog listings.

**MISSISSIPPI PIPPIN:** David Beverage of Buckeye, West Virginia, says his great-great-great grandfather bought the original tree before the Civil War from a tree peddler. His single surviving tree, a graft from the original and over a hundred years old, was found by Dr. L. R. Littleton.

Fruit medium or above, round; skin pale green, often with a faint reddish blush on the sunny side; stem medium length in a brownish, russeted cavity. Ripe September. No catalog listings.

**MISSOURI PIPPIN** (Missouri Keeper, Missouri Orange, Missouri, Stone's Eureka): In 1839 Brinkley Hornsby was one of the first settlers in western Missouri, in what is now Johnson County. Like many other pioneers, he carried with him and planted seeds of various fruits. His first apple orchard consisted entirely of seedling trees. Some of these trees bore fruit that seemed to be useful, so Mr. Hornsby started a nursery. Knowing the potential value of seedling apple trees, he was careful to carry into fruiting those seedling rootstocks on which the grafts had failed. One of these rootstocks resulted in the Missouri Pippin, which first fruited in 1854. Mr. Hornsby first called it his "dollars and cents apple" but later named it Missouri Pippin. It was being propagated in St. Louis by 1869 where it was called Missouri Keeper, and it was under this name that it first was described by Warder (1867).

The tree is a very early bearer, often having apples the second or third year. Because of this precocity, Missouri Pippin was recommended as a "filler" tree in new apple orchards before being cut out to allow the primary trees room to grow. The apple is handsome and a good keeper and was grown commercially in many places, including the South. Several references indicate Missouri Pippin is adapted to the piedmont region of the South and up to 3,000 feet in the mountains. The tree is quite susceptible to fire blight.

Gene Wild, a friend from Indianapolis, is a discriminating grower of old and new apple varieties. This is what he wrote in *Pomona* magazine a few years ago: "Missouri Pippin is a good apple to eat. It is firm, crisp, juicy with a mild flavor—a good, common, all-around apple flavor. The best apples are supposed to be tender but a number of people seem to enjoy the firm, crisp apple you have to work at to eat, and which cracks when you succeed in getting into a good bite."

Fruit medium or above, roundish, flattened on the ends, somewhat conical; skin thick, tough, smooth, mostly shaded, and striped with light and dark red, often quite dark red in the sun, sometimes with a thin grayish bloom; dots conspicuous, large and small, russet and gray; stem short to medium in a large, deep, thinly russeted cavity; calyx closed or nearly so; basin abrupt, deep, somewhat corrugated; flesh whitish tinged with yellow, slightly coarse, breaking, subacid. Ripe October/November. Catalog listings: MD, VA, NC, AL, LA, TN, KY, TX, AR (1870–1926).

**MITCHELL:** I received a fascinating letter in 1993 from James Hall of Logan, West Virginia. He has established an orchard of antique apple varieties and writes:

> It was a local apple that kindled my interest in older apples. My family and friends call it the Mitchell apple.
>
> I grew up in Mitchell Heights in Logan County, which is on the site of the Henry Mitchell farm. Henry was a Confederate soldier wounded at Seven Pines and again at Gettysburg. You may recall the famous Hatfield-McCoy feud. The Hatfield clan

was in Logan County, and its feared patriarch was "Devil Anse" Hatfield. Henry Mitchell married Bridget Hatfield, the sister of Devil Anse, and sometime between 1880 and 1890 Henry and his wife Biddy built a house on the Guyandotte River. It was here he established his orchard. The last living tree of this orchard was in our front yard, and, as it began to die in 1970, my dad succeeded with two grafts to insure its future. This Mitchell apple may have been a seedling . . . but may also be a named variety from the past.

The tree bears consistent heavy crops of medium to large apples. The largest I measured three years ago was 14 inches in circumference. . . . The apples are red on the sunny side with some faint striping. The shaded side is greenish. Here by the 15th of October it looks to be ripe; *it isn't*! Only at the end of October and 12 days into November is it acquiring a good taste. At first it has a moderate, not sweet and not tart, flavor and a medium amount of juice and is good for pies, fried apples, or out-of-hand eating. But November 7 through 12, when I allow individual large specimens to be placed on a board and ripened in a cool, shaded, moist environment (in a tiny hollow), they take on a sweet, juicy quality under that tough skin that I believe to be outstanding. Not just sweet only as in some sweet apples, but a sweetness with a true apple flavor. When you are really hungry, you will eat these apples with such gusto, you must be careful not to bite your own fingers as you indulge.

This apple definitely doesn't ripen properly in modern refrigeration systems. They seem to shrivel and never get that special flavor. We always picked up Mitchell apples from the ground under the tree for our Thanksgiving apple pie. I hope you will help me pass on the Mitchell apple to the future.

Fruit above medium to large, roundish, slightly conical; skin tough, mostly covered with orangish red with some broken red stripes; dots numerous, rather large, mostly russet, but smaller and white near the calyx end; stem short or medium length in a deep, russeted cavity; calyx open or almost closed; flesh yellowish, fine-grained, moderately crisp, juicy, mild subacid to almost sweet. Ripe October/ November. No catalog listings.

**MITCHELL SWEET:** This is a Mitchell family apple probably named for John Mitchell, who lived in the late 1800s in the Cheatham Ford community of Alexander County, North Carolina. A tree belonging to Wayne Wooten of Hiddenite was found by Tom Brown and identified by Harold Mitchell, great grandson of John Mitchell.

Fruit medium or below, roundish; skin tough, rough, pale yellow with a faint pinkish blush on the sunny side with blotches of light tan russet; dots large, irregular, tan russet; stem medium to long, ending in a knob, in a deep, russeted cavity; calyx closed or slightly open; flesh pale yellow, chewy, slightly juicy, sweet. Ripe late August/ September. No catalog listings.

**MONGOLIAN:** Sold in the early 1900s by the Pores Knob Nursery of Wilkes County, North Carolina. A single limb grafted onto a large tree was found by Tom Brown in 2002 in Troutdale, Virginia, belonging to Leslie Call.

Fruit above medium to large, oblate, and quite irregular in shape; skin bright red, waxy; flesh subacid. Ripe September.

**MORGAN'S CHRISTMAS** (Morgan, Morgan Seedling): Originated on the farm of J. W. Morgan of Otter Creek, Rutherford County, North Carolina, before 1880. Sold by two Virginia nurseries in 1894 and 1928 and described here. A few years ago Tom Brown found an old tree in Wilkes County, North Carolina, identified as "Morgan's Christmas" that closely fits the best description we have.

Fruit above medium to large, roundish, often oblique, flattened on the ends; skin dark red to almost black at the stem end, fading to yellow at the blossom end, often with a bloom; dots numerous, large, gray; stem long in a large, deep, russeted cavity; calyx open; basin wide, shallow; flesh yellowish, fine-grained, moderately crisp and juicy, sweet. Ripe September. ❖ **Plate 34.**

**MOSEY:** An old local apple grown by Herbert Childress in Dunnville, Kentucky. He describes it as follows: "A conical, green apple with pale pink or red stripes. It used to be the ultimate apple to smoke (with sulfur fumes). Not too tart and just average for eating out of hand." No catalog listings.

**MOTHER** (Gardener's Apple, Queen Anne, American Mother, Bolton Mother): A Massachusetts apple well adapted to the South and popular around 1900. It was recommended for growing in the mountains, piedmont, and coastal plains by a 1908 North Carolina agricultural bulletin. In 1909, the USDA noted: "Its behavior . . . indicates its adaptability to conditions as widely different as New England, New York, North Carolina. . . ." The tree is rather small, vigorous, productive, blooms late, and often is a biennial bearer. The fruit needs thinning to be of good size, tends to ripen all at once, and is not a good keeper. The apples are excellent for fresh eating and cider but become bland if left on the tree too long.

Mother originated early in the nineteenth century in Bolton, Massachusetts, on the farm of General Stephen P. Gardner. It was brought to notice in 1844 when exhibited to the Massachusetts Horticultural Society.

The Mother apple may have been responsible for the many commercial apple orchards established in Rabun County, Georgia, in the early 1900s. The pioneer Rabun County orchardist, Colonel John P. Fort, started his orchards there in 1906 and later wrote in a memoir: "Through Demorest [Georgia] there used to pass covered wagons full of apples on their way to Athens [Georgia]. I was struck with the beauty of these apples, especially an apple called the 'Mother' apple which was capable of a very high polish and was very free of blemish. On talking to the wagoneers I found that they came down from Rabun County . . . and that they grew their apples with very little care or cultivation. I was so interested that I went up to Rabun County to study the apple question."

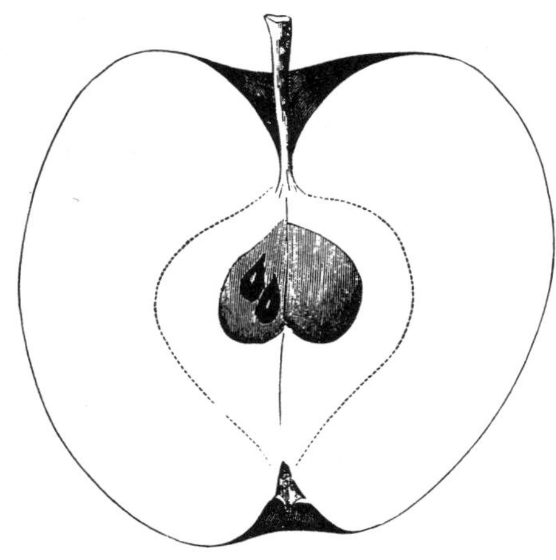

MOTHER

Fruit medium, roundish conical, sometimes slightly oblong; skin thin, smooth, nearly covered with red with deeper red stripes; dots very numerous, minute, gray; stem short to medium length and rather stout in a cavity of varying shape and size, often russeted; calyx closed; basin greenish, narrow, somewhat wrinkled; flesh yellow, fine-grained, tender, juicy, mild subacid with a distinctive aroma. Ripe August/September. Catalog listings: VA, NC, SC, GA, KY (1855–1915). ❖ **Plate 35.**

**MOTHER BUD:** In Avery County in the mountains of western North Carolina, there are many people who remember this apple. A letter to me says: "It was a good eating apple and made the most delicious applesauce and pies." Tom Brown found a tree belonging to Pershing Cuthbertson. No description except ripe August/September. No catalog listings.

**MOUNTAIN BEAUTY:** Originated with Stephen Ferguson near Keswick Depot, Virginia. This is probably the same apple as the Mountain Beauty mentioned in an 1855 issue of *The American Gardener* magazine. Tree vigorous and a biennial bearer. A tree of this name was found by Tom Brown in 2002. Its fruit pretty much fits the description below.

Fruit medium or below, oblate; skin smooth, whitish shaded with light and dark red, purplish red in the sun, some obscure stripes; dots many, light colored, some areole; stem very short and rather stout in a broad, moderately deep, russeted cavity;

basin broad, smooth; flesh white, tender, juicy, mild subacid to almost sweet. Ripe December/January. No catalog listings.

❦ **MOUNTAIN BOOMER** (Mount Boomer, Seek No Further): The Virginia State Horticultural Society described Mountain Boomer in 1900 as a new variety, and it was listed by two Tennessee nurseries from 1905 to 1916. John and Mary Creech, of Turkey Hollow Nursery in Kentucky, rediscovered this apple. Mary found the old, almost dead tree in an abandoned orchard, and John described the fruit as huge, with flavor and texture exceptional for such a large apple. The tree is susceptible to fire blight.

Fruit large to very large, roundish conical; skin pale yellow or greenish yellow, occasionally with a blush; stem short to medium in a russeted cavity; calyx closed; flesh firm, juicy, sometimes with watery streaks near the skin. Ripe August/September.

❦ **MOUNTAIN ROSE:** Discovered in Wilkes County, North Carolina, a few years ago by my friends and nurserymen Suzanne and Ron Joyner.

Fruit below medium, roundish; skin lemon yellow with a faint blush on one side; stem medium length in an abrupt, russeted cavity; calyx closed; flesh yellowish white, tender, crisp, juicy. Ripe September. No catalog listings.

❦ **MRS. BRYAN** (Bryan, Lady Bryan?): This large, showy apple was grown from seed in the 1870s by Robert Boatman near Dillon, Georgia. It was named for Mrs. J. W. Bryan of Lookout Mountain, Georgia, who was an esteemed member of the Georgia Horticultural Society. (In 1880 she exhibited thirty varieties of vegetables at a meeting of the society.) The tree is a heavy and regular bearer. One Texas catalog describes this apple as "always recognized by a peculiar dimple on every apple," but Texas nurseries confused Mrs. Bryan with an apple called San Jacinto. (*See* San Jacinto.) Like Carter's Blue, Mrs. Bryan was extinct in the United States for many years, but I found a tree in the fruit collection of the National Fruit Trust, Kent, England, and imported scionwood into the United States.

Fruit large, roundish to slightly oblate, conical, often lobed, and irregular; skin pale greenish, blushed with orange or pale red, with broken darker stripes; dots numerous, russet and gray; stem short to medium in a russeted cavity; calyx open; basin broad, rather deep; flesh creamy white, tender, coarse, not very juicy. Ripe August/September. Catalog listings: NC, GA, TX, AR (1889–1909). ❖ **Plate 36.**

❦ **MUNSON SWEET** (Orange Sweet, Ray Apple, Meacham Sweet, Orange, Rag Apple, Northern Sweet): Probably originated in Massachusetts before 1849 and sold by several southern nurseries at the turn of the twentieth century. Rediscovered when noticed by nurseryman Ron Joyner in a catalog of Seed Savers Exchange. Scions were obtained from Oregon. The tree is an abundant bearer.

Fruit medium to large, roundish oblate to oblate, often ribbed; skin thick and separates easily from the flesh, smooth, green becoming pale yellow, often blushed; dots minute; stem short and rather thick in a medium to large, lightly russeted cavity; calyx closed; basin shallow, narrow, furrowed; flesh yellowish, fine-grained, tender, moderately juicy, very sweet. Ripe August. Catalog listings: MD, VA, TN (1895–1916).

❦ **MUSKMELON SWEET:** The late T. Blaine Poole of Fries, Virginia, wrote me a letter in 1986 about a nearby Muskmelon Sweet apple tree. When I visited him, Mr. Poole (then almost ninety) related that when he was a boy, Muskmelon Sweet was his favorite apple. The only tree nearby belonged to neighbors who stored boxes of Muskmelon Sweet apples in an unused room in their house. On his way home from school, Mr. Poole would fashion a long spear out of a stick and would then detour by the neighbor's house. He would spear apples through a missing window pane until he had eaten his fill. As far as he knew, the neighbors never figured out where those Muskmelon Sweet apples were going to.

Fruit above medium to large, sometimes very large, roundish conical, very irregular and prominently ribbed; skin dull, pale greenish yellow; dots large, whitish, numerous, some areole; stem short to medium length in a narrow, deep, lumpy, russeted cavity with the russet over the top of the apple; calyx closed or usually open; basin corrugated; flesh greenish white, fine-grained, not very crisp or juicy, sweet. Ripe late September/October. No catalog listings.

❧ **NEWTOWN PIPPIN** (Albemarle Pippin, Green Winter Pippin, New York Pippin, Virginia Pippin, Back Creek, Large Newtown Pippin, Petersburg Pippin, Yellow Pippin, Pippin, Yellow Newtown Pippin, Green Newtown Pippin, Green Ohio Pippin, Green Winter Pippin, Hunt's Fine Green Pippin, Mountain Pippin): There are two Newtown Pippin apples—Green Newtown Pippin and Yellow Newtown Pippin. One is certainly a seedling or a sport of the other, but which one came first is impossible to know because of the antiquity of both apples. Yellow Newtown Pippin is synonymous with Albemarle Pippin, one of the truly great apples of the South, which grows to perfection in certain soils in Virginia, North Carolina, and Georgia.

Before 1817 there is no record of more than one type of Newtown Pippin. Coxe (1817), in his great book on American fruit, described a "Large Yellow Newtown Pippin" and a "Green Newtown Pippin." Both apples have been grown in the South, but Yellow Newtown Pippin has always predominated under its southern name of Albemarle Pippin or, very often, simply Pippin.

The original Newtown Pippin tree stood on the farm of the Moore family near Newtown Village, Long Island, New York. It is family tradition that this tree was brought from England and planted about 1666 by the first member of the Moore family in America, but whether as a seed or graft or scion or young tree is unknown. The original tree stood until 1805. Thomas Sorsby's nursery in Surry County, Virginia, advertised Newtown Pippin trees for sale in 1761.

Some Newtown Pippin apples were sent to Benjamin Franklin while he was in London in 1759. The quality of these apples so astonished the British that a demand for their import quickly developed. Considerable numbers of Newtown Pippins were being exported to England by the 1770s, most of them from orchards in New York and Pennsylvania. By 1800 southern-grown Yellow Newtown Pippins, known as Albemarle Pippins, became important in the export trade.

The United States ambassador to England in 1837 was Andrew Stevenson from Albemarle County, Virginia. He presented Queen Victoria with several barrels of Albemarle Pippins, which so delighted the queen that she removed from this single variety a small crown import tax. The British willingly paid premium prices for these American apples. Southern orchardists were getting up to seven dollars a barrel for Albemarle Pippins in 1851, which sold for a phenomenal twenty dollars per barrel in London. This was over three times the selling price of other apples at that time. In 1898 Albemarle Pippins sold for thirty-six cents a pound in England. Overseas demand for Albemarle Pippins made it one of the leading commercial apples in the South throughout the nineteenth century, along with Winesap, Ben Davis, and York Imperial. The British tried to grow their own Newton Pippins but failed for lack of proper climate and soils.

Virginians long considered Albemarle Pippin a Virginia apple and thought it originated as a seedling near North Garden, Virginia. In 1857, Franklin Davis, the prominent Virginia pomologist and nurseryman, proved Albemarle Pippin to be identical to Yellow Newtown Pippin. Subsequent investigations established a historical connection between Albemarle Pippin and Newtown Pippin as follows: In 1755, Dr. Thomas Walker of Castle Hill, Albemarle County, Virginia, accompanied Virginia troops serving with British General Braddock's army during the French and Indian War. General Braddock suffered a disastrous defeat in his attack on Fort Duquesne, and the remnants of his army retreated back to Philadelphia. Dr. Walker then left the army and returned to Virginia, bringing some apple scions with him in his saddlebags. The land on which the supposed original Albemarle Pippin tree grew, near North Garden, Virginia, belonged to Dr. Walker's stepdaughter, Mildred Meriwether. It is most probable that this original Albemarle Pippin tree was, in fact, a graft using a scion of Yellow Newtown Pippin brought home by Dr. Walker from Pennsylvania.

More so than any other apple, the quality of Newtown Pippin fruit is influenced by the soil. It has been grown successfully in only a few areas, notably the lower Hudson River Valley; the upper piedmont and mountains of Virginia, North Carolina, and Georgia; and portions of California, Oregon, and Washington. In the South, certain soils were known to favor the growth of Albemarle Pippin apples. Chief among these soils was Porter's Black Loam, a soil found in limited areas of the South and that came to be known as "pippin soil." Other soils can also grow the Albemarle Pippin if they are of high fertility and of a loose, friable texture. Excellent soil and air drainage have always been recognized as necessary to grow top-quality Albemarle Pippins. In the South, except in those few favored areas, Albemarle Pippin fruit is smaller, of lower quality, more subject to disease, and may drop prematurely.

Albemarle Pippin steadily decreased in commercial importance in the South after 1900. It has some real drawbacks to commercial production. Trees on seedling rootstock seldom bear crops for ten or twelve years or even longer, and the trees are often biennial bearers. The variety is susceptible to fire blight and bitter rot and requires good cultural practices to grow well. Today the main commercial area for this variety is northern California where four million bushels were produced in 1990, about 2 percent of American apple production.

The eating quality of Newtown Pippin improves with storage. John Creech, of Turkey Hollow Nursery in Kentucky, wrote: "When our Newtown tree had its first crop, I attempted to eat the apples right off the tree. For a couple of years the fruit was considered worthless and was mixed in with cider. Then one spring, when cleaning out the cellar, I ran across a peck of Newtown Pippins and absently bit into one. What a revelation! Needless to say, no more Newtowns have gone into cider; they are jealously guarded until mid-March and then rationed out until the first of June. Sadly, our growing conditions and/or soil are not very well suited to this fine old variety, and production has been very low. Still, I believe everyone with a long enough growing season (about 160 days) should try a tree of Newtown on the chance that it might do well. It is worth the gamble."

The Green and Yellow Newtown Pippins are quite alike in both tree and fruit. Both are good keepers, although Yellow Newtown is somewhat better, keeping in good cellar storage until at least March. Both are tops for cooking and both make a clear, high-quality cider. In the mid-1800s it was remarked that the tree of the Green Newtown had a peculiar roughness of the bark that easily distinguished it from Yellow Newtown. Later descriptions do not mention this bark roughness but say that the tree of Green Newtown has a more drooping growth habit than Yellow Newtown. In commercial orchards in the South, only Yellow Newtown Pippin apples were grown because of their larger size, brighter color, and better keeping quality.

*Green Newtown Pippin*: Fruit medium to large, variable in shape and color. The shape is usually roundish oblate, often oblique, sometimes elliptical; skin rather tough, smooth or slightly roughened with russet dots, grass green at harvest but turns much more yellow when stored, often with some brownish or pinkish color near the stem end; dots white, submerged, more numerous near the blossom end; stem short or medium length in a deep, acute, often russeted cavity; basin medium in width and depth, furrowed; flesh yellowish or tinged green, firm, crisp, tender, rather fine-grained, juicy, sprightly, aromatic, subacid. Ripe October and keeps until February or later. Catalog listings as Green Newtown Pippin: VA, NC, KY (1845–1901).

*Yellow Newtown Pippin*: Very similar in most respects to Green Newtown Pippin but perhaps slightly larger. At harvest, Yellow Newtown is more yellow and has more pink tones near the stem end. Less highly colored fruit often has streaks of light green showing through, giving a slightly striped effect. The flesh of Yellow Newtown usually has a more yellowish tinge, is milder or less sprightly, and is more aromatic. Catalog listings as Albemarle Pippin or Yellow Newtown Pippin: VA, NC, GA, KY (1761–1924). *See also* Brooke Pippin. ❖ **Plate 37.**

❦ **NICKAJACK** (Summerour, Berry, Wall, Aberdeen, Ruckman's Red, Red Horse, Jackson Red, Hubbard, Big Hill, Carolina Spice, Red Pippin, Howard,

Mobbs, Cheataw, Pound, Accidental, Edward Shantee, Trenham, Cheatham Pippin, Winter Rose, Red Hazel, Wander, Forsythe's Seedling, Allegheny, Cheltram Pippin, Gowden, Walb, Graham's Red Warrior, Winter Horse, Missouri Pippin, Missouri Red, Leanham, World's Wonder, Grogg, Gowdie?, Dahlonega?, Carolina, Caroline, Edwards, Hollman, Holman, Tranham?, Chatham Pippin): In 1846 Silas McDowell, the great North Carolina pomologist, sent scions and fruit of this apple to his friend and fellow apple enthusiast Mr. Camack of Georgia. McDowell described it as a seedling that originated with the Cherokee Indians, near Nickajack Creek in Macon County, North Carolina. A different version of its origin is that it came from the seedling orchard of Colonel John Summerour of either Lincoln or Burke County, North Carolina, where it was first called Winter Rose and later Summerour. It is probable that Summerour and Nickajack were, in fact, two different apples closely resembling each other, and that eventually lost their separate identities. Although its eating quality is only average at best, southerners prized Nickajack for its large size, reliable bearing, and good keeping ability. In 1908 the USDA found Nickajack to be prolific when grown on clay or sandy loam soils of the upper piedmont and mountains.

Downing (1878) remarks that "on branches two, three or four years old, there are woody knobs or warts of various sizes which, when cut from the branch, are found to contain kernels entirely detached from the regular grain of the wood." Other early sources describe the tree as "a vigorous but open grower; requires severe shortening in until well formed." By this is meant that young branches of Nickajack should be shortened (usually by cutting off one-fourth of the new growth) each winter to make a more bushy tree. Nickajack is susceptible to cedar-apple rust. Scions were obtained from Lawson's Nursery in Georgia.

Fruit above medium to large, roundish or roundish oblate, slightly conical; skin greenish yellow shaded with red, usually described as dull red or brick-dust red, with indistinct darker stripes, a thin bloom gives a grayish appearance to the fruit; dots large, numerous, red and yellow; stem short to medium, about one-half inch long, in an acute, large, regular-shaped, slightly russetted cavity; calyx greenish; basin shallow to medium depth, wide, slightly corrugated; flesh slightly yellowish, firm, juicy, briskly subacid. Ripe October. Catalog listings: MD, VA, NC, GA, AL, MS, LA, TN, KY, TX, AR (1858–1917). *See also* Wall *and* World's Wonder.

❦ **NORTH CAROLINA KEEPER** (Bullet?, Yates?, Carolina Keeper): Sold by two North Carolina nurseries from 1886 to 1902. One catalog says: "A new variety introduced from Davidson County, North Carolina. Superior keeping qualities, retaining its fine, rich flavor and crisp, juicy texture all through the winter and spring; slightly subacid when fully mellow. Size medium, yellow covered with beautiful red stripes. A strong grower and extremely productive bearer, fruit growing in perfect clusters along the limbs. Season January to May." An 1890 letter to the USDA says North Carolina Keeper is probably a seedling of Gilpin, which it much resembles.

A letter to me in 1996 from Hazel Baker of Marshville, North Carolina, says, "My mother had an apple tree called Carolina Keeper. We would gather the apples in the fall and store them in the attic where they would keep all winter. I have never tasted an apple to compare since that time."

In 1993, Mrs. Lee Dale Edwards, who lives in the New Salem area of Union County, North Carolina, found a single old tree of this apple in her community and sent me scions. Fruit from Mrs. Edwards' trees closely resemble and are probably Yates.

Fruit medium or below, roundish to oblate, conical; skin almost entirely covered with red with some indistinct darker red stripes; dots numerous, light-colored and russet; stem usually long in a rather wide, gradually sloped, medium depth, russeted cavity; calyx closed; basin medium depth; flesh yellowish, crisp, juicy, subacid. Ripe September/October. ❖ **Plate 38.**

❦ **NORTHERN SPY** (Northern Spice, Spy, Adair Red, King Apple): I do not begrudge northerners their fine heirloom apples—Baldwin, McIntosh, Rhode Island Greening, and others. After all, down South we have our Magnum Bonum, Blacktwig, and

Shockley. Northern Spy, however, I regret not being able to grow well in my lower Zone 7 climate. When I go to the Virginia or North Carolina mountains in the late fall, I try to visit friends who have a big, old Northern Spy tree near their house. Mountain grown or northern grown, it is truly a great apple. Grown in warmer areas it lacks crispness and flavor and often rots on the tree.

Northern Spy has many admirable qualities. Very important to those who live in a frosty location in the mountains is the fact that it is a late bloomer, often two weeks later than most others. The fruit is a good keeper, even in ordinary cellar storage, and is excellent for cooking (but too juicy for drying). The roots of the tree are quite resistant to the woolly apple aphid and, for this reason, Northern Spy has been used in breeding several important dwarfing apple rootstocks.

On the negative side, Northern Spy is notorious for being tardy in coming into bearing, often taking ten years or longer when grafted on seedling rootstock. Best fruit color and flavor develop only when the dense foliage of the tree is carefully pruned to let sunlight into the interior of the tree. Finally, Northern Spy trees are very susceptible to apple scab and fire blight, and the fruit bruises easily.

Northern Spy originated from seeds planted about 1800 in East Bloomfield, New York, in the same seedling orchard of Heman Chapin that produced the Early Joe and Melon apples. Root sprouts of the original tree were dug up and replanted by Chapin's brother-in-law, Humphrey Roswell, which turned out to be a fortuitous action because the original tree was killed by mice or rabbits before bearing. The value of this variety became apparent about 1840, and within a few years it was being sold by nurseries all over the United States. My scions are from a Northern Spy tree selected by Dr. Oberle for apple-breeding work at Virginia Polytechnic Institute in the 1940s and 1950s.

The unusual name of this apple has caused speculation over the years. A letter to a gardening magazine in 1853 from Rochester, New York, had this to say: "To the Editor: In reply to Mrs. B. who inquired about the naming of the Northern Spy apple, everybody here knows it was named for the hero of that notorious dime novel *The Northern Spy*, but no one will come out and admit it."

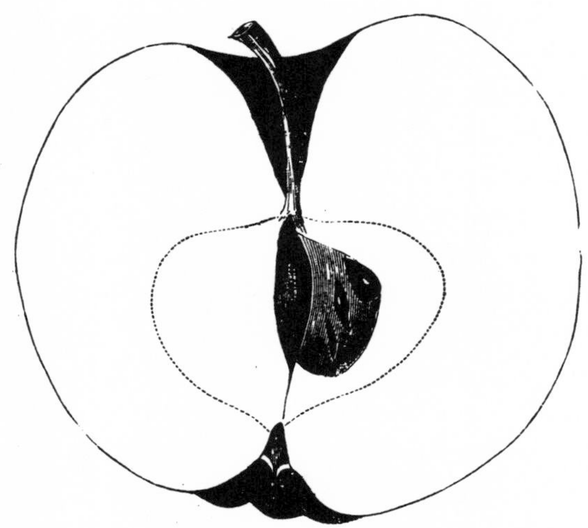

NORTHERN SPY

According to the late Conrad Gemmer, an apple hunter and collector in Pennsylvania, "*The Northern Spy* was written anonymously, published sub-rosa, and circulated among radical hard-core abolitionists circa 1830." The hero of the novel set up safe houses and helped runaway slaves escape to Canada.

Fruit large, roundish, sometimes oblong, flattened at the stem end, conical, often ribbed; skin thin, smooth, mostly greenish or yellowish in the shade but fruit exposed to the sun is nearly covered with light and dark red stripes, often overspread with a thin white bloom; stem medium to long in a very wide, acute, deep, usually russeted cavity; calyx closed; basin narrow, abrupt, usually furrowed; flesh yellowish, rather fine-grained, tender, juicy, crisp, aromatic, spicy subacid. Ripe October and an excellent keeper. Catalog listings: MD, VA, NC, SC, AL, LA, TN, KY, AR (1853–1928). ❖ **Plate 39.**

❧ **NORTHWESTERN GREENING:** Valued mainly for the hardiness of the tree and the keeping qualities of the fruit. Beach (1905) rates the fresh-eating qualities of Northwestern Greening much inferior to Rhode Island Greening, but the apples are excellent for cooking, especially apple pies.

Northwestern Greening originated in Waupaca

County, Wisconsin, and was introduced in 1872. It was mostly grown in those northern states where winter hardiness is important.

Fruit medium to large but variable in size and form, usually roundish but sometimes oblong or oblate; skin smooth, clear pale yellow or greenish, sometimes faintly blushed; dots usually whitish and submerged; stem medium to short in an acute, often lipped, russeted cavity; basin usually abrupt, moderately deep, furrowed; flesh tinged yellow, medium in texture and crispness, juicy, mild subacid. Ripe October and a good keeper. Catalog listings: MD, VA, AL, TN, KY, AR (1899–1928).

❦ **NOTLEY P. NO. 1** (Notly Pippin No. 1, Knotty Pea, Knotley Pea, Notnepee?): Some years ago I found an apple tree near Spruce Pines, North Carolina, called by the owner "Knotty Pea" that is the Notley P. No. 1. An 1855 North Carolina nursery catalog has the only description: "Very large, has weighed 27 ounces; one of the best large apples; flesh coarse, pleasant flavor; tree upright, moderate bearer. October and November." An 1863 Pennsylvania nursery catalog credits the origin of this apple to North Carolina. Notley P. No. 1 appears identical to Gloria Mundi. Catalog listings: VA, NC (1855–1904). *See* Gloria Mundi.

❦ **OLD ENGLISH MILAM:** Greg Lam lives in the mountains of Virginia and has rediscovered several old apple varieties. In 1997 he wrote me that he had found several huge old trees of Old English Milam in the backyard of Bobby Comer near Shenandoah. The trees were big when Mr. Comer was a child sixty years ago. Old English Milam apples "are gone before the Milams get ripe."

Fruit medium or slightly larger, oblate; skin pale green mostly covered with dull red with faint darker stripes; dots numerous; calyx open or closed. Ripe August. No catalog listings.

❦ **OLD NONSUCH:** Found in West Virginia in 1998 by Dr. L. R. Littleton. This may be Red Canada, which has the synonym of Old Nonsuch. No description. No catalog listings.

❦ **OLIVER** (All-over Red, Oliver's Red, Senator): In the Arkansas fruit exhibit at the World's Columbian Exposition in Chicago in 1893, there was a brilliant red apple with conspicuous, large, light-colored dots. This was Oliver's Red, grown for many years in the Ozarks of Arkansas. Stark Bro's Nursery began selling this variety in 1895 under the name Senator, a name trademarked by them.

This apple originated in the early 1800s on the farm of John Oliver, seven miles south of Lincoln in Washington County, Arkansas. It was first propagated about 1850 by a local nurseryman, John Holt, who called it Oliver's Red or All-over Red.

Beach (1905) characterizes Oliver as "an attractive dark red apple of good size and good quality." The fruit hangs well on the tree and keeps in ordinary cellar storage until Christmas. The tree is healthy, vigorous, productive, and an annual bearer.

Fruit medium or above, varying in shape from roundish to slightly oblate; skin thick, smooth and glossy, mostly covered with red with many broken stripes of darker red; dots large and very conspicuous, whitish, sometimes areole; stem usually short in a narrow, russeted cavity; calyx open; basin large, wide, deep, greenish; flesh yellowish often stained red, rather fine-grained, crisp, juicy, mild subacid. Ripe September/October and an excellent keeper. Catalog listings: MD, AR (1899–1920).

❦ **OOTEN:** In February 1998 I received scions from James R. "Sammy" Hall of Logan, West Virginia, and I quote at length from his accompanying letter:

> The Ooten apple has been in the Trace Creek and Pigeon Creek areas of Mingo County since prior to 1895, when Mingo was part of Logan County. The name comes from the family who discovered, maintained and shared this majestic apple with friends and neighbors. This first Ooten apple tree and others in the small orchard, so proudly maintained, are now gone. They are victims of strip mining, which left the little hollow and surrounding hills looking like photos beamed back from Mars.
>
> Locally this green apple, colossal in size, ripens in mid-late August. When the green skin takes on a yellowish tint, they

should be picked. If not, these gargantuan apples will drop, creating apple sauce on the ground. A larger and, in my opinion, a better apple than Wolf River, the Ooten, before overly ripe, is a good eating apple and a very useful cooking apple. The awesome spectacle of the behemoths hanging on a tree make this variety worthy of preservation. It is not impossible that my single tree is the last of its kind.

No catalog listings.

❦ **OPALESCENT:** According to Virginia apple historian, Tom Burford, Opalescent originated in the 1800s with George Hudson of Barry County, Michigan. He found it as a seedling while clearing oak stumps from a piece of land and named it Hudson's Pride of Michigan. It was later renamed Opalescent by the Dayton Star Nursery and introduced in 1899 by the McNary and Gaines Nursery of Xenia, Ohio. Sold by Virginia and Maryland nurseries in the 1920s and 1930s. A letter to me a few years ago from Ralph Johnson of New Wilmington, Pennsylvania, urged me to grow this apple for its quality.

Fruit above medium to large, roundish conical, sides sometimes unequal; skin nearly covered with dark red; dots small and large, irregular-shaped, yellowish and russet, often submerged, sometimes the skin shows flecks of russet; stem short to medium length in a deep, partly russeted cavity; calyx greenish, closed or slightly open; basin abrupt, fairly deep; flesh yellowish, crisp, juicy, aromatic, mild subacid. Ripe August/September and becomes greasy in storage. ❖ **Plate 40.**

❦ **OPHIR:** Sometimes an apple hunter is lucky and gets a letter like the one I received in 1987 from Nellie L. Williams of Kittrell, North Carolina. She wrote, "I read with interest of your search for old apple varieties. My husband was a minister before his recent retirement, and one church he served was in the Ophir community near the Uwharrie Mountains. Mr. and Mrs. Robert Saunders of Ophir are retired and have an apple tree set out by Mrs. Saunders' parents when they first married. This tree bears medium-size, rosy-red apples which do not require much sugar when used for cooking and make the best tasting and beautiful pinkish applesauce and also a very good pie. At the time I first saw this old tree, which is not in good shape, I thought what a shame to lose this apple. God bless your efforts."

I visited Mrs. Saunders to cut scions. She told me her father dug up a small seedling tree at an abandoned sawmill seventy-five years ago and planted it near the house. She and I agreed to call the apple "Ophir" (pronounced OH-fur).

Fruit medium, roundish or slightly oblate, lobed; skin mostly covered with red; dots small, gray; stem medium to long in an irregular, deep greenish cavity; calyx closed or open; basin abrupt, deep, round; flesh crisp, very juicy, mild subacid. Ripe late August/September. No catalog listings.

❦ **ORTLEY** (White Bellflower, Ortley Pippin, Detroit, Greasy Pippin, Hollow Core Pippin, Ohio Favorite, Woolman's Long Pippin, Yellow Pippin, Crane's Pippin, White Detroit, Willow Leaf Pippin, Woodward's Pippin, Green Bellflower, Marrow Pippin, White Pippin, Melting Pippin, Inman, Spice Pippin, Cleopatra, Tom Woodward Pippin, Van Dyne?, Davis, Todd's Golden Pippin, Warren Pippin): An old New Jersey apple first described by Coxe (1817) under the name Woolman's Long Pippin. It was better known in the South as White Bellflower, White Detroit, or White Pippin. The fruit is similar to Yellow Bellflower but less acid in flavor and bruises more easily. The tree has brittle wood and is susceptible to apple scab and bitter rot.

Fruit medium to large, roundish to oblong, conical; skin waxy or greasy, greenish yellow becoming yellow at maturity, sometimes with greenish stripes, occasionally with a slight blush; stem slender, medium length in a deep, acute, greenish russeted cavity; calyx closed; basin abrupt, somewhat corrugated; flesh white or creamy, fine-grained, tender, juicy, subacid. Ripe October. Catalog listings: MD, VA, NC, SC, GA, AL, TN, KY, TX (1853–1904).

❦ **OZARK BEAUTY:** Herbert Childress of Dunnville, Kentucky, has sent me scions of several antique apples from his preservation orchard. This is one of them, but I believe it may be a modern apple, although I cannot find any reference to it anywhere. I taste Golden Delicious in it, and it is shaped somewhat like a Golden Delicious. I keep it for its quality and because my friend sent it to me.

A friend of mine in South Carolina is reasonably sure Ozark Beauty is actually Ozark Gold, an apple developed at the Missouri State Agricultural Station in 1970, using Golden Delicious as one parent.

Fruit medium or above, roundish conical, flat on the ends; skin tough, lemon yellow with a faint reddish blush on the sunny side; dots faint, numerous, russet or greenish; stem medium length in a tan russet, deep cavity with russet spilling out over the top of the apple; calyx greenish, closed or slightly open; basin wide, corrugated; flesh whitish, juicy, crisp, sweet. Ripe August/September. No catalog listings.

❧ **PARKS' PIPPIN** (Gilmer Pippin): This apple, sold by Jim Lawson's nursery in Georgia for years, originated on the farm of Monroe Parks in Gilmer County, Georgia. Howard Parks, a descendent of Monroe Parks, told Jim Lawson this: "Monroe Parks killed a wild goose in Gilmer County back in the mid 1800s and found a bunch of corn in its craw. He planted the corn to see if it was some unusual variety. In the row of corn a little apple sprout came up, and he let it grow. It turned out to be this apple." The apples are suitable for apple butter, cider, and jelly. The fruit is large, green to greenish yellow often with a blush, and very tart until fully ripe. It ripens mid-September and is a good keeper.

❧ **PARMER** (Parmar, Yellow Flat): This old Virginia apple is not mentioned in any pomological references or nursery catalogs. I first encountered Parmer when Roy Wood of Stuart, Virginia, sent me some apples, urging me to make applesauce from them (a unique sauce, very dense and dark yellow in color). Later I found a tree in the heritage orchard at the Eli Whitney homestead near Steele's Tavern, Virginia. Harriet Allen, who lived near Floyd, Virginia, called this apple Yellow Flat and remembered that it was used mostly to make apple brandy. She recalled that if you had several Parmer trees in your orchard, neighbors knew you were making illegal brandy. The flesh of Parmer is the darkest yellow of any apple I know.

Fruit small to medium, oblate, slightly conical; skin deep yellow, russeted at the stem end and with irregular russet patches all over; stem long and slender in a deep, rather broad, corrugated cavity; calyx green; basin shallow, green, wrinkled; flesh very yellow, (darkest yellow just under the skin), fine-grained, brisk subacid. Ripe July/August. No catalog listings.

❧ **PAW:** Leona Price of Taylorsville, North Carolina, has a tree over eighty years old, and others remember Paw apple trees elsewhere in Alexander County at one time. Tom Brown found this apple in 2000 and describes the apple as medium size, oblate; skin yellow blushed with red on the sunny side; flesh crisp, juicy, subacid. Ripe early September. No catalog listings.

❧ **PENNOCK** (Pennock's Red Winter, Red Pennock, Winter Penick, Big Romanite, Large Romanite, Pelican, Phoenix, Neisley's Winter, Prolific Beauty, Red Ox, Pennsylvania Pennock, Benton Red, Broad Apple, Penick, Crooked Red, Foster's Best, Massac Pippin): A large, showy, good-keeping apple of mediocre eating quality, first grown by Joseph Pennock before 1817 in Delaware County, Pennsylvania. In the South, Pennock was grown in the mountains and piedmont, doing well on both black loam and red clay soils at elevations above 1,000 feet. The tree bears abundantly, but the fruit is susceptible to a dry rot called "Baldwin spot" or bitter speck. I obtained scions from Lou Tams in Utah, who got his start from the late Art Hontz of Pennsylvania. Early Pennock is a different apple, not of southern origin and little grown in the South.

Fruit large, roundish oblate but sometimes roundish oblong, often oblique; skin thick, tough, smooth, mostly mottled and striped with deep red, sometimes described as dull red; dots numerous, large, gray or yellow, often areolar; stem short and rather thick in an acute, deep, green or russeted cavity; basin somewhat abrupt, often furrowed; flesh yellow, tender, juicy, coarse, subacid to almost sweet. Ripe late. Catalog listings: MD, VA, DC, NC, TN, KY (1824–1904). *See also* Vandevere, North Carolina Beauty *and* Romanite. ❖ **Plate 41.**

❦ **PERKINS:** A Tom Brown discovery near Statesville, North Carolina, where a single old tree belongs to Ruth Harmon. This is almost certainly the same apple as Perkins of North Carolina discussed in the chapter on extinct varieites. Tom describes the apple as large, oblate to oblong; skin dark red to almost black with prominent dots; flesh crisp, juicy, subacid. Ripe September/October.

❦ **PERRY RUSSET** (Golden Russet [incorrectly], Russet Greening, Pineapple Russet, Rhode Island Russet): This northern apple, now very rare, has never been grown in the South as far as I can determine. Scions were sent to me in 1996 by the late Conrad Gemmer, a fellow antique apple collector living in Pennsylvania. As fruited by me, it is a lovely yellow apple that I keep because of its rarity and its delectable taste and texture.

Beach in *Apples of New York* (1905) says it originated in the early 1800s either in New York or Rhode Island, and "the tree is very hardy, healthy and a reliable cropper."

Fruit medium, roundish, often oblique; skin rough, pale greenish yellow shading to orangish on the sunny side and with some black and russet blotches; dots fairly numerous, medium size, whitish and blackish, areole; stem medium long in a russeted cavity; calyx closed or open; basin round, russeted; flesh pale yellow, crisp and juicy, mild subacid. Ripe late September/October. No catalog listings.

❦ **PEWAUKEE:** Pewaukee resulted from a cross of Northern Spy × Duchess of Oldenburg made by George P. Peffer of Pewaukee, Wisconsin, and was first brought to notice in 1870. It is considered one of the "Ironclads" or winter-hardy apple varieties. Pewaukee was sold by southern nurseries as a productive tree bearing good-keeping apples suitable for market fruit. The eating quality of Pewaukee is only fair at best, and the fruit often drops prematurely.

Fruit medium to large, varying in shape but usually roundish oblate, ribbed; skin smooth, striped and mottled with light and dark red over most of the surface, often with a gray bloom; dots pale gray or white, some large and areolar; stem usually short and fleshy under a fleshy lip in a variable shape and size cavity that is sometimes barely developed at all; basin usually abrupt, medium to shallow, wrinkled; flesh yellowish white, moderately firm, juicy, subacid. Ripe October/November. Catalog listings: MD, VA, NC, GA, AL, TN, KY, AR (1884–1928).

❦ **PHIFER:** Fifty years ago, Elmer Knox's father grafted him a Phifer apple tree from an old tree dating back to the 1800s. Tom Brown found this remaining tree at the old Phifer homeplace near Statesville, North Carolina. Described as medium size, oblate; skin whitish yellow often with a pinkish blush; flesh acid. Ripe August/September. No catalog listing.

❦ **PILOT** (Virginia Pilot): "As I have said that the apple is the great fruit of all fruits, the Pilot Apple, a natural seedling of Nelson County, Virginia, is the great apple of all apples in our acquaintance. The tree is a magnificent grower, absolutely hardy. The fruit is large, handsomely formed and of the finest flavor, both for dessert and for cooking." So said Professor J. Dinwiddie of the University of Virginia in 1872.

For years I searched for Pilot, which was high on my "Ten Most Wanted List." It was a great disappointment to me to discover that both trees in the heritage orchard at the Eli Whitney Homestead, Steele's Tavern, Virginia, were dead. Tom Burford, of Monroe, Virginia, rediscovered Pilot in 1989.

Pilot originated about 1830 on the farm of John Lobban (or Lobbin), at the base of Pilot Mountain, in northern Nelson County, and seems best suited to the upper piedmont and mountains on rich, friable soils. On heavy clays at less than 1,000 feet of elevation, Pilot has been reported to be a poor bearer and usually a biennial bearer.

The fruit is a good keeper. In 1908 the USDA reported that some Virginia growers would pile up Pilot apples under the trees and cover them with leaves or straw. In spring, the apples would be uncovered, packed in barrels, and sold for satisfactory prices.

Fruit large, roundish or slightly oblate, often oblique; skin striped and shaded with dull red; dots numerous, large, whitish, areolar; stem short in a rather large cavity; basin large and deep; flesh yellowish, fine-grained, rather firm, tender, juicy, slightly aromatic, mild subacid. Ripe October and an excellent keeper. Catalog listings: MD, VA, NC (1869–1904).

❦ **PINEAPPLE:** Dave Hughes, age 90, had an old Pineapple tree at his home over forty years ago and identified this apple for Tom Brown. Described as medium size, oblate; skin rough, whitish yellow with a light reddish blush on the sunny side; flesh firm, crisp, acid. Ripe late September. No catalog listings.

❦ **PINKY:** A tree of this variety was brought from Virginia to North Carolina at the end of the Civil War by a man named Alfred Harris Smith. The Smith family grew this apple first in Cabarrus County, North Carolina, then later in the community of Cornelius in Mecklenburg County. Trees are still being grown by members of the Smith family, and Frank Smith brought scions to me.

Fruit medium size, roundish conical; skin partly to mostly covered with bright to purplish red; stem medium to long in a slightly russeted cavity; dots numerous, irregular, russet; calyx open or closed; basin gradually sloped, broad, leather-cracked. Ripe for cooking mid-August, fully ripe September/October. No catalog listings.

❦ **POLLY EADES:** Discovered in 1884 by W. A. Sandefur, Sr., owner of a nursery in Robards, Kentucky, and sold by Kentucky nurseries from 1915 to 1925. The original tree grew on the farm of Polly Eades, two and a half miles east of Robards and was thought to be a seedling of Horse. The tree is a late bloomer, resistant to fire blight (but the fruit is very susceptible to summer rots), and bears early and heavily.

Fruit above medium, roundish or slightly oblate, conical; skin tough, light greenish yellow with a bronzy or red blush or indistinct stripes on the sunny side; dots mostly submerged but a few are rather large with russet centers; stem long in a faintly russeted cavity; calyx slightly open or closed; basin smooth and shallow; flesh yellowish, juicy, tender, aromatic, subacid to rather tart, browns quickly. Ripe July/August. ❖ **Plate 42.**

❦ **POLLY SWEET:** Elwood Smathers, who died in 2001 at age ninety-five, said the original tree grew up in the woodpile at the abandoned homesite of Polly Cook at the head of Dutch Cove, near Canton, North Carolina. This tree was very large in 1915. At least two trees of Polly Sweet still exist in the Canton area where one was found by Tom Brown.

Fruit medium, roundish; skin pale greenish yellow; dots numerous, pale with russet centers; stem almost long in a rather shallow, russeted cavity; flesh juicy, barely sweet. Ripe late July/August. No catalog listings.

❦ **POMME GRISE** (Gray Apple, Pomme Gris d'Or, Pomme Gris, Pleasant Valley Pippin): This russet apple probably originated in Canada, but Downing (1878) says it may have been brought from France or Switzerland by early settlers. Although Pomme Grise was little grown in the South, it seems to be well adapted to much of the southern piedmont and mountains. Peter Horowitz, an apple hobbyist in Maryland, rates this apple very highly, with fruit quality improving as the tree gets older. The tree bears heavy annual crops.

Fruit medium or smaller, roundish oblate; skin thick, tough, greenish gray, partly or entirely covered with brown, knobby russet, rarely with a faint red cheek on the sunny side; dots inconspicuous, greenish or whitish; stem usually medium to long in a large, deep, broad, and folded cavity; calyx closed; basin variable, usually wide, deep and furrowed; flesh yellowish, firm, crisp, fine-grained, juicy, subacid. Ripe late August/September. Catalog listings: GA, KY (1858–70).

❦ **PORTER** (Jennings, Yellow Summer Pearmain): First grown about 1800 by Rev. Samuel Porter of Sherburne, Massachusetts. Unlike many northern apples, Porter retains its fine qualities when grown in the South. It was introduced to several generations of American women by being highly recommended in early editions of the famous *Fanny Farmer Boston Cookbook*. When cooked, the fruit keeps its flavor and shape remarkably well. It is also a good apple for fresh eating and canning. The tree is a biennial bearer and often has apples ranging from small to large on the same tree. The fruit ripens on the tree over a two-month period.

Fruit small to large, mostly almost large, roundish to slightly oblong, conical; skin rather thin and smooth, clear greenish yellow, sometimes with an orangish blush, often very obscurely striped; dots medium to small, green with whitish centers, sometimes russet; stem medium to short in a deep, acute, usually russeted cavity; calyx closed; basin narrow, shallow to deep, abrupt, furrowed; flesh yellow, fine-grained, tender, crisp, juicy, aromatic, subacid. Ripe August/September. Catalog listings: MD, VA, NC, KY (1845–1904).

**POTOMAC** (Browning Beauty): Discovered by Frank Browning in 1962 near Wallingford, Kentucky. Later sold by Bountiful Ridge Nurseries, Princess Anne, Maryland.

Fruit medium to large, roundish, often oblique; skin bright red blushed with purple; dots numerous, large and small, grayish; stem medium in an abrupt, deep, slightly russeted cavity; calyx usually closed; basin round, medium size; flesh firm, tart. Ripe late September and keeps extremely well.

**POTTS** (Red Potts, Brushy): A Potts apple was briefly discussed without description in the chapter on extinct varieties in the previous edition of this book, said to have been grown in the Brushy Mountains of North Carolina and prized for making apple brandy. Tom Brown found an apple called Red Potts that almost certainly is the same apple as Potts. Three trees were found in Statesville and Taylorsville, North Carolina, including a tree in Henry Tevepaugh's orchard in Alexander County. Described as large, roundish conical; skin yellow with a dull red blush; flesh dry, slightly acid. Ripe September. No catalog listings.

**POUND** (Longshore Pound, Carroll County Pound): The Collinsville Nursery of Alabama sold this apple in the 1920s and later, but its origin is unknown. It appears to be different (and better in quality) than several other apples called Pound. The late W. M. Longshore of Anniston, Alabama, worked in the Collinsville Nursery as a young boy and is responsible for saving this excellent apple, which is one of my favorites. He, in turn, passed it on to Joyce Neighbors of Gadsden, Alabama.

Fruit above medium to large, roundish, slightly conical; skin pale yellow, faintly blushed, and striped with red on the sunny side; dots large and small, dark gray; stem medium length in a russeted cavity; calyx open in a corrugated basin. Ripe late August/September.

**POUND PIPPIN:** I have received several letters from southerners extolling Pound Pippin and asking if it is available. Pound Pippin is a synonym of Fall Pippin, and I believe that Fall Pippin is the variety people actually mean when they ask about Pound Pippin. There is considerable confusion concerning apples beginning with the name Pound. Ragan (1905) lists no less than fifteen different varieties beginning with the name Pound and eighteen synonyms beginning with Pound. Fall Pippin is a fine old apple and is available. *See* Fall Pippin.

**PRIMATE** (Rough and Ready, July Apple, Scott, Powers, Sour Harvest, North American Best, Highland Pippin, Ryerson, Early Baldwin, Early Tart Harvest, Harvest Apple, Jenkins Summer, Belle Rose): In New York, Primate was considered a high-quality yellow apple best suited for the home orchard because it ripens over a period of several weeks and bruises very easily. The fruit was praised as grown in Blacksburg, Virginia, in 1900.

Primate originated about 1840 on the farm of Calvin D. Bingham in Camillus, New York, and was distributed throughout the state by traveling grafters.

Fruit medium or above, roundish oblate, conical, often ribbed; skin thin, greenish yellow, often slightly blushed on the sunny side, sometimes with a few red streaks near the basin; stem short in an acute, deep, brown, furrowed cavity; calyx closed; basin abrupt, medium to narrow in width, furrowed; flesh white, tender, juicy, crisp, aromatic, sprightly subacid. Ripe August/September in the North, but July in most of the South. Catalog listings: MD, VA, NC, TN, KY (1858–1904).

**PRISSY GUM:** Found by that tireless apple hunter (and my good friend) the late Dr. L. R. Littleton. Three old trees belong to Doreen Ralston of Vanderpool, Virginia. She says it is named for Priscilla Wade Gum, wife of Abraham Gum, who moved to Virginia in the late 1700s from a place called Sugarlands in Maryland. Ms. Ralston says the apples are tart and have a wonderful texture when cooked. They ripen in August. No catalog listings.

**PRYOR'S RED** (Big Hill, Prior's Red, Pitzerhill, Red Russet, Prior, Bersford, Bonford, Concord, Pryor's Pearmain, James River, Conford, Deacon's Pryor?): A common belief among apple growers a hundred years ago was that an apple variety could go downhill over a period of a century or so and become "played out." Pryor's Red was considered a "played out" variety in 1908 when investigated by the USDA. Southern catalogs of the period said such things as "once of fine quality but of latter years has become diseased" or "of late years has not been profitable to the orchardist in some localities." There is no genetic basis, however, for believing that a fruit variety becomes "played out." Because Pryor's Red is known to be very susceptible to cedar-apple rust and other fungal diseases, a possible explanation is that diseases built up in orchards over many years, to the particular detriment of Pryor's Red.

Another anomaly about Pryor's Red is that virtually all early pomological texts and references state that the origin of this apple is either unknown or "probably Virginia." In fact, there is good information in the files of the USDA about the origin of Pryor's Red. This apple originated about 1775 on the top of a "considerable eminence" or hill on a farm in Botetourt County, Virginia, owned by a man named Pitzer. The original name of Pryor's Red was Pitzerhill from the facts of this origin. Later the farm was purchased by Luke Pryor, and this apple became known as either Big Hill or Pryor's Red. It seems to have been much better known in Virginia by the name Big Hill. Pryor's Red was introduced into Illinois in 1823 by a Mr. Dennis, using scions brought from Virginia, and it became popular in Illinois, Indiana, and Ohio, as well as in most southern states. Several references state that it is adapted to the piedmont of the South and eastern Virginia as well, requiring a deep, rich, warm soil for best results.

Writing for *Tilton's Journal of Horticulture* in 1869, a Kentucky orchardist describes Pryor's Red in these glowing terms: "that fine, aromatic, nutty flavor possessed by the incomparable Pryor's Red, which is the most luscious apple, to our taste, known to pomology."

An interesting observation concerns the variability of Pryor's Red when grown on different soils in different climates. Southern-grown fruit is almost always heavily russeted, whereas fruit grown in New York has little or no russet. Warder (1867) remarks that when grown near the Ohio River the fruit is quite flat, but on limestone soils in Indiana, Pryor's Red is round in shape. Northern-grown fruit is often striped, while southern fruit is mostly dull red under the russet. A distinctive feature is a cracking around the calyx in the basin, which seems to be present in all Pryor's Red apples.

I found two apple trees called Big Hill, one belonging to Lewis Umbarger of Wytheville, Virginia, and the other to Rev. M. D. Hart of West Jefferson, North Carolina. The apples are identical and are Pryor's Red.

Fruit medium to large, shape variable but usually roundish oblate, often oblique with unequal sides; skin thick, greenish or brownish yellow mostly overspread with dull red that is often broken into shades and streaks and dots and mostly covered with russet; stem short and thick in an acute, small, russeted cavity; calyx closed; basin small, shallow, brownish, cracked; flesh yellowish, tender, often not very juicy, fine-grained, subacid. Ripe October and a good keeper. Catalog listings: MD, VA, NC, SC, GA, AL, MS, LA, KY, TX, AR (1845–1906).

❖ **Plate 43.**

**PUMPKIN SWEET** (Pound Sweet, Lyman's Large Yellow, Lyman's Pumpkin Sweet, Round Sweet, Vermont Sweet, Rhode Island Sweet, Yankee Apple, Sweet Pumpkin): There are at least three apples named Pumpkin Sweet, but southern nurseries sold the apple described here.

Pumpkin Sweet and Pound Sweet are the same apple, which originated before 1834 in the orchard of S. Lyman of Manchester, Connecticut. The name comes from the large size and yellow skin of the fruit.

Downing (1878) calls Pumpkin Sweet "a very valuable apple for baking," and Beach (1905) says "one of the best sweet apples of its season for baking and for canning or stewing with quinces." Bernice Lawson, wife of Georgia nurseryman Jim Lawson, preferred "Pound Sweet" for apple preserves and also to fry. The tree is a biennial bearer, a tip bearer, and susceptible to fire blight. The fruit is not a very good keeper.

Fruit large to very large, roundish to roundish conical, sometimes oblong, often ribbed; skin thin, tough, smooth, pale green becoming yellow with whitish streaks near the stem, sometimes with a faint brownish red blush, often russeted in the South; dots conspicuous, whitish, more numerous near the calyx; stem very short and stout, often inserted under a lip, in a variable-shaped, russeted cavity; calyx open; basin small to medium in size, often wrinkled; flesh white tinged with yellow, firm, not very juicy, very sweet. Ripe August. Catalog listings as Pumpkin Sweet and Pound Sweet: MD, VA, NC, KY (1836–1904).

❧ **QUEEN:** This is one of several different apples called Queen or having the word Queen in the apple's name. This Queen comes from John Creech of Kentucky, who sent me scions from a tree in an old orchard about to be destroyed by a strip mine. It is a favorite of mine for fresh eating.

Fruit above medium to large, roundish conical, often lopsided, flattened on the ends; skin partly to mostly covered in red with darker, broken red stripes; dots russet, some areole; stem medium to long in a deep, narrow, russeted cavity, often with rays of russet over the top of the apple; calyx open; basin rather deep, corrugated; flesh yellowish, juicy, moderately crisp, subacid. Ripe September. No catalog listings.

❧ **RABUN BALD:** (Rabun): Listed as extinct in the first edition of this book. The rediscovery of Rabun Bald is one of the great delights of my apple-hunting career. Its rediscovery started with an article about old Georgia apples that I wrote for the free monthly magazine distributed to rural customers by Georgia Rural Electric Co-ops. A short time later I received a letter from Caroline Montague of Clayton, Georgia, telling me she had a seventy-year-old Rabun Bald apple tree in her yard. Her tree, there when she purchased the house, was identified by Louis Speed, who has lived next door since 1941. The Andy Hamby place, where Rabun Bald originated, is only three miles away. Caroline Montague's tree was started as a root sprout from an old Rabun Bald tree at the Hamby place and was planted at her house about 1932 by Howard Ledford, who lived where Ms. Montague now lives. Mr. Ledford's son confirmed these facts.

The 1906 *USDA Yearbook* calls Rabun Bald "one of the most promising new apples for the lower Appalachian region (western North Carolina, eastern Tennessee, and northern Georgia)." The original tree was found about 1890 by Andy Hamby while he was clearing land on his farm thirteen miles northeast of Clayton, Georgia. This location is a spur of Rabun Bald Mountain in Rabun County. Over two thousand trees of Rabun Bald had been planted by 1906 in commercial orchards around Clayton, Georgia, but it was unknown elsewhere and slowly died out. Its eating quality is highly praised in several references.

The tree is stocky, vigorous, and quite spreading in growth habit. The fruit is largely borne on spurs along older branches. Rabun Bald seems to be a heavy, biennial bearer with about half a crop in "off" years.

Fruit above medium to large, roundish oblate, slightly ribbed, often oblique; skin tough, smooth, mostly a rich yellow on shaded fruit but heavily splashed and striped with crimson on fruit exposed to the sun; dots numerous, often irregular in shape, russet; stem short and stout in a large, deep, russeted cavity; calyx closed or partly open; basin large, deep, gradually sloped, furrowed; flesh yellowish, fine-grained, breaking, juicy, mild, subacid. Ripe September/October. Catalog listings: NC, GA (1910–24). ❖ **Plate 44.**

❧ **RAINBOW:** A Missouri apple sold by Stark Bro's Nursery around 1900 and listed by a Virginia nursery from 1898 to 1901. Tom Burford found Rainbow some years ago.

Fruit very large, conical; skin yellow with stripes and splashes of scarlet and red; flesh yellow, fine-grained, juicy. Ripe August/September.

**RALLS JANET** (Rawle's Janet, Geneton, Neverfail, Rawle's Genet, Jeniton, Gennetting, Jannetting, Rock Rimmon, Rock Remain, Raul's Genet, Rollings Jenneting, Rock of Remon, Jefferson Pippin, Red Neverfail, Royal Janette, Winter Genneting, Yellow Janette, Rock of Ammon, Rholl, Winter Neverfail, Gray Romanite, Missouri Janet?, Copper Schmidt, Indiana Jannetting, Lauback): The origin of this great southern apple caused much comment among pomologists in the mid-1800s. What is known without question is that it first came to notice in this country in the 1790s, being grown by Caleb Ralls (1750–1823) in Amherst County, Virginia. Caleb Ralls operated a small nursery on his farm, and the question is whether Mr. Ralls originated/found this apple locally or received it from somewhere else. (Incidentally, the spelling of the name Ralls was also disputed for a hundred years—usually being spelled Rawles or sometimes Raules in old catalogs and references. In 1903 the USDA wrote to the clerk of Amherst County for clarification. He dug up a deed from Caleb Ralls, dated September 1802, on which the name in the body of the deed and the signature were both spelled R-A-L-L-S.)

Caleb Ralls came from an apple-growing family. His grandfather, John Ralls, listed his Virginia farm for sale in a 1771 Virginia newspaper, "The Plantation is in good order with a very fine apple orchard from which are made seven or eight thousand gallons of cider a year. (That quantity has been made on average ever since the year 1756.) The trees are of the best kind of fruit, and the cider as good as any on the continent."

The most conservative and believable theory concerning the origin of Ralls Janet is that it originated as a seedling on the farm of Caleb Ralls or somewhere nearby and was named Janet by him. As far as is known, Mr. Ralls left no records about this apple. The name Janet may be a spelling variation on the old English name Jennet or Genit, which originally meant a crossbreed or hybrid. The English had several apples called Genit and some of these were grown in colonial times in America. For example, in 1786 George Washington planted a "Booth's Genitan" on his farm in Virginia. It is worth noting that Reuben Ragan, a noted Ohio pomologist and father of W. H. Ragan (who authored *Nomenclature of the Apple*, 1905), placed early Kentucky nurseryman Edward Darnaby and the Ralls Janet apple in central Kentucky in 1790. Reuben Ragan's date of 1790 contradicts Dr. W. M. Howsley's date of 1795 for the introduction of Ralls Janet into Kentucky. See Dr. Howsley's explanation below.

A more implausible theory is that Ralls Janet originated in France. This idea was first advanced in an 1853 letter to the *Western Horticultural Review* magazine, signed only with the initials J. S.:

> I will give you the history of what I presume you call the Rawles Geneting, as related to me by Mr. John Brown, one of the present U.S. Senators from the State of Kentucky. His statement was this—that it was introduced into this country from Normandy in France, by Mr. Genet, the French Minister, about sixty years ago, during the administration of George Washington. Mr. Genet married a daughter of Gov. Clinton of New York and settled on a farm near Albany. He noticed that the apples there were very often killed by spring frosts, and as this apple puts forth its blossoms about two weeks later than other kinds, he concluded that it could be advantageously introduced into American orchards. Senators Brown and Breckenridge introduced it into Kentucky, and it soon became so popular as to constitute the greater portion of the orchards in that state. If the history I send is correct, (of which there is not a doubt) the tree should be called the Normandy Geneting.

Dr. W. M. Howsley, president of the Kansas Horticultural Society, presented to the 1871 meeting of the American Horticultural Society a full-blown explanation of the origin of Ralls Janet:

> Rawles' Genet is the proper spelling of the name of this apple, and not Janet,

as it is usually spelled. We derive the name of Rawles' Genet in the following manner. During the administration of Gen. Washington, M. Genet was sent to Washington as minister of the government of France. [*Note*: M. Genet arrived in this country in 1793.] Mr. Thomas Jefferson, being at the time Secy. of State for General Washington, was frequently thrown into the company of M. Genet, especially at their dinner parties. By this means Mr. Jefferson became acquainted with and so admired this apple, which M. Genet had sent from France for his own use, that he, Jefferson, procured scions of this variety. He handed them over to Mr. Rawles, a nurseryman and fruit grower in Virginia, for propagation. Mr. Rawles grew trees from these scions and introduced the fruit to the public under the name of Genet Apple. Scions of this apple were brought to Kentucky in the year 1795 by a nurseryman named Edward Darnaby, who commenced a nursery not far from Harrodsburg, and within a mile or two of a gentleman by the name of Robert Ragan, the father of the late lamented Reuben Ragan, of Fillmore, Indiana. When Mr. Darnaby introduced it into Kentucky, the apple was called Genet, afterwards Genit, and about the year 1810 it was called Geniton. Never, until after 1810, was it called Rawles' Janet, and not until after this time was the last half of the name commenced with Ja instead of Ge. Within our own recollection this apple was, in the vicinity of Lexington, Kentucky, called by the name of Jefferson Pippin, this showing the connection of Mr. Jefferson with the introduction of this apple to public notice. Many of the foregoing facts are within our own knowledge, others we obtained from Mr. Ragan during his lifetime, and the balance from Dr. Thompson, who was raised in Lexington, Kentucky, and to whom we are indebted for many of the facts in regard to the history of this fine apple. We, therefore, consider that from the part which Mr. Rawles performed in introducing this apple to the fruit growers of the Southwest, that it is highly appropriate to prefix his name to the apple and spell it properly, R-a-w-l-e-s' G-e-n-e-t.

In concluding this discussion on the origin of Ralls Janet, it must be pointed out that there is a complete lack of substantiation for the idea that Ralls Janet was brought to this country by M. Genet and given to Thomas Jefferson or anyone else. None of the three major players—Caleb Ralls, Thomas Jefferson, or M. Genet—left any written records to back up this theory. Thomas Jefferson in particular was vitally interested in agriculture and was a careful keeper of journals. It is inconceivable that he would not have commented on the origin of Ralls Janet, which had become a very popular apple before Mr. Jefferson died in 1824. Furthermore, there is no record of an apple identical to Ralls Janet ever having been grown in Normandy, France. Finally, the name Jefferson Pippin most likely originated because the apple was widely grown in Jefferson County, Kentucky.

The major area for growth of Ralls Janet during the 1800s more or less coincided with the area later usurped by Ben Davis, a wide swath extending from Virginia westward through the Ohio Valley and on into Kansas, Missouri, and Arkansas. In this area, Ralls Janet had the reputation of being a good keeper of fine eating quality and attractive enough to be a market apple. In this area also, Ralls Janet was completely displaced by Ben Davis by 1900. Further south, although widely grown, Ralls Janet was often less successful, sometimes rotting badly on the tree. The conventional wisdom advanced in old references is that Ralls Janet requires deep, rich, loamy soils to do well. However, in 1908 the USDA found that Ralls Janet did quite well on clay soils. Stark Bro's Nursery sold Ralls Janet under the name Jeniton in the 1920s. They also sold a Giant Jeniton at the same time, touted as larger than Ralls Janet but with the same appearance and flavor. Giant

Jeniton originated in Lewis County, Missouri, by J. W. Johnson.

When grown on seedling rootstocks, the tree of Ralls Janet is smaller than most and bears heavily almost every year. This heavy bearing tends to make the fruit small so that considerable thinning of young fruit is required to have apples of marketable size. A most valuable characteristic of Ralls Janet is its tendency to bloom and leaf out very late, thus often escaping late frosts. This late-blooming trait gives Ralls Janet its synonym of Neverfail, a name better known to many rural southerners than the name Ralls Janet. It was this late blooming, plus the quality of the fruit, that led to the use of Ralls Janet as one parent of the popular apple Fuji, from a cross made by the Japanese in 1940 at an agricultural experiment station in northern Japan and introduced in 1962. Ralls Janet is susceptible to fire blight and has a twiggy growth habit that requires careful, annual pruning.

Fruit below to above medium, larger if properly thinned, roundish oblate, conical; skin yellow or greenish, blushed and mottled pinkish red and striped with darker red or crimson on the sunny side, often with a light bloom that gives the fruit a dull appearance; dots numerous, small, whitish or russet; stem medium to long and slender in a deep, brown, often furrowed cavity, sometimes with a fleshy protuberance; calyx usually open; basin rather wide, often shallow, cracked; flesh whitish yellow, fine-grained, crisp, juicy, mild subacid. Ripe October and an excellent keeper. Catalog listings: MD, DC, VA, NC, SC, GA, AL, LA, TN, KY, TX, AR (1824–1926). ❖ **Plate 45.**

❦ **RAMBO** (Bread and Cheese, Romanite of New Jersey, Terry's Red Streak, Seek-No-Further, Delaware, Fall Romanite, Gray Romanite, Striped Rambo, Trumpington, Winter Rambo): This quotation from an 1878 Virginia nursery catalog pretty well sums up Rambo: "One of the best early winter apples for the piedmont and [Shenandoah] Valley districts, and stands at the head of the list of autumn apples in the Tidewater section." From studying old southern catalogs, it appears that Rambo was little grown south of North Carolina. When grown in the North or in the mountains, Rambo is smaller, more solid, and keeps better than when grown in warmer areas. The trees bear moderate crops annually.

Several early references say Rambo originated in Delaware but others cite Pennsylvania. It became very popular in the 1800s in Pennsylvania and throughout the Ohio Valley. Some believe it originated with John Chapman, better known as "Johnny Appleseed," but this is very doubtful.

Recent information has shed new light on the origin of the Rambo, and I thank Peggy C. Troxell of Hillsborough, North Carolina, for bringing it to my attention. She is a direct descendent of Peter Gunnarson Rambo. Her information is as follows: "In 1640, the twenty-seven-year-old Swede, Peter Gunnarson Rambo, arrived in the Swedish colony of New Sweden on the Delaware River. In his pocket were seeds of a Swedish apple from which the Rambo apple originated. Peter Rambo became a man of prominence and served under Swedish, Dutch, and English governments in Delaware. His apple was first mentioned and its origin described in a supplement to the book *Travels in North America, 1747–1751*, written by the noted Swedish naturalist Per Kalm."

In 2008, scions of the Rambo apple were sent to Sweden as a gift from Swedish-Americans. Trees were grafted in Sweden and planted at several important cultural and historical locations.

Fruit medium or above, usually roundish to rather oblate, but sometimes may be roundish oblong; skin thin, mottled with red and striped with carmine, often mostly red, often with a bloom; dots numerous, rather large, conspicuous, whitish or russet; stem medium length in an acute, wide, deep, usually greenish or russeted cavity; calyx closed; basin wide, often furrowed; flesh greenish white, firm, fine-grained, very crisp, tender, juicy, aromatic, subacid. Ripe September/October. Catalog listings: MD, DC, VA, NC, AL, TN, KY, TX, AR (1824–1928).

❦ **RATTLE CORE** (Rattler, Rattle-Box?, Hollow Core Pippin?): From West Virginia to western North Carolina, one can find peculiar apples that have loose seeds in a hollow core that make an audible rattle when the fruit is shaken. In West Virginia it is the Rattler; in North Carolina it is Rattle Core. From 1869 to 1904 the Franklin Davis Nursery in Richmond listed but did not describe an apple called Hollow Core Pippin, and Downing (1878) describes what is probably this same apple under the name Rattle-Box. Jonah Parker of Moravian Falls, North Carolina, has an apple named Rattle Core and gave me scions. It is described as follows.

Fruit medium, roundish, prominently lobed from top to bottom; skin pale yellow thinly striped with red; dots few, russet; stem short to medium length in a slightly russeted cavity; calyx prominent, closed; basin shallow, corrugated; flesh white, tender, juicy, mild subacid. Seeds rattle audibly when the apple is shaken. Ripe July.

❦ **RAWLEY** (Raleigh): Rawley Duncan Stallard (1771–1856) played a fife to entertain Revolutionary War soldiers in Virginia when he was nine years old. He later amassed considerable land on the Clinch River in Virginia. Family lore is that Rawley Stallard planted seven "clusters" of apple trees on his land and named the clusters for his seven sons. One cluster was Samuel, one Peter, one Rawley (or Raleigh), etc. The Rawley trees produced far above the others, and the apple became popular in Scott County. An undated newspaper article says: "The home orchard which lasted more years than any other in Scott County was the cluster of trees planted by Rawley Stallard on the farm now owned by William Banner. It is a documented fact that some six or eight apple trees, without any expert care such as pruning or spraying, there grew and bore a bumper crop for more than one hundred and fifty years. This apple, the Raleigh apple, was named for Rawley Stallard, an early pioneer of Scott County."

Fruit medium, round, flattened on the ends; skin yellow, partly to mostly covered with bright red; dots almost large, scattered, whitish; stem medium to long in a wide, greenish or russeted cavity. Ripe September. No catalog listings.

❦ **REASOR GREEN** (Resor Green): From the 1887 catalog of Silver Leaf Nurseries, Lee County, Virginia: "New. Originated with Peter Reasor, Esq., of this county. Fruit above medium, roundish ovate, green with a faint blush, flavor mild subacid and excellent. The fruit dries when wounded instead of rotting; a reliable keeper. Highly valued where known. November to April."

The short discussion above, quoted from the chapter on extinct varieties in the first edition of this book, led directly to the rediscovery of the Reasor Green apple by Tim Hensley of Bristol, Virginia. (Tim's great-great-grandfather started and operated Silver Leaf Nurseries.) Reading that Reasor Green was considered extinct, Tim became determined to find it. This he was able to do with the help of Harold Jerrell, the agricultural extension agent for Lee County. Mr. Jerrell knew of a tree of Reasor Green still bearing fruit on the farm of Hap Slemp of Dryden, Virginia.

Tim Hensley now sells Reasor Green and many other heirloom apple trees through his small nursery in Bristol called The Urban Homestead.

❦ **REBEL** (American Rebel, America): A 1908 USDA report says: "The fine appearance and good dessert quality of the Rebel apple make it worthy of more general testing. In the middle piedmont region on Cecil clay, it does well and is of value." Rebel is a lovely apple, eliciting such comments in old nursery catalogs as "the prettiest apple that grows" and "one of the most showy apples in cultivation." Rebel originated about 1850 on the farm of Captain Charles B. Wood of Rappahannock County, Virginia.

Melvin Naumann of Flint Hill, Virginia, sent me some apples in 1999 with a note: "Would you please confirm that these are the 'Rebel' apple variety?" They were, indeed, the Rebel, matching an existing color plate and written description very closely. Mr. Naumann grafted four trees in 1997 from a single old Rebel tree belonging to a Mr. Jenkins and called Rebel by him. Mr. Naumann provided me with scions.

Fruit medium, round to roundish oblate; skin red on a yellow background, often heavily striped, usually with a bloom; dots numerous, small, gray; stem medium to almost long in a wide, deep, russeted cavity; basin wide, corrugated, usually shallow; flesh yellowish white, subacid. Ripe September. Catalog listings: MD, VA, NC, AL, TN, AR (1894–1923). ❖ **Plate 46.**

❦ **RED ASTRACHAN** (Red Ashmore, Early Rus, Deterding's Early, Abe Lincoln, Red Astracan, Astrakan, Astrachan Red, Hamper's American, American Red, Captain, Red Astragen?, Mississippi Red?, Mannington?, Early Red): With the single exception of Winesap, no other apple variety was more widely sold by southern nurseries than Red Astrachan. It is listed in old nursery catalogs from every southern state including Florida. Around 1900 Red Astrachan was certainly the most widely distributed apple variety in the world. It was popular in the United States, Canada, Sweden, Norway, Poland, Germany, England, Belgium, France, and Russia.

Many old references state emphatically that Red Astrachan is the best of the very early apples. It is a lovely red apple with skin usually quite smooth and clear, covered with a heavy white bloom. Its earliness and red color make Red Astrachan a good apple for local markets, but its ease of bruising limits its ability to be shipped. For an early apple it has fair eating quality but quickly becomes mealy when overripe. Most people would probably consider Red Astrachan a bit tart for fresh eating but a superior cooker, especially good for pies. Applesauce from this apple has a delicate reddish tinge. It develops a strong quince flavor when cooked, and this flavor comes through in jelly made from Red Astrachan apples. Like many other early apples, the tartness of Red Astrachan is subdued when it is fully ripe, at which time it is acceptable for fresh eating. The tree is vigorous, a late bloomer, and an annual bearer but is susceptible to apple scab and often has light crops.

Red Astrachan apples develop a distinct "bloom" or powdery coating on the skin of each apple. Writing about Red Astrachan in 1870, a man said: "The fruit must be ripened on the tree or else it will soon rot. If picked before the bloom is fully matured, it will decay before it mellows, and even before the decay, the flavor will be deficient. Its ripeness may be ascertained correctly by the finished ripeness of the bloom."

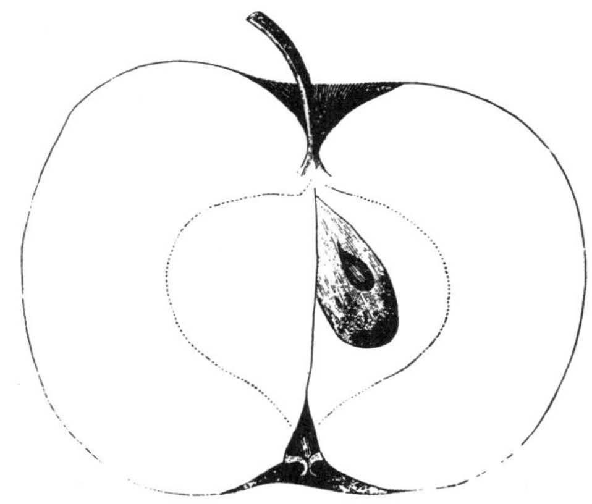

RED ASTRACHAN

This popular American apple originated in Russia. It was subsequently grown in Sweden and from there trees were imported into England before 1816. Red Astrachan was one of the first Russian apple varieties to reach America, being received by the Massachusetts Horticultural Society from London in 1835. A mere ten years later it was listed by a nursery in Kentucky.

Fruit below to above medium, roundish to slightly oblate, usually lobed; skin thin, smooth, nearly covered with bright red, sometimes with indistinct crimson stripes, with a heavy bloom much like a plum; dots numerous, prominent, white; stem medium to long in an acute and russeted cavity with the russet often extending well out over the top of the apple; calyx closed; basin shallow, often broadly lobed; flesh white often tinged red, rather coarse, crisp, moderately juicy, aromatic, acid to brisk subacid. Ripe June/July. Catalog listings: MD, VA, NC, SC, GA, FL, AL, MS, LA, TN, KY, TX, AR (1845–1928). ❖ **Plate 47.**

❦ **RED BIETIGHEIMER** (Beitigheimer, Bietigheimer, Bodenheimer): This old German apple was brought to this country before 1880. In Europe, Red Bietigheimer was first described in 1598, where it was known by the name Roter Stettiner. The fruit is notable mostly for its large size and lovely color as its coarse, rather tough flesh makes it mainly a cooking apple. Because of their large size, the apples tend to drop badly before ripening.

Fruit large to very large, roundish to roundish

oblate, slightly conical, lobed; skin thick, tough, smooth, mostly covered with light and dark red with some obscure stripes; dots numerous, prominent, grayish or light-colored; stem short to medium and thick in an acute, broad, sometimes furrowed, lipped, russeted cavity; calyx closed; basin varies from shallow to deep, somewhat wrinkled, often with prominent knobs; flesh white, firm, coarse, not very juicy, somewhat tough, briskly subacid. Ripe August/September. Catalog listings: MD, NC, VA, GA, AL, LA, TN, KY (1884–1925).

**RED CANADA** (Steele's Red Winter, Canada Redstreak, Old Nonsuch, Red Winter, Winter Nonsuch, Nonsuch, Nonesuch, Richfield Nonsuch, Poland, Bullman, Donahoe, Real Nonsuch, Welch's Spitzenburg, Washington Pearmain): Although eleven southern nurseries sold this variety before 1904, there is no information on its performance in the South. As grown in New York and described by Beach (1905), Red Canada is a lovely apple of superior eating quality, suitable as a market fruit. In New York it was found to be best adapted to fertile soils, and the fruit was of poorer quality when the trees were grown on heavy clay soils.

The origin of Red Canada is obscure, but it probably originated in New England before 1822. It was grown extensively in New York and Michigan around 1900, and in Michigan it was called Steele's Red Winter.

Fruit medium, sometimes larger, roundish to oblate, somewhat conical; skin mostly covered with red, with red stripes particularly on the sunny side; dots numerous, conspicuous, gray and greenish, often areolar; stem short to medium length in a broad, deep, often russeted cavity; calyx closed; basin small, narrow, furrowed; flesh white, tender, crisp, very juicy, rather fine-grained, aromatic, subacid. Ripe September/October and a good keeper but tends to shrivel in storage. Catalog listings: MD, VA, NC, AL, KY (1855–1904).

**RED CATHEAD** (Cathead): A Virginia apple first described in 1853 and listed by Virginia nurseries from 1873 to 1880. Said by Downing (1878) to have been grown extensively in eastern and southwestern Virginia. Tree bears regularly and heavily.

Fruit large, roundish conical; skin partly to completely shaded with red, sometimes with faint stripes; dots numerous, prominent, whitish and russet, some areole; stem short to medium length in a deep russeted cavity; calyx open; basin large; flesh yellowish, tender, juicy, subacid. Ripe September/October.

**RED CHEESE:** Sold by North Carolina nurseries from 1853 to 1902. I rediscovered this variety in 1989 in an old mountain orchard near Fries, Virginia, belonging to John and Val Green, two bachelor brothers over eighty years old. The orchard, which contained several rare apple varieties besides Red Cheese, was grafted and set out by their mother before 1900. The brothers said Red Cheese makes superior apple butter and the tree is very productive.

Val Green was blinded by a dynamite blast in 1934 while working on a road crew. Even so, he stood on his porch where he pointed out to me and named every tree in the old orchard down the hill from the house. *See* San Jacinto.

Fruit medium, roundish conical, occasionally nearly oblong, often oblique; skin smooth, mostly covered with red and some darker stripes; dots small, numerous, white or russet; stem short to almost long in a deep, russeted cavity; calyx closed; basin medium size; flesh yellowish white, crisp, juicy, subacid. Ripe July and sometimes early August. ❖ **Plate 48.**

**RED DELIGHT** (Dixie Red Delight, Red Joy?): Oren T. Bowman, Sr., of Sylacauga, Alabama, was a minister who practiced horticulture as a hobby. He grew this apple probably from a seed of Yellow Transparent, and it was patented in 1960 by the Commercial Nursery Company of Dechert, Tennessee. Trees were sold by the Hastings Seed Company of Atlanta in the 1960s and 1970s. Writing in *Pomona* magazine, a man said: "Red Delight fruits are sprightly, crisp, sweet and all the other things a good apple should be. The spring blossom is an ornamental pink. Fireblight can be a problem." The trees are vigorous and tend to bloom late. A tree was found some years ago by Alabama nurserywoman Joyce Neighbors.

Fruit above medium to large, roundish to oblate, lobed; skin smooth, mostly covered with a dark reddish blush; dots numerous, whitish, large at the stem end but smaller near the basin; stem short in a narrow, deep, greenish cavity; calyx open; basin small, acute, deep, greenish; flesh white, firm, juicy, mild subacid. Ripe September/October.

❦ **RED DETROIT** (Norga, Cherokee): There are two different apples, a northern apple called Detroit Red and a southern apple called Red Detroit, which has caused considerable confusion. The northern apple, Detroit Red, probably was introduced by early French settlers into the area around Detroit, Michigan. As grown in Ohio, Michigan, and New York, this apple is of high quality with a mild flavor, but this northern apple has never been important in the South.

The southern apple called Red Detroit is of unknown origin but has been grown for almost a century in north Georgia, especially around the town of Blue Ridge. It is still grown commercially to some extent in northern Alabama and southeast Tennessee. This southern apple was examined by USDA pomologists in 1924 and found to be different from the northern Detroit Red. At that time the USDA suggested the name of Cherokee for this southern apple to avoid confusion with the northern apple, but this name never caught on with growers who sometimes call this apple Norga. The Red Detroit tree blooms late, and the fruit is excellent for drying. *See* Cherokee Red.

Fruit medium, roundish, flattened on the ends, often oblique; skin almost covered with dark red except where shaded by a leaf; dots numerous, small, reddish and gray; stem long in a narrow, slightly russeted cavity; calyx greenish, closed; basin medium size, shallow, sometimes corrugated; flesh whitish, coarse, moderately crisp and juicy, subacid. Ripe late August/September. No catalog listings.

❦ **RED HACKWORTH:** Likely a seedling of Hackworth originating about 1900 in either Morgan County or Cullman County, Alabama. It was introduced about 1925 by the Empire Nursery and Orchard of Baileyton and is considered well adapted to Alabama soils and climate. Red Hackworth often has been propagated by root sprouts. Joyce Neighbors found two trees of Red Hackworth in 1998 being grown by Lowell Landers, who lives only a few miles from Cullman, Alabama. The fruit is smaller, firmer, and redder than Hackworth.

Fruit medium or below, roundish; skin mostly covered with medium red and faint, darker stripes; dots numerous, large, pale; stem medium in a narrow, russeted cavity; calyx closed; basin lobed; flesh yellowish, fine-grained, moderately crisp and juicy, sweet. Ripe August/September.

❦ **RED INDIAN:** An apple of this name was sold in 1858 by Staunton Nurseries of Staunton, Virginia, without description. An apple named Red Indian Sweet, of North Carolina origin, was sold by Lawson's Nursery in Georgia in the 1980s, but nothing is known of its origin.

❦ **RED REBEL:** Nurserywoman Joyce Neighbors of Gadsden, Alabama, found a tree called Red Rebel in an orchard planted in the 1930s on her sister-in-law's farm near Wedowee, Alabama. No one knows where this variety originated. The tree is very productive and appears to be disease-resistant. The skin can be rather bitter, and the apple should be peeled.

Fruit medium or below, round; skin thick, mostly to entirely covered with purplish red and occasionally some inconspicuous stripes; dots numerous, small, gray; stem almost long and often pushed to one side in a small, narrow, russeted cavity; calyx closed; basin abrupt, corrugated; flesh greenish white, fine-grained, moderately juicy and crisp, subacid. Ripe August/September. No catalog listings.

❦ **RED REESE** (Reese?, Reese Red): A Reese apple, said to have originated before 1915 with C. W. Ewing of Mountainboro, Alabama, is described as medium, roundish conical; irregular; skin greenish yellow splashed with red; flesh mild subacid; ripe September in Alabama. This is certainly the same apple as the Red Reese that originated in Randolph County, Alabama, and that first fruited in 1911. Tree is said to be very disease-resistant with the fruit resembling a small Red Delicious apple. Joyce Neighbors found Red Reese in the orchard of Doyle Baker, Fayette County, Alabama.

Fruit medium or above, roundish to oblong and very conical; skin partly to mostly covered with lovely red; dots numerous, small to medium size, gray and russet; stem medium length in a narrow, deep, russeted cavity with some russet sometimes over the top of the apple; calyx partly open; basin round, very corrugated; flesh almost sweet. Ripe early October. No catalog listings.

❦ **RED WINTER SWEET:** Although sold only by a Kentucky nursery in 1870, Downing (1878) says it originated in Virginia or Maryland. There are records of a cider apple named Red Sweet being grown in Virginia in colonial times. An apple named Red Winter Sweet is grown in western North Carolina. The description here is taken from Downing.

Fruit medium, roundish conical; skin yellow mostly covered with deep red with indistinct stripes; dots large and small, light-colored; stem short in a small cavity; calyx closed; flesh yellow, slightly coarse, very sweet. Ripe late.

❦ **REGENT:** The Tennessee apple hunter and my late friend, Don Stocker, found Regent trees several places in his state. It is not a very old apple but is rare in the South. Regent originated as a cross of Red Duchess × Delicious made in 1924 at the University of Minnesota Fruit Breeding Farm. The quality of the fruit and its keeping ability, plus a vigorous, high-yielding tree, all recommend Regent. Some people detect a banana flavor and aroma from Regent apples.

Fruit medium, roundish to oblong, conical; skin tough, glossy, light yellow with bright red and redder stripes, often completely red; dots white or corky, rather small; stem medium length in a wide, shallow, russeted cavity; calyx closed; basin small, deep, bumpy; flesh creamy white, crisp, very juicy; "flavor suggestive of Delicious but more sprightly." Ripe September/October. No catalog listings.

❦ **REPUBLICAN PIPPIN:** Originated in Lycoming County, Pennsylvania, and sold by nine southern nurseries. The tree has a crooked growth habit and is moderately productive. The fruit is good for cooking and drying. An apple called Republican was grown by Swanzie Shepherd in his old orchard in Ashe County, North Carolina. The tree blew over in 1998, but scions were obtained the year before by my friend Jim Yates.

Fruit large, oblate, irregular; skin mostly shaded with red, obscurely striped and marbled; dots few, large and gray; stem long and slender; calyx closed; flesh whitish, tender, juicy, subacid. Ripe September. Catalog listings: VA, NC, SC, KY (1855–1904).

❦ **REVEREND MORGAN:** This southern apple is not old, but its quality and adaptability to warmer areas of the South make it worthy of preservation. It originated in 1972 in Houston, Texas (Zone 9) and is named for Rev. Herman T. Morgan (b. 1894), the Methodist minister who first grew this apple. It is believed to be a seedling of Granny Smith and seems to be resistant to several apple diseases. In 1983, Jim Lawson of Ball Ground, Georgia, was the first person to propagate and sell Reverend Morgan apple trees. He heard about the apple from the Agricultural Extension Agent in Houston.

Fruit medium or above, roundish conical; skin pale greenish mostly covered with pinkish red; dots numerous, rather large, whitish; stem slender and medium length in a deep, abrupt, tannish russeted cavity; calyx open; basin wide, round; flesh whitish, crisp, juicy, fine-grained, mild subacid. Ripe August. No catalog listings.

❦ **REXRODE BEAUTY:** In 1993 I wrote a letter to the Elkins, West Virginia, newspaper asking readers to let me know if they had old apple varieties. Walter Lesser, a wildlife biologist who works for the state of West Virginia, wrote me back listing a number of old varieties he had in his orchard (which I already had) including Rexrode Beauty (a new discovery!). The family with the remaining Rexrode Beauty tree tells the story of an ancestor who walked thirty miles from Elkins to Buckhannon to obtain scions. Rexrode, incidentally, is a West Virginia family name.

Fruit almost large, roundish, flattened on the ends; skin mostly covered with light red or an orangish red blush; dots large and small, numerous, whitish; stem long in a wide, deep, slightly russeted cavity; basin broad, gradually sloped, irregular. Ripe October. No catalog listings.

❦ **RHODE ISLAND GREENING** (Rhode Island, Burlington Greening, Greening, Hampshire Greening, Jersey Greening, Russine, Green Winter Pippin): In 1900 this apple was second only to Baldwin in commercial orchard acreage in New York. Like Baldwin, Rhode Island Greening is a famous northern apple that does well in the South only at higher elevations. When northern grown, the fruit is a good keeper and shipper and one of the best cooking apples in America. Additionally, Rhode Island Greening is a fine apple for fresh eating, its tartness being preferred by many people. It is the American equivalent of the Granny Smith apple (which originated in Australia), only much, much better.

The tree is best adapted to friable, well-drained soils and is a biennial or, if properly thinned, an annual bearer. It is very susceptible to apple scab, and in warmer areas of the South the fruit often drops from the tree before ripe or rots on the tree. The USDA said in 1908: "In most southern locations, it lacks nearly all points of merit."

The generally accepted story is that Rhode Island Greening originated before 1700 in a seedling orchard near Newport, Rhode Island, belonging to a tavern keeper named Green. People who stopped at the tavern so appreciated this unique apple that the original tree was killed by excessive cutting of scions for grafting.

Fruit large, uniform in size and shape, roundish, slightly flattened on the ends; skin waxy, dark green becoming greenish yellow when ripe, sometimes with a brownish red blush near the stem, sometimes russeted when grown in the South; dots numerous, gray; stem medium length in an acute, medium-size, sometimes russeted cavity; calyx closed; basin small to medium size, sometimes slightly furrowed; flesh yellow, fine-grained, tender, crisp, juicy, aromatic, sprightly subacid. Ripe September/October and keeps well. Catalog listings: MD, VA, NC, SC, AL, KY, AR (1824–1928).

❦ **ROANOKE:** This is another apple variety bred by Dr. George D. Oberle at VPI. A cross of Red Rome × Schoharie introduced in 1967. The tree is productive and blooms late.

Fruit round; skin almost entirely red; flesh firm, mild subacid. Ripe September. No catalog listings.

❦ **ROBERTSON RED** (Robertson's Red, Robertson's Red Streak?, Roberson Red, Robinson Red, Red Robinson): This apple originated in Robertson County, Tennessee, and was grown in Kentucky, Indiana, and Illinois in the 1870s. It was sold by a Kentucky nursery in 1870: "A better keeper than Rome Beauty or Ben Davis."

Fruit medium, roundish, flattened on the ends; skin mostly covered with a dark red blush and some obscure stripes; dots scattered, whitish; stem short in a narrow, abrupt, deep, russeted cavity; calyx closed; basin smooth, gradually sloped. Ripe October and an excellent keeper.

❦ **ROMANITE** (Broad River, Little Red Romanite, Southern Romanite, Romanite of the South, Sweet Romanite?): Romanite is so confounded with Gilpin in the South that it is often impossible to disengage the two varieties. Although Romanite and Gilpin are different apples, the brief descriptions in old southern catalogs can fit either one, and the name Romanite was often listed as a synonym of Gilpin in old catalogs and pomological references. Romanite was used also as a synonym of Rambo and Pennock. To further muddy the waters, southerners often confused Romanite with Shockley because the two have very similar fruit. The branches of the Romanite tree are said to be pendant and short-jointed, and the tree is a heavy, regular bearer.

Fruit small to almost medium, roundish to oblong, conical; skin mostly overspread with clear red; dots few, indistinct, light colored; stem slender in a fairly deep, acute, smooth cavity; basin wide, abrupt, and almost shallow; flesh yellowish, fine-grained, juicy, mild subacid to almost sweet. Can be used in July for cooking but usually ripe in September/October. Catalog listings as Romanite (but many of these listings are probably Gilpin): MD, VA, NC, DC, GA, MS, TN, KY, AR, TX (1824–1925).

❦ **ROMAN STEM:** I keep this old New Jersey apple because it is a good apple on a very productive tree. It originated before 1868 and was sold by a nursery in Arkansas in the early 1900s.

Fruit medium, roundish; skin pale greenish, often with bronzing or pale pink on the sunny side and often with some russet patches; stem medium to almost short in a cavity that is usually russeted and sometimes contains a fleshy protuberance; basin corrugated; flesh tender, juicy, almost sweet. Ripe September. ❖ **Plate 49.**

❧ **ROME BEAUTY** (Rome, Gillett's Seedling, Foust's Rome Beauty, Press Ewing?, Phoenix, Royal Red, Starbuck, Roman Beauty): Rome Beauty has been an important commercial apple in the eastern United States for over fifty years. Many people think of it as not the best apple for fresh eating but excellent for cooking. Although considered by Beach (1905) to be best adapted to the Ohio Valley, Rome Beauty is commercially grown in the South, from Alabama northward, usually in orchards at elevations of 1,000 feet or higher. Its commercial importance is rapidly waning.

From a commercial viewpoint, Rome Beauty has many good attributes. It is a large, beautiful apple that keeps very well and stands rough handling. The tree blooms late, begins bearing when young, usually is an annual bearer, and holds its apples well. On the negative side of the ledger, the tree is somewhat susceptible to apple scab and fire blight.

In the spring of 1817, Zebulon and Joel Gillett and their brother-in-law, Nathanial Pritchard, bought some fruit trees from Israel Putnam, a nurseryman in Marietta, Ohio. The young trees were carried by flatboat to newly purchased land in Quaker Bottom, Rome Township, Lawrence County, Ohio. Because Mr. Putnam's practice was to graft very low and pull dirt up over the graft, many of the young trees had thrown up sprouts from the seedling rootstock below the graft. The legend is that Joel Gillett pulled off a partially rooted sprout from the rootstock and handed it to his young son Alanson. Alanson planted the ungrafted root sprout in the corner of the orchard, and within a few years it began bearing large, red apples. It was named Rome Beauty for Rome Township and was first described in an 1846 issue of *The Magazine of Horticulture*. The original tree was washed away by the Ohio River in 1860. Since then, many redder sports or mutations of Rome Beauty have been found with several of them now commercially important.

Fruit large, sometimes very large, usually roundish but sometimes oblate or oblong, conical; skin thick, tough, smooth, almost entirely covered with bright red and striped with carmine; dots numerous, whitish or russet; stem long and slender in a wide, usually deep, greenish cavity; basin rather narrow, deep, abrupt; flesh yellowish, firm, rather crisp, juicy, sprightly subacid. Ripe September/October and keeps well. Catalog listings: MD, VA, NC, GA, AL, LA, TN, KY, TX, AR (1858–1928).

❧ **ROXBURY RUSSET** (Boston Russet, Putnam Russet, Howe's Russet, Belpre Russet, Marietta Russet, Russet Golden, Sylvan Russet, Warner Russet, Leather Coat, Shippen's Russet, Russet, Warren Russet): The russet apple, once so popular in America, is now an outcast in the marketplace. Americans of today, bombarded by the perfect, waxy, shiny apples in supermarkets, would consider a russet apple to be diseased and ugly. What a shame; a whole class of wonderful apples condemned by ignorance. Even beyond the often delicious flavor, the feel of the rough skin of a russet apple in the hand is a textural delight.

Although not of southern origin, Roxbury Russet was a widely grown russet in the South. Old trees are still encountered in the mountains of North Carolina and Virginia, bearing their rough, long-keeping fruit.

Roxbury Russet is the oldest American apple, originating in Roxbury, Massachusetts, within twenty years of the arrival of the Pilgrims. It was taken to Connecticut in 1649, and in the late 1700s was introduced into the Ohio Valley under the names Putnam Russet, Marietta Russet, and other synonyms. In the South outside the mountains, it is only a moderately good keeper, but mountain-grown and northern-grown Roxbury Russets are excellent keepers. The tree bears heavily annually, is healthy, and is said to be resistant to several apple diseases, including cedar-apple rust and scab. The fruit is often used for making cider.

Fruit medium, sometimes larger, variable in shape but usually roundish conical; skin dull green mostly

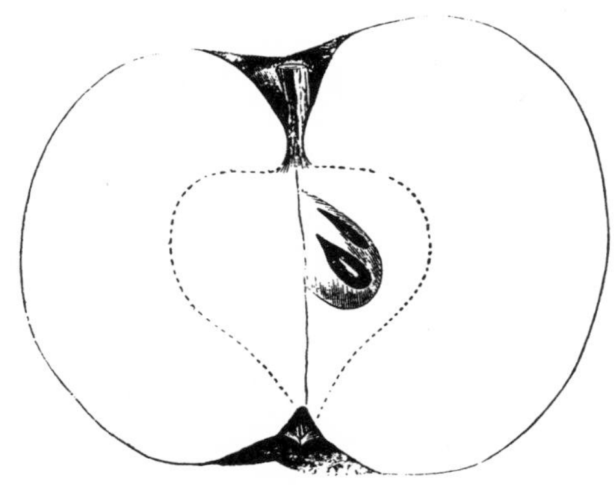

ROXBURY RUSSET

covered with a rough yellowish brown russet, sometimes with a bronze or reddish blush on the sunny side; dots numerous, tan; stem short to medium in an acute, narrow, sometimes lipped cavity; calyx closed; basin varies but usually is round and medium in width and depth; flesh greenish white, moderately juicy, firm, somewhat coarse, breaking, sprightly subacid. Ripe September/October. Catalog listings: MD, VA, NC, SC, GA, KY, TX (1845–1928).

❦ **RUSTY COAT:** There are many kinds of russet apples—American Golden Russet, Roxbury Russet, Sweet Russet, Keener Seedling, Pomme Grise, and others. Sooner or later, when the original name was forgotten, southerners would call any russet apple Rusty Coat. The confusion is increased because none of the old pomological references, such as Downing, Thomas, or Beach, lists or describes an apple named Rusty Coat, and the only southern catalog listing is by a 1916 Tennessee nursery. There may be a true and distinct Rusty Coat apple because a listing of apple trees planted in 1843 at the Snow Hill plantation near Durham, North Carolina, includes Rusty Coat. I found an old apple tree near Andrews Store in my county, called Rusty Coat by its owner, that I grow under the name Rusty Coat (Andrews). It appears to be different from other Rusty Coat apples and is described here.

Fruit small, roundish; skin covered with a tan russet; dots not visible; stem long in a small, shallow, corrugated cavity; calyx greenish, partly open; basin shallow and wide; flesh fine-grained, crisp, moderately juicy, mild subacid. Ripe late July.

❦ **SALLY GRAY:** Years ago, while waiting for a haircut, I struck up a conversation with the man sitting beside me. We began talking about apples, and he told me his uncle, Raymond Ferrell, in neighboring Wake County, North Carolina, had an apple tree called Sally Gray. I tracked the tree down and found that it had been grafted from a much older tree planted around 1900 by Mr. Ferrell's great uncle. This apple was grown in eastern North Carolina at one time because Frances Hinton, who lives in Nashville, North Carolina, remembers Sally Gray trees on her farm when she was young. Among other uses, her family dried the apples. Ragan (1905) lists a Sally Gray apple, which he thought was possibly of Kentucky origin.

We know that Sally Gray is a very old apple because it was listed for sale by a nursery in the November 4, 1763, *Virginia Gazette* newspaper. It was also included in the 1849 listing of a nursery in Stone Mountain, Georgia.

Fruit medium or below, roundish oblate; skin rough, light yellow, russeted at the stem end, with faint red stripes on the sunny side but much more red on fruit fully exposed to the sun; dots scattered, irregular, russet; stem short to long in a wide, medium depth, greenish cavity; calyx usually open; basin wide and rather shallow, often cracked; flesh crisp, juicy, brittle, fine-grained, compact, almost sweet. Ripe late July/August.

❦ **SALOME:** Originated about 1853 in a nursery in Ottawa, Illinois, and introduced in 1884. The tree is healthy, productive, hardy, resistant to scab, and holds its fruit well. As grown in the Ohio valley, the apples keep exceptionally well and are of good eating quality. The rather small size and poor color of the fruit doomed Salome for commercial production.

Fruit medium or below, roundish oblate, conical, often ribbed; skin tough, smooth, pale yellow mottled with pinkish red and obscurely striped with carmine, usually with a whitish bloom and often having some russet blotches and streaks; dots conspicuous, whitish or pale gray, often areolar with russet points; stem medium to long in an acute, deep, broad, thinly russeted cavity; calyx closed;

basin usually abrupt, rather narrow, furrowed; flesh tinged yellow, firm, crisp, tender, juicy, sprightly subacid. Ripe October. Catalog listings: MD, VA, KY, AR (1897–1925).

❦ **SAM APPLE:** Fay Farrow of Eastanollee, Georgia, wrote me in 1993: "I have two trees of this apple. It has been in my family over 100 years. The apples are medium size, yellow with red streaks and get ripe in July and August. We have always called it the Sam Apple. I am 83 years old and it has always been my favorite. I could send you some scions, if you wanted them."

Fruit medium, roundish conical; skin almost covered with brick red that is darker on the sunny side; dots rather numerous, gray, protruding, some with russet centers; stem medium length in a narrow, deep, greenish, slightly cracked cavity; calyx greenish, open; basin large, abrupt, deep; flesh crisp, moderately juicy, collapsing, mild subacid. Ripe August/September. No catalog listings.

❦ **SAM HUNT:** I quote from a letter written to me in 1995 by Sylvia Walker of Jackson, Mississippi: "After receiving your letter I decided to walk through the woods where our old orchard used to be. I was amazed to find a giant, gnarly apple tree still alive but consumed by the forest. We call it Sam Hunt because we got it from our uncle Sam. My mother says this very tree was old when she went there in 1929. I cut some young growth in hopes that you might be able to graft some trees."

Fruit medium or above, roundish, often oblique; skin partly to mostly covered with red and some obscure stripes; dots numerous, large and small, gray; stem medium length in a greenish or tan russeted cavity. Ripe September/October. No catalog listings.

❦ **SAM WHITSON:** Originated with Sam Whitson (1859–1952) on his farm on Bean's Creek in Mitchell County, North Carolina. Local farmers in the Honeycutt community prize this apple for applesauce and apple butter. An old tree was tracked down by the late Maurice Marshall, whose aunt was a granddaughter of Sam Whitson.

Fruit above medium to large, roundish conical; skin heavily striped with two shades of red; stem almost short; dots scattered, large, whitish. Ripe September. No catalog listings.

❦ **SAN JACINTO:** Some years before 1900, Dr. A. M. Ragland of Pilot Point, Texas, bought some apple trees labeled Mrs. Bryan from the Fruitland Nursery, Augusta, Georgia. Both he and the Munson Nursery of Denison, Texas, grafted and sold trees from these Georgia trees, calling them Mrs. Bryan. A few years later Dr. Ragland realized that the trees obtained from Georgia had been mislabeled and were not Mrs. Bryan at all, but were an unknown variety not identifiable by Fruitland Nursery or anyone else. Dr. Ragland then renamed this apple San Jacinto. Texas nursery catalogs usually described San Jacinto as a very large, Red June–type apple, ripening a week or ten days after Red June, and "regarded as one of the best varieties in north Texas, New Mexico and southern Kansas. Tree very prolific and holds its fruit well." As grown here and in South Carolina, San Jacinto appears identical to the old North Carolina apple Red Cheese.

Fruit medium, roundish, often oblique, sometimes slightly oblong, lobed; skin smooth, partly to mostly covered with pinkish red with broken darker red stripes; dots tiny, numerous, grayish, often areole; stem medium to long in a narrow, shallow, russeted, lumpy cavity; calyx large, green, open or closed; basin often irregular in shape, corrugated; flesh whitish, fine-grained, moderately crisp and juicy, mild subacid. Ripe July. ❖ **Plate 50.**

❦ **SCHELL** (Schull, Shell): A West Virginia apple first described in 1839 and sold in 1871 by the Fruitland Nursery, Augusta, Georgia. It is certainly the same apple as Schull, listed without description from 1869 to 1904 by the Franklin Davis Nursery of Richmond, Virginia.

Seldom do I encounter someone as persistent and enthusiastic about finding old apple varieties as I am. Dr. L. R. Littleton of Raleigh, North Carolina, was such a man. In January 1993 Dr. Littleton spotted some old apple trees while driving a back road near Maysville, West Virginia. He stopped to question a man on a tractor who directed him to some very old trees near a family cemetery. These ancient trees were the Schell apple, still being grown by Delmer Schell and Mr. and Mrs. Clarence Schell.

Fruit medium or above, roundish; often oblique and lobed; skin clear yellow, sometimes with a slight pinkish blush on the sunny side; dots few, submerged or russet; stem medium length and slender in a wide, deep, russeted cavity with the russet spilling out over the top of the fruit; calyx closed; basin rather small, medium depth; flesh yellowish, fine-grained, juicy, moderately crisp, mild subacid, very aromatic. Ripe August/September.

❧ **SCHUMACHER** (Shoemaker): T. C. Moss of Cameron, South Carolina, wrote me in 1996: "The story is that in the late 1700s a Mr. Shoemaker came from Germany and brought this apple with him when he settled in our area. A distant cousin of mine, a country doctor making his rounds, noticed the apple tree and asked for a sprout. He then propagated the Shoemaker apple and it has come down through the generations in our family." Another letter, from Wade Fairey of Rock Hill, South Carolina, gives more information: "This apple was given to my great-grandfather, Dr. Joseph Fairey, or to his wife's family, by the Schumachers, a German family who lived south of Crestor. My grandfather made sure each of his children and grandchildren received rootings from this family tree." Comparison proves Shoemaker and Schumacher are the same.

Fruit almost large, roundish conical, often irregular and oblique; skin yellow, partly to mostly covered with bright red with faint darker red stripes; dots numerous, faint, whitish or russet; stem short with a thickened end in a deep, narrow, lumpy, greenish or russeted cavity; calyx closed or open; basin abrupt, wide; flesh pale yellow, moderately crisp and juicy, subacid. Ripe late July/August. No catalog listings.

❧ **SCOTT'S WINTER** (Scott's Red Winter, Wilcox's Winter): A very hardy apple that originated about 1864 in Newport, Vermont. Sold by several southern nurseries as a red, good-quality, long-keeping apple that could be substituted for Roxbury Russet in commercial orchards.

Fruit medium or below, roundish; skin mostly covered with bright red and darker red stripes; dots inconspicuous, whitish or with russet centers; stem short in a narrow, deep, greenish cavity; calyx closed; basin abrupt, narrow, deep; flesh yellowish, juicy, not very crisp, fine-grained, subacid. Ripe September/October. Catalog listings: MD, VA, AR (1902–20).

❧ **SHEEPNOSE:** There are at least six apples named Sheepnose, and it is a synonym for several others. Any apple very pointed on the blossom end probably received this name (or perhaps "Ladyfinger") sooner or later. Yellow Bellflower is often called Yellow Sheepnose, and Black Gilliflower has been called Red Sheepnose. American Golden Russet has the synonym of Sheepnose.

Several Virginia nurseries listed a summer apple named Sheepnose from 1910 to 1928: "We have fruited it for several years and pronounce it the best eating apple we have seen for August. Fruit large at the base, tapering to the apex, covered with brown russet red. Tender and fine. Tree rather a crooked grower; said to live to a great age." This apple sounds like the Black Gilliflower.

An apple named "Sheepnose of Virginia" was tested at the Illinois Agricultural Experiment Station in the 1870s to 1890s, and was described as "above medium, oblong conical, pale lemon yellow, mild subacid, very good in quality, keeps through the winter." This apple has not yet been found and may be extinct.

❧ **SHELL:** It is hard to believe that down at the southern end of Alabama, just above the Florida panhandle, an apple industry developed in the late 1800s. The following information is from the *History of Escambia County Alabama* by Annie C. Waters:

> Green Shell was an enterprising agriculturist who was born in 1841. He planted an apple orchard near the intersection of present day highways 49 and 40, about 10 miles north of Brewton, Alabama. This enterprise developed into a business that gave the town its name—Appleton.
>
> His apple business had a large grading shed complete with shipping barrels and a

cider press. During harvest, Mr. Shell's son, Andrew, made two trips a day by wagon to deliver barrels of apples to the freight office in Brewton. They were shipped to northern markets as "Shell Apples." Culls were used for making jelly or cider.

Mr. Shell also grafted young trees, and soon nearly every other farm over a wide area had at least one "Shell" apple tree producing apples for family use. A few very old trees are believed to have survived in the area.

Daniel Mullins, Agricultural Extension Agent for Santa Rosa County, Florida, found an old Shell apple tree about 1995 and sent me scions from it in 2006. He also provided the above historical information. Here in central North Carolina, a two-year-old Shell apple tree bloomed in mid-February! Obviously it is a low-chill variety, but this young tree bore several truly delicious apples ripe in mid-July.

Fruit medium or above, roundish to oblate, conical, very irregular shaped; skin yellowish mostly covered with a bright red blush; dots very small, often areolar; stem very long in a narrow, deep, russeted, often lipped and irregular cavity; basin wide, surrounded by broad protrusions; flesh pale yellow, moderately crisp, juicy, almost sweet with a faint pear flavor. Ripe July. No catalog listings.

❦ **SHENANDOAH:** In the 1940s and 1950s, Dr. George D. Oberle did apple-breeding work at the Virginia Polytechnic Institute (VPI) in Blacksburg, Virginia. Shenandoah is a cross of Winesap × Opalescent made in 1942. Dr. Oberle thought this apple would be excellent for commercial applesauce and canning, but it never became popular and now is quite rare.

Fruit round, conical; skin waxy, tough, almost solid red; flesh firm, sprightly subacid to almost acid. Ripe September. No catalog listings.

❦ **SHERRILL:** Listed without description in 1902 by the Startown Nursery, Newton, North Carolina. Harold O. Punch of Hickory, North Carolina, sent me scions of this apple in 1988, but I later lost the only tree I had. In the year 2000, Tom Brown found an eighty-year-old tree of Sherrill in Catawba County, North Carolina, which had been cut down that very day and was lying on the ground. Tom obtained scions from the doomed tree and this old apple was saved.

Fruit medium, roundish conical; skin smooth, dull, almost covered with red and obscure stripes; dots numerous, rather large, grayish russet; stem medium to almost long in a wide, russeted cavity; calyx open or closed; basin wide, deep, abrupt; flesh quite yellowish, crisp, moderately juicy, rather coarse, mild subacid. Ripe October/November.

❦ **SHOCKLEY** (Waddell Hall, Sweet Romanite, Neverfail, Horse Bud, Dixie): If you study old southern apples, you eventually realize there were a few that could be counted on, year after year, to provide southern farm families with apples for eating, cooking, drying, and cider. These favorite varieties were sold continuously by nurseries as other apple fads rose and fell. Horse Apple and Winesap lead the list; Buckingham is there and Red June. Shockley, too, is one of this inner circle of apples that were grown all over the South. Many other apple varieties were of higher eating quality (Albemarle Pippin comes to mind), but for one or several reasons they never made it into this select group of reliable favorites.

The USDA said about Shockley in 1908: "It possesses many characteristics of merit in nearly the entire piedmont region from Virginia to Georgia. . . . Its abundant and regular bearing proclivities under most piedmont conditions and its unusually good keeping qualities make it worthy of consideration." The keeping ability of Shockley apples was legendary in the South at one time. An article in 1872 in *Carolina Farmer* magazine says: "The specimens we have are yet in perfect preservation this 6th day of August and are only a little shriveled, but of a color so intense that they look to be almost artificial. Mr. W. H. Thurmond, whose reputation as a horticulturist makes him a first rate authority, tells us he has known Shockley apples which were preserved two years." Shockley was said to be the best-keeping winter apple grown in Mississippi in 1877.

Shockley originated with a Mr. Shockley of Jackson County, Georgia, and was brought to public notice when exhibited at the Georgia State Fair in 1852. The tree has an upright growth habit and is very productive annually. The fruit hangs well on the tree.

Fruit medium size or often below, roundish; skin tough, smooth, mostly to almost completely overspread with bright red; dots few, gray; stem medium to long and slender in a deep, narrow, acute, slightly russeted cavity; calyx half closed; basin shallow and corrugated; flesh yellowish white, crisp, juicy, mild subacid to almost sweet. Ripe October. Catalog listings: MD, VA, NC, SC, GA, AL, MS, LA, TN, KY, TX, AR, FL (1856–1928). ❖ **Plate 51.**

❧ **SHORT CORE** (Garden Red, Short Core Winesap?): Originated before 1850 in an orchard belonging to a Mrs. Todd near Berea, Kentucky. Described by the USDA as a good dessert-quality apple borne on a small, productive tree.

This is from a letter to the USDA written in 1894 by W. L. Morgan, Canes Store, Pulaski County, Kentucky: "I would plant this for a winter apple. The size is small and it is short through the core. The color is dark red. It is an all-purpose apple. The tree and limbs grow upright and the wood is rather brittle and splits very easily. I have known these apples to fall on the ground, and in the spring we could pick them up by the bushels. Bruising don't seem to hurt them about keeping. They are small to be marketable, but there is no better variety for home use."

Another letter to the USDA written in 1894 from Putnam County, Tennessee, says: "I recommend them on account of their keeping until June. They never get soft or watery after freezing like other apples. The tree bears young and abundantly. This apple was brought here from Adair County, Kentucky, forty years ago."

Catherine Yaden wrote me that her family has grown a dark red, winter-keeper apple called Shortcore Winesap for over sixty years near Pioneer, Tennessee. From her description I believe this apple is identical to the Short Core described above.

Fruit medium, roundish or slightly oblong, flattened on the ends, often irregular in shape; skin mostly deep or purplish red; dots numerous, white; stem short to medium in a narrow, deep, slightly russeted cavity; calyx closed; basin large, abrupt, corrugated, and quite deep, which causes the core to be short; flesh fine-grained, yellowish, juicy, subacid. Ripe October. No catalog listings.

Apple collector Herbert Childress of Dunnville, Kentucky, had Short Core in his orchard and provided me with scions, describing it as having a unique taste. Mr. Childress also discovered another old apple called Yellow-fleshed Short Core that may be a different variety although very similar in size, shape, and color.

❧ **SINE QUA NON** (Cornel's Early): An early apple rather widely grown in the South until well into the 1900s. It originated before 1831, probably in or near the famous nursery of William Prince on Long Island, New York. Considered extinct in 1989, Sine Qua Non was rediscovered in Pennsylvania by Conrad Gemmer of Susquehanna. The late Mr. Gemmer had a collection of over 450 apple varieties, including many rare old American apples, which he collected during a lifetime of studying and searching for old apples.

Fruit medium, roundish; skin smooth, pale yellow, sometimes with a brown blush; dots gray; stem slender; flesh white, fine-grained, tender, juicy, aromatic, sprightly subacid. Ripe July. Catalog listings: MD, VA, NC, SC (1836–1919).

❧ **SLABSIDE:** Last year (2009), when the Slabside tree in the Southern Heritage Apple Orchard had its first fruit, I was astonished at the quality of the apples. My memory and notes failed me when I tried to recall where I got this apple. Tom Brown reminded me that I got scions as a result of a talk I gave about old apples at a museum in Old Fort, North Carolina.

Fruit medium, roundish conical, lopsided; skin tough, pale greenish but mostly covered with bright red and a few broken red stripes; dots numerous, small, gray; stem short in a wide, russeted cavity; calyx closed; basin small, lobed; flesh fine-grained, moderately crisp and juicy, whitish, mild subacid to sweet. Ripe August. No catalog listings.

❧ **SLOPE:** A single tree dating back to the 1920s was found by Tom Brown belonging to Jack Harold of Hays, North Carolina. Described as medium to large, roundish to slightly oblate, often oblique; skin covered in red; flesh firm, crisp, fine-grained, mildly acid. Ripe October. No catalog listings.

❦ **SMITH SEEDLING:** Originated before the Civil War with the Smith family near Francisco in Stokes County, North Carolina. It was a seedling that grew up near the front porch of Annie Boles' great-grandmother's house. It was grown there around 1900 in the orchard of Garland Smith (d. 1926) that contained over 2,300 apple trees. Mr. Smith would take apples by mule and wagon to tobacco auctions in Winston-Salem and Mount Airy and sell them from his wagon. He also used them to make large quantities of cider vinegar, which he sold to local merchants for fifty cents a gallon. Thanks to his granddaughter, Annie Boles, a Smith Seedling tree was found and this fine old variety has been saved. Mrs. Boles wrote to me: "Smith Seedling is a very tasty apple, a good keeper, and especially good to fry since they don't cook to a mush. Mama used to make preserves of them. There is a Smith Seedling tree at my mother's house in front of the chicken house."

Fruit medium, roundish, flattened on the ends; skin mostly covered with brick red that is heavier on the sunny side, overlaid with a few, obscure, darker red stripes with some apples having russet veinings; dots numerous, large, light-colored, often with russet centers; stem sometimes pinkish, medium length to long in a deep, narrow, usually russeted cavity; calyx open; basin wide, almost shallow, corrugated; flesh yellowish, fine-grained, moderately juicy, moderately crisp, subacid. Ripe September/October and a good keeper. No catalog listings.

❦ **SMITH'S CIDER** (Smith, Poplar Bluff, Popular Bluff, Fuller's Cider, Fowler, Pennsylvania Cider, Choice Kentuck, Jackson Winesap, Smith's, Oregon Spitzenburg, Buck's County Cider, Smith's Choice?, Smith's Superb, Cider, Kentucky Choice, Poplar Block?): Despite its name, this is not exclusively a cider apple but is also good for cooking and fresh eating. As early as 1857 it was recommended that the word "cider" be dropped from its name because it gives a false impression. When grown on friable soils, even clay loams, Smith's Cider is a prodigious biennial or sometimes annual bearer, well-adapted to many areas of the piedmont and mountains of the South. The wood is brittle and limbs can break under heavy fruit loads. The tree blooms late.

Smith's Cider supposedly originated in Bucks County, Pennsylvania, and is almost certainly the apple written about in 1905 in *The American Cultivator* magazine:

> A specimen fruit from an historic orchard tree is forwarded to this office by A. A. Sharp of Baltimore, Maryland. This tree is 130 years old. When Gen. Howe, the English commander during the Revolutionary War, approached Philadelphia in his march from Chesapeake Bay, a number of the leading citizens of Philadelphia were arrested (by American patriots), charged with being loyal to the English king, and sent to the American prison at Winchester, Virginia, as political prisoners. It was feared they would give information to Gen. Howe. These prisoners were allowed parole with families of the neighborhood.
>
> Mr. Sharp's great-grandfather accompanied three of these political prisoners in 1776, and while they were in Winchester they planted an apple orchard, which since then has been bearing fruit known as the Smith apple, supposedly named for one of the prisoners. No other trees of this variety are known in that section. It is a large yellow apple with a red cheek, flat at the ends, and of excellent subacid quality.

Smith's Cider was widely grown throughout the South (often under the name Poplar Bluff) and in the Ohio Valley. Even as far south as Alabama and Mississippi, Smith's Cider was extensively grown for both market and home use, though these apples lose flavor and texture after long storage.

Fruit medium, larger when well grown, roundish conical; skin tough, smooth, mostly shaded and striped with pale red; dots few, large, distinct, gray; stem usually medium length and slender in a deep, acute, russeted cavity; calyx closed or half open; basin broad and rather shallow; flesh white or tinged yellowish, tender, breaking, juicy, crisp, mild subacid. Ripe October. Catalog listings: MD, DC, VA, NC, GA, AL, LA, TN, KY, AR (1824–1910).

❦ **SMITH'S SEEDLING OF MISSISSIPPI** (Smith Apple): L. Hiram Smith of Woodville, Mississippi, originated this apple before 1874, and it was grown in southwest Mississippi until the 1950s under the name "Smith Apple." It was listed as extinct in the first edition of this book. George Flowers, who married the great-granddaughter of Hiram Smith, searched for and found a single old tree of "Smith Apple" belonging to Leno McFarland and passed it on to my friend and Mississippi apple hunter, Jack Herring. Smith's Seedling of Mississippi has always been propagated by root sprouts.

Fruit almost large, oblate, slightly angular; skin pale greenish yellow with a rosy blush on the sunny side; stem short in a shallow to medium-depth cavity; calyx open; basin medium depth, slightly corrugated; flesh whitish yellow, slightly coarse, tender, moderately juicy, mild subacid. Ripe July. No catalog listings.

❦ **SMOKEHOUSE** (Mill Creek, Red Vandevere, English Vandevere, Gibson's Vandevere, Mill Creek Vandevere): When a Smokehouse tree that I planted beside the gravel road in my community bore its first apples twenty years ago, I took apples to a neighbor, a level-headed woman not given to false praise. After chewing her first bite, she looked at me and said, "This is the best apple I have ever eaten." If you like a dense, chewy, tasty apple, Smokehouse is for you. A bonus to southerners is the fact that Smokehouse is adapted to much of the South and grows well on clay soils in the piedmont as well as on more porous soils in the mountains. Smokehouse is an excellent cooking apple, too, and can be used for baking from July until it is fully ripe. The tree has a crooked growth habit, tends to be a biennial bearer, and is susceptible to cedar-apple rust and fire blight. The fruit closely resembles and often is confused with Vandevere.

The original tree grew up beside the smokehouse on the farm of William Gibbons near Lancaster, Pennsylvania, and was brought to public notice about 1836. In Pennsylvania it ripens late enough to be kept until late winter, but southern-grown Smokehouse apples ripen much earlier and require refrigeration to keep for any length of time.

Fruit above medium, oblate; skin greenish yellow shaded and striped with red; dots few, large, gray and russet; stem almost short in an acute, narrow to wide cavity; calyx closed; basin wide, rather shallow, slightly corrugated; flesh yellowish, firm, crisp, juicy, aromatic, subacid. Ripe August/September. Catalog listings: MD, VA, NC, GA, LA, TN, TX, AR (1855–1928). ❖ **Plate 52.**

❦ **SNUFF:** Miney Hensley, over eighty years old at the time, remembered Snuff apple trees at her homeplace and other nearby homes when she was young. Tom Brown found a tree there at the head of Fox Creek in Yancey County, North Carolina.

Fruit small to medium size, roundish conical; skin mostly covered with bright or purplish red; dots few, large, gray with russet centers; stem medium length in a wide, brownish russeted cavity; flesh firm, crisp, acid. Ripe October and a good keeper. No catalog listings.

❦ **SOPS OF WINE** (Hominy, Homony, Homomy June, Lane, Saps of Wine, Bennington, Washington, Dodge's Early Red, Warden's Pie Apple, Sopsavine, Bell's Early, Bell's Favorite, Sapson, Summer Queen [in Kentucky], Horning, Sops-in-wine, Early Washington): An old English apple variety that does quite well in the South, where it was grown mostly under the names Hominy or Homony. Sops of Wine was said to be an excellent summer market apple as grown in Illinois in 1871, but the USDA described Sops of Wine in 1908 as inferior to several other early apples, including Williams Favorite. The tree is productive and an annual bearer.

Fruit medium or larger, roundish conical; skin mostly covered with dark red, sometimes obscurely striped, sometimes with a thin white bloom; dots few, small, light or russet; stem short and slender in an acute, narrow, usually russeted cavity; calyx closed; basin shallow and furrowed; flesh yellowish, stained pink, tender, not very juicy, aromatic, mild subacid. Ripe late June/July. *See also* Williams Favorite. Catalog listings: VA, NC, GA, AL, LA, MS, TN, KY, TX, AR (1855–1909).

**SOUR JUNE:** Probably a local apple grown mostly in Beaufort and surrounding counties in extreme eastern North Carolina.

Sherry R. Everett of Pinetown, North Carolina, sent me several apples and wrote: "My mother-in-law moved here in 1933 and said that her neighbors had very large Sour June trees then. She remembers the trunks being very thick. That is as far back as I can trace them in our area. Most of the old folks have died who would know about Sour June. If you wait til these apples get much of a blush before picking them, they are overripe. They are very tart, and we enjoy applesauce made from them. We also freeze them to cook with. We still have a few trees of Sour June on our farm."

Fruit medium or below, roundish or slightly oblate; skin light green or pale yellow with a light red, grainy wash, and a few broken, red stripes on the sunny side; dots few, russet, some areole; stem short to medium length in a deep, acute, russeted cavity; calyx usually open; basin shallow to medium depth, wide, corrugated; flesh slightly greenish, fine-grained, crisp, juicy, acid. Ripe July. No catalog listings.

**SPARGER:** The original tree grew up in the 1800s from a Limbertwig seed beside the smokehouse on the Murlin Sparger farm on Crossingham Road, five miles from Mount Airy, North Carolina. The Sparger family called it their Smokehouse apple. I received a letter from Elizabeth Smith of Mount Airy in 1988 telling me that a Sparger tree, planted by her father in 1905, was alive and bearing apples in her backyard. She used the fruit for apple butter, applesauce, and fried apples. Miss Smith said it is an excellent keeper and "can be raked out of the snow and eaten." A letter from Josie Seal of Mount Airy says Sparger apples were "gathered in the Fall and kept in a log tobacco barn covered with leaves until Spring." Sparger was sold from 1900 to 1915 by the J. Van Lindley Nursery in Greensboro and grown commercially in Surry County, North Carolina, and surrounding counties in North Carolina and Virginia until about 1940.

Fruit medium or below, round or roundish oblate, often oblique; skin thick, light green, washed with dull red with purplish stripes and overlaid with gray scarfskin; dots numerous, large, white with russet centers; stem medium length and thick in a greenish brown russeted cavity; calyx open or closed; basin shallow, sometimes greenish, corrugated; flesh greenish or white, moderately juicy, firm, subacid. Ripe late September/October or even later and an excellent keeper. ❖ **Plate 53.**

**SPOTTED PIPPIN:** Ed Douglas of Bakersville, North Carolina, owns a tree of Spotted Pippin, an apple dating back to the early 1900s that Tom Brown found in 2000. Trees of Spotted Pippin are very prolific.

Fruit below medium, roundish, often slightly oblique; skin smooth, bright yellow, sometimes with a bronzing on the sunny side; dots prominent and often protruding slightly; stem medium length in a greenish or orangish tan russeted cavity; flesh juicy, crisp, subacid. Ripe August/September. No catalog listings.

**ST. CLAIR:** In 1972 the *Register of New Fruit and Nut Varieties* (Brooks and Olmo) said of St. Clair: "Originated in St. Clair County, Illinois, by John J. Lizakowsky. Introduced in 1947. Parentage unknown; raised from the seed of an apple purchased from a train vendor in 1913 or 1914. Fruit resembles Wealthy; large; quality good; matures in summer; skin nearly solid red when grown in the southern states." St. Clair was recommended by the Alabama Agricultural Extension Service for central and north Alabama. Joyce Neighbors, a nurserywoman in Gadsden, Alabama, found this apple in four different locations in Alabama as it was sold by the Eva Nursery in Morgan County in the years before 1960. St. Clair is one of my favorite July apples for fresh eating.

Fruit above medium, round, occasionally slightly oblate; skin smooth, pale yellowish, partly to mostly covered with bright red and broken red stripes, but less red near the stem end; dots few, small, gray, and submerged greenish; stem short in a deep, abrupt, irregular, sometimes greenish russeted cavity; calyx usually closed; basin large, wide, deep; flesh fine-grained, moderately crisp, juicy, subacid. Ripe mid to late July over several weeks.

**STAFFORD:** An apple of this name was listed in 1853 by Lindley's Nursery in Greensboro, North Carolina, and by two Virginia nurseries from 1859 to 1869. I found this obscure apple still being grown by Stafford family descendants in Alamance County, North Carolina. Agnes Garrison, whose grandfather was James Stafford, has two trees of the Stafford apple. *See also* Stafford's Russet.

Fruit medium or above, roundish oblate, slightly conical; skin thin, light yellow with broken darker red stripes on lighter red; dots small, scattered, whitish; stem medium length ending in a knob; calyx greenish, closed; basin rather shallow; flesh whitish tinged yellow, tender, fine-grained, juicy, subacid. Ripe early July.

**STARK** (Robinson, Starke, Yeats, Winter King): Probably originated in Stark County, Ohio, as it was widely grown there by 1869. It was sold by many southern nurseries as a good-quality, late-keeping apple suitable for marketing. The fruit withstands commercial handling and shipping well because of its firmness and thick skin. The tree is vigorous, healthy, annually productive but susceptible to fire blight. In warmer areas the fruit often rots on the tree.

Fruit medium to large, roundish or oblong, conical, ribbed; skin overlaid with dull red or purplish streaks and splashes, sometimes almost entirely red, often with a bloom; dots numerous, light brown and whitish; stem medium to long in a rather deep, russeted cavity; calyx closed; basin shallow, rather wide, slightly wrinkled; flesh yellowish, crisp, coarse, firm, moderately juicy, mild subacid. Ripe September. Catalog listings: MD, VA, NC, GA, AL, TN, KY, TX, AR (1884–1928).

**STARR** (Star in the East?, Star?, Early Greening): Downing (1878) describes Star and Starr as different varieties and both were listed by southern nurseries. Even so, the apple listed as Star in southern catalogs is an exact match of the New Jersey apple named Starr as described by Beach (1905), and it must be the same apple. Starr was touted in some southern catalogs as "the largest early apple known, measuring 10 to 12 inches in circumference." Starr apples were picked unripe and sold under the name Early Greening as a cooking apple. The tree originated before 1878 as an accidental seedling on the farm of John Starr of Woodburg, New Jersey.

Fruit large to very large, oblate to roundish oblate; skin pale greenish yellow, sometimes faintly blushed in the sun; dots numerous, small and large, pale or russet; stem short to medium length, sometimes swollen, in an acute, broad cavity; calyx closed; basin medium depth, narrow, abrupt, furrowed; flesh tinged yellow, moderately fine-grained, tender, crisp, very juicy, aromatic, sprightly subacid. Ripe late June/July in North Carolina and a good keeper for an early apple. Catalog listings as Star and Starr: MD, NC (1898–1928).

**STAYMAN** (Stayman Winesap): Some years ago a man in north Georgia wrote this: "What can I say? This is Stayman country and rightly so. A Stayman grower is a benefactor to all mankind." Like its Winesap parent, Stayman is a great apple adapted to much of the South. Redder sports of the original Stayman, with names such as Staymared, Stayman Double Red, and Stayman Newred, are grown in commercial orchards at higher elevations in several southern states, and the fruit is popular for fresh eating, sauce, baking, and pies. The trees are strong growers with luxuriant foliage and are resistant to apple scab and cedar-apple rust. The fruit hangs well on the tree. Like Winesap, Stayman has sterile pollen and cannot be used to pollinate other apple trees.

This apple originated with Dr. J. Stayman who planted some seeds of Winesap at Leavenworth, Kansas, in 1866. When the seedling trees were two years old, Dr. Stayman selected the best dozen young trees and moved them near his house. The tree now called Stayman bore its first fruit in 1875, and the other seedlings fruited soon thereafter. Dr. Stayman sent out scions of several of the most promising of these seedlings to nurserymen in various states for further testing. The numbering system Dr. Stayman used for these scions produced considerable confusion at first, but this one variety was so superior that it eventually became known as Stayman's Winesap. The original tree in Leavenworth was destroyed by a storm in 1899.

The high quality of Stayman was first recognized about 1890 by the nurseryman J. W. Kerr of Denton, Maryland, and it was being planted extensively in the South by 1902. In 1990, Stayman accounted for about 2 percent of American commercial apple production. Many commercial growers are now replacing Stayman trees with newer varieties because of splitting or cracking of almost ripe apples on the tree, especially if heavy rains just precede ripening. *See also* Magnate.

Fruit medium to large, roundish to roundish oblong, conical, sometimes oblique; skin smooth, virtually covered with rose red and indistinct stripes of crimson, often lightly russeted; dots gray and russet, many areole; stem medium length and stout in a large, deep, russeted cavity; calyx closed, basin corrugated and shallow; flesh yellowish, rather fine-grained, firm, breaking, juicy, sprightly subacid. Ripe October and a good keeper. Catalog listings: MD, VA, NC, SC, GA, AL, MS, LA, TN, KY, TX, AR (1890–1928). ❖ **Plate 54.**

❦ **STRIPED EARLY HARVEST:** Charles Jordan of Roaring River, North Carolina, has the only known tree, which came from a much older tree at his grandfather's home. He says Striped Early Harvest is much superior in flavor to Early Harvest. Found by Tom Brown in 2000 and described as large to sometimes very large, oblate; skin pale yellow partially striped with red; flesh tender, juicy, subacid. Ripe late July. No catalog listings.

❦ **STRIPED JUNE:** A glance at the "Index of Apple Names and Synonyms" in the back of this book will show at least five apple varieties carrying the name or synonym of Striped June. Any striped apple ripening in June has always been a candidate to be called Striped June, and there are a host of different apples out there so called. I grow a Striped June apple from Paul Dobbs of Chattanooga, Tennessee. It is no better or worse than other Striped Junes I have found over the years.

Fruit small, round, slightly conical; skin smooth, greenish, mottled and striped with bright to purplish red; dots few, rather large, whitish; stem almost long in a shallow, cracked, and russeted cavity; calyx closed; basin shallow, corrugated; flesh fine-grained, soft, not very juicy, greenish, browns quickly, tart. Ripe June. *See* Early Red Margaret.

❦ **STUMP:** There are at least three apples named Stump, all of which probably acquired the name when the original seedling tree grew up near an old stump. A Stump apple was briefly mentioned in a horticultural magazine in 1846 as having originated in the garden of the Shakers of Union Village, Ohio. This may be the same as the Stump apple sold in 1870 by a Kentucky nursery as "a seedling of the Newtown Pippin which it much resembles." This apple is extinct.

Downing (1878) describes a Stump apple of supposedly Delaware origin: Fruit medium size, oblate; skin yellow shaded or blushed with light red over much of the surface. This apple was not sold by southern nurseries and also is extinct.

Another Stump apple originated before 1875 in Chili, New York, and was sold by several southern nurseries as a high-quality, early-autumn apple of brilliant color. Beach (1905) says the fruit bruises easily and requires several pickings. This apple is available and described as follows.

Fruit medium or below, roundish to slightly oblong, conical; skin smooth, washed, and mottled with pinkish red that is deep red in some apples, indistinctly striped with carmine; dots numerous, areolar with russet or white points; stem short in an acute, rather shallow, unsymmetrical, furrowed, sometimes lipped, usually russeted cavity; basin shallow, narrow, abrupt; flesh whitish, rather fine-grained, tender, juicy, aromatic, sprightly subacid. Ripe September. Catalog listings: MD, VA, NC, GA, AL, KY (1885–1904).

❦ **STUMP THE WORLD:** Listed without description in 1905 by the Robbins Nursery Company of Powells Station, Tennessee. In 1999 Tom Brown found an apple of this name near Roan Mountain, Tennessee, belonging to Raymond Dugger. This apple is described below. Another apple named

Stump *of* the World (still available) was once rather widely grown in Avery County, North Carolina, but it appears to be a different apple. Full identification of this Avery County apple is ongoing.

Fruit large, roundish conical, somewhat lobed; skin yellow with faint bronzing on the sunny side; dots numerous, large and small, russet, some areole; stem short to almost medium in a deep, russeted cavity; calyx greenish, closed; basin corrugated; flesh rather coarse, whitish, moderately juicy, mild subacid. Ripe October.

❦ **SUGAR APPLE:** Grown in eastern North Carolina near Grantsboro. I received scions from Mrs. C. F. Hall, who described the apple as "no good for cooking but extremely good to eat. Very sweet, sort of crumbly white flesh."

Fruit medium, roundish conical; skin mostly covered in dark red; dots numerous, small, gray; stem short in a russeted cavity. Ripe October. No catalog listings.

❦ **SUGAR LOAF PIPPIN** (Early Sugar Loaf, Sugar Loaf Greening, Hutching's Seedling, Sugar Loaf?): Elliot (1858) and Downing (1878) say this apple is of foreign origin (possibly England but more likely Russia). Sugar Loaf Pippin was widely grown in the Ohio Valley around 1880, having been brought there from Pennsylvania about 1824. It was listed by a North Carolina nursery in 1855. Olin Warner gave scions to Dr. L. R. Littleton from an old tree in West Virginia.

Fruit medium to large, oblong conical; skin variously described as "pale yellow becoming nearly white on one side when fully ripe" or "dull greenish yellow, brownish in the sun"; stem short; flesh white, firm, slightly acid or subacid, moderately juicy. Ripe July to September.

In 1888 an apple called "Sugar Loaf" was listed by an Alabama nursery and briefly described as large, red, oblong, ripe August. This Alabama apple is obviously different from Sugar Loaf Pippin and is probably extinct.

❦ **SULSER RED:** When a single unidentified tree was found by Dr. L. R. Littleton in West Virginia in 1996, belonging to Harry Sulser, Dr. Littleton named it Sulser Red for the family and the apple's color. For several years now it has been one of my favorite apples for fresh eating in September and early October. This apple closely matches the description of Via's Seedling, considered extinct, and may be identical to it. *See* Via's Seedling.

Fruit medium or slightly above, roundish, often oblique; skin smooth, almost entirely red with virtually no stripes and with a heavy whitish bloom on the skin; dots numerous, small, gray; stem short to medium length in a round, greenish, rather deep cavity; calyx closed; basin round, deep, slightly corrugated; flesh pale yellow, crisp, moderately juicy, mild subacid. Ripe September/October. No catalog listings.

❦ **SUMMER BANANA** (White Summer?, Summer Banana Sweet?): The original tree grew in Marion County, South Carolina. Summer Banana was sold from 1890 to 1925 by two North Carolina nurseries and was trademarked about 1900 by the J. Van Lindley Nursery of Greensboro: "We paid $75 for the original tree and control of same." David Vernon, a nurseryman and friend near Reidsville, North Carolina, grows Summer Banana to perfection in his orchard, grafting from an old tree on his family farm.

Fruit medium or above, roundish, slightly conical; skin yellow sometimes with light red and pink stripes; dots numerous, russet; basin shallow; flesh has faint banana aroma. Ripe September. *See also* White Summer.

❦ **SUMMER CHAMPION** (Holland, Kincaid): About 1921 two trees of an unknown apple variety were noticed in the home orchard of J. W. Kincaid, five miles south of Weatherford, Texas. First named Kincaid, this variety was renamed Holland for G. A. Holland, a prominent citizen of Weatherford. Holland was once grown commercially in the West Cross Timbers area of Texas because the trees are productive and the fruit matures early. The trees are susceptible to fire blight.

Stark Bro's Nursery began selling this Texas apple in the 1930s and renamed it Summer Champion, a name almost universally used today. Many southerners remember this apple, and old trees can still be found. Womack Nursery of DeLeon, Texas, sells this apple under the name Holland.

Fruit medium or above, round, slightly conical; skin yellow, mostly covered with pink and red stripes; dots small, inconspicuous; stem medium length in a russeted cavity; calyx closed; flesh light yellow, crisp, juicy, subacid. Ripe August. No catalog listings. *See* Lonnie's Summer Giant. ❖ **Plate 55.**

❦ **SUMMER CHEESE:** This may be the Summer Cheese described in the chapter on extinct varieties, but more time is needed for proper identification. Tom Brown found a tree in Traphill, North Carolina, owned by Dean Mathis, that was grafted from a much older tree about forty years ago. Fruit described as medium to large, oblate; skin yellow, occasionally blushed on the sunny side; flesh juicy, acid. Ripe August/September.

❦ **SUMMER KING** (King, Bounty, Kentucky Summer Queen, Puckett's Summer, Cheese, Puckett, Summer Cheese, Summer King of Kerr, August Apple): Introduced into Kentucky by settlers from North Carolina, perhaps as early as 1807. It was called King in Kentucky and was an important apple in Warren and Todd counties around 1850. Dr. Howsley, president of the Kansas Horticultural Society, grew this variety about 1860 and renamed it Summer King to distinguish it from other apples named King. Scions of this apple were sent in 1884 to the Maryland nurseryman J. W. Kerr under the name Kentucky Summer Queen, and he sold it from his nursery for several years under that name. In 1895 the USDA identified Kentucky Summer Queen as identical to Summer King.

The 1912 *USDA Yearbook* highly praises this apple: "On account of the beauty and high quality of the fruit and the productiveness of the tree, it is worthy of a more prominent place in the early apple industry of the middle latitudes and the South." The tree tends to be rather small, bears heavily biennially, and is susceptible to fire blight "unless grown on dry or thin land."

Alabama nurserywoman Joyce Neighbors was taken to a single tree of Summer King by her friend, the late W. M. Longshore of Anniston. This tree was grafted on Siberian crab rootstock about 1935 by Mr. Longshore when he worked as a boy for the Collinsville Nursery in Alabama owned by his uncle.

Fruit medium to large, roundish conical; skin tough, smooth, washed and marbled with mixed red and striped with broken crimson, overspread with a gray bloom; dots numerous, yellowish or light gray, sometimes russet; stem medium to almost long in an abrupt, deep, narrow, greenish or russeted cavity; calyx closed; basin abrupt, narrow, deep; flesh whitish yellow, fine-grained, tender, brittle, juicy, mild subacid. Ripe late July/August and keeps for six weeks. Catalog listings: MD, TN, KY (1889–1913). ❖ **Plate 56.**

❦ **SUMMER LADYFINGER:** Found in 1994 in an old orchard near Fries, Virginia. Apples with Ladyfinger in their name are usually oblong.

Fruit large, quite oblong conical; skin smooth, light green to yellowish with pinkish red and broken, darker red stripes on the sunny side and with some scarf skin; dots numerous, small, gray and whitish; stem short in an abrupt, deep, wide, lightly russeted cavity; calyx closed; basin wide, deep, corrugated; flesh fine-grained, moderately juicy and crisp, subacid. Ripe mid-July. No catalog listings.

❦ **SUMMER ORANGE:** In the late 1980s, while picking strawberries at a U-Pick farm near my home in Chatham County, North Carolina, I spotted an old apple tree nearby. The owners, Mr. and Mrs. Marion Glosson, identified the tree as Summer Orange, planted by Mrs. Glosson's father about 1910. Mrs. Glosson prized the apples for making apple pies. Summer Orange was listed from 1920 to 1928 or later by a small nursery in Julian, North Carolina. A close comparison shows conclusively that Summer Orange is identical to Fall Orange. *See* Fall Orange.

❦ **SUMMER PIPPIN** (Sour Bough, Champlain, Nyack Pippin, Large Golden Pippin, Underdunk, Walworth, Paper Apple, Calkin's Pippin, Tart Bough, Geneva Pearmain, Haverstraw Pippin): Probably of New York origin and sold in the South mostly by Virginia nurseries. The fruit is good for fresh eating, excellent for cooking and ripens over several weeks.

Fruit medium to large, variable in shape but

usually roundish oblong, conical, sides unequal; skin smooth, yellow or pale yellow sometimes with a delicate blush; dots green and grayish; stem variable in length in a deep, abrupt, lightly russeted cavity; calyx closed; flesh white, very tender, moderately juicy, subacid. Ripe July/September. Catalog listings: MD, VA, NC (1836–1902).

❦ **SUMMER POUND ROYAL** (Pound Royal, Orange, Orange Pie Apple, Summer Rhode Island Greening, Summer Pound): Of unknown (but not southern) origin, sold by southern nurseries mostly under the name Pound Royal. The tree begins bearing at an early age.

Fruit large, roundish to roundish oblate, conical; skin greenish yellow sometimes with a pink blush; dots green or light-colored; stem rather short in a large, deep, slightly russeted cavity; calyx closed; basin abrupt and deep; flesh white, fine-grained, tender, juicy, mild subacid. Ripe July/August. Catalog listings: MD, VA, AL, KY, TX (1845–1915).

❦ **SUMMER QUEEN** (Early Queen, Lancaster Queen, Orange Apple, Pole Cat, Queen, Sharpe's Early, Swett's Harvest, Sweet's Harvest)/**LARGE SUMMER QUEEN:** A very popular apple in the South at one time and listed in southern nursery catalogs for over 130 years. Coxe (1817) describes Summer Queen, and it may be of New Jersey origin, although an apple of this name was listed by a Delaware nursery in 1791. Most old references say that Summer Queen has sufficient acid for cooking and drying but can be used for fresh eating because of its rich, spicy flavor. The tree is quite productive annually, blooms late, and has somewhat drooping branches.

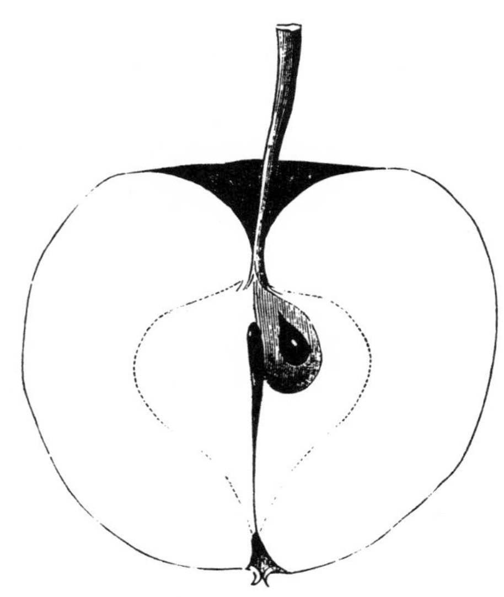
SUMMER QUEEN

The defining physical characteristic of Summer Queen fruit is a very shallow to almost non-indented basin. All the old pomological references point this out. I have found several old trees called Queen or Summer Queen, but none of them has fruit with a very shallow basin. The description here is for the Summer Queen described in old references.

Fruit medium to large, roundish conical; skin pale to deep yellow striped with red, which is sometimes described as dull red or dark crimson; dots small, yellow; stem long in a rather deep cavity that often has protuberances; basin very shallow to almost flat, furrowed; flesh yellow, aromatic, juicy, slightly coarse, spicy subacid. Ripe July/August. Catalog listings: DE, MD, VA, DC, NC, SC, GA, AL, MS, LA, TN, KY, TX, AR (1791–1924).

An apple called Large Summer Queen was described to the 1883 meeting of the American Pomological Society as a North Carolina apple. This apple generally fits the description of Summer Queen except it is large to very large in size and has white flesh. It was sold by North Carolina and Virginia nurseries from 1853 to 1904. Lawson's Nursery in Georgia sold an apple called Summer Queen in the 1990s that more closely fits the description of Large Summer Queen.

❦ **SUMMER RAMBO** (Summer Rambo of Pennsylvania, Frank Rambo, Rambour d'Ete, Rambour Franc, Summer Rambour, Imperial Rambo, Striped Rambo?, Redsumbo): An old French apple very popular in Maryland and Virginia and states further north and west until World War I. It reportedly originated in the early 1600s in the French village of Rembures in Picardy and was being grown in England in 1665. It has probably been in this country since colonial times. I find Summer Rambo trees in many old orchards in western Virginia, where it usually ripens in August. The apples can be picked while still green, beginning in early to mid-July, for frying, pies, and outstanding applesauce. Mrs. Sammie Stoneman of Galax, Virginia, gave me scions from her old tree in 1989.

The tree of Summer Rambo is vigorous and healthy (although susceptible to fire blight), often attaining a large size when grown on seedling rootstock. It is a dependable, annual bearer of lovely fruit. Stark Bro's Nursery sold Summer Rambo in the 1920s under the name Imperial Rambo. There is a red sport of Summer Rambo called Redsumbo that originated in Indiana, and another red sport called Red Summer Rambo that originated in Pennsylvania.

Fruit above medium to sometimes large, roundish oblate to oblate, ribbed, sides often unequal; skin thick, smooth, washed and mottled with pinkish red and striped with carmine, particularly on the sunny side; dots numerous, usually small and submerged, but some large, brown or russet; stem short to medium length, rather thick, in a broad, rather deep, sometimes lipped, russeted cavity; basin usually deep, abrupt, smooth; flesh greenish yellow, tender, breaking, somewhat coarse, very juicy, mild subacid. Ripe August/September. Catalog listings: MD, VA, MS, TN, AR (1858–1928). ❖ **Plate 57.**

❧ **SUMMER ROSE** (Simm's Harvest, Glass Apple, Lippincott, Lippincott's Early, Lodges' Early, Wolman's Harvest, Woolman's Early, Woolman's Striped Harvest, French Reinette, Harvest Apple, Symm's Harvest, Striped June?): A New Jersey apple first mentioned in 1806. Although sold by many southern nurseries over a long period, I seldom find any old trees named Summer Rose in my apple searches, and I suspect it is often hidden under the catch-all name of Striped June. It ought to be resurrected under its own name and grown more in the South as a good-quality, early apple for fresh eating. Summer Rose holds its own in eating quality when compared to Yellow Transparent, Red June, Early Harvest, and Red Astrachan, the other important heirloom early apples in the South.

The tree often bears fruit in clusters with apples ripening over a period of a month or longer beginning in late June in warmer areas. Because Summer Rose blooms late, it may escape late frosts. The tree is a slow grower but quite productive when grown on good soils.

Fruit small to almost medium, sometimes roundish but usually oblate; skin smooth, waxen, mostly blushed and striped with bright red on the sunny side, sometimes completely red; dots very small, white, reddish or green; stem usually short and stout in a small, narrow, russeted cavity; basin wide, abrupt; flesh white, fine-grained, tender, crisp, juicy except when overripe, sprightly subacid. Ripe July. Catalog listings: MD, VA, NC, SC, GA, TN, KY, TX (1824–1915).

❧ **SUNDAY SWEET** (Buffalo Sweet?): Elkton, Virginia, apple hunter, Greg Lam, sent me scions of this apple saying: "Sunday Sweet, or Sweetning as some call it, was grown by many in my area in earlier times. I have found only one tree but have heard older folks talk about this apple. This surviving tree was planted by my great-great-grandfather Gilbert Bailey. His son Marvin Bailey, who died last year at age eighty-eight, told me about the tree. It is the best early eating apple that I have tried."

The late Henry Morton, a nurseryman in Gatlinburg, Tennessee, sold Sunday Sweet in the 1980s. His catalog says, "Medium in size, round and a very aromatic sweet apple. Was widely grown here and a favorite for fresh eating. This is the best apple for frying I have ever tasted. It is still chunky when fried with a very spicy, aromatic taste." Henry Morton's Sunday Sweet was lost after his death and has only recently been recovered. It is too early to tell if Greg Lam's apple is the same as Henry Morton's apple.

Warder (1867) very briefly describes a Sunday Sweet apple, which he thought was possibly of Illinois origin. An 1894 letter to the USDA from C. S. Scott, Monroe County, Virginia, describes a Sunday Sweet: "Season July and August. Planted to some extent in this section. The origin is unknown to me, but it is no new variety. The tree is productive and does not grow very large. The fruit is like Sweet Bough but smaller, firmer, richer, of the same shape and color."

Fruit small or slightly above, roundish or a little oblong; skin light yellow partly covered with russet splotches and irregular, large dots; stem medium to long, sometimes thick, in a russeted cavity. Ripe late July/August.

❦ **SURPRISE** (Yellow Surprise, Red Core): Surprise is a small, red-fleshed apple with yellow skin, of European origin. It was sold by nurseries in Washington, D.C., Virginia, and Kentucky from 1824 to 1870. As grown in most of the South, Surprise seldom has red flesh, but the flesh may be pale pink.

❦ **SUTTON BEAUTY** (Beauty, Morris Red, Sutton, Steele's Red): Originated about 1757 in Sutton, Massachusetts, and grown commercially in New York around 1900 as a high-quality, dessert apple. The tree is productive but usually a biennial bearer and susceptible to fire blight. Sutton Beauty is the earliest-blooming variety in my orchard.

Fruit medium or above, roundish, conical; skin waxen, shaded and obscurely striped with crimson; dots numerous, whitish with russet centers; stem rather short in an acute, rather deep, greenish cavity; basin medium in width, acute, leather-cracked; flesh whitish tinged yellow, crisp, juicy, fine-grained, sprightly subacid. Ripe August/September. Catalog listings: MD, VA (1895–1928).

❦ **SWAAR** (Hardwick): A discerning apple friend in Maryland has written me: "The Swaar can be a great delight and a prized variety, but I think you have to give it good soil and fertility." These observations echo those in an 1858 Virginia nursery catalog: "Requires a deep, rich, sandy loam to bring it to perfection." Downing (1878) calls Swaar "a truly noble American fruit" and "one of the finest flavored apples in America."

Swaar is an eating apple with too little acid to be valuable for cooking. Many people find its flavor rather unpleasant when the apples are eaten directly off the tree. After storage, however, the fruit softens and the flavor becomes exquisite. The tree is only moderately productive, usually biennially, and often drops much fruit before it is ripe. Bitter rot and fire blight can be problems.

Swaar was first grown by Dutch settlers in the 1700s in the Hudson River Valley and was advertised by a Long Island nursery in 1771. Its name means "heavy" in Low Dutch.

Fruit above medium to large, usually roundish but varying from slightly oblate to somewhat oblong, often ribbed; skin tough, rough, greenish yellow when picked but changing to a deep yellow when ripened in storage, often shaded with a bronze or gray russet; dots numerous, greenish or russet; stem medium length and slender in an acute, round, rather deep, often furrowed and russeted cavity; calyx closed or partially closed; basin usually rather shallow, wide and slightly furrowed; flesh yellowish, fine-grained, firm becoming rather tender, juicy, aromatic, mild subacid. Ripe October, with flavor improving in storage. Catalog listings: MD, VA, NC, KY, TX (1845–1902).

❦ **SWEET BOUGH** (Large Yellow Bough, Sweet Harvest, Bough, Early Sweet Bough, Washington, August Bough, August Sweeting, Boughsweet, Bow, Cane Mash, Early Sweet, Early Sweetheart, July Bough, Large Bough, Large Early Bough, Large Sweet Bough, Niack Pippin, Pound's July, Yellow Bough, Watermelon?, Summer Bough?): An old American apple first described by Coxe (1817). Several southern nursery catalogs call it "the earliest sweet apple worth cultivation." Some references praise Sweet Bough both for fresh eating and cooking, but Warder (1867) says it is tasteless when cooked. The tree is often a poor grower, slow to begin bearing, only moderately productive and susceptible to fire blight. The fruit needs to be picked when firm-ripe.

Fruit above medium to large, round to oblong, conical with a flat base, sides often unequal; skin smooth, pale greenish yellow to almost white, occasionally faintly blushed; stem rather long in a deep, usually smooth but sometimes furrowed or compressed cavity; basin rather small, medium to shallow, narrow; flesh white, very tender, juicy, crisp, and very sweet when ripe but bitter when unripe. Ripe late July. Catalog listings: MD, VA, NC, GA, AL, MS, LA, TN, KY, TX, AR (1853–1928).

❦ **SWEET DIXON:** Recollections by elderly men and women show that this apple was widely grown in Watauga County, North Carolina, early in the 1900s. Inadene Hampton of Watauga County had an old tree that was cut down to make room for growing Christmas trees. Although over eighty years old when my wife and I visited her, Miss Hampton promised us that she would find another Sweet Dixon tree in her area, and find it she did! Both this apple and Dula's Beauty owe their rediscovery to Miss Hampton, and I am indebted to her. For some strange reason, Sweet Dixon was never sold by North Carolina nurseries but was listed in 1905 by the Comal Springs Nursery of New Braunfels, Texas.

Fruit medium or below, roundish to slightly oblate and sometimes oblique; skin pale yellow with scattered, broken, pale reddish stripes, with some apples mostly red; dots inconspicuous, numerous, gray, some with russet centers; stem medium length in a russeted cavity; calyx closed; basin abrupt, small; flesh whitish, moderately crisp and juicy, barely sweet. Ripe September.

❦ **SWEET LANNIE:** Lona Akers of Max Meadows, Virginia, had the last remaining three trees, but Sweet Lannie was once widely grown in her area. Dr. L. R. Littleton found this apple in 1996.

Fruit medium or below, roundish conical; skin yellow with some russet dots and patches and a russeted cavity. Ripe July/August. No catalog listings.

❦ **SWEET RUSSET** (Sweet Rusty Coat?, Rusty Sweeting?): There are at least three different apples with this name and five others with Sweet Russet as a synonym. Sweet Russet was listed by several southern nurseries, usually with no descriptions or very abbreviated ones, making identification difficult. The Forest Nursery in Fairview, Kentucky, listed a Sweet Russet in 1870: "Fruit small, greenish white, flesh sweet and good. Ripe winter." This is probably the Sweet Russet of Kentucky origin described by Warder (1867): "Fruit small, conical, truncated, rough, dark russet. Dots minute, white, prominent. Flesh yellowish white, fine-grained, not tender, sweet. Scarcely good. December-February." In 1989 I found a tree of Sweet Russet in Burnsville, North Carolina, belonging to Troy Cooper, but it does not match the above description and may be the same apple as Sweet Rusty Coat, once widely grown in Watauga, Alleghany, and Wilkes counties in western North Carolina. It is described as follows.

Fruit medium, roundish conical, flattened on the ends; skin light green, heavily russeted and with a bronze tinge on the sunny side; dots white and russet; stem short in a deep cavity; calyx open; basin small, rather shallow; flesh crisp, juicy, sweet. Ripe July/August in central North Carolina. Catalog listings: VA, DC, NC, KY (1824–1904).

❦ **SWEET WINESAP** (Henrick Sweet, Henry Sweet, Ladies Sweet, Red Sweet Winesap, Sweet Pearmain, Rose Sweet, Hendrick): Originated in Pennsylvania and grown commercially in New York around 1900 for shipment to southern markets as a high-quality, good-keeping apple. Sweet Winesap was little grown in the South as it was listed by only three Virginia nurseries between 1858 and 1928. The tree is slow to begin bearing and susceptible to fire blight.

Fruit medium or above, roundish conical, often oblique; skin almost entirely overspread with red and narrow carmine stripes, often with a thin bloom and scarf skin; dots medium, whitish or russet; stem short to long in an acute, greenish, almost deep, cavity; calyx greenish, closed; basin very abrupt, rather large and deep, sometimes furrowed; flesh white, moderately crisp, fine-grained, tender, juicy, very sweet. Ripe September and a good keeper. ❖ **Plate 58.**

❦ **TALIAFERO** (Taliaferro, Tallafero, Robinson?, Gloucester White?): From *The New American Orchardist* (1841) by William Kendrick: "The fruit is the size of a grape shot, or from one to two inches in diameter; of a white color, streaked with red; with a sprightly acid, not good for the table, but apparently a very valuable cider fruit. This is understood to be a Virginia fruit, and the apple from which Mr. Jefferson's favorite cider was made." Thomas Jefferson said of it: "The most juicy apple I have ever eaten," and he described its cider as "with a taste more like wine than any liquor I have ever tasted which was not a wine."

The Taliafero (pronounced Tolliver) originated in Gloucester County, Virginia, about 200 years ago. For perhaps a hundred years it has been missing from the cider orchard planted by Thomas Jefferson at Monticello.

In 1994, Dr. Connie Anderson discovered an unidentified apple tree growing in the orchard of Conley Colaw in Virginia. She sent some of the apples to Tom Burford, well-known apple historian in Amherst County, Virginia, and he has tentatively identified the tree as the long-missing Taliafero. Peter Hatch, Director of Gardens and Grounds at Monticello, has said: "I think we will plant it, but the judge is still out. It may be close enough to make a good Taliafero substitute, if it is not actually Jefferson's mystery apple."

The Taliafero is said to ripen in late September in western Virginia. The tree drops its leaves early in the fall.

❦ **TANNER'S WINTER** (Tanner, Tanner No. 1): Listed as extinct previously but recently found as a single old tree in Warsaw, North Carolina. The story is that this variety was propagated and spread by an itinerant grafter/handyman named Tanner who worked in eastern North Carolina in the 1800s.

Tanner's Winter was said by Downing (1900) to be "considerably grown in Granville County, Georgia, where it succeeds and is prized as a winter fruit for general use." There is no Granville County, Georgia; I am sure Mr. Downing meant to say Granville County, *North Carolina,* as this apple was sold by North Carolina nurseries from 1870 to 1877.

Fruit medium, oblate, slightly conical, slightly angular; skin whitish yellow, shaded and obscurely striped with pale purplish red; stem short in a broad, deep, sometimes russeted cavity; basin large, very deep, almost smooth; flesh whitish or slightly yellow, coarse, moderately juicy, mild subacid. Ripe October.

❦ **TANYARD SEEDLING:** An old apple from the mountains of north Georgia sold by Lawson's Nursery in Georgia. The tree blooms late.

Fruit medium size, oblate; skin greenish with a faint blush on the sunny side; dots numerous, russet, areolar; cavity wide, rather shallow, russeted; calyx partly open; basin round, slightly russeted; flesh pale greenish, chewy, juicy, subacid. Ripe October. No catalog listings.

❦ **TARBUTTON:** Like Tanyard Seedling, above, Jim Lawson was brought scions of Tarbutton by customers to graft and then put it in his orchard and nursery catalog. It is an old Georgia apple that originated with Humphrey Tarbutton in the 1800s in the Cherry Grove area, and root sprouts were used for many years to propagate it. Jim Lawson describes it as small to medium size, red-striped, often borne in clusters. Good for cooking, drying, jelly, and fresh eating. Ripe August.

❦ **TAYLOR SWEET:** A local apple from Yancey County, North Carolina. Arnold Proffitt and his sister Audrey Davenport brought this apple to my attention. Mr. Proffitt says Taylor Sweet was grown on his farm when his father was a boy, which would make it at least a hundred years old.

Fruit medium, roundish, often lopsided; skin pale yellow partly covered with pale red and darker red stripes; dots scattered, russet; stem short in a narrow, russeted cavity; calyx open; basin round, shallow; flesh fine-grained, moderately crisp and juicy, mild subacid. Ripe August. No catalog listings.

❦ **TEN OUNCE:** Grown in the 1930s and 1940s in North Carolina near the Wilkes-Alexander County line. Tom Brown found a tree belonging to James Ford near Taylorsville, North Carolina.

Fruit medium size, roundish conical, often oblique; skin tough, mostly washed and striped with light red; dots small, numerous, russet and white; stem short in a greenish or russeted cavity; calyx open; basin sometimes leather-cracked; flesh juicy, somewhat chewy, almost fine-grained, mild subacid. Ripe September/October. No catalog listings.

❦ **TENDERSKIN** (Tender Peeling, Thin Skin?, Tender Rind?): Probably of South Carolina origin and useful for eating, cooking, and cider. The tree is healthy, annually productive, and holds its fruit well. I believe there may be several different southern apples called Tenderskin. This Tenderskin, sold by Lawson's Nursery in Georgia, is from Gilmer County, Georgia.

Fruit medium, roundish to roundish oblate, conical; skin smooth, light yellow, striped and splashed with red, which is darker on the sunny side, often with a bloom; dots scattered, gray with russet centers; stem long in a wide, green cavity; calyx closed; basin abrupt and rather shallow; flesh yellow, very tender, juicy, fine-grained, aromatic, sprightly subacid. Ripe October. Catalog listings: VA, GA, KY (1858–70).

❦ **TERRY WINTER** (Terry, Terry Winter Pippin, Hastler): Terry Winter joins Shockley, Yates, Hall, and Winesap (and a few others) as a high-quality apple, adapted to southern conditions, which keeps extremely well. The 1903 *USDA Yearbook* recommends Terry Winter for the piedmont and coastal plains of the South. In 1908 one Georgia grower got eighteen bushels "of perfect apples" from one eleven-year-old tree. The fruit will be small unless heavily thinned, and it hangs well on the tree. To me the apples have a unique "nutty" flavor.

Terry Winter originated before the Civil War on the farm of a Mr. Terry in Fulton County, Georgia. It was first grafted and sold by a local nurseryman in 1868, and by 1886 it was being sold by several Georgia nurseries and was spreading from Georgia to neighboring states. Terry Winter was grown commercially in the early years of the 1900s in Habersham and nearby counties in Georgia, but the small size of the fruit limited its commercial success. I got scions in 1989 from my friend Gene Wild of Indianapolis, Indiana.

Fruit medium or below, roundish, flattened on the ends, sometimes oblique; skin thick, tough, covered with dull strawberry red with a few broken stripes and a heavy gray bloom; dots numerous, medium size, whitish and russet, many areole; stem medium to long and slender in a narrow, deep, abrupt, russeted cavity; calyx open or partially open; basin medium size, deep, abrupt, greenish, furrowed; flesh almost white, fine-grained, crisp, juicy, mild subacid. Ripe October/November and an excellent keeper. Catalog listings: NC, SC, GA, TX (1891–1928).

❦ **TETOFSKY** (Russian Crab, Tetofski): A Russian apple noted for bearing heavily even on very young trees and for fruit that ripens almost as early as Yellow Transparent. It is mostly a cooking apple as the flesh is acid until fully ripe. Beach (1905) says Yellow Transparent apples are larger and of better quality than Tetofsky. Tetofsky was first imported into this country from England in 1835 by the Massachusetts Horticultural Society. It is considered an Ironclad apple suitable for growing in severe winter areas. The tree tends to be small.

Fruit medium, roundish to slightly oblate, conical; skin smooth, striped and splashed with red and overspread with a whitish bloom; dots inconspicuous, pale, or greenish, submerged; stem medium length in a rather deep, furrowed cavity; calyx closed; basin shallow, furrowed; flesh white, tender, juicy, slightly coarse, acid until fully ripe. Ripe June/July. Catalog listings: MD, VA, NC, GA, AL, LA, TN, TX (1871–1914).

❦ **THOMPSON OF MISSISSIPPI:** Scions of this old Mississippi apple were sent to me by Sylvia Walker of Jackson, Mississippi: "We call it the Thompson apple because we got it originally from a Mr. Thompson. It has been in my family well over a hundred years. It cooks very smooth and is good for drying. The tree is not grafted and produces sprouts around the tree from time to time. That is how we have passed it around in my family. I have three trees growing in my backyard." This is not the Thompson apple discussed in the chapter on extinct varieties.

Fruit medium, round, slightly oblate, sometimes lopsided; skin light green mostly covered with blotches of golden russet and a pale red blush; dots numerous, russet, large, irregular; stem medium length in a deep, greenish russeted cavity; calyx closed; basin deep, abrupt, corrugated; flesh yellowish, fine-grained, not very juicy or crisp, brisk subacid. Ripe late July/August. No catalog listings.

❦ **TOLMAN SWEET** (Tallman Sweeting, Brown's Golden Sweet, Tolman's Sweeting, Tolman): Thatcher (1822) first described Tolman Sweet but was unable to determine its origins. It was widely grown in home orchards in New England and New York around the turn of the twentieth century and was sold by a number of southern nurseries but was never important in the South. Downing (1878) calls it a second-rate apple borne on a tree that is very hardy, productive, and that blooms late. It bruises easily and is susceptible to fire blight. Tolman Sweet is considered a good cider apple because its juice has a high specific gravity.

A professor at Duke University, Durham, North Carolina, wrote me to take issue with Downing's comment about the Tolman Sweet as second-rate:

> Downing has given you a bum steer about the Tolman Sweet. He must have tried to eat it raw, in which case "second-rate" would be a very charitable judgment. Turnips would make a better table apple.
>
> The Tolman Sweet, however, is not meant to be eaten that way. It is a specialized fruit, a steaming apple, the only one I have ever encountered. When steamed it provides a culinary experience so rare that I hardly know how to describe it. To judge it as a dessert apple, or a sauce apple, or a baking apple, is as unreasonable as it would be to eat Twenty Ounce raw or use a Yellow Transparent for winter keeping.
>
> My mother, who was an excellent cook, learned how to steam Tolman Sweet. I learned to do it myself, and I have been trying to remember just how. I think that we used a cake-baking dish. Perhaps a second dish was inverted over it to contain the steam. We must have kept the apples out of the water somehow. I believe that steaming was done in the oven, but it may have been on top of the stove. Perhaps a little sugar was sprinkled over the apples. In any case, they were steamed until they were no longer hard. I hesitate to say soft, because one of the features of a steamed Tolman Sweet was that it retained its integrity through the cooking process, with no tendency to degenerate into a split-skinned heap of mush like some baked apples do. The apples were cored, but not peeled. In fact the steamed peeling was the best part.

Fruit below to above medium, round; skin whitish yellow, sometimes faintly blushed, often roughened with faint russet, often with a suture line from the cavity to the basin; dots small, inconspicuous, pale yellow or russet; stem rather long and slender in a wide, deep (Downing says shallow), often russeted cavity; basin small, often oblique, medium in width and depth, rather abrupt and furrowed; flesh white, firm, fine-grained, not tender or crisp, moderately juicy, sweet. Ripe September. Catalog listings: MD, VA, NC, AL, TN, KY, AR (1853–1928).

❦ **TOM JONES SEEDLING:** Taron Jones, who owns an orchard near Asheville, North Carolina, wrote me in 1997: "This is a seedling discovered in my grandfather's orchard 50 or 60 years ago. Many people buy this apple from me year after year because of its quality. It is a medium to large apple, green in color with a slight bronze or reddish blush when ripe. The flesh is firm and crisp until overripe. The taste is slightly tart but good for eating and very good for applesauce." Ripe late August. No catalog listings.

❦ **TOMMY:** A local apple of the Martha community in Randolph County, North Carolina. Charles Nance and his wife took me to three old trees and say the Tommy apple is grown only within a five-mile radius of Salem Church near their home. This apple has always been propagated by root sprouts. Local lore says the original tree was grown by a man named Tommy Johnson over 150 years ago. The tree is very fruitful.

Fruit above medium, roundish, flattened on the ends, sides often unequal; skin dull greenish turning to light green when ripe, without any blush or stripes; dots numerous, large and small, irregular, russet and submerged green; stem short in a narrow cavity, which is occasionally russeted; calyx closed; basin rather small and shallow, gradually sloped; flesh greenish, fine-grained, tender, juicy, subacid. Ripe August/September and a good keeper. No catalog listings.

❦ **TOMPKINS KING** (King, King of Tompkins County, King Thompson, Flat Spitzenburg, King Apple, Tompkins County King, Toma Red, Tommy Red, Tom's Red, Winter King): This northern apple has outstanding eating quality but was seldom grown in the South. Certainly the merits of Tompkins King are such that if it could have been grown in the South, it would have been grown here. The fact that it was sold by relatively few southern nurseries is convincing evidence that Tompkins King is poorly adapted to southern soils and climate, except possibly in the mountains. In 1900 it was fourth in orchard acreage in New York behind Baldwin, Rhode Island Greening, and Northern Spy. That same year a USDA observer noted that Tompkins King was not much grown in the South.

Beach (1905), while highly praising the appearance and qualities of the fruit as grown in New York, notes that the tree of Tompkins King has several faults, being subject to collar rot and less cold-hardy than many northern apples. Additionally, the tree is only moderately productive, usually a biennial bearer, and rather susceptible to fire blight.

The original tree grew in Warren County, New Jersey, where it attracted little attention. Jacob Wycoff carried scions to Tompkins County, New York, about 1804 and grafted them onto rootstocks there. By the 1840s it had acquired the name King apple and was being sold extensively by New York nurseries. In 1856 the American Pomological Society listed this apple as Tompkins King to distinguish it from other apples named King. Its cultivation spread through New England, New York, Michigan, New Jersey, Pennsylvania, Ohio, and as far as the West Coast by 1900.

Fruit large, roundish to slightly oblate, slightly conical; skin washed with red, splashed and striped with crimson; dots numerous, conspicuous, white or russet; stem usually short and stout in a large, irregular, often russeted cavity; calyx usually closed; basin rather deep and slightly corrugated; flesh yellowish, rather coarse, crisp, tender, aromatic, juicy, subacid. Ripe September. Catalog listings: MD, NC, GA, AL, LA, KY, TX (1875–1924).

❦ **TONY APPLE:** Tony Apple was once widely grown in Rowan, Stanly, and Cabarrus counties in central North Carolina where it was considered unsurpassed for sauce, apple butter, pies, and drying. A few old trees still exist there, and Benjamin Brown of Brown's Nursery, Rockwell, North Carolina, grafted a few trees each year until the 1990s. The late Norman Liske of Siler City, North Carolina, spent an entire day guiding me to several old Tony Apple trees. The fruit is borne in clusters and needs heavy thinning to increase its size. The apples ripen over a month or longer and often hang on the tree until November.

There are two different stories concerning the origin of the Tony Apple. One legend is that this apple originated from seeds carried to Mount Pleasant in Cabarrus County by a Confederate soldier wounded at Gettysburg in 1863. While walking home, he picked an apple to eat and pocketed the seeds, later planting them in his garden. Another story is that this apple originated with a wealthy, antebellum, North Carolina landowner named Drew Morgan. One day while out riding over his lands with his manservant, a slave named Tony, a small, seedling apple tree was found. Tony replanted the tree near the main house and it was named "Tony's Apple" when it began bearing excellent fruit.

Fruit small to below medium, roundish conical; skin light greenish yellow, usually lightly blushed on the sunny side; dots few, large, whitish and russet; stem long in a wide, deep, occasionally russeted cavity; calyx closed; basin very shallow, sometimes corrugated; flesh fine-grained, white, moderately juicy and crisp, subacid. Ripe September/October. No catalog listings.

❦ **TUCKER** (Tucker Everbearing): Listed as extinct previously with the following quote from the 1920 catalog of the J. Van Lindley Nursery of Greensboro, North Carolina: "A new sort called to our attention three summers ago. Begins to ripen in June and continues all through the summer. Tucker is really the nicest ever-bearing apple we have ever seen."

In 1997 Miriam Kivett introduced me to Harry Tucker Smith of Pleasant Garden Road, Vandalia, North Carolina (a suburb of Greensboro), who was then eighty-two years old and is now deceased. The Tucker apple originated there with his grandfather, John R. Tucker, and Mr. Smith had three large trees in his yard. The tree is very fruitful.

Fruit medium, roundish, flattened on the ends, often lopsided; skin smooth, light yellow with a rosy blush and a few faint, darker stripes on the sunny side; dots inconspicuous, gray or russet; stem medium length in a deep, greenish cavity; calyx usually closed; flesh light yellow, fine-grained, moderately crisp and juicy, subacid. Ripe July/August/early September.

❦ **TURLEY WINESAP** (Turley): A seedling of Winesap bred in Orleans, Indiana, about 1910 by Joe E. Burton. It is excellent for cooking but not as good as Stayman for fresh eating. Does not crack like Stayman.

Fruit medium or above, roundish, flattened on the ends; skin almost covered with red without any stripes; dots medium size to large, whitish, few to many; stem medium to long in a greenish tan, russeted cavity; calyx usually open; basin wide, rather shallow, greenish; flesh pale green, crisp, juicy, subacid. Ripe September/October. No catalog listings. ❖ **Plate 59.**

❦ **TWENTY OUNCE** (Aurora, Blessing, Cayuga Red Streak, Coleman, Congress?, Dunlap's Aurora, Eighteen Ounce, Governor Seward, Lima, Morgan's Favorite, Wine): A different apple, named Twenty Ounce Pippin, is inferior to Twenty Ounce and was not sold by southern nurseries. Both originated in New York or New England in the early 1800s. As grown in the South, Twenty Ounce is often quite large and showy, excellent for cooking, but only fair for fresh eating as it is not highly flavored. Beach (1905) says the tree is very susceptible to sunscald and canker and requires careful pruning to keep the top open. It is also susceptible to fire blight and bitter pit.

Fruit very large, roundish, sometimes slightly conical; skin thick, tough, washed and splashed with red (sometimes purplish red) and striped with carmine; dots small to large, grayish or russet; stem short to medium in a very deep, sometimes russeted cavity; calyx usually closed; basin often oblique, rather abrupt, broadly furrowed; flesh whitish tinged yellow, coarse, moderately tender, juicy, subacid. Ripe August/September and does not store well. Catalog listings: MD, VA, NC, AL, LA, TN, TX, AR (1875–1928).

❦ **VANDEVERE** (Fall Vandevere, Gibbon's Smokehouse, Gray Vandevere, Green Vandevere, Vandiver, Imperial Vandevere, Lasting Vandevere, Mill Creek, Old Vandevere, Ox Eye, Pennsylvania Vandevere, Red Vandevere, Staalcubs, Stalcubs, Striped Ashmore?, Striped Vandevere, Vandervere, Watson's Vandevere, White Vandevere, Yellow Vandevere, Longbottom?, Little Vandevere): Praised in many old southern nursery catalogs and said to be well adapted for growing in the South. For example, the following is from a North Carolina catalog: "This well-known old variety I had nearly dropped, but in the winter of 1882 I received specimens of it for identification from Sparta, Georgia, and Chester, South Carolina. Both parties said it was a fine keeper and succeeded better in their localities than any other variety." The appearance and quality of Vandevere have been compared to another great apple, Smokehouse, but Vandevere ripens later and keeps longer in storage. Coxe (1817) remarks upon the high-quality cider made from Vandevere apples, and it also makes superior apple butter.

The faults of Vandevere are few. The wood is brittle and branches sometimes break under heavy fruit loads. On clay soils deficient in calcium, the apples are subject to bitter rot. The fruit occasionally drops prematurely in late summer. Most old southern references advised planting Vandevere on "deep vegetable loams."

This is the most likely history of the Vandevere apple: Swedish settlers built Fort Christiana about 1653 (near what is now Wilmington, Delaware) and a "plantering" of fruit trees brought from Sweden was made or commissioned by Governor Risingh. A year later the Dutch captured the fort, and most of the Swedish settlers moved away. A Swede by the name of Johan Andersson Stalcop (or Stahlkop) remained and probably took over the Swedish orchard. At this time one apple became known as Stalcop or Stalcub. At least one Stalcop daughter married into the Dutch family Vander Veer, perhaps to the Dutch soldier of fortune Jacop V'D'Veer, and the orchard passed into that family. The Stalcub apple then became known as Vandevere or variations on that spelling.

The noted New York nurseryman William Prince

advertised an apple called Vandevel in 1771, likely the Vandevere. One must be careful in identifying any apple called Vandevere because considerable confusion exists. Another and inferior apple, Vandevere Pippin, can be confused with Vandevere. Pennock was often sold in the South under the names Vandevere and Vandeveer as it closely resembles the true Vandevere. Finally, the name Vandevere was commonly used in New York for the Newtown Spitzenburg.

Fruit medium, oblate; skin greenish yellow with faint red stripes but more red on the sunny side, becomes greasy in storage; dots numerous, yellow or green; stem about an inch long in a deep cavity; calyx closed; basin round; flesh yellow, firm, juicy, tender, mild subacid to almost sweet. Ripe September/October. Catalog listings: MD, VA, DC, NC, AL, TN, KY (1824–1915). ❖ **Plate 60.**

**VANDEVER JUNE** (Vandever, July, Crouch, Shook?): Tom Brown says two small nurseries near Statesville, North Carolina, sold this apple in the late 1800s and early 1900s. Mr. Kessler of Kessler Nursery originated Vandever June and named it for a friend. It was prominent at one time in Iredell County and is still being grown there. Tom found several trees near Statesville and cut scions from a tree owned by Buster Holton.

Fruit medium size, roundish or occasionally slightly oblong, often oblique; skin pale greenish or yellow, washed and striped pinkish and grainy red under heavy scarf skin; stem barely medium length. Ripe July/August.

**VANHOY** (Van Hoy's No Core, Van Hay's No Core): This unusual apple originated in Forsyth County, North Carolina, and is notable for its very small core, usually having few seeds. It is highly praised in old North Carolina catalogs as "one of the best large winter apples" and "an extra good keeping apple of first quality." Beach (1905), however, rates Vanhoy as unattractive and only fair in quality as grown in New York. There is some mystery concerning this apple, as several rural North Carolinians have told me that Vanhoy is identical to York Imperial, an apple known to have a small core. A tree identified as Van Hoy No Core has been found in an old orchard near Valle Crucis, North Carolina. Family lore is that a scion was transported to Watauga County in the early 1800s and was kept alive by being stuck in a potato. *See* Johnny No Core.

Fruit medium or large, roundish, slightly conical; skin smooth, thick, mostly overspread with dull red and stripes of darker red; dots conspicuous, pale yellow or russet; stem medium to long and rather thick in an acute, deep, often compressed, sometimes russeted cavity; calyx closed; basin corrugated; flesh yellowish, firm, crisp, juicy, slightly coarse, mild subacid. Ripe late. Catalog listings: VA, NC (1875–1902). ❖ **Plate 61.**

**VINE** (Vine Apple, Large Vine?): Sold from 1895 to 1910 by the J. Van Lindley Nursery of Greensboro, North Carolina. It originated in Patrick County, Virginia, and was grown mostly in the piedmont along the Virginia-North Carolina line. Its name comes from its thin, wiry, new growth.

After searching for several years, I finally found trees of the Vine apple in three different places in North Carolina and Virginia, and I thank those people who helped seek it out for me, especially Roy Wood near Stuart, Virginia. Annie Boles, of Francisco, North Carolina, sent me scions from a tree behind her sister's old house. "Most of the limbs are high and out of reach, but I finally found some water sprouts I could get to. I'm sending these sprouts hoping some will be worthwhile."

Fruit medium or above, round to oblong, conical, distinctly lobed; skin rough, yellow, sometimes with a blush on one side; heavily dotted with large, irregular, russet dots and cracks, which are often areole; stem very long and slender in a rather deep, russeted cavity; calyx closed or partially open; basin medium depth with some russeting; flesh yellowish, fine-grained, juicy, crisp, subacid. Ripe October and keeps rather well.

**VIRGINIA BEAUTY** (Zach's Red): If (Red) Delicious had not come along at about the same time, I believe Virginia Beauty would have become an important commercial apple in the South. As it turns out, Virginia Beauty was pushed aside and is now a rare variety. Its mild flavor and glossy, dark red color make it a fine eating apple, and it keeps well enough to be successfully marketed in the late fall and early winter.

Virginia Beauty is adapted to much of the South. A 1908 North Carolina agricultural bulletin recommends it for growing in the mountains, piedmont, and coastal plains. Also in 1908, a USDA observer noted Virginia Beauty growing well on clay soils in the piedmont. The tree is moderately productive and stocky with limbs that grow at wide angles from the trunk, a very desirable growth trait. It seems to me to be resistant to fire blight, and I consider well-colored Virginia Beauty apples to be the most beautiful apples in my orchard.

Virginia Beauty is a good example of an apple grown for many years in a local area before its qualities became widely recognized and larger nurseries began selling it. The original tree grew from a seed planted about 1810 in Zach Safewright's yard in the Piper's Gap District of Carroll County, Virginia (at that time still part of Grayson County). This original tree began bearing apples about 1820. A man named Martin Stoneman, who did grafting for local people, took scions from the tree and grafted it throughout Carroll, Grayson, Wythe, and Pulaski counties. It was first called Zach or Zach's Red, but about 1850 it become known as Virginia Beauty. It was not until 1869 that a major nursery, the Franklin Davis Nursery of Richmond, began selling Virginia Beauty and extolling its many good qualities. The original tree stood until 1914.

Ralph Ward, great-great-great grandson of Newell Stoneman, younger brother of Martin Stoneman, discussed Virginia Beauty with me in 1996. Family lore is that it was Newell Stoneman who renamed Zach's Red, calling it Virginia Beauty. In 1985 I got scions of Virginia Beauty from Frank Reese of Taylorsville, North Carolina. He wrote: "I grafted my tree forty years ago from an old tree set at my spring about 1850 by my great grandmother Annie Watts Echert. My tree will have 25 bushels in a good year."

The following tribute to this wonderful apple was written to the USDA in 1914 by F. H. LaBaume, a Virginia farmer and fruit grower: "The Virginia Beauty seems the very acme of deliciousness among eating apples. Others, as rich in flavor, do not have its sprightly juiciness. No other apple that I know combines in the same degree its rich, red beauty and delicious eating quality. It has a distinctive flavor all of its own that clings to the palate and lingers in the memory for a lifetime."

Fruit medium to large, variable in shape, but usually roundish conical, often lopsided; skin smooth, entirely covered with purplish or bronzish red, rarely showing dim, darker red stripes; dots numerous, variable in size, light-colored and russet, some indented; stem short to medium and rather thick in a greenish tan, russeted cavity with the russet spilling out over the top of the apple; calyx closed or partly open; basin shallow, slightly furrowed and lumpy; flesh pale yellow, fine-grained, tender, juicy, mild subacid to almost sweet. Ripe September/October. Catalog listings: MD, VA, NC (1869–1920). ❖ **Plate 62.**

❧ **VIRGINIA GREENING** (Green Mountain Pippin, Ross Greening, Rose Greening, Virginia Pippin?, Virginia Apple, Virginia Winter?, Virginia Blush): The origin of this very old apple is unknown, but certainly it originated in Virginia in the 1700s. It was briefly described in an 1829 issue of *New England Farmer* magazine from apples received from Virginia. Virginia Greening was never sold by Virginia nurseries under this name, but it was sold by nurseries in five other southern states. Two Virginia nurseries listed Ross Greening, a synonym

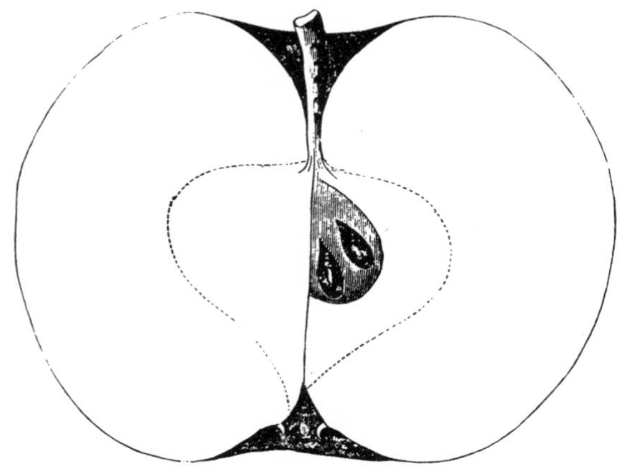

VIRGINIA GREENING

of Virginia Greening, from 1858 to 1869 without description. Warder (1867) says Virginia Greening is subject to bitter rot. Tom Burford of Virginia sent me scions.

Fruit medium to large, oblate or roundish; skin thick, tough, green changing to greenish yellow with a light blush or bronzing on the sunny side; dots scattered, large, usually irregular russet or reddish; stem short to medium in a large, wide, russeted cavity; calyx open; basin wide, shallow, abrupt, corrugated; flesh yellowish, compact, breaking, coarse, subacid but almost sweet when ripe. Ripe late September/October. Catalog listings as Virginia Greening and Ross Greening: VA, TN, AL, LA, KY, TX (1858–1890).

❦ **WALTER TIBBS:** Dr. L. R. Littleton found "a very old and almost dead tree north of Mountain Grove, Virginia, set out by Uncle Walter Tibbs' father who was a slave."

Fruit medium, roundish conical, often oblique; skin light green washed with pale red with darker red, broken stripes; dots scattered, gray, often with tiny russet centers; stem medium to long in a greenish or brown russeted cavity; calyx open or closed; basin wide. Ripe September/October. No catalog listings.

❦ **WATERMELON:** Found by Tom Brown in Haywood County, North Carolina, and almost certainly different from the Water Melon listed in the chapter on extinct varieties.

Fruit medium or below, roundish; skin greenish yellow covered with a heavy bloom over light and darker red blotches that cover most of the apple; stem medium to long ending in a swelling. Ripe September. No catalog listings.

❦ **WEALTHY:** Originated about 1860 with Peter M. Gideon of Excelsior, Minnesota, from seeds of the Cherry Crab and widely sold by southern nurseries as an attractive apple borne on a hardy, healthy, productive tree. One Maryland nursery recommended Wealthy as a "filler" tree in orchards because it bears fruit on very young trees. As grown in the North, Wealthy is a late fall apple keeping in cold storage until January or later. In warmer areas of the South it ripens as early as July or August and is not a good keeper. In 1908 the USDA found Wealthy to be well adapted to much of the South. The tree tends to be a biennial bearer and is susceptible to fire blight, scab, and cedar-apple rust.

Fruit medium or above, roundish to roundish oblate, conical; skin shaded and striped with red; dots numerous, small, pale or russet; stem usually short to medium length and slender in an acute, rather deep, lightly russeted cavity; basin medium to deep, abrupt; flesh white, sometimes stained pink near the skin, moderately fine-grained, crisp, tender, very juicy, subacid. Ripe August. Catalog listings: MD, VA, AL, LA, TN, KY, TX, AR (1887–1928).

❦ **WESTERN BEAUTY** (Beauty of the West, Big Rambo, Musgrove's Cooper, Ohio Beauty, Grosh, Wells, Mammoth Rambo, Large Summer Rambo, Summer Rambo [incorrectly]): First described in 1829 in Ohio but probably originated with John Grosh in Marietta, Pennsylvania, about 1815. The fruit very closely resembles Summer Rambo but ripens somewhat later. A 1904 Maryland nursery catalog says: "Never water cores and not disposed to rot; one of the best fall apples."

Fruit medium to large, roundish oblate; skin thin, nearly covered with red and striped with darker red; dots numerous, gray; stem medium length in a deep cavity; calyx closed or half open; basin large, broad, slightly corrugated; flesh yellowish, moderately juicy and tender, mild subacid. Ripe August. Catalog listings: MD, VA, NC, AL, KY (1870–1914). ❖ **Plate 63.**

❦ **WHITE WINTER PEARMAIN** (Campbellite, Griffin's Pearmain [in Texas], Michael Henry Pippin?, White Pearmain): Warder (1867) gives the history of this high-quality apple: "This favorite fruit was brought to Indiana by . . . saddlebag transportation. In one lot of grafts, two varieties, having lost their labels, were propagated and fruited without name. Being Pearmain shaped, they were called respectively, Red and White Winter Pearmains. The former proved to be Esopus Spitzenburg; the latter has never yet been identified, though believed to be an old eastern variety."

White Winter Pearmain was widely sold and praised by southern nurseries for its annual yield and excellent eating quality. In 1870 one North Carolina nursery said: "Regarded by leading pomologists of this state as the highest flavored apple in cultivation. The soil must be rich to perfect the fruit."

Southern nurseries often listed Michael Henry Pippin as a synonym of White Winter Pearmain as did Elliott (1858), Downing (1878), and the USDA in 1869. Beach (1905), however, says that there is convincing evidence that Michael Henry Pippin (an old New Jersey apple) and White Winter Pearmain are different apple varieties. The descriptions of these two apples are an extremely close fit.

Fruit medium or above, roundish to slightly oblong, conical, often oblique; skin smooth, waxy, greenish turning to pale yellow, sometimes with a faint blush or bronzing, perhaps clouded with darker green in splotches or spots; dots numerous, small, pale or russet, elongated around the cavity; stem short to almost medium length; cavity acute, deep, somewhat furrowed, sometimes russeted; calyx closed; basin usually furrowed; flesh white or yellowish, tender, crisp, juicy, fine-grained, aromatic, subacid to almost sweet. Ripe September/October and a fairly good keeper. Catalog listings: MD, VA, NC, KY, TX, AR (1853–1926). ❖ **Plate 64.**

❦ **WILLIAMS FAVORITE** (Williams, Williams Apple, Williams Early Red, Ladies Apple, Queen, Williams Red, Southern Queen, Summer Queen [incorrectly], Early Red, Red, Favorite, Motto?): A tree full of Williams Favorite apples is a sight to behold with the bright red apples contrasted against the green foliage. From the large number of southern nurseries that listed Williams Favorite, it was grown widely in the South around 1900. The USDA reported in 1908: "Recently it has disclosed its special merit as a summer apple for both home use and market in portions of North Carolina and South Carolina where few northern varieties succeed. . . . Some of the finest specimens of this variety seen in recent years have been grown in Delaware, Virginia, North Carolina and South Carolina." The USDA successfully experimented with shipping Williams Favorite apples to England in the early 1900s, noting that the apples possess the firm flesh and tough skin necessary for market transportation. The fruit, at first glance, very closely resembles a Red Delicious, but Williams Favorite is brighter red and ripens months earlier. In warmer areas of the South the fruit tends to be red mostly on the sunny side rather than all over. The tree is said to be resistant to fire blight.

The original tree grew on the farm of Captain Benjamin Williams in Roxbury, Massachusetts, about 1750. The fruit was known there as Queen or Ladies Apple. It was introduced to public notice by being exhibited to the Massachusetts Horticultural Society in 1830 where it was renamed Williams Favorite. It gradually worked its way into the South in the late years of the nineteenth century. Some southern nurseries, knowingly or unknowingly, sold trees of Sops of Wine under the name of Williams Favorite.

Fruit medium or above, roundish to oblong, conical, often lobed, sometimes angular; skin smooth, heavily washed and striped with two shades of bright red, darker red on the sunny side; dots scattered, inconspicuous, small, white and russet, some areole; stem about an inch long and rather thick, often pushed to one side, in a wide, often russeted and lipped cavity; calyx closed; basin rather deep, slightly furrowed; flesh yellowish white, stained red at the core line, breaking, tender, moderately juicy, mild subacid. Ripe July. Catalog listings: MD, VA, NC, GA, TN, KY, TX (1853–1928). ❖ **Plate 65.**

❦ **WILLOW TWIG** (Willow, James River, Willow Leaf?, Maryland Red Streak?, Missing Link?, Red Willow Twig): Beach (1905) cites Willow Twig as representative of many southern winter apples that are not of the highest quality but that are "good long keepers." His description of Willow Twig is reinforced by the following exchange, which took place between several delegates to the 1860 meeting of the American Pomological Society:

Warder, of Ohio: I propose the Willow Twig, known also as Willow or James River. A large sized apple, one of our best market fruits. Thousands of dollars have been brought back for years and years by those who have taken this apple in large quanti-

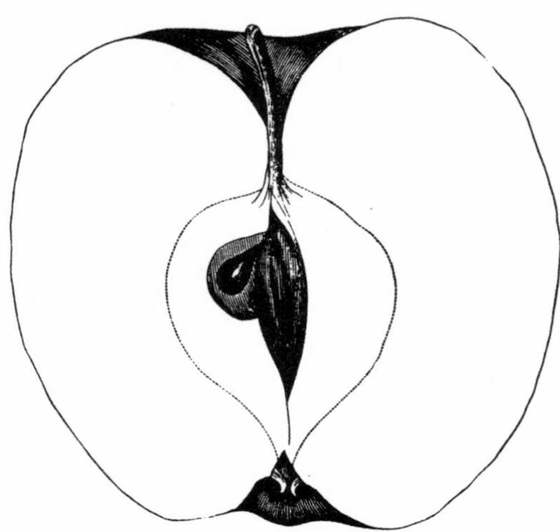

WILLOW TWIG

ties down the Mississippi. It is known all along the banks of the Ohio, though I believe it of southern origin, from Virginia. The tree is a good bearer, though not heavy.

Bissel, of Pennsylvania: Willow Twig apples have been kept in the neighborhood of Pittsburgh for two years. Fair but not a high flavored apple.

Stewart, of Illinois: It is considered by our market dealers as the most valuable fruit of the apple species. It will keep twelve months. Hangs on the tree until late in the season. Bears a uniform crop and when properly packed will keep all winter. It is salable to the last of June.

The origin of Willow Twig is unknown. Warder attributed its origin to Virginia (but did not cite a source for his information), and Willow Twig was first mentioned in an 1845 West Virginia (then Virginia) nursery catalog. It was an important commercial apple in orchards along the Ohio River (as well as in Missouri, Arkansas, and Kansas) for shipment to southern markets, particularly New Orleans. Its susceptibility to apple scab, fire blight, and other diseases proved to be its downfall, and by 1900 Willow Twig had been entirely replaced by Ben Davis. In 1908 the USDA reported it to be well adapted to the piedmont and mountains of the South at elevations of 1,200 to 3,800 feet.

A red sport of Willow Twig, named Red Willow Twig, was found in an orchard in Calhoun County, Illinois, and was grown to some extent in the 1930s. Red Willow Twig is available. Another mutation, Red Willow, was discovered in Columbiana County, Ohio, in 1939 by E. E. Leeper.

Fruit usually medium but sometimes larger, roundish to roundish oblate, conical, faintly ribbed; skin smooth, mottled and blushed with dull red and irregularly striped and splashed with darker red; dots numerous, rather large, russet or yellowish; stem short and slender in an acute, deep, often compressed or lipped, usually green cavity; calyx closed or partially closed; basin abrupt, wide, irregular or compressed, sometimes wrinkled; flesh yellowish green, coarse, not very tender, crisp, juicy, subacid. Ripe October. Catalog listings: MD, VA, SC, GA, AL, LA, TN, KY, TX, AR (1845–1923).

**WILSON:** Two years ago my friend Bruce Ingram, on a wild turkey hunt in West Virginia, found two old apple trees on the Roger Wilson farm in Fayette County. Family lore is that this apple was brought from Scotland in the 1740s when the family purchased the land that Roger Wilson still occupies. From the late 1800s to the 1920s the Wilson apple was grown commercially in the area. "It is a great variety for apple butter and general stovetop cooking," Roger Wilson says. "My family likes it in fried pies, and we dry the apples for the winter, too. It keeps fine for six months." My thanks to Bruce Ingram for the above information.

An apple named Wilson was sold from 1858 to 1869 by two Virginia nurseries without description, probably this very variety. No description.

**WILSON JUNE** (Wilson Red June?, Mammoth June?): This apple could be confused with Wilson's June and Wilson's Summer, both of which are also summer apples of southern origin. With Wilson's June and Wilson's Summer, both apparently extinct, there is no way to compare the fruit to help clear up the confusion.

Wilson June can be traced back to Arkansas. A man named Earle Holt, who had a small nursery there, died just prior to the Civil War. His nursery was completely neglected during the War, but afterwards the surviving apple trees were sold off. Some of these were grafted trees, but a large number were seedlings, probably originally grown for rootstocks.

About a thousand trees from Holt's nursery were planted in 1865 on the William Wilson farm, five miles northwest of Prairie Grove, Arkansas. In 1867 one tree bore fruit that attracted local attention, being unrecognized as an existing variety by anyone in that area. Grafts were taken and trees were sold through two local nurseries that called this apple Wilson June. Wilson June fell into obscurity in the 1880s but was rediscovered by W. M. Norwood, who began selling it in his nursery about 1890. There is sketchy information indicating that Wilson June was called Lady Sweet in Benton County, Arkansas, about 1880, but this is improbable as Wilson June is not a sweet apple. (Lady Sweet is a synonym of Howard Sweet, an apple that also originated in Earle Holt's nursery.) Wilson June is not the same apple as Carolina Red June. Carolina Red June is a medium-size, red-blushed apple, whereas Wilson June is a larger, darker red apple with faint stripes.

Stark Bro's Nursery sold an apple called Wilson Red June. Their 1928 catalog states that they found this apple in an orchard near Farmington, Arkansas, and that it is "almost as large and as brilliantly red as Black Ben. Ripe mid-summer." Certainly this is the same apple as Wilson June.

Fruit medium to almost large, roundish conical, sometimes slightly oblong, ribbed; skin almost entirely purplish red with faint darker stripes sometimes visible; dots small, scattered, gray and russet; stem medium length in a medium-depth, russeted cavity; basin usually shallow and wide; flesh white, juicy, crisp, subacid. Ripe July/August. ❖ **Plate 66.**

❦ **WINE** (Hay's Winter, Winter Haze, English Redstreak, Pennsylvania Red Streak, Winter Wine, Wine Apple, Hollow Crown Pearmain, Redstreak, Winter Red, Fine Winter, Hays Wine, Wine of Pennsylvania, Large Winter Red): A Delaware apple first described by Coxe (1817) and well adapted to growing in the South. Elliot (1858) says, "Strong heavy clay loams produce the largest fruit, while best quality fruit is grown on sandy loams." The tree grows very large on seedling rootstock and has small, curled leaves. This apple should not be confused with Fall Wine, which is somewhat smaller, ripens a month earlier, and has coarse flesh.

Fruit above medium to large, roundish, flattened on the ends, sides often unequal; skin smooth, mostly covered with splashes and broken stripes of deep red, but more yellow when the fruit is shaded; dots scattered, large, gray; stem short in a smooth, deep, russeted cavity; flesh yellowish white, juicy, firm, crisp, subacid. Ripe October. Catalog listings: MD, VA, NC, GA, AL, KY, TX (1827–1925).

❦ **WINESAP** (Holland's Red Winter, Royal Red, Texan Red, Old Fashion Winesap, Blacktwig, Potpie, Refugee, Winter Winesap, Wine Sop, Dukes Winesap?, Banana): Historically, no other apple even comes close to being as popular in the South as the Winesap. By a large margin it is the apple variety listed in old southern nursery catalogs more often than any other. Let the following quotes from old catalogs speak for the Winesap:

> "This apple stands unrivaled, combining more excellent qualities than any other we know of for cider and for table use. As a good keeper it is unsurpassed, and we earnestly recommend it to all." (Tennessee, 1887)

> "We can scarcely find words sufficiently strong to express the high opinion we have of this fruit, possessing as it does so many excellent qualities." (Virginia, 1872)

> "We believe it is the finest apple that grows in America. If we were setting out an orchard of a thousand trees, eight hundred of them would be Winesaps." (South Carolina, 1845)

> "More largely planted than any apple grown in this state and deservedly popular." (Kentucky, 1897)

> "Named for its delicious, sprightly, winy flavor. Universally popular, known to everyone and liked by everybody. No one can go amiss when he plants Winesaps." (North Carolina, 1910)

> "This is to winter what the Horse apple is to summer. There is nothing to surpass it." (North Carolina, 1879)

What are the qualities of Winesap that have earned such praise by southerners for so many years? Perhaps most importantly, it grows well on most southern soils, even clays. An 1893 Tennessee catalog says it best: "There is no winter apple that will do better than the Winesap on second or third rate land with ordinary culture." There is some evidence that Winesap apples are bigger and color better when grown on clay soils in the upper piedmont rather than on richer soils in the mountains. Second only to this wide adaptability is the fine eating quality of Winesap. It seems to have a flavor most southerners like, with a "twang" or snap to it that lingers in the memory.

To Winesap's adaptability and eating quality, add that elusive trait so sought by southerners in the days before refrigeration—keeping ability. Winesap is a great keeper even when southern-grown. Almost anywhere in the South it will keep until March or April when carefully picked and stored. Commercially grown Winesaps in the late 1800s were often the last apples to be marketed each year, sometimes as late as May or June.

The last important trait of Winesap is its productiveness. The tree usually bears heavily every year, and the fruit hangs well on the tree. Even in bad years Winesap trees will often have a light crop when other apples fail entirely, probably because the tree blooms rather late. Winesap is almost immune to cedar-apple rust and is moderately resistant to fire blight.

No apple has only good qualities, and Winesap is no exception. The tree is a straggling and drooping grower. The fruit can often be rather small unless care is given to pruning, thinning, and fertility. The pollen of Winesap is sterile and worthless for pollinating other apple varieties.

Winesap certainly originated in New Jersey before 1800. It was first described, as a cider apple, by Dr. James Mease in a book published in Philadelphia in 1804. He makes no mention of the origin of Winesap, noting only "cultivated by Samuel Coles, of Moore's Town, New Jersey." William Coxe (1817), in his great book on American fruit, describes and illustrates the Winesap and says, "becoming the most favorite cider fruit in West Jersey." By 1824 Winesap was being sold as a cider and eating apple by a Washington, D.C., nursery.

Winesap has given rise to many seedlings that have become important southern apples. Chief among these are Kinnaird's Choice, Stayman, Blacktwig, Arkansas Black, and Turley Winesap. It is strange that all of these famous Winesap seedlings originated west of the Appalachian Mountains. I grow a Winesap I found under the name "Old Fashion Winesap" being grown by the late E. Lloyd Curl of Alamance County, North Carolina.

Up until about 1950 Winesap was one of the leading commercial apple varieties in the United States. Since then its commercial production has rapidly diminished because cold storage and "controlled atmosphere" storage allow the late marketing of other apple varieties that normally would not keep as long as Winesap.

Many mutations or sports of Winesap have been found and exploited over the years because they have a redder color than the original Winesap. A whole-tree sport having dark red fruit was found in 1922 in the Garland Orchards near Troutville, Virginia. This sport was named Virginia Winesap and was sold by Stark Bro's Nursery until the late 1940s. Many old trees of Virginia Winesap are still bearing fruit in the South.

Fruit medium, usually roundish but sometimes rather oblate, conical, flattened at the base; skin tough, mostly covered with splashes and occasionally stripes of dark red, sometimes with patches of yellow near the stem, sometimes with a faint bloom, often with a fine russet netting especially near the stem end; dots small or medium size, scattered, whitish and russet; stem about medium length in an acute, deep, narrow, russeted cavity; calyx closed; basin usually shallow, rather small, corrugated; flesh yellow, firm, crisp, very juicy, fine-grained, sprightly subacid becoming sweeter in storage. Ripe September/October and a good keeper. Catalog listings: DC, MD, VA, NC, SC, GA, AL, LA, TN, KY, TX, AR (1824–1928).

❦ **WINTER BANANA** (Banana, Flory): My friend Elwood Fisher of Harrisonburg, Virginia, at one time had over a thousand varieties of apples growing in his backyard. He says Winter Banana is his favorite, but admits he is prejudiced because it is the apple he fondly remembers from his youth. Winter Banana is a fine eating apple, aromatic, and mild-flavored, with some people discerning a banana perfume. It is generally considered too mild in flavor to be useful for cooking. The tree blooms late, alternates large and small crops, and often bears fruit the second or third year after planting. The fruit bruises easily, and the tree is suceptible to fire blight and cedar-apple rust.

Winter Banana originated about 1876 on the farm of David Flory, Cass County, Indiana, and was introduced in 1890.

Fruit usually above medium to large but not uniform in size or shape, roundish to oblong but sometimes oblate, conical, often ribbed and oblique, often with a suture line; skin smooth, tough, waxy, bright pale yellow, usually with a blush that is sometimes dark pinkish red on well-colored apples; dots numerous, whitish or with russet points; cavity rather large, acute, broad, furrowed; basin often oblique, usually narrow, furrowed; flesh whitish, crisp, tender, juicy, aromatic, fine-grained, subacid. Ripe September. Catalog listings: MD, VA, NC, SC, GA, AL, LA, TN, KY, TX, AR (1890–1928).

❦ **WINTER CHEESE:** Introduced by E. R. Turnbull of Brunswick County, Virginia, and briefly mentioned in an 1853 horticultural magazine. Sold by Virginia nurseries from 1858 to 1904. George Wood of Meadows of Dan, Virginia, wrote me of his Winter Cheese tree in 1990.

Fruit medium, oblate; skin yellow or orangish striped with red, some apples are mostly red; dots russet; stem short to medium in a medium-size, russeted cavity; basin rather deep; flesh very juicy, crisp, subacid. Ripe October. ❖ **Plate 67.**

❦ **WINTER JON** (Winter John, Sour Jon): A mountain apple of unknown origin grown in the southern Appalachians for many years but not described in any old catalogs or other pomological literature. It is excellent for cider and jelly, ripens very late, and often hangs on the tree until December. Tart as a lemon in October, it mellows on the tree. I like to pick and eat Winter Jon apples off the tree in late November and even December, the last apples hanging in my orchard.

Fruit small, often very small, roundish conical; skin pale dull yellow, often heavily leather-cracked, occasionally blushed; dots few, large, irregular, russet; stem medium to almost long in an irregular, russeted cavity with russet extending over the top of the apple, calyx closed; basin round, leather-cracked; flesh whitish, a little tough, juicy, briskly subacid with an unusual flavor all its own. Ripe late October to mid-November or even later. No catalog listings. ❖ **Plate 68.**

❦ **WINTER MAY:** This apple was listed in the 1910 catalog of the W. H. Crawford Nursery of Statesville, North Carolina. In 2000 Tom Brown found a single old tree owned by Diana King of Statesville.

Fruit medium, slightly oblong conical, often oblique; skin greenish yellow occasionally with a faint pink blush on the sunny side; dots small, whitish with russet centers; stem short to medium, ending in a large knob in a russeted cavity; basin deep, corrugated; flesh fine-grained, firm, juicy, mild subacid. Ripe October.

❦ **WINTER SWEET PARADISE** (Paradise Winter Sweet, Winter Paradise, Grandmother, Honey Sweet, Wine Sweet, Pennsylvania Sweet Paradise, White Robinson, Paradise Sweet?): Fruit of this variety was sent to A. J. Downing about 1842 along with Summer Sweet Paradise by a Mr. Garber of Columbia, Pennsylvania. It probably originated near Paradise, Lancaster County, Pennsylvania.

In 1908 the USDA reported it to be a popular, local market apple in Virginia, where it frequently sold for high prices. Winter Sweet Paradise grows well at altitudes of 1,200 to 1,500 feet in the piedmont and mountains. At higher altitudes, the fruit is often smaller and of poorer dessert quality. The fruit is subject to bitter rot.

Fruit above medium to large, roundish oblate; skin dull green, becoming lighter green or yellowish

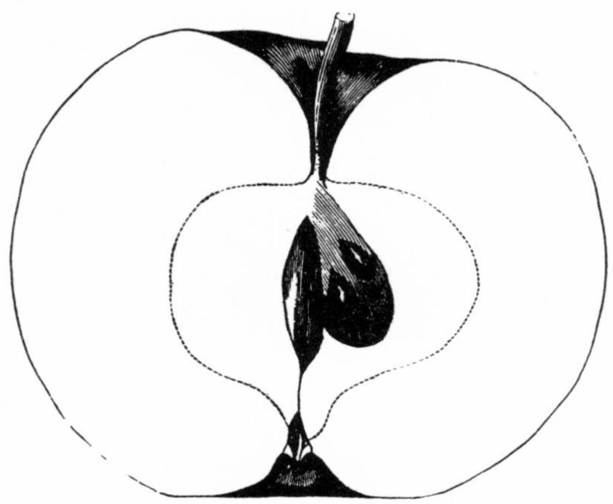

WINTER SWEET PARADISE

at maturity, sometimes slightly blushed with dull brownish or purplish red on one side; stem short in a round, deep, often russeted cavity; calyx closed; basin abrupt, corrugated; flesh white, fine-grained, juicy, tender, aromatic, sweet, sometimes said to have a pear flavor. Ripe September or later and a good keeper. Catalog listings: MD, VA, NC, SC, KY (1853–1928). *See also* Robertson's White. ❖ **Plate 69.**

❦ **WOLF RIVER:** The fruit of Wolf River is very large, often enormous. It was (and still is to some extent) very popular in western North Carolina and Virginia, where old trees still can be found. The fresh eating quality of Wolf River is only fair at best, but it is a good cooking and drying apple. It is prized for making apple butter, and the flesh cooks to a smooth applesauce.

Wolf River originated with William A. Springer, a Québec lumberman. About 1856 Mr. Springer moved his family by wagon from Canada to Wisconsin. On the way, on the shore of Lake Erie, he bought a bushel of large apples, probably Alexander. Mr. Springer saved some seeds and planted them when he reached his new farm, which was located on a little stream called Wolf River near Fremont, Wisconsin. The Wolf River apple originated from one of these seeds. Mr. Springer is reported to have sold the tree (and probably his farm) to a man named Henry Riflen before it fruited. Wolf River resembles Alexander but is usually larger and flatter. The tree is a vigorous grower, does not bear early, and is productive biennially or almost annually. As grown in much of the South, it is an early autumn apple and does not keep well. If allowed to get overripe on the tree, the fruit becomes mealy and tends to rot quickly. Wolf River is susceptible to fire blight but resistant to scab and mildew.

Fruit large to very large, roundish oblate to oblate, flattened on the ends, often irregular, angular, ribbed; skin mostly covered with bright red with splashes and broad stripes of carmine, often with a thin whitish bloom; dots large, whitish and russet; stem usually very short and rather thick in a deep, acute, medium-width, russeted cavity; calyx open; basin medium to deep, narrow, abrupt, wavy; flesh whitish, coarse-grained, soft, tender, moderately juicy, subacid. Ripe September. Catalog listings: MD, VA, NC, GA, AL, TN, KY, TX, AR (1895–1928).

❦ **WORLD'S BEST:** An apple grown in and around Robbinsville, North Carolina, since at least 1900. A tree belonging to Floyd Sherrill was found by Tom Brown in 2000.

Fruit below medium, oblate; skin covered with red and darker red stripes; dots numerous, gray; stem almost long in a gradually sloped, shallow cavity; calyx partly open; basin greenish, wide, round; flesh grainy, moderately crisp and juicy, mild subacid. Ripe August. No catalog listings.

❦ **WRIXPARENT:** Wrixparent originated about 1920 as a seedling in an orchard of Yellow Transparent apples belonging to Wrixham McIlvain, near Magnolia, Delaware. The tree is an annual and heavy bearer of bruise-resistant apples that ripen one to two weeks before Yellow Transparent. The tree seems to have some resistance to fire blight and other diseases and is a rare tetraploid (having extra chromosomes) like Levering Limbertwig. Thirty other tetraploid apple varieties are known, but Wrixparent is the only one of any importance.

Fruit usually large, oblate; skin light green without any markings; flesh white, crisp, fine-grained, sprightly subacid. Ripe June. No catalog listings.

❦ **YANKEE SWEET** (Yankee?): Popular at one time in Floyd County and around Roanoke, Virginia, but very rare now. I found Yankee Sweet when I received a letter in 1990 from Harriet S. Allen, who lived about eight miles north of Floyd, Virginia. The day I spent with her looking for old apples is a very fond memory for me. Mrs. Allen was an excellent guide although almost blind from macular degeneration. She said the apples are good for canning and make excellent apple preserves and apple marmalade.

Fruit medium, roundish conical, flattened on the ends; skin yellowish or light green, never blushed; dots numerous, rough, russet, often with a green areole; stem long in a narrow, deep, russeted cavity with the russet often extending out over the top of the apple; calyx usually closed; basin small, rather shallow; flesh whitish tinged yellow, fine-grained, juicy, moderately crisp, mildly sweet. Ripe August/September. No catalog listings. ❖ **Plate 70.**

❧ **YATES** (Yates Winter, Red Warrior, Jates, Ferguson Late): Yates is among the elite of southern apples, being sold continuously by southern nurseries for 130 years and still listed by several nurseries. At first glance you might ignore such a small apple, but its good qualities have kept it a southern favorite. Yates certainly is a small apple, being as small as some crab apples. For the fruit to make any size at all, the apples need to be severely thinned when they are pea-sized. The juicy apples make excellent winter cider, which can be pressed late because the apples keep so well. Often dropped fruit can be gathered under trees in December, or even later, in perfectly good condition. Even in the warmer coastal plains of the South, Yates keeps until spring with little care if, as one old catalog puts it, "you can keep the children from them." According to an article in an 1874 horticultural magazine, "insect punctures do not cause it to dry rot."

Yates originated about 1844 with Matthew Yates of Fayette County, Georgia, and was often called Red Warrior in the South.

Fruit small, roundish to oblate; skin mostly covered with shades and stripes of dark red; dots numerous, gray or russet; stem medium to long in a large, russeted cavity; calyx closed; basin wide and shallow, slightly corrugated; flesh white, sometimes stained red near the skin, tender, juicy, aromatic, mild subacid to almost sweet. Ripe October/November. Catalog listings: MD, VA, NC, SC, GA, AL, MS, LA, TN, KY, TX (1861–1928).

❧ **YELLOW BELLFLOWER** (Fall Bellflower, Belle Fleur, Bellflower, Lady Washington, Warren Pippin, Yellow Sheepnose, Sheepnose, Lincoln Pippin, Mrs. Barron, Bishop Pippin): There is conflicting information in old references whether Yellow Bellflower is widely adapted to the South. *The Southern Apple and Peach Culturist* (1872) says it is well adapted to Tidewater Virginia (where it is a fall apple) as well as the Shenandoah Valley (where it is a good-keeping winter apple). On the other hand, an 1880 Richmond catalog says Yellow Bellflower is not adapted to the Richmond area but is "very profitable in the Valley and Western Virginia." A Delaware grower reported in 1856 that the fruit dropped prematurely. The USDA found it growing in all parts of Virginia in 1908, but "there is nothing to recommend it in any of these situations." In any case it was listed by forty-six southern nurseries over a hundred-year period, so many southerners must have liked and grown Yellow Bellflower. The fruit is excellent for pies and cider and outstanding for applesauce.

Coxe (1817) describes Yellow Bellflower and says the original tree grew in Burlington, New Jersey. This variety does not get very high marks from Beach (1905), who describes the tree as susceptible to apple scab, not very productive, and often bearing a high percentage of undersize fruit. According to several old references, Yellow Bellflower requires a light, well-drained soil to do well, and the trees are often slow to begin bearing. I find it susceptible to fire blight. Mr. and Mrs. Ray Delp of Woodlawn, Virginia, gave me scions from an old tree in Mrs. Delp's father's orchard.

Fruit variable in size, small to large, sometimes very large, oblong conical, but often barrel-shaped and ribbed with prominent knobs at the calyx end, sides usually unequal; skin smooth, pale lemon yellow, often blushed with brownish red or pinkish red; dots conspicuous, whitish or russet, small at the basin end but larger and more irregular at the stem end; stem usually medium to long and slender in an acute, deep, furrowed, sometimes compressed or lipped, usually russeted cavity; calyx usually closed;

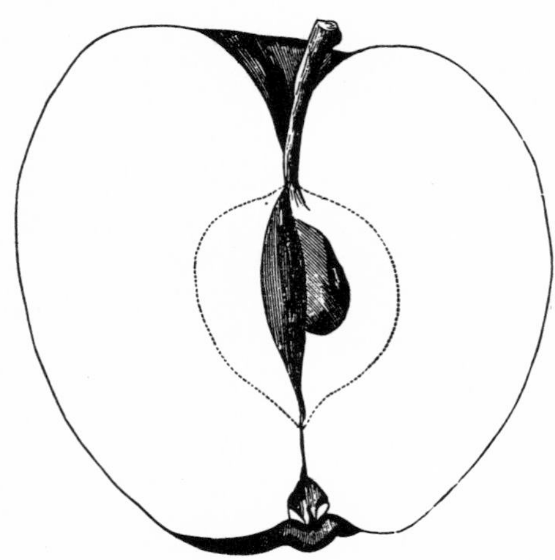

YELLOW BELLFLOWER

basin small, abrupt, narrow, ridged; flesh whitish tinged pale yellow, firm, crisp, rather tender, juicy, aromatic, acid when first picked but becoming less acid later. Ripe September. Catalog listings: MD, VA, DC, NC, SC AL, LA, TN, KY, TX, AR (1824–1928).

❦ **YELLOW HARDIN** (Yellow Flat?, Yellow Hard?): Found by Tom Brown in 2002 in Wilkes County, North Carolina, and probably the same apple as Yellow Flat, which I found in Woolwine, Virginia, in the 1990s. Tom says, "A famous Wilkes brandy apple which made the most brandy per bushel, a quart more."

Fruit below medium, oblate, slightly conical, flat on the ends; skin bright, waxy yellow, sometimes faintly blushed; dots irregular in shape, russet; stem short in a wide, russeted cavity; calyx closed. Ripe August/September. No catalog listings.

❦ **YELLOW JUNE** (White Juneating?, Hoover June): A southern apple of unknown origin that ripens the same time as Carolina Red June. It should not be confused with Yellow Sweet June, which is a synonym for Hightop Sweet. Yellow June is probably identical to White Juneating. Many apples called Yellow June are actually Early Harvest, which has the synonym of Yellow June.

Fruit medium, roundish to roundish oblate; skin thin, pale yellow or greenish yellow; dots numerous, large, green and brown; stem long and slender in a slightly russeted cavity; calyx open; flesh whitish yellow, tender, juicy, brisk subacid. Ripe late June/July. Catalog listings: VA, NC, SC, GA, AL, MS, TN, KY, AR (1845–1925).

❦ **YELLOW POTTS:** Several trees were found in Taylorsville, North Carolina, by Tom Brown. Old trees up to eighty-five years old were in the area. The apple is described as medium size, oblate conical; dull yellow, rough skin; very acid. Ripe late August. No catalog listings.

❦ **YELLOW TRANSPARENT** (Grand Sultan?, Russian Transparent, White Transparent?, Charlottenthaler?, Thaler?, Early Transparent, Early June Transparent): Of the hundreds of Russian apple varieties brought to the United States in the late 1800s by the USDA, this apple caught on with southerners better than any other, and old trees are common in rural areas. The reasons for its popularity are not hard to find. Yellow Transparent trees bear when very young and bear heavy crops. The apples ripen early (often ten days before Early Harvest) and can be kept for a couple of weeks, thus making local marketing possible. The fruit is rather pretty for a yellow apple and a good cooker (making absolutely wonderful applesauce). Last, but certainly not least, Yellow Transparent can be successfully grown all over the South, even in the coastal plains areas, and is quite resistant to cedar-apple rust and scab. Its weaknesses include a high susceptibility to fire blight, biennial bearing, and fruit that is only fair for fresh eating. The flesh rapidly becomes dry in overripe fruit.

There is a mutation of Yellow Transparent (still available) named Perrine Yellow Transparent or Giant Transparent, discovered about 1930 by D. B. Perrine in Centralia, Illinois. Its fruit is larger, somewhat better in quality, and ripens a week earlier than Yellow Transparent. It is also reported to be less susceptible to fire blight. The trees are very compact.

Many southerners grow the Lodi apple, which is similar to Yellow Transparent (perhaps a little larger) and ripens a week or so later. Lodi is a cross of Yellow Transparent × Montgomery from the New York Agricultural Experiment Station, introduced in 1924. It has been sold by Stark Bro's Nursery for many years.

Yellow Transparent was imported into this country by the USDA in 1870 from St. Petersburg, Russia (although it originated in the Baltic region) in the search for cold-hardy apples for the Great Plains. It is the most widely planted summer apple in Europe.

Fruit medium, but above medium to large on young trees or if properly thinned, roundish, conical; skin smooth, transparent, clear white becoming pale yellow when ripe; dots white or greenish, often submerged and obscure; stem short to medium and slender in an acute, rather deep, usually greenish russeted cavity; calyx closed; basin narrow, rather shallow, corrugated; flesh white, tender, juicy, fine-grained, acid to sprightly subacid. Ripe June/July. Catalog listings: MD, VA, NC, GA, AL, LA, TN, KY, TX, AR (1887–1928). ❖ **Plate 71.**

❦ **YORK IMPERIAL** (Johnson's Fine Winter, York, Shep): If you use store-bought apple sauce, canned apple slices, or cider vinegar, the chances are good that they have been made from York Imperial apples grown in Virginia or Pennsylvania. York Imperial has been an important commercial processing apple in Virginia, as well as in Pennsylvania, for many years. While considered mainly a processing apple, York Imperial apples can sometimes be found in supermarkets in the winter and are excellent eating apples. These fresh apples are mostly one of several redder sports or mutations developed from the original York Imperial. About five million bushels of Yorks are produced in this country each year, 2 percent of American commercial apple production.

Until 1930 York Imperial was grown mostly for export to England, but import restrictions were imposed by Great Britain and huge quantities of these apples could not be sold. Seeing this, the apple-processing industry opened factories in Pennsylvania and Virginia to utilize surplus apples. The demand has now increased to the point that new orchards are being planted to provide apples for processing. York Imperial is particularly good for processing as it makes a desirable yellow sauce, the slices keep their shape when canned, and the core is small, thus yielding more usable flesh per apple.

York Imperial originated as a chance seedling that grew up by a turnpike near York, Pennsylvania, on the farm of a Mr. Johnson. Mr. Johnson was an invalid and spent time at his window watching people on the road. He noticed that schoolboys would stop at the seedling tree in early spring to gather apples under the leaves on the ground. Fascinated with this keeping ability, Mr. Johnson notified a local nurseryman named Jonathan Jessup, who began grafting and selling trees about 1820 under the name of Johnson's Fine Winter. There were few buyers for this new fruit the first year, so Mr. Jessup discarded surplus trees near a road on his place. Farmers scavenged up the discarded trees and soon realized the many good qualities of this apple. About 1850 Johnson's Fine Winter was brought to the attention of the famous pomologist Charles Downing, who pronounced it "the Imperial of Keepers" and suggested it be named York Imperial. (Even so, many southern nurseries continued to sell it under the name Johnson's Fine Winter until the early 1900s.) In 1871 the American Pomological Society publicized the merits of York Imperial, and it began being sold by many nurseries, becoming the leading variety in Maryland, Pennsylvania, Virginia, and West Virginia by 1895. It was grown as a high-quality, good-keeping apple to compete with Ben Davis, then flooding eastern markets from the Midwest and Arkansas.

A bronze plaque commemorating York Imperial is located in the Apple Hill Medical Mall in York, Pennsylvania. This site was part of Jonathan Jessup's farm and nursery.

York Imperial is easily recognized by its shape. The apples usually are noticeably oblate and oblique or lopsided, but apples of different shapes are found on the same tree. The tree is quite susceptible to cedar-apple rust, fire blight, and cork-spot. Serious rotting and premature dropping of York Imperial apples occur in the South below elevations of about 1,000 feet. The tree often is a biennial bearer unless the fruit is thinned each year.

Fruit medium to large, usually oblate and oblique, but may be oval or oblong and flattened on the ends; skin heavily splashed and striped with two shades of brownish red, sometimes with russet patches; dots few, gray, often areolar; stem short in a deep, wavy, narrow, russeted cavity; calyx nearly closed; basin wide, shallow, furrowed, abrupt; flesh yellow, firm, juicy, slightly coarse, crisp, sprightly subacid. Ripe September/October. Catalog listings: MD, VA, NC, GA, AL, TN, KY, TX, AR (1858–1928).

## SIX

# Extinct Southern Apples

**AARON HOLT:** A fall or late-ripening apple that originated in east Texas and that was listed in 1896 by the Austin Nursery, Austin, Texas. Tree said to be vigorous, yielding large crops of excellent apples. No description of fruit.

**ABBOTT YELLOW SEEDLING** (Abbott Seedling?): Listed but not described in the 1916 catalog of J. A. Holder & Company, Concord, Tennessee. Probably the same apple as Abbott Seedling described as follows by Elliot (1858): "Fruit medium, roundish, slightly conical, dull green tinged with red; flesh tender, juicy, wants flavor. Winter." *See also* Fenley.

**ACCOMACK PIPPIN:** Originated before 1899 in Accomack County, Virginia.

Fruit medium or above, roundish, flattened on the ends; skin light yellow speckled with many russet dots; stem short in an acute, deep, russeted cavity; basin wide and deep; flesh whitish. Ripe August. No catalog listings.

**ACORN** (Acorn Greening): Listed from 1824 to 1827 by the Linnean Hill Nursery, Washington, D.C. No description except ripe August.

**ADA RED:** Found by A. G. Philpott before 1921 as a seedling in a fencerow near Springtown, Washington County, Arkansas, and named for his daughter Ada. Susceptible to fire blight.

Fruit medium or above, roundish; skin yellow, nearly covered with red with broken stripes of purplish crimson; flesh whitish, tender, fine-grained, mild subacid. Ripe August. No catalog listings.

**ADDY'S WINTER:** A South Carolina apple listed in 1860 by Pomaria Nurseries of South Carolina.

Fruit medium size, green, ripe November and keeps until April.

**ADMIRAL PIPPIN:** Listed in 1916 by J. A. Holder & Company, Concord, Tennessee. No description except a winter apple.

**AKESON'S WINTER SWEET:** A southern apple of unknown origin briefly mentioned in an 1853 horticultural magazine.

Fruit sweet, late ripening. No catalog listings.

**ALABAMA BEAUTY:** Apples sent to the USDA in 1908 by W. J. Willoughby, Ashland, Clay County, Alabama.

Fruit above medium, roundish oblate; skin light yellow, mostly covered with crimson with broken darker red stripes; dots numerous, russet; stem nearly short in a wide, russeted cavity; basin wide, gradually sloped; flesh white. No catalog listings. **❖ Plate 72.**

**ALABAMA QUEEN:** Ragan (1905) lists but does not describe this variety, giving its origin as Illinois, which defies logic and is certainly an error. Alabama Queen is not listed in any Alabama nursery catalogs, which further adds to the mystery. It was listed from 1893 to 1902 by the J. Van Lindley Nursery of Greensboro, North Carolina: "A few years ago we obtained this variety from Alabama and after fruiting and testing it here, it proved so fine that we have decided to offer it to the general public. Similar to and ripens with the Summer Pearmain. Striped with red; a good bearer; above medium size; very fine quality."

**ALABAMA WINTER:** Described by Warder (1867) only as a large, late-ripening Alabama apple. Listed by a Virginia nursery in 1896.

**ALAMANCE BEAUTY** (Troxler): From an 1884 letter written by the prominent North Carolina nurseryman, J. Van Lindley, to Charles Downing: "Alamance Beauty is an old apple from Alamance County, North Carolina, known as the Troxler apple. Some parties, fruit growers in that county, a year since, concluded as it was so fine, to give it a new name and so named it Alamance Beauty and dropped the local name."

The Troxler apple was listed from 1855 to 1860 in two North Carolina nursery catalogs. From 1893 to 1895 this same apple was again listed, this time by the J. Van Lindley Nursery under the name Alamance Beauty. Fruit large; skin yellow striped with red. Ripe August.

❦ **ALBRIGHT'S PEARMAIN:** A North Carolina apple sold by a North Carolina nursery from 1853 to 1867.

Fruit medium size, conical; skin pale greenish yellow. Ripe October–March.

❦ **ALL PURPOSE:** Apples sent to the USDA in 1900 by the North Carolina nurseryman, J. Van Lindley.

Fruit above medium, roundish oblate; skin light green with a blush on the sunny side; dots few, large and small, russet; stem medium length in a deep, russeted cavity; basin rather wide and deep; flesh whitish. Ripe September. No catalog listings.

❦ **ALL SUMMER** (All Summer Ripe?): How can two Georgia nurseries, in the same year, each list and describe an apple called All Summer completely unlike each other? In its 1924 catalog, Crawford Nurseries of Concord, Georgia, describes this All Summer apple: "Originated in middle Alabama. Fruit medium to large; beautiful red. Begins to ripen last of May and continues until September, thus giving fruit from the same tree all summer. Recommended for garden or orchard but not for commercial planting. Ripe June, July, August." It is probable that this apple is the Hackworth, an Alabama apple with the synonym of All Summer.

Also in 1924, the catalog of Cureton Nurseries of Austell, Georgia, describes a different apple named All Summer: "Rather small, roundish, greenish-white; flesh white, crisp, pleasant. July and August."

Ragan (1905) lists an apple called All Summer that supposedly originated in Pennsylvania before 1867. From his brief description, it seems probable that this All Summer apple is the same apple as the one sold by Cureton Nurseries. In 1928, a Tennessee nursery listed but did not describe an apple called All Summer Ripe. *See* Moon.

❦ **ALLEGHANY SEEDLING** (Allegheny): Originated in Alleghany County, North Carolina, and introduced in 1871 by N. L. Williams of Yadkin County, North Carolina. Sold by Cedar Cove Nurseries of Yadkin County from 1875 to 1902. The tree bears abundantly. This comment was made in an editorial in an 1883 North Carolina newspaper: "Mr. Hiram Shore of Yadkin County kindly handed me three of the largest and finest white apples that have come under the observation of my peepers this season. He called them the Alleghany apple. They averaged in weight a little more than one pound each."

Fruit very large, roundish oblate; skin bright yellow with green blotches; flesh moderately coarse, juicy, rich, subacid. Ripe November–February.

❦ **ALLEN'S PIPPIN** (Allen's Sweet?): According to Downing (1878), Allen's Pippin originated in Chatham County, North Carolina, and was first described in an 1853 North Carolina nursery catalog. Ragan (1905), however, lists the origin of Allen's Pippin as either North Carolina or Georgia, and an "Allen Pippin" was listed in 1912 by the Georgia Horticultural Society as a Georgia apple. The description of this Allen Pippin is almost exactly the same as the Allen's Pippin of North Carolina origin, and it is obviously the same apple.

Fruit medium or large, oblate (also described as oblong); skin greenish yellow, perhaps with pale red streaks; flesh white, tender, mild subacid. Ripe October–December. Catalog listings: NC, AL (1853–88).

❦ **ALLEY** (Alley's Red): A Tennessee apple sold in 1859 by a Virginia nursery. Fruit very large; red striped. Ripe August–November.

❦ **ALPINE** (Alpine Crab): First grown before 1897 by D. C. Swadley of Johnson City, Tennessee.

Fruit small to medium, oblate; skin yellow washed with red and striped with darker red; dots conspicuous, large, raised, yellow, some with dark centers; stem slender and about an inch long in a wide, deep, russeted cavity; basin medium size, abrupt, furrowed and cracked; flesh yellowish, fine-grained, breaking, juicy, mild subacid. Ripe winter. No catalog listings.

❦ **ALTON:** Apples sent to the USDA in 1903 by R. M. Groin, Waverley, Tennessee.

Fruit medium, roundish oblate; skin light yellow

streaked with pinkish red; dots inconspicuous; stem medium length in a medium-size, russeted cavity; basin wide; flesh whitish. No catalog listings.

❧ **AMLIN:** A Virginia apple listed in the 1859 catalog of Hopewell Nurseries, Fredericksburg, Virginia. No description.

❧ **AMMOND KANE:** Described in an 1863 Ohio nursery catalog as an apple of southern origin. Fruit below medium size; skin nearly covered with dull rusty red; flesh yellow, crisp, tender, subacid. Ripe winter and keeps until May.

❧ **AMOS JACKSON** (Amos, Jackson): Beach (1905) says he received this apple from Illinois where it was believed to be of southern origin. An 1863 Pennsylvania nursery catalog also describes it as being of southern origin. The tree is productive.

Fruit medium size, roundish oblate, symmetrical; skin yellow, often with a brownish blush; dots scattered, russet; stem long, often pushed to one side in an acute, shallow to moderately deep, usually russeted cavity; calyx open; basin shallow or moderately deep, sometimes corrugated; flesh nearly white, hard, rather coarse, moderately juicy, sprightly subacid. Ripe November–March. It should be noted that the Pennsylvania nursery catalog describes Amos Jackson as a red apple.

❧ **ANDERSON:** A South Carolina apple listed in 1860 by Pomaria Nurseries of South Carolina. "Medium, red, beautiful and good." Ripe October.

❧ **ANDERSON'S SOUTHLAND:** From the 1920 catalog of the Parker Brothers Nursery, Fayetteville, Arkansas: "The best sweet apple grown. Fine delicious flavor. The original tree from which our scions are cut is the oldest apple tree in Northwest Arkansas and has borne annual crops since it was planted before the War." (In the South, "the War" refers to the Civil War.)

❧ **ANDREW'S WINTER** (Andrews): From the 1888 catalog of Jamestown Nurseries, Greensboro, North Carolina: "Another new apple introduced by Mr. G. P. O'Neal, a thorough and enterprising agriculturist of Abbeville County, South Carolina. It is an apple of fine size and good quality; color dark red, faint stripes. In appearance much like Mattamuskeet. A winter apple. Keeps well in South Carolina." Sold by North Carolina nurseries from 1888 to 1895.

Fruit small to medium, roundish to oblong, conical, often irregular; skin tough, somewhat waxy, dull yellowish green partly overlaid with a dull, dark red with indistinct stripes; dots numerous, pale, rather conspicuous; stem short and thick, often obliquely inserted in an acute, moderately shallow to rather deep, furrowed, sometimes lipped cavity; calyx closed; basin abrupt, medium size, furrowed; flesh greenish, firm, moderately fine-grained, somewhat crisp. Mild subacid. Ripe winter. ❖ **Plate 73.**

❧ **ANDREWS FROST PROOF:** A winter apple listed but not described in the 1872 catalog of Joshua Lindley of North Carolina.

❧ **ANGEL'S FAVORITE** (Angell's Favorite): Introduced by Mr. D. D. Angell of Yadkin County, North Carolina, and sold by North Carolina nurseries from 1886 to 1902. The tree is hardy, a good grower, and bears some apples every year but heavier crops every other year.

Fruit medium to large; skin yellow splashed and marbled with bright red; flesh white, tender, juicy, mild subacid. Ripe November–April.

❧ **ANNIE FRANK:** Apples sent to the USDA in 1905 by A. B. Collingsworth, Wilna, Harford County, Maryland.

Fruit above medium, oblate; skin yellowish, almost covered with two shades of bright red; dots few, russet, some areole; stem very short in a wide, russeted cavity; basin wide, gradually sloped; flesh whitish. No catalog listings.

❧ **AR-JO-MA:** This apple with the strange name was described in the 1920 catalog of the Parker Brothers Nursery, Fayetteville, Arkansas: "A seedling of our own introduction. Has borne eleven crops in succession. A better keeper than the Arkansas Black, equal in color and bearing to the Jonathan and far superior to the Mammoth Black Twig in hardiness and flavor."

❧ **ARCHIBALD:** First described in an 1897 Tennessee agricultural experiment station bulletin. Brought to attention by Archibald Knight, Valley Home, Hamblen County, Tennessee. Described by the USDA as "a most excellent sweet apple and very beautiful." The original tree stood on the Richard Thornhill farm in Hamblen County and was about twenty-five years old in 1897.

Fruit large, slightly oblong; skin thin, smooth, bright red and dark crimson; stem short and stout in a small to medium size, abrupt, slightly russeted cavity; calyx open; basin medium size, abrupt, ribbed; flesh white, very fine-grained, tender, melting, sweet. Ripe late July–August. No catalog listings. ❖ **Plate 74.**

❦ **ARKANSAS BEAUTY:** Probably originated in Johnson County, Arkansas, and introduced by Colonel E. F. Babcock (a major figure in the Blacktwig controversy), who saw this apple at a fair in Fort Smith, Arkansas, in 1886. He was struck by its beauty, visited the original tree, and was convinced it was a seedling. Stark Bro's Nursery carried this apple in their catalogs around the turn of the century. Tree very productive. Note that there is a different apple named Early Arkansas Beauty.

Fruit above medium to large, roundish, sometimes conical; skin tough, smooth, rather glossy, pale green or yellow with mostly light crimson in the shade but darker in the sun, indistinct splashes and stripes of dark crimson over the entire surface (northern-grown apples apparently have much less red); stem sometimes medium length but usually quite long and rather slender in a small, acute, deep, broad, slightly furrowed cavity; calyx closed or partly open; basin medium in depth and width, somewhat furrowed; flesh fine-grained, firm, tinged with red and yellow, moderately crisp, tender, juicy, subacid. Ripe November–January, often later. Catalog listings: NC, GA, TN, KY (1890–1923). ❖ **Plate 75.**

❦ **ARKANSAS BELLE:** An undated note (circa 1900) in the USDA files states: "D. Branchcomb, Rhea, Arkansas, says it is a seedling. The old tree is standing in his seedling orchard." Ragan (1905) describes it only as large, red, and late-ripening and says it may be the same apple as Gano. No catalog listings.

❦ **ARKANSAS GLOBE:** Developed by Louis Hubach of the Hubach and Hathaway Nursery, Judsonia, Arkansas, and sold by that nursery in 1903. Said to be a cross of Yellow Bellflower × Ben Davis. Described in the nursery catalog only as large, mottled yellow, subacid flavor; ripe winter. The blossoms of Arkansas Globe are said to be very large. In 1929, an apple named Arkansas Globe was briefly described by an Illinois Agricultural Experiment Station as yellowish green with a blush; ripe August. Probably the same apple in spite of the differences in description.

In 1903, nurseries charged about twenty-five cents for young apple trees; Hubach and Hathaway priced the Arkansas Globe at five dollars!

❦ **ARKANSAS JUNE:** Like the Arkansas Globe, this variety was originated by the Hubach and Hathaway Nursery, Judsonia, Arkansas. Described in their 1903 catalog as "a cross bred seedling apple, white with red streaks, free from specks, sweet flavor, ripe June."

❦ **ARKANSAS PIPPIN** (Mammoth Pippin): Sold by Stark Bro's Nursery in 1891. Said to be a showy fruit, very large, acid flavor. Ripe September/October.

❦ **ARKANSAS PROLIFIC:** Yet another apple variety originated by Louis Hubach of the Hubach and Hathaway Nursery, Judsonia, Arkansas, and described in their 1903 catalog. Fruit said to hang long on the tree. Fruit medium size, oblong conical; skin red with some stripes. Ripe October and a winter keeper.

❦ **ARKANSAS QUEEN:** Mentioned but not described at the 1877 meeting of the American Pomological Society. No catalog listings.

❦ **ARKANSAS RED:** An Arkansas apple that originated before 1899, probably in Washington County, Arkansas. An old watercolor in the USDA National Agricultural Library shows a rather small apple with bright red stripes on a yellow background, closely resembling Striped June. No catalog listings.

❦ **ARMINTROUT:** Noticed in 1873 growing in the Blue Ridge mountains of Virginia and introduced by A. Bolen of Kimball, Virginia. Tree a slow grower but an annual bearer that holds its fruit well.

Fruit medium, oblate, slightly conical; skin thin, tough, lemon yellow, almost completely washed and striped with red; dots numerous, russet, some with raised centers; stem short to medium in a wide,

# The USDA Pomological Watercolor Collection

The United States Department of Agriculture (USDA) established a Division of Pomology in 1886 to collect and disseminate information to fruit growers. Almost instantly it was overwhelmed with boxes of fruit from the public with cover letters asking "what kind of apple (or pear or peach or cherry) is this?" By 1888, the Division of Pomology had received over 10,000 fruit specimens for identification!

Accurate depiction of American fruit became necessary to aid in the task of identification. With color photography a distant invention, the division hired a series of accomplished watercolor artists, beginning in 1887, to paint pictures of American fruit. By the time this effort ended around 1940, over 7,700 paintings had been made of fruits and nuts. Some of these paintings were reproduced in USDA publications such as the annual *Yearbook of Agriculture*, but most were filed away and faded from public view.

USDA artists were both men and women. Listed below are some of these artists and the years they worked for the USDA: William Prestele, 1887–95, Frank Muller, 1891–97, Deborah Passmore, 1892–1911, Bertha Heiges, 1896–1907, Amanda Newton, 1896–1928, Elsie Lower, 1900–09, Ellen Schutt, 1904–14, Royal Steadman, 1916–31.

The recent burgeoning interest in heirloom fruits has renewed the public's desire to see the pomological watercolors. A monetary grant from a private source in 2009 allowed the USDA's National Agricultural Library in Beltsville, Maryland to convert the watercolors to digital format and make the files available to the public. The images in this book are the result of the digital conversion. I thank the staff of NAL's Special Collections, led by Susan Fugate, for their efforts to provide timely scans of the watercolors needed for this book.

For more information about the library or access to the USDA Pomological Watercolor Collection, see their excellent website at http://www.nal.usda.gov/speccoll/index.shtml.

Plate 1: **Abram**

Artist: Deborah Griscom Passmore, 1910

PLATE 2: **American Beauty**
Artist: Amanda Almira Newton, 1912

PLATE 3: **Arkansas Sweet**
Artist: Deborah Griscom Passmore, 1906

PLATE 4: **Ball's Choice**
Artist: Deborah Griscom Passmore; Bertha Heiges, 1896

PLATE 5: **Ben Davis**
Artist: Amanda Almira Newton, 1912

PLATE 6: **Benham**
Artist: M. Strange, 1914

PLATE 7: **Buncombe**
Artist: Ellen Isham Schutt, 1905

PLATE 8: **Chenango Strawberry**
Artist: Ellen Isham Schutt, 1911

PLATE 9: **Coffelt Beauty**
Artist: Deborah Griscom Passmore, 1901

PLATE 10: **Cullasaga**
Artist: Amanda Almira Newton, 1909

PLATE 11: **Disharoon**
Artist: Deborah Griscom Passmore, 1904

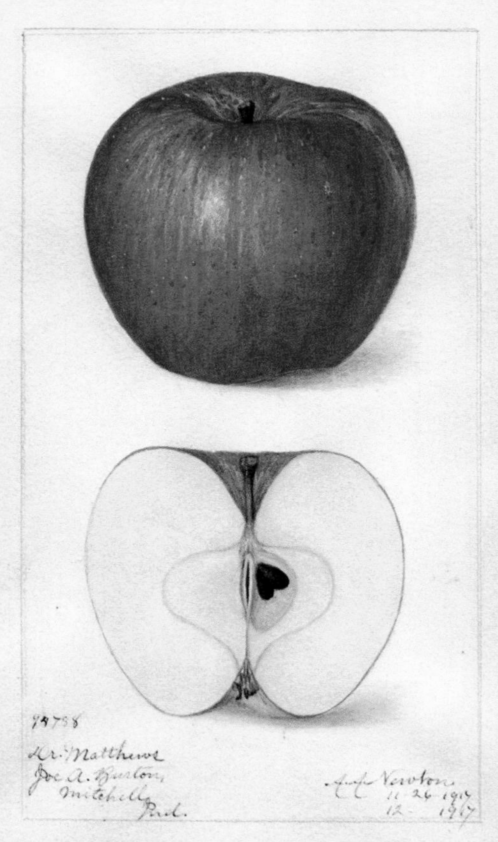


PLATE 12: **Doctor Matthews**
Artist: Amanda Almira Newton, 1917

PLATE 13: **Dula's Beauty**
Artist: Bertha Heiges, 1903

Plate 14: **Early Harvest**
Artist: Ellen Isham Schutt, 1912

Plate 15: **Early Strawberry**
Artist: Amanda Almira Newton, 1921

Plate 16: **Fall Pippin**
Artist: Ellen Isham Schutt, 1905

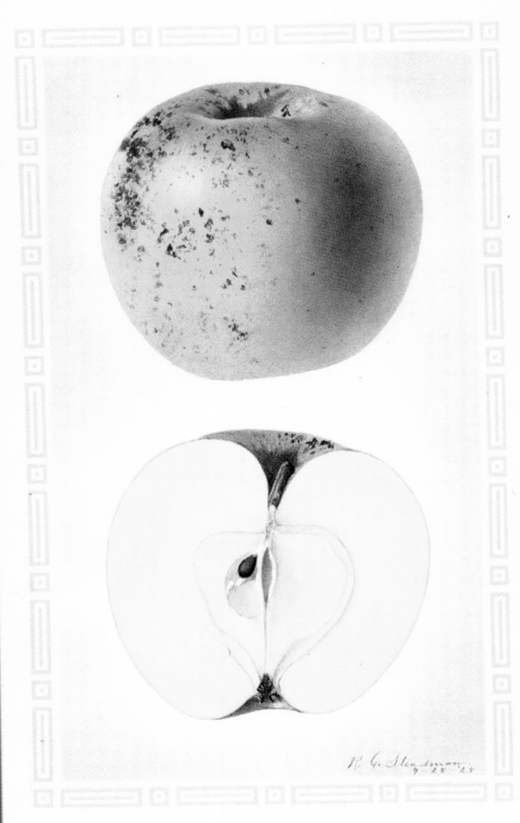

Plate 17: **Fallawater**
Artist: Royal Charles Steadman, 1925

Plate 18: **Fanny**
Artist: Ellen Isham Schutt, 1907

Plate 19: **Fyan**
Artist: L. C. C. Krieger (Louis Charles Christopher), 1937

Plate 20: **Gloria Mundi**
Artist: Amanda Almira Newton, 1912

Plate 21: **Hackworth**
Artist: Deborah Griscom Passmore, 1906

Plate 22: **Henry Clay**
Artist: Royal Charles Steadman, 1919

Plate 23: **Huntsman's Favorite**
Artist: Royal Charles Steadman, 1918

Plate 24: **Ingram**
Artist: Mary Daisy Arnold

PLATE 25: **Kane**
Artist: Ellen Isham Schutt, 1908

PLATE 26: **Kinnaird's Choice**
Artist: Royal Charles Steadman, 1928

PLATE 27: **Lady Sweet**
Artist: Deborah Griscom Passmore, 1898

PLATE 28: **Lawver**
Artist: Amanda Almira Newton, 1909

Plate 29: **Lewis Green**
Artist: Deborah Griscom Passmore, 1905

Plate 30: **Royal Limbertwig**
Artist: Ellen Isham Schutt, 1905

Plate 31: **Magnum Bonum**
Artist: Deborah Griscom Passmore, 1905

Plate 32: **Mattamuskeet**
Artist: Ellen Isham Schutt, 1911

PLATE 33: **Milam**
Artist: Deborah Griscom Passmore, 1906

PLATE 34: **Morgan's Christmas**
Artist: Ellen Isham Schutt, 1912

PLATE 35: **Mother**
Artist: Ellen Isham Schutt, 1909

PLATE 36: **Mrs. Bryan**
Artist: Ellen Isham Schutt, 1907

**Plate 37: Newtown Pippin**
Artist: Deborah Griscom Passmore, 1896

**Plate 38: North Carolina Keeper**
Artist: Amanda Almira Newton, 1915

**Plate 39: Northern Spy**
Artist: Ellen Isham Schutt, 1905

**Plate 40: Opalescent**
Artist: Amanda Almira Newton, 1913

Plate 41: **Pennock**
Artist: Mary Daisy Arnold, 1916

Plate 42: **Polly Eades**
Artist: Mary Daisy Arnold, 1915

Plate 43: **Pryor's Red**
Artist: Ellen Isham Schutt, 1911

Plate 44: **Rabun Bald**
Artist: Amanda Almira Newton, 1905

PLATE 45: **Ralls Janet**
Artist: Deborah Griscom Passmore

PLATE 46: **Rebel**
Artist: Mary Daisy Arnold, 1912

PLATE 47: **Red Astrachan**
Artist: Amanda Almira Newton, 1905

PLATE 48: **Red Cheese**
Artist: Amanda Almira Newton, 1905

PLATE 49: **Roman Stem**
Artist: Amanda Almira Newton, 1913

PLATE 50: **San Jacinto**
Artist: James Marion Shull, 1933

PLATE 51: **Shockley**
Artist: Amanda Almira Newton, 1912

PLATE 52: **Smokehouse**
Artist: Deborah Griscom Passmore, 1895

PLATE 53: **Sparger**
Artist: Amanda Almira Newton, 1905

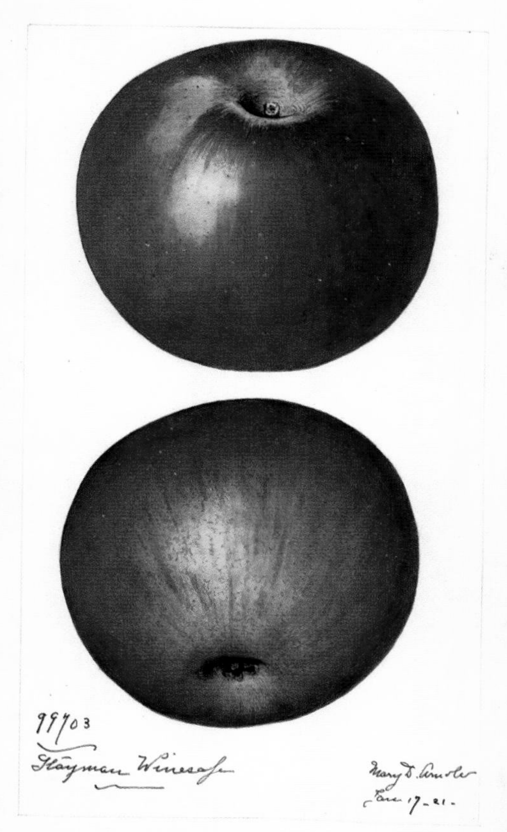


PLATE 54: **Stayman**
Artist: Mary Daisy Arnold, 1921

PLATE 55: **Summer Champion**
Artist: Mary Daisy Arnold, 1911

PLATE 56: **Summer King**
Artist: William Henry Prestele, 1893

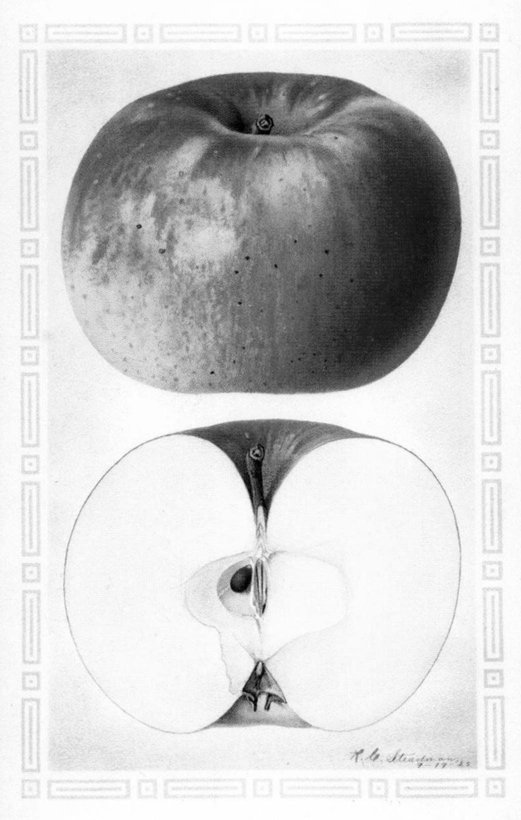

**PLATE 57: Summer Rambo**
Artist: Royal Charles Steadman, 1925

**PLATE 58: Sweet Winesap**
Artist: Amanda Almira Newton, 1912

**PLATE 59: Turley Winesap**
Artist: L. C. C. Krieger (Louis Charles Christopher), 1939

**PLATE 60: Vandevere**
Artist: Amanda Almira Newton, 1912

PLATE 61: **Vanhoy**
Artist: Royal Charles Steadman, 1925

PLATE 62: **Virginia Beauty**
Artist: Amanda Almira Newton, 1906

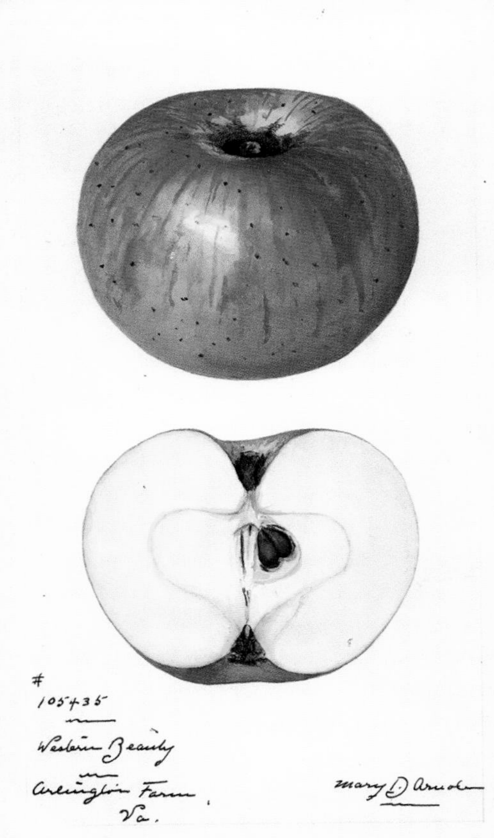


PLATE 63: **Western Beauty**
Artist: Mary Daisy Arnold, 1924

PLATE 64: **White Winter Pearmain**
Artist: Ellen Isham Schutt, 1906

Plate 65: **Williams Favorite**
Artist: Deborah Griscom Passmore, 1903

Plate 66: **Wilson June**
Artist: Deborah Griscom Passmore, 1907

Plate 67: **Winter Cheese**
Artist: Ellen Isham Schutt, 1907

Plate 68: **Winter Jon**
Artist: Amanda Almira Newton, 192?

Plate 69: **Winter Sweet Paradise**
Artist: Royal Charles Steadman, 1929

Plate 70: **Yankee Sweet**
Artist: Amanda Almira Newton, 1920

Plate 71: **Yellow Transparent**
Artist: Royal Charles Steadman, 1918

PLATE 72: **Alabama Beauty**
Artist: Bertha Heiges, 1903

PLATE 73: **Andrew's Winter**
Artist: Deborah Griscom Passmore

PLATE 74: **Archibald**
Artist: Deborah Griscom Passmore

PLATE 75: **Arkansas Beauty**
Artist: Bertha Heiges

PLATE 76: **Avera's Favorite**
Artist: Mary Daisy Arnold

PLATE 77: **Baltzley**
Artist: Deborah Griscom Passmore, 1910

PLATE 78: **Beauty of Kent**
Artist: Deborah Griscom Passmore, 1901

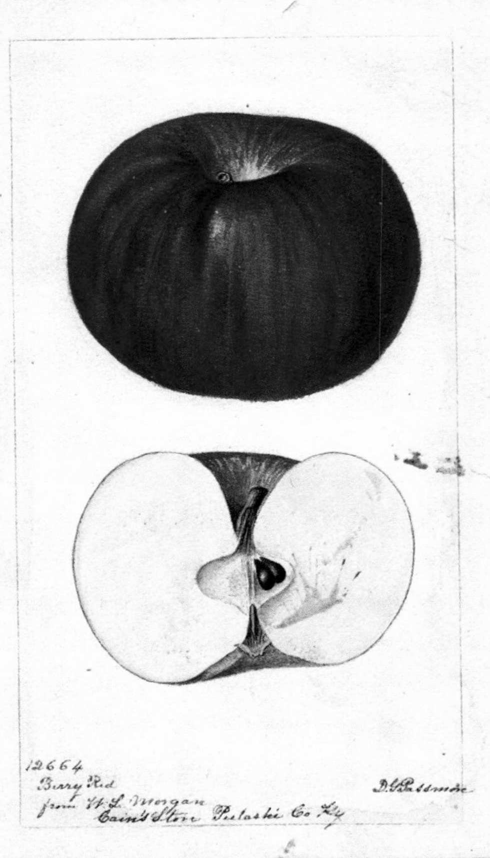


PLATE 79: **Berry Red**
Artist: Deborah Griscom Passmore, 1896

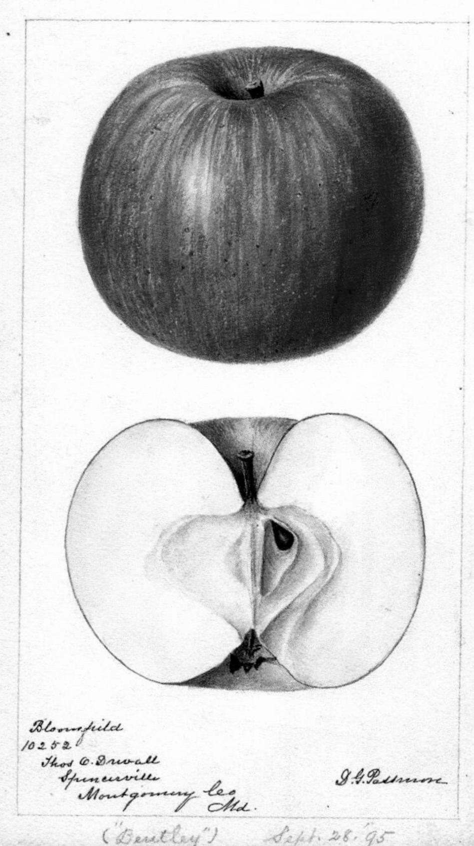


PLATE 80: **Bloomfield**
Artist: Deborah Griscom Passmore, 1895

PLATE 81: **Carolina Beauty**
Artist: Deborah Griscom Passmore, 1895

PLATE 82: **Catline**
Artist: Deborah Griscom Passmore, 1895

PLATE 83: **Doctor Walker**
Artist: Amanda Almira Newton, 1905

Plate 84: **Early Cluster**
Artist: Bertha Heiges, 1898

Plate 85: **Eckel**
Artist: Deborah Griscom Passmore, 1900

Plate 86: **Elkhorn**
Artist: Bertha Heiges, 1901

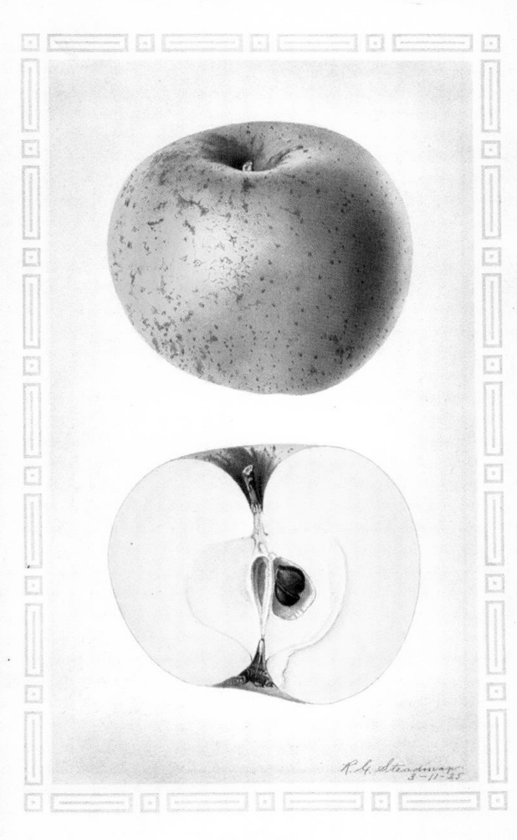

Plate 87: **Ferdinand**
Artist: Royal Charles Steadman, 1925

Plate 88: **Fort's Prize**
Artist: Ellen Isham Schutt, 1910

Plate 89: **Frazier's Hard Skin**
Artist: Deborah Griscom Passmore, 1897

Plate 90: **Glendale**
Artist: Amanda Almira Newton, 1914

Plate 91: **Glenloch**
Artist: Amanda Almira Newton, 1912

PLATE 92: **Goosepen**
Artist: Ellen Isham Schutt, 1907

PLATE 93: **Gray Hills**
Artist: Bertha Heiges, 1900

PLATE 94: **Heidemeyer**
Artist: Royal Charles Steadman, 1924

PLATE 95: **Helm**
Artist: Amanda Almira Newton, 1914

PLATE 96: **Huff**
Artist: Deborah Griscom Passmore, 1899

PLATE 97: **Kentucky Red**
Artist: Amanda Almira Newton, 1911

PLATE 98: **Lankford Seedling**
Artist: Elsie E. Lower, 1910

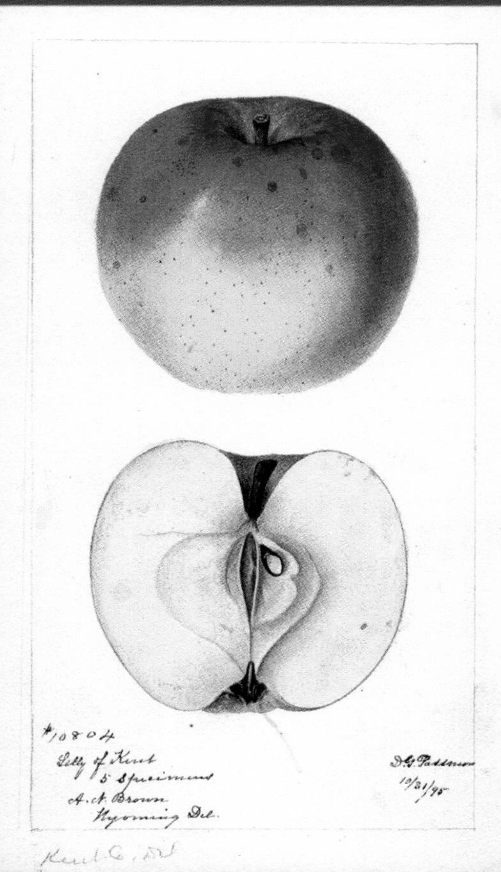

PLATE 99: **Lillie of Kent**
Artist: Royal Charles Steadman, 1895

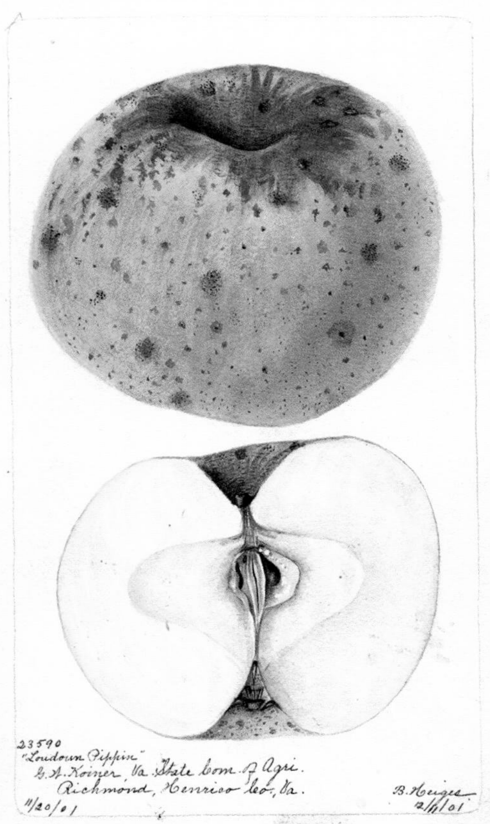


**Plate 100: Loudon Pippin**
Artist: Bertha Heiges, 1901

**Plate 101: Loy**
Artist: Amanda Almira Newton, 1905

**Plate 102: McCroskey**
Artist: Bertha Heiges, 1896

**Plate 103: McMullen**
Artist: Deborah Griscom Passmore, 1904

Plate 104: **Mitchell's Favorite**
Artist: Bertha Heiges, 1904

Plate 105: **Nansemond Beauty**
Artist: Bertha Heiges, 1899

Plate 106: **Oconee Greening**
Artist: Deborah Griscom Passmore, 1899

Plate 107: **Pine Stump**
Artist: Bertha Heiges, 1897

Plate 108: **Pride of Tennessee**
Artist: Mary Daisy Arnold, 1912

Plate 109: **Randolph**
Artist: Royal Charles Steadman, 1933

Plate 110: **Rutledge**
Artist: Mary Daisy Arnold, 1912

Plate 111: **Sandbrook**
Artist: Royal Charles Steadman, 1928

**Plate 112: Scarlet Cranberry**
Artist: Bertha Heiges, 1901

**Plate 113: Sewell's Favorite**
Artist: Deborah Griscom Passmore, 1896

**Plate 114: Shackleford**
Artist: Amanda Almira Newton, 1912

**Plate 115: Shirley**
Artist: Deborah Griscom Passmore, 1901

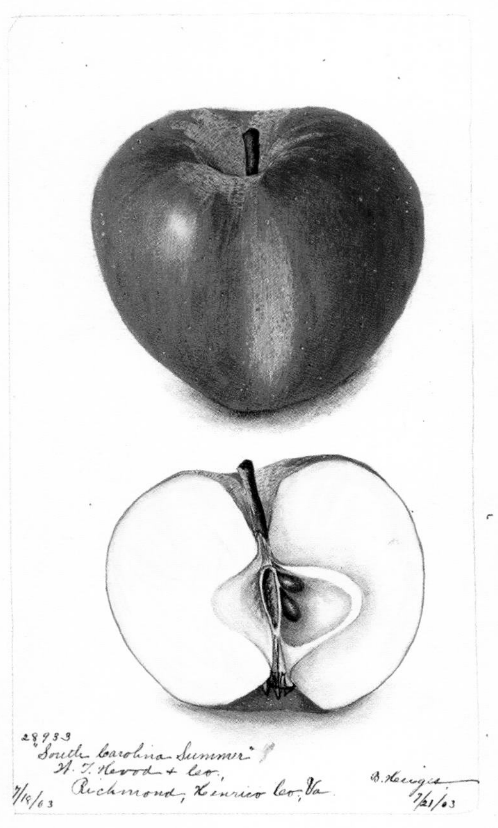


PLATE 116: **South Carolina Summer**
Artist: Bertha Heiges, 1903

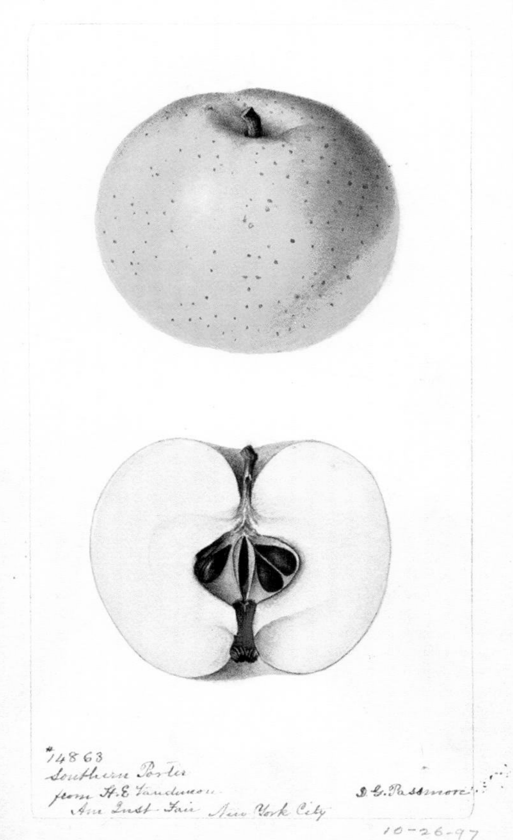


PLATE 117: **Southern Porter**
Artist: Deborah Griscom Passmore, 1897

PLATE 118: **Springdale**
Artist: Deborah Griscom Passmore, 1902

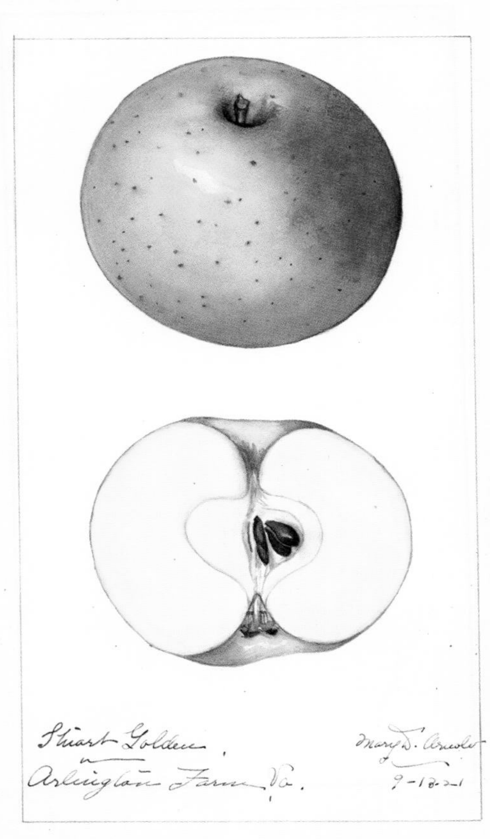


PLATE 119: **Stuart's Golden**
Artist: Mary Daisy Arnold, 1921

Plate 120: **Texas Red**
Artist: Amanda Almira Newton, 1905

Plate 121: **Via's Seedling**
Artist: Bertha Heiges, 1897

Plate 122: **Water Melon**
Artist: Elsie E. Lower, 1909

Plate 123: **White Catline**
Artist: Ellen Isham Schutt, 1910

deep, gradually sloped, slightly russeted cavity; calyx closed; basin medium size, abrupt, russeted; flesh whitish, fine-grained, juicy, moderately tender, subacid. Ripe October–March. No catalog listings.

❦ **ARNOLD:** Originated before 1900 on the farm of Rollins Evans in Kinney's Bottom, Lewis County, Kentucky. Different from the Arnold apple in Beach (1905), which originated in Ontario, Canada. No description. No catalog listings.

❦ **ARNOLD'S CHEESE:** Described only as a summer apple in the 1894 catalog of Spring Hill Nurseries, Prince Edward County, Virginia.

❦ **AROMATIC CAROLINA** (Aromatic, Aromatic Calville): Ragan (1905) made a mistake by listing two southern apples named Aromatic as well as a third apple named Aromatic Carolina. An examination of all southern catalogs that list these varieties, as well as other references, shows conclusively that these are all the same apple.

Originated as a seedling grown by Johannes Miller in South Carolina and was first listed in 1856 under the name Aromatic Carolina by Pomaria Nurseries, Pomaria, South Carolina. By 1859, several Virginia and Georgia nurseries were selling this apple using the name Aromatic. These two names were used interchangeably by southern nurseries during the nearly forty years this variety was sold, which no doubt led to Ragan's mistake.

Fruit medium or larger, roundish oblate, slightly conical, sides sometimes unequal; skin greenish yellow striped with pale or dull red, often with a white bloom; stem short and fleshy in a deep, wide cavity; calyx open; basin wide and shallow; flesh yellowish, tender to moderately firm (also described as melting), highly aromatic, subacid. Ripe July/August. Catalog listings: VA, SC, GA, MS, KY (1856–94).

❦ **ASH BLACK** (Black Ash): A Kentucky apple that originated before 1905. No description. No catalog listings.

❦ **ASHTON:** Quoted from an 1898 Arkansas agricultural experiment station bulletin: "A small to medium red apple of value where a sweet apple is desired. The original tree stands in Mr. Marshall's orchard a few miles east of Cincinnati, Arkansas. It is very productive, bearing heavy crops annually. The tree resembles the Winesap somewhat, but it branches more freely, and the branches are more slender; is a good grower.

"Fruit medium size, roundish or roundish oblate, uneven; stem medium to long; cavity medium, usually marked with a lip, russeted; color light and dark red on yellow ground, very highly colored, sometimes nearly black; skin thick, oily, surface covered with minute light dots; core small to medium; flesh fine-grained, white to slightly yellow, tender; flavor sweet, good to very good. Season, early winter." No catalog listings.

❦ **ATKINS:** From *The Southern Apple and Peach Culturist* (1872): "Origin, Powhatan County, Virginia. Medium to large; round; skin fine red; flesh pale yellow; flavor subacid and rich. This fine apple is raised by Geo. B. Atkins, Esq.; December to May." No catalog listings.

❦ **AUGUSTINE:** Originated in South Carolina before 1858 and sold by a Georgia nursery in 1861.

Fruit medium to large, roundish conical or perhaps slightly oblong; skin yellow splashed and striped with red; flesh moderately juicy, not crisp, tender, sweet. Ripe August/September.

❦ **AUNT GINNIE** (Ginnie): Originated in Clarke County, Virginia, and sold by a North Carolina nursery from 1884 to 1898.

Fruit large, oblate, slightly conical; skin bright crimson. Ripe October.

❦ **AUNT PEGGIE:** Quoted from an 1874 letter from Joshua Lindley to Charles Downing: "Originated near the dwelling of an old lady named Peggie Hownis who was always called Aunt Peggie. It undoubtedly grew from a seed of our Neverfail as the fruit and tree resemble that fruit considerably. The original tree is standing a little over a mile from here and a half mile from New Garden Meeting House."

Fruit medium, roundish or slightly oblong, conical; skin greenish yellow striped with red; flesh white. Keeps until late spring. No catalog listings.

❦ **AUNT SUSAN'S FAVORITE:** Said to be a Maryland apple but first described in 1863 by the Missouri Horticultural Society.

Fruit large, roundish oblate; skin greenish yellow with red stripes; flesh white, tender, juicy, subacid. Ripe June/July. No catalog listings.

❦ **AUSTIN SWEET:** Apples sent to the USDA in 1915 by the Mountain View Nursery Company, Williamsport, Maryland.

Fruit above medium, roundish, slightly conical; skin light yellow with a blush; dots scattered, russet; stem short in a medium size, russeted cavity; calyx closed; basin shallow; flesh yellowish. Ripe winter. No catalog listings.

❦ **AUTUMN APPLE:** Originated in a seedling orchard planted about 1820 on the farm of a Mrs. McAllister near Clarksville, Georgia.

Fruit medium, oblate, ribbed; skin russeted around the stem; stem very short in a deep cavity; calyx open; flesh white, rather hard, sweet. Ripe August. No catalog listings.

❦ **AUTUMN BEAUTY:** Listed from 1912 to 1926 by the Clingman Nursery, Keithville, Louisiana.

Fruit large, oblate; skin rich red to maroon; flesh white, mild subacid. Ripe late winter.

❦ **AVERA'S FAVORITE** (Averoe's Favorite?): Probably of North Carolina origin. Sold from 1887 to 1893 by the J. Van Lindley Nursery of Greensboro, which obtained it from a Mr. W. H. Avera. Tree an annual bearer. Fruit useful for fresh eating, drying, or cider.

Fruit above medium to large, roundish oblate to oblate; skin yellow mostly covered with dull red sprinkled with white or russet specks; stem medium to long in an abrupt, deep cavity; basin medium in depth; flesh yellow, juicy. Ripe early August to the last of September. ❖ **Plate 76.**

❦ **BABBIT** (Western Baldwin): Originated about 1838 from seeds of Baldwin in Tazewell County, Illinois. Sold by several southern nurseries around 1900, often under the name Western Baldwin. Reportedly a large and beautiful apple, but too acid to be anything but a cooker until after January when its acid subsides. The tree was a shy bearer in Maryland in 1900.

Fruit large, roundish oblate, somewhat irregular; skin yellow mostly mottled and striped with carmine; stem short in a moderately shallow, rather broad cavity; calyx nearly closed; basin rather deep, somewhat furrowed; flesh whitish or a little yellow, fine-grained, rather crisp, sprightly subacid to acid. Ripe October–April. Catalog listings: MD, VA, KY, TX (1897–1910).

❦ **BACCOLINUS** (Bacalinus): A southern apple sold by two Virginia nurseries from 1858 to 1869.

Fruit small, roundish to slightly oblong, flattened on the ends, rectangular; skin white flushed and specked with two shades of red; dots few, small; stem medium to long and slender in a deep, russeted cavity; calyx closed; basin shallow and wide; flesh yellow, firm, fine-grained, juicy, subacid. Ripe December–March.

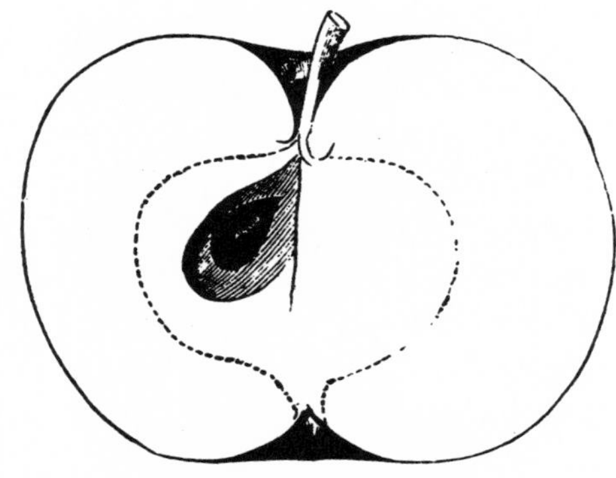

BACCOLINUS

❦ **BAKER:** A winter apple listed in 1875 by the Middletown Nursery of Virginia. No description.

❦ **BALLARD:** Apples sent to the USDA in 1908 by the prominent North Carolina nurseryman, J. Van Lindley.

Fruit medium or above, oblate; skin almost covered with red and darker red stripes with several russet warts or bumps; dots numerous, large, russet; stem short in a narrow, russeted cavity; calyx open; basin wide and rather shallow; flesh whitish. Ripe October–December. No catalog listings.

❦ **BALLENGER:** Sold in 1926 by the Taylor Nursery and Fruit Farm, Greer, South Carolina: "An old time green apple, small, mealy, very prolific. Keeps well for a summer apple."

❦ **BALTZLEY** (Baltzby?, Baltzley's Sweet): Although Downing (1878) and Ragan (1905) list Baltzley and Baltzby as two separate varieties, they are so similar in name and description they must be the same apple. Virginia and Maryland nurseries all sold an apple called "Baltzley." Downing (1878) credits the origin of Baltzley to Pennsylvania and Baltzby to Virginia.

Fruit large, oblate, somewhat angular; skin smooth, pale yellow or yellowish white, sometimes with a faint blush on the sunny side; dots small, scattered, white; stem medium size, green in a brown, wavy cavity; basin rather deep, abrupt, wavy; flesh white, firm, somewhat tough and spongy, juicy, rich, almost sweet (also described as very sweet). Ripe September–November. Catalog listings: MD, VA (1858–1904). ❖ **Plate 77.**

❧ **BANANA PIPPIN** (Summer Banana?): Sold in 1923 by the Western Home Nursery, Wetherford, Texas: "Fruit greenish yellow, sweet and mellow, fine flavor. Season June 1–10." Probably the same as Summer Banana.

❧ **BAPTIST:** Originated with W. M. Samuels of Clinton, Kentucky, and first described by Downing (1900). Tree an abundant bearer on alternate years.

Fruit medium, roundish oblate, sides sometimes unequal; skin smooth, thick, entirely covered with dark red or maroon; dots numerous, yellowish and brown; stem short to medium length and stout in a broad, deep, russeted cavity; calyx half open; basin large, broad, deep, slightly wrinkled; flesh white, rather fine-grained, tender, moderately juicy, mild subacid to almost sweet. Ripe December–February. No catalog listings.

❧ **BAR SEEDLING** (Bar's Seedling): Downing (1878) describes a Bar apple of Rhode Island origin and another apple, Bar Seedling, of unknown origin. Bar Seedling probably originated in North Carolina as several southern nursery catalogs describe it as popular in eastern North Carolina and a good winter cider apple.

Fruit medium to small; skin streaked and splashed with red; flesh yellow, juicy. Ripe October–April. Catalog listings: VA, NC (1872–1904).

❧ **BARKER'S LINER** (Ezell in Marshall County, Tennessee; Baltimore in Sumner County, Tennessee): I quote the following rather long story that was presented to the Illinois Horticultural Society in 1871 by William A. White of Marion, Illinois:

> We have two very meritorious apples to introduce to the state and the world. One of them is the "Barker's Liner" which in my judgement, and that of all others who have tested its merits, has no equal. It was grown from seed when none but seedlings were grown in the state of Virginia. The circumstances of its origin and name are these: There were two men having land adjoining and there was a small piece of land equally owned by them which they agreed to set in trees and share the profits. Mr. Barker, who was one of the parties, planted one tree on the line which divided their land, and it bore the apple under description. It was known after it came into bearing as Barker's Line tree. The only probable reason why this apple is not disseminated all over the world must be the fact that this was in a day when grafting was not practiced, and but little known. Before the original tree died, however, there was a man by the name of William Jenkins who moved to Tennessee, and carried some scions with him. I moved from there to this county (Williamson) in 1859 bringing scions and grafting them in a nursery, and today this apple is in greater admiration than any other variety. It is perfectly hardy in tree and fruit. It is a very large, flat, showy apple and a good keeper. The tree is a regular and abundant bearer, and I do not remember to have ever seen a broken limb caused by the load of fruit, as the limbs are stiff and tough.

Grown extensively in colonial Virginia and Maryland as an eating and cider apple, and first mentioned as "Barker Line" in Campbell County, Virginia, in 1788. Listed in the 1893 catalog of Smith's Nursery, Franklin, Tennessee, which suggested that Barker's Liner may be the same apple as Gilpin, a Virginia apple that it somewhat resembles.

Fruit medium to large (also described as small), oblate, somewhat oblique; skin striped with red or purple; flesh very juicy and high-flavored. Ripe November–March and improves in storage.

❦ **BARLEY'S SWEET:** Listed in the 1895 catalog of T. W. Wood and Sons, Richmond, Virginia. Described only as a good, sweet, summer apple.

❦ **BARNES' FANCY:** Listed from 1824 to 1827 by the Linnean Hill Nursery, Washington, D.C. No description except ripe October/November.

❦ **BARNETT'S RED:** Listed in 1915 by the New Cumberland Nursery Company of Sawyer, Kentucky. Described only as a winter apple.

❦ **BARNSLEY:** Apples sent to the USDA in 1906 by F. L. Milford, Blowing Rock, Watauga County, North Carolina.

Fruit medium, roundish, flattened on the ends; skin bright yellow with a blush; dots large, russet, some reddish; stem long in a deep, narrow cavity; basin shallow; flesh white, tinged yellow under the skin. Ripe December. No catalog listings.

❦ **BARROW'S SEEDLING:** Listed by an 1863 Pennsylvania nursery as a Virginia apple. No description except ripe February.

❦ **BASS' RED WINTER:** Listed in the 1870 catalog of the Forest Nursery, Fairview, Kentucky: "Fruit above medium, yellow mostly covered with red."

❦ **BASSEER:** Described in an 1888 issue of *The American Gardener* magazine as a seedling grown by L. T. Sanders of Collingsburg, Louisiana.

Fruit rather small, oblate, slightly uneven sides; skin smooth, yellow; stem medium length and slender in a wide, gradually sloped cavity; basin wide, medium depth; flesh fine-grained, juicy, subacid, with the aroma of pineapple. Ripe end of September and keeps until April or later. No catalog listing.

❦ **BATINGME** (Bartingme): From the 1897 catalog of Green River Nurseries, Bowling Green, Kentucky: "Tree found near Cedar Hill, Tennessee, in the spring of 1883, by the senior member of our firm. The fruit is the largest we have ever seen; color bright red on yellowish ground; flesh white, moderately acid but good; tree hardy and vigorous. Ripens last of July." This apple is probably Red Bietigheimer.

❦ **BATTLEFIELD** (Guilford Battlefield): The original tree grew on the farm of Ellis Hoskins, which was part of the Revolutionary War battlefield of Guilford County Courthouse, Greensboro, North Carolina.

Fruit medium size or sometimes larger; skin striped with red but dark red in the sun; dots white; flesh yellow, firm, crisp, juicy, fine-grained, aromatic. Ripe December–April. Catalog listings: VA, NC, SC, GA (1855–1904).

❦ **BATTYAM:** Apples sent to the USDA in 1908 by J. A. McLaughlin, Fauquier County, Virginia.

Fruit medium, oblate, irregular; skin greenish yellow; dots red and gray, large and small; stem long and thick in a gray, often lipped cavity; basin wide, corrugated; flesh yellowish. Ripe September. No catalog listings.

❦ **BEAHM** (Brahm?): Apples sent to the USDA in 1899 by A. Bolen, Kimball, Page County, Virginia.

Fruit medium, roundish conical; skin yellow mostly covered with two shades of red and with a light bloom; dots few, white; stem short in a wide, greenish cavity; calyx closed; basin medium size; flesh white. Ripe September. No catalog listings.

❦ **BEARDEN'S IMPROVED SHOCKLEY:** Mentioned but not described in an 1898 report of the South Carolina Agricultural Experiment Station. No catalog listings.

❦ **BEAUTY OF KENT** (Graves' Red): A showy English apple, mainly for cooking, sold by several southern nurseries. Still in the apple collection in Brogdale, England.

Fruit large to very large, roundish conical; skin smooth, greenish yellow and bright red with large broken stripes of purplish red; stem short in a round, russeted, corrugated cavity; basin shallow and narrow; flesh whitish yellow, juicy, crisp, tender, subacid to acid. Ripe October/November. Catalog listings: VA, NC, SC (1853–1904). ❖ **Plate 78.**

❦ **BECKER:** Dr. Eduard F. Becker, a native of Westphalia, Germany, moved to Frelsburg, Texas, about 1854, bringing some seeds of German apples with him. From these seeds, he obtained a variety that became widely planted in central and southern Texas, known as the Becker apple. One Texas nursery catalog says, "This is the only apple that has given satisfactory results in the coast country." While the Becker was generally described as hardy, prolific, and adapted to any soil, one old reference says "requires watering in hot, dry summers." Sold by Texas nurseries from 1903 to 1924.

Fruit medium size; skin yellow striped with light and darker red and having white flecks; flesh firm, "well flavored." Ripe July.

❦ **BEDFORD:** Listed as a new Georgia apple in the 1871 catalog of the Fruitland Nursery, Augusta, Georgia. Fruit large, red. Ripe August.

❦ **BEEFSTAKE:** A summer apple listed but not described in the 1872 catalog of Joshua Lindley's nursery of North Carolina.

❦ **BELL'S SEEDLING** (Bell Apple?, Kentucky Bell?): Originated with Mr. Z. Bell near Adairville, Kentucky, and sold by a Kentucky nursery in 1870. This is probably the "Bell Apple" described by an Ohio nursery in 1863 as "new from Louisville, Kentucky." Downing (1878) says: "Rarely fails to produce a crop of fair fruit."

Fruit medium to large, roundish to slightly oblong, slightly angular; skin yellow, mostly covered with light red, splashed and striped with darker red; dots few, light-colored; stem short and slender in a deep, acute, russeted cavity; calyx closed or partly open; basin almost deep, medium size; flesh white, rather fine-grained, tender, juicy, sprightly subacid. Ripe September/October.

❦ **BEN TILLMAN** (Ben Tel Man): A South Carolina apple described in a 1905 South Carolina agricultural experiment station bulletin and was being grown in 1910 in Westminster, South Carolina. Eating quality highly praised. Named for a governor of South Carolina.

Fruit small to medium, roundish oblate; skin rich yellow covered with red that becomes lighter red toward the basin; dots few, large, gray; stem short to very long and slender in a wide, deep, gradually sloped, russeted cavity; calyx partly open; basin small, shallow, and smooth; flesh yellow, tender, fine-grained, subacid. Ripe October–February. No catalog listings.

❦ **BENDER'S RED STRIPED:** Listed by two Virginia nurseries from 1858 to 1869. Downing (1900) gives Bender as a synonym of Shaffer, a Pennsylvania apple. The Shaffer, a red-blushed apple, is probably a different apple than Bender's Red Striped. No description except the clues given by its name.

❦ **BENTON COUNTY BEAUTY:** Apples sent to the USDA in 1900 by F. M. Bates of Benton County, Arkansas.

Fruit large, roundish; skin bright red; dots small, gray; stem medium length in a deep, abrupt, russeted cavity; basin wide; flesh whitish. Ripe October. No catalog listings.

❦ **BERKELEY** (Berkeley Red, Berkely, Winter Berkeley): Originated in the Shenandoah Valley and listed by three Virginia nurseries from 1858 to 1896. Fruit oblate, red-striped; flesh acid. Ripe winter.

❦ **BERRY RED:** Originated about 1812 on the farm of John Berry of Meadow Creek, Whitley County, Kentucky. The original tree was said to have averaged over forty bushels of apples per year and was still alive in 1894. The apple named Berry (with the synonym Berry Red) described by Warder (1867) and Ragan (1905) is certainly Nickajack, a different apple.

Fruit large, roundish oblate, slightly conical; skin dark shiny red with indistinct darker red stripes; dots scattered, whitish and russet, many areole; stem medium to rather long in a moderately deep, abrupt, russeted cavity; basin almost shallow, wide; flesh cream-colored, juicy, subacid. Ripe winter and a good keeper. Catalog listings: MD, VA, KY (1887–1914). ❖ **Plate 79.**

❦ **BETSY'S FANCY:** Origin unknown, but mentioned by Warder (1867) and still being grown in Virginia in 1897.

Fruit below medium, roundish oblate; skin greenish with faint red streaks near the stem; dots few, red and russet; stem medium to long in a russeted cavity; calyx closed; basin rather shallow; flesh whitish tinged green, coarse, tender, mild subacid. Ripe September/October or later. No catalog listings.

❦ **BEVERLEY'S RED** (Beverly Red): Originated before 1830, probably in Virginia, and sold by two Virginia nurseries from 1858 to 1904. Fruit large;

skin smooth and crimson; flesh very white, subacid. Ripe winter and a good keeper.

❧ **BEWIES EARLY:** Described only as ripe June/July by a Washington, D.C., nursery in 1824.

❧ **BIBLE:** Apples sent to the USDA in 1902 by L. C. Ayres, Midway, Greene County, Tennessee.

Fruit medium, roundish conical; skin greenish yellow with heavy red striping on the sunny side; dots scattered, light and dark; stem medium length and thick in a shallow, russeted cavity; calyx open; basin abrupt; flesh yellowish. Ripe August. No catalog listings.

❧ **BIDWELL'S FAVORITE:** An autumn apple mentioned in an 1891 Tennessee agricultural experiment station bulletin as suited to "the highland rim of middle Tennessee." No description. No catalog listings.

❧ **BIG RED SWEET:** A southern apple of unknown origin mentioned by Warder (1867). No description. No catalog listings.

❧ **BIGGER'S LATE RED:** A southern apple sold by a Virginia nursery in 1869. No description.

❧ **BIGGERSTAFF:** A chance seedling found on the farm of G. M. Biggerstaff of Cleveland County, North Carolina, and sold by a North Carolina nursery from 1893 to 1902. Tree a heavy, annual bearer.

Fruit large, red-striped; flesh yellow, sweet. Ripe September/October.

❧ **BILL ARP** (Doolittle): Undoubtedly named for the famous southern humorist. Described in the 1924 catalog of the Newton Nursery, Newton, Mississippi, as "the best late apple I have ever grown."

Fruit large; skin yellow, mostly covered with deep crimson; dots white; flesh yellow, tender, sweet. Ripe September/October.

❧ **BILL SMITH:** Sold from 1884 to 1898 by Guilford Nurseries, Greensboro, North Carolina. No description.

❧ **BILLINGS JULY:** Listed in the 1916 catalog of J. A. Holder and Company, Concord, Tennessee. No description.

❧ **BILLY BARKER** (Barker): Originated before 1860 on the farm of William Barker, Wake County, North Carolina.

Fruit large, roundish conical; skin green (perhaps with red stripes); flesh yellow, juicy, tender, brisk or acidic. Ripe August. No catalog listings.

❧ **BILLY GEORGE:** A winter apple listed in 1875 by the Middletown Nursery of Virginia. No description.

❧ **BIRD SEEDLING:** Listed in 1916 by the Mountain Top Home Nursery, Mena, Polk County, Arkansas. No description.

❧ **BIZZELL'S SEEDLING:** A Georgia apple sold by Georgia and South Carolina nurseries from 1861–72. No description except ripe September.

❧ **BLACK ANNETTE** (Annette Black): There are three apples about which much confusion exists—Black Annette, Black's Annette, and Annette. Comparing what we know about each of these apples, it is obvious that Black Annette is distinct from the others. It is the only one of the three that is a red apple. Elliott (1858) calls it dark red and an 1863 Ohio nursery catalog describes it as dull red. This clearly differentiates Black Annette from the other two apples that have "whitish yellow" or "greenish yellow" skin. Black Annette originated before 1858 in Bourbon County, Kentucky. Annette and Black's Annette are discussed under the name Black's Annette.

Fruit medium or smaller, roundish oblate; skin dull or dark brownish red with darker splashes; dots conspicuous, large, whitish and russet; stem medium to long in an obtuse, green and russet cavity; calyx open; basin wide, shallow, smooth, sometimes cracked; flesh white, fine-grained, tender, juicy, subacid. Ripe November and an excellent keeper.

❧ **BLACK COAL** (Black Cole?, Baltimore Red, Welcome?, Black Ann, Hoover?, Cranberry Pippin): The 1836 catalog of Clairmont Nurseries, Baltimore, Maryland, describes a new apple introduction called Black Coal, of large size, ripe October–April, "a superior apple." This may be the same apple as the Welcome, which is thought to have originated or been brought to notice before 1844 by Welcome Johnson of Rhode Island. The Welcome apple has been described as medium size, round, very dark red, flesh stained red.

Kendrick (1841) describes a Black Coal apple that he received from Baltimore: "a most beautiful and singular fruit, of a fine black or reddish black color; of large size or 3½ inches in diameter. It keeps until April." Around 1900, two Virginia nurseries listed but did not describe an apple called Black Cole. For many years, North Carolina nurseries carried a large, dark red apple called Baltimore Red.

Ragan (1905) and others suppose Black Coal to be a synonym of Hoover, a large, dark red apple generally accepted as having originated in South Carolina. If Black Coal and Hoover are the same apple, it is likely that scions or young trees of Black Coal were introduced from Baltimore (or perhaps Rhode Island) into South Carolina around 1840, there to be resurrected under the new name of Hoover. *See* Hoover.

Fruit above medium to large, round (sometimes described as roundish oblate, conical); skin smooth, glossy, light red mostly overspread with deep red stripes, sometimes with a bloom; dots numerous and white; stem short in a deep, slightly russeted cavity; calyx closed; basin open; flesh white, slightly tinged with red, almost coarse, moderately juicy, crisp, rather acid. Ripe November–February, but also listed as ripe September–November. Catalog listings as either Black Coal, Black Cole, or Baltimore Red: MD, VA, NC (1836–1904).

❦ **BLACK TOM:** A Maryland apple briefly described by Warder (1867).

Fruit medium, oblate; flesh acid. Ripe August/September. No catalog listings.

❦ **BLACK WARRIOR:** An Alabama apple. Tree said to be vigorous, prolific, and a regular bearer.

Fruit medium, round, slightly conical; skin green with some light russet and faintly blushed on the sunny side; dots few and gray-colored but lighter in color around the basin; stem very short and stout in a rather narrow, deep, acute, russeted cavity; calyx closed; basin deep and smooth; flesh yellowish tinged greenish, compact, tender, spicy subacid. Ripe November–February. Catalog listings: VA, GA, AL, AR (1858–1909).

❦ **BLACK'S ANNETTE** (Cornell, Cornell's Early, Cornell's Favorite, Cornell's Fancy)/**ANNETTE** (Bettie Brooks, Old Bettie, Annate): Downing (1900) lists and describes separately both Annette and Black's Annette. The two descriptions are rather similar, and I believe these are the same apple. Downing's descriptions are quoted here to let readers decide for themselves:

*Black's Annette*: "Of unknown origin, supposed to be Virginia; tree vigorous, spreading, very productive on alternate years.

Fruit medium or below, roundish oblate conical; skin whitish yellow; stalk short to long, slender; cavity large, deep; calyx small, closed; basin rather small, slightly corrugated; flesh white, fine, tender, moderately juicy, sprightly subacid; core small. August." Catalog listings: VA (1870–1904).

*Annette*: "Of unknown origin, received from John Dollins, Greenwood, Virginia, who informs us that it was found in that locality in the late Nicholas Merritt's orchard a half a century ago; tree vigorous, with an upright, round, compact head, requiring but little pruning—one of the most valuable of its season for its locality.

Fruit medium, oblate, sides sometimes unequal, slightly angular; skin pale greenish yellow, rarely with a blush; stalk very short, small; cavity large, deep, slight russet; basin broad, deep, a little uneven; flesh white, half fine, brittle, tender, moderately juicy, mild, pleasant, subacid. September, October." No catalog listings.

❦ **BLACK'S HARDTIMES:** Praised but not described in 1872 by Professor T. Dinwiddie of the University of Virginia. No catalog listings.

❦ **BLACK'S LATE SWEET** (Black's Sweet): Originated in Georgia and sold by Georgia and Kentucky nurseries from 1858 to 1870. This apple is distinct from Black Sweet, an Illinois apple. No description.

❦ **BLACKBURN:** There is much confusion about this variety. Warder (1867) describes a Blackburn apple (large, red-striped, ripe fall) of possible Kentucky origin, but no Kentucky nursery catalogs ever listed it. Beginning about 1890, three North Carolina nurseries listed a Blackburn apple, but their descriptions differ from each other markedly. One of these nurseries said the Blackburn apple was a seedling that originated in Lincoln County, North Carolina.

I tend to agree with most old references that the Blackburn apple is probably the Buckingham under one of its many synonyms.

❦ **BLACKSHEAR:** Originated in Laurens County, Georgia, by a Colonel Blackshear and sold from 1858 to 1861 by South Carolina and Georgia nurseries.

Fruit large to very large, oblate; skin dull white or yellow, perhaps faintly red-striped; flesh yellow or white; crisp, juicy, rich. Ripe October–January.

❦ **BLEDSOE** (Bledsoe's Favorite, Cleveland?): The book *Horticulture and Horticulturists in Early Texas* (1945) credits the origin of this apple to James Bledsoe of Grayson County, Texas. This is contradicted by a letter written to the USDA in 1894 by T. V. Munson, the prominent owner of a nursery in Denison, Texas. He says this apple originated about 1874 in the orchard of Judge Joseph Bledsoe of Sherman, Texas, as a shoot that came up below a failed graft. Specimens of this apple were examined by USDA pomologists at the turn of the century and were found to be different from the apple Bledsoe Pippin. Texas nursery catalogs listed Bledsoe from 1894 to 1928, describing it as dependable and prolific in north Texas and the western, high-plateau region. This apple closely resembles the Cleveland, also a Texas apple, and may be identical to it.

Fruit large, roundish to slightly oblate, conical, sometimes angular; skin mostly greenish with some red splashes and stripes; dots scattered, russet, areole; stem short to medium in a deep, narrow, greenish cavity; basin gradually sloped, medium depth; flesh white, subacid. Ripe August and continuing until October.

Another apple named Bledsoe, this one from Virginia, was sent to the USDA about 1900 by G. W. Robinette of Flag Pond, Virginia. This apple is distinct from the other apples called Bledsoe or Bledsoe Pippin. No description. No catalog listings.

❦ **BLEDSOE PIPPIN:** Originated with John Bledsoe of Carroll County, Kentucky. Tree moderately vigorous, productive.

Fruit large, roundish conical, flattened at the base; skin greenish yellow, sometimes very obscurely striped with red, light bronze at the base; dots brownish; stem short in a deep, slightly russeted cavity; calyx closed; basin shallow and furrowed; flesh white, fine-grained, tender, juicy, crisp, mild subacid. Ripe December–March. Catalog listings: VA, SC, KY (1858–70).

❦ **BLEEK:** A Georgia apple listed in 1859 by Hopewell Nurseries of Fredericksburg, Virginia. No description.

❦ **BLOOMFIELD** (Bentley's Seedling, Bloomfield Bentley): A chance seedling that began bearing about 1880 at Bloomfield, the farm of Richard T. Bentley of Sandy Spring, Montgomery County, Maryland. Widely grown at one time in orchards on both the Maryland and Virginia sides of the Potomac River. Prior to 1894 it was called Bentley's Seedling, but the name was changed at the behest of the USDA to avoid confusion with the apple named Bentley's Sweet. Said to resemble the English Red Streak and considered a seedling of that apple. Tree vigorous and an abundant annual bearer of fruit that was popular for both cooking and fresh eating in Washington, D.C., markets at the turn of the century.

Fruit large, roundish or barrel-shaped; skin thin, tough, smooth, yellowish almost entirely washed with crimson and striped with darker red, overspread with gray; dots conspicuous, sometimes triangular, protruding, russet; stem short and rather stout, often knobbed; cavity large, deep, abrupt, russeted; calyx open; basin wide, deep, furrowed; flesh yellow, rather fine-grained, tender, juicy, subacid. Ripe September–November but can be cooked in July. No catalog listings. ❖ **Plate 80.**

❦ **BLURTON'S ICE CORE:** Sold in 1889 by Planters Nurseries, Humboldt, Tennessee. Described as "large, fine, one of the best. Ripe fall."

❦ **BLUSH PIPPIN:** Apples of this name were sent to the USDA in 1901 by a Mr. Donaldson of Cherrydale, Virginia.

Fruit medium, oblate, very irregular; skin yellow with patches of blush; dots numerous, russet; stem very long in a wide cavity; calyx closed; basin wide, corrugated; flesh whitish. Ripe November/December. No catalog listings.

❦ **BOA EXCELSIOR** (Boyer's Excelsior, Bowman's

Excelsior, Boas): A note in the USDA files excerpts two letters written in 1893 by two men from Bedford City, Virginia. These excerpts seem to say that this apple and the others listed as synonyms are the same apple, first raised by a Benjamin F. Key of Peaksville, Virginia. *See* Bowman's Excelsior.

❦ **BOATMAN'S LARGE:** A South Carolina apple sold by South Carolina and Georgia nurseries in 1860–61. No description except ripe November.

❦ **BOB DON:** Listed but not described by two Virginia nurseries from 1858 to 1869.

❦ **BOHANNAN** (Buchanan, Bohanon): The 1857 report of Indiana to the American Pomological Society recommends the "Summer Pearmain of Mount Bohannan or Bohannan." Most old catalogs say this apple originated in Kentucky, but Elliot (1858) thought it was probably of Virginia origin. Tree a regular bearer of fruit resembling Maiden's Blush.

Fruit almost large, roundish oblate, conical, sometimes ribbed; skin smooth, whitish or yellow with a crimson cheek on the sunny side; dots minute; stem slender in a narrow, uneven, slightly russeted cavity; basin narrow, deep, abrupt; flesh yellow (Warder says white), tender, juicy, spicy, aromatic, subacid. Ripe July–September. Catalog listings: VA, NC, GA, KY (1858–1904).

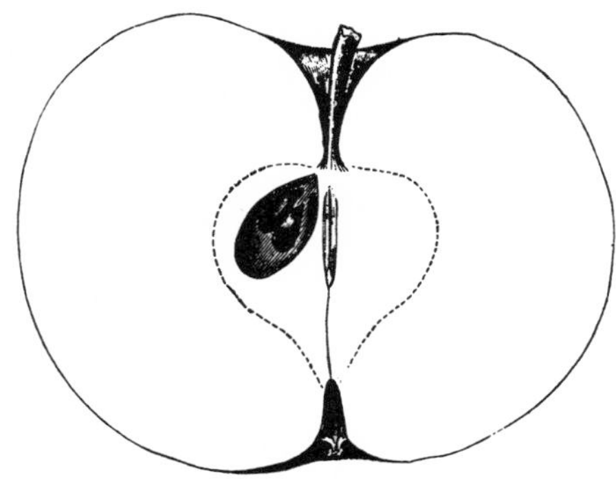

BOHANNAN

❦ **BOLAND'S RED WINTER** (Boland's Late?): A South Carolina apple listed from 1860–78 by Pomaria Nurseries of South Carolina.

Fruit medium size, deep red, juicy. Ripe January.

❦ **BONNER CHOICE:** Originated in Texas by Dixon Henry Lewis Bonner (1825–1917). Described only as a yellow apple. No catalog listings.

❦ **BONUM RED JUNE:** Found in 1919 as a mislabeled tree in the orchard of the Alabama Polytechnic Institute, Auburn. Parentage unknown.

Fruit small, roundish to somewhat oblong, flattened on the ends; skin entirely bright red. Ripe June–August. No catalog listings.

❦ **BORAN'S WINTER:** Originated before 1869 on Alfred Boran's farm about a mile north of New Garden, Guilford County, North Carolina, and sold in 1877 by a North Carolina nursery.

Fruit medium to large, roundish oblate; skin greenish yellow striped with red; flesh rich, juicy, slightly acid. Ripe midwinter.

❦ **BOSMAN:** A South Carolina apple listed in 1860 by Pomaria Nurseries of South Carolina. Fruit large, ripe November.

❦ **BOSSIER GREENING:** Originated about 1880 by L. T. Sanders, Collingsburg, Bossier Parish, Louisiana. Described only as ripe the middle to the last of September. No catalog listings.

❦ **BOSTICK QUEEN** (High Lo Jack; Bostic): Listed by Stark Bro's Nursery in its 1891 catalog. The only southern listing is the 1893 catalog of Smith's Nursery, Franklin, Tennessee: "Tree similar to Fall Queen but a more vigorous grower. Fruit resembles Fall Queen but larger and more highly colored. Sells higher in Nashville than any apple of the same season. September."

❦ **BOSWELL:** Listed in 1890 by Jamestown Nurseries of Greensboro, North Carolina.

Fruit medium size, conical; skin yellow; flesh mealy. A good winter keeper.

❦ **BOSWORTH:** Probably of Kentucky origin before 1905.

Fruit red. Ripe winter. No catalog listings.

❦ **BOTSFORD RED:** Described in the 1845 catalog of the Joel Wood Nursery, Wheeling, West Virginia, (then Virginia) as large, round, red. Ripe October–January.

❦ **BOUNDER:** Listed but not described by three Virginia nurseries from 1858 to 1904.

❦ **BOWKER:** Probably of Virginia origin before 1857.

Fruit medium, roundish, flattened on the ends,

slightly conical, angular; skin pale yellow tinged with crimson; dots few, brown and gray; stem short and slender in a medium-size cavity; calyx closed; basin rather shallow and corrugated; flesh white, tender, juicy, mild subacid. Ripe October. No catalog listings.

❦ **BOWLING'S SWEET:** Originated by Louis Bowling of Spotsylvania County, Virginia, and listed from 1859 to 1873 by Hopewell Nurseries, Fredericksburg, Virginia.

Fruit medium, roundish; skin dull red on yellow; flesh juicy, sweet, "entirely free from acid." Ripe October–January.

❦ **BOWMAN'S EXCELSIOR** (Boyer's Red?): Origin unknown, but listed by six North Carolina and Virginia nurseries from 1867 to 1904. *See* Boa Excelsior.

Fruit large, roundish oblate, slightly conical; skin mostly deep red in the sun but striped and blotched with red on yellowish green otherwise; flesh yellowish, rather coarse, juicy. Ripe November–March.

❦ **BOYD** (Clayton?): Originated before 1869 on the McPherson farm in Monroe County, Kentucky, and introduced by Alfred and Thomas Boyd. A letter to Charles Downing in 1878 describes the Boyd as "a fine bearer with fruit of great solidity and weight." Sold in 1870 by the Forest Nursery of Fairview, Kentucky. Ragan (1905) says Boyd may be a synonym of Clayton, an apple that it closely resembles. *See* Clayton.

Fruit large, oblate, slightly conical; skin yellow, shaded with light and dark red but mostly deep red in the sun; dots light and brown; stem short in a large, broad, deep, often russeted cavity; calyx closed or half-closed; basin rather large and smooth; flesh yellowish, slightly coarse, rather firm, moderately juicy, slightly aromatic, subacid. Ripe January–April.

❦ **BOYD'S SEEDLING:** Awarded an "honorable mention" at the 1874 Atlanta exhibition of the Georgia State Horticultural Society in the category "Georgia Seedling Winter Apple." No description. No catalog listings.

❦ **BRACKEN EARLY:** Quoted from an Ohio delegate to the 1850 meeting of the American Pomological Society: "Found as a seedling in 1812 on Bracken Creek, Bracken County, Kentucky, by Hon. William Pitt Putnam of Washington County, Ohio. Introduced into his nursery and extensively disseminated thence by him and from other nurseries by others. It is our earliest apple, ripening in June and July. It has been confounded with Prince's Early Harvest and White June. The leaf, wood, tree, and fruit in all their peculiarities are the same as those of Prince's Early Harvest, brought from Prince's Nurseries, New York. It is strictly a dessert fruit and not very good for the kitchen. Where each limb leaves its supporting stem, there is a navicular projection which it is claimed is peculiar to both these varieties." Listed by the Forest Nursery, Fairview, Kentucky, in 1870.

Fruit medium, oblate conical, angular; skin yellow; dots scattered and dark; stem large and knobby in a wide, deep, brown cavity; calyx closed; basin abrupt, medium size, folded; flesh white, very tender, fine-grained, mild subacid. Ripe June/July.

❦ **BRACKETT** (Nanny's Seedling): Apples sent to the USDA in 1901 by A. F. Morgan of Otter Creek, Rutherford County, North Carolina.

Fruit medium, oblate; skin yellow, mostly covered with crimson; dots numerous, russet; stem very short in a russeted cavity; calyx closed; basin rather wide; flesh whitish. Ripe January. No catalog listings.

❦ **BRADFORD'S BEST** (Kentucky Red Streak, Kentucky Streak, Bradford, Winter Red Streak): This apple is listed in ten southern nursery catalogs, all of which give Kentucky Red Streak or Kentucky Streak as synonyms. Both of these synonyms are also synonyms of Ben Davis. The sketchy catalog descriptions of Bradford's Best also generally fit the Ben Davis. This apple was sold throughout Georgia in the 1850s by Hiram Bradford, a nurseryman of Brownsville, Tennessee.

Ragan (1905) lists an apple called Bradford Best of Texas origin. This is an error, as Texas nursery catalogs list Bradford's Best and give Kentucky Red Streak or Kentucky Streak as synonyms. Catalog listings: VA, GA, AL, TX (1859–1903). Ben Davis is available.

❦ **BRANCH:** In 1900, J. W. Beard of Boone's Mill, Franklin County, Virginia, wrote to the USDA:

"The Branch apple is a chance seedling discovered by Mr. A. D. Wray in 1864 on his farm near a branch or small stream, hence its name. The original tree still stands, though badly broken from overbearing. It has been propagated quite extensively in the neighborhood. The tree is a vigorous and symmetrical grower and a heavy annual bearer. The apple is about the size of the Winesap, a little more flat or less conical. Its season extends from the middle of July to the first week in September."

Fruit below medium, roundish oblate, conical; skin yellow, heavily striped with red on the stem end; dots large, numerous; stem medium length, slender; flesh whitish. Ripe July–September. No catalog listings.

Another letter to the USDA about a Branch apple, dated 1894, from H. T. Vose, West Point, White County, Arkansas, says: "This apple tree is on the Haywood Branch place, former owner now deceased. The tree is, I suppose, thirty years old." No catalog listings. No description.

In addition to these two apples bearing the name of Branch, there is an apple, still available, named Branch from eastern North Carolina. *See* Branch *in chapter 5.*

❦ **BRANDENBURG'S KEEPER:** Listed in 1889 by Planters Nurseries of Humboldt, Tennessee: "Similar to the Hughs' Virginia. Good eating, very late."

❦ **BRANDY:** Listed from 1858 to 1861 by South Carolina and Georgia nurseries. No description except "of North Carolina origin, ripe October." From its name, this apple was mainly used for making apple brandy. The Golden Harvey, an apple of English origin, has the synonym "Brandy Apple" and was occasionally grown in the South. *See* Golden Harvey.

❦ **BREAKFAST:** Listed from 1824 to 1827 by the Linnean Hill Nursery, Washington, D.C. No description except ripe August.

❦ **BRECKINRIDGE:** Probably a Tennessee apple that originated before 1906.

Fruit medium, roundish, flattened on the ends, ribbed, sides unequal; skin almost smooth, pale yellow; dots variable in shape and size, brown, raised; stem long and slender in a wide, very deep, abrupt, russeted cavity; calyx almost closed; basin large, regular, deep, furrowed and lumpy; flesh white, satiny, fine-grained, tender, juicy, subacid. Ripe September. No catalog listings.

❦ **BREWINGTON PIPPIN** (Breckenridge): Originated about 1870 with James Brewington of Garfield, Kentucky. Tree blooms late and bears heavily on alternate years.

Fruit medium to large, roundish oblate, conical, slightly angular, often ribbed; skin yellow, shaded with pale red, striped and splashed with crimson over most of the surface; dots numerous, large, yellow, some areolar; stem short and small in a medium-size, russeted cavity; calyx closed; basin somewhat abrupt, quite deep, slightly corrugated; flesh white, rather fine-grained, tender, juicy, subacid inclining to sweet. Ripe February/March. No catalog listings.

❦ **BRIAR:** Listed in 1879 by Raleigh Nurseries, Raleigh, North Carolina. Tree moderately productive.

Fruit large, smooth, conical; skin yellow, slightly russeted; flesh rich, not very juicy, aromatic. Ripe October–February.

❦ **BRIDE:** From the 1880 catalog of Virginia Nurseries, Richmond, Virginia: "Medium, oblong, striped red, handsome; flesh white, fine-grained, crisp, tender and juicy. A first rate new variety; origin supposed to be Bedford County, Virginia. October to November."

❦ **BRIGHTWATER:** From a letter to the USDA, undated but circa 1900, from McHenry Bryan, Bentonville, Arkansas: "The Brightwater apple is supposed to be a seedling of the Limbertwig, the trees bearing a striking resemblance and the fruit being somewhat similar, though the Brightwater is much brighter red. The flavor is also better than the Limbertwig, and like the latter it is a great bearer and good keeper, and about the same size. This apple is now grown extensively in the immediate vicinity in which it originated, Brightwater, Benton County, Arkansas, twenty years ago. The tree was a seedling and grew up in one of the streets of the above village."

Fruit medium, round, conical; skin thick, greenish yellow, somewhat mottled with russet, heavily splashed, striped and shaded with dull red; dots minute, yellow and brown; flesh greenish yellow, fine-grained, juicy, subacid. A winter apple and a good keeper. No catalog listings.

**BRILLIANT:** Old records of the USDA indicate an apple named Brilliant originated on the farm of Lindsay F. Thomas, Lewis County, Kentucky, nine miles above Quincy, Kentucky, and three miles below Portsmouth, Ohio, near the Ohio River. Downing (1900) describes this apple as having its origin "near Portsmouth, Ohio." Ragan (1905) lists this apple and also lists another apple called Brilliant with an Iowa origin (not described).

Fruit medium to large, oblate, slightly angular; skin somewhat waxy, pale yellow blushed pale red if exposed to the sun; dots few, grayish; stem short and rather small in a large, deep, often russeted cavity; calyx open; basin large, broad, deep, slightly corrugated; flesh white, slightly coarse, tender, juicy, subacid. Ripe October–January. No catalog listings.

**BRILLIANT OF GEORGIA:** An apple named Brilliant, said to be of Georgia origin, was sold in 1923 by Excelsior Nurseries of Rome, Georgia.

Fruit medium to large, slightly oblong; skin bright yellow partially covered with bright red; flesh subacid. Ripe August.

**BRINKLEY SEEDLING** (Brinkley White Sweet, Brinckley Seedling?): Probably originated on the Delaware-Maryland peninsula before 1833, but Downing (1878) describes an apple called Brinckley Seedling as an English apple.

Fruit medium or below, roundish oblate; skin whitish green; flesh white, crisp, tender, juicy, sweet. Ripe fall or perhaps later. No catalog listings.

**BROADNAX** (Broadax?): Originated on the farm of a man named Broadnax in Rockingham County, North Carolina, and sold by Virginia and North Carolina nurseries from 1877 to 1904.

Fruit medium or larger, roundish oblate; skin clear pale yellow; flesh yellowish, rich, juicy. Ripe winter and keeps until late spring.

**BROADWATER** (Wheatyard): Originated before 1900 on the farm of Colonel Charles Broadwater, Vienna, Virginia.

Fruit below medium, oblate; skin smooth, yellowish white with some pale red in the sun; stem short and small in a medium-size, slightly corrugated cavity; flesh whitish, fine-grained, tender, juicy, subacid. Ripe September. No catalog listing.

**BROCK'S PIPPIN:** A large Virginia winter apple listed in 1860 by a South Carolina nursery.

**BROOK'S FAVORITE:** Listed in 1916 by the Mountain Top Home Nursery, Mena, Polk County, Arkansas. No description.

**BROOKE PIPPIN** (Broke's Pippin?): In the year 1905, two great American pomologists had different ideas concerning the identity of Brooke Pippin. S. A. Beach, in his two-volume work *The Apples of New York*, includes Brooke Pippin among the synonyms of Newtown Pippin and says, "Brooke Pippin is possibly identical with Green Newtown." The same year, W. H. Ragan, in his USDA Bulletin *Nomenclature of the Apple*, lists and describes Brooke Pippin as a separate apple variety under its own name with the notation "very similar to Yellow Newtown." Furthermore, in a note written in 1902 in the files of the USDA, Mr. Ragan says, "My father, the late Reuben Ragan, obtained the Brooke Pippin direct from Mr. Brooke. Although of the same type, it was distinct in tree and fruit from the Yellow Newtown."

The following is from the 1852 proceedings of the American Pomological Society and quotes H. R. Robey of Fredericksburg, Virginia:

"The tree from which this apple was taken was found upon the farm when Mr. Brooke purchased it about forty years ago. It was then about the size of a coach whip. He thinks it is a seedling. The tree is now very large—bears regular and large crops of fruit, always fair, of the largest size—keeps well till May—fine yellow flesh, juicy and rich, and of the finest flavor. The tree grows in a warm, sandy soil. Mr. Brooke has nearly all the known varieties of the Pippins, which very rarely come to perfection."

Elliot (1858) gives a full description of Brooke Pippin with this notation: "bearing abundantly every year in localities where the Newtown Pippin, to which it bears some resemblance, does not succeed."

Before 1870, southern nursery catalogs listed

and described Brooke Pippin as a distinct variety; after 1870, Brooke Pippin was most often listed as a synonym of Yellow Newtown Pippin. At the present time, with the Brooke Pippin apparently extinct, the distinction (if any) between Brooke Pippin and the Yellow or Green Newtown Pippins will remain a mystery. *See* Brooks.

Fruit large, roundish inclining to conical, obscurely ribbed; skin greenish yellow with a faint blush; stem short and rather stout in a deep, irregular, russeted cavity; basin small, shallow, sometime furrowed; flesh crisp, juicy, fine-grained, aromatic. Ripe November–March. Catalog listings: MD, VA, GA, KY (1857–1904).

❦ **BROOKS ROW APPLE:** Listed from 1824 to 1827 by the Linnean Hill Nursery of Washington, D.C. No description except ripe June and July.

❦ **BROWN JUNE:** Described in an 1863 Pennsylvania nursery catalog as a Virginia apple, medium size, ripe June.

❦ **BROWN'S SEEDLING:** Listed in 1872 as a Virginia apple. No description.

❦ **BROWNITE** (Brown's Winter, Brown Knight): Said by Coxe (1817) to be of Delaware origin.

Fruit below medium, roundish oblong (also described as oblate), conical; skin red-streaked; flesh tender, crisp, sprightly. Ripe midwinter. No catalog listings.

❦ **BRUCE'S SUMMER:** Probably a Georgia apple, as it was first listed by the Fruitland Nursery of Augusta, Georgia, in the 1850s. A cooking and eating apple. Tree a regular and heavy bearer.

Fruit large to very large; skin greenish yellow with a blush cheek; flesh crisp, juicy, firm, high-flavored. Ripe July/August. Catalog listings: GA, AL, MS, TX (1858–94).

❦ **BRYANT:** Originated about 1820 near Vienna, Virginia. The original tree was standing and bearing on the farm of B. W. Bryant in 1893. The fruit was highly praised and pictured in the 1893 Report of the U.S. Secretary of Agriculture. Sold from 1899 to 1913 by Eastern Shore Nurseries, Denton, Maryland. Tree described as not productive in Virginia in 1900.

Fruit medium to large, roundish to roundish oblate, conical, often oblique; skin rather smooth, pale greenish yellow, shaded and splashed with dull red and striped with darker red, often covered with a gray bloom; dots numerous, large, russet, with protruding centers; stem short and stout in a large, deep, abrupt, russeted cavity; calyx open; basin very large, deep, gradually sloped, folded; flesh yellow or white, firm, juicy, mild subacid. Ripe winter.

❦ **BRYANT'S MAMMOTH:** Listed in 1890 by Jamestown Nurseries, Greensboro, North Carolina: "Origin Wilkes County, North Carolina. Now grown by Robert Bryant of Guilford County. Mr. Bryant has actually sold apples at 25 cents each. Extra large, yellow, nearly round, of good flavor. Oct. to Jan."

❦ **BUCKMAN:** First briefly described in 1865 and listed as a southern apple in the 1870 catalog of the Forest Nursery, Fairview, Kentucky.

Fruit medium size or below; skin yellow mostly covered with red. Ripe autumn.

❦ **BUDD'S SWEETING:** Described only as ripe in July in the 1856 catalog of Pomaria Nurseries, Pomaria, South Carolina.

❦ **BULL RUN BEAUTY:** Listed but not described in the 1928 catalog of Westcott's Nursery, Falls Church, Virginia.

❦ **BULLET** (Bullett, Green Abram, North Carolina Keeper?): Sold from 1856 to 1901 only by North Carolina nurseries, then for several years by a Virginia nursery. In 1878, Downing said it was formerly much grown in Virginia, Kentucky, and North Carolina but had been superseded by "better sorts." Bullet was grown primarily for its extraordinary keeping qualities, keeping its flavor and crisp texture through the winter to the following June. The tree is rather slender, drooping, productive, and "succeeds well only on deep vegetable loam." The description of the fruit is similar to the description of Yates, and the two apples may be identical.

Fruit medium size or below, roundish oblate to oblate, oblique, sometimes rectangular; skin greenish, mostly overspread with stripes and shades of red and grayish russet (also described as dingy red with indistinct stripes); flesh white, firm, moderately juicy, "peculiar subacid." Ripe January–June. Catalog listings: NC, VA (1856–1904).

❦ **BULLOCK HEART:** Sold from 1824 to 1827 by the Linnean Hill Nursery of Washington, D.C. No description except ripe September.

❦ **BUNCH APPLE** Listed in 1862 by Pomaria Nurseries of South Carolina. A Georgia apple, small, fruit borne "in clusters," ripe October.

❦ **BURROW** (Giles Beauty): A Tennessee apple first grown about 1878 by J. H. Burrow of Lynnville, Giles County, Tennessee.

Fruit large, roundish, slightly conical; skin thick and rather rough with russet marbling, yellow almost covered with dark or dull red; dots numerous, large, gray and russet; stem short to medium length in a medium to deep, russeted cavity; calyx open; basin medium size, corrugated; flesh yellowish, coarse, tender, juicy, subacid. Ripe early October and keeps until January. No catalog listings.

❦ **BURTON CATHEY:** From an 1883 letter from W. H. Hargrove, Pigeon River, Haywood County, North Carolina, to Charles Downing: "The local name is Burton Cathey. It originated on the farm of a very worthy gentleman by that name on the Pigeon River. I think it is a fine little apple, thrifty grower, good bearer, and keeps splendidly." No catalog listings.

❦ **BUTTER:** Ragan (1905) lists no fewer than seven apples with this name, which was commonly applied to any apple, usually aromatic and sweet, that made good apple butter. The Butter apple listed in Virginia nursery catalogs from 1858 to 1904 is probably of Pennsylvania origin and is described as rather large, red-striped (also said to be yellow), sweet, ripe September.

Elliot (1858) describes a Butter Apple, also of Pennsylvania origin, which differs from the above description. Fruit below medium, roundish; skin yellow overspread with red marbling; dots few, yellow russet; stem long and slender in a narrow, deep, russeted cavity; basin abrupt, ribbed; flesh yellowish white, tender, sweet. Ripe November–February.

❦ **CADDO** (Brooks): Apples sent to the USDA in 1898 from Marion County, Texas.

Fruit medium, oblong, flattened on the ends; skin yellowish striped with two shades of red and having russet warts; dots numerous, gray; stem long in a rather narrow and shallow cavity; calyx open; basin wide; flesh whitish. Ripe July–September. No catalog listings.

❦ **CALBREATH'S SWEETING:** Listed but not described in the 1869 catalog of Richmond Nurseries, Richmond, Virginia.

❦ **CALEB** (Caleb Sweet): A Pennsylvania apple sold by several Virginia nurseries from 1858 to 1904 as a cooking apple.

Fruit medium, oblate conical; skin yellow blushed with red; flesh yellow, crisp, sweet. Ripe August.

❦ **CANDID:** From the 1904 catalog of Riverside Nurseries, Greenville, North Carolina: "There is no better fall apple than the Candid. The tree is a vigorous grower and bears as full as a huckleberry. The fruit is about the size of the May Apple, striped with red. Ripens in October."

❦ **CANE CREEK SWEET:** Originated on Cane Creek in Burke County, North Carolina.

Fruit medium, roundish or ovate; skin pale greenish yellow with a shade of brown; stem long and slender in a deep cavity; calyx closed; basin narrow; flesh white, rather firm, tender, sweet, juicy when ripe but mealy when overripe. Ripe July/August. Catalog listings: NC, AL (1863–88).

❦ **CAPITOLA:** Originated or introduced before 1905 by John Steele Kerr, owner of the John S. Kerr Nursery, Sherman, Texas.

Fruit large, roundish, broadly ribbed; skin light green with broad stripes of two shades of red; dots numerous, gray; stem medium length and thick in an abrupt, medium-depth, greenish cavity; basin rather small; flesh white tinged with pale yellow. Ripe September/October or perhaps later. No catalog listings.

❦ **CAPTAIN MOSES:** Originated about 1850 near Turin, Coweta County, Georgia, and was being grown there as a market fruit in 1894. Sold by a Georgia nursery from 1894 to 1896. The apples hang on the tree until Christmas.

Fruit medium, roundish conical; skin yellow, overspread with red; flesh juicy, crisp, sweet. Ripe November and keeps until May.

❦ **CAPTAIN RANDALL:** From the 1912 catalog of the Clinton Nursery, Clinton, Kentucky. "This beautiful red apple is the largest of all apples. It netted $3.00 per bushel on the Chicago market in 1910. A plate of these apples will perfume a room. Six of these apples weigh nine pounds. Get in on the ground floor and buy an orchard of this fruit. Ripens August and September."

❦ **CARBAL:** A North Carolina apple listed in 1859 by Hopewell Nurseries of Fredericksburg, Virginia. No description.

❦ **CARNATION:** Described in 1855 as a seedling tree growing on the farm of Mrs. McAlister near Clarksville, Georgia, from seed planted about 1820 by Richard Cook.

Fruit medium size; skin dark red splashed with russet; cavity and basin very deep; flesh white, juicy, brittle, subacid. Ripe August. No catalog listings.

❦ **CAROLINA BEAUTY:** Originated in eastern North Carolina in Johnston County and was sold by North Carolina nurseries from 1884 to 1915. Tree a regular bearer. *See* North Carolina Beauty.

Fruit medium to large, oblate, slightly conical (also described as roundish oblong); skin smooth except for numerous russet knobs, yellow mostly washed with crimson with some darker red stripes; dots inconspicuous, gray; stem medium length in a deep, greenish cavity; basin quite shallow to medium depth; flesh whitish or yellowish, rather fine-grained, crisp, juicy, aromatic, subacid. Ripe September–November and can be kept until March. ❖ **Plate 81.**

❦ **CAROLINA FALL:** A North Carolina apple sold in 1860 by Pomaria Nurseries of South Carolina. "Large, productive, good. Ripe September."

❦ **CAROLINA FAVORITE:** A winter apple of North Carolina origin that keeps until May. Listed by North Carolina and Georgia nurseries from 1855 to 1861. No description.

❦ **CAROLINA PEARMAIN:** A South Carolina apple listed in 1860 by Pomaria Nurseries of South Carolina. "Small, very productive, a seedling of Clark's Pearmain. Ripe November."

❦ **CAROLINA QUEEN** (Carolina Winter Queen): From 1855 to 1860, two North Carolina nurseries listed an apple named Carolina Queen, described only as ripe August and September. Elliot (1854) and Thomas (1897) both describe an apple by this name or its synonym as an early winter apple. Their descriptions closely fit the Buckingham, which is ripe in August and September in warmer regions but ripens later in the mountains and in the North. A description is given here of the Carolina Queen, but it is probably the same apple as Buckingham.

Fruit rather large, roundish or slightly oblate, slightly conical; skin greenish yellow stained and streaked with red, which is heavier at the stem end; dots few, faint; stem three-fourths of an inch long and slender in a wide, deep, russeted cavity; basin round, ribbed; flesh yellowish, crisp, juicy, sprightly subacid. Ripe November–January or perhaps earlier.

❦ **CAROLINA RED** (Carolina Red Winter?, North Carolina Red?): An apple named Carolina Red was described by a Pennsylvania nursery in 1863 as a North Carolina apple, medium size, ripe January. An 1875 letter in the USDA files says a Carolina Red Winter was carried to Indiana from North Carolina by Addison Coffin of Hadley, Hendricks County, Indiana. A pre-1905 Illinois agricultural experiment station bulletin describes the apple called North Carolina Red this way: "Fruit medium, oblate; skin dark red; flesh mild subacid." These are probably all the same apple, originally from North Carolina.

❦ **CAROLINA RUSSET:** Probably originated in South Carolina and sold by South Carolina and Georgia nurseries from 1856 to 1871.

Fruit medium, roundish oblate; skin russeted; flesh subacid, "vinous flavor." Ripe October–December.

❦ **CAROLINA SUMMER:** From the 1928 catalog of the Titus Nursery Company, Waynesboro, Virginia: "Ripens with Early Harvest. Medium size, red stripes with yellow background. Subacid. Excellent for home use and export. Bears two years after planting."

❦ **CAROLINA SWEET:** From Downing (1878): "Fruit rather large, roundish, a little flattened, yellow, slightly shaded in the sun. Flesh yellow, dry, sweet. Poor. August." No catalog listings.

❦ **CAROLINA WATSON:** Sold extensively by Georgia nurseries, which advertised it as a good market apple. Tree an excellent bearer.

Fruit large, oblate conical; skin green striped with dull red, often with a red cheek; dots large, light-colored with dark centers; flesh white, crisp, aromatic, sweet (Downing says mild subacid). Ripe July in Georgia. Catalog listings: NC, GA, AL, MS, TX (1861–1909).

❦ **CARPENTER NORTH CAROLINA:** Described to the 1877 meeting of the American Pomological Society.

Fruit large, oblate, oblique; skin greenish yellow slightly blushed and russeted; flesh yellow, firm, tender, juicy, sprightly subacid. Ripe winter. No catalog listings.

❦ **CARPIP:** A Virginia apple sold in 1859 by Hopewell Nurseries of Fredericksburg, Virginia. No description.

❦ **CARR'S POUND SWEET** (Carr Sweet): Briefly described in the 1889 catalog of Planter's Nurseries, Humboldt, Tennessee, as "large, yellow, sweet." Ripe September/October.

❦ **CARR'S RED** (Carr): From the 1889 catalog of Planter's Nurseries, Humboldt, Tennessee: "Large to very large, red and green, good bearer." Ripe July.

❦ **CARR'S WINTER** (Carr's Late): From the 1853 catalog of the North Carolina Pomological Gardens, Greensboro, North Carolina: "Fruit large, oblate, green." Ripe February–May.

❦ **CARROL'S STRIPED/CARROL'S WHITE:** Both of these apples were listed from 1824 to 1827 by the Linnean Hill Nursery of Washington, D.C. No description except ripe October/November.

❦ **CARTER OF VIRGINIA** (Carter Apple, Carter, Royal Pippin?): Almost all southern catalogs that list the Carter are referring to the Mangum, a red-striped apple. There are, however, several brief references to another Carter apple with white or yellowish skin. This apple was mentioned at the 1860 meeting of the American Pomological Society by the Virginia delegate and also was briefly described by Thomas (1897). It was reported to have been widely grown in Spotsylvania County, Virginia, in 1852. Tree very prolific.

Fruit medium or below, conical; skin whitish or yellowish; flesh tender, juicy, subacid. Ripe late summer or fall. Catalog listings: VA, KY (1858–70).

❦ **CARTER OF ARKANSAS:** An 1899 Arkansas agricultural experiment station bulletin describes an apple named Carter that appears to be distinct from the Carter of Virginia and Carter's Blue.

Fruit medium to large, roundish; skin smooth, yellow covered with bright red, very highly colored; dots indistinct; stem short and stout in an irregular, medium-size, abrupt, russeted cavity; calyx closed; basin small and corrugated; flesh yellowish, fine-grained, mild subacid. Ripe winter. No catalog listings.

❦ **CASS** (Cass Red): Probably originated in Georgia before 1843 and was sold by two Virginia nurseries from 1858 to 1869.

Fruit medium size, red; flesh rich, juicy. Ripe November–May.

❦ **CASTNOR** (Castner): Described in 1860 by Pomaria Nurseries of South Carolina as a medium-size winter apple of North Carolina origin.

❦ **CATAWBA'S FAVORITE:** Listed as a "new and rare" apple in the 1902 catalog of Startown Nursery, Newton, North Carolina. No description.

❦ **CATFACE:** A Kentucky apple described by Elliot (1858).

Fruit large, oblate conical, flattened at ends; skin greenish yellow streaked with light and dark red; stem long and slender in a deep, wide cavity; calyx prominent in a deep basin; flesh white, tender, brisk, subacid. Ripe February to April or May. No catalog listings.

❦ **CATHEY:** Originated about 1900 by Frank Cathey of Mountain City, Rabun County, Georgia.

Fruit medium to large, oblate, often conical, irregular, often ribbed; skin thick, tough, waxy, green to pale yellow, sometimes russet-streaked; dots raised, russet to black, areolar; stem medium length in a medium to deep, narrow, usually russeted, furrowed, sometimes lipped cavity; basin abrupt, medium to deep, much furrowed; flesh rather coarse, sometimes mealy, rather dry, aromatic, subacid. No catalog listings.

❦ **CATLINE** (Gregson, Winter Grixon, Winter Grickson, Catlin, Winter Catline?, Cataline?, Cataling?): Coxe (1817) describes Catline in his great book on American apples, but, even in 1817, there was disagreement as to whether it originated in Delaware or Maryland. Thatcher (1822) says, "A Delaware autumn cider fruit and considered a pleasant eating apple in its season. The tree is very productive."

Fruit medium or sometimes smaller, roundish oblate, conical, sides often unequal; skin smooth, greenish yellow with red mottling and streaks and a red cheek in the sun; dots numerous, dark; stem short to medium length and thick in a moderately deep, greenish cavity; basin somewhat narrow, furrowed; flesh pale yellow, tender, juicy, nearly sweet. Ripe October–December. Catalog listings: VA, NC, SC (1855–1904). ❖ **Plate 82.**

❧ **CATO:** Probably originated in Maryland and described by Downing (1878).

Fruit small, oblate; skin white, shaded and splashed with bright red, deeper red in the sun; dots few, light-colored; flesh white, often stained red near the skin, tender, sprightly subacid. Ripe January–March. No catalog listings.

❧ **CATOOGA** (Cattoogaja, Cuttugaja, Cattugaja, Corbin, Raw Bread): A North Carolina apple first described in 1859. Downing (1878) says it is a cooking apple, but southern writers described it as being "of fine flavor."

Fruit large to very large, nearly round but irregular and ribbed, broadest at the base, sides unequal; skin pale yellow mottled with dark specks and sprinkled with green flecks; stem slender, medium length in a very deep cavity; basin deep; flesh yellowish, tender, juicy, mild subacid. Ripe October–January. No catalog listings.

❧ **CEDAR FALLS:** Originated in Forsyth County, North Carolina, and sold by South Carolina and Georgia nurseries from 1861 to 1878. Described as "a Number 1 apple, flavor exquisitely aromatic" in the book *Gardening for the South* (1885).

Fruit medium to large, slightly oblate; skin deep yellow nearly covered with purplish red and having a large patch of russet around the stem; flesh yellow, firm, aromatic, subacid. Ripe November and keeps until February.

❧ **CELLAR APPLE** (Swain): Listed from 1824 to 1827 by the Linnean Hill Nursery, Washington, D.C. No description except ripe August.

❧ **CENTER'S SEEDLING** (Centers): Warder (1867) gives North Carolina as the state of origin, but two early nursery catalogs credit South Carolina.

Fruit medium, conical; flesh subacid. Ripe July in South Carolina. Catalog listings: NC, SC, (1856–63).

❧ **CHAMPAGNE CRAB:** From the 1887 catalog of Grand Central Nurseries, Nashville, Tennessee: "This apple was brought to notice by Joe Phillips who has several trees. The apples remained on the trees this year until after two very hard freezes without the slightest injury. He then made them into cider, samples of which he submitted to the best judges in Nashville, who pronounced it equal to the best American champagnes. The apple is of good size, beautiful bright red color and delicious flavor, but does not become mellow and fit for eating until very late in the spring. Mr. Phillips has been offered $20 per barrel for all the cider he can produce from this apple."

The Champagne Crab is listed in an 1863 Pennsylvania nursery catalog as a South Carolina apple that ripens in November.

❧ **CHANCELLER'S RED** (Chancellor's Red): From an 1874 letter to Charles Downing from Franklin Davis, the prominent Virginia nurseryman: "It has been grown for many years by Capt. Henry B. Jones of Brownsburg, Virginia, but I cannot tell from what source he procured it. It is distinct from anything I have seen." A subsequent letter from Captain Jones calls it a Virginia apple. Sold by a Virginia nursery in 1859. No description.

❧ **CHAPMAN'S HORSE:** Listed in 1872 as a summer apple by Pomaria Nurseries of South Carolina. No description. Probably identical to Chapman's Large Flat Horse.

❧ **CHAPMAN'S LATE/CHAPMAN'S LARGE FLAT HORSE:** Two South Carolina apples listed in 1860 by Pomaria Nurseries of South Carolina. Both described as large, ripe October/November.

❧ **CHARLEY'S WINTER:** Raised before 1869 by H. R. Robey of Fredericksburg, Virginia.

Fruit medium or below, oblate inclining to conical; skin pale yellow, often shaded with red in the sun; flesh yellow, compact, juicy, crisp, brisk subacid. Ripe January/February. No catalog listings.

❦ **CHATTAHOOCHEE** (Chattahoochee Greening): Originated in Georgia near the Chattahoochee River and sold by Georgia nurseries from 1871 to 1898.

Fruit medium, roundish oblate, conical, oblique; skin yellowish green with a faint pinkish or brownish blush in the sun; dots small, numerous, russet, green or pink, some indented; stem very short (also described as long) in a deep, somewhat russeted cavity; basin deep (also said to be shallow), slightly furrowed; flesh yellowish white, crisp, tender, brisk subacid. Ripe November–January.

❦ **CHEESE:** There are many apples called Cheese or having the word Cheese in their name or synonym. The word "Cheese" in the name of an apple probably refers to fruit having a pronounced oblate or flat shape, looking somewhat like a wheel or hoop of cheese. Warder (1867) lists two apples named Cheese, one from Pennsylvania and one that he received from Lewis Sanders of Grass Hill, Gallatin County, Kentucky. This Kentucky apple is described here.

Fruit medium or small, oblate; skin smooth, yellowish green with stripes and splashes of deep red and purplish red; dots scattered, gray and purple; stem long and slender in a wide, brown cavity; calyx closed; basin shallow or deep in different apples; flesh subacid. Ripe December/January.

❦ **CHEOEE:** Originated before 1863 in either North Carolina or Georgia and sold by a Georgia nursery in 1871. Fruit medium size. Ripe January and a fine keeper.

❦ **CHEROKEE RED** (Cherokee): A large apple of north Georgia origin. Tree bears heavily biennially. The description closely fits the description of Red Detroit.

Fruit large, round to slightly oblong; skin striped and splashed with light and dark red with some russet near the stem; dots numerous, large, irregular, gray; stem long and slender in an acute, russeted cavity; basin abrupt, almost deep, smooth; flesh yellowish, coarse, rather dry, subacid. Ripe October–January. Catalog listings: VA, NC, SC (1856–69). *See* Red Detroit.

❦ **CHESTATEE** (White Apple): Probably originated in Georgia. Said to be too acid for fresh eating but good for cooking. Tree drooping and a tip bearer.

Fruit medium to large, roundish oblate, slightly conical; skin pale yellow, often with a slight blush in the sun and with spots and small flecks of black at the stem end; stem short and slender in a deep cavity; flesh white, juicy, slightly acid. Ripe September and October and keeps until December. Catalog listings: GA, KY (1857–70).

❦ **CHESTER DAVIS:** Sold in 1927 by the Thompson Nursery of Waco, Texas: "A very early bearer of fine quality apples. Originated in south Texas." No description.

❦ **CHESTOA** (Rabbit's Head, Chestooa): Probably of North Carolina origin, as it was introduced by the North Carolina pomologist, Silas McDowell. Sold by South Carolina and Georgia nurseries from 1860 to 1871. An outline of this apple in *Gardening for the South* (1885) shows a very lopsided apple somewhat resembling the head of a rabbit.

Fruit medium or above, oblong conical, but often distorted so one side is much smaller than the other; skin greenish or yellow mostly splashed and striped with red or dark crimson; dots minute and dark; stem short and slender in a slightly russeted cavity; flesh whitish or yellowish, crisp, juicy, aromatic, "pleasantly acid." Ripe November and keeps until January or perhaps later.

❦ **CHRISTIANA:** Originated by John R. Brinckle of Wilmington, Delaware, and first fruited in 1855.

Fruit medium, oblate or perhaps roundish, conical; skin yellow, nearly covered with bright red; stem half an inch long in a deep and rather narrow cavity; basin deep, moderately wide, corrugated; flesh yellowish white, fine-grained, rather juicy, sprightly subacid. Ripe November. No catalog listings.

❦ **CHURCH'S LATE SWEET:** Downing (1878) says this is a southern apple of unknown origin.

Fruit medium, roundish conical; skin yellow, occasionally with a blush in the sun; flesh yellowish, compact, mild subacid, almost sweet. Ripe February–May. No catalog listings.

❦ **CILLAGOS:** Probably a foreign apple mentioned in an 1898 Alabama agricultural experiment station bulletin. No description. No catalog listings.

**CLAGHEAD:** Briefly mentioned in a Maryland agricultural experiment station bulletin before 1905. No description. No catalog listings.

**CLAMPETT** (Clampit, Clampet): Probably of North Carolina origin but resembles the Benoni.

Fruit medium size; skin striped and nearly covered with light red; flesh yellow. Ripe August/September. Catalog listings: NC, TN (1855–89).

**CLARK:** There are several southern apples named Clark, but none of them was ever listed by a southern nursery catalog. A Clark apple has been found by Tom Brown in Burnsville, North Carolina, but it has not yet been further identified.

*Clark* (of Georgia): A seedling found before 1853 growing on the lot of Robert Campbell of Clarksville, Habersham County, Georgia. Fruit large; skin green with russet around the stem; flesh subacid. Ripe mid-August in Georgia.

*Clark* (of Kentucky): Originated before 1874 on the farm of a Mr. Clark, Madison County, Kentucky. Tree an annual bearer. Fruit small to medium, roundish oblate, slightly conical; skin greenish yellow, mostly covered and striped with dull purplish red mixed with gray; flesh yellowish white, very tender, juicy, mild subacid. Ripe September–December.

*Clark Seedling*: The original tree grew from a seed planted in 1855 and bore its first crop in 1866 near Asheville, North Carolina. Fruit large to very large, roundish conical, ribbed; skin deep yellow; flesh yellowish white, firm, juicy, aromatic, mild subacid. Ripe winter.

**CLARK'S GREENING:** A Virginia apple briefly described by Warder (1867).

Fruit oblate; skin green; flesh subacid. No catalog listings.

**CLARK'S DELAWARE:** Originated before 1878 by John C. Clarke of Maryland.

Fruit medium, roundish, slightly oblong, oblique; skin smooth, yellow, shaded orange-red in the sun; dots numerous, gray; flesh white, moderately tender, juicy, mild subacid. Ripe December–March. No catalog listings.

**CLAYTON:** Supposedly of Indiana origin but sold by six southern nurseries. Tree moderately productive and bears early. *See* Boyd.

Fruit large, roundish conical, flattened on the ends; skin greenish yellow covered with stripes and splashes of dull red; dots minute, scattered; stem medium length, stout, in a wide, deep, acute, waxy, green cavity; calyx closed; basin narrow and abrupt; flesh yellow, crisp, subacid. Ripens late and keeps until January or later. Catalog listings: MD, VA, GA, TN, KY (1871–1913).

**CLEVELAND** (Grover Cleveland): This is not the Cleveland of Ohio (or perhaps Kentucky) origin but is a Texas apple originated by Dr. W. W. Stell of Paris Nurseries, Paris, Texas. Said to be very showy. Sold by Texas nurseries from 1885 to 1904.

Fruit large, oval; skin yellow, nearly covered with red and deeper red stripes; flesh very juicy, subacid or perhaps sweet. Ripe August. *See* Bledsoe.

**CLOTZ:** Described to the 1877 meeting of the American Pomological Society by Natt Atkinson of Asheville, North Carolina.

Fruit large, roundish oblate, conical, oblique; skin greenish yellow with a dull, deep red blush, some russeting; flesh yellowish white, tender, fine-grained, juicy, spicy, sprightly subacid. No catalog listings.

**CLOUD:** A South Carolina apple sold by a Georgia nursery in 1861.

Fruit oblate, red-striped, subacid. Ripe winter.

**COBB:** A Georgia apple listed in the 1859 catalog of Hopewell Nurseries, Fredericksburg, Virginia. No description.

**COBIA** (Cohea): A South Carolina apple listed from 1860 to 1878 by Pomaria Nurseries of South Carolina. "Very large, yellow striped red; high flavor; ripe November-December. A seedling produced near Pomaria, South Carolina."

**COCHRAN:** The original tree was carried from Burke County, North Carolina, to Blount County, Tennessee, about 1825 by a William Cochran. In 1897, it was known only in Blount County where it was brought to attention by Samuel Dunlap. Fruit keeps well for a summer apple and is useful for fresh eating, cooking, and drying.

Fruit medium to large, roundish to slightly oblong, slightly conical, somewhat oblique; skin thin, rather smooth, golden yellow, somewhat russeted, with a light red blush; dots numerous, brown; stem long and slender in a large, abrupt, russeted cavity; calyx partially closed; basin large, rather deep, abrupt, with a few furrows; flesh yellowish, fine-grained, tender, juicy, subacid. Ripe early July. No catalog listings.

❧ **COE'S GOLDEN:** Coe's Golden is described in the 1884 catalog of Guilford Nurseries, Vandalia, North Carolina (At that time, Vandalia was three miles from Greensboro, North Carolina.): "Brought into notice by W. A. Coe, near my place. He says the original tree was three feet in diameter and his father gathered one hundred bushels of apples in one season from it. Apples of this variety were used to make the word 'Guilford' at the State Exposition. Fruit medium to large, fine golden yellow with some russet. Flesh tender and mild subacid when well ripe. One of the very best for cooking and evaporating. Tree bears annual crops ripening with and after the Magnum Bonum."

This apple is different from the English apple Coe's Golden Drop. *See* Coe.

❧ **COFFMAN** (Summer Red, Koffman June, Red July, Summer Neverfail, Coffman June): The original tree grew before 1855 on the farm of W. L. Coffman, Lauderdale County, Tennessee, and trees were spread throughout western Tennessee, northern Alabama, and into Arkansas by farmers using root sprouts. Coffman was sold by small local nurseries around 1888 and was listed by Georgia nurseries from 1909 to 1928. Coffman is widely adapted to southern growing conditions, the tree is an abundant annual bearer, and the fruit is suitable for summer marketing. It resembles the Carolina Red June, and is probably a seedling of it. Praised as grown in Mississippi in 1860. *See* Summer Red.

Fruit above medium to large, roundish to oblong conical, tapering toward the base, often oblique; skin rather thick, smooth, glossy, pale yellow washed almost entirely with mixed red (often very dark red) and striped with purplish red, thinly overspread with a gray bloom; dots numerous, pale; stem short in a small to medium-size, deep, lipped, russeted cavity; calyx closed; basin medium size, abrupt, furrowed; flesh yellowish, often tinged with red, rather fine-grained, juicy, crisp, sprightly subacid. Ripe late June through July in Tennessee.

❧ **COLE DAVIS** (Cole Ben Davis): Originated about 1898 in a Ben Davis orchard in Lincoln, Arkansas, belonging to S. T. Cole. The fruit is of higher color than Ben Davis but otherwise quite similar. Sold by Stark Bro's Nursery for a few years around 1900.

❧ **COLLOT'S APPLE:** Listed in the 1824 catalog of the Linnean Hill Nursery, Washington, D.C. No description except a winter apple.

❧ **COLSON:** Listed as a new Alabama apple in 1871 by the Fruitland Nursery, Augusta, Georgia. No description except ripe fall and a good keeper.

❧ **COLTON** (Early Colton): Originated before 1840 on the farm of Mr. Colton, Rowe, Massachusetts, and highly extolled when it first became available in the South because of its extreme early ripening. It ripens in late May in parts of the South, ten days ahead of Early Harvest and Red Astrachan. Described as "sufficiently acid to be good for cooking and not too sour to be first class for eating."

Fruit medium, roundish, slightly ribbed; skin pale greenish yellow, sometimes with a brownish red blush; dots large, numerous, gray; stem stout; cavity small, shallow, narrow; calyx nearly closed; basin shallow, wrinkled; flesh whitish green, rather coarse, crisp, juicy, sprightly subacid. Ripe June/July. Catalog listings: MD, VA, NC, TN, KY (1893–1928).

❧ **COLUMBIAN RUSSET** (Browne's Imperial Russet, Bowne's Imperial Russet): This may be another synonym of Clarke's Pearmain. It is so listed by Downing (1878), and Warder (1867) remarks upon the resemblance. Its description, however, indicates it is more russeted than Clarke's Pearmain.

Fruit medium to large (Warder says medium to small), roundish oblate; skin smooth greenish yellow overspread with russet; dots minute, scattered, prominent; stem long and slender in an acute cavity; calyx open; basin medium size; flesh yellow, fine-grained, moderately juicy, aromatic, mild subacid. Ripe October–December or perhaps later. Catalog listings: MD, NC, KY (1836–70).

❧ **COMFORT:** Listed by two Virginia nurseries in 1858 and 1869. No description.

❦ **COMPANION:** A southern apple of unknown origin briefly described by Warder (1867).

Fruit oblate, subacid. No catalog listings.

❦ **COMPETITOR:** Originated by E. N. Sword of Chandler, Virginia, and first fruited in 1893. A large, striped apple resembling McAfee. Season early winter in southwestern Virginia. No catalog listings.

❦ **CONE:** Listed as a North Carolina apple in the 1859 catalog of Hopewell Nurseries, Fredericksburg, Virginia. No description.

❦ **CONEY CREEK SWEET:** Mentioned but not described in an 1889 Texas agricultural experiment station bulletin. Grown at that time in Chambers County, Texas. No catalog listings.

❦ **CONN:** From the 1916 catalog of Corinth Nurseries, Corinth, Mississippi: "This is a fine winter keeper. Conn was found in Prentiss County and was first grafted by Mr. Belcher, an old Confederate soldier who died a few years ago in the Old Soldier's Home. This was his special winter apple." No description.

❦ **COOK'S RED** (Cook's Red Winter): Originated before 1858 by Jacob Cook of Edisto, South Carolina, and sold by South Carolina and Georgia nurseries in the 1860s. Tree a regular bearer.

Fruit medium to large. Ripe October and keeps well.

❦ **COON:** Originated before 1860, probably in Kentucky.

Fruit large, green, subacid. Ripe July-August. No catalog listings.

❦ **COONER:** Mentioned at the 1860 meeting of the American Pomological Society as a large Mississippi apple. No description. No catalog listings.

❦ **COOPER** (Beauty Red, Lady Washington): An old apple, perhaps of New England origin, that was introduced into Ohio in 1796 and became popular in that area. Sold by several southern nurseries.

Fruit large, often very large, roundish oblate; skin greenish yellow with stripes and blotches of red; stem short and slender in a deep cavity; calyx closed; basin deep; flesh yellowish, crisp, juicy. Ripe September and keeps up to two months. Catalog listings: VA, SC, KY, TX (1845–1904).

❦ **COOPER'S PRIDE:** An Arkansas apple that originated before 1905.

Fruit medium, oblong conical; skin greenish yellow. Ripe September/October. No catalog listings.

❦ **COOPER'S YELLOW:** A seedling apple first grown before 1873 by Major Mark A. Cooper of Etowah Iron Works, Cass County, Georgia. This apple and the better-known variety, Etowah, originally grew near each other, both being seedlings of Shockley.

Fruit large, oblate, regular; skin yellow with a faint red cheek; calyx closed; basin shallow, corrugated; flesh slightly coarse, brittle, crisp, almost sweet. Ripe October–January. No catalog listings.

❦ **CORLEY'S LATE:** Listed as a winter apple in the 1878 catalog of Pomaria Nurseries, Pomaria, South Carolina. No description.

❦ **CORNELIA:** A South Carolina apple listed in 1860 by Pomaria Nurseries, Pomaria, South Carolina. "Medium, green, ripe December, keeps till April."

❦ **CORNFIELD:** A southern apple that originated before 1850. Brought to notice in Kentucky and listed in 1870 by the Forest Nursery, Fairview, Kentucky.

Fruit medium, roundish oblate, regular; skin smooth, yellow, mostly covered with red and red stripes; dots small and numerous; stem short in a wide, acute cavity; calyx open; basin abrupt, deep, cracked; flesh yellow, fine-grained, tender, rather dry, subacid. Ripe December.

❦ **COTTER:** Apples sent to the USDA in 1905 from Baxter County, Arkansas.

Fruit above medium, roundish to slightly oblate; skin crimson with faint darker red stripes; dots numerous, mostly areole with dark centers; stem short to medium length in a deep, russeted cavity; basin large, corrugated; flesh yellowish. Ripe October–January. No catalog listings.

❦ **COVE:** A Tennessee apple that originated in either Williamson or Davidson County as a cross of Red Limbertwig and Kinnaird's Choice and sold by a Kentucky nursery in 1897. Described as "lacking the flavor of a good eating apple but sells well late in the winter on account of its beauty and keeping qualities." Tree a shy bearer and susceptible to borers and fire blight.

Fruit large, roundish, slightly conical, irregular; skin yellow, mostly covered with streaks and stripes of two shades of red; dots inconspicuous; stem medium length in a narrow, irregular cavity; basin medium in width and depth, corrugated; flesh tinged yellow, firm, mild subacid. Ripe winter and an outstanding keeper, often keeping until August.

**COVINGTON:** Mentioned at the 1860 meeting of the American Pomological Society as a Mississippi apple that ripens in August. No description. No catalog listings.

**CRADDOCK:** Originated before 1896 with A. Davis of Woodville, Haywood County, Tennessee.

Fruit large, roundish oblate; skin thin, whitish yellow overspread with brownish gray and with some russet patches; dots conspicuous, brown; stem short and stout in a large, deep cavity with dark russet markings; basin medium size, furrowed, and with "mammiform lumps"; calyx nearly closed; flesh whitish, rather fine-grained, tender, juicy, subacid. Ripe August/September. No catalog listings.

**CRANBERRY:** The Cranberry is a Georgia apple described by Elliot (1855). The Cranberry Pippin is a different apple, from New York. The Scarlet Cranberry is a Virginia apple. The description here is for the Cranberry.

Fruit medium, roundish conical; skin yellow striped with light red on the shady side and deep red on the sunny side; dots numerous, gray and russet; cavity narrow and russeted; calyx closed; flesh white. No catalog listings.

**CRATCHFIELD:** A Virginia winter apple mentioned by a New England magazine in 1832. No description. No catalog listings.

**CRAVEN'S WINTER:** Origin unknown but sold in 1870 by the Forest Nursery of Fairview, Kentucky: "Fruit small, yellowish covered with russet; sweet, good."

**CRAWFORD** (Crawford Pippin, Crawford's Fall?, Cranford?): This apple originated about 1850 on the farm of W. D. Crawford, Washington County, Arkansas. I believe this is the same man as William Crawford, who was involved in the Paragon–Mammoth Blacktwig controversy. Like the Mammoth Blacktwig, the Crawford was noticed by Colonel E. F. Babcock when he was searching for seedling Arkansas apples to display at the 1884 New Orleans World Exposition. This apple is distinct from the Ohio apple named Crawford Keeper, which is described by Downing (1878), and Crawford's Seedling, which is from North Carolina. This may be the same apple as Crawford's Fall, mentioned in an 1891 Tennessee agricultural experiment station bulletin as adapted to east Tennessee. Tree not a heavy bearer and susceptible to scab.

Fruit medium to large, slightly oblate; skin smooth, deep yellow, often with a blush and splashed with red; dots numerous, medium size; stem almost long and stout in a narrow, medium-depth cavity; calyx open; basin medium depth to shallow, smooth; flesh yellowish, moderately juicy, fine-grained, subacid. Ripe December–March. Catalog listings: GA, KY (1890–97).

**CRAWFORD'S SEEDLING:** Originated by the owner of Crawford and Company, a nursery in Statesville, North Carolina, and listed by them in 1915.

Fruit very large, cream-colored; flesh tender, juicy, subacid.

**CRAYTON** (Crayton's Seedling?): A South Carolina apple listed from 1860 to 1878 by Pomaria Nurseries of South Carolina. "Medium, best quality. Ripe December and keeps until April. Origin B. F. Crayton of Anderson, S.C."

**CRITTENDEN:** Crittenden originated about 1864 on the farm of Winn Green of Shelby County, Kentucky. It was named for John C. Crittenden, a Kentucky statesman.

Fruit medium, roundish, somewhat rectangular; skin dull red on yellow; flesh juicy, very sweet. Keeps until May or June. No catalog listings.

**CROCKETT COUNTY KEEPER** (Crockett): Sold in 1889 by Planters Nurseries, Humboldt, Tennessee: "Hangs on the tree until freezing; good late." No description.

**CROSS:** Originated before 1846 with Robert Cross

of Fair Play, Maryland, and sold in 1909 by Eastern Shores Nurseries, Denton, Maryland. Tree a heavy bearer on alternate years.

Fruit large to very large, roundish oblate; skin greenish white, thinly striped, splashed and mottled with light and dark red; dots few, light colored and gray; stem very short in a large, deep cavity; basin large, deep, slightly furrowed; flesh white, tender, juicy, mild subacid. Ripe August/September.

**CROTCHER:** Originated in Dorchester County, Maryland, before 1867.

Fruit medium, oblate conical; skin whitish, somewhat waxy, often with a slight blush; dots few, light-colored and green; stem short in a large, deep, russeted cavity; basin rather large, slightly uneven; flesh white, crisp, tender, juicy, subacid. Ripe July/August. No catalog listings.

**CRUMPTON:** Described in 1895 as a new seedling variety from Henrico County, Virginia, and sold by three Virginia nurseries from 1895 to 1910.

Fruit medium, oblate; skin very dark red. Ripe August and a good keeper for a summer apple.

**CRYDER:** An autumn apple listed in 1875 by the Middletown Nursery of Virginia. No description.

**CULLAWHEE:** This apple is described in several old catalogs as being of immense size, "perhaps the largest apple known." One apple is said to have been twenty-one inches in circumference. Downing (1878) and others, however, describe Cullawhee as medium size or above. Unless a living tree is discovered, we will never know just how big the apples were. The description below very closely fits the description of Red Bietigheimer except for time of ripening.

Cullawhee was first mentioned in 1857 and was thought to be a seedling of the Buff (another huge apple), which it resembles. It originated in Jackson County, North Carolina, where it was found growing in the woods. Described as "resembling a huge pomegranate in shape, being much ribbed, with the calyx only slightly sunk." The immense size of the fruit often caused it to drop prematurely, so this variety was recommended for growing only as a curiosity.

Fruit large to very large, oblate, slightly conical, ribbed; skin yellow, mostly shaded and striped with dull and light red; dots dark colored; stem short and fleshy; basin shallow; flesh white, coarse, tender, juicy, brisk subacid or rather acid. Ripe November–March. Catalog listings: VA, SC GA, KY (1857–72).

**CULLODEN:** A southern apple listed from 1859 to 1861 by the Fruitland Nursery, Augusta, Georgia.

Fruit conical, red-striped, subacid. Ripe winter.

**CUMBERLAND:** From the 1897 catalog of Green River Nurseries, Bowling Green, Kentucky: "Originated near Clarksville, Tennessee, and introduced by F. N. Downer in 1886. Specimens remain in perfect condition till the first of May. Form roundish oblate with basin depressed; core very short; color dark red; about the size of the Wine Sap; surface smooth and glossy; flesh white and quality very good." This is probably Dodge's Crimson, which has the synonym Cumberland Black.

A different apple named Cumberland, of Pennsylvania origin, was sold by one Virginia nursery circa 1900.

**CUMMING'S RED** (Cummin's Red): Originated before 1873 by Enos Cummings near New Garden, Guilford County, North Carolina, and listed by North Carolina nurseries from 1888 to 1890. Tree an abundant bearer.

Fruit large, roundish oval, somewhat conical; skin deep red; flesh juicy, rich. Ripe October.

**CUNNINGHAM'S CHEESE** (Cunningham): Originated about 1865 by Jacob Cunningham of Prince Edward County, Virginia, and grown in that vicinity around 1900 as an eating, cooking, and cider apple. An 1893 letter from Thomas J. Garden of Gardenia, Virginia, says: "Let these mellow thoroughly and you will find the flavor peculiar and delightful. The fruit grows in bunches." Sold by a Virginia nursery in 1894.

Fruit medium, oblate; skin thick, smooth, greenish yellow almost covered with different shades of red washes and stripes; dots raised, slightly russet; stem short and rather stout in a large, deep cavity marked with yellowish brown russet; calyx closed; basin large, nearly round, deep, nearly smooth; flesh yellowish, firm, juicy, mild subacid. Probably a winter apple.

❦ **CURLESE'S SWEET:** Originated before 1863 in Mason County, Kentucky, and listed in 1870 by the Forest Nursery, Fairview, Kentucky. Fruit medium, skin very white, flesh sweet. Ripe summer.

❦ **CURRY'S RED WINTER** (Carry's Late?, Curry's Striped Winter?): Originated in eastern North Carolina and first described in 1869.

Fruit medium, oblong; skin yellow nearly covered with pale red; dots yellow and russet; stem short and slender in a small cavity; calyx open; basin large; flesh white, solid, aromatic, subacid. Keeps until January. No catalog listings.

❦ **CURTIS:** In 1829, apples of this name were sent to William Prince, the noted nurseryman on Long Island, New York, by J. B. Russell of Virginia. Described by Kendrick (1841). "Skin smooth, red; flesh juicy. Ripe mid to end of August." A Curtis Superb was listed in 1873 by Hopewell Nurseries of Virginia.

❦ **DABNEY:** Grown by S. H. Stepp of Dry Creek, Tennessee, and highly praised in an 1896 Tennessee agricultural experiment station bulletin.

Fruit large, roundish oblate, sometimes oblique; skin thick, rather smooth, greenish yellow washed with red and striped with crimson, overspread with russet or gray; dots conspicuous, yellow or brown, some indented; stem medium to long and stout in a large, russeted cavity; calyx open; basin large, deep; flesh yellowish, "satiny," almost fine-grained, tender, juicy, subacid. Ripe September. No catalog listings.

❦ **DAHLONEGA:** Dahlonega is listed as a distinct variety by Ragan (1905); however, it is probably Nickajack under one of its many synonyms.

Fruit medium, roundish conical; skin light greenish yellow shaded and marbled with crimson and having a light bloom; dots numerous, light-colored; flesh whitish, moderately tender, juicy, subacid. Ripe February/March. Catalog listings: GA, KY (1858–70).

❦ **DAPPER:** A Georgia apple that originated before 1853. Fruit small, roundish oblate; skin yellow clouded with dull green with crimson specks in the sun; calyx small, closed. No catalog listings.

❦ **DAVIDSON** (Davidson's Mutton, Mutton): A Virginia apple sold from 1869 to 1904 by the Franklin Davis Nursery, Richmond, Virginia.

Fruit medium size, yellow. Ripe August.

❦ **DAVIS** (Davis October): Ragan (1905) lists four apples named Davis. One of these is an apple from Mississippi that originated before 1849. All we know is that it is a large green, sweet apple that ripens in October and keeps until January or later. Catalog listings: VA, SC (1856–69). It is barely possible this is the same apple as Captain Davis (also a Mississippi apple), but neither the history nor the description is a good match.

❦ **DAWSON:** From an 1876 letter from James Fitz, Albemarle County Virginia: "It grew near a fence many years since on Benjamin Childress' land since bought by his grandson Benjamin H. Dawson. He called my attention to the tree as a heavy bearer of fine fruit. I found it to be a good apple if taken from the tree before it was mellow. It keeps well and is of good size. I gave it the name of Dawson." No catalog listings.

❦ **DAWSON'S CLUSTER:** An Ohio apple sold from 1898 to 1903 by the Austin Nursery, Austin, Texas: "Early Joe, Little Romanite and Dawson's Cluster. Nearly all apples do well on Cypress Creek in the northern part of Travis County. Of all the old varieties, these three are the most profitable and are in great demand. If you have apple land, plant some of these."

Fruit medium, oblong conical; skin yellow with a light blush on the sunny side; dots scattered, gray; stem long in an acute, wavy cavity; calyx closed; basin abrupt; flesh yellowish white, fine-grained, tender, juicy, subacid. Ripe August in Texas.

❦ **DEASON:** Listed in 1871 as a new Alabama apple by the Fruitland Nursery, Augusta, Georgia. No description except ripe winter.

❦ **DEFIANCE:** A wild seedling found about 1850 growing in the orchard of Peter Ray, Habersham County, Georgia, and sold by Virginia, North Carolina, and Georgia nurseries from 1858 to 1872. Different from the Defiance of Ohio origin.

Fruit medium size, sweet. Ripe July.

❦ **DEGRUCHY** (Degrucy): Warder (1867) briefly describes Degruchy as a southern winter apple, large and subacid. Sold by two Virginia nurseries from 1858 to 1869.

❦ **DELASURE:** A southern apple of unknown origin sold by two Virginia nurseries from 1858 to 1869. Described only as round and subacid.

❦ **DELAWARE BOTTOM:** A cooking apple probably of Maryland origin before 1868.

Fruit oblate; skin yellow with a blush; flesh subacid. Ripe October/November. No catalog listings.

❦ **DELAWARE LATE SPICE:** Probably of Delaware origin before 1905. No description. No catalog listings.

❦ **DELAWARE SUPERIOR:** Probably a Delaware apple that originated before 1850. No description. No catalog listings.

❦ **DEMOREST:** A Georgia apple that originated before 1895 in Habersham County.

Fruit medium, roundish oblate; skin yellow washed with pale red and striped with crimson; dots minute, brown; stem half an inch long and slender in a large, deep cavity; basin abrupt, deep, overspread with russet, furrowed; flesh white, tender, juicy, medium subacid. Ripe June/July. No catalog listings.

❦ **DEMURRY PIPPIN:** A southern apple sold by two Virginia nurseries from 1858 to 1869. No description.

❦ **DENNISON:** Listed from 1824 to 1827 as a winter apple by the Linnean Hill Nursery, Washington, D.C. No description.

❦ **DINWIDDIE** (Dinwiddie's Seedling): In 1864, a North Carolina Confederate soldier found an apple sprout in Dinwiddie County, Virginia. He took it home with him to Johnston County, North Carolina, planted it, and thus originated this variety. A 1902 North Carolina nursery catalog says, "Tree healthy, free from blight and disease, medium to late bloomer and a full annual bearer. Fruit medium, dark green color with a deep blush next to the sun, shading to a deep red by September. Hangs on the tree until November. Very juicy and melting; flesh yellow and of fine quality. This is a splendid family apple." Ripe September. Catalog listings: VA, NC (1901–15).

At the 1871 meeting of the American Pomological Society, there was brief mention of a different apple named Dinwiddie grown by W. W. Dinwiddie of Albemarle County, Virginia. No description. No catalog listings.

❦ **DIXIE:** Not surprisingly there are several southern apples named Dixie or having Dixie as a synonym. J. W. Fitz in his book *The Southern Apple and Peach Culturist* (1872) describes the Virginia apple called Golden Dixie. (*See* Golden Dixie.) Dixie also is a synonym of the southern apple named Lowry. (*See* Lowry.) Dixie Red Delight is a synonym of Red Delight, and Dixie is a synonym of Shockley.

The 1920 catalog of the Texas Nursery Company, Sherman, Texas, describes an apple named Dixie: "This beautiful yellow apple originated from the seed of some Kentucky apples planted by Mrs. Emiline Burge of Ector, Texas, in her garden in 1898. The fruit is a beautiful clear yellow, round, smooth, fine-textured, subacid and is excellent for cooking or eating. Ripe last of June."

❦ **DOBBIN'S EVERBEARING:** Described in the 1878 catalog of Pomaria Nurseries of South Carolina: "A South Carolina apple; medium to large, striped, commencing ripening early May and continues in bearing for three months; a great acquisition."

❦ **DOCTOR BERRY'S LATE:** Listed from 1872 to 1878 by Pomaria Nurseries of South Carolina. A winter apple of southern origin.

❦ **DOCTOR BRIGGS:** From the 1897 catalog of Green River Nurseries, Bowling Green, Kentucky: "A new seedling originating on the farm of Dr. Jason A. Briggs, near this city. Size large, resembling the Rome Beauty, and is possibly a seedling of this noted apple."

Fruit medium or above, roundish oblate, conical; skin light yellow, heavily striped and shaded with crimson; dots inconspicuous; stem medium length in a narrow, russeted, medium depth, acute cavity; basin rather wide and deep; flesh whitish tinged with creamy yellow. Ripe October.

❦ **DOCTOR FULCHER:** A seedling found on the farm of a Dr. Fulcher of Fairview, Kentucky, and listed in the 1870 catalog of the Forest Nursery, Fairview, Kentucky. Tree an annual and abundant bearer.

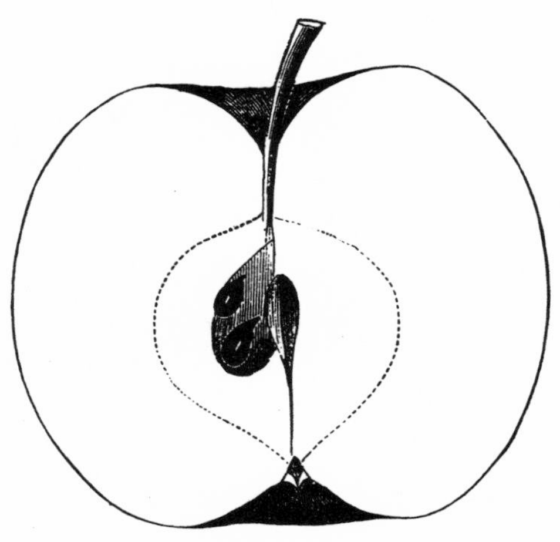

DOCTOR FULCHER

Fruit below medium, roundish to roundish oblate, flattened on the ends, sometimes a little oblique; skin yellow, shaded and mottled over most of its surface with light and dark red and with a grayish bloom; dots few, light-colored; stem short (Warder says medium to long) and small in a rather large, slightly russeted, wavy cavity; basin medium size, slightly corrugated; flesh white (or perhaps yellow), sometimes stained red near the skin, fine-grained, tender, juicy, subacid. Ripe November and keeps until about January.

❧ **DOCTOR HUTCHENS:** Listed as a winter apple in the 1870 catalog of the Forest Nursery, Fairview, Kentucky: "Fruit small, skin greenish striped with dull red."

❧ **DOCTOR WALKER** (Litsey, Geneton Improved): Originated about 1870 on the farm of John Litsey near Springfield, Kentucky. A seedling of Ralls Janet, but the tree is hardier and the fruit brighter red, better quality, and at least as good a keeper as Ralls Janet. A late bloomer like its parent and an annual bearer. Popular in northern Kentucky around the turn of the century. Said to resemble the Stayman Winesap in appearance and quality.

Fruit medium, oblate, inclining to conical, sometimes oblique; skin pale yellow, mostly shaded and striped with light and dark red; dots few, light colored; stem short and small in a medium size, greenish cavity; calyx closed; basin rather large, moderately deep, slightly corrugated; flesh whitish, tender, juicy, mild subacid. Ripe February–May. Catalog listings: TN, KY (1893–97). ❖ **Plate 83.**

❧ **DODGE'S CRIMSON** (Cumberland Black): Originated with J. W. Dodge of Pomona, Tennessee, and sold by a Georgia nursery from 1859 to 1861. The tree has slender limbs that droop under a load of fruit. *See also* Cumberland.

Fruit medium, roundish conical; skin a deep, almost purplish red; dots few, small, light-colored; flesh white, sometimes stained red near the skin, fine-grained, tender, juicy, sprightly subacid. Ripe November–January.

❧ **DOE:** Originated by S. H. Stepp of Dry Creek, Carder County, Tennessee, and described in an 1897 Tennessee agricultural experiment station bulletin.

Fruit medium to large, oblate, oblique, irregular; skin rather thick, tough, smooth, slight leather crackings, greenish yellow blushed with red; dots numerous, small, gray with green areoles; stem medium length and rather stout in a very deep, abrupt cavity; calyx closed; basin wide, abrupt, slightly wavy, leather-cracked; flesh pale yellow, fine-grained, firm, mild subacid. Ripe late fall. No catalog listings.

❧ **DONAHOO'S SEEDLING** (Donahue): A Maryland apple described by Downing (1869).

Fruit medium or below, roundish oblate; flesh subacid. Ripe October/November. No catalog listings.

❧ **DONAHUE:** Originated before 1900 with Mr. P. Donahue, near Cumberland, Kentucky. Resembles Dodge's Crimson.

Fruit medium or below, oblate, slightly conical, regular; skin deep red, purplish in the sun, sprinkled with light dots; stem short and small in a broad, sometimes greenish cavity; calyx closed; basin large; flesh white, fine-grained, tender, moderately juicy, mild subacid. Ripe October–January. No catalog listings.

❧ **DONNELL'S WINTER:** Listed in 1870 by Ridgeway Nurseries, Warren County, North Carolina. No description.

❧ **DORCHESTER** (Tripp, Mitchell of Dorchester): Discussed at the 1900 meeting of the Maryland

Horticultural Society as originating in Dorchester County, Maryland, and one of the most popular apples in that county. "It is a beautiful, small to medium sized winter apple, highly scented and flavored. It requires moderately stiff, rich land and is worthless in poor land with neglect. It is one of the handsomest yard apple trees." No catalog listings.

❦ **DORLING:** Listed by a North Carolina nursery in 1855 and 1856. No description except ripe August and September.

❦ **DOUGHERTY:** Described as a new winter apple in 1871 by the Fruitland Nursery, Augusta, Georgia. No description.

❦ **DOWDY'S RED WINTER:** Sold in 1870 by the Forest Nursery, Fairview, Kentucky: "Size medium, skin yellow striped with red, good."

❦ **DOYLE** (Doil, Doil's Autumn): A Texas apple grown in Tyler and Smith counties in 1889 and listed from 1898 to 1903 by T. V. Munson and Sons Nurseries, Denison, Texas.

Fruit medium or above, roundish; skin yellow mostly covered with crimson; dots numerous, large, gray; stem medium length in a gradually sloped cavity; basin wide and somewhat shallow; flesh yellow. Ripe October.

❦ **DRUMORE:** Listed by three Virginia nurseries from 1858 to 1901. Fruit medium size, red. Ripe winter.

❦ **DUCK:** Listed in 1869 by Richmond Nurseries, Richmond, Virginia. No description.

❦ **DUCKETT:** A North Carolina apple probably first grown by Silas McDowell of Macon County, North Carolina. This apple was still being grown twenty years ago near Spruce Pines, North Carolina, but recent attempts to locate it have failed.

Fruit medium or above, oblate; skin light waxen yellow, often with a red cheek; stem short in a deep cavity; basin deep; flesh white, tender, juicy, fine-grained, aromatic, subacid. Ripe October/November, or perhaps later. Catalog listings: VA, GA, KY (1859–70).

❦ **DUKE APPLE:** Listed in 1877 by the Old North State Nursery, Wilson, North Carolina. No description except ripe October to April.

❦ **DULIN'S RED** (Dulin): Raised by Lodd Dulin of Hopkinsville, Christian County, Kentucky, and listed in 1870 by the Forest Nursery, Fairview, Kentucky. Tree productive in alternate years.

Fruit medium, oblate, slightly conical, sides sometimes unequal; skin light red striped with dark red; dots numerous, light and brown; stem short in a large and deep cavity; basin medium size; flesh yellowish, slightly coarse, breaking, tender, moderately juicy, slightly aromatic, subacid. Ripe December–February.

❦ **DUNBAR:** Introduced by R. N. Pollard of Stevensville, King and Queens County, Virginia. Listed by three Virginia nurseries between 1859 and 1902 as a rich-flavored and long-keeping apple.

Fruit large, oblate; skin dull red with dark brown splashes; flesh yellow, aromatic. Ripe January–June.

❦ **DUNCAN:** From an 1895 letter to the USDA from W. M. Samuels, Clinton, Hickman County, Kentucky: "I found a single tree of this apple at George Puckets, 10 miles south of Hickman, with a fine crop of firm, good fruit. He called it Duncan. Mr. Pucket, now dead, was a large fruit grower in that section. The tree bears every other year and originated about 1872."

Fruit medium to large, round; skin red-striped. Ripe winter. No catalog listings. This apple is different from the Duncan described by Downing (1878).

❦ **DUNLAP'S JULY:** Listed in 1888 by the Planter's Nursery, Humboldt, Tennessee: "Large, sold in 1886 at $1.00 per peck." No description.

❦ **DURHAM'S WINTER** (Durham Winter Pearmain?): Originated in Marcus, Georgia, by J. C. Justice. This is probably the Durham Winter Pearmain briefly described by Warder (1867).

Fruit medium, round; skin mostly bright red; flesh sweet. Keeps until May. No catalog listings.

❦ **DUTCH BUCKINGHAM:** Probably of North Carolina origin, as it was sold only by the J. Van Lindley Nursery, Greensboro, North Carolina, from 1899 to 1915: "This is one of the most showy apples of recent introduction; large, bright red all over, with darker red broad stripes; one of the highest colored apples in our entire collection; a perfect beauty; flesh yellow, high color. Ripens at the same season as Old Buckingham."

❦ **EARGLES WINTER:** Listed around 1920 by Fayette County Nurseries, Fayetteville, Georgia: "Originated from a seedling in Douglas Co., Ga. Ripens in Nov. and will keep through the winter. Apples all large and very fine flavor. Tree a vigorous grower and full bearer. One of the best market apples for the South."

❦ **EARLY AMBROSIA:** An apple sold about 1915 by the Continental Plant Company of Kittrell, North Carolina. No description.

❦ **EARLY ARKANSAS BEAUTY:** Listed from 1888 to 1894 by the Planter's Nursery, Humboldt, Tennessee: "Large, yellow tinged with red. Resembles Astrachan but better quality. Highly perfumed. July."

❦ **EARLY CIDER:** A North Carolina apple ripening in June and was listed from 1858 to 1861 by the Fruitland Nursery, Augusta, Georgia. Warder (1867) briefly describes it as medium size, conical, subacid.

❦ **EARLY CLEARDRINKING:** Listed from 1824 to 1827 by Linnean Hill Nursery, Washington, D.C. No description except ripe June/July.

❦ **EARLY CLUSTER:** Sold from 1900 to 1904 by Bonham Nurseries, Bonham, Texas. In 1898, the owner of Bonham Nurseries wrote a letter to the USDA: "I would plant for family use. The fruit is small, round, striped red on yellow, flavor peculiar to itself, use table and market. It was secured from an old orchard 25 years ago. I know nothing of its history. It was named by us because of its habit of bearing in large clusters. Season June 15th to July 1st." ❖ **Plate 84.**

❦ **EARLY COLDIN:** Probably a Virginia apple, as it was listed by two Virginia nurseries from 1858 to 1869. Good for culinary use.

Fruit large, conical, red-striped; flesh white, subacid. Ripe August.

❦ **EARLY DELLINGER:** A summer apple listed in 1875 by Middletown Nursery, Virginia. No description.

❦ **EARLY FLY** (Fly Apple): A summer apple, probably of North Carolina origin, which was sold by a North Carolina nursery from 1856 to 1872. Mr. Grimes Conrad, of Davidson County, North Carolina, remembers this as a good-sized, golden yellow apple "with fly specks all over it" and an excellent eating apple. Mr. Conrad says that neighbors would stop their wagons near a Fly Apple tree on the road and fill up buckets with fruit.

❦ **EARLY NORFOLK:** A Virginia apple first described in 1891. Fruit above medium, oblate; skin yellow with red stripes; flesh white, subacid. Ripe June/July. No catalog listings.

❦ **EARLY MOOR'S:** A Georgia apple listed in 1860 by Pomaria Nurseries of South Carolina.

Fruit medium size, ripe June.

❦ **EARLY PEAR APPLE:** A North Carolina apple that originated before 1905.

Fruit medium to large; skin yellow with red stripes. Ripe June/July. No catalog listings.

❦ **EARLY RED:** This is a synonym for several different apples including Early Red Margaret, Early Red Bird, and Red June, and some years ago I found Red Astrachan being grown in Virginia under this name. Ragan (1905) lists three apple varieties named Early Red: one from New York, one a Russian apple, and the other possibly from Pennsylvania. The Franklin Davis Nursery of Richmond, Virginia, listed an Early Red in its 1901 and 1904 catalogs without description. An apple by this name was grown in Indiana in 1856: "Medium size, red with a white bloom, flattened at the base, nearly sweet, firm and rather dry. July."

❦ **EARLY SOUTHERN PEARMAIN:** Listed in the 1853 catalog of the North Carolina Pomological Garden and Nurseries.

Fruit small, conical, skin red on yellow. Ripe July/August.

❦ **EARLY UPTON:** Listed in 1845 by the Holly Springs Nursery, Bloomfield, Kentucky.

Fruit large, round, striped. Ripe July.

❦ **ECKEL** (Eckle's Summer, Eckel's Summer, Sweet Red June, Eckel's Red Sweet June, Eccle's Summer, Red Sweet June): Originated on the farm of Eugene Eckel, Guilford County, North Carolina, and sold by North Carolina nurseries from 1893 to 1925. Tree productive and bears for four to five weeks. *See also* June Sweeting.

Fruit medium to large, roundish oblong, conical; skin solid dark red; dots very indistinct; stem medium to long in a small, shallow, russeted cavity; calyx open; basin rather shallow, abrupt; flesh white, crisp, juicy, aromatic, sweet. Ripe July/August. ❖ **Plate 85.**

❦ **EDWARD'S EARLY** (Early Edward, Early Seek-No-Further): A summer apple grown in Virginia as a market and farm orchard apple. Originated about 1810 with Edward French in Moorestown, New Jersey, and introduced into Virginia about 1855. Tree prolific, an annual bearer, and the fruit does not bruise as easily as most other summer apples.

Fruit medium, roundish conical; skin yellow striped with bright red; flesh yellowish, juicy, subacid. Ripe July. Catalog listings: VA, NC, SC, (1872–1904).

❦ **EL DORADO:** Listed in 1861 by Fruitland Nursery, Augusta, Georgia. Fruit round, subacid.

❦ **ELARKEE** (Elarkie, Alarkee, Eluskee): Originated in Macon County, North Carolina, and introduced by the great North Carolina pomologist Silas McDowell.

Fruit medium, oblong, slightly conical; skin yellow, mostly striped and covered with red, sometimes described as dark red to almost black; flesh yellowish, firm, "with sufficient juice," acid when picked but becoming subacid in storage. Ripe October/November and said to keep until June. Catalog listings: VA, GA, LA, KY (1857–88).

❦ **ELDRIDGE:** Listed but not described in the 1872 catalog of Joshua Lindley, Greensboro, North Carolina.

❦ **ELGIN PIPPIN** (Elgin, White Spanish Reinette?): This apple variety was found growing in Mississippi and was sold for forty years by the Fruitland Nursery of Augusta, Georgia. This nursery considered Elgin Pippin to be identical to the White Spanish Reinette, which it very closely resembles. The tree reportedly grows to immense size, is moderately productive, and tends to bloom late.

Fruit large to very large, oblate, perhaps conical; skin bright yellow or orange yellow; calyx open; basin deep; flesh yellow, subacid. Ripe August/September. Catalog listings: SC, GA, AL, LA (1858–98). *See* White Spanish Reinette.

❦ **ELKHORN:** The following account of the origin of the Elkhorn apple is taken from a letter written to the USDA in 1886 by G. F. Kennan, Brightwater, Arkansas: "When the Civil War was closed, the farm of Jesse Cox was destitute of improvements and very much grown up in sassafras sprouts. Mr. Cox and others were grubbing out the brush when someone pointed out an apple sprout about an inch in diameter. Mr. Cox pulled it out of the brush heap and set it out where he was starting an orchard. The following year it bore two nice apples. The tree was propped up for several years as it did not during those years take very strong root. That apple sprout was taken up from the battleground of Pea Ridge, Arkansas, where the Federal battery was planted that contended against General Price's battery that was on top of Elk Horn Mountain." Sold by a Texas nursery in 1900.

Fruit large to very large, often four inches in diameter and weighing 18 ounces, roundish to oblate; skin yellowish, mostly covered with dull red with darker stripes; dots numerous, large, light gray on lighter bases; stem short and slender in a deep, russeted cavity; basin large; flesh yellowish, firm, slightly coarse, juicy. Ripe November to late spring. ❖ **Plate 86.**

❦ **ELLIJAY:** Originated before 1858 in Clarksville, Georgia, and introduced by the southern pomologist Silas McDowell. Mainly a cooking apple.

Fruit large, roundish or somewhat oblong, conical, oblique; skin pale yellow with a blush cheek in the sun and patches of greenish russet; dots small, black; stems short in a narrow cavity; calyx closed (or perhaps open) in a rather shallow basin; flesh white, fine-grained, tender, juicy, subacid. Ripe November/December. No catalog listings.

❦ **ELLIS EVER-BEARING:** Listed from 1910 to 1915 by the Continental Plant Company, Kittrell, North Carolina: "The Ellis Ever-bearing comes nearer bearing all the time than any fruit we have seen. It begins to ripen in June and extends through July and August. The apples are large, of a beautiful golden color, and of a most excellent flavor. The tree bears an enormous crop and never fails to bear. Instead of having half a dozen varieties to supply you with fruit throughout the summer, to get all that from one tree is a wonder in the apple world. We have exclusive control of this valuable apple."

❦ **ELLWILL'S LATE** (Elwell's Late, Ellwell's Large?): Grown in Thomas County, Georgia, from about 1870 to 1900, and listed by the Georgia Horticultural Society in 1912 as a "Georgia Native Apple." Said to be adapted to southern Georgia and northern Florida.

Fruit medium to rather large, green or yellowish often with red stripes (or a red blush); flesh rather acid. Ripe late and keeps until April. Catalog listings: GA, KY (1858–98).

❦ **ENE'S WINTER SWEET** (Ene, Enis Winter Sweet): In 1835 or 1836, Enos Harned of Christian County, Kentucky, dug up some apple seedlings and planted them in an orchard on his farm. The Ene's Winter Sweet was one of those seedlings. Listed by a Kentucky nursery in 1870.

Fruit medium, oblate conical; skin rough, uneven, greenish yellow blushed in the sun, russeted; dots numerous, minute, russet; stem medium length in a wide, wavy, brown cavity; calyx open; basin abrupt, cracked; flesh yellow, fine-grained, very sweet. Ripe December.

❦ **ENGLAND'S SEEDLING** (English Seedling): Originated about 1860 by a Mr. England, who was a nurseryman near Sparta, Tennessee.

Fruit medium to large, roundish oblate, conical; skin light yellow mostly covered with light red; flesh yellowish white, slightly coarse, tender, juicy, sweet. Ripe October. No catalog listings.

❦ **ENGLISH CODLIN** (Codling, Old English Codling): An ancient English apple, mainly a cooking apple. Tree vigorous and productive. Fruit ripens gradually on the tree. Sold for over a hundred years by a few southern nurseries.

Fruit medium to large, oblong conical; skin clear lemon yellow with a faint blush on the sunny side; stem short and stout; flesh white, tender, subacid. Ripe July–November. Catalog listings: MD, VA, NC, DC (1824–1928).

❦ **ENGLISH GOLDEN PIPPIN** (English Golden): An old English dessert apple sold by Maryland, Washington, D.C., and Virginia nurseries from 1824 to 1869.

Fruit small to medium, roundish; skin yellow; flesh yellow, rich, subacid. Ripe winter.

❦ **ENGLISH PIPPIN:** Ragan (1905) lists three apples having this name or synonym, but two of these are Russian apples imported into this county about 1870. These cannot be the English Pippin listed by North Carolina nurseries from 1853 to 1884. More likely, this English Pippin is probably Golden Reinette, which has a synonym of English Pippin. Golden Reinette is available.

Fruit medium, oblate; skin red on yellow. Ripe September–November.

❦ **ENGLISH RUSSET** (Poughkeepsie Russet, Winter Russet, Long-limbed Russet): This is one of the best keeping apples known, often keeping for twelve months when grown in the North or cooler areas of the South. English Russets grown in warmer areas apparently will keep until about March. In spite of its name, the English Russet is almost certainly an American apple of New York or New England origin before 1842. It much resembles and has been confused, even by experts, with Golden Russet, which has the synonym English Golden Russet. The Bullock or American Golden Russet is yet another apple often confused with English Russet.

Fruit medium, roundish to oblate, slightly conical; skin dull greenish yellow mostly covered with russet that is thickest at the stem; stem small, short, about even with the surface of the fruit, in a deep, narrow, smooth cavity; calyx small, closed; basin round, even, moderately deep; flesh yellowish white, firm, crisp, tender, mildly subacid. Ripe January–March or perhaps later. Catalog listings: VA, NC, TN, KY (1853–94).

❦ **ENORMOUS:** A Russian apple that first fruited in this country in Vermont in 1879. Sold by Alabama and Louisiana nurseries from 1886 to 1898.

Fruit very large, red-striped, poor quality. Ripe September/October.

❦ **EPER:** Mentioned but not described in an 1898 Alabama agricultural experiment station bulletin. No catalog listings.

❦ **EPTING'S PREMIUM:** From the 1860 catalog of Pomaria Nurseries, Pomaria, South Carolina: "Large, greenish with red stripes; flesh juicy and excellent, retaining its flavor well; ripe in November and keeps until March. This variety received a premium of $10 from the So. Ca. State Agricultural Society as the best late seedling. A seedling produced at Pomaria, S. C.; tree vigorous and productive."

❧ **EPTING'S RED WINTER:** A South Carolina apple that originated before 1858 and that was sold by South Carolina and Georgia nurseries until 1878.

Fruit large, "beautiful red resembling Red June"; flesh yellow, slight pineapple flavor, juicy. Ripe October.

❧ **ERNST:** A North Carolina apple sold in 1859 by Hopewell Nurseries, Fredericksburg, Virginia. No description.

❧ **ESTHER:** Listed as a "new and rare" apple in the 1902 catalog of the Startown Nursery, Newton, North Carolina. No description.

❧ **ETOWAH** (Cooper's Red): Like the Cooper's Yellow, this apple originated before 1873 from a seed of the Shockley in the garden of Major Mark A. Cooper, Etowah Iron Works, Glen Holly, Georgia. The fruit is more highly colored than Shockley and, like Shockley, a good keeper. Tree healthy and an abundant bearer.

Fruit nearly medium, oblate conical, slightly oblique; skin pale yellow, almost completely covered with bright red with some obscure stripes; dots few, large, light colored; stem very short and small in a large, deep, often russeted cavity; basin large and very deep; flesh whitish, tender, moderately juicy, subacid to almost sweet. Ripe November–March. Catalog listings: VA, GA, AL, AR (1885–1906).

❧ **ETRIS:** First fruited near Bentonville, Arkansas, in the orchard of A. K. Etris, the trees having been purchased from the nursery of John Breathwait. Quite similar and perhaps identical to Gano. Extensively grown in Benton County, Arkansas, about 1910. No catalog listings. *See* Gano.

❧ **EVANS** (Walker's Sweet): From an 1898 Arkansas agricultural experiment station bulletin: "This is a sweet apple of considerable merit. It is a good keeper, keeping until spring without any trouble. Mr. C. Walker, of Lowell, Arkansas, furnished specimens of this variety from the original tree, which is now standing near Lowell and bearing good crops of fruit. It is a good sized apple, form oblate conical; cavity medium, irregular, deep; stem medium to long, stout; basin large, regular, slightly furrowed, slope abrupt; surface smooth; skin yellow, splashed and striped with a very thin covering of red, giving the apple a light color; gray dots scattered over the surface; flesh yellowish, firm, rather tough; it is called a sweet apple, but it is pronounced to be mild subacid by some. Season, late winter." No catalog listings.

❧ **EVEN'S RED:** A winter apple listed but not described in 1872 by Joshua Lindley's Nursery, Greensboro, North Carolina.

❧ **EVERBEARING RED JUNE** (Everbearing, Simmon's Red?): Two nurseries sold this apple. The J. Van Lindley Nursery of North Carolina listed it from 1893 to 1895 and seemed to attribute its origin to Arkansas. The Commercial Nursery Company of Tennessee listed it from 1910 to 1917 and said it was a Georgia apple. Everbearing Red June is probably the same apple as Simmon's Red.

Fruit medium to large; skin red with darker stripes; flesh crisp, juicy. Ripe June/July.

❧ **EVERGREEN:** An apple of southern origin sold by Pomaria Nurseries of South Carolina from 1872 to 1878. "Large, red, crisp; pleasant and very fine. Ripe from November till February. A seedling of North Carolina."

❧ **EXCELSIOR:** Ragan (1905) lists three apples named Excelsior. One of these is a Maryland apple sold from 1894 to 1913 by Eastern Shore Nurseries of Denton, Maryland: "A peninsula variety (origin Queen Anne County, Maryland). Above medium size; generously overspread with two shades of red. Tree vigorous, upright. A very productive fall apple."

❧ **EXTRA BEN DAVIS:** An Arkansas apple sold by Stark Bro's Nursery before 1905. Fruit large, yellow with red stripes. Ripe winter.

❧ **FAIL NOT:** A North Carolina apple sold in 1859 by Hopewell Nurseries, Fredericksburg, Virginia. No description.

❧ **FAIR SWEETING:** Listed by two Virginia nurseries from 1858 to 1869. No description.

❧ **FALL AMBROSIA:** From the 1915 catalog of the Continental Plant Company, Kittrell, North

Carolina: "Superior in flavor even to the Early Ambrosia, that is, if such a thing is possible. Very large, brilliant red. Ripens in the fall and keeps all winter."

❦ **FALL CHEESE:** The name Fall Cheese is a well-known synonym of the old and widely disseminated southern apple called Mangum. It is apparently also the name of a Virginia apple that differs from the Mangum in several respects. This Fall Cheese is usually large, while the Mangum is a medium-sized apple, and is most often described as having white flesh, whereas the Mangum has yellow flesh.

In Virginia, especially in and around Albemarle County, any apple called Fall Cheese is probably the Virginia apple that is described here. Elsewhere in the South, an apple called Fall Cheese is most likely to be the Mangum.

Fruit large, probably oblate; skin green striped with red; flesh white, subacid, aromatic. Ripe September–December. Catalog listings as Fall Cheese (most are probably Mangum): VA, KY, TX (1869–1928).

❦ **FALL CLUSTER:** Sold from 1895 to 1898 by Clingman Nurseries, Homer, Louisiana: "Medium, green and dull red with white specks; very productive and a long keeper."

❦ **FALL RED:** Probably a Kentucky apple, as it was sold by a Kentucky nursery in 1870. Fruit large; skin greenish striped with red; keeps well.

❦ **FALL STRIPE:** Sold from 1900 to 1904 by Bonham Nurseries, Bonham, Texas. Described by them as a local variety, so it probably is different from the New England apple of the same name.

Fruit medium size, bright red striped. Ripe September.

❦ **FALL SWEETING:** Origin unknown. Sold by Virginia and North Carolina nurseries from 1853 to 1858.

Fruit large, round, pale yellow; flesh sweet. Ripe September/October.

❦ **FALL WINESAP:** Origin unknown. First mentioned in 1861 and sold by two Virginia nurseries from 1897 to 1910.

Fruit medium, roundish conical; skin yellow with a blush on the sunny side; flesh tender, juicy, subacid. Ripe September–November.

❦ **FAMILY** (McLoud's Family, McCloud's Family): This was once a widely grown and popular Georgia apple that ripens over a period of six weeks or more. The tree is very productive and an annual bearer. Although a summer apple in most of the South, it ripens in September in Illinois and even later further north.

Fruit medium, roundish to oblate, conical, sides often unequal; skin yellowish, much shaded and striped with dull red, with narrow stripes; dots numerous, faint green or white; stem short (Beach says long) in a large, slightly russeted cavity; calyx closed or slightly open; basin medium to shallow, wrinkled; flesh white (Beach says yellowish tinged with red), crisp, juicy, tender, subacid. Ripe early July/August. Catalog listings: VA, SC, GA, AL, MS, TN, KY, AR (1858–1906).

❦ **FARINGTON:** Listed as a Georgia apple in an 1863 Pennsylvania catalog. No description.

❦ **FARLEY'S RED:** Originated before 1855 in Oldham, Kentucky. Tree healthy and productive.

Fruit medium or smaller, roundish oblate (also described as roundish oblong), slightly conical; skin yellow, shaded and striped with deep or dull red; dots small, indented, light colored or purplish; stem medium length in a deep, acute, wavy, brown cavity; calyx closed; basin shallow, corrugated; flesh whitish, fine-grained, firm, crisp, juicy, subacid. Ripe January–April. No catalog listings.

❦ **FARRAR'S SUMMER** (Farrar, Farrens Summer, Robinson's Superb): Most references, including Ragan (1905), say Farrar's Summer originated in Virginia. The oldest catalog listing, however, a Virginia nursery listing of 1859, cites Georgia as the state of origin. An 1874 letter from W. P. Robinson of Atlanta, Georgia, states that Farrar's Summer originated before 1850 with John Farrar of Putnam County, Georgia. It was listed as a Georgia apple in 1860 by Pomaria Nurseries of South Carolina.

Fruit large to very large; flesh crisp, juicy. Ripe September/October or perhaps earlier in Georgia. Catalog listings: VA, GA, SC, AL, LA (1859–88).

❦ **FAUST'S RUSSET:** Listed but not described in the 1872 catalog of Joshua Lindley, Greensboro, North Carolina.

❧ **FAVORITE:** A Kentucky apple that originated before 1854. Fruit small, roundish; skin yellow, striped and splashed with red; flesh yellow, juicy, subacid. Ripe November–January. No catalog listings.

❧ **FELT'S STRAWBERRY:** Described to the 1858 meeting of the American Pomological Society: "From Mr. Felt of Bayou Sara, Louisiana. Medium size, conical; yellow striped with red; flesh tender, juicy, good." Ragan (1905) has the origin of this apple incorrectly attributed to New York. No catalog listings.

❧ **FENLEY** (Finley, Findley): A Kentucky apple discussed at the 1860 meeting of the American Pomological Society, where it was described as superior to Early Harvest and Maiden's Blush.

At the 1863 meeting of the Indiana Horticultural Society, one member identified a "Finley" apple as being identical to Abbott and useful mainly for cooking. Its description does not fit the Abbott Seedling described by Elliot (1858). *See* Abbott Yellow Seedling.

Fruit large, roundish oblate, slightly conical; skin smooth, pale yellow sprinkled with a few brown (Warder says gray) dots; stem short in a broad, russeted cavity; calyx closed; basin rather large; flesh yellow, crisp, juicy, subacid. Ripe September, but can be used for cooking in July and August. No catalog listings.

❧ **FERDINAND:** A seedling grown by Adam Minnick of Pomaria, South Carolina, and named for his father. First fruited in 1848. Tree moderately productive and usually an annual bearer. Described in 1852 by William Summer of Pomaria Nurseries of South Carolina as "the best winter apple for our climate, large and fine flavored."

Fruit almost large, roundish to oblate, conical, flattened at the base; skin rather thin, yellow or orange-yellow, sometimes deepening to red, sometimes russeted; dots numerous, white or russet; stem short and thick, often with a fleshy protuberance; cavity acute, rather narrow, usually russeted, sometimes lipped; basin often oblique, usually shallow but varies; flesh yellowish, tender, juicy, rather fine-grained, slightly acid becoming subacid. Ripe October/November and keeps well. Catalog listings: VA, NC, SC, GA, MS, KY (1856–78). ❖ **Plate 87.**

❧ **FERRIS:** From the 1852 meeting of the American Pomological Society: "A seedling raised by Benjamin Ferris, Wilmington, Delaware, and an apple of great merit. It is medium to large, same shape as the Newtown Pippin, and a beautiful red. A first rate kitchen apple, not equal to Baldwin for eating, and a long keeper. Bears every year, one half of the tree at a time." No catalog listings.

There is another apple named Ferris, which probably originated in New York about 1854.

❧ **FILLMORE** (Fill?): A North Carolina apple sold by North Carolina and Georgia nurseries in 1860 and 1861. No description. An apple named "Fill" was listed by a Georgia nursery in 1849 and 1851 without description.

❧ **FINNICK:** Listed in 1870 by the Forest Nursery, Fairview, Kentucky: "Fruit large, skin yellowish striped with red, handsome and good." Ripe winter.

❧ **FIRKIN:** A southern winter apple mentioned in 1858. No description. No catalog listings.

❧ **FIXLIN:** A South Carolina apple sold from 1856 to 1860 by Pomaria Nurseries of Pomaria, South Carolina, and described as "a variety of Calville."

Fruit large, oblate, red-striped. Ripe August.

❧ **FLAMINGO:** Listed by two Virginia nurseries from 1858 to 1869.

Fruit oblong, red-striped, sweet.

❧ **FLANIGAN'S LATE** (Flanigan's Yellow?): Listed as an autumn apple in the 1872 catalog of Pomaria Nurseries of South Carolina. No description.

❧ **FLAT CODLING:** Listed in 1853 by the North Carolina Pomological Gardens and Nurseries, Guilford County, North Carolina.

Fruit large, round, pale yellow. Ripe July/August.

❧ **FLORA:** A southern apple, origin unknown. Fruit medium, oblate; skin yellowish, shaded and mottled with red or crimson; flesh whitish, mild subacid. Ripe August. Catalog listings: GA, KY (1858–70).

A note in USDA files, dated 1890, mentions another apple named Flora, which originated with F. H. Horne of Latham, Van Buren County, Arkansas. Described only as smooth, pale red. No catalog listings.

❦ **FLORENCE:** An Arkansas apple commercially grown near Bentonville, Arkansas, in 1896.

Fruit medium, roundish, slightly oblong; skin yellow, covered and somewhat striped with dark red; dots numerous, small, white; stem short in a narrow and slightly russeted cavity; calyx closed; basin narrow, abrupt, medium in depth; flesh yellowish, tinged red under the skin, tender, very fine-grained, mild subacid. Ripe September/October and keeps well. Catalog listings: AR, TX (1918–20).

❦ **FLORY** (Flora's Bellflower, Sheepshire): Originated about 1869 in Montgomery County, Ohio, and sold by Virginia and Maryland nurseries from 1898 to 1904.

Fruit medium, roundish conical; skin golden yellow with small patches of russet and minute raised russet dots; flesh yellowish, tender, moderately juicy, subacid. Ripe September/October in Maryland.

❦ **FLOYD** (Huff's Seedling)/**FLOYD KEEPER:** From a letter written in 1900 to the USDA by Charles H. Huff, Huffville, Floyd County, Virginia: "The original tree that produced the Floyd apple was found on my farm about fifteen years ago. I dug it up and transplanted it in my yard because of its peculiar and beautiful shape. It has fewer branches growing out from the body of the tree than any other variety I have ever seen. I have kept the apples until May at which time the flesh is golden yellow and of fine flavor. The skin is greenish yellow with a very few, small, red stripes."

Fruit large, roundish oblong; dots gray, areole; stem long in a narrow, lipped cavity; basin small; flesh yellowish.

About 1901, an apple named Floyd Keeper, which also originated in Floyd County, Virginia, was sent to the USDA by Benjamin Buckman of Farmingdale, Illinois. No description. No catalog listings.

In 1905, the Georgia Horticultural Society listed an apple named Floyd as a Georgia apple. No description except ripe June–September. No catalog listings.

❦ **FOGLE:** Sold in 1925 by the Austin Nursery Company of Austin, Texas: "Originated in Austin. Extra healthy growing tree. Fruit large, flat, yellow. Ripe summer."

❦ **FONVILLE:** Originated in Alamance County, North Carolina, and listed from 1872 to 1915 by the J. Van Lindley Nursery, Greensboro, North Carolina.

Fruit medium to large, roundish oblong; skin yellow mostly covered with "glistening" red, sprinkled with small (or perhaps large) white dots; flesh yellowish, tender, aromatic. Ripe December–January.

❦ **FORD** (Parker): From the 1924 catalog of Newton Nurseries, Newton, Mississippi: "Large, red striped, medium quality, ripens last of September or first of October; origin unknown; grown by W. M. Ford of Bezer, Smith County, Mississippi, who says the tree came from Texas many years ago. Known around Laurel as Parker. Growth of tree and fruit resembles Ben Davis."

❦ **FORT'S PRIZE** (Jim Kell Thinskin?): Fort's Prize is perhaps the most interesting apple in this book, and it is one for which we have much information. In addition, the National Agricultural Library has three full-size watercolors of Fort's Prize apples, painted in 1909 and 1910, which show the beauty of this dark red apple with white dots.

Our knowledge of Fort's Prize comes almost entirely from a booklet written by John P. Fort, whose name graces this apple, and who was the founder of the apple-growing industry in north Georgia just after 1900. (*See* Mother *for more historical information.*) We are indebted to John P. Fort's grandson, Tomlinson Fort of Franklin, Tennessee, who has a continuing interest in finding a living tree of Fort's Prize and perpetuating this outstanding apple variety. He provided me with a copy of the booklet written by John P. Fort. I can do no better than to quote at considerable length from this booklet:

> The Story of an Apple
>
> Jno. P. Fort
>
> In pursuance of a long contemplated desire, I purchased in 1906 fifty acres of land near Rabun Gap, in Northeast Georgia, for the purpose of planting an apple orchard.

The position chosen was within a mile and one-half of Rabun Gap, on the Tallulah Falls railroad. The place was known as Turkey Cove, on Black's Creek, forming the head waters of the Tennessee River.

There were upon the place about fifty apple trees that had been planted fifteen or twenty years previous. They were overgrown with wild vines, and presented a very neglected appearance. I had the old trees cared for and I planted a young orchard of twelve hundred trees on the place, of approved varieties of apples.

I was influenced in this enterprise by the continued rain fall in which I considered a favored section of our State. The annual rainfall being greater than any section of the States East of the Mississippi River—near twenty inches per annum more than any other section of Georgia.

The young apple trees that I planted grew, and the old trees responded to the care given them. After the first year's care and cultivation, there appeared among the old trees in the orchard four trees that produced a red apple that surprised me with its splendid appearance. They ripened about the 1st of November, 1908.

About this time I received by mail a pamphlet showing that there was to be held in Spokane, Wash., the first National apple show. A prize was offered for the best two barrels or six boxes of apples grown in the sixteen Southern States. This prize was called the Southern States Special and was divided into first, second, and third prizes. I conceived the idea of sending six boxes of my apples to contest for the Southern States Special. I had about twenty-five bushels from the four trees. I shipped six boxes by express to the secretary of the National apple show to enter for the premium. In return I received a check for $50 for the second best apples, North Carolina receiving first prize, my apples from Georgia the second and apples from Oklahoma the third prize.

Being elated with my success I had my four apple trees specially cared for. On November 1st, 1909 they presented an appearance superior to any similar sight I ever beheld. The National apple show was again held in Spokane in November, 1909. I again competed for the first prize in the Southern States Special with superior apples to my entry in 1908. They were awarded the first prize above all competition. The chairman of the committee making the award was the most renowned pomologist in our country—Mr. H. E. Van Deman of Washington, D.C. Besides I obtained a diploma for the best new variety of apples.

The cancelled check one hundred dollars for this prize was applied for by a trustee of Mr. Ritchie's School, near Rabun Gap, and is now framed and hung upon the schoolhouse wall, to remind the children that their county can produce the best of apples.

This apple, having been pronounced a new variety and worthy of being put upon the pomological books at Washington, was listed and given the name of Fort's Prize.

The apple having demonstrated those qualities that make a financial success, such as appearance, color, taste, and above all, keeping without decay until the spring time, I at once began to investigate its origin. I was fortunate in finding the man who had grafted and planted the four apple trees whose products had made so much commotion among the apple growers. The originator of this apple is named Kell. He lives near Clayton in Rabun County, Georgia. His story is this: About sixteen years prior to 1908 he lived at Turkey Cove. At this time while on a visit to his uncle near the source of War Woman's Creek in Rabun Co., he noticed an apple tree growing from behind the chimney of his uncle's cabin, upon which was a beautiful red apple. His uncle informed him that the tree was a seedling and that he had named it after his niece, Mollie.

From this tree Mr. Kell cut a switch and from grafts made upon young trees planted the four trees in Turkey Cove.

May we not surmise that the continuous supply of potash and phosphoric acid from the ashes from the fireplace of this cabin may have produced this superior apple? The cabin has fallen down upon the old tree and it is dead. The four trees in Turkey Cove are its only known products so far as I have any knowledge.

Anticipating that an orchard of the new variety will be valuable, I have obtained grafts from the old trees and have put out an orchard of three hundred of them.

As can be seen from John Fort's writing above, Fort's Prize originated with a Mr. Kell (almost certainly Jim Kell) in Rabun County, Georgia. There is good reason to believe that another Rabun County apple, named Jim Kell Thinskin, is identical to Fort's Prize. Several elderly people in Rabun County familiar with Fort's Prize have said it is the same apple as Jim Kell Thinskin, including George Kell who knew both apples.

I have obtained scions of Jim Kell Thinskin from Caroline Montague of Clayton, Georgia, and anxiously await the fruiting of the three trees I grafted. Ms. Montague is the same woman who found and saved the Rabun Bald apple, another great Rabun County apple on the verge of extinction.

Fruit above medium to large, round to slightly oblate; skin dark red; dots small to medium size, scattered, conspicuous, grayish, sometimes irregular; stem medium length in a narrow, deep, russeted cavity; calyx usually open; basin wide and shallow; flesh pale yellow. Ripe October and a good keeper. Catalog listings: TN (1917–23). ❖ **Plate 88.**

**FRANKLIN** (Franklin Pippin?): Ragan (1905) lists five apples named Franklin. This apple, which is also named Franklin, is probably different from any of the five Franklin apples listed by Ragan.

From an 1872 letter from C. W. Westbrook, owner of a North Carolina nursery, to Charles Downing: "No one could give me any positive information as to the origin of the Franklin apple. The oldest trees known are in Warren County, North Carolina, on the farm of Dr. C. L. Sims, near Ridgeville. The trees were planted in 1840 by an old fruit grower named Charles Davis. The impression seems to be among local people that Charles Davis originated the Franklin, as he originated several other apple varieties." Sold by a North Carolina nursery from 1888 to 1895.

Fruit medium to large, roundish; skin greenish yellow when picked but turns to a golden yellow later in the winter; flesh yellow, juicy, fine-grained, subacid. Ripe December–April.

**FRANKLIN'S SEEDLING:** Originated about 1885 with J. R. W. Franklin, Epps, Habersham County, Georgia, and subsequently took a premium at the Georgia State Horticultural Fair.

Fruit very large, oblong conical; skin red-striped. Ripe early July. No catalog listings.

**FRAZIER'S HARD SKIN** (Frazer Hardskin): Listed from 1893 to 1895 by the J. Van Lindley Nursery, Greensboro, North Carolina. No description. ❖ **Plate 89.**

**FREEDLE:** Listed as a North Carolina apple in 1859 by Hopewell Nurseries of Fredericksburg, Virginia. No description.

**FREEMAN'S BEAUTY:** Listed in the 1915 catalog of New Cumberland Nursery Company, Sawyer, Kentucky. No description except ripe fall.

**FRENCH PIPPIN** (Newark Pippin?): Ragan (1905) lists four apples named French Pippin, and it is a synonym of six other apples. French Pippin is listed in nine southern nursery catalogs before 1869, without any description. My guess is that most or all of the southern listings are actually the Newark Pippin, for which French Pippin is a synonym. Catalog listings: DC, VA, GA (1824–69).

**FREY:** Originated in South Carolina before 1858. No description except ripe November. No catalog listings.

**FRY'S LARGE FINE SUMMER/FRY'S CRAB:** Fry's Large Fine Summer was listed in 1863 by a

Pennsylvania nursery as a very large southern apple. Ripe August–October. This same nursery also listed a Fry's Crab as a southern apple.

Fruit small, red, excellent for table or cider.

❦ **FULKERSON:** Originated on the farm of William Ford, Claiborne County, Tennessee, and described in an 1897 Tennessee agricultural experiment station bulletin.

Fruit medium or below, oblate, angular; skin rather rough, thick, greenish yellow marbled with russet; dots numerous, large, russet; stem short and stout in a medium size, abrupt cavity; calyx nearly closed; basin rather large, medium depth, gradually sloped; flesh yellowish, fine-grained, firm, juicy, subacid. Ripe winter and a good keeper. No catalog listings.

❦ **GABRIEL** (Ladies Blush?, Garden [of Indiana]): Said by Warder (1867) be to a southern apple, and its description somewhat matches the southern apple called Ladies Blush.

Fruit medium, conical; skin smooth, greenish yellow with stripes of pale red; dots small; stem medium length and slender in a greenish cavity; calyx closed; basin medium size; flesh fine-grained, tender, juicy, aromatic, subacid to sweet. Ripe August/September or later. No catalog listings. *See* Ladies Blush.

❦ **GARDEN:** Originated before 1853 by Hezekiah Ellis of Spotsylvania County, Virginia, and sold by a Virginia nursery in 1859. Greg Lam of Elkton, Virginia, has recently found an old apple called locally "Merica or Garden" that is probably this apple. More time is needed for full identification.

Fruit small, oblate; skin yellow, shaded and striped with two shades of red over most of the surface; dots moderate in number, light and gray; stem long and slender in a medium-size, thinly russeted cavity; calyx closed; basin abrupt and slightly corrugated; flesh white, stained red near the skin, crisp, juicy, subacid. Ripe October–December.

❦ **GARDEN SWEET:** A North Carolina apple that originated before 1869.

Fruit medium, roundish oblong, conical; skin yellow with crimson; flesh yellowish white, tender, juicy, rather sweet. Ripe August/September. No catalog listings.

❦ **GARDEN WALK:** Originated before 1905 by James Garrett, Woodford County, Kentucky.

Fruit medium to large; skin pale greenish yellow with red stripes. Ripe September. No catalog listings.

❦ **GARDENIA:** A seedling apple found about 1885 on the farm of C. A. Price of Prince Edward County, Virginia. Tree an annual and heavy bearer.

Fruit medium or above, roundish, flattened on the ends; skin thin, rather smooth, yellow covered with dull red and obscure stripes of darker red, finely russeted; dots small to large, yellow and russet, often star-shaped; stem short in a shallow, russeted cavity; basin medium size; flesh yellowish, rather fine-grained, juicy, mild subacid. No catalog listings.

❦ **GARFIELD:** Listed in 1912 by the Georgia Horticultural Society as a Georgia apple. Fruit large, oblong conical; skin greenish with red stripes; flesh yellowish white, crisp, fine-grained, subacid. Ripe late. No catalog listings.

❦ **GARRETT:** From the 1916 catalog of Corinth Nurseries, Corinth, Mississippi: "This is a very fine summer apple; very large and red-striped. Ripens about the same time as the Horse and is a much better apple. This apple was brought from Alabama by Mr. M. E. Garrett and everyone that sees it wants trees. Ripens in August."

❦ **GARST:** Originated about 1885 on the farm of Prof. T. C. Garst of Blizzard, Washington County, Tennessee. The tree is vigorous and bears heavy crops annually.

Fruit above medium to large, roundish oblate, prominently ribbed; skin thick, tough, smooth, yellow, almost entirely washed and mottled with light red and crimson; dots gray; stem medium length in a deep, ribbed, irregular, abrupt, slightly russeted cavity; basin wide, irregular, large, gradually sloped, deeply furrowed; flesh yellow stained with red near the skin, fine-grained, tender, juicy, subacid. Ripe June/July. No catalog listings.

❦ **GARVIS:** An apple shown at the 1858 meeting of the American Pomological Society by the North Carolina nurseryman S. W. Westbrook. Fruit very large, yellow. No catalog listings.

❦ **GASTON'S SEEDLING:** Originated by A. L.

Gaston in South Carolina and taken by him to Texas in 1869 where he operated a small nursery.

Fruit very large, conical, ribbed; skin green with gray russet specks and a large patch of russet around the stem; stem one inch long and slender in a large, open cavity; calyx closed; basin narrow, ribbed; flesh white, juicy, subacid. Ripe middle of September and keeps for two months. No catalog listings.

**GEM:** From the 1901 catalog of Greensboro Nurseries, Greensboro, North Carolina: "In 1891, we offered a premium for the best seedling apple. A committee appointed by the State Horticultural Society awarded the premium to an apple offered by Mr. Perry of Chatham County. We pronounced the apple a 'Gem' and secured it for our customers. It is medium to large, roundish oblate, clear yellow; flesh rich, golden, with a very delicate, fine flavor. July and August."

**GENERAL HASKELL:** Originated in Graves County, Kentucky, and listed in the 1870 catalog of the Forest Nursery, Fairview, Kentucky.

Fruit medium; skin greenish, mostly covered with red. Ripe late and a good keeper.

**GENERAL MARION:** Originated with Henry Lyons of Columbia, South Carolina, and sold in 1870 by the Forest Nursery of Fairview, Kentucky.

Fruit medium or below, roundish oblate, conical, slightly angular; skin pale yellow or green, shaded and obscurely striped with two shades of red over nearly the entire surface; moderately sprinkled with light and gray dots; stem short in a medium or small cavity; basin rather narrow, deep, slightly wrinkled; flesh whitish, compact, moderately juicy, mild subacid. Ripe January–April.

**GEORGIA MAMMOTH:** A winter apple listed from 1872 to 1878 by Pomaria Nurseries of South Carolina and in 1872 by a North Carolina nursery. No description.

**GEORGIA TRIUMPH:** Mentioned but not described in a 1928 Mississippi agricultural experiment station bulletin. No catalog listings.

**GHIO:** Sold in 1904 by Paris Nurseries, Paris, Texas.

Fruit extra-large; skin yellow, almost entirely covered with red and sometimes with a few darker red stripes. Ripe July.

**GIANT WINESAP** (Keep Late): Originated by a Mr. Dillard in Virginia and sold in 1921 by the Continental Plant Company, Kittrell, North Carolina: "Similar to the famous Winesap in color and flavor but much larger and a much better keeper. In fact, one of the very best keepers of all apples."

**GIBBS** (Gibbs Apple): A seedling that originated on the farm of Benjamin Gibbs near Middletown, Kent County, Delaware, probably in the 1870s or before. Tree a strong grower, bearing full crops on alternate years. Not a high-quality apple but a good cooker and an excellent keeper. As grown near Fayetteville, North Carolina, in 1894, the Gibbs was an unhealthy tree with small fruit.

Fruit medium or above, nearly round, flattened on the ends; skin light yellow or greenish shaded with red or brownish red on the sunny side; dots numerous, russet; stem almost long in a medium-size, even cavity; basin medium in width and depth; flesh whitish, subacid. Ripe late winter or spring and keeps through the summer if properly stored. Catalog listings: MD, VA (1889–1901).

**GIBSON** (Gibson Red, Red Horse): The original tree grew before 1850 on the farm of a Mr. Gibson, north of Campbellsville, Tennessee, and was first brought to notice about 1870 by Charles E. Abernathy at a fruit show in Pulaski, Tennessee. An 1894 letter from Jason E. Abernathy of Buford, Tennessee, says: "It does not resemble the Horse apple in tree or fruit. I suppose it was first called Red Horse on account of its time of ripening. The Giles County Farmers Association changed its name a few years ago to Gibson Red. It somewhat resembles the Red June but is much larger, the tree has darker foliage, and it grows more vigorously. The apple when ripe is nearly red all over. It turns red on the tree some days before ripening. It is the firmest red apple I know of and valuable for shipping. Quality not the best but fair. A few barrels sent to Cincinnati several years ago attracted much attention and brought the highest price in that market. I know of no other apple ripening in August so attractive."

No catalog listings as Gibson, but Red Horse was listed in NC, AL, TN (1890–95). An apple called Red Horse is available, but positive identification has not been made because Red Horse is a synonym of Buckingham and also is the name of an entirely different apple. *See* Red Horse.

❧ **GILBERT** (Blacktwig Junior, Blacktwig Seedling, Gilbert's Seedling): Grown from a seed of Winesap planted about 1835 by Washington Wilson of Lincoln County, Tennessee. The original tree was still bearing full crops in 1885. Many trees in neighboring orchards were grafted from the original tree and the fruit was marketed and popular in Huntsville, Alabama. Probably a cross of Winesap × Red Limbertwig. Dr. Moores of Cyruston, Tennessee, named this apple (he also named the Paragon) as follows: "An old Negro man, a slave of Mr. Wilson, brought me these apples when I was a little fellow. He called it Blacktwig Seedling. The old slave's name was Gilbert, and out of memory for his kindness to me when I was a boy, I named the apple Gilbert." Dr. Moores considered the Gilbert to be a "twin brother" of Paragon but of better quality. Fruit holds well on the tree. Sold by a Maryland nursery from 1899 to 1913.

Fruit large, roundish oblate, slightly conical, sides unequal; skin yellowish washed with dark red and indistinctly striped; dots distinct, large, brown or gray; stem short to medium length in a medium to wide, deep, russeted cavity; flesh greenish yellow, rather coarse, crisp, juicy, subacid. Ripe January–June.

❧ **GILL'S BANANA:** A South Carolina apple listed in 1860 by Pomaria Nurseries: "Medium, exquisite flavor, rich, excellent. Ripe November."

❧ **GILL'S BEAUTY** (Gill): An Arkansas apple described in an Arkansas agricultural experiment station bulletin in 1899. Susceptible to bitter rot.

Fruit large, roundish oblate; skin smooth, tough, greenish yellow nearly covered with bright red; dots small and dark; cavity narrow, medium depth, rather abrupt, greenish; calyx closed; basin almost shallow and slightly corrugated; flesh white, coarse, juicy, mild subacid. No catalog listings.

❧ **GILMER PIPPIN:** Listed in 1917 as a winter apple by the J. A. Withrow Nursery of Ellijay, Georgia. No description.

❧ **GILMORE:** Sold from 1898 to 1901 by the Franklin Davis Nursery, Richmond, Virginia: "Originated in Rockbridge County, Virginia. Large, red winter apple; first class keeper; valuable for market. The parent tree bore 35 bushels in 1885. December to March."

❧ **GIPSON'S KENTUCKY SEEDLING:** Originated before 1867 with A. Gipson of Calhoun County, Kentucky.

Fruit below medium, roundish, sides unequal; skin greenish with dark red in the sun; flesh pale yellow, juicy, sprightly subacid. Ripe January–April. No catalog listings.

❧ **GIVENS** (Arkansas Baptist): Originated on the farm of John Givens, Benton County, Arkansas, probably about 1880. Tree productive.

Fruit below to above medium, roundish conical, sometimes flattened on the ends, often lopsided; skin tough, smooth, greenish, nearly covered with dark red with inconspicuous darker stripes; dots small, whitish, inconspicuous, some areole; stem long or very long in a wide, deep, acute, often russeted cavity; basin rather deep, medium-wide, wrinkled; flesh tinged with yellow, firm, rather fine-grained, not very crisp or tender, moderately juicy, mild subacid. Ripe January–May. No catalog listings.

❧ **GLADNEY RED:** A Mississippi apple borne on a healthy and productive tree.

Fruit medium or below, roundish oblate; skin pale green turning light yellow when ripe, shaded and obscurely striped with red over most of the surface; stem long and slender; calyx closed; flesh yellowish, rather firm, juicy, slightly aromatic, subacid. Ripe November and keeps until February or later. Catalog listings: NC, VA, SC, GA (1857–72).

❧ **GLASS' FAVORITE SWEET:** From an 1893 letter to the USDA from G. W. Robinette, Flag Pond, Scott County, Virginia: "The best cooking apple and the best bearer we have ever had here; also a great keeper. It came up from seed of unknown stock in 1862 or 1863 on the farm of George Glass, Lee County, Virginia. Tree is healthy, low, spreading, a free grower."

Fruit medium, roundish; skin dull green with a dull red blush and faint stripes over about half the apple; dots indistinct, some areole; stem medium length and slender in a corrugated cavity; calyx closed; basin narrow, rather deep; flesh white. Ripe December/January. No catalog listings.

❦ **GLEN ALPINE:** First grown before 1900 by George E. Murrell of Coleman's Falls, Bedford County, Virginia.

Fruit below medium, roundish oblate; skin mostly striped with red; dots gray; stem very short in a shallow, green cavity; basin rather shallow and wide; flesh creamy, stained red under the skin. Ripe September. No catalog listings.

❦ **GLENDALE:** From an 1883 letter to *The Farmer's Home Journal* from J. W. Smith: "Fifty or sixty years ago a man named Quinn or Gwinn brought some apple sprouts from Virginia (I think Berkeley County) and set them out in the northern part of Hardin County, Kentucky. From these trees were taken sprouts which were set out in Larue County, and from these trees I obtained sprouts. It has always been propagated from sprouts or suckers. The Mississippi Valley Horticultural Society gave it the name of Glendale." Fruit said to resemble Ben Davis but a better keeper and does not rot on the tree.

Fruit large, roundish conical; skin yellow shaded nearly all over with red; flesh subacid. Ripe winter. Catalog listings: GA, KY (1890–97). ❖ **Plate 90.**

❦ **GLENLOCH:** Originated before 1896 by H. M. McCroskey of Glenloch, Monroe County, Tennessee, who also originated the McCroskey apple. The Glenloch is said to closely resemble the York Imperial, but supposedly is a seedling of Winesap or Red Limbertwig. Tree very productive.

Fruit large, roundish, flattened on the ends; skin moderately smooth, tough, yellow washed with red with dark crimson stripes, a very thin gray bloom; dots numerous, yellowish or gray; stem medium length and rather stout in a very deep, large, abrupt, russeted cavity; basin wide, large, deep, corrugated; flesh yellowish, fine-grained, breaking, juicy, subacid. Ripe early winter. No catalog listings. ❖ **Plate 91.**

❦ **GLOBE:** From the 1891 meeting of the American Pomological Society: "Exhibited by the Rev. Joseph A. Buck, Rock Creek, District of Columbia. Size good medium; roundish, slightly conical; color dull red, striped darker, yellowish towards the calyx; quality good; season winter." No catalog listings.

❦ **GLOBE GIANT:** Listed in the 1923 catalog of J. M. Lewis and Son, Cascade, Virginia. No description.

❦ **GLOUCESTER WHITE** (Settle's Superb White?, White Gloucester): I believe this is one of the lost apple varieties grown by Thomas Jefferson in his orchard at Monticello. If so, its rediscovery would be a superb find. It was sold by southern nurseries until the early years of the twentieth century, so an old tree may still survive somewhere.

One can do no better than to quote the description written by Coxe in 1817: "This apple is of middling size, of a shape not very uniform, varying from oblong to flat; the color when ripe is a bright yellow with clouds of black spots; the flesh is yellow, rich, breaking, and juicy; of a fine flavor as a table apple and producing cider of an exquisite taste. The stalk is of ordinary length, inserted in a cavity of medium depth; the crown is moderately deep. The time of ripening is about the first of October, after which the fruit soon falls and is fit for cider. It does not keep long, but while in season is a delicious table apple. The tree is very thrifty, hardy, and vigorous, of a regular and beautiful form, and very productive. It is much cultivated in the lower counties of Virginia, from whence I procured it, as an apple of high reputation." Some fruit of Gloucester White has a pinkish blush. Catalog listings: MD, DC, VA, KY (1824–1904).

❦ **GLYMPH:** A South Carolina apple listed from 1860 to 1878 by Pomaria Nurseries of South Carolina. A large, winter apple.

❦ **GOIN:** A Tennessee apple that originated before 1895 on the farm of Ely Goin, Claiborne County, Tennessee.

Fruit large, roundish oblate; skin thick, tough, smooth, yellow nearly covered with purplish red and distinct red stripes; dots large, light gray; stem medium length and rather slender in a large, deep, abrupt, russeted cavity; calyx closed; basin small and shallow; flesh yellow, fine-grained, tender, subacid to acid. Ripe late winter. No catalog listings.

❦ **GOLD** (Gold Apple): An Arkansas apple that originated before 1896.

Fruit medium or above, oblong conical, rather pointed; skin golden yellow covered with russet dots; cavity large, medium to deep, gradually sloped, russeted; basin shallow; flesh yellow, fine-grained, tender, juicy. Ripe early winter. No catalog listings.

❦ **GOLDEN BANANA:** Listed from 1884 to 1898 by Guilford Nurseries, Vandalia, North Carolina. No description.

❦ **GOLDEN BURCH:** Listed from 1824 to 1827 by the Linnean Hill Nursery, Washington, D.C. No description except ripe August.

❦ **GOLDEN DIXIE:** Originated before 1872 in the seedling orchard of James Fitz, Keswick Depot, Albemarle County, Virginia. Tree vigorous and an abundant bearer on alternate years.

Fruit medium to large, oblate to roundish oblate, slightly conical; skin light golden yellow, deeper yellow on the sunny side; stem short and small in a medium size, often slightly russeted cavity; calyx closed; basin rather abrupt, deep, slightly corrugated; flesh whitish yellow, somewhat firm, juicy, slightly aromatic, brisk subacid. Ripe August. No catalog listings.

❦ **GOLDEN DROP:** A southern apple listed from 1858 to 1904 by three Virginia nurseries. No description.

❦ **GOLDEN LADY:** Listed from 1824 to 1827 as a winter apple by the Linnean Hill Nursery, Washington, D.C. No description.

❦ **GOLDEN ROSE:** Said by Warder (1867) to be a southern apple. No description. No catalog listings.

❦ **GOLDEN WILDING** (Golden Wild, Golden Willow?): Originated in Cumberland County, near Fayetteville, North Carolina, and used by Thomas Jefferson as a cider apple from his orchard at Monticello in 1796. Mr. Jefferson mixed the juice of Golden Wilding with that of Hewe's Crab to make a superior cider. The tree is a heavy bearer. Described in 1888 as "one of the most beautiful and perfect of apples, a good and long keeper."

Fruit medium, roundish oblate, slightly oblique; skin golden yellow (one reference says with a faint dull blush), sprinkled with brown dots; stem rather short and small in a deep, russeted cavity; calyx open; flesh yellow, firm, crisp, brisk subacid. Ripe October–December or perhaps later. Catalog listings: VA, NC (1853–1904).

❦ **GOLDEN WINTER:** A Jackson County, Georgia, apple (or perhaps from New York) sold by several North Carolina nurseries from 1867 to 1902.

Fruit large, roundish or roundish oblate; skin deep golden yellow; flesh firm, juicy, subacid (sweet according to Ragan). Ripe October–February or later.

❦ **GOLDEN WYLIE:** A North Carolina apple sold from 1855 to 1860 by Guilford Pomological Nurseries of Greensboro, North Carolina. No description except ripe October–January.

❦ **GOLDEN YELLOW:** Originated in Lincoln County, Tennessee, and sold from 1886 to 1890 by Huntsville Nurseries of Huntsville, Alabama. Said to be the best winter keeper of any apple where it originated. Fruit medium to large; skin golden yellow. Ripe winter.

❦ **GOLDFINCH:** A seedling of the Lord Botetourt apple, very similar in appearance and quality, but the tree is a better grower. Ripe winter. Listed in 1895 by Munson Hill Nurseries of Falls Church, Virginia.

❦ **GOOSEPEN:** Described in *The Southern Apple and Peach Culturist* (1872): "Somewhat resembling the Wine Sap and by no means its inferior; November to March." Sold by a Virginia nursery from 1901 to 1904. This apple closely resembles Royal Limbertwig, which has a synonym of Goosepen, and may be identical to it.

Fruit medium or above, roundish oblate, sides slightly unequal; skin light yellow, mostly striped with two shades of red; dots rather large, russet; stem almost long in a deep, russeted cavity; calyx open; basin wide, shallow; flesh creamy white. Ripe December–February. ❖ **Plate 92.**

❦ **GORDON'S CLUSTER:** Fruit sent to the USDA by J. W. Kerr of Denton, Maryland, and described in the 1891 *USDA Annual Report*: "Of medium size, globular in form, red with stripes of darker red; very good quality for an early apple (received August 4), and a profuse bearer." No catalog listings.

❦ **GORDON'S SEEDLING** (Gordon): Originated in Gates County, North Carolina. An 1877 letter from Suffolk, Virginia, calls it an old apple variety in the Tidewater area of Virginia, grown there for over twenty-five years. Also popular in eastern North Carolina.

Fruit medium to large, oblate, perhaps conical; skin red or red-striped with white dots; flesh subacid. Ripe November and keeps until Christmas. Catalog listings: VA, NC, GA (1859–98).

❦ **GORE:** Origin attributed to either South Carolina or Mississippi. Described only as a large apple. Ripe August. Catalog listings: NC, SC, GA (1856–61).

❦ **GORIN'S RUSSET** (Gorin's New Russet): Originated before 1871, probably in Hartford County, Kentucky.

Fruit medium size; skin dull crimson and russeted. Ripe winter. No catalog listings.

❦ **GOSESEY** (Goshen?): Listed without description in 1849 by a nursery in Stone Mountain, Georgia. May be the same as "Goshen" listed by the same nursery in 1851 and described as "large, striped, ripe in October."

❦ **GOSS' YELLOW:** Listed as an autumn apple in the 1878 catalog of Pomaria Nurseries of South Carolina. No description.

❦ **GOVERNOR HOGG:** From the 1903 catalog of the Austin Nursery, Austin, Texas: "Gov. Hogg spoke to me at different times about 'the best apple on earth'—an old seedling growing in the orchard of his father-in-law, Mr. Stinson of Wood County. I put in all the grafts I could get after receiving a letter from Mr. Stinson. I give it in part: 'The seed was planted twenty-five years ago by my little son. It has been in bearing some twenty years without missing a single crop. I think the seed was taken from a Shannon Pippin. It ripens the last of August until the first of October. Above average size, yellow, somewhat flat, sprightly, crisp. Has taken two blue ribbons at two fairs at Mineola. The tree is thrifty and branching in its habit.'"

❦ **GRAHAM WHITE:** Graham White was listed from 1895 to 1902 by the Munson Hills Nursery of Falls Church, Virginia. No description.

❦ **GRAHAM'S WINTER:** In 1863, a Pennsylvania nursery listed a Graham's Winter as an Alabama apple. No description except ripe November–April.

❦ **GRAND REPUBLIC:** Quoted from a 1920 salesman's book of the Georgia Nursery Company, Concord, Georgia: "It comes from southern Georgia and is described as follows by the originator: 'It is a chance seedling. I have two large trees about 30 years old and they never fail to bear a full crop of large apples.' Its ripening season is July 15 to Aug. 15. It is of extra large size, unexcelled in quality and equally good for cooking, eating or other purposes."

❦ **GRAND SULTAN:** This is a Russian apple imported into the United States about 1870 by the USDA and thoroughly confused from its earliest days with the Yellow Transparent. As described in several southern nursery catalogs it very much resembles the Yellow Transparent, which is also a Russian apple, and it is possible that scions of Grand Sultan and Yellow Transparent were mixed up when sent out by the USDA for testing.

Fruit medium to large, roundish oblong; skin smooth, waxen, greenish white changing to pale transparent yellow when ripe; flesh soft, mellow, slightly aromatic, subacid. Ripe June.

An 1895 report of Pennsylvania State College describes the following Russian apple named Grand Sultan. This apple, completely different from the Yellow Transparent, may be the true Grand Sultan. Fruit medium, roundish oblate; skin whitish yellow when ripe, sometimes striped and blotched with carmine over pink; dots light and gray; stem very short (also said to be long) in a medium-size, russeted cavity; calyx usually closed; basin very shallow; flesh white, tender, juicy, subacid. Ripe early August in Pennsylvania. Catalog listings: MD, NC, GA, AL, LA (1886–1902).

❦ **GRAND SYR:** Listed as a North Carolina apple in 1859 by Hopewell Nurseries, Fredericksburg, Virginia. No description.

❦ **GRANTHAM:** Described in an 1863 Pennsylvania nursery catalog as an apple received from Georgia. Fruit large, red, juicy, ripe November to April.

❦ **GRASSY MOUNTAIN:** From an 1894 letter to the USDA from George E. Murrell, Coleman's Falls, Bedford County, Virginia:

> A large, red, oblong, ovate, conical apple; the handsomest of 45 varieties. Season Fall. A seedling originating on top of a small mountain in Bedford County, Va. When discovered by me the tree had been blown up by the roots and was in a dying condition. This was in the fall of 1892. I took some of the fruit, then mature, to the Virginia State Exposition, and I took first premium for seedling of general merit. Upon my return home, I succeeded in getting enough wood to make several root grafts and top-work one or two young trees just commencing to bear. The original tree is now dead, but I can furnish specimens in a year or two from the grafted trees. The fruit, in color, is a beautiful red ground, covered with minute white specks, and takes a brilliant polish. In flavor it is not quite up to the best of our fall apples, being rather too acid when first gathered; but in other respects it may prove of value worthy of dissemination. As a designation more than a name, I call it Grassy Mountain from the locality where it was found.

Fruit large, rather oblong; skin light yellow mostly covered with two shades of red; dots small, gray; stem short in a greenish cavity; calyx open; basin wide, deep, prominently corrugated; flesh creamy white. Ripe October. No catalog listings.

❦ **GRAVE'S RED:** An autumn apple mentioned but not described in an 1891 Tennessee agricultural experiment station bulletin. Adapted to the east Tennessee valley. No catalog listings.

❦ **GRAY:** Sold by two Texas nurseries from 1898 to 1903. From the catalog of the Austin Nursery, Austin, Texas: "An old variety we have been unable to name. The parent tree is growing in the orchard of Mr. Gray, San Saba County, Texas. Its many merits make it sought and demanded by all who have seen it." No description.

❦ **GRAY HILLS:** Carried from North Carolina to Bedford County, Virginia, in 1850 by Z. J. Wheat. The original tree bore up to fifty bushels each year. The fruit keeps until February or March and is good for apple preserves, as it does not cook to pieces.

Fruit almost large, oblate; skin yellowish, almost covered with red and indistinct darker stripes; dots numerous, dark, areole; stem short in a greenish cavity; calyx open; basin rather wide; flesh greenish white. Ripe winter. No catalog listings. ❖ **Plate 93.**

❦ **GRAY RUSSET:** Sold by two Virginia nurseries from 1858 to 1904. No description.

❦ **GRAY'S SEEDLING:** Sold in 1870 by the Forest Nursery, Fairview, Kentucky: "Fruit large, yellow striped with red, flesh juicy."

❦ **GREAT HENSON:** Listed without description in 1849 by a nursery in Stone Mountain, Georgia.

❦ **GREAT KEEPER:** Sold by several Virginia nurseries from 1858 to 1904. Briefly described by Warder (1867) as oblong, russet, subacid, late-ripening.

❦ **GREAT UNKNOWN** (Unknown): Like the Cullasaga and Nickajack, this apple originated with or was first introduced by the southern pomologist Silas McDowell of Macon County, North Carolina. He wrote in 1858 that he did not know where the Great Unknown came from or from whom he got it—hence its name. The last known tree, on Peaks Creek in Macon County, North Carolina, was cut down about 1960. Listed in 1871 by the Fruitland Nursery, Augusta, Georgia.

Fruit large, roundish oblate, conical; skin waxen, yellow or pale green shaded and marbled with red; stem fleshy and short (Downing says slender) in a medium-size cavity; calyx open; basin small and smooth; flesh yellowish (also said to be white), very tender, juicy, subacid. Ripe September and keeps until Christmas.

❦ **GREEN FLATS** (Green Flat): Sold by two Virginia nurseries from 1858 to 1904.

Fruit oblate, greenish yellow, subacid. Ripe autumn.

❦ **GREEN FLOUR** (Green Flower): Perhaps of Pennsylvania origin but sold by two Virginia nurseries from 1858 to 1869.

Fruit conical, greenish yellow, subacid.

❦ **GREEN MOUNTAIN PIPPIN:** A Georgia apple first described in 1848.

Fruit medium, roundish oblong; skin greenish

yellow; flesh white, crisp, tender, juicy, subacid. Ripe October/November. No catalog listings.

❦ **GREEN RUSSET** (Winter Sweet): This apple was taken to Indiana from North Carolina in the 1820s by Joshua Lindley, who started a nursery in Morgan County, Indiana. Similar to, but distinct from Green Cheese. Mainly a cooking apple.

Fruit large, roundish oblate; skin greenish and russeted with a blush; flesh subacid. Ripe October/November. No catalog listings.

❦ **GREEN SWEET** (Honey Sweeting, Honey Greening, Poppy Greening, Green Winter Sweet): Sold in the South mostly by North Carolina nurseries without description. Ragan (1905) lists four apples named Green Sweet with the notation that some may be the same as Victuals and Drink, a late-summer apple of New Jersey origin. The apple in southern catalogs is a winter apple and is probably the Green Sweet of Massachusetts origin, described below. Valued for baking.

Fruit medium or smaller, usually oblate, sometimes conical; skin smooth, greenish yellow, perhaps with a brownish red blush; dots whitish with green bases; stem long in a wide, brown cavity; calyx open; basin rather shallow and wavy; flesh very tender, fine-grained, juicy, very sweet. Ripe December–March. Catalog listings: NC, KY (1855–1902).

❦ **GREENE'S CHOICE** (Green's Choice): A Pennsylvania apple sold by two Virginia nurseries from 1858 to 1869.

Fruit medium, roundish conical; skin yellow with red stripes; flesh tender, juicy, mild subacid. Ripe August/September.

❦ **GREGORY** (Gregory's Red): Sold from 1869 to 1904 by Virginia and North Carolina nurseries. From the 1904 catalog of Emporia Nurseries, Emporia, Virginia: "A fine cider apple, medium size, striped red. Bears young and abundantly, ripening in August. A good many Virginians prefer this apple to all others for cider."

❦ **GREYHOUSE** (Grayhouse, Big Romanite, Black Jack, Black Pennock, Black Vandevere, Gray Romanite, Hard Red, Hoopes, Hoops, Hopsey, Hopson, Keystone, Lopside, May Seek-No-Further, Pilliken, Red Everlasting): A very old Pennsylvania or New Jersey apple that was widely grown at one time because it makes good cider and is a very good keeper. Tree productive.

Fruit medium, oblate; skin thick, dull red with faint stripes; flesh firm, dry, coarse, subacid. Ripe February–May. Catalog listings: MD, DC, VA (1824–69).

❦ **GRIFFIN'S PROLIFIC:** Listed in the 1878 catalog of Hermitage Nurseries, Richmond, Virginia: "Origin Brunswick County, Virginia. Medium to small, red, oblong, mealy, good quality and possessing the remarkable and useful characteristic of having the fruit in several stages of ripe, half grown, and immature on the same tree at the same time. Ripens in succession from June to September."

❦ **GRIMES:** Not Grimes Golden, but probably the same as Pattie Grimes. From the 1900 meeting of the Maryland Horticultural Society: "The Grimes, also coming from Dorchester County, is described as a fine, large, red, early winter apple, a good bearer, fine flavor, ripens up smoothly, a fine market apple; requires light, good land." No catalog listings. *See* Pattie Grimes.

❦ **GROSS** (Gross Seedling): A seedling grown by Dr. J. Gross of Jackson County, Georgia. The tree bears abundantly nearly every year. Fruit very large; skin red; flesh yellow, crisp, juicy. Ripe December and keeps until March or later. Catalog listings: VA, NC (1855–72).

❦ **GUILFORD RED:** Originated in Guilford County, North Carolina, by a man named Edwards. The tree is an annual bearer. Sold by three North Carolina nurseries from 1872 to 1898.

Fruit medium, roundish oblong (Downing says oblate), slightly conical, sides often unequal; skin almost entirely red, but purplish crimson on the sunny side; dots moderate in number, yellowish; stem short in a large, deep, sometimes russeted cavity; calyx closed; basin medium size, corrugated; flesh pale yellow, rather firm, juicy, slightly aromatic, subacid. Ripe January–March.

❦ **GUINEA:** A variety originated by Louis Hubach of the Hubach and Hathaway Nursery, Judsonia, Arkansas, and listed in their 1903 catalog. Fruit medium size, red with white specks. Ripe September but keeps well.

❦ **GULLY:** In old southern catalogs and other references, the name Gully or Gulley is most often a synonym of that great old southern apple Mangum. There is also a Pennsylvania apple that originated before 1852 in Lancaster, Pennsylvania, named Gully Apple. A Gully apple is mentioned in 1793 in Dinwiddie County, Virginia.

There is another southern apple named Gully that differs significantly from the above two apples and must be a separate variety. It is briefly described in the 1869 *USDA Annual Report*: "Origin Granville County, North Carolina; fruit medium size; form oblong; color pale yellow nearly covered with lively red, thinly sprinkled with gray dots; flesh rich, tender, juicy, subacid; keeps till April; tree of vigorous, upright growth, valued where known." Catalog listings unknown because of confusion concerning apples named Gully.

❦ **GUY'S WINTER:** Listed in 1870 by the Forest Nursery, Fairview, Kentucky.

Fruit medium; skin green; flesh tender, juicy. Ripe winter.

❦ **HABERSHAM LATE:** Probably a Georgia apple from Habersham County. Mentioned but not described in an Alabama agricultural experiment station bulletin before 1905. No catalog listings.

❦ **HABERSHAM PEARMAIN:** A Georgia apple that originated in Habersham County before 1853.

Fruit medium, egg-shaped; skin bright crimson; stem short and slender; flesh white, rather dry, firm, brisk subacid. Ripe mid-July (Downing says September). No catalog listings.

❦ **HAGLOE CRAB:** An English cider crab sold from 1858 to 1869 by two Virginia nurseries. Recommended in *The Southern Apple and Peach Culturist* (1872) for both cider and vinegar. Described by Thatcher (1822) as having "soft and woolly flesh," yielding a small amount of clear juice that makes a rich, dark cider. Also said to be an excellent cooking apple. Not the same apple as the Summer Hagloe.

Fruit small, irregular-shaped, usually roundish oblate but sometimes oblong; skin yellow in the shade but russet red in the sun; flesh soft, rather acid. Ripe August/September.

❦ **HALE COUNTY BEAUTY:** Sold from 1920 to 1926 by the Plainview Nursery, Plainview, Texas: "A red apple with yellow background, of the most delicious flavor. In flavor it is sweet, slightly touched with acid, but only enough to make it all the more pleasing, with an aroma delightfully fragrant; the flesh is fine-grained, very crisp, exceedingly juicy; an extra good keeper."

❦ **HALSTEAD:** Listed in the 1906 catalog of Yarbrough Brothers, Stephens, Arkansas: "Originated in North Louisiana. A vigorous grower and good keeper; one of our best southern seedlings. Ripens in September." No description.

❦ **HAMES** (Hames' Seedling, Haines Seedling): Originated by Henry S. Hames and first fruited about 1872 in West Point, Troup County, Georgia. Said to be a seedling of the Carolina Red June and the largest early apple grown in the South. In 1893, the USDA commented, "It does not seem to have received the attention it deserves from apple growers in the southern states." Tree productive, vigorous and an annual bearer with dark green foliage.

Fruit large to very large, roundish to roundish oblate; skin thick, tough, smooth, pale yellow with a crimson cheek and darker red stripes, often the fruit is almost entirely red; moderately sprinkled with yellowish and brown dots, areolar and indented; stem medium, stout, fleshy at both ends in a rather large cavity; calyx closed; basin medium size, gradually sloped, corrugated; flesh white, firm, juicy, rather coarse, acid to brisk subacid. Ripe June in Georgia, August in Maryland. Catalog listings: MD, NC, SC, GA, AL, TN, TX (1884–1920).

❦ **HAMETER'S LATE/HAMETER'S RED WINTER** (Hemater's Green and Red?): South Carolina apples listed in 1861 by Pomaria Nurseries of South Carolina. No description except ripe winter.

❦ **HAMILTON** (Wonder?): Originated in Cass County, Georgia. Resembles Buckingham.

Fruit large, roundish, irregular, somewhat ribbed; skin smooth, yellow, mostly covered with red stripes and splashes, sometimes almost purple; dots scattered, large, yellow or white; stem medium to long and knobby in a deep, wavy, brown cavity; calyx open; basin deep, abrupt, folded; flesh yellow, rather juicy, breaking, high-flavored, subacid. Ripe September/October. Catalog listings: VA, GA, AL, SC (1858–96).

**HANDY APPLE-TREE:** From a description written in 1900 by Powhatan Bouldin of Marion, Virginia:

> About seven miles from Stuart, in Patrick County, is the Handy Apple-tree, measuring ten feet around the trunk where the limbs branch out about five feet from the ground. It has four prongs, averaging from four to six feet in circumference, is fifty-two feet high and has a spread of seventy-one feet. Over eighty-five years ago, Colonel Joseph Martin and Samuel Hairston came to Patrick County on a deer hunt. Shortly after, Mr. Jesse Hooker, who owned the land they camped on, found a small apple tree growing on the camp site. The soil was exceedingly rich and the tree grew rapidly and, in course of time, became the most celebrated tree in the county. It is a winter apple and has produced a crop of over one hundred and ten bushels in a single season, from which was made over forty gallons of high-grade brandy, in addition to those that were used for eating. The tree gets its name from the present owner of the land on which it grows, Mr. Sparrel Handy, and he states that, from present indications, it should live for at least twenty years more.

No description. No catalog listings.

**HANNER'S FAVORITE:** A Georgia apple listed in 1860 by Pomaria Nurseries of South Carolina. A large apple, ripe August.

**HARBOUR** (Harbor's Winter): The following letter was written to the USDA in 1887 by B. F. White of Mebane, Alamance County, North Carolina:

"This variety originated in Alamance County many years ago and is doubtlessly a seedling of the Father Abraham hybridized with one of the many well known crabs which were grown for cider making. It resembles the Abram very much in shape, size, and color, and the tree is very similar. It is a much better apple in all respects, however.

"The great temperance reformation that took place many years ago pretty generally put an end to planting fruit trees for cider and brandy. There being no nurseries nearby, this old variety came near becoming extinct. Harrison Harbour, who was greatly interested in the improvement and cultivation of fine fruit, succeeded in getting some buds from a very old tree and budded them himself on some seedlings. The buds grew and in a few years bore fruit. He supplied a nurseryman with grafts, and the nurseryman named the apple Harbour's Winter. It is preeminently a winter apple, and in all respects the best winter apple in this section.

"It matures the middle of October and hangs on the tree till freezing weather. It is not injured by being lightly frozen if thawed out slowly. It mellows in December and keeps sound in a cool cellar till apples come again. The acid taste gives way as it mellows, and the flavor becomes very fine.

"The growth of the tree is slow and the limbs are twiggy. The apples are evenly distributed over the tree, firmly set and not easily blown off. Its slow growth is compensated for by a long life."

Fruit small (2 to 2¾ inches), oblate or perhaps roundish; skin smooth, yellow, almost entirely covered by bright red with indistinct stripes and a light bloom; dots small, indistinct, yellowish gray; stem short, slender, straight, in a medium to shallow cavity; calyx open; basin abrupt and deep; flesh yellow, crisp, firm, juicy, subacid. Ripe December to late spring. No catalog listings.

**HARDISON'S JULY:** From a letter written to the USDA in 1897 by J. J. Hardison of Medina, Gibson County, Tennessee: "About ten or twelve years ago I planted seed of good apples for the purpose of grafting them for my own use. I cut the seedlings off at ground level and set scions in clefts. About two years later a roguerish ram ventured to trespass my orchard and quickly removed the bark from about a half dozen of my nicest trees. This one tree put out buds below the graft and eventually bore fruit. The name was given it by a nurseryman.

"The fruit is streaked with dark red, and when thoroughly ripe it is nearly a dark red apple. It is a little flat and uniform in size. The fruit has good flavor and cooks well. The apples begin to ripen the last of June and continue for about a month. They will not drop off till well ripened and have to be pulled off to pick for market. The skin is a little thick, and it ships well. I have shipped to Kansas City, Pittsburgh, and St. Paul with returns of good prices. My trees have never failed a single year. The limbs never grow thick and are at right angles with the body."

Sold by Tennessee nurseries from 1889 to 1894.

**HARGROVE:** The Hargrove originated in the orchard of W. Campbell on the headwaters of Jonathan Creek, Haywood County, North Carolina. Fruit was exhibited at the 1891 meeting of the American Pomological Society. Highly praised in the catalogs of the Fruitland Nursery, Augusta, Georgia: "Possesses exceptional merits."

Fruit medium to large (about 3½ inches in diameter), nearly round to oblate, conical; skin smooth, golden yellow with a crimson bronze cheek and faint stripes at the stem end and a little russet; dots numerous, brown, some areole; stem short in a small, shallow, russeted, lipped cavity; calyx protuberant and open, surrounded by corrugations; basin shallow, furrowed, russeted; flesh white, brittle, crisp, "pearmain flavor," subacid. Ripe October and keeps until January. Catalog listings: NC, GA, AL, AR (1893–1909). *See also* Haywood.

**HARMAN'S SEEDLING:** Sold from 1869 to 1904 by the Franklin Davis Nursery, Richmond, Virginia. No description.

**HARNED'S SWEET:** Described as a summer apple in the 1870 catalog of the Forest Nursery, Fairview, Kentucky: "Medium size, greenish yellow, sweet, juicy, good."

**HARPER:** Originated in western Tennessee and sold by a Georgia nursery in 1890.

Fruit medium to large, oblate, slightly conical; skin whitish yellow, shaded and almost entirely striped with light and dark red; dots large and small, light-colored, some areolar; stem rather short and slender in a large, deep, yellowish cavity; basin rather large, wrinkled; flesh whitish, tender, juicy, subacid. Ripe October–January or later.

**HARPER'S SEEDLING:** Listed by the Cedar Cove Nursery of Yadkin County, North Carolina, from 1886 to 1902: "A new and very interesting apple; originated on the premises of the late Edgar Harper of Forsyth County, North Carolina; perhaps combines more good qualities than any other one of our fall apples (unless it be Magnum Bonum or Merritt). Similar to Rome Beauty."

Fruit medium, oblong, flattened on the ends; skin dark red with dots and streaks of russet; stem medium length in a deep, narrow, russeted cavity; calyx closed; basin deep and russeted; flesh yellow. Ripe August/September.

**HARRAH** (Billie's Favorite): A Virginia apple that originated about 1882 near Thornton's Gap. Tree a rapid grower with large, glossy leaves.

Fruit large, roundish oblate, conical; skin yellowish, washed and striped with two shades of crimson; dots prominent, variable in size with some very large, yellow and brown; stem short in a wide, deep, russeted cavity; calyx open; basin large, deep, abrupt, furrowed; flesh yellowish white, fine-grained, tender, juicy, subacid. Ripe September–November or often later. No catalog listings.

**HARRISON OF MONTGOMERY COUNTY:** Presumably originated in Montgomery County, Maryland. Sold in 1880 by Saul's Nursery of Washington, D.C.: "Fruit large, elongated, conical, striped with bright red, tender, juicy, subacid. Productive and very popular. Ripe October."

**HARTNESS:** Sold in 1915 by Crawford and Company, Statesville, North Carolina: "Of medium size and oblong shape. The color is light red; flesh rich, tender and mildly subacid. Tree a heavy bearer. September."

**HASKELL'S SWEET** (Sassafras Sweet): There is confusion concerning the origin of this apple. Warder (1867) says it was found growing in the orchard of Dr. George Haskell of Rockford, Illinois. Downing (1878) says it originated on the farm of Deacon Haskell, Ipswich, Massachusetts.

Fruit medium or above, oblate; skin greenish yellow, sometimes with a bronze blush; dots russet; stem short in a broad, deep cavity; calyx closed; basin broad, medium depth; flesh yellowish, tender, juicy, very sweet, aromatic. Ripe September/October. Catalog listings: VA, KY (1858–1901).

❦ **HATCHER** (Hatcher's Seedling): Originated on the farm of O. C. Hatcher near Franklin, Tennessee, and was popular in middle Tennessee around 1870. Tree vigorous, moderately productive and an annual bearer.

Fruit medium (or perhaps small), roundish, slightly conical, slightly angular; skin very dark red, almost purplish; dots few, light colored; stem short and rather small in a medium size, slightly russeted cavity; calyx open; basin medium size; flesh yellow, fine-grained, compact, juicy, subacid to almost sweet. Ripe January/February. Catalog listings: AL, KY (1870–90).

❦ **HATHAWAY:** Said to be a seedling of Yates × Ben Davis. Originated by Louis Hubach and listed in the 1903 catalog of Hubach and Hathaway, Judsonia, Arkansas.

Fruit large and red; keeps all winter in Arkansas.

❦ **HATLEY:** Originated before 1890 in Latham, Arkansas. The 1890 *Report of the Secretary of Agriculture* calls Hatley "An excellent apple to eat from the hand."

Fruit medium, oblate, conical, often lopsided and oblique; skin yellow, nearly covered with bright and dark red, splashed with russet; dots numerous, prominent, russet; stem short to medium and slender; cavity deep, abrupt, green or russet; calyx closed; basin abrupt, leather-cracked; flesh yellow, fine-grained, tender, juicy, subacid. Ripe October/November and a fair keeper. No catalog listings.

❦ **HAUPE STRIPE:** Sold from 1869 to 1904 by the Franklin Davis Nursery, Richmond, Virginia. No description.

❦ **HAW:** A Virginia apple sold in 1859 by Hopewell Nurseries, Fredericksburg, Virginia. No description.

❦ **HAWKINS:** From the 1906 catalog of Yarbrough Brothers Nursery, Stephens, Arkansas: "Everbearing. Original tree was produced by ex-senator Hawkins of Columbia County, Arkansas. Begins to ripen June 1st and continues through July and August. One of the finest eating and cooking apples known." No description.

❦ **HAYDEN'S FAVORITE:** Sold in 1921 by the Tucker-Mosby Seed Company of Memphis, Tennessee: "Hardy tree, sure bearer." No description.

❦ **HAYES FALL:** Listed in 1872 by Joshua Lindley's Nursery, Greensboro, North Carolina.

Fruit large, roundish, flattened on the ends; skin greenish yellow with stripes and blotches of dull red; flesh pale yellow, coarse. Ripe September/October.

❦ **HAYWOOD** (Queen of Haywood): Originated before 1890 in Haywood County, North Carolina, and possibly identical to Hargrove. Listed from 1893 to 1909 by the Fruitland Nursery, Augusta, Georgia.

Fruit large, oblate; skin yellowish striped with crimson; flesh white, brisk, subacid. Ripe October or later.

❦ **HEBRON'S SURPRISE:** Grown before 1855 by John Hebron of LaGrange, Warren County, Mississippi. No description except ripe summer. No catalog listings.

❦ **HEIDEMEYER:** An apple variety brought to Texas from Stuttgart, Germany, about 1850 by a Mr. Heidemeyer. Sold from 1894 to 1924 by the Comal Springs Nursery of New Braunfels, Texas. Tree an annual and prolific bearer and said to be a good variety for southwest Texas with the fruit having very high eating quality.

Fruit small to medium, roundish to slightly oblate, slightly conical, ribbed; skin golden yellow, often heavily russeted, sometimes with very faint red stripes; dots widely scattered, brown; stem short to medium in a rather deep, narrow, russeted cavity; calyx closed; basin medium in width and depth; flesh yellowish, fine-grained, crisp, juicy, aromatic, subacid. Ripe August. ❖ **Plate 94.**

❦ **HEIGES** (Red Limbertwig, erroneously): Listed in an 1898 Arkansas agricultural experiment station bulletin as an Arkansas seedling apple that resembles the Red Limbertwig. Tree very productive annually. Considerably grown in Arkansas at the turn of the century. Listed by a Maryland nursery in 1899.

Fruit medium to large, roundish, flattened on the ends, slightly conical; skin yellow covered with red or purplish red, sometimes highly colored; dots minute, numerous, very thick near the calyx; stem slender, medium to long in a medium-size, sometimes russeted cavity; calyx closed; basin small to medium in width, shallow, furrowed; flesh yellow, fine-grained, tender, juicy, mild subacid. Ripe November–January.

❦ **HEINE:** Originated in Burnet County, Texas, on the farm of Henry Heine. Introduced by Otto Locke of Comal Springs Nursery, New Braunfels, Texas, and sold by several Texas nurseries from 1895 to 1903: "Fruit large to very large, oblong, depressed at one end; skin a beautiful yellow with a slight blush where exposed to the sun. Flesh firm, white and excellent quality. Ripens in September and keeps till January."

❦ **HELEN:** Originated or introduced in the late 1800s by Frank T. Ramsey, a Texas horticulturist. No description. No catalog listings.

❦ **HELM:** Sold from 1910 to 1924 by the Austin Nursery of Austin, Texas: "The old mother tree has been bearing for thirty-five years down in Lee County. Suckers jerked off from around the collar of the tree and planted by neighbors are making the same record. The greatest point in its favor is that the Helm seems to be unaffected by root rot, the disease that kills cotton, the one great obstacle in the way of apple growing in central and southern Texas. The fruit is of the highest quality, bright red with cream colored flesh. We named it after the owner of the original tree and believe it will guide Texas apple growers into the haven of success. Ripens through July."

Fruit medium, round to roundish oblate, slightly conical; skin smooth, light green, mostly covered with shades and stripes of medium and dark red; dots numerous, gray; stem long in a rather wide, russeted cavity; basin medium depth, broadly corrugated; flesh whitish yellow. Ripe July/August. ❖ **Plate 95.**

❦ **HEMPHILL:** Originated in Person County, North Carolina, and was listed in 1859 by Hopewell Nurseries of Fredericksburg, Virginia. Tree a prolific bearer.

Fruit above medium, roundish (Downing says oblate), slightly conical; skin pale yellow shaded with red and thickly sprinkled with gray dots; flesh yellowish, solid, mild subacid. Ripe November and keeps until May.

❦ **HEN HOUSE:** A Virginia apple that originated before 1829. Skin pale gold. Ripe mid-July to mid-August. No catalog listings.

❦ **HENDRIX:** A South Carolina apple listed in 1860 by Pomaria Nurseries.

Fruit very large. Ripe November.

❦ **HENLEY:** Probably of Georgia origin and was sold from 1857 to 1870 by Georgia and Kentucky nurseries.

Fruit medium, conical; skin deep red; flesh sweet. Ripe November–February.

❦ **HEREFORDSHIRE PEARMAIN** (Red Pearmain, Winter Pearmain, Green Winter Pearmain?): Listed for many years without description, mainly by Virginia nurseries. It is probably the English apple of the same name, which is much confused in England with an older apple called Autumn Pearmain.

Fruit medium or slightly smaller, roundish conical; skin yellow with orangish red streaks and darker red stripes, often the fruit is mostly red; dots large, numerous, russet, areole; stem medium length in a rather shallow, narrow cavity; calyx closed; basin wide and shallow; flesh yellowish, very juicy, subacid to almost sweet. Ripe October–February. Catalog listings: VA, NC, SC (1853–1904).

❦ **HERR'S WINTER:** Listed in the 1856 catalog of Pomaria Nurseries, Pomaria, South Carolina. No description except ripe December.

❦ **HERSCHAL COX:** Sold from 1900 to 1902 by the Comal Springs Nursery, New Braunfels, Texas: "A new winter apple from Tennessee. Fruit and tree resemble Ben Davis but fruit smaller, better quality, better keeper."

Fruit above medium, roundish conical, sides often unequal; skin light yellow with faint stripes in the sun; dots scattered, dark, some areole; stem long in a deep, narrow, abrupt, russeted cavity; calyx closed; basin abrupt, deep, narrow; flesh white. Ripe winter.

❦ **HESLEP** (Haslep): Originated in Polk County, Georgia. Described as an improvement of the Shockley, which it much resembles, with the Heslep having better eating quality.

Fruit medium or smaller, roundish conical; skin yellow overspread with crimson. Ripe late. Catalog listings: VA, GA (1890–1901).

❦ **HICK'S WHITE** (Settle Pippin, Settle's Superb, Adams' White, Hex's White, Superb White, Hix White): Originated before 1872 in Loudoun County, Virginia, and was sold from 1875 to 1902 by Virginia nurseries. Called Settle's Superb in most old nursery catalogs. Popular at one time in the Winchester area of Virginia and the lower part of the Shenandoah Valley. Tree vigorous, productive, and an annual bearer. This apple is different from the Hicks (synonym Buckram), probably of New York origin, described in the 1868 *American Horticultural Annual* as a sweet apple with yellow flesh.

Fruit medium, roundish oblate, conical; skin white with a cheek slightly tinged with red; dots few, brown; stem short in a rather large, deep cavity; calyx closed; basin almost shallow, broad, corrugated; flesh very white, fine-grained, crisp, tender, juicy, subacid. Ripe September–November.

❦ **HICKS' TEXAS KEEPER** (Hicks): From the 1885 catalog of Paris Nurseries, Paris, Texas: "This wonderful keeping apple is named after the originator, Mr. W. T. Hicks of Lamar County. The fruit is medium size; green with red streaks. Introduced by us."

❦ **HIGHFILL** (Highfill Blue?, Highfill Seedling?): A seedling of Ben Davis originated by Mr. Hezikiah Highfill in his nursery near Springtown, Arkansas, from a seed planted about 1875. The tree resembles Ben Davis, is an early bearer and is very productive annually.

Fruit medium to large, roundish conical; skin yellow splashed and covered with red, and often highly colored, and has a heavy bloom; stem medium length in a deep, lipped, russeted cavity; basin deep, narrow, abrupt; flesh white to yellow, tender, mild subacid. Ripe winter. No catalog listings.

❦ **HILEY'S EUREKA** (Hyler's Eureka): The original tree was found before 1879 growing in the woods on the farm of Jacob Hiley, Macon County, Georgia. Sold by two Georgia nurseries from 1887 to 1898.

Fruit medium, roundish or oblate; skin deep orange nearly covered with dull red, russeted near the cavity and basin; dots numerous, light colored; stem slender in a narrow and deep cavity; calyx closed; basin shallow; flesh white, brittle, firm, juicy, somewhat acid. Ripe November and keeps until April.

❦ **HILL:** From a 1920 salesman's book of the Georgia Nursery Company, Concord, Georgia: "Came from Meriweather County, Georgia. Growth rank and spreading; free from disease; early and prolific bearer. Ripens October 1st and keeps all winter. Flesh fine-grained, very juicy, and melting. Large size, nearly solid red with small dots over entire surface. One of the finest of winter apples for the South."

❦ **HINES:** Listed in the 1859 catalog of Hopewell Nurseries, Fredericksburg, Virginia. No description.

❦ **HOCKETT'S SWEET** (Hocket's Sweet): A North Carolina apple highly praised in an 1872 *Southern Gardener* magazine: "Fruit always fair and sound."

Fruit medium to large, roundish oblate; skin yellow mostly covered with red and striped with darker red; flesh yellowish white, slightly coarse, crisp, moderately juicy, sweet. Ripe September/October and keeps until February. Catalog listings: VA, NC, GA, MS, TX (1859–96).

❦ **HOG SNOUT:** A North Carolina apple sold in 1824 by the Linnean Hill Nursery of Washington, D.C.

Fruit medium to large, round, red-striped, subacid.

❦ **HOGEL'S IMPERIAL/HOGEL'S SEEDLING:** Two apple varieties listed in 1863 by a Pennsylvania nursery as "received from South Carolina." No descriptions.

❦ **HOLLADAY'S SEEDLING** (Hollady's Seedling, Halliday?): First raised by John Hollady of Spotsylvania County, Virginia, before 1852.

Fruit medium or above, oblate; skin yellow with gray or russet spots, sometimes with a faint blush; flesh yellowish, compact, tender, highly aromatic, probably almost sweet. Ripe November–March. Catalog listings: VA, SC, GA, KY (1858–70).

❦ **HOLLY** (Persimmon, Simmon, Hardskin, Hollis Red): Originated in Georgia before 1846. In 1874, the Kansas Horticultural Society said: "Tree erect, very hardy and healthy, a regular bearer. The most valuable of all sweet apples for keeping, but rather small in size." (*See also* Holly *in chapter 5.*)

Fruit small to medium, roundish oblate, slightly conical; skin smooth, yellow, mostly covered with mixed red and indistinct stripes; dots minute; stem medium length, thick or knobby, in a wide and green cavity; calyx closed; basin abrupt and folded; flesh yellow, firm, fine-grained, juicy, aromatic, "sprightly sweet." Ripe November–February or later. Catalog listings: VA, SC, GA, MS, KY (1858–87).

**HOLT'S BISCUIT/HOLT'S FRYING:** Two apples listed as being planted in 1863 in a North Carolina orchard. Both are said to be "superior August and September fruit for the table, frying and pastry." No description. No catalog listings.

**HOLT'S SEEDLING** (Holt): Originated about 1860 on the Earle Holt farm near Fayetteville, Arkansas.

Fruit large, oblate conical; skin greenish yellow washed with dull red and striped with darker red; dots numerous, small, brown and yellow, some areole; stem medium length in a wide, deep, abrupt, irregular, russeted cavity; calyx closed; basin large, deep, narrow, abrupt, slightly furrowed; flesh greenish yellow, coarse (also described as fine-grained), solid, crisp, moderately juicy, subacid. Ripe winter. No catalog listings.

**HONEST JOHN:** Found about 1865 growing near Brahm's Gap, Virginia.

Fruit above medium, oblate conical; skin thick, rather smooth, yellow washed with mixed red and striped with crimson; dots conspicuous, russet; stem short in a large, deep, russeted cavity; calyx open or partially closed; basin medium size, gradually sloped, furrowed, and cracked; flesh yellowish white, fine-grained, crisp, juicy, mild subacid. Ripe October and a good keeper. No catalog listings.

**HONEY:** A Honey apple was sold by the Dayton Nursery of Dayton, Virginia, from 1870 to 1896. This is probably an apple of the same name described by Warder (1867) as being of Pennsylvania origin, but it was popular and grown in Rockingham County, Virginia, making a superb sweet cider. No description. *See also* Honey Sweet.

**HOPBOLE:** Sold from 1858 to 1904 by the Franklin Davis Nursery, Richmond, Virginia. Certainly the same as Hoopbole, an Ohio apple. No description.

**HOPKINS:** Downing (1878) describes an apple named Hopkins, "supposed origin, Maryland," as medium or below, roundish oblate, mottled light and dark red, ripe October/November. This is certainly the same apple as the Hopkins in the 1836 catalog of Clairmont Nurseries, Baltimore, Maryland: "Favorite for table and cider on the Eastern Shore of Maryland. Ripe November–March."

**HOPKINS RED** (Monmouth Pippin?, Hopkins Large?): The 1880 catalog of the Saul Nursery, Washington, D.C., lists an apple called Hopkins Red that does not match the description of the Hopkins apple described above: "Large, elongated, conical, bright red striped, tender, juicy and rich, very productive. October." This apple is probably Monmouth Pippin, a New Jersey apple with the synonym of Hopkin's Red Cheek.

**HOPPER:** A South Carolina apple listed by South Carolina and Georgia nurseries from 1856 to 1861.

Fruit large, roundish, flattened on the ends, sides unequal; skin greenish yellow with a brownish orange cheek in the sun, russeted around the stem; flesh white, firm, moderately juicy, subacid. Ripe August.

**HOPPER PIPPIN:** Listed in the 1917 catalog of J. A. Withrow, Ellijay, Georgia. No description except as a winter apple.

**HORACE:** Originated before 1912 with L. C. H. Ayers, Midway, Tennessee.

Fruit medium to large, roundish oblate; skin lemon yellow. Ripe August. No catalog listings.

**HORN** (North Carolina Vandevere, Leech's Red Winter, Horne's Winter Wine?): Originated as a seedling by William Rutherford of Culloden, Monroe County, Georgia, and first brought to notice when exhibited at the Georgia State Fair in 1852. This is thought by some to be identical to the popular old apple named Vandevere, but Horn seems to have more red color. A Georgia nursery catalog says "here and further south dark crimson; further north green with a red cheek."

Fruit medium or below, quite oblate, sides unequal and sometimes lumpy; skin whitish yellow mostly shaded and obscurely striped with red, but green with a red cheek in cooler areas; dots numerous, large, light colored; stem almost short in a medium to wide, wavy, russeted cavity; calyx open; basin abrupt, rather shallow, russeted; flesh yellowish white, solid, moderately juicy, subacid to almost sweet. Ripe November–February. "Hard as a billiard ball and will keep eternally." Catalog listings: VA, GA, AL, LA, MS, AR (1858–1909).

**HORNBEAK'S SWEET:** Listed as a new apple in 1915 by the New Cumberland Nursery Company of Sawyer, Kentucky. No description except ripe winter.

**HORTON:** The Horton is listed in the 1898 catalog of Easterly Nurseries, Cleveland, Tennessee: "This new southern winter apple originated at Cleveland, Tenn., and is without doubt the most valuable winter apple for the middle and lower South. It is not affected by the heat of autumn, and holds its fruit until cold weather, when it can be gathered perfectly firm and sound and kept until the following May or June in good condition. Large, of good shape, color yellow, nearly overspread with bright red and crimson stripes. Core very small; flesh fine, juicy, rich, with a sprightly subacid flavor, of good quality. Tree a strong vigorous grower, with a spreading habit, forming a beautiful, robust, healthy tree. Keeping qualities unexcelled, has been kept with ordinary care until June. Mr. Horton, the originator and an experienced fruit grower, says the Horton apple is decidedly the best winter apple in his orchard."

**HORTON'S SWEET:** Not the same apple as the Horton described above and probably originated in Ohio. Described as a summer apple in 1870 by the Forest Nursery, Fairview, Kentucky: "Medium size, skin greenish yellow, sweet, good."

**HOWARD SWEET** (Lady Sweet?): The original tree grew on the farm of Mr. Howard near Cincinnati, Arkansas, the tree having been purchased from the Earle Holt Nursery around the end of the Civil War. Extensively planted about 1900 in the vicinity of Cincinnati, Arkansas, where it was claimed by some to be the same as Lady Sweet.

Fruit large, oblong conical; skin mostly covered with red; flesh sweet. Ripe October/November. No catalog listings.

**HOYAL'S GREENING:** From the 1869 *USDA Annual Report*: "Of southern origin; fruit medium, roundish conical; color green, rarely blushed; flesh white, rich, juicy, very agreeable; keeps very well during the winter; tree very luxuriant in growth and bears abundantly after a few years." No catalog listings.

**HOYLE'S BRIDGE** (Hoyle's Nonpareil?, Hoyles Large?): A North Carolina apple.

Fruit medium, oblate; skin yellow mostly covered with red or red stripes; flesh subacid. Catalog listings: SC, GA, KY (1858–78).

**HUBACH'S FAVORITE:** Sold in 1903 by the Hubach and Hathaway Nursery, Judsonia, Arkansas.

Fruit very large, "green with red and streaked blush." Ripe August.

**HUBBARD'S SUGAR:** Originated in Guilford County, North Carolina.

Fruit medium, oblate; skin greenish yellow striped with red; flesh yellowish white, juicy, fine-grained, sugary. Ripe August–October. Catalog listings: VA, NC, GA (1853–69).

**HUFF:** From a letter written in 1899 by A. F. Morgan of Otter Creek, Rutherford County, North Carolina: "Originated near the house of one Huffstutler in 1877, hence the name Huff. Tree is a vigorous grower and resembles the pippin tree of this section. Fruit a good keeper."

Fruit medium, roundish oblate, slightly conical; skin dirty green with russet, especially at the stem end; dots inconspicuous; stem short in a deep, wide cavity; calyx open; basin deep and wide; flesh greenish white. Ripe February. No catalog listings.

❖ **Plate 96.**

**HULL'S WINTER RAMBO:** Apples sent to the USDA in 1893 by Otho Hull of Lowry, Virginia.

Fruit below medium, oblong conical; skin yellowish, mostly covered with purplish red and having some bloom; dots inconspicuous; stem quite long and slender in a shallow, corrugated cavity; calyx open; basin shallow; flesh greenish white. Ripe December. No catalog listings.

**HUNT EVER-BEARING:** Briefly described in the 1915 catalog of the Continental Plant Company, Kittrell, North Carolina: "A medium sized apple of most delicious flavor; ripening all through June, July, and August."

❧ **HURNE:** Originated before 1895 in the orchard of E. Hurne, Weddington, Arkansas. Tree dwarfish with drooping branches. A poor grower in the nursery.

Fruit medium, roundish; skin yellow washed with red and striped with crimson, overspread with gray around the stem end; dots conspicuous, russet, indented; stem short in a medium size, russeted cavity; calyx nearly closed; basin medium size, furrowed and cracked; flesh yellowish, almost fine-grained, crisp, juicy, subacid. Ripe autumn. No catalog listings.

❧ **HUTCHESON** (Hutchinson): Originated in Logan County, Kentucky, and sold by two Kentucky nurseries from 1870 to 1897. Tree a slow grower but productive.

Fruit medium, roundish, slightly conical; skin yellow overspread with red; dots large and light-colored; stem short in a narrow cavity; calyx closed; basin abrupt and deep; flesh white, moderately juicy, mild subacid to almost sweet. Ripe December–April.

❧ **HYATT'S WONDERFUL** (Hyatt's Seedling, Hiatt's Wonderful, Gloria Mundi?): Supposedly a North Carolina apple that originated before 1845 and that was listed from 1861 to 1878 by South Carolina and Georgia nurseries.

Fruit large, oblate, yellow, subacid. Ripe November. In 1896, an Illinois agricultural experiment station found this apple to be identical to Gloria Mundi.

❧ **HYCO SWEET:** A North Carolina apple sold in 1859 by Hopewell Nurseries, Fredericksburg, Virginia. No description.

❧ **HYDER SWEET** (Hyder?): From the 1895 meeting of the American Pomological Society: "Grown by F. N. Hyder, Gap Run, Tennessee. Fruit above medium, roundish conical, sides unequal; skin smooth, yellow washed with light red and slightly striped with crimson; flesh yellow, fine-grained, crisp, juicy, sweet, rich. Ripe autumn." This is probably the same apple as the Hyder, which supposedly originated with S. H. Stepp of Carter County, Tennessee. This apple is described as large with rather coarse, dry flesh. No catalog listings.

❧ **IMPERIAL SWEETING:** Listed by two Virginia nurseries from 1858 to 1869. No description.

❧ **INDIAHOMA:** Described in the 1920 catalog of the Texas Nursery Company, Sherman, Texas: "Originated in the old Indian Territory. Large, oblong, of excellent flavor; red. Well adapted to southwestern planting. Ripe in July. Trade-marked."

❧ **INDIAN WINTER** (Moultrie's Winter?): Probably the same as Moultrie's Winter, although the abbreviated and only description is not a good fit.

Fruit large, conical, yellow, subacid. Ripe October–December. Catalog listings: GA, MS, KY (1861–78).

❧ **INGRAHAM'S WINTER:** Originated in Richmond County, North Carolina, and sold in 1861 by the Fruitland Nursery, Augusta, Georgia. Tree moderately productive.

Fruit medium, roundish conical; skin yellow shaded with red on one side; stem short and fleshy in a small cavity; calyx closed; basin small; flesh white, firm, juicy. Ripe early October and keeps until January.

❧ **IRON:** Warder (1867) briefly describes this as a southern apple.

Fruit round, yellow, subacid. No catalog listings.

❧ **IRON BLACK:** A north Georgia apple described in a 1905 South Carolina agricultural experiment station bulletin. Tree very productive.

Fruit below medium to small, roundish conical; skin very dark red to almost black; dots large, numerous, gray, more concentrated near the basin; stem almost short, stout in a wide, regular cavity; calyx partly open; basin shallow and smooth; flesh creamy white often stained red, firm, tender, crisp, coarse, mild subacid. Ripe December–April. No catalog listings.

❧ **IRON PIPPIN:** A Kentucky apple listed in 1870 by the Forest Nursery, Fairview, Kentucky.

Fruit medium or above, round; skin greenish, striped with dull red; flesh subacid. Ripe winter.

❧ **IRONSIDES:** A North Carolina apple sold in 1861 by the Fruitland Nursery, Augusta, Georgia. No description except medium size, ripe January.

**IVANHOE:** Originated in Prospect, Albemarle County, Virginia, and thought to be a seedling of Newtown Pippin. Won special premiums at the Lynchburg and Richmond fairs in 1886 and sold by Virginia nurseries from 1887 to 1904. The fruit hangs on the tree until Christmas and keeps exceptionally well. The tree bears when very young, abundantly, and every year. One catalog says the apples keep in cellar storage until mid-September of the following year. "Has been tested side by side in the same box with Roxbury Russet, Romanite and Winesap and outkept them all."

Fruit medium to large, round, conical; skin light golden yellow when ripe, sometimes with a slight blush in the sun; cavity shallow; basin shallow; flesh tender, crisp, juicy, sprightly subacid, "pippin flavor." Ripe October/November and keeps well.

In 1920, the Texas Nursery Company of Sherman, Texas, sold an Ivanhoe apple: "A light cream, oblong apple of unusually fine quality. Ripens in late fall. Originated in Grayson County, Texas." Probably the same apple as the Ivanhoe from Virginia, in spite of its supposed Texas origin.

**JACKSON:** Ragan (1905) lists five apples named Jackson and four others with Jackson as a synonym. At least two are southern apples.

From a letter written to the USDA in 1893 by P. Emerson of Wyoming, Delaware:

> Regarding the history and origin of the Jackson Apple would state that the original tree is still in good and fruitful condition upon the farm of Thomas Jackson near here. It was purchased of a local nurseryman by his father for Winter Grixon in 1847 and planted out with and among same. It always excelled the others in fruitfulness. It shows today a much hardier nature and more fruitful condition and bids fair to far out-live them. It really seems to be a cross between the Grixon and Grindstone as the flavor is decidedly similar to Grixon while the grain is identically the same as that of Grindstone. It keeps well until April and those who have them pronounce them profitable. The trees hold all their fruit exceedingly well and late, therefore the fruit can all be picked at one time. It has received high endorsement at our horticultural meetings as a late keeper of rich flavor, good size and productiveness.

Another old reference describes this apple as "not attractive in color, a dull, brownish red, but of very good quality and the flesh is very firm and fine-grained." No catalog listings.

Warder (1867) briefly describes a different Jackson apple of either Virginia or Georgia origin.

Fruit oblate, yellow, subacid. No catalog listings.

**JACKSON RED** (Jackson's Red): This is a synonym of three southern apples—Buckingham, Nickajack, and Buncombe. It has been used most often as a synonym of Buncombe.

**JACKSON SEEDLING:** A Georgia apple that originated before 1881.

Fruit medium, oblate; skin yellowish with red; flesh white, tender, juicy. Ripe October. No catalog listings.

**JACKSON'S BEAUTY:** Listed from 1889 to 1894 by the Planters Nursery of Humboldt, Tennessee: "Large, fine color and shape, good eating and market, keeps till May."

**JAMES MOORE APPLE TREE:** An apple tree of unknown variety was carried in the late 1700s from Rockbridge County, Virginia, to Abb's Valley, Tazewell County, Virginia, by Captain James Moore. The "Moore Family Massacre" occurred here in 1786 when eight members of the family were killed by a Shawnee Indian raiding party. The old apple tree was still bearing apples in 1931 but was subsequently cut down. No description. No catalog listings.

The much-missed Dr. L. R. Littleton, who died in 2004, brought this history to my attention during his years as an invaluable apple hunter.

**JAMES SPURLIN:** An apple sold around 1920 by the Fayette County Nurseries of Fayetteville, Georgia: "We introduce this new apple as one of the best Georgia has produced. It was originated by Judge James Spurlin on his farm in Fayette County, Georgia, near Lowery. Fruit color of Yates. Twice as large, with yellow flesh and flavor of Shockley. Ripens in Nov. and keeps sound and firm until May."

❦ **JARKER:** A North Carolina apple listed in 1859 by Hopewell Nurseries, Fredericksburg, Virginia. No description.

❦ **JENE'S FAVORITE:** Mentioned but not described in an 1889 Texas agricultural experiment station bulletin. Grown at that time in Victoria and Jackson counties. No catalog listings.

❦ **JENNINGS** (Jennings' Florida): This is the only old apple variety known to have originated in Florida. It probably originated in Baker County, where it was grown for many years as a local variety. In 1896, the Jennings was said to succeed farther south than any other apple, as far south as the coast of Texas. In 1898, the Jennings and Red Astrachan were the only apples recommended for growing in Florida by the Florida Horticultural Society. Tree a heavy, annual bearer. *See* Shell.

Fruit large, skin green turning yellowish green when fully ripe; flesh white, juicy, subacid. Ripe July. Catalog listings: FL, GA, TX (1896–1916).

❦ **JERSEY SWEET** (American, July Branch): An old American apple considered valuable for dessert, cooking or feeding to farm animals. The tree is productive, an annual bearer, and ripens its fruit over several weeks.

Fruit medium, roundish or oblate, conical, sides often unequal; skin thin, greenish yellow becoming clear yellow, mottled and washed with brownish red with narrow red stripes; dots inconspicuous, greenish, submerged; stem medium length in a narrow to medium-width cavity; calyx closed; basin small, almost shallow, ribbed and wrinkled; flesh yellowish, fine-grained, crisp, tender, juicy, sweet. Ripe August/September. Catalog listings: MD, VA, NC, SC, KY (1853–1914).

❦ **JESSE:** A Georgia apple that originated about 1875 on the farm of Jesse Morrison, Habersham County, Georgia. Tree an annual bearer.

Fruit small to medium, roundish oblate, sides unequal; skin yellow, russeted; dots small, russet and black, in clusters; stem three-fourths of an inch long in an abrupt, narrow, deep, russeted cavity; calyx open; basin medium size, wavy; flesh yellow, fine-grained, firm, mild subacid. Ripe October. No catalog listings.

❦ **JEWETT'S BEST** (Jewett's Striped, Jewett): Originated before 1857 on the farm of S. W. Jewett near Weybridge, Vermont. Sold for many years by the Fruitland Nursery, Augusta, Georgia, and for a few years by a Mississippi nursery. Not to be confused with the New Hampshire apple known as Jewett's Red (or Nodhead).

Fruit large, oblate or nearly round; skin greenish yellow with a red cheek; stem short in a large cavity; calyx closed; basin very small; flesh yellowish, juicy, very tender, subacid. Ripe July/August in Georgia. Catalog listings: GA, MS (1871–98).

❦ **JILES:** A medium-size winter apple, "a great favorite in Tidewater Virginia" in the early 1800s. No catalog listings.

❦ **JOE SHAVER'S SWEETING:** Sold about 1900 by Faught Branch Nurseries of Rockingham County, Virginia: "Large; yellow with spots of red all over; flesh tender and juicy; very sweet; valuable and one of the best; tree hardy and lives to a great age; the original tree, we suppose, is seventy-five years old; September and October."

❦ **JOHN ELLIS:** Included in an 1889 list of apple trees growing at the North Carolina agricultural experiment station. No description. No catalog listings.

❦ **JOHN HUNT:** An Alabama apple that ripens in early July in Mississippi. Briefly mentioned at the 1860 meeting of the American Pomological Society. No description. No catalog listings.

❦ **JOHN MILLER:** An apple once grown in extreme eastern North Carolina. Mrs. C. F. Hall of Grantsboro, who helped me find the Little Benny and Sugar apples, recalls the John Miller apple, but apparently no living trees now exist. No description. No catalog listings.

❦ **JOHN STEWART'S RED:** Listed by a Pennsylvania nursery in 1863 as a small Georgia apple, excellent for dessert. Ripe November–May.

❦ **JOHNSON'S RED** (Brazil Crab, Johnson Red): Sold from 1893 to 1895 by the J. Van Lindley Nursery, Greensboro, North Carolina. Said to be similar to the Hall and a great favorite in eastern North Carolina.

Fruit small, very juicy. Ripe late.

❦ **JOHNSON'S RED WINTER** (Johnson): From a letter written to the USDA in 1893 by Wesley Johnson: "The Johnson apple originated on my plantation near Jackson, Mississippi, some fifteen years ago, and the tree bears a very heavy crop each year. Its merits were brought before the public at the New Orleans Cotton Exposition (in 1885) where it took the premium as a winter apple over all competitors, Arkansas included. It has been considerably disseminated through this county but cannot say how much farther. The apples will keep in a state of perfect soundness until spring. Its merits are not alone due to its flavor which is most excellent. It was named for me, in my absence, at the New Orleans Exposition."

Fruit medium or below, round; skin greenish with red; ripe late. No catalog listings.

❦ **JOHNSTON'S CIDER** (Johnson's Cider?): Described in the 1870 catalog of the Forest Nursery, Fairview, Kentucky: "Fruit of medium size, conical; skin white, shaded with patches of russet; flesh compact, a little coarse and unpleasant, but tree is hardy and the fruit keeps long. Valuable for winter or spring cider."

❦ **JONATHAN OF EASTERN NORTH CAROLINA:** Sold in 1894 by Old Dominion Nurseries of Richmond, Virginia: "Large, white, subacid; very popular. September."

❦ **JONES CIDER:** Listed from 1877 to 1893 by the J. Van Lindley Nursery, Greensboro, North Carolina: "From Richmond County, North Carolina. Said to make the finest cider, keeping sweet through the entire winter." No description.

❦ **JONES FAVORITE:** Listed as a Georgia apple in the 1860 catalog of Pomaria Nurseries of South Carolina, but was being grown in Texas about 1880. This is not the same apple as Jones Favorite of New York origin found as a seedling about 1950.

Fruit medium to large, oblong; skin green. Ripe June.

❦ **JONES GOLDEN:** Listed in 1927 by the C. M. Fitts and Son Nursery of Dahlonega, Georgia. No description.

❦ **JONES' SEEDLING** (Allison): May have originated in South Carolina before 1863, but its origin is usually attributed to Williamson County, Tennessee. Believed to be a seedling of Red Limbertwig crossed with "striped pearmain" (probably McAfee). Tree hardy, a late bloomer, and an abundant bearer. One old catalog says, "This apple requires a good grade of limestone soil. Will not be successful on high, poor, free-stone land."

Fruit medium to large, roundish oblate, slightly conical, sometimes angular; skin rather smooth, yellow with shades and stripes of pale and darker red; dots numerous, brown and gray, some areole; stem short and stout in an irregular, broad, deep, russeted cavity; calyx open; basin abrupt, furrowed, russeted, medium depth; flesh yellowish, almost fine-grained, tender, juicy, spicy, subacid to almost sweet. Ripe late and an excellent keeper. Catalog listings: NC, GA, AL, TN, KY (1890–97).

❦ **JOY:** Sold in 1903 by the Hubach and Hathaway Nursery, Judsonia, Arkansas: "Tree finest grower of all. Fruit medium size, red. Ripens in October and will keep all winter. Originated by Louis Hubach."

❦ **JULIAN** (Julien, Julin, Juling, Thurmond, Franklin's June): The first we hear of this fine southern apple is a brief article in an 1853 issue of the *Western Horticultural Review* magazine: "This is one of the very best early apples; far better than the vaunted Early Harvest apple of the North. It ripens about the 10th of July and is rich, juicy, fine flavored, and very crisp and tender fleshed and white. It is a beautiful looking fruit, rather above medium size, tapering somewhat towards the eye, and beautifully marbled and striped with carmine. I am informed that it was first introduced into Pendleton, South Carolina, by Mr. John Juling, from Virginia, and from him it has been widely disseminated through South Carolina and Georgia and is justly a favorite. It is in keeping till 1st of September." Other southern references mince no words: "The best summer apple known" and "fine flavored, of best quality" are typical descriptions. These and similar encomiums make one hope against hope that this old southern variety will be rediscovered.

In 1894, J. Van Buren, the southern pomologist,

made this observation about Julian: "It has the peculiarity of rarely being attacked by the worm of the coddling moth, or any other." The tree is vigorous, productive, blooms late, and bears when young. The fruit also is valuable for cider and cooking. Susceptible to cedar-apple rust.

Fruit medium or below, roundish or oblique, conical, sides often unequal; skin thin, waxen, greenish yellow to yellowish white, striped and marbled with crimson in the sun; dots large, few; stem three-fourths to one inch long (Downing says short) in a moderate to deep, narrow, sometimes russeted cavity; calyx usually closed; basin round, broad, smooth or slightly corrugated, medium to deep; flesh white or tinged yellow, tender, juicy, sprightly subacid. Ripe July/August. Catalog listings: VA, NC, GA, AL, MS, LA, TN, KY (1858–1904).

❦ **JULY CLUSTER:** Sold from 1893 to 1902 by the J. Van Lindley Nursery, Greensboro, North Carolina: "Medium size, whitish yellow; very juicy and fine flavored; bears in clusters, whence its name. The apples of each cluster ripen at different times, making a succession of fruit for some weeks. Originated in Albemarle County, Virginia. Introduced and described by Rev. Richard W. Anderson, Princess Anne County, Va., he considering it the best summer apple."

❦ **JULY QUEEN:** Originated before 1900 in the nursery of Newman Taunton, near Ophelia, Georgia. Tree vigorous and an annual bearer.

Fruit medium, roundish, slightly conical; skin pale yellow and thinly striped with pale red on exposed fruit but little red on shaded fruit; dots few, light-colored and brown; stem short and sometimes lipped in a small, russeted cavity; calyx closed; basin small; flesh whitish, tender, juicy, slightly aromatic, mild subacid. Ripe July/August. No catalog listings.

❦ **JULY SWEET:** Listed in 1893 by the J. Van Lindley Nursery, Greensboro, North Carolina. No description.

❦ **JUNALUSKEE** (Junaliska, Junaluska): Silas McDowell, the noted southern pomologist who lived in the 1800s in Macon County, North Carolina, wrote this in an undated letter to Charles Downing: "The original tree was owned by a Cherokee Chief of the above name, residing in Macon or Cherokee County, N.C., I do not now recollect which. When the state purchased of the Indians this portion of their territory, Chief Junaluskee refused to part with his lot on which grew his favorite tree. To induce him to part with it, the Commissioners agreed to allow him $50 for his apple tree."

An 1857 issue of the *Magazine of Horticulture* discusses the Junaluskee apple: "A magnificent apple from the orchard of Stephen Whitaker, Esq., of Cherokee County, North Carolina. It is of an irregular globular form with numerous warts of russet color on it. It is of a dull yellow color, much speckled with dark russet, marbled and spotted with pale red on the sunny side. Flesh yellow, juicy, tender, rich and of a pleasant, mild, subacid flavor. Size from large to very large, sometimes weighing from one to one and one half pounds; stem half an inch long and fleshy; cavity quite small and dark green within; calyx of common size, closed, in a small, smooth basin. Ripens in November and keeps until March. Quality best." Catalog listings: VA, GA, AL, MS, KY (1858–94). *See* Junaluska.

❦ **KANSAS QUEEN:** A Kansas apple that originated before 1870 and that resembles Wilson June. Tree hardy and very productive.

Fruit medium, roundish conical; skin yellow, nearly covered with two shades of red, sometimes almost purplish in the sun; dots small, light and gray; stem short in a deep, narrow cavity; calyx closed; basin medium deep, corrugated; flesh white, fine-grained, juicy, subacid. Ripe July/August. Catalog listings: MD, GA, AL (1885–1928).

❦ **KEAN'S KITCHEN:** Listed in 1904 by the Franklin Davis Nursery, Richmond, Virginia. No description.

❦ **KEEPSAKE:** Listed in the 1900 catalog of Bonham Nurseries, Bonham, Texas. No description. There is also a modern apple named Keepsake that is an entirely different variety.

❦ **KEEP FOREVER:** A Tennessee apple listed in 1860 by Pomaria Nurseries of South Carolina. "A fine variety of Limbertwig."

❦ **KEICHER** (Pleasant Garden): Originated before

1895 in Pleasant Garden, Washington County, Tennessee.

Fruit small, roundish conical; skin smooth, thin, tough, greenish yellow with dull red stripes; dots numerous, yellow; stem short and rather thick in a medium-size, abrupt, russeted cavity; calyx partly closed; basin medium size, abrupt, russeted, furrowed; flesh yellow, firm, tender, mild subacid. Ripe September/October. No catalog listings.

❦ **KENTUCKY** (Summer Pippin): From an 1874 letter to Charles Downing from David Leonard of Iowa: "We found it on the place when we came here in 1842. It had been set the year before. As near as we could make out it originated in Kentucky and was grafted and sold by a little nursery above Burlington, Iowa. Grafts of it were scattered throughout Iowa and Illinois. Illinois horticulturists decided to call it Kentucky." Another 1874 letter, from a pomologist in Illinois, says, "I got my scions from a bearing tree in Knox County, Illinois, of a farmer named Alfred Brown. He said it was a seedling in his father's orchard in Kentucky."

Fruit large, roundish, slightly conical; skin yellow, marbled with dull red in the sun, with irregular greenish splashes or specks; flesh juicy, tender, subacid to rather acid. Ripe October or probably earlier. No catalog listings.

❦ **KENTUCKY CREAM:** Originated before 1861 in Todd County, Kentucky, and was listed by a Kentucky nursery in 1870. Tree an abundant bearer said to succeed best on thin, dry soils.

Fruit medium to large, roundish to somewhat oblong, largest at the calyx end and tapering toward the stem end; skin yellowish, smooth, glossy, mostly covered with clear red; dots numerous, large, areole; stem slender in a narrow, acute, grayish cavity; basin broad, deep, somewhat corrugated; flesh yellowish, breaking, not very juicy, mild subacid. Ripe December–March.

❦ **KENTUCKY KING:** A Kentucky apple described by Warder (1867).

Fruit above medium, oblate; skin yellow, mixed and striped with red; dots scattered and minute; stem medium to long in a medium-size, russeted cavity; calyx open; basin medium size; flesh yellow, breaking, fine-grained, juicy, aromatic, subacid. Ripe December–February. No catalog listings.

❦ **KENTUCKY LONGSTEM:** Originated in Kentucky and sold by Kentucky nurseries from 1870 to 1897. Tree slow to begin bearing but productive. Said to do best on dry, sandy soils.

Fruit medium to large, oblate conical, sides often unequal and ribbed; skin yellow, mostly covered with shades and stripes of red; dots inconspicuous; stem almost long in a deep, russeted cavity; basin broad; flesh yellow (also described as white), firm, juicy, fine-grained, tender, mild subacid to sprightly. Ripe December–March.

❦ **KENTUCKY RED** (Red Crab, Castor Crab, Red Cider Crab, Beeler's Crab?): This crab apple was highly prized in Kentucky and Indiana for cider and preserving. From a letter written in 1882: "They were grafted from a tree that grew in the orchard of John Harpool, eight miles from Bowling Green, Kentucky. The tree is still living and is not less than seventy years old." Kentucky Red was discussed at the 1888 meeting of the Indiana Horticultural Society: "It has the same quality as Hewes' Crab but is four times larger. The cider is rich and will keep without any reducing. The fruit when cooked and sweetened is as good, without cooking down, as apple butter. Naturally it is puckering in taste and the cider has the same quality at first."

Fruit very large for a crab apple, almost round or slightly oblate; skin almost entirely deep red; dots numerous, large, russet; stem long and slender in a greenish cavity; basin medium size; flesh white, stained red under the skin, crisp, very juicy, tannic, acid. Ripe September/October. Catalog listings: AL, TN, KY (1897–1923). ❖ **Plate 97.**

❦ **KENTUCKY SWEET:** In 1867, Warder said, "This is an apple of Kentucky or southern origin, found in many parts of the western country among the emigrants from Dixie Land, with whom it is a great favorite on account of abundant fruitage and rich sweetness."

Fruit medium, conical; skin smooth, almost entirely deep red with obscure stripes; dots scattered, large, yellow; stem short to medium length in an acute, brown cavity; calyx open; basin narrow

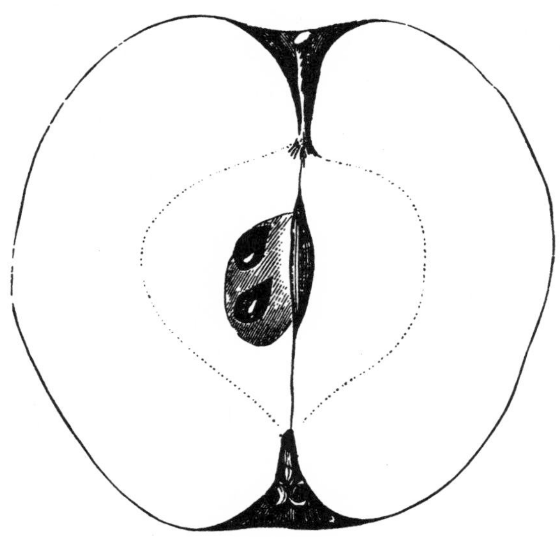

KENTUCKY SWEET

and cracked; flesh yellow, tender, fine-grained, juicy, aromatic, very sweet. Ripe November–January. No catalog listings.

**KENTUCKY WONDER:** Origin unknown. Sold in 1890 by the Jeff Nursery, Jeff, Alabama: "Medium to large, a little flattened at the ends; striped with pale red. Quality good. Annual bearer. Ripens first to middle of August."

**KENWORTHY:** Originated before 1897 with Dr. C. J. Kenworthy of Tryon, North Carolina. "Of the Shockley type."

Fruit above medium, oblate; skin dark crimson with a few faint stripes; flesh yellowish, tender, sugary. Ripe November and a good keeper. No catalog listings.

**KERCHEVAL'S SWEET:** A summer apple listed in 1875 by the Middletown Nursery of Virginia. No description.

**KERNODLE** (Kernodle's Winter, Kernoodle's Seedling): Originated before 1885 by L. L. Kernodle of Gibsonville, Guilford County, North Carolina.

Fruit medium to large, roundish oblong; skin pale yellow, splotched, and striped with light red; flesh whitish, juicy. Ripe December–April, or later. Catalog listings: VA, NC (1893–1904).

**KERR GREENING:** The original tree was found before 1894 in a thicket by the noted Maryland nurseryman J. W. Kerr of Denton, Maryland.

Fruit medium, roundish to slightly oblate; skin roughened by russet, thick, greenish yellow, sometimes with a blush; dots numerous, green; stem short to medium length in a shallow cavity; basin wide and deep; flesh yellowish white, very firm, breaking, subacid. Keeps until spring. No catalog listings.

**KESTNER:** Originated with Marcus Kestner, Hickman, Kentucky, and called a new apple in 1900. Tree an annual bearer.

Fruit medium, oblate, slightly oblique; skin whitish yellow, nearly covered with pale red and obscure darker stripes; dots few, light and gray; stem very short in a slightly russeted cavity; calyx closed; basin rather large, corrugated; flesh yellow, tender, juicy, subacid. Ripe December–March. No catalog listings.

**KEY EARLY** (Key's Early White): Originated before 1875 in Madison County, Tennessee, as a chance seedling. No description. No catalog listings.

**KEY'S RED** (Key's Red Winter): Originated with Martin Key of Clay Brook, Madison County, Tennessee, and sold by a Tennessee nursery in 1889. Tree an annual bearer.

Fruit medium, roundish oblate, slightly conical; skin greenish yellow, nearly covered with dark red; dots numerous, large, yellowish, areole; stem short in a rather deep and russeted cavity; calyx open; basin almost large, deep; flesh whitish, slightly coarse, juicy, slightly aromatic, subacid. Ripe October–February.

**KIMBALL** (Dr. Dunn's Sweeting, Dunn's Sweeting): Originated about 1860 near Brahm's Gap, Virginia, on the east side of the Blue Ridge Mountains. Kimball was being grown in 1899 in Page County, Virginia.

Fruit medium or below, roundish to roundish oblate; skin greenish yellow, mostly covered with stripes of two shades of red; dots numerous, gray and russet, many areole; stem very long in a rather deep, narrow, russeted cavity; calyx open; basin medium to small, shallow, furrowed; flesh whitish, fine-grained, crisp, moderately juicy, sweet. Ripe October/November. No catalog listings.

**KING/KING APPLE:** Maryland and Virginia

nurseries used King as a synonym of Tompkins King. Georgia and South Carolina nurseries used King as a synonym of Buckingham.

Elliot (1858) describes a King Apple from Mason County, Kentucky: Fruit oblong, flattened at the stem end; skin yellow mostly covered with dull red; stem short and slender in a narrow cavity; basin shallow; flesh white, tender, juicy, subacid. Ripe January/February. No catalog listings.

**KING LADY:** Listed in 1925 by Willadean Nurseries of Sparta, Kentucky. No description.

**KING OF THORPE:** Sold by two Virginia nurseries from 1858 to 1869. No description.

**KING OF TITUS COUNTY:** Originated with Marcus G. Black, a nurseryman in Titus County, Texas, and sold in 1912 by the Vine Hill Nursery Company, Mt. Pleasant, Texas. Tree vigorous and productive.

Fruit large to very large; flesh tender, yellow, subacid. Ripe summer.

**KINNEY** (Kinney's Seedling?): Sold in 1870 by the Forest Nursery, Fairview, Kentucky.

Fruit medium, roundish conical; skin greenish yellow with some russet; dots numerous, gray; stem long and slender; calyx closed; flesh yellowish, firm, moderately juicy, subacid. Ripe November/December.

**KINNEY'S WINTER:** A North Carolina apple sold in 1871 by the Fruitland Nursery, Augusta, Georgia.

Fruit medium; skin red. Ripe winter and a fine keeper.

**KIRTLEY'S HANG-ON** (Kirtly's Hangon): From the 1897 catalog of Green River Nurseries, Bowling Green, Kentucky: "Found on the farm of Sam'l Kirtley, near this city, and attracted attention because of the fruit having been found hanging on the tree till nearly Christmas. Mr. Kirtley claims for this variety superiority in quality to Wine Sap. Of dark red color; about the same size and general appearance as Wine Sap. Tree a thrifty grower and bears abundantly. A long keeper."

**KITTAGESKEE** (Kettageskie): Originated in North Carolina or Georgia. Beach (1905) says Kittageskee probably originated with the Cherokee Indians in western North Carolina and was introduced into Georgia about 1851. Described as one of the surest bearers in the piedmont region of the South. Tree healthy, bears early and heavily, and has a brushy growth habit.

Reading old southern nursery catalogs, one would not single out Kittageskee as an exceptional apple. It receives the usual glowing praise often seen in catalogs. Beach, however, a great pomologist and a man stingy with his praise, has this to say about Kittageskee: "Fruit too small to be valuable for market, but its quality is excellent and it is attractive in appearance, being of uniform size, symmetrical form and bright yellow color. It is desirable for dessert use, especially because it retains its texture, flavor, quality and color remarkably well till very late in the season. The tree comes into bearing rather young, is an annual bearer or nearly so, yielding moderate to heavy crops. The fruit hangs well to the tree. In the South it has the reputation of being vigorous, very prolific and almost free from blight."

Beach also says that Kittageskee trees were sent to France from Georgia in 1860 and the fruit, as grown in France, was considered to be of first quality. There are reports that Kittageskee was still in French collections until World War II. Because this apple was sold by southern nurseries until the early years of the twentieth century, old trees may still exist. Apple fanciers the world over can only hope an old tree will be rediscovered and thus restore this fine variety to the first rank of dessert apples.

Fruit small to medium, varying in shape but usually roundish or oblate, slightly conical; skin thin, smooth, rich or light yellow with a tinge of bronze or brown in the sun; dots few, dark or russet; stem slender and rather short (Beach says usually long) in a sometimes russeted, usually shallow cavity of varying shape; calyx usually open; basin broad, usually very shallow, and furrowed; flesh yellow, firm, tender, crisp, juicy, aromatic, mild subacid becoming nearly sweet (also described as "brisk acid"). Ripe November–February or often later. Catalog listings: VA, SC, GA, TX (1858–1904).

**KNIGHT:** Originated in Union County, South

Carolina, and described in the 1893 *USDA Annual Report*.

Fruit below medium, oval, flattened on the ends; skin smooth, thick, glossy, greenish yellow almost entirely covered with two shades of red; dots numerous, large, conspicuous; stem medium length in a medium-size, abrupt, deep cavity; basin large and rather deep; flesh white tinged with red, mild subacid. Ripe winter and a good keeper. No catalog listings.

❦ **KNIGHT'S RED JUNE:** A Kentucky apple mentioned by Warder (1867).

Fruit medium to large; skin red. Ripe June. No catalog listings.

❦ **KNOTT:** Originated on the Knott Ranch near Harper, Texas. Sold by the nursery of L. A. Mosty and Sons, Center Point, Texas, in 1916. No description.

❦ **KNOWLES' EARLY** (Knowls' Early, Oat Harvest, Potter's Early): Origin uncertain, probably Pennsylvania. Ripens with Red Astrachan, but said to be more valuable because of its productiveness and early bearing.

Fruit small (also said to be large), roundish oblate (Warder says oblong conical); skin smooth, pale greenish yellow with dull crimson stripes; stem long and slender in an acute cavity; calyx closed; basin shallow; flesh whitish, tender, moderately juicy, mild subacid. Ripe June/July. Catalog listings: VA, GA, NC (1858–95).

❦ **KOLB'S WINTER:** A southern apple sold in 1869 by Richmond Nurseries, Richmond, Virginia. No description.

❦ **KOSCIUSKO:** Originated about 1898 by Whitman Davis of Kosciusko, Mississippi. Fruit large, red. No catalog listings.

A Mississippi apple of this name is described in the *Register of New Fruit and Nut Varieties* (1972): "Parentage unknown; discovered about 1922 in Kosciusko, MS, by J. C. C. Price, Mississippi Agricultural Experiment Station. Recommended for home gardens in 1938. Fruit large, oblate, skin dark red, calyx open. Ripens July 15 to August 15."

❦ **KOSSOTH:** An Arkansas apple that originated before 1889.

Fruit small to medium, oblate; skin greenish with some red; flesh white, tender, crisp, subacid. Ripe late. No catalog listings.

❦ **LACKEY'S SWEET** (Lackey's Green): Listed by a Kentucky nursery in 1870 and a Tennessee nursery in 1916.

Fruit medium size; skin green; flesh sweet. Ripe summer.

An apple named Lackey has been found by Tom Brown belonging to Hal Brown of Stony Point, North Carolina, but it does not fit the brief description of Lackey's Sweet.

❦ **LADIES BLUSH** (Lady's Blush): The origin of this apple is disputed. Ragan (1905) lists two apples by this name, one from Pennsylvania and one from the South. A magazine article in 1853 says: "A specimen of Lady's Blush was presented by Z. R. Jones, Esq., from Dekalb County, Georgia; said to have been brought originally from Ohio." Perhaps the confusing origin of Ladies Blush can be explained by this article written by a Georgian for an 1869 issue of *The Southern Cultivator* magazine: "This is one of the largest and most beautiful apples we have ever raised. Its nativity we are unable to give with any certainty. It is reported to have been disseminated by itinerant grafters who, from time to time, have perambulated the country. The trees are enormously productive and very beautiful; fruit large to very large, nearly round in form and slightly conical; color greenish yellow, striped and marbled with dark red with a large patch of russet above the stem; cavity narrow and deep; stem three fourths of an inch long and slender; basin of a medium size; calyx medium size with the segments reflexed; flesh white, fine-grained, juicy, and of pleasant flavor; an early winter fruit and will rank as second quality." Catalog listings: GA, KY (1857–70).

The Georgia apple described above is certainly different from the Lady Blush or Ladies Blush of Pennsylvania origin, which has been described as having yellow skin with a blush, dry flesh, ripe August.

❦ **LADIES CHOICE:** Listed in 1915 by the New Cumberland Nursery Company of Sawyer, Kentucky. No description except ripe fall.

**LADIES FAVORITE:** Listed by Virginia, Georgia and Kentucky nurseries from 1845 to 1904. Almost always a synonym of Buckingham, but sometimes a synonym of McAfee.

**LADY LYONS:** Listed in 1901 by the Franklin Davis Nursery, Richmond, Virginia. No description. May be identical to Lyons Seedling.

**LAKIN'S CHOICE:** Listed from 1901 to 1904 by the Franklin Davis Nursery, Richmond, Virginia. No description.

**LANDRUM:** A Georgia apple sold in 1859 by Hopewell Nurseries, Fredericksburg, Virginia.

Fruit medium, conical; skin deep crimson (also described as yellow); flesh rather coarse, sweet. Ripe October/November.

**LANIER** (Lannier): This apple was exhibited at the Cotton States Fair in 1870 and 1871 and attracted much attention because of its large size and lovely appearance. It originated about 1858 with Thomas P. Shaw of Edgefield, South Carolina. Tree vigorous and a good bearer.

Fruit large to very large, roundish to oblate; skin yellow, much streaked with carmine and with a purplish carmine cheek on the sunny side, a few green blotches on the stem end; stem short to medium length and slender in a wide, deep cavity; calyx small, open; basin shallow, regular; flesh whitish, crisp, brittle, rather coarse-grained, sugary, mild subacid. Ripe late October/November. Catalog listings: MD, GA (1889–98).

**LANKFORD SEEDLING** (Lankford, Langford Seedling, Vickers): From an article in a 1902 issue of *The American Agriculturist* magazine, written by Thomas Vickers, Kent County, Maryland: "About sixty years ago a little seedling was taken up from a fence row on my place and planted by an old Negro. It was planted on very poor land and was the only apple tree around. It was never pruned or thinned but grew to a fine, large tree. When about six or eight years old it bore two bushels of apples. I found it so fine that I bought 600 Winesap trees and top-grafted them with this new apple. It does splendidly in this section, and I will plant no other apple till I find a better one. The original tree was blown down two years ago. The apple is well known locally and is popular for family use." Tree vigorous and annually productive. The original tree grew near Lankford Bay, Maryland, hence the name. A tree called Langford has been recently found, but has not yet fruited for me.

Fruit medium to large, roundish to slightly oblong, flattened at the ends; sides sometimes unequal; skin pale greenish yellow shaded with pale and darker red over half or more of its surface; moderately sprinkled with large light-colored and gray dots, many areole; stem short to medium and slender in a large, deep, greenish cavity; basin large, rather deep, slightly corrugated; flesh whitish, slightly coarse (another reference says fine-grained), tender, moderately juicy, mild subacid to almost sweet. Ripe December–May. Catalog listings: MD, VA (1889–1914). ❖ **Plate 98.**

**LANSINGBURG** (Rock Apple, Lansingburgh Pippin): An old variety known for its keeping ability, probably of New York origin. Warder (1867) says "common about Cincinnati and along the Ohio River for many years." Primarily a cooking apple as its eating quality has been described as "scarcely good." A Tennessee catalog says: "Very hard, keeps two years."

Fruit medium, roundish oblate, sides often unequal; skin thick, tough, yellow or greenish, mostly covered with a red blush and stripes; stem short in an acute, deep, russeted cavity; basin medium to wide, furrowed and wrinkled; flesh firm, compact, rather coarse, rather dry, mild subacid. Ripe December–June. Catalog listings: MD, VA, TN, KY (1889–1904).

**LARGE HALL** (Big Hall): Called Large Hall by North Carolina nurseries and Big Hall by Virginia nurseries. Probably of North Carolina origin. No description except ripe October–March. Ragan (1905) guesses this may be Nickajack or Pryor's Red, but there is nothing in any other reference to confirm this. Catalog listings: VA, NC (1855–1904).

**LARGE JUNE:** Sold in 1885 by the Paris Nursery, Paris, Texas: "Large, nearly covered with red; subacid, well flavored and a good bearer. Ripe last of June and continues through July. Good market apple."

❦ **LARGE MAY** (Large White May?): The Large May was sold from 1869 to 1904 by the Franklin Davis Nursery, Richmond, Virginia. No description. This is probably the same apple as the Large White May that was discovered by J. B. Johnson of Johnston County, North Carolina, and described in the 1888 catalog of Jamestown Nurseries, Greensboro, North Carolina: "Large, yellowish white, very tender skin, almost skinless. Flesh very tender and remarkably juicy and luscious. Flavor rich, sugary, and most excellent for so early an apple. Tree quite productive and bears annual crops."

❦ **LARGE WHITE SWEET:** Sold by two North Carolina nurseries from 1855 to 1867. No description except ripe August.

❦ **LARGE WINTER RED** (Big Red, Winter Red, Pottinger): This apple almost certainly originated in North Carolina and then was taken to Indiana about 1830 by Joshua Lindley when he emigrated from Chatham County, North Carolina, and started a nursery in Morgan County, Indiana. Its only southern listing is a brief description in an 1853 catalog of a North Carolina nursery. Ragan (1905), in a personal recollection found in the USDA files, says: "Planted in pioneer orchards of Indiana generally under the names Big Red, Winter Red or Large Winter Red, seldom under its true name of Pottinger. It was a vigorous, hardy and fruitful tree, surviving almost any kind of abuse and neglect. The fruit was really poor in quality but, on account of its hardy fruitful habit, was very popular with the sturdy, uneducated classes that were paving the way for our present civilization."

Fruit large, roundish or roundish oblate; skin rough, yellow, shaded and striped with dull red; dots prominent, small, rough; stem medium to short in a wide, russeted cavity; calyx closed; basin wide, medium depth; flesh yellow, granular, juicy, aromatic, subacid. Ripe October–February. *See* Big Red.

❦ **LARUE'S BIG GREEN** (Larue): Originated before 1878 in Hardin County, Kentucky, and said to be "superior for cooking."

Fruit very large, yellow, sprightly subacid. Ripe February/March. No catalog listings.

❦ **LATE HARVEST** (Long Stem): Listed as a summer apple in the 1870 catalog of the Forest Nursery, Fairview, Kentucky: "Fruit large, skin yellow, flesh subacid, good." *See also* Long Stem.

❦ **LATE QUEEN** (Brown's Late Queen): Several North Carolina nurseries listed this apple from 1853 to 1898, often listing Buckingham in the same catalog. Even so, the descriptions in the catalogs are close enough for me to believe that Late Queen is Buckingham under another one of its many synonyms. The detailed description of Late Queen in Elliott (1858) also closely matches Buckingham.

❦ **LAURENS' GREENING** (Lawrens' Greening): Originated in Laurens County, Georgia.

Fruit medium to large, oblate; skin greenish, sometimes tinged red in the sun; flesh white, crisp, juicy, acid. Ripe September–November. Catalog listings: GA, MS (1857–91).

❦ **LEAPHEART'S ROSE/LEAPHEART'S SEEDLING:** Two South Carolina apples listed in 1860 by Pomaria Nurseries of South Carolina. No description except both ripe late.

❦ **LEATHERBERRY'S FAVORITE:** Probably of Mississippi origin, as it was briefly mentioned in 1855 as one of the best summer apples for Mississippi. No description. No catalog listings.

❦ **LEE'S FROST PROOF** (Frost Proof?): Sold before 1905 by the J. Van Lindley Nursery, Greensboro, North Carolina. No description except "blooms thirty days after Winesap, resembles Rusty Coat." This may be the same apple as Frost Proof (still available) found or first grown in 1930 by Max Bazzanella of Mineral, Virginia, and introduced in 1947.

❦ **LETOREY** (Leterey): A Tennessee apple that originated before 1895 on the farm of William Ford, Goin, Claiborne County, Tennessee.

Fruit medium to large, oblate (also described as oblong); skin thin, smooth, yellow, almost covered with solid dull red, some indistinct stripes; stem short and stout in a large, deep, wavy, slightly russeted cavity; calyx closed; basin deep, broad, wavy; flesh yellow, fine-grained, juicy, subacid. Ripe winter and a good keeper. No catalog listings.

❦ **LEVEL'S FINE KEEPER:** Sold about 1900 by Faught Branch Nurseries of Rockingham County, Virginia: "Large to medium; fruit lemon color splashed on one side with crimson dots; handsome form; round, quite smooth; December to May."

❦ **LEVER** (Leever, Leaver, Leavel's Red?): A seedling that originated near Pomaria, South Carolina. "Tree remarkably vigorous. Fruit of second quality but a fine keeper."

Fruit medium, roundish, slightly conical; skin yellow, shaded and obscurely striped with red; stem slender; calyx nearly closed; flesh yellowish, fine-grained, crisp, juicy, subacid. Ripe November–March. Catalog listings: VA, NC, SC, GA (1856–78).

This may be Leavel's Red, listed in 1859 by Hopewell Nurseries, Fredericksburg, Virginia. No description.

❦ **LEVETT'S:** A Kentucky apple mentioned but not described by Warder (1867). No catalog listings.

❦ **LEXINGTON:** Ragan (1905) lists three apples named Lexington without any information concerning their origin. The 1860 catalog of Pomaria Nurseries of South Carolina lists a new apple named Lexington, origin South Carolina. No description except ripe December.

❦ **LILLIE OF KENT:** From a letter written in 1903 to the USDA by P. Emerson of Wyoming, Kent County, Delaware: "I have driven to the James Anderson farm a few miles from here and learned from the family the following particulars: About 30 years ago several boys of the family secured some seedling apple trees that were growing along the head rows or division fences, to plant near the old mansion. This tree is the only profitable result of their effort. I found the tree still standing in good health, loaded with a bountiful crop of apples."

Fruit large, round, conical; skin light green or yellow, usually partially blushed with light red or bronze; dots very small, dark; stem medium length in a narrow, russeted cavity; calyx closed; basin shallow, corrugated; flesh greenish yellow, fine-grained, juicy, mild subacid. Ripe late October and keeps all winter. No catalog listings. ❖ **Plate 99.**

❦ **LINAS:** A Virginia apple listed in 1859 by Hopewell Nurseries, Fredericksburg, Virginia. No description.

❦ **LINCOLN:** A seedling from Victoria County, Texas, sold by Texas nurseries from 1894 to 1924.

Fruit medium, oblate; skin pale green, becoming almost entirely red just before ripening; flesh cream-colored, subacid. Ripe August/September.

❦ **LINCOLN'S WONDER:** Originated before 1879 in either Alabama or Kentucky. No description. No catalog listings.

❦ **LINDLEY'S NONPAREIL** (Lindley, Lyndley): Raised from seed perhaps as early as 1770 by Thomas Lindley of Chatham County, North Carolina. Like the Large Winter Red, this apple was taken about 1830 from North Carolina to Morgan County, Indiana, by Joshua Lindley, who started a nursery there. In 1840, *The Indiana Farmer* magazine called it "the finest apple of its season . . . with a rich aromatic flavor equalled by few and surpassed by none." The tree is described as having a "delicate" appearance, bearing young and abundantly but susceptible to fire blight. Reuben Ragan, the father of the great pomologist W. H. Ragan, grew this apple in Illinois in the 1840s and considered it to resemble Maiden's Blush but "of much finer and more delicate quality."

Fruit medium or below, oblate; skin deep yellow when ripe (Downing says with a blush); flesh yellow, crisp, tender, aromatic, subacid to nearly sweet. Ripe August/September. Catalog listings: VA, NC, KY (1853–70).

❦ **LINER:** From the 1906 catalog of Yarbrough Brothers, Stephens, Arkansas: "One of the best southern apples ever introduced. Originated in North Louisiana. Original tree is now 50 years old and still bearing good crops of fruit. A remarkable keeper. Ripens in October." The name suggests this may be Barker's Liner. No description.

❦ **LIVELY'S CHOICE:** Sold in 1923 by the Plainview Nursery, Plainview, Texas: "Fruit golden yellow beautifully striped and shaded with bright red; flesh firm, juicy, subacid; said to be a good keeper. Tree fruits early."

❦ **LOCKHART** (Lockart): Originated in southeast Texas and considered well adapted to Texas and Louisiana.

Fruit medium size; skin smooth, waxy, yellow (perhaps striped with red); flesh crisp, juicy. Ripe early August in Louisiana. Catalog listings: LA, TX (1920–25).

❧ **LOCUST GROVE:** Sold from 1869 to 1904 by the Franklin Davis Nursery, Richmond, Virginia. No description.

❧ **LOGAN** (Logan County Streak?): In 1898, an apple named Logan, said to be an Arkansas seedling, was described as follows: Fruit medium, roundish oblate; skin smooth, oily, yellow mostly covered with bright crimson; stem rather short to medium in a deep, usually lipped cavity; basin medium with gradually sloping sides, ribbed; flesh yellowish, solid, nearly acid. A winter apple and a good keeper. No catalog listings.

In 1870, the Forest Nursery, Fairview, Kentucky, briefly described an apple called Logan County Streak, which is almost certainly the same apple as Logan. "Fruit medium, yellowish nearly covered with red." Ripe winter.

❧ **LOGAN BERRY:** Described as a North Carolina apple in an 1858 issue of *The Horticulturist* magazine.

Fruit large, oblate; skin yellow; flesh sweet. Ripe August.

❧ **LOGAN'S SWEETING** (Logan Sweet?): Listed but not described in 1869 by Richmond Nurseries, Richmond, Virginia. Several years later a Wisconsin nursery described a Logan Sweet, which must be the same apple.

Fruit large, ovate, somewhat one-sided, slightly ribbed; skin yellow, a little russeted with a brownish cheek; dots crimson; stem short in a rather narrow and irregular cavity; calyx large and open in a medium basin; flesh yellowish white, juicy, crisp, pleasant subacid. Ripe December.

❧ **LOLLER:** Listed from 1824 to 1827 by the Linnean Hill Nursery, Washington, D.C. No description except ripe October/November.

❧ **LOMBARD:** Listed in the 1859 catalog of Hopewell Nurseries, Fredericksburg, Virginia. No description.

❧ **LONG ISLAND PEARMAIN** (Autumn Pearmain, Hollow Crown Pearmain, Winter Pearmain): Origin uncertain, but not southern. Described by Coxe (1817) and confused by some with White Winter Pearmain. Sold from 1853 to 1860 by a Greensboro, North Carolina, nursery.

Fruit large, roundish oblong with a large hollow basin; skin yellow, splashed and streaked with red and with faint russet spots; flesh coarse, tender, somewhat dry, aromatic. Ripe October–December.

❧ **LONG ISLAND RUSSET:** Beach (1905) describes two different American apples with this name. Both are old varieties considerably grown at one time in New York. Virginia and Maryland nurseries listed a Long Island Russet for many years, but the exact variety cannot be identified. The 1869 catalog of Richmond Nurseries, Richmond, Virginia, gives the synonym Golden Russet of Massachusetts, an entirely different apple, for the Long Island Russet listed in their catalog. Catalog listings: MD, VA (1836–1904).

❧ **LONG'S RED WINTER:** A seedling found growing in a forest about fifteen miles from Fredericksburg, Virginia, and listed in 1859 by Hopewell Nurseries of Fredericksburg.

Fruit medium to large, roundish oblate; skin yellow, striped and splashed with red; dots few, brown; flesh yellowish, tender, crisp, juicy, subacid. Ripe December–February.

❧ **LONG'S RUSSET:** Originated by J. S. Long of Fairview, Kentucky, and listed in 1870 by the Forest Nursery, Fairview, Kentucky. Tree large, vigorous, and annually productive.

Fruit medium to large, oblate, slightly oblique; skin greenish, nearly covered with rough, dull russet; stem very short in a rather broad, deep cavity; calyx open; basin medium size, regular; flesh white with a greenish tinge, moderately juicy, rather tender, subacid. Keeps until March or April.

❧ **LONG'S YELLOW:** Listed in 1859 by Hopewell Nurseries, Fredericksburg, Virginia. No description.

❧ **LORD BOTETOURT:** From the 1895 catalog of Munson Hill Nurseries, Falls Church, Virginia: "This variety was found in Botetourt County, Virginia, and is a large, round, red apple; mild subacid and a fine keeper. Highly recommended as one of the best grown in that county."

❧ **LORICK CLUSTER** (Smith's Cluster): Probably originated in South Carolina. "Uncommonly productive, producing its fruit in strings or clusters." Listed as a cider apple in 1872 by a South Carolina nursery. Fruit described as "valuable only for its long keeping."

Fruit small, roundish conical; skin pale green or yellowish with a brownish tinge in the sun; flesh greenish white, subacid. Ripe December–April. Catalog listings: VA, NC, SC, GA, KY (1856–70).

❦ **LORSEAU/LORTON:** Both varieties were listed as Virginia apples in the 1859 catalog of Hopewell Nurseries, Fredericksburg, Virginia. No description.

❦ **LOUDON PIPPIN** (White's Loudon Pippin, Loudoun, Lady Washington?, London Pippin?, Loudon White?, Loudon Sweet?): For some reason, almost all the early pomologists who discussed this apple misspelled the county of its origin—it should be spelled Loudoun, not Loudon. The tree originated on the farm of Levi White, Loudoun County, Virginia. In 1871, the original tree was said to have produced eighty bushels of marketable apples.

Fruit large, roundish (Downing says oblate), slightly conical; skin smooth, waxy, yellow, sometimes blushed in the sun; dots scattered, gray; stem short, reddish color, in a wide, russeted cavity; basin wide and rather deep; flesh yellowish (Elliott says greenish white), tender, breaking, juicy, subacid. Ripe December–February. Catalog listings: VA, NC (1853–1902). ❖ **Plate 100.**

❦ **LOUGH:** Listed from 1893 to 1895 by the J. Van Lindley Nursery, Greensboro, North Carolina. No description. This may be the same apple as Lowe.

❦ **LOUISIANA:** Apples sent to the USDA in 1897 by L. T. Sanders & Sons, Plain Dealing, Bossier Parish, Louisiana.

Fruit large, bright yellow with some light green at the stem end; dots pale, inconspicuous; stem short in a greenish cavity; calyx closed; basin very shallow; flesh greenish white. Ripe September. No catalog listings.

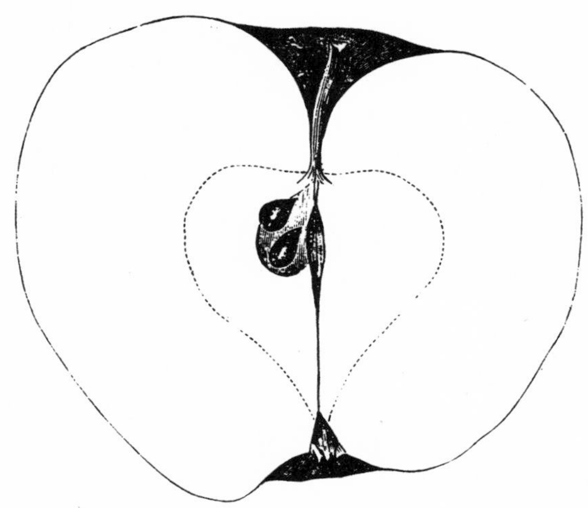

LOUDON PIPPIN

❦ **LOVE'S LARGE RED:** A North Carolina apple listed in 1860 by Pomaria Nurseries of South Carolina. "Very large, resembles Buff; excellent. Ripe November."

❦ **LOWE** (Lough?): Sold from 1900 to 1910 by Greensboro Nurseries, Greensboro, North Carolina: "An apple that has been in cultivation in the southeast corner of Guilford County, North Carolina, for some time. It is medium, dull red on yellow ground; quality the best and will keep until May." Described elsewhere as a large apple on an early-blooming tree.

❦ **LOY** (Rankin, Loy's Seedling): Originated on the farm of George Loy, eighteen miles south of West Plains, Missouri. Mr. Loy planted seeds of some Arkansas apples about 1870, and this variety grew in that seedling orchard. The fruit was exhibited at the New Orleans World Exposition (1884) under the name Rankin, where it won first prize for Best New Apple. As grown in Maryland in 1900, the Loy was found to be susceptible to apple scab and required spraying to give marketable fruit. Resembles the Willowtwig apple in shape and color.

Fruit medium to large, oblong conical, flattened on the ends; skin yellow with a red cheek that deepens into a bronze or russet; dots minute; stem short; flesh yellow, fine-grained, juicy. Ripe December and an excellent keeper. Catalog listings: MD, VA, NC, GA, TN, TX, AR (1890–1904). ❖ **Plate 101.**

❦ **LUCY:** From a letter written to the USDA in 1898 by John C. Chilton of Byrdstown, Picketts County, Tennessee: "A seedling that originated on the farm of Mrs. Lucy Riley some 60 years ago. It has been propagated but little and only from root sprouts. The original tree is dead. My tree is third removed from the original. I like the apple for cooking, drying and eating from hand. Though not showy, it is good. I cannot understand why it has not been more planted." No description. No catalog listings.

This apple is probably distinct from the Lucy and the Lucy Red described by Ragan (1905).

❦ **LUD:** Sold from 1824 to 1827 by the Linnean Hill Nursery, Washington, D.C. No description except ripe June/July.

❦ **LUKE BALLOW'S WHITE:** Listed in 1915 by the New Cumberland Nursery, Sawyer, Kentucky. No description except ripe fall.

❦ **LUMMSDEN'S BEST:** An apple exhibited at the 1914 meeting of the Georgia Horticultural Society. No description. No catalog listings.

❦ **LUPTON:** In a circa 1900 letter to the USDA, John S. Lupton of Winchester, Virginia, wrote: "The fine red apple in the bottom of the box is from a seedling; the seeds were planted by myself."

The USDA Pomologist, H. E. Van Deman, wrote back to Mr. Lupton: "The seedling variety being of very good size and quality and red in color would lead me to think that it might prove of some value for market. If you decide to give it a name, let me suggest that you call it Lupton." No catalog listings.

❦ **LUSTER:** A winter apple mentioned in an 1891 Tennessee agricultural experiment station bulletin as being adapted to the valley of east Tennessee. No description. No catalog listings.

❦ **LUTE'S GREAT KEEPER:** Listed as a "new and rare" apple in the 1902 catalog of Startown Nursery, Newton, North Carolina. No description.

❦ **LYNN:** A Kentucky apple briefly described by Warder (1867).

Fruit medium to large, oblong; skin red stripes on yellow; flesh subacid. Ripe late. No catalog listings.

❦ **LYONS SEEDLING:** Originated before 1900 on the Lyons farm near Ivanhoe, Virginia, and grown at the Virginia Polytechnic Institute until 1959. Said to be a disease-resistant tree bearing highly colored fruit. No catalog listings. *See also* Lady Lyons.

❦ **MACK** (Uncle Jack): Originated on the farm of Rev. A. J. Harris about 1840 and grown only near Demorest, Georgia.

Fruit large, oblate conical, sides unequal; skin greenish yellow washed with red and striped with crimson; dots numerous, large, russet; stem short and slender in a large, deep, russeted cavity; calyx open; basin medium size; flesh greenish yellow, fine-grained, juicy, crisp, sweet. Ripe September–January. No catalog listings.

❦ **MADISON SWEET:** Sold by Tennessee nurseries from 1910 to 1920. Fruit "large, yellow, sweet and juicy."

❦ **MADOX:** From an 1899 letter to the USDA from J. R. Johnson, Dallas, Texas: "Originated at Longview, Texas, by an old man named Orland Madox who died several years ago. It is a regular, annual and heavy bearer. The fruit is very large, rather flat, deep colored, striped, somewhat resembling Ben Davis in color. It is a most excellent eating apple, good from September till Christmas here in the South. The tree stands the southern climate better than any other apple I know of." No catalog listings.

❦ **MAE:** Sold in 1859 by Hopewell Nurseries, Fredericksburg, Virginia. No description.

❦ **MAGNATE** (Magnet, Stayman's No. 1, Stayman's Superior, Stayman's No. 2): Originated from Winesap seeds planted in 1866 by Dr. J. Stayman of Leavenworth, Kansas, who originated the Stayman Winesap from the same batch of seeds. Dr. Stayman, a medical doctor and a noted pomologist, bequeathed his extensive collection of notes and other data to the USDA when he died in 1903. Magnate was sold only by Eastern Shore Nurseries of Denton, Maryland, from 1899 to 1909 under the names Stayman's No. 1, Stayman's No. 2, and Magnate. *See* Stayman.

Fruit medium to large, round to roundish conical; skin smooth, glossy, rich yellow washed with crimson over almost the entire surface and indistinctly striped with purple, usually with a whitish bloom; dots numerous, variable in size, yellow or red; stem slender, short, curved in a large, deep, furrowed, faintly russeted cavity; calyx closed; basin medium in width and depth, gradually sloped, furrowed; flesh yellowish stained with red, fine-grained, juicy, subacid. Ripe September–December in Kansas.

❦ **MAGNOLIA:** Apples were sent to Charles Downing before 1878 by the prominent Tennessee nurseryman J. W. Dodge.

Fruit large, roundish oblate, somewhat conical; skin yellow striped and splashed with red.

Flesh yellow, slightly coarse, juicy, aromatic. Ripe December/January. No catalog listings.

**MAGYUR:** Mentioned but not described in an 1898 Alabama agricultural experiment station bulletin. Probably of Hungarian origin. No catalog listings.

**MALONEY** (Rosedale Pippin): Originated about 1870 by I. Keicher of Conklin, Washington County, Tennessee. In 1897, this apple was described both by the American Pomological Society and by a Tennessee agricultural experiment station bulletin. These descriptions differ so markedly that portions of both are given here for comparison.

Tennessee agricultural experiment station bulletin: Fruit above medium, roundish, oblate; skin thick, tough, smooth, yellow washed, striped and splashed with dark crimson; dots conspicuous, yellow, indented; stem medium length and rather stout in a large, deep, russeted cavity; calyx closed or partly open; basin almost small, shallow, furrowed; flesh yellowish, rather fine-grained, tender, juicy, subacid. Ripe autumn.

American Pomological Society: Fruit above medium to large, roundish to roundish oblate, conical, oblique; skin rough with russet patches and knobs, yellow and greenish with golden russet; flesh yellowish, rather fine-grained, tender, juicy, sweet. Ripe autumn. No catalog listings.

**MAMMOTH GREENING:** Origin unknown. Sold in 1912 by Clinton Nurseries, Clinton, Kentucky: "This splendid winter apple is adapted to lowlands as well as to highlands. These monster apples, when ripe, are a beautiful yellowish green and are fit for kings to eat. The demand takes them as fast as we can grow them." This is probably Gloria Mundi under another of its many synonyms.

Fruit very large, roundish oblate, conical; skin greenish yellow mixed with green; flesh white, tender, juicy, sprightly subacid. Ripe November/December.

**MAMMOTH JUNE:** Supposedly originated in Christian County, Kentucky, and sold in 1870 by the Forest Nursery, Fairview, Kentucky. This apple generally fits the description of Wilson's Summer.

Fruit medium, roundish oblate, conical; skin whitish yellow striped and splashed with two shades of red; dots light-colored; flesh very white, tender, moderately juicy, subacid (also said to be acid). Ripe July/August.

**MANGUM** (Cheese, Fall Cheese, Small Fall Cheese, Summer Cheese, Gully, Carter's Winter, Carter, Carter of Alabama, Alabama Pearmain, Patton, Sam Wingard, Seago, Sego, Macksfield, Mangham, Maxfield, Johnston's Favorite, Blakely, Billy Lewis Gully, Peak's Fall?, Hard's Limbertwig?, Gloucester Cheese?, Maiden's Favorite, Magnum [incorrectly]): Mangum is one of a handful of great southern apples and also is the most confusing. The confusion arises because Mangum has been known more often by its synonyms of Fall Cheese, Carter, and Gully. This is indeed unfortunate as these are also the names or synonyms of other, completely different apples. Thus, when an old reference discusses Gully or Fall Cheese, is it Mangum or is it another apple that is being discussed? Sometimes the answer to this question can be deduced, and sometimes it remains unclear.

The confusion deepens with the synonym Gully or Gulley. This is the name of one other apple, almost certainly the name of two other apples, and quite possibly the name of three other apples!

From the many synonyms of Mangum, this must be a very old variety, perhaps dating back to the early 1800s. The first reference to Mangum is a brief magazine article in 1853: "Said to be a native of Jackson County, Georgia, and exhibited by William H. Thurmond, Esq., of Atlanta at the state fair in 1852. An excellent apple of medium size which keeps well until March. Tree very prolific; certain of a crop."

Mangum is well adapted to southern soils and climate. It has the three prerequisites rural southerners looked for in an apple—excellent eating quality, good keeping ability, and a healthy, productive tree that blooms late. Let us continue to hope that somewhere in the South an old Mangum tree still lives and this variety can be resurrected.

Fruit medium, oblate conical; skin yellowish striped and shaded with red, perhaps a russet red;

dots numerous, whitish or bronze; stem short and small in a broad, russeted cavity (one reference says a small cavity); basin shallow and corrugated; flesh yellow, very tender, juicy, aromatic, mild subacid (two references say fine-grained). Ripe October. It should be noted that several descriptions of Mangum differ markedly, particularly the description by Warder (1867) of an apple he received from Alabama under the name Patton. Catalog listings as Mangum: VA, NC, SC, GA, AL, MS, LA, TN, KY, AR (1856–1915).

❦ **MARKET:** A Virginia apple sold from 1858 to 1869 by two Virginia nurseries.

Fruit round, red-striped, subacid.

❦ **MARL BANK:** Sold from 1869 to 1904 by the Franklin Davis Nursery, Richmond, Virginia. No description.

❦ **MARSH:** Grown from a seed of the Buff apple planted in 1876 by Mr. Marsh of Blount County, Tennessee.

Fruit medium, round, slightly angular; skin smooth, dull green with dull red stripes and clouds; dots gray, numerous; stem rather stout, five-eighths of an inch long, in a medium-size, irregular, abrupt cavity, knobbed on one side; basin large, round, shallow, gradually sloped; flesh greenish white, moderately tender, very juicy, mild subacid. Ripe winter. No catalog listings.

❦ **MARTHA WASHINGTON:** An Arkansas apple that originated before 1896.

Fruit large; skin yellow with red stripes; flesh subacid. Ripe winter. No catalog listings.

❦ **MARTIN:** Charles A. Martin discovered this apple in Natchitoches Parish, Louisiana, in 1936, and patented it 1943. Possibly fire-blight-resistant.

Fruit medium to large, round; skin thick, waxy, glossy, mostly yellow blotched with red; dots large; flesh yellowish, firm, tender, crisp, aromatic, mild subacid. Ripe mid-August. No catalog listings.

❦ **MARY BELL:** A seedling found about 1805 in Lincoln County, Kentucky, by a woman named Mary Bell and was being grown in Missouri around 1870. No description. No catalog listings.

❦ **MARY CHESTER:** A southern apple of unknown origin briefly described by Warder (1867).

Fruit oblate; skin red-striped; flesh subacid. No catalog listings.

❦ **MARY GOLD:** Listed but not described in 1872 by Joshua Lindley's Nursery of North Carolina.

❦ **MARY MOYER** (Mary Mayer): A Georgia apple.

Fruit large, oblate, red stripes on yellow background; flesh subacid. Ripe September–November. Catalog listings: SC, GA, MS, (1858–78).

❦ **MARY WOMACK** (Womack): A chance seedling found before 1867 on the farm of George Womack near Middletown, Kentucky, and named for his wife by the Kentucky Horticultural Society. Probably a seedling of Rambo. Tree bears full crops on alternate years with small crops in between. Sold by a Kentucky nursery in 1897.

Fruit medium, oblate; skin whitish faintly striped and splashed with red on the sunny side; dots numerous, small and large, brown; stem short in a large, deep cavity; calyx closed; basin large, shallow, slightly corrugated; flesh whitish yellow, fine-grained, tender, moderately juicy, mildly sweet. Ripe August/September in Kentucky.

❦ **MARYLAND** (Maryland June, Maryland Beauty, Maryland Red Streak): A Maryland cider apple that originated in colonial times and was planted by George Washington in the 1760s. An apple of this name has been found by Tom Brown in Clemmons, North Carolina, but has not yet fruited for me.

Fruit medium to large, roundish oblate; skin yellow, mostly covered with dark red stripes when fully ripe; flesh yellow (Ragan says white), juicy, tender, coarse, subacid. Ripe late June–August, but one reference says October. Catalog listings: NC, KY (1870–1902).

❦ **MARYLAND MAIDEN'S BLUSH** (Maryland Maid, Maiden's Blush): Sold from 1898 to 1912 by Eastern Shore Nurseries of Denton, Maryland: "This is an exceedingly fine fall apple, and it is a pity that it has to be burdened with so much name, but it carries the name suggested by that eminent pomological authority—the lamented Charles Downing, who added the prefix Maryland in order to avoid confusion with the other fine Maiden's Blush variety. It is a product of this peninsula and is known to everyone here as Maiden's Blush. Above medium size when well grown; yellow with a distinct blush; flesh white, fine-grained, tender, and of excellent quality. Tree vigorous, bearing while quite young. Very productive."

Fruit medium to large, roundish oblate; skin smooth, easily bruised, creamy white with a delicate, faint blush; cavity wide and deep; basin wide and shallow; flesh creamy white, tender, juicy, very fine-grained, subacid. Ripe August.

❧ **MARYLAND SPICE:** Listed in 1913 by Eastern Shore Nurseries, Denton, Maryland.

Fruit medium, skin red. Ripe midsummer.

❧ **MASON'S STRANGER** (Mason Pippin, Izzard, Old Field Apple): From an article in an 1868 issue of *The Southern Planter and Farmer* magazine: "This apple was discovered about thirty years ago by some gentlemen in a fox chase on the Sandy Grove plantation of Dr. George Mason of Greenville County, Virginia. It was growing in an old field remote from any habitation, and this circumstance has caused some parties to call it the Old Field Apple. A Mr. Izzard grafted from it and from him it was called the Izzard Apple. Dr. Mason has always called it the Stranger Apple, and by that cognomen I propose to introduce it to the public at large as Mason's Stranger Apple."

Mason's Stranger is thought to be a seedling of the Yellow Newtown Pippin and was said to be superior to that fine apple when grown in central and eastern Virginia.

Fruit below medium to large, oblate, sometimes angular; skin smooth, greenish or bright yellow, usually bronzed or lightly blushed in the sun; dots few, light brown; stem medium to long (Downing says short) in a deep, acute, large, brown cavity; calyx open; basin large, deep, wavy (Downing says smooth); flesh whitish, firm, juicy, mild subacid. Ripe December–March or April. Catalog listings: MD, VA, NC, GA (1869–1904).

❧ **MASSEY'S WINTER** (Massay's Seedling?): A southern apple of unknown origin described only as "small, handsome, long keeping, of good quality." Catalog listings: GA, KY (1861–70).

❧ **MATHEWS:** Originated before 1875 on the farm of Hugh Foster near Alton Depot, Nelson County, Virginia, where it was popular for family use. The tree bears heavily in alternate years.

Fruit medium, roundish oblate, slightly conical; skin smooth, whitish shaded with pale dull red where exposed to the sun; dots numerous, large, light-colored, a few areole; stem short and small in a medium-size cavity; calyx closed; basin rather abrupt, deep, slightly corrugated; flesh white, fine-grained, tender, juicy, subacid. Ripe October–January. No catalog listings.

❧ **MATILDA:** Apples of this name were sent to the 1871 meeting of the American Pomological Society by the Dollins and Brothers Nursery of Albemarle County, Virginia. No description. No catalog listings.

❧ **MATLOCK'S SUMMER** (Mattock's Summer?): Probably of Georgia origin.

Fruit large, oblate; skin red-striped; flesh tender, juicy, almost sweet. Ripe July. Catalog listings: GA, KY (1857–70).

❧ **MATTY:** Apples sent to the USDA in 1910 by W. R. Ballard of College Park, Maryland.

Fruit below medium, roundish oblate, sides unequal; skin yellow, mostly covered with two shades of red; dots small, russet; stem medium length in a rather narrow cavity; calyx closed; basin abrupt, medium size; flesh whitish tinged with red. Ripe September/October. No catalog listings.

❧ **MAVERICK'S SWEET** (Maverack Sweet, Sweet Mavarack): Raised by Dr. Samuel Maverack, Pendleton District, South Carolina, and widely grown in the South. A sweet apple on a late-blooming tree with a flavor often described as rich, but one catalog says, "In certain localities it is apt to be too sweet and without flavor."

Fruit large, roundish oblate, angular, ribbed; skin russet green or yellow with a dark red cheek (also described as mostly red), sometimes with a bloom; dots few, gray, sometimes dotted with black near the stem; stem short in a large, open, russeted cavity; calyx open; basin deep, corrugated; flesh yellowish, rather coarse, crisp, very juicy, sugary, sweet. Ripe October–February. Catalog listings: VA, GA, SC, NC, AL, MS, KY, TX (1857–1904).

❧ **MAXEY** (Maxey Red, Maxley): A good-keeping

Kentucky apple sold by Kentucky nurseries from 1870 to 1897. The tree is an annual bearer.

Fruit above medium, roundish to somewhat oblate (but pictured in an 1869 magazine as a slightly oblong apple), slightly conical; skin smooth, light green, mostly covered with mixed red and broken stripes; dots few, small, mostly dark, but some light-colored; stem short or medium length in a deep, acute, lightly russeted, sometimes lipped cavity; calyx open; basin shallow, broad, regular; flesh yellow (Downing says whitish), rather firm, juicy, (Downing says not very juicy), subacid. Ripe March and keeps until May or even later.

❦ **MAYBERRY SEEDLING:** Listed in 1869 by Richmond Nurseries, Richmond, Virginia. No description.

❦ **MAYBIN:** Listed in 1863 by a Pennsylvania nursery as a South Carolina apple. No description except ripe July.

❦ **MAYNARD NO. 1:** Said by Warder (1867) to be a Kentucky apple. No description. No catalog listings.

❦ **McAFEE** (McAfee's Nonsuch, McAfee's Red, Large Striped Winter Pearmain, Large Striped Pearmain, Striped Pearmain, Stine, Stein, Striped Winter Pearmain, Striped Sweet Pippin, Snorter, Nonesuch, Uncle Zeeke, Missouri Superior, Gray's Keeper, Storr's Wine, Vallandigham, White Crow, New Missouri, Parks' Keeper, Indian, Russian, Stephenson's Pippin, Wyandotte, Zeeke, Pride of Texas?, Loge, Starr Apple, Winter Pearmain, Missouri Keeper, Gray Apple, Ladies Favorite, Mississippi Superior?, Missourian): With the exception of Nickajack, no southern apple has as many synonyms as McAfee, clear testimony to its early origins and wide popularity. McAfee is a fascinating apple because, in spite of being over two hundred years old, much is known of its origins and early history. This knowledge comes from a concerted effort by pomologists in 1869 and 1870 to sort out its history. These pomologists included Dr. Warder of Ohio, author of the book *American Pomology: Apples* (1867), Dr. Howsley, president of the Kansas Horticultural Society, and Reuben Ragan, a prominent farmer and horticulturist in Indiana and father of the great pomologist W. H. Ragan.

The following is an account of the origin of McAfee written by Dr. Howsley in 1871: "A colony from Virginia of five brothers named McAfee, together with other persons, moved to Kentucky in 1779. They erected a fort on the banks of the Salt River five miles below Harrodsburg, Kentucky. After clearing some land, the McAfee brothers planted peach pits and apple seeds. From the apple seeds thus sown sprang the tree under consideration. They planted orchards from the seedlings and this tree stood in the orchard of George McAfee, the oldest of the five brothers. Col. John McAfee, the grandson of George McAfee, now lives on the old homestead. He says in letters to us that the original tree was a seedling and was called McAfee's Nonsuch after it commenced to spread through the country."

A personal recollection of W. H. Ragan in the USDA files, dated 1902, has this to say about the McAfee: "My father, the late Reuben Ragan of Indiana, was raised near McAfee's Station in Kentucky. In 1820, he removed to Putnam County, Indiana, bringing the McAfee with him where he introduced it largely in that section. A friend of his, John Burford, in removing to Missouri, took scions of McAfee to Missouri where it thrived under a number of synonyms, among them Parks' Keeper and Large Striped Pearmain."

In an 1870 issue of *The Gardener's Monthly* magazine, Dr. Howsley explained the origin of several synonyms of McAfee: "Large Striped Pearmain is the McAfee, having received the name from Col. Allen of Holly Spring Nursery in Nelson County, Kentucky. Col. Allen thought Large Striped Pearmain was more descriptive of the apple, hence he called it that. Winter Pearmain is the same, also having been called that by Col. Allen about 1836. Park's Keeper is also the McAfee, it having acquired that name in Kentucky also."

In 1908, a USDA observer reported that the McAfee was growing and fruiting well in the southern piedmont and mountains, often producing fruit when others failed. He noted that its dull color limited the usefulness of the McAfee as a market fruit.

In North Carolina, McAfee was commonly called Stine or Stein. Tom Brown recently found a Stine apple being grown by Ora Burnette near Canton, North Carolina, which needs more time for identification.

Fruit medium to large, roundish oblate, slightly conical; skin yellow, mostly covered with light and dark red, yet showing the yellow background through the red, often with a thin bloom making the apple look gray, some russet; dots few, gray, some areole; stem medium (Downing says short to long) in a large, open, deep, often russeted cavity; calyx closed; basin shallow; flesh yellowish, juicy, rather coarse, crisp, mild subacid inclining to sweet. Ripe October–February or later. Catalog listings: MD, VA, GA, AL, LA, TN, KY, TX (1824–1917). *See also* Pride of Texas.

❦ **McALISTER:** Sold in 1916 by the Greenville Nursery Company of Greenville, South Carolina: "Large, red-striped apple. Begins ripening last of August and will hang until frost. Sure bearer."

❦ **McBRIDE'S WAXEN:** A conical, yellow, sweet apple of unknown origin sold in 1861 by the Fruitland Nursery, Augusta, Georgia.

❦ **McCORD** (Arlington Queen): Originated in the Pleasant Valley community of Giles County, Tennessee, perhaps as early as 1815, in a seedling orchard planted by Jesse Abernathy (1778–1852). He called it Arlington Queen. Arlington was the name he gave to his farm and house. Probably a seedling of Buckingham. Tree vigorous and productive but slow to begin bearing. Fruit ripens over a six-week period.

Fruit large, oblate; skin thin, smooth, greenish white with faint pinkish stripes near the stem on the sunny side; dots few, small, brown or greenish; stem short or medium length in a deep, wide cavity; calyx open; basin abrupt, large, deep; flesh yellow, fine-grained, tender, juicy, subacid. Ripe August/September. No catalog listings.

❦ **McCROSKEY:** Originated from Winesap seeds planted about 1875 by H. M. McCroskey, Glenloch, Monroe County, Tennessee. Highly praised in an 1896 Tennessee agricultural experiment station bulletin: "We consider this the most valuable new seedling apple that has been brought to our notice in this state. Its main points of merit are productiveness, vigor in growth, symmetry, beauty of fruit and quality." The USDA Pomologist in Washington, D.C., also praised the McCroskey: "This is one of the finest apples sent to the Division of Pomology from Tennessee. It looks like a highly colored York Imperial but is far superior in quality to that variety. I should be pleased to receive a few scions for my own orchard in Pennsylvania."

In spite of its obvious quality, this fine apple was not listed in any old southern nursery catalogs, and the McCroskey now is almost certainly extinct.

Fruit medium, roundish, flattened on the ends, very symmetrical; skin thick, smooth, yellow, nearly covered with bright red (one reference says light and dark red); stem rather long in a regular, medium-size, deep, abrupt, somewhat russeted cavity; calyx open; basin medium size, deep, abrupt, slightly corrugated; flesh yellowish, crisp, very juicy, mild subacid. Ripe winter and has been kept until June. No catalog listings. ❖ **Plate 102.**

❦ **McCULLERS' WINTER:** In 1880, Mr. J. J. L. McCullers of Wake County, North Carolina, wrote this letter to a Raleigh nurseryman: "This apple originated on my farm as an accidental seedling. It is in every respect a first class fruit, being a little above medium size, red with a yellow background, speckled, oblong. The tree was discovered by my boys while opossum hunting three years ago. It keeps without care until April. It will keep better than any apple I ever saw. Its greatest fault is that it takes too long to get mellow—usually about the first of March. The tree bears full crops annually. The original tree stands in a piney old field, and there are at least a dozen large pines within 20 feet of it." Another description says McCuller's Winter is almost entirely dark red.

A description in a catalog says that fruit grown in 1879 was still in good condition in February 1881 "with no signs of decay." Several old catalogs recommended this apple for growing in the coastal plains of the South. Catalog listings: VA, NC (1884–1915).

❦ **McDONALD'S RED** (MacDonald): A Georgia apple.

Fruit medium to large; skin mostly red-striped. Ripe November–March. Catalog listings: MD, VA, SC (1859–89).

❦ **McDOWELL'S SWEET** (McDowell's Neverfail?, McDowell's Winter, McDowell's Red?): Originated in North Carolina.

Fruit medium to large, roundish oblate; skin yellow, mostly shaded with light and dark red, almost purplish in the sun; stem short; calyx closed; basin narrow, corrugated; flesh whitish, tender, juicy, mildly sweet. Ripe October–December. Catalog listings: VA, GA, SC, KY (1856–71).

❦ **McGREW SWEET:** Sold in 1845 by the Joel Wood Nursery, Wheeling, West Virginia (then Virginia).

Fruit medium, roundish, pale yellow. Ripe December–March.

❦ **McGWIRE:** From a letter written to the USDA in 1898 by Dr. S. Wolf of Grandview, Rhea County, Tennessee: "Mr. McGwire (for such he spells his name) bought land 5 or 6 miles from Crossville, Cumberland County, Tennessee, in 1867 and found an apple tree growing on the place, supposed to be a seedling. It has been propagated by top grafting and through one nursery. The tree is a thrifty grower, a young and abundant bearer, upright, open."

Fruit large, roundish conical; skin yellow, heavily striped with light and dark red; dots numerous, whitish; stem very short in a wide, greenish cavity; basin wide, abrupt, deep; flesh whitish. Ripe October. No catalog listings.

❦ **McKINLEY** (McKinley's Green, McMillin): The following was written in 1892 by William Hy Smith, owner of Smith's Nursery, Franklin, Tennessee:

"Learning from friends in Nashville that there was a valuable new apple near Pekin, Putnam County, Tennessee, I visited the owner a few days since. The original tree is gone, but there are eleven bearing trees in the orchard, all of them grown from sprouts from the original tree. I would take them to be at least forty years old. They range from six feet to six feet ten inches in circumference. They are situated on a very high ridge at an old tavern [known as Raulston's Stand and built in 1795] on the main thoroughfare from Nashville to Cookeville. The trees are upright and spreading, of very distinct habit, with one peculiarity more plainly marked than I have seen anywhere before. Many of the main limbs and much of the best young growth crooks back and forth at nearly every bud, giving them a wavy appearance, which enables the close observer to distinguish the trees at a glance. The apple is very large, light green, becoming a rich yellow in winter, of fine flavor, good in August and keeps well all winter, and cooks well. It is called McKinley after the originator [R. B. McKinley, 1830–1918], and is certainly a seedling of Putnam County, Tennessee."

Fruit large, roundish; skin smooth, thick, greenish yellow with a suggestion of a blush on the sunny side; dots brown or gray, some areole; stem short to medium length in a medium-size, gradually sloped, somewhat russeted cavity; calyx open; basin medium in size and depth, gradually sloped with shallow furrows; flesh greenish yellow, rather coarse, tender, juicy, subacid. Ripe late winter. Catalog listings: TN, KY, TX (1893–1902).

❦ **McMULLEN:** In 1888, Joe McMullen of Stonewall, DeSoto Parish, Louisiana, purchased several unknown apple trees from a traveling nursery peddler. One tree bore excellent fruit and was named McMullen about 1905. Described in a 1908 Louisiana agricultural experiment station bulletin as "the best one grown so far in Louisiana."

Fruit medium to large, roundish oblate; skin greenish washed with two shades of dark red; dots few but conspicuous; stem short, rather stout and knobbed in a broad, abrupt, often lipped cavity; basin wide and deep, slightly furrowed; flesh yellowish, almost fine-grained, tender, juicy, subacid. Ripe September/October. No catalog listings. ❖ **Plate 103.**

❦ **McMURRY'S FAVORITE** (McMurry): Originated on the Clark or McMurry farm about 1845 in Robertson County, Tennessee. Tree productive. Fruit ripens over a period of about a month.

Fruit medium, roundish oblate; skin thin, smooth, yellowish, nearly entirely washed, striped and splashed with light and dark red; dots small, numerous; stem short, stout, downy, in a broad, shallow, lightly russeted cavity; calyx closed; basin broad, shallow, gradually sloped; flesh nearly white, fine-grained, tender, juicy, mild subacid. Ripe July/August. No catalog listings.

❦ **McNASH:** A Maryland apple sold from 1894 to 1899 by Eastern Shore Nurseries of Denton, Maryland.

Fruit medium size; skin greenish yellow with a blush. Ripe winter and a good keeper.

❦ **MEAD'S KEEPER** (Meade): A Virginia apple.

Fruit medium size; skin red; flesh tender, juicy. Ripe November–June. Catalog listings: VA, DC, SC (1856–78).

❦ **MEADOW WOODS:** A South Carolina apple listed in 1860 by a South Carolina nursery. A medium-size apple; ripe November.

❦ **MEALING:** Mentioned but not described at the 1914 meeting of the Georgia Horticultural Society. No catalog listings.

❦ **MEBANE:** A North Carolina apple listed in 1860 by West-Green Nurseries, Greensboro, North Carolina. No description except ripe fall.

❦ **MECKLENBURG:** Sold from the 1893 to 1895 by the J. Van Lindley Nursery, Greensboro, North Carolina: "Originated on the farm of T. A. Squires, Mecklenburg County, North Carolina. Medium size, faint stripes; flesh yellow with a rich aroma. Its appearance and quality is nearest that of the Esopus Spitzenburg, the best flavored apple of the northwestern states. It is a new North Carolina seedling and a good keeper."

❦ **MENTZER:** From a letter to the USDA written in 1894 by John Martin, Jr., Smithburg, Maryland: "Fruit hardly eatable until late spring. As near as I can learn, this variety originated on the farm of George Mentzer, dec'd, many years ago. The original tree is dead, but quite a number of persons have grafts from the parent tree. About the most that can be said in its favor is its long keeping qualities. I have heard of them being kept two years. Its extreme acidity prevents its use until late spring, when it tones down, and is then an apple of fair quality." No catalog listings.

❦ **MERCER:** W. H. Lewis of Pike County, Mississippi, wrote this description in an 1872 issue of *The Southern Gardener* magazine: "Jeremiah Smith, one of the first and most successful fruit raisers in Pike County, obtained grafts of it from a Baptist minister by the name of Mercer, about fifty years ago, hence the name. Proving to be a valuable apple, it has been cultivated on all kinds of soils with uniform success. The tree is a strong grower, bears young, and has abundant and regular crops. The apple is above medium size, varying from flat to conical; skin thin, yellow with pale red streaks in the shade but the apple is almost red in the sun; flesh fine-grained, white, and a peculiarly rich subacid flavor. Time of ripening, all the month of July. Indispensable in any collection of apples." No catalog listings. This apple is different from the apple (or crabapple) named Mercer that was developed in South Dakota about 1892 and used mainly for cooking and jelly.

❦ **METALBI/METELL:** Two apples mentioned but not described in an 1898 Alabama agricultural experiment station bulletin. Certainly of foreign origin and probably the same apple. No catalog listings.

❦ **METTS:** Listed in 1923 by Lenoir Nurseries of La Grange, North Carolina. No description.

❦ **MEXICO** (Mexican?): From the 1924 catalog of the Cibolo Nursery, Cibolo, Texas: "A wild apple found in the Mexican mountains; a strong, healthy grower and a heavy bearer of good sized, fine flavored red apples; stands our hot sun better than any other apple on our grounds." This apple is different from the Mexico apple of Connecticut origin, but is probably the same as an apple named Mexican that was listed by an Arkansas nursery in 1916.

❦ **MILBURN** (K's Seedling): Originated before 1896 on the farm of John K. Beale, Greene County, Tennessee.

Fruit large, oblong, flattened on the ends; skin thin, rather smooth, bright yellow; stem medium length in an abrupt, medium-size cavity; basin regular, medium depth; flesh white, fine-grained, tender, juicy, mild subacid. Ripe late winter. No catalog listings.

❦ **MILES:** Originated prior to 1915 by L. C. H. Ayers, Midway, Tennessee.

Fruit medium to large, roundish conical; skin yellowish; flesh mild subacid. Ripe summer. No catalog listings.

❦ **MILLBROOK:** Described to the American Pomological Society in 1897 as a chance seedling that grew up on a town lot in Wyoming, Delaware.

Fruit medium, roundish oblate; skin smooth, bright red striped with darker red; dots numerous, light yellow; stem short in a medium-size, green cavity; calyx closed; basin medium size, corrugated; flesh yellowish white, fine-grained, crisp, subacid. Ripe early winter. No catalog listings.

❦ **MILLS:** Described in the 1902 catalog of the J. Van Lindley Nursery, Greensboro, North Carolina: "We obtained this apple from Mr. Eli Bradley of Polk County, North Carolina. He says it originated in his section. Resembles Grimes Golden but is much more prolific. Mr. Bradley says it bears more fruit than any other tree he has ever seen unless it be the Abundance Plum. Color light yellow; quality good; tree a good grower and an annual bearer. Autumn." In 1860, a South Carolina nursery catalog listed a Mills apple from South Carolina, ripe December. Probably the same apple.

❦ **MIMS:** A very showy apple on a productive tree that originated with Robert Mims of Edgefield County, South Carolina. Described at the 1883 meeting of the American Pomological Society.

Fruit above medium, oblate; skin orange covered with crimson and splashes of buff; dots numerous; stem one-half inch long and slender in a moderately deep cavity; calyx closed; basin shallow, regular; flesh white, fine-grained, juicy, sweet. Ripe October/November. No catalog listings.

❦ **MISSISSIPPI WINTER SWEET:** Briefly mentioned in 1855 as a good winter apple for Mississippi. No catalog listings. No description except ripe winter.

❦ **MITCHELL'S CIDER:** Described in 1889 by the Georgia Department of Agriculture as a summer cider apple adapted to the southern and coastal regions of Georgia. No description. No catalog listings.

❦ **MITCHELL'S FAVORITE:** Apples of this name, grown by George E. Murrell of Fontella, Virginia, were exhibited at the St. Louis Exposition in 1904.

Fruit large, roundish conical; skin light yellow, almost covered with purplish red and having a light bloom; dots scattered, russet; stem medium length in a deep, narrow, greenish cavity; basin rather wide; flesh creamy white. Ripe winter and a good keeper. No catalog listings. ❖ **Plate 104.**

❦ **MOCK OF ARKANSAS** (Mock's Winter): This apple originated before 1897 on the farm of James Mock near Prairie Grove, Arkansas.

Fruit large, roundish, sides often unequal; skin almost smooth, greenish yellow, almost entirely covered with red with indistinct darker red stripes; dots numerous, yellow; stem long (also described as short) and stout in a medium-size, russeted cavity with a very large lip on one side; basin medium size, furrowed; flesh yellowish tinged with red, fine-grained, crisp, moderately juicy, subacid. Ripe winter. No catalog listings.

❦ **MOCK OF SOUTH CAROLINA** (Fall Mocks?): This is probably the same apple as the Fall Mocks, listed without description in 1863 by a Pennsylvania nursery as a South Carolina apple.

In 1867, Westbrook Nurseries of Greensboro, North Carolina, listed a different apple also named Mock: "Large, roundish, oblate, yellow with beautiful stripes of bright red intermingled with a brownish bronze in the sun; flesh firm and well flavored. Tree upright and prolific. October and November."

❦ **MOLLY** (Mollie Fancy?, Reinette Molly, Pomme Molly): Originated in Augusta, Georgia, and first described in 1859.

Fruit small, oblate, rather rectangular; skin yellow with brown dots; flesh white, firm, crisp, very sweet. Ripe late winter. This is probably the apple from the Mollie Fancy briefly mentioned in 1914 at the meeting of the Georgia State Horticultural Society: "Resembles Fort's Prize. Season early winter." No catalog listings.

❦ **MONOCACY** (Hoop, Bill Baumgardner, Baumgardner, Smith, Maryland): The original tree was a "wilding" that first fruited before 1849 on the farm of William Baumgardner on the Monocacy River in Carroll County, Maryland. In the fall, the fruit was so hard that local people would leave the apples on the tree until Christmas, thaw them out, and eat them. About 1860 a tenant on the Baumgardner farm put several bushels of these apples in a pit.

By spring, when no one else had any good apples, the apples in the pit were found to be sound and of high quality. A local nurseryman began selling trees of this variety, known locally as the Baumgardner or Hoop apple, and it was widely grown in Frederick and Carroll counties, Maryland. It acquired the name Monocacy about 1897 and this name gradually supplanted the other names. Monocacy was pictured and highly praised in the 1912 *USDA Yearbook*. In 1918, it was renamed Maryland by Westminster Nurseries in Maryland to obtain a more easily pronounced name.

Fruit medium to large, roundish, occasionally slightly oblate; skin smooth, yellowish green, almost entirely covered with dark crimson and striped with darker crimson; dots yellowish white, numerous, large and conspicuous; stem short in a medium to large, deep, abrupt cavity; calyx closed; basin medium in size and depth, gradually sloped, slightly furrowed; flesh yellowish white, sometimes tinted red, juicy, rather fine-grained. Ripe winter.

❦ **MOON:** A chance seedling found on the farm of W. J. Moon of Monroe, Walton County, Georgia, which first fruited in 1873. Described to the 1877 meeting of the American Pomological Society: "A very showy fruit, of good quality, with the peculiarity of having its fruit to commence ripening June 10th and continuing through the entire summer to last ripening about October 10th. Ripe and green apples on the tree indiscriminately during four months." Sold by the Fruitland Nursery of Augusta, Georgia, from 1889 to 1896, and it is quite possible that this is the same apple as the All Summer sold by a Georgia nursery in 1924.

Fruit above medium to large, roundish oblong, conical; skin tough, smooth, waxy, light yellow washed with crimson and with deeper crimson stripes; dots small and inconspicuous; stem very short in a narrow cavity; calyx closed or partially open; basin deep and narrow; flesh white tinged yellow, brittle, juicy, mild subacid. Ripe June–October.

❦ **MOORE'S BLIGHT PROOF:** Originated near Enterprise, Mississippi, before 1880 and was sold in 1921 by the Citronelle Orchard and Nursery Company, Citronelle, Alabama.

Fruit large, roundish, slightly oblate; skin red-striped; flesh very acid. A good keeper.

❦ **MORRIS WINTER** (Morris?): Originated in Hanover, Virginia, and considered a good apple for sandy soils. Sold by two Virginia nurseries from 1858 to 1869, without description. This probably is the same apple as the Morris briefly described by Warder (1867) as grown in Illinois.

Fruit large, oblong, russeted, subacid. Ripe winter.

❦ **MORTON:** A North Carolina apple sold in 1859 by Hopewell Nurseries, Fredericksburg, Virginia. No description.

❦ **MORVEN:** A small dessert apple, usually a brilliant scarlet color, which originated before 1889 on the Morven Fruit Farm near New Castle, Delaware. Thought to be a cross of Lady × Carthouse. The fruit is borne in bunches. The tree bears heavily in alternate years with lighter crops between.

Fruit small, oblate, five-sided; skin thin, smooth, glossy, pale yellow, mostly washed and striped with scarlet; dots large and gray; stem medium length in a russeted cavity; basin rather shallow, regular; flesh white, fine-grained, very juicy, sprightly subacid. Ripe winter. No catalog listings.

❦ **MOTT'S MAMMOTH** (Mott's Sweet?): Probably a Virginia apple.

Fruit large; skin greenish striped with red; flesh sweet. Ripe fall. Catalog listings: VA, KY (1859–70).

❦ **MOULTRIE'S WINTER** (Moultree, Indian Winter?): An Alabama apple.

Fruit medium to large, very flat; skin dull green with dull red stripes; dots russet; flesh whitish, fine-grained, crisp, juicy, aromatic, subacid or perhaps sweet. Ripe October–January in Georgia. Catalog listings: SC, GA, MS (1856–96). *See* Indian Winter.

❦ **MOUNT PLEASANT** (Mount Pleasant Sweet): Listed in 1845 by a West Virginia (then Virginia) nursery and in 1870 by a Kentucky nursery.

Fruit below to above medium, round, pale green, sweet. Ripe August.

❦ **MOUNTAIN BELLE:** The original tree was found in an old Indian field in Habersham County, Georgia, by the southern pomologist J. Van Buren. The fruit is not of high eating quality but is an excellent keeper. Listed in 1871 and 1872 by Georgia and South Carolina nurseries.

Fruit medium to large, oblate conical; skin orange shaded and striped with red; stem short in a wide, deep cavity; basin medium size, smooth; flesh white, hard, juicy, tough, subacid. Ripe November–May.

❧ **MOUNTAIN JUNE:** Originated prior to 1890 on the grounds of the Industrial School, Fountain Head, Tennessee. Tree productive but susceptible to fire blight.

Fruit medium size, red. Ripe early July. No catalog listings.

❧ **MOUNTAIN RED** (Kiss Me Quick): Apples sent to the USDA in 1914 by N. R. Wills of Mount City, Tennessee.

Fruit medium, roundish oblate; skin almost covered with bright red; dots numerous, areole with dark centers; stem long in a deep, russeted cavity; basin medium size; flesh white. Ripe October. No catalog listings.

❧ **MOUNTAIN SPROUT:** A North Carolina apple described in an 1853 issue of the *Magazine of Horticulture* and in an 1870 Kentucky nursery catalog.

Fruit medium or larger, oblong conical; skin greenish striped with red; dots numerous, white; flesh subacid. Ripe September/October.

❧ **MOUNTAINEER:** Mountaineer is a synonym of three apples, none of them of southern origin. It is also the name of the apple described here that was sold from 1884 to 1898 by several North Carolina nurseries. Origin unknown.

Fruit medium to large, roundish oblate; skin yellowish green, mostly covered with red or dark red; flesh yellow, fine-grained. Ripe midwinter.

❧ **MRS. de CARADEUC** (Mrs. Caradeuc's Apple, Caradeuc): A South Carolina apple sold by South Carolina and Georgia nurseries from 1858 to 1878.

Fruit small, oblate; skin yellow covered with russet; flesh subacid, high flavor. Ripe October/November.

❧ **MRS. RICHARDSON:** Sold in 1921 by Thompson's Nurseries of Waco, Texas: "Fruit large, yellow."

❧ **MULBERRY GREENING:** An apple of southern origin sold by Pomaria Nurseries of South Carolina in 1872: "Medium size, greenish yellow; excellent. Ripe December till February. A seedling of Mr. Kirbo on Mulberry River, Georgia, and a very productive variety."

❧ **MUNCH:** A South Carolina apple listed in 1860 by a South Carolina nursery. No description except a large apple, ripe August.

❧ **MUNROE** (Monroe?): Sold in 1870 by the Forest Nursery of Fairview, Kentucky.

Fruit large; skin yellow, mostly covered with red; flesh subacid. Ripe winter.

❧ **MURFREESBOROUGH:** A winter apple mentioned but not described in an 1891 Tennessee agricultural experiment station bulletin. Adapted to the valley of east Tennessee. No catalog listings.

❧ **MURKY GREEN:** Origin unknown. Listed from 1869 to 1904 by the Franklin Davis Nursery of Richmond, Virginia. No description.

❧ **MURRAY:** From a description in an 1853 issue of *Western Horticultural Review* magazine: "This fine specimen was brought into notice by Mr. Murray of Whitfield County, Georgia, and was named after him by the examining committee at the State Fair in 1852. Size from medium to large; flavor fine and brisk, being a pleasant subacid. Said to keep well until March. Tree said to be very prolific and its habit pendant; the fruit borne principally from the ends of the limbs. Local origin not known."

Fruit medium to large, oblong conical; skin yellow; flesh subacid. Ripe winter. No catalog listings. An apple named Murray was developed in Canada about 1980 and is obviously a different apple.

❧ **MY SWEETHEART:** Listed in the 1901 catalog of the Franklin Davis Nursery of Richmond, Virginia. No description.

❧ **MYERS:** A Virginia apple listed in the 1880 catalog of John Saul's Nursery, Washington, D.C.

Fruit large, juicy, sweet, and rich. Ripe July and August.

❧ **MYRICK:** Described in the 1909 catalog of Harrison's Nurseries, Berlin, Maryland: "We do not know of any other sort that would approach it from the standpoint of beauty. Prominent pomologists have pronounced it most meritorious. In prime during November and December. Round, oblate, and of good size. Rich yellow overlaid with pinkish red. The flesh is of fine texture and very juicy, subacid."

**NALE APPLE:** Listed from 1824 to 1857 by two Washington, D.C., nurseries. No description except ripe August.

**NALL'S WINTER** (Nall's Golden Pippin?): An apple named Nall's Winter was listed but not described in 1912 by Clinton Nurseries, Clinton, Kentucky. This may be the same as Nall's Golden Pippin, said in 1904 to be a new apple from Hardin County, Kentucky. No description.

**NANSEMOND BEAUTY** (Nanson Beauty?, Nansyman Beauty?): The first we hear of this apple is the following description presented to the 1875 meeting of the American Pomological Society by Franklin Davis, the prominent Virginia nurseryman: "Originated in Nansemond County, Virginia, and named by the Chuckatuck Agricultural Club for its appearance. It is a red winter apple as large or larger than the Winesap. Color bright, approaching carmine; excels Winesap in keeping qualities; excellent for market and dessert. It is regarded as a great acquisition where it originated as there is a scarcity of good winter apples in that part of the state."

In 1908, the USDA reported Nansemond Beauty to be widely grown in the piedmont of Virginia and North Carolina. Under good growing conditions, the fruit was "very highly colored and of good size." The USDA report then says, "It is so very poor in dessert quality that it is not a popular apple, though it is frequently very beautiful in appearance and sometimes sells at good prices." On poor soils, Nansemond Beauty apples have been found to be less brilliant in color. The fruit tends to drop before maturity.

An apple called "Manson Beauty," which is very similar in sound to the synonym Nanson Beauty, has been found in North Carolina by Tom Brown on the Jackson-Macon county line. This apple has fruited for me only once and closely resembles the description below but ripens in late August/September. More time is needed for full identification.

Fruit medium, roundish oblate, slightly conical; skin pale yellow, mostly covered with light and dark red, sometimes obscurely striped; stem short and small in a quite large, slightly russeted cavity; basin large, deep, slightly corrugated; flesh white, crisp, tender, juicy, subacid. Ripe January–April. Catalog listings: MD, VA, NC, AL, TN, KY (1880–1910). ❖ **Plate 105.**

**NANTAHALEE** (Nantahala, Maiden's Bosom, Yellow June?): Found before 1855 by Dr. W. O. Baldwin on an old Indian farm eight miles from Montgomery, Alabama, and subsequently given its name by the southern pomologist J. Van Buren. The tree has a straggling, drooping growth habit and blooms late.

Fruit medium to large, oblate conical, ribbed; skin yellowish green or yellow; dots few, gray; cavity large and uneven; calyx closed; basin small, corrugated; flesh white, tender, juicy, sprightly acid. Ripe July or later. Catalog listings: SC, GA, MS (1858–98).

**NASH** (Nash's Seedling): Originated before 1860 on the farm of Upton (or Arthur) Nash of Union County, Tennessee. Nash was the favorite apple in that county around 1900 and very successful elsewhere in east Tennessee. Its keeping qualities have been described as follows: "It ripens in September, remains mellow two or three months, then literally dries up, resembling brown sugar. It is good for dessert, cooking or drying."

Fruit large, roundish oblate or oblate, ribbed, sides often unequal; skin smooth, thin, tough, greenish yellow, mostly covered with dull red and striped at the apex with bright red; dots russet; stem medium length and slightly curved in a narrow, deep, russeted cavity with the russet spreading out over the top of the apple; calyx open; basin medium wide, deep, abrupt, green, ribbed; flesh yellow, greenish at the core, rather fine-grained, subacid. Ripe September–November. No catalog listings.

**NASHVILLE MAMMOTH** (Nashville): A Tennessee apple with some specimens reported to be sixteen inches in circumference and weighing as much as 22½ ounces. A good keeper for an early apple, "free from rot." Tree vigorous, drooping.

Fruit very large; skin deep yellow; flesh yellow, crisp, juicy, mild subacid. Ripens throughout July. Catalog listings: TN, TX (1887–1904).

**NEBO:** Sprouted from below the graft of a

"Jennette" tree (Ralls Janet) on the farm of George Collins near Rhea's Mill, Arkansas. Described in 1895 by the USDA Pomologist as "quality very good to best."

Fruit large, elongated, conical, sides often unequal; skin tough, moderately smooth, yellow washed with red with indistinct crimson stripes, overspread with a thin russet and with fine russet patches over much of the surface; dots conspicuous, russet; cavity medium size, irregular, gradually sloped, lipped, russeted; calyx open; basin medium size, regular, abrupt, furrowed, russeted; flesh whitish, satiny, fine-grained, tender, moderately juicy, sweet. Ripe early winter. No catalog listings.

❧ **NECTAR:** Originated before 1860 near Raleigh, North Carolina.

Fruit medium, oblate; skin green; calyx closed; stem short; flesh yellowish, juicy, sweet. Ripe August. No catalog listings.

❧ **NELSON ROCK** (Rock Apple): A seedling that grew before 1872 next to a large rock on the farm of Henry G. Roberts, near Greenfield, Nelson County, Virginia. Tree bears heavy and light crops in alternate years.

Fruit medium to large, oblate, slightly conical; skin pale greenish white but shaded, striped and splashed with light and dark red over most of its surface; dots light and gray; stem short and small in a large, deep cavity; calyx closed; basin rather broad, shallow, slightly corrugated; flesh whitish yellow, tender, juicy, mild subacid. Ripe December–March. No catalog listings.

❧ **NEQUASSA** (Nequasse, Nequassa Sweet): Originated near Franklin, Macon County, North Carolina.

Fruit large, oblate, prominently ribbed at the calyx end; sides often unequal; skin yellow-striped with red (also described as yellow flushed with brown and flecked with carmine); dots russet; stem medium length in a large, open cavity; basin smooth and open; flesh white, tender, rather fine-grained, very sweet. Ripe November–January. Catalog listings: SC, GA, KY (1861–78).

❧ **NERO:** Nero originated in Princeton, New Jersey, probably as a seedling of Romanite. The tree is well adapted to the piedmont and mountains of the South and bears large crops of attractive, good-keeping apples.

Fruit above medium, roundish, slightly conical; skin tough, glossy, greenish yellow, mostly covered with bright red overlaid with numerous, narrow, carmine stripes; dots small, whitish or russet; stem short to medium length and rather thick in an acute, medium-size, often russeted cavity; calyx usually closed; basin rather wide and sometimes gently furrowed; flesh yellowish, firm, moderately coarse, somewhat crisp, moderately juicy, mild subacid to almost sweet, aromatic. Ripe September and keeps well. Catalog listings: MD, VA, NC (1884–1913).

❧ **NEW FALL SWEETING:** Called a new apple in 1853 and sold by the North Carolina Pomological Gardens of Guilford County, North Carolina.

Fruit large, flat, pale green. Ripe September/October.

❧ **NEW RIVER BOAT APPLE** (New River): Originated before 1871 by Robert Porter, Sr., of Porter's Ferry, Virginia. Tree vigorous and a biennial bearer.

Fruit medium, oblate, sometimes oblique; skin bright yellow, rarely blushed; stem very short in a rather large cavity; calyx closed; basin medium size and slightly corrugated; flesh whitish, tender, moderately juicy, mild, "peculiar subacid," almost sweet. Ripe October–December. No catalog listings.

❧ **NEWBOLD'S EARLY:** Listed in the 1836 catalog of Clairmont Nurseries, Baltimore, Maryland. No description except ripe August.

❧ **NEWCOMER:** A Virginia apple listed by two Virginia nurseries from 1858 to 1904.

Fruit oblate, yellow, subacid.

❧ **NINE PARTNER'S LITTLE RUSSET** (Partners): Origin unknown.

Fruit small, roundish oblong; skin greenish, russeted. Ripe October–December. Catalog listings: MD, VA, NC (1836–56).

❧ **NIX GREEN** (Queen Apple, Nix, Nix's Green Winter, Carolina Winter, Carolina Winter Queen, Nick's Green): A seedling found growing in the orchard of John Nix, Habersham County, Georgia. Sold by two Virginia nurseries from 1859 to 1904.

Fruit large to very large (some references say medium), oblate, very conical; skin smooth, greenish yellow; dots numerous, light-colored; stem short; calyx closed; flesh white, firm, tender, subacid. Ripe November–January.

❦ **NIXON'S RED:** A winter apple listed in 1875 by the Middletown Nursery of Virginia. No description.

❦ **NIX'S LARGE RED STREAK:** Described in an 1863 Pennsylvania nursery catalog as a Georgia apple.

Fruit large; skin striped; flesh reddish. Ripe November–May.

❦ **NONSUCH SWEET WINTER:** Described in the 1863 catalog of a Pennsylvania nursery: "A valuable and popular apple from Virginia, resembling Ribston Pippin." No description.

❦ **NORTH CAROLINA BEAUTY:** From a letter that accompanied some apples sent to the USDA in 1899 by Thomas Coffey of Kelsey, Watauga County, North Carolina: "Originated about 20 years ago on Thomas Wright's farm in Caldwell County. It is now grown by many farmers. This apple will keep until spring. The tree is a very rapid grower, a good bearer and needs but little pruning. The acid of this apple is fine." The fruit was examined at the USDA and was thought to be Pennock or quite similar to it. No catalog listings. *See also* Carolina Beauty.

❦ **NORTH CAROLINA SWEET:** Listed in 1870 by the Forest Nursery of Fairview, Kentucky: "Fruit large, skin green, flesh rich and sweet." Ripe summer.

❦ **NORTH CAROLINA YELLOW:** Listed as a large, autumn apple in the 1878 catalog of Pomaria Nurseries of South Carolina. No description.

❦ **NORTH VIRGINIA MAMMOTH:** A Virginia apple that originated before 1905. No description. No catalog listings.

❦ **NORTON APPLE:** From an 1852 issue of *The Southern Cultivator* magazine: "A truly beautiful and good fruit, of large size, and said to keep until May. Tree vigorous and prolific. Exhibited by Colonel William Murray of Whitfield County, Georgia. Supposed to have originated with the Indians." No catalog listings.

❦ **NORTON PIPPIN** (Norton): Described by Downing in 1900, who said it originated with James Brewington of Freedom, Kentucky. Tree a biennial bearer.

Fruit medium or above, roundish, flattened on the ends; skin whitish yellow shaded with light and dark red over almost all the surface, some obscure stripes; dots few, light-colored, some areole; stem short to medium length in a medium-size, slightly greenish cavity; calyx closed; basin large, round, deep; flesh white, tender, juicy, subacid. Ripe November/December or perhaps earlier. No catalog listings.

❦ **NOVEMBER:** An apple listed by a North Carolina nursery from 1855 to 1860. No description except ripe November–January.

❦ **NUBA:** From the minutes of the 1897 meeting of the American Pomological Society: "Origin unknown; somewhat grown in Pulaski County, Kentucky. Named for Squire Nuba, near Somerset. Fruit small, oblate, sides unequal; skin yellow splashed and striped with crimson; subacid; very good; summer." No catalog listings.

❦ **NUNN:** From the 1904 catalog of Bonham Nurseries, Bonham, Texas: "A very large, oblong, dark red apple, of good quality. None better in size and color. Discovered in Fannin County, Texas, and introduced by me. Those who have seen it class it at the top. Ripens July and August."

❦ **O'BRIAN'S ORANGE:** From the 1886 catalog of Raleigh Nurseries, Raleigh, North Carolina: "A new apple from Granville County, North Carolina, introduced by Mr. Sollie O'Brian. This is a remarkable apple in that it commences to ripen in July and continues for three months, thus embracing almost the whole summer season. It is of fine size and appearance, roundish, orange color, with occasional dark splotches, flesh yellow, flavor approaching sweet, a novelty in fragrance, a single apple being sufficient to perfume a whole room. I consider this quite an acquisition. It is very popular in its native home and much sought after. Vigorous grower."

❦ **O'NEAL'S EARLY:** Sold from 1884 to 1888 by two North Carolina nurseries. Introduced by G. P. O'Neal of Abbeville, South Carolina, who also introduced Andrew's Winter: "Of fine size, striped with red on yellow ground. Quality fine.

Commences to ripen about the last of May and continues for several weeks."

❦ **OAT STACK:** Originated before 1850 by Madison Crisp on Peak's Creek in Macon County, North Carolina. The original tree grew where oats had been stacked up for drying.

Fruit small, red-striped, very juicy, and good for cooking and drying. Ripe September and a good keeper. No catalog listings.

❦ **OCONEE GREENING** (Oconee): Originated on the banks of the Oconee River just below Athens, Georgia, in an area now called Whitehall. Said to resemble the Disharoon in appearance, but a better keeper and more acid in flavor. Tree vigorous and a heavy bearer. "The best greening for the South," says one catalog.

Fruit medium or sometimes larger, roundish, flattened on the ends (also described as oblate); skin yellow or greenish with a brownish blush in the sun; dots scattered, russet; stem very short in a deep, russeted cavity; calyx open; basin wide, shallow, furrowed; flesh yellow, crisp, juicy, fine-grained, very aromatic, subacid. Ripe September–February. Catalog listings: GA, AL, MS, LA, KY (1858–96). ❖ **Plate 106.**

❦ **OCTOBER APPLE:** One of the varieties sold in 1920 by the Collinsville Nursery, Collinsville, Alabama, and named for the months of the year (*see* August Apple). "A large black apple with a yellow tint. The tree is hardy, thrifty, an annual bearer. These apples have been kept from October until June in perfect condition. They ripen after being gathered during the fall. Hard and firm. Bears handling and makes a fine seller."

❦ **ODOM:** An Alabama apple that was sold in 1871 by the Fruitland Nursery, Augusta, Georgia. No description except ripe November.

❦ **OGLEBY** (Ogilby, Oglesby, Oglevie?, Ogilby Superior): Described to the 1852 meeting of the American Horticultural Society by H. R. Robey of Fredericksburg, Virginia: "Raised by an old colored man from seed of a red fall apple. The tree has borne this the third year. The fruit is fine yellow, very rich, a little spicy. Specimens have been kept till February, and I suppose they would keep longer." Sold by North Carolina, Virginia, and South Carolina nurseries from 1858 to 1872.

Fruit medium or below, roundish oblate to oblate; skin greenish yellow, sometimes bronzed; dots medium size, scattered, gray and green; stem medium length, yellow, in an acute, brown cavity; calyx closed; basin abrupt and rather deep; flesh light yellow, juicy, breaking, crisp, subacid. Ripe October–February.

❦ **OKOLONA:** Originated in 1880 by S. H. Stepp of Dry Creek, Tennessee. Tree vigorous and a rapid grower.

Fruit large, oblate, sides often unequal; skin greenish yellow washed with pale red and striped with darker red; dots conspicuous, russet, many with dark centers; stem varies from short to long and slender to thick in a wide, deep, russeted cavity; basin medium size; flesh white, satiny, fine-grained, tender, sweet, dry when overripe. Ripe August/September. No catalog listings.

❦ **OLD DOMINION:** A winter apple listed in 1875 by the Middletown Nursery of Virginia. No description.

❦ **OLD HICKORY:** Listed in 1853 by the North Carolina Pomological Gardens, a nursery in Guilford County, North Carolina.

Fruit medium size, round, red. Ripe January–May.

❦ **OLD TOWN CRAB** (Spice Apple, Virginia Spice?): Origin credited to Virginia and first described in 1851. Almost certainly identical to Virginia Spice.

Fruit small, greenish yellow with brown specks; flesh greenish white, crisp, juicy, sweet. Ripe December–March. No catalog listings. Virginia Spice is available.

❦ **OLIVE:** Originated in Wake County, North Carolina, probably in the Olive community in extreme western Wake County where the Olive family was prominent. Sold by North Carolina nurseries from 1867 to 1895. Fruit borne in clusters.

Fruit small to medium, roundish to somewhat oblong, slightly conical; skin thick, tough, entirely dark red or crimson or mottled with red and striped with carmine; dots numerous, pale or gray, often large, conspicuous, areolar; stem short to medium (Downing says long) in a rather small, acute, moderately deep, narrow, usually russeted and furrowed cavity; calyx open; basin abrupt, almost shallow, often wrinkled; flesh tinged deep yellow, rather coarse, crisp, rather tough, juicy, aromatic, mild subacid to nearly sweet. Ripe November–January.

❦ **ONSLOW:** Originated in Onslow County, North Carolina, and sold from 1910 to 1921 by the J. Van Lindley Nursery, Greensboro, North Carolina.

Fruit above medium, roundish oblate; skin entirely dark red with light specks and faint darker stripes; flesh yellow. Ripe winter and a fine keeper.

❦ **OOLTEWAH:** Originated before 1895 by Mrs. Jennie Fowler of James County, Tennessee.

Fruit large, roundish oblate, sides sometimes unequal; skin thick, tough, greenish yellow, ripening to a golden yellow with russet patches and veinings; dots numerous, variable, russet; stem medium length in a large, deep, abrupt, russeted cavity; basin small, gradually sloped, shallow, furrowed; flesh yellowish, coarse, tender, juicy, subacid. Ripe August. No catalog listings.

❦ **OOSTANAULA** (White Sweet): Found growing in the center of a twenty-acre field in 1886 by I. F. Fisher of Apison, James County, Tennessee. Tree vigorous and a heavy bearer. Fruit valuable for fresh eating, cooking, and drying.

Fruit medium to large, roundish oblate; skin thin, smooth, glossy with fine russet markings near the basin, color greenish yellow with a faint blush on the sunny side; dots light colored with green bases; stem short to medium length in a large, deep, abrupt, russeted cavity; calyx open; basin abrupt, large, deep; flesh yellowish, satiny, tender, moderately juicy, sweet. Ripe July/August. No catalog listings.

❦ **ORANGE:** Several southern nurseries sold apples named Orange, usually without descriptions. Most of these are probably the Lowell, which has the synonym of Orange. One Maryland nursery listed Orange as a synonym of Summer Pound Royal. Catalog listings: MD, DC, VA, GA (1824–1904).

❦ **ORANGE PIPPIN:** Listed by five southern nurseries without description. There are two apples described under this name by Beach (1905). One is a European apple, ripe summer. The other is a New Jersey apple, ripe autumn. Catalog listings: MD, VA, KY (1836–1904).

❦ **ORRICK:** Origin unknown. Listed by a Kentucky nursery in 1897.

Fruit very large, roundish oblate, ribbed; skin yellow, mostly covered with red and sprinkled with small, gray dots; flesh yellow, subacid. Ripe winter and a good keeper.

❦ **OSBORNE'S CHEESE/OSBORNE'S PIPPIN:** These two varieties were listed as Georgia apples in an 1863 Pennsylvania nursery catalog.

*Osborne's Cheese*: Large; bright yellow; juicy. Ripe November–April.

*Osborne's Pippin*: Large; red-striped. Ripe November–February.

❦ **OSZI-VAJ:** Origin unknown, but certainly a foreign apple imported by the USDA. Mentioned in an 1898 Alabama agricultural experiment station bulletin.

Fruit medium, roundish conical; skin light green with red stripes on the sunny side; stem medium length in a corrugated cavity; calyx closed; basin deep, narrow, corrugated; flesh greenish. Ripe July/August. No catalog listings.

❦ **OYSTER BAY:** Listed in 1858 by Staunton Nurseries, Staunton, Virginia. No description.

❦ **OZARK** (Gano?): In 1884, the top died on an old Ben Davis tree on the farm of Thomas Marchal, Jr., Crowell, Benton County, Arkansas. The roots of the tree sent up some sprouts, and Mr. Marchal dug up a finger-sized sprout about three feet from the old trunk. Three years after he planted the root sprout, it bore a bushel of nice red apples that Mr. Marchal named Ozark. The description of the fruit is almost identical to the Gano, and some references list Ozark as a synonym of Gano. Sold by a Texas nursery from 1900 to 1904.

Fruit large, round, sometimes with unequal sides; skin smooth, light yellow, almost covered with carmine; dots small, light colored on raised bases; stem short and slender in a wide, deep, slightly russeted cavity; calyx closed or nearly so; basin abrupt, deep, wide; flesh white, tender, subacid. Ripe November/December.

❧ **OZONE** (Martin's Red, Red Russet): Here is a letter written to the USDA in 1888 by F. M. Farris of Ozone, Johnson County, Arkansas.

"This apple is known as Martin's Red or Red Russet. The latter name is more generally known here in Johnson County. The apple has been grown here for perhaps 35 years. It is said to have been raised from seed by one Mr. Martin who once lived in a backwoods district in the south part of Madison County, Ark. by some means unknown to us. One characteristic of the tree is that it sends up an abundance of sprouts from the main trunk near the ground which can be rooted and produce the same fruit. This apple was grown to some extent by a local nurseryman by the name of John Gimlin but was never generally introduced until taken up by the Ozone Nurseries. There is surely no better apple grown in the southwest. We consider it the richest apple grown by us. It is very hardy and has a longer season than any other apple grown here. Its productiveness and market qualities compare very favorably with the best Ben Davis and Winesap. Mr. L. Wood, an old orchardist here who has grown them for 20 years says that he would not give up the Red Russet for any apple that he has ever seen. His trees, while they have borne heavy crops, have never had a limb break with the fruit. The tree is an upright grower when young, bending and spreading as it fruits. The apple is surely an Arkansas Seedling and has never to our knowledge been introduced beyond the state."

Apparently the USDA Pomologist objected to the names Martin's Red and Red Russet and suggested this apple be named Ozone. Another letter from Mr. Ferris in 1888 says: "We will be pleased to call this apple Ozone."

Fruit above medium, roundish conical, flattened on the ends, sides sometimes unequal; skin tough, yellow splashed with crimson, sometimes with darker stripes, sometimes partly russeted; dots numerous and conspicuous, yellow or gray; stem short to medium and stout in a medium-size, deep, abrupt, green cavity; basin medium size, slightly furrowed; flesh yellowish, fine-grained, very tender, juicy, mild subacid. Ripe fall and early winter. No catalog listings.

Several Virginia catalogs listed a Red Russet apple from 1858 to 1901. This is probably Pryor's Red, which has the synonym Red Russet.

❧ **PAINTED LADY:** Listed in 1899 by the J. Van Lindley Nursery, Greensboro, North Carolina: "Similar to the Lady Apple and from its name is one of the most fancy colored apples." No description.

❧ **PAINTER:** Listed in 1869 by Richmond Nurseries, Richmond, Virginia. No description.

❧ **PALMER** (Pear Apple): An old Georgia variety that was being grown in Washington and Hancock counties in 1825 or earlier, where it was esteemed for its quality and market value. Flavor described as "almost the exact flavor of the pear" in one old catalog. The fruit is variously described in old references as resembling American Summer Pearmain (but larger) or Rhodes Orange (but matures a month earlier). Ripens a week or two after Red Astrachan.

Fruit medium to large, roundish oblate, slightly conical; skin light yellow, striped and splashed rather thinly with pale red over most of the surface; dots numerous, large, light-colored; stem medium length and slender in a medium-size, slightly russeted cavity; calyx closed or nearly so; basin large and deep; flesh whitish yellow, somewhat firm, juicy, slightly aromatic, subacid. Ripe mid-June in Georgia. Catalog listings: GA (1889–98).

This apple is probably different from the Pear Apple supposedly of Pennsylvania origin. In 1903, an Arkansas nursery named Hubach and Hathaway listed a Pear Apple that is also a different variety: Fruit large, yellow with a red cheek. Ripe winter.

❧ **PAOLO ALTO** (Paoli?): An apple described only as foreign, ripe August. Sold by the Fruitland Nursery, Augusta, Georgia, from 1858 to 1861.

❧ **PAPAW:** Described in an 1863 Pennsylvania nursery catalog: "Large, beautiful, sweet, rich, excellent. A winter apple received from Georgia." This must be a different apple than the Pawpaw of Michigan origin.

❧ **PARKER'S GREENING** (Parker?): A late-ripening Georgia apple listed by a Pennsylvania nursery in 1863 and a South Carolina nursery in 1872. No description. May be Park's Pippin.

**PARKER'S WINTER SWEET:** Originated in northwest Arkansas and introduced in 1925 by the John Parker and Son Nursery, Fayetteville, Arkansas.

Fruit large, red, sweet.

**PASMAN:** Origin unknown, but certainly foreign. Mentioned in an 1898 Alabama agricultural experiment station bulletin.

Fruit small, roundish oblate; skin almost entirely striped bright red; dots gray, some areole; stem long in a narrow, russeted cavity; basin very shallow; flesh creamy white. Ripe July/August. No catalog listings.

**PATTIE GRIMES:** Originated in Wicomico County, Maryland, and sold in 1889 by Snow Hill Nurseries, Snow Hill, Maryland: "Light red; flesh white, juicy, fine flavor; keeps well until May." *See* Grimes.

**PAUL:** A seedling that originated before 1884 on the farm of John Paul, Boone County, Arkansas, and extensively sold by local nurserymen in that area around 1900. "A very fine apple as to quality, size and flavor, taking the premium wherever exhibited." Tree an annual bearer.

Fruit very large, reddish, subacid. No catalog listings.

**PAYNE'S EARLY:** Origin unknown. Sold for a few years in the 1920s by H. F. Hillenmeyer and Sons, Lexington, Kentucky. Quality said to be excellent. No description.

**PAYNE'S WINTER:** Originated before 1869 on the farm of a Mr. Payne in Guilford County, North Carolina.

Fruit medium, roundish oval, somewhat conical; skin green, turning pale yellow when ripe, sometimes with a blush; flesh juicy, fine-flavored. A good keeper. No catalog listings.

**PEACH POND SWEET** (Peach Pound Sweet): A high-quality, sweet apple of New York origin sold by several Virginia nurseries from 1858 to 1904.

Fruit medium or below, roundish oblate; skin yellow, striped and splashed with two shades of red; stem long and slender in a deep, russeted cavity; calyx closed; basin narrow; flesh yellow, tender, fine-grained, moderately juicy, very sweet. Ripe September/October.

**PEACH RIDGE:** A seedling that originated about 1850 on the Castle Hill Farm in southwestern Virginia. A good-keeping dessert apple. No description. No catalog listings.

**PEAKE'S FALL** (Peak Fall, Hard's Limbertwig)/ **PEAKE'S YELLOW/PEAKE'S RED WINTER** (Peak): All are of South Carolina origin. Listed from 1860 to 1872 by Pomaria Nurseries of South Carolina.

Peake's Fall is described as above medium, oblate conical; skin whitish yellow with red stripes; stem rather long and slender in a deep cavity; calyx partially open; basin shallow and small; flesh white, brittle, very juicy, sprightly acid. Ripe October in South Carolina.

The same Pennsylvania nursery that listed Peake's Fall also listed Peake's Yellow and Peake's Red Winter as South Carolina apples, both ripe December.

**PEEBLES:** Originated by William M. Samuels near Clinton, Kentucky, and described at the 1895 meeting of the American Pomological Society.

Fruit above medium, oblong, flattened on the ends, slightly oblique; skin rather smooth, greenish yellow with a dull blush on the sunny side and some russet patches; dots light russet, many erupted; stem short in a deep, russeted cavity; calyx partly open; basin large, deep, abrupt, furrowed, cracked; flesh yellowish, breaking, juicy, subacid. Ripe early winter. No catalog listings.

**PENDLETON'S WINTER:** Origin unknown. Sold in 1870 by the Forest Nursery, Fairview, Kentucky: "Fruit below medium, yellow, shaded and striped with red." Ripe winter.

**PENINGTON RED:** An autumn apple listed but not described in 1872 by Joshua Lindley's Nursery, Greensboro, North Carolina.

**PENNSYLVANIA BLACK** (Penn Black): Sold by two Alabama nurseries from 1886 to 1890: "A local variety from Lincoln County, Tennessee." No description except ripe winter.

**PERKINS:** Originated with Judge Perkins of Cumberland County, Virginia, and sold by Virginia nurseries from 1895 to 1928. A seedling of Maiden's Blush, but larger and higher in quality. Several old catalogs describe it as "best quality" and "has no superior for August."

Fruit above medium to large; skin pale yellow; flesh white, tender. Ripe August/September.

Warder (1867) briefly describes a southern apple named Perkins that is somewhat similar to this apple. Fruit small, round; skin yellow; flesh subacid. Ripe October/November.

**PERKINS** of North Carolina (Perkins Red, Forney, Fleming): Upon comparing descriptions in old southern catalogs, it becomes obvious that there are at least two and probably three entirely different southern apples named Perkins. There are the Perkins from Virginia and the Perkins apple listed by Warder (both described just above), and this apple, which may have been rediscovered recently. *See* Perkins *in chapter 5*.

This Perkins apple originated before 1843 in Burke County, North Carolina, and was esteemed there for its lovely appearance, eating quality, and suitability as a market apple. It was being grown commercially in Lincoln County, North Carolina, in 1871. Downing (1900) describes this apple under the name Forney.

Fruit rather large, roundish to slightly oblong, somewhat conical, a little oblique; skin whitish, shaded and striped with light and dark red; dots numerous, small and large, light-colored, some areole; stem short in a rather narrow and deep cavity; calyx closed; basin large, round, wrinkled; flesh white, tender, moderately juicy, mild subacid. Ripe October/November. Catalog listings: NC, SC, GA (1853–61).

**PERVIS** (Pervis Winter, Pervis Red?): Originated in eastern North Carolina and considered a better keeper than Winesap.

Fruit medium or above; skin tough, red, russeted; flesh rich, melting when fully ripe. Ripe winter. Catalog listings: NC, KY (1870–1901).

**PETER THE GREAT:** Sold by two Kentucky nurseries from 1916 to 1925. No description. May be the Russian apple named Peterhof.

**PETREE'S FAVORITE:** Sold in 1870 by the Forest Nursery, Fairview, Kentucky: "Fruit rather small, yellowish red, rich, juicy and good." Ripe autumn.

**PHARR** (Pharr's Seedling): Probably of North Carolina origin. Described to the 1877 meeting of the American Pomological Society.

Fruit large to very large, roundish oblate, conical, oblique; skin deep yellow with some russet; flesh yellowish white, tender, juicy, mild subacid. Ripe November/December. No catalog listings.

**PICKETT** (Picket's Late, Pickett): Grown about 1840 by William Pickett of Ballard County, Kentucky, from the seed of an apple bought from a flatboat that landed at Fort Jefferson, Kentucky. The tree is vigorous, an early and abundant bearer. Sold by a Tennessee nursery in 1893. *See* Branch.

Fruit medium to large, roundish oblate to oblate; skin pale yellow, nearly overspread with light and dark red (also described as purplish red), and having some obscure stripes and grayish bloom; dots light-colored and brown; stem very short in a large, deep, slightly russeted cavity; calyx open; basin deep, round, slightly wrinkled; flesh whitish yellow, fine-grained, tender, juicy, subacid. Ripe December–April.

**PIEDMONT:** In 1915, the catalog of Crawford and Company of Statesville, North Carolina, described an apple named Piedmont that is a different variety from the Piedmont Pippin, described below: "Rather above medium, a beautiful apple, striped with red on pale yellow, juicy, subacid and fine-grained. Very prolific and fine for market, lasting nearly a month. June and July."

**PIEDMONT PIPPIN** (Dollins Pippin): Originated before 1875 on the farm of James Woods of Rockford, Virginia. Supposedly a seedling of the Albemarle Pippin, which it resembles. A high-quality, long-keeping dessert apple. Tree vigorous, dwarfish, a "forky grower," bearing heavily on alternate years.

Fruit large, roundish oblate, conical, sometimes oblique; skin greenish yellow with a bronze blush on the sunny side; dots few, brown, some areole; stem short in a very large, deep, slightly russeted cavity; calyx nearly closed; basin large, wide, deep, slightly corrugated; flesh pale yellow, crisp, tender, juicy, aromatic, subacid. Ripe November–March. Catalog listings: MD, VA, NC (1880–1904).

**PINE APPLE RUSSET** (Pine Russet, Hardingham's Russet): An English apple sold by several southern nurseries.

Fruit medium or below, roundish conical, angular; skin whitish yellow with faint stripes, russeted; stem long and slender in an uneven, slightly russeted cavity; calyx closed; basin shallow and corrugated; flesh whitish, juicy, tender, slightly aromatic, subacid. Ripe September/October. Catalog listings: VA, NC, KY (1853–70).

**PINE STRAWBERRY:** Probably of Kentucky origin and said to be a new variety in 1863. Sold by a Kentucky nursery in 1870.

Fruit medium to large, roundish oblate, conical; skin pale yellow blushed and splashed with light carmine; dots scattered, large, yellow; stem short and thick in a wide, green or brown cavity; calyx open; basin medium size; flesh yellow, tough, juicy, sweet. Ripe winter.

**PINE STUMP:** Originated in Granville County, North Carolina, and well adapted to the piedmont and coastal plains of the South. Resembles Clarke's Pearmain with showy fruit of excellent eating quality. Tree healthy, productive, and an annual bearer. This fine variety was sold by southern nurseries until 1928 or later, and an old tree, as yet undiscovered, may still be alive somewhere.

Fruit medium or larger in the piedmont but below medium in the North and when mountain-grown, roundish or somewhat oblate, slightly conical; skin deep orange with a brownish crimson cheek on the sunny side, streaked in the shade, sometimes entirely dark red; dots numerous, tan; stem short in a narrow, russeted cavity; calyx open; basin shallow and corrugated; flesh yellow, crisp, juicy, sugary, mild subacid. Ripe mid September–December. Catalog listings: NC, GA, AL (1884–1928). ❖ **Plate 107.**

**PINNACLE** (Red Pippin): Apples sent to the USDA in 1900 by N. F. Morgan of Otter Creek, Rutherford County, North Carolina.

Fruit large, roundish, heavily ribbed at the stem end, sides unequal; skin bright red; dots few, small, gray; stem short in a deep, wide, russeted cavity; calyx closed, basin wide and shallow; flesh white, tinged yellow. Ripe December. No catalog listings.

**PIPER'S FALL BEAUTY** (Fall Beauty): Originated before 1893 on the farm of R. N. Emerson, Clinton, Kentucky, and listed in the 1912 catalog of the Clinton Nursery Company. Tree susceptible to fire blight.

Fruit above medium, roundish oblate; skin greenish yellow, heavily striped with two shades of red, especially on the sunny side; dots scattered, white and russet, some areole; stem medium length in a medium-size, russeted cavity; basin gradually sloped, rather wide; flesh yellowish, slightly subacid. Ripe August/September.

**PIPER'S RED JUNE** (Piper's Best?): Listed in the 1912 catalog of the Clinton Nursery Company, Clinton, Kentucky. No description.

**PIRCE:** A South Carolina apple listed in 1860 by Pomaria Nurseries of South Carolina. "Medium, green, best keeper. Ripe February."

**PITT'S IMPROVED WINESAP:** From the 1890 catalog of Jamestown Nurseries, Greensboro, North Carolina: "Of the same character as the common Winesap only a little larger and more perfectly colored; tree a good strong grower."

**PLANTERS' FAVORITE:** Sold from 1889 to 1894 by Planters' Nurseries, Humboldt, Tennessee.

Fruit large, oblong; skin orange-yellow; flesh juicy, "flavor like a banana."

**POKEBERRY RED:** From an 1890 letter to the USDA written by G. W. Robinett, Flag Pond, Scott County, Virginia: "This apple is known here as the finest apple we have. Some think it is a seedling of the Neverfail as it is the same shape, but I think it is a seedling of the Rocky Mountain. One tree of Rocky Mountain grew within a short distance of where the Pokeberry Red came up. I make it my choice, and you would too if you had one of the fine ones to try your teeth on. I believe it will keep until spring in a cool place."

Fruit below medium, oblate; skin covered with red with darker red stripes; dots numerous, russet; stem short in a medium-size, russeted cavity; calyx closed; basin rather deep, corrugated; flesh whitish, stained red under the skin on the sunny side. Ripe winter. No catalog listings.

**POLLARD'S EARLY:** From the 1880 catalog of

Virginia Nurseries, Richmond, Virginia: "Medium, pale yellow, flesh white and firm, sprightly, refreshing, subacid. Bears transportation long distances. This is a native of King and Queen County, Va. July."

❦ **POLLY BRIGHT** (Polly?): Probably of Virginia origin before 1853 and sold by a Kentucky nursery in 1870.

Fruit medium to large, oblong conical; skin light yellow shaded with carmine and obscurely striped (also described as striped with red); stem medium length in an acute, russeted cavity; basin small and furrowed; flesh tender, juicy, rather acid. Ripe September/October or perhaps earlier.

❦ **POMARIA GREENING** (Pomera, Pommaria Greening): Originated by William Chapman near Pomaria, Newberry County, South Carolina, and sold by Pomaria Nurseries from 1856 to 1874.

Fruit large, green; flesh juicy with a sprightly flavor. Ripe October–December.

❦ **PONYIK:** Probably Ponyik Alma, a Hungarian apple that originated before 1872. Mentioned in an 1898 Alabama agricultural experiment station bulletin, and specimen apples were sent to the USDA in 1898 by Q. B. Ramsey of Lebanon, Tennessee.

Fruit large, round; skin yellowish, almost covered with dark red; dots small, scattered, whitish; stem short in a narrow, rather shallow, russeted cavity; calyx closed; basin medium size; flesh white. Ripe August. No catalog listings.

❦ **POOLE:** Originated in Alabama and first described by the Mississippi delegate to the 1860 meeting of the American Pomological Society: "As a winter apple it has no superior in Mississippi or elsewhere."

Fruit large, deep yellow, "equal in flavor to the Newtown Pippin." No catalog listings.

❦ **POORHOUSE** (Suwanee, Winter Green, Winter Queen): From an 1895 letter to the USDA written by B. A. Craddock, Curve, Lauderdale County, Tennessee: "Originated in Sumner County, Tennessee, as an accidental seedling found on the grounds of the poorhouse. It was first propagated by Dr. Bains of Haywood County to which county he brought five scions about 1860 and grafted a few trees for his own planting. The fruit ripens in late autumn and keeps better than Ben Davis. Some specimens weigh one and a half pounds. Baskets of the fruit often average one pound to the apple. The tree is a heavy, annual bearer and holds its fruit well."

The Poorhouse was grown mostly in Tennessee, Kentucky, and Georgia as a high-quality apple for both market and home use. In 1920, it was sold by a Georgia nursery under the name Suwanee.

Fruit large, roundish to slightly oblate; skin pale yellowish green to yellow with numerous russet dots; stem short in a narrow, deep, russeted cavity; basin medium size, abrupt; flesh yellowish, compact, moderately juicy, mild subacid. Ripe November–February, but keeps much longer in good storage. Catalog listings: GA, TN, KY (1893–1920).

❦ **POPOFF'S STREAKED** (Papoff's Streaked): A Russian apple imported by the USDA about 1870. From a North Carolina nursery catalog: "Large, yellow, beautifully streaked with red. Considered the best flavored of all the Russian apples. Very prolific. Ripens last of June." Catalog listings: NC, AL, LA (1886–93).

❦ **PORTLAND SEEDLING:** Apples sent to the USDA in 1910 by John Daniels of Nashville, Tennessee.

Fruit medium, slightly oblong, flattened on the ends; skin almost covered with red to purplish red; dots light gray; stem medium length in a shallow cavity; basin narrow; flesh whitish. Ripe June/July. No catalog listings.

❦ **POTOMAC JUNE:** (Potomac?) Listed in the 1880 catalog of John Saul's Nursery, Washington, D.C. No description. Different from the modern apple named Potomac.

❦ **POUND CAKE** (North Carolina Pound, Royal Pearmain?): While I include a description of Pound Cake, which was thought to be a North Carolina apple, I believe it is identical to Royal Pearmain. Described in an 1858 issue of *The Southern Cultivator* magazine.

Fruit large, roundish oblate, conical; skin deep yellow mottled and shaded with red, with some patches and netting of greenish russet; stem thick, short in a broad, shallow cavity; calyx small, open; basin small, regular; flesh yellowish, rather crisp, tender, juicy, mild subacid. Ripe November/ December. No catalog listings.

❦ **POUND'S JULY** (Early Pound): Originated on the farm of George Seaton, Jefferson County, Kentucky, from seeds planted about 1800. Sold by a Kentucky nursery in 1870.

Fruit large, roundish conical, sides unequal; skin greenish white with a dull blush; dots few, brown; stem very short in a deep and russeted cavity; calyx closed; basin small and narrow; flesh white, fine-grained, tender, not very juicy, sweet. Ripe July/ August.

❦ **PREMIUM** (Prize Sweet): An Alabama apple mentioned by Warder (1867).

Fruit medium, roundish; skin yellow with red markings; flesh sweet. Ripe early autumn. No catalog listings.

❦ **PRESH'S WINTER:** Originated by the Forest Nursery of Fairview, Kentucky, and described by Downing in 1900. Tree productive but a biennial bearer.

Fruit medium to large, roundish conical; skin pale yellow, shaded dark red in the sun, but much less red and thinly striped in the shade; dots few, light-colored; stem short in a medium-size, russeted cavity; calyx open; basin large, deep, smooth; flesh yellowish, fine-grained, crisp, juicy, subacid. Ripe December–March. No catalog listings.

❦ **PRESIDENT:** The following is a personal recollection of the great American pomologist, W. H. Ragan, written in 1902: "Lewis Shell, late of Putnam County, Indiana, brought this apple from Tennessee in about 1830. Shell was a veteran of Andrew Jackson's army in the battle of New Orleans, and as that hero was then president, Shell gave it the rank of his late chief. The variety was poor in quality but fine in the habits of the tree and in the appearance of the fruit. The fruit was large, highly colored and almost perfect in form, being obtuse conical. It was enormously productive and took the markets where unknown, but because of its poor quality, the producer was under the necessity of finding a new customer each time he went to market." Listed by a North Carolina nursery in 1853.

Fruit very large, roundish conical; skin yellow, mostly covered with dark red stripes; flesh somewhat coarse, very white, mild subacid. Ripe October/ November.

❦ **PRESS EWING** (Ewing, President Ewing, Press): Originated about 1800 with Benjamin Harned near Fairview, Kentucky. Ragan (1905) gives Press Ewing as a synonym of Rome Beauty, but Rome Beauty is a completely different apple. Sold in 1870 by a Kentucky nursery. Tree vigorous, healthy, and productive.

Fruit medium or above, roundish oblate; skin smooth, yellow, nearly covered with shades and stripes of red or dull red; dots numerous with dark centers; stem medium to long in a broad, deep, russeted cavity; calyx closed (Warder says open); basin abrupt, deep, uneven; flesh yellowish, fine-grained, juicy, crisp, tender, aromatic, mild subacid. Ripe October and a good keeper with quality improving in storage.

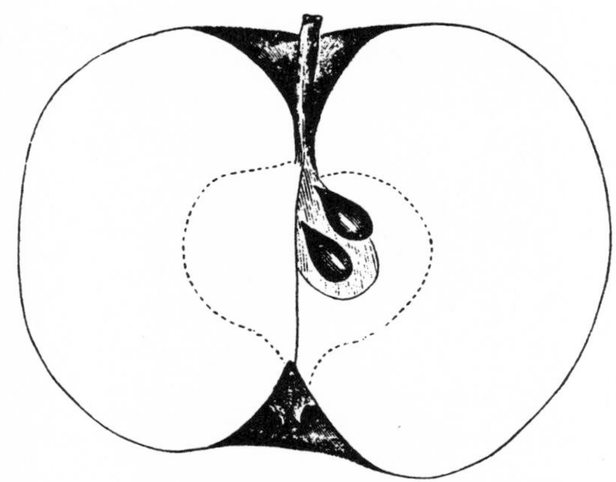

PRESS EWING

❦ **PREWIT:** Originated on the farm of William Prewit, Rock Spring Church, Kentucky, and described by Downing (1900). Tree an annual bearer. Fruit said to be "chiefly valuable for its long keeping."

Fruit medium, oblate conical, sides unequal; skin yellow, shaded and faintly striped with light and dark red; stem very short in a large, deep, russeted cavity; calyx closed; basin deep; flesh yellowish, tender, moderately juicy, mild subacid. Ripe January–May. No catalog listings.

❦ **PRICE** of South Carolina (Price's Sweet?, Price's Winter Sweet): There are two southern apples named Price. This apple, of South Carolina origin, is the older of the two. Mentioned by a South Carolina nurseryman in 1858 and briefly described by Warder (1867).

Fruit medium to large, roundish conical; skin red-striped (also described as greenish yellow); flesh subacid to almost sweet. Ripe fall or winter. Catalog listings: VA, TX (1895–1917).

❦ **PRICE** of Virginia: A seedling apple found about 1885 growing near a "water furrow" on the farm of C. A. Price, near Gardenia, Virginia. Tree an annual and heavy bearer. No description. No catalog listings.

❦ **PRIDE OF GREENVILLE:** Originated in Greenville County, Virginia, and listed in 1878 by Hermitage Nurseries, Richmond, Virginia. Introduced by Dr. George Mason, who first grew the Mason's Stranger apple. Fruit "medium red with light streaks." Ripe December–March.

❦ **PRIDE OF NORTH CAROLINA:** Listed in 1902 by the Startown Nursery, Newton, North Carolina, and in 1920 by another nursery in Newton.

Fruit above medium, flattened on the ends; skin yellow with red stripes; flesh yellow, fine-grained, pleasant subacid.

❦ **PRIDE OF SUMMER:** Apples sent to the USDA in 1911 by Q. L. Patterson, Blairsville, Union County, Georgia.

Fruit above medium, roundish; skin yellowish green with scattered red stripes mostly near the stem end; dots few, large, russet; stem medium length in a medium-size, abrupt cavity; basin almost shallow, wide, corrugated; flesh yellowish white. Ripe August. No catalog listings.

❦ **PRIDE OF TENNESSEE:** Originated near Humboldt, Gibson County, Tennessee. Listed in 1894 by Planter's Nursery of Humboldt and named by this nursery: "Sells for fancy prices, holds six weeks in shipping and will bear transportation to England."

Fruit medium, roundish oblate, skin almost entirely covered with red with darker red stripes; dots large, russet; stem long in a medium-size, russeted cavity; calyx closed; basin shallow; flesh white, tinged red under the skin "with wine streaks through the white meat inside." Ripe June/July. ❖ **Plate 108.**

❦ **PRIDE OF TEXAS (TEXAS):** This apple was sold by several North Carolina nurseries from 1884 to 1893 under the name Pride of Texas. One catalog says: "This fruit was sent to me from near Sherman, Texas, under this name. A dozen or more specimens received in September and kept on a shelf in my office until January were still solid and sound." From 1893 to 1902, this apple was listed as McAfee by North Carolina nurseries with Pride of Texas as a synonym. *See* McAfee.

❦ **PRIDE OF THE SOUTH:** Originated about 1863 in Tangipahoa Parish, Louisiana, by W. D. Lewis and widely grown there in the 1870s. An 1878 letter to the USDA from the brother of W. D. Lewis says, "Pride of the South does not please me as well as it did on account of its rotting before maturity." No description. No catalog listings.

❦ **PRINCE JOHN:** From a circa 1890 letter to the USDA from Thomas J. Garden, Prospect, Virginia: "A little red seedling apple very much admired here. It originated in Lunenburg County, Va., coming up near an old cabin. I have named it Prince John. It is a very late keeper." No catalog listings.

❦ **PRINCESS ANNE BEAUTY** (Anne): From the 1880 catalog of Virginia Nurseries, Richmond, Virginia: "A new variety originating in Princess Anne County, Va. Of fair size and good quality, much esteemed on account of its keeping qualities. December to April." No description.

❦ **PROGRESS** (Miller's Best, Esquire Miller's Best Sort): Originated in Middlefield, Connecticut, and sold in the South mostly by Virginia nurseries.

Fruit medium, roundish oblate; skin smooth, yellow with a blush cheek; dots scattered, gray; stem short in a russeted cavity; flesh white, tender, crisp, juicy, subacid or almost sweet. Ripe October–April. Catalog listings: VA, KY (1858–1904).

❦ **PROTHER'S WINTER** (Prother's Large?): A North Carolina apple sold from 1858 to 1871 by the Fruitland Nursery, Augusta, Georgia.

Fruit medium, conical; skin yellow with a red cheek; flesh sweet (Warder says subacid); ripe November and a good keeper.

❦ **PUSHMATAHA** (Sloan's Seedling, Sloan's Beauty): Originated near Tuscaloosa, Alabama, and described by Downing in 1869. Tree an abundant bearer.

Fruit medium or below, roundish oblate, conical; skin pale yellow, mostly covered with red; dots few, brown; stem medium length, slender; calyx closed; flesh yellowish white, juicy, mild subacid. Ripe November–January. No catalog listings.

❦ **PUTNAM KEEPER:** A Kentucky apple sold by a Kentucky nursery in 1870.

Fruit large, oblate; skin yellowish, striped with red; stem rather long; calyx closed; flesh yellowish, crisp, juicy, subacid. Ripe December–March.

❦ **QUEEN OF ALBEMARLE:** Listed in 1919 by Old Dominion Nurseries of Richmond, Virginia. No description.

❦ **QUEEN OF THE SOUTH** (Pumpkin): Originated about 1860 as a wild seedling ten miles south of Greensboro, North Carolina. Resembles the Buckingham but larger and more oblong. Listed in 1872 by Joshua Lindley's Nursery of Greensboro.

❦ **QUEEN PIPPIN:** Sold by two North Carolina nurseries from 1877 to 1895: "From western North Carolina. Large, roundish, slightly oblate; covered with red on greenish yellow; flesh yellow, fine-grained, rich. October–November." A Queen Pippin has been found by Tom Brown but has not yet fruited.

❦ **QUEEN'S DELIGHT:** Listed in 1862 by Pomaria Nurseries of South Carolina. A South Carolina apple, ripe October.

❦ **RABUM:** Listed as a Georgia apple in 1859 by Hopewell Nurseries, Fredericksburg, Virginia.

Fruit oblong, red-striped; flesh subacid.

❦ **RAGAN'S YELLOW** (Regan's Yellow): From the 1893 catalog of Smith's Nursery of Franklin, Tennessee: "A beautiful yellow apple, larger and finer than Horse. Really an improved Horse. July 15th to 30th. We continue to grow some trees of the old Horse apple but this is better in tree and fruit."

Fruit medium, roundish conical; skin greenish yellow; flesh yellow, fine-grained, moderately juicy, subacid. Ripe July/August.

❦ **RAGLAND:** Apples of this name were sent to the 1871 meeting of the American Pomological Society by Dollins and Brothers Nursery, Albemarle County, Virginia. No description. No catalog listings.

❦ **RALPH:** A Georgia apple sold in 1861 by the Fruitland Nursery, Augusta, Georgia.

Fruit oblate, yellow, subacid. Ripe November.

❦ **RANDOLPH** (Unknown, Bibbing?): The original tree was found growing in a forty-year-old orchard on land purchased by Randolph Peters in 1869 near Farnhurst, Delaware. No pomologists of the time could identify this apple so Mr. Peters named it "Unknown" and sold it through his small nursery. The fruit is described as of good quality and beautiful in color, being borne singly or in pairs on fruit spurs, so it never overbears. Randolph was grown commercially in Maryland and as far away as Arkansas and Nebraska around the turn of the century as a good summer apple that ships well. The tree is healthy and an annual bearer.

Fruit usually medium, sometimes larger, oblate; skin smooth and glossy, very light green washed with crimson and striped with darker red; dots few, gray, indented; stem short to medium in a medium-size, gradually sloped, russeted cavity; calyx closed; basin abrupt, slightly furrowed, lumpy; flesh yellowish, rather fine-grained, very firm, breaking, moderately juicy, mild subacid. Ripe July in Delaware. No catalog listings. ❖ **Plate 109.**

❦ **RANKIN'S FAVORITE:** A North Carolina apple sold by Virginia and Georgia nurseries from 1859 to 1861. No description except ripe September.

❦ **RANSOM:** A Georgia apple exhibited in 1908 at a Georgia Horticultural Society meeting. Different from the Connecticut apple of the same name. No description. No catalog listings.

❦ **RAPER'S FALL** (Raper): A North Carolina apple sold by Virginia and Georgia nurseries from 1859 to 1861. No description except ripe September.

❦ **RAWL'S SEEDLING/RAWL'S NO. 2:** South Carolina apples listed in 1860 by Pomaria Nurseries of South Carolina. Both "large, fine flavored, new. Ripe late."

❦ **REAGAN** (Day, Clark, Boler, Jack): Reagan is a synonym of the Black Ben Davis. It is also the name of a Mississippi apple described in the 1924 catalog of Newton Nurseries, Newton, Mississippi: "Medium to large, red striped, tender, juicy and sweet; immense bearer; one of the best eating apples known; ripens July and August and lasts six weeks. This apple is known over the state under many different local names, Day, Clark, Boler and Jack." I believe this is the same apple as Jim Day, which has been recently rediscovered in Mississippi.

❦ **REBECCA** (Daddy?): Rebecca is probably a seedling of Maiden's Blush and originated in Honeycomb, Delaware, two miles northeast of Wilmington. It was brought to notice in 1856 by J. P. Jeffries and named by him for his wife. Some notes found in Charles Downing's files upon his death seem to indicate this apple may have been grown first by a Swedish family named Stidhouse or Stidham around 1812 or so: "Called locally the Daddy apple because daddy prohibited children from taking its fruit." Daddy was introduced into Indiana around 1835. There is some doubt whether Daddy and Rebecca are the same apple.

Fruit medium to large, roundish oblate; skin whitish yellow, sometimes with a faint orange and red blush, occasionally a deeper red blush; stem very short and fleshy in a deep, narrow cavity; calyx closed; basin wide and deep; flesh fine-grained, tender, juicy, subacid. Ripe August/September. No catalog listings.

❦ **RED AND GREEN SWEET** (Large Red and Green Sweeting, Virginia Sweet, Red Bough, Red Pound Sweet, Bedford Sweet, Large Early Red, Large Red Sweeting, Sallie Sweet, Wheelock Sweet, Prince's Large Red, and Green Sweet): A very large apple of unknown origin first described by Coxe (1817). Not high in eating quality but suitable for baking. Tree a heavy annual bearer.

Fruit very large, oblong conical, ribbed; skin smooth, greenish white partly overspread with pinkish red with stripes of bright red; cavity deep, broad, furrowed, sometimes lipped and russeted; basin medium to deep, wrinkled; flesh white, fine-grained, very tender, moderately juicy, sweet. Ripe July/August. Catalog listings: MD, NC (1836–1902).

❦ **RED BANANA:** An Arkansas apple that first fruited before 1877. Said to resemble Esopus Spitzenburg.

Fruit large, slightly conical; skin a rich red; flesh yellow, juicy, almost sweet with a banana flavor. No catalog listings.

❦ **RED CEDAR:** Origin unknown, but perhaps Ohio, where it was growing in 1849. Sold in 1870 by the Forest Nursery of Fairview, Kentucky: "Fruit rather small, roundish; skin dark red; flesh yellowish, compact, mild subacid, rich and pleasant. Valuable for its keeping qualities and winter cider."

❦ **RED EVERLASTING:** Originated before 1872 by Thomas J. Bouldin of Charlotte County, Virginia, and listed in 1878 by Hermitage Nurseries, Richmond, Virginia.

Fruit medium to small, oblong, red, juicy, sweet. Ripe January–June.

❦ **RED HORSE** (Carden Flat): Brought to Kentucky from South Carolina by a group of settlers in 1793. Resembles Buckingham, but smaller, less juicy, and a better keeper.

Fruit medium, oblate, ribbed; skin mostly dark red with obscure stripes and some russet netting; dots numerous, gray; stem short in a large, irregular cavity; calyx open; flesh yellowish, crisp, tender, rather juicy, aromatic, mild subacid. Ripe October–January.

There are several southern catalog listings of Red Horse, but these listings are almost certainly for the Gibson, which has Red Horse as a synonym.

❦ **RED HOUST** (Houst): From the 1893 catalog of Planter's Nursery, Humboldt, Tennessee: "Large, fine, showy, commands the best prices and will last a week in transit. Early." This may be a misspelling of Red Horse, a synonym of Gibson.

❦ **RED HUB:** Originated before 1893 in an old pine field on the farm of J. Hub Frazier of Forsyth County, North Carolina. Sold by the J. Van Lindley Nursery, Greensboro, North Carolina, from 1898 to 1902: "It is a large, summer apple, blushed and striped with red; juicy and fine in quality. One of the best July apples; far superior to the old Summer Queen." Fruit sent to the USDA was found to resemble Kansas Queen.

❧ **RED IONE:** Mentioned but not described in an 1889 Texas agricultural experiment station bulletin as being grown in Hancock County, Texas. No catalog listings.

❧ **RED JEWELL** (Red Limbertwig?): According to Downing (1878), this apple originated in Todd County, Kentucky, and it was listed in 1870 by a Kentucky nursery. A later Illinois agricultural experiment station bulletin says Red Jewell turned out to be Limbertwig (presumably Red Limbertwig). Perhaps so, but the description of Red Jewell is not a close match of the Red Limbertwig; however, it is a close match of Oliver. An apple named Red Jewel is in the collection of the National Clonal Germplasm Repository at Geneva, New York, but it is not this apple.

Fruit medium or below, roundish oblate, sides often unequal; skin dark red with many conspicuous white dots; stem slender; flesh yellowish, fine-grained, compact, juicy, mild subacid. Ripe December–February.

❧ **RED JULY:** From the 1904 catalog of Paris Nurseries, Paris, Texas: "Large, round or conical, yellow nearly covered with dark crimson, with a few stripes on the shady side; fine, showy for market. July 1st to 10th."

❧ **RED MAY:** The following is taken from the 1888 catalog of Langdon Nurseries, Mobile, Alabama: "A native fruit found on most of the old settlements in this section; very hardy and uniformly productive, and hence its value; fruit variable in size from large, medium to small, nearly covered with red on a yellow background; flavor quite acid. Ripens last of May and early June." Catalog listings: NC, AL, LA (1872–98).

❧ **RED OX:** Red Ox is a synonym of the Pennock, but according to the following comments made to the American Pomological Society in 1879, by a Mr. McWhorter of Tennessee, it is also a distinct southern apple variety: "The Red Ox apple of the South has been erroneously confounded with the Pennock. I have the Red Ox in bearing which I obtained from a very reliable source. It is distinct from the Pennock. It is brighter in color and a much better apple. The tree growth of the two is wholly distinct; the Red Ox having peculiar crooked shoots." Listed by a Kentucky nursery in 1870. No description.

❧ **RED ROBINSON:** Origin unknown, but sold by two Virginia nurseries from 1858 to 1904.

Fruit medium, oblate or round; skin red-striped; flesh subacid or acid. Ripe winter. This is probably Robertson Red.

❧ **RED ROWDEN:** Thought to have been brought into Mississippi from Alabama in the early years of that state by a man named Rowden. It was grown locally around Columbus, Mississippi, for many years and tested at the Mississippi Agricultural Experiment Station in the 1940s.

Fruit medium, roundish to slightly oblong; skin red, often striped; flesh tinged with red and mealy when ripe. No catalog listings.

❧ **RED SEEDLING:** Listed in 1916 by the Mountain Top Home Nursery, Mena, Polk County, Arkansas. No description.

❧ **RED STREAK** (Herefordshire Red Streak, Johnson, Scudamore's Crab, Scudamous Crab): Herefordshire Red Streak is a famous old English apple used for both cider and fresh eating. Old references say it thrives in the "middle states" of this country, and it was listed by a South Carolina nursery in 1856. Downing (1878) says: "Makes a rich, high flavored, strong liquor." Thatcher (1822) says: "When used for pies, they need not be pared." Red Streak is a synonym of several other popular southern apple varieties, including Wine and Domine.

Fruit medium to large, roundish; skin yellow, mostly covered with red streaks and splashes; calyx small; basin rather deep; flesh yellow, fine-grained, juicy (Downing says dry), subacid.

❧ **RED TYLER:** Listed in 1849 without description by a nursery in Stone Mountain, Georgia.

❧ **RED WARRIOR:** Red Warrior is a synonym of Yates and Nickajack, both important southern apples. It is also the name of another southern apple variety, as shown by this 1855 letter from Dr. William O. Baldwin of Montgomery, Alabama:

"The Red Warrior is a good winter apple, very large, red and striped with yellow, sometimes weighing twenty ounces and upwards. This Red Warrior is a native Indian seedling. I first traced its history and gave it its name." Listed by a Georgia nursery in 1871.

Fruit large to very large, nearly round to roundish oblate; skin yellow, striped and marbled with two shades of red; russet specks and spots; stem three-fourths of an inch long in a medium-size cavity; calyx closed; basin even and deep; flesh white, juicy, moderately acid. Ripe November–March.

Another apple named Red Warrior was found as a seedling near Warrior Mountain in Maryland about 1929. This large red apple is part of the collection of the National Clonal Germplasm Repository in Geneva, New York, and still available.

❦ **RED WINTER** (Red Winter Cluster?, Kinnaird's Choice?): Red Winter was listed from 1898 to 1903 by Munson Nurseries of Denison, Texas, and described only as "good, prolific; red; medium; fine, table and market." In the 1920s, an apple called Red Winter Cluster, further identified as Kinnaird's Choice, was sold by the Plainview Nursery, Plainview, Texas. It seems probable that the Red Winter sold by Munson Nurseries was also Kinnaird's Choice.

❦ **RED WINTER KEEPER:** Listed in 1904 by the Maryland Nursery Company, Baltimore, Maryland: "Fine grower and keeper; one of the best winter apples." No description.

❦ **REID'S SUMMER:** Sold in 1915 and 1916 by Blue Grass Nurseries of Lexington, Kentucky: "This is an apple that we named after Allen Reid, Owensboro, Kentucky. Mr. Reid is one of the best fruit growers in Kentucky. He knows a good apple when he sees it and raises it. He says this is one of his best. For those who know him, that's enough."

Fruit large; skin tender, yellow with a faint or bright pink blush; flesh somewhat acid and loses flavor if stored. Bruises easily. Ripe late July/August.

❦ **REINETTE TRIOMPHANTE** (Victorious Reinette)/**REINETTE VAN MONS:** These European apple varieties were sold by North Carolina and Virginia nurseries from 1858 to 1904. The Reinette Triomphante is large, oblong; skin pale yellow; flesh yellow, juicy, subacid. Ripe winter. No description for Reinette Van Mons.

❦ **RENSHAW'S BEAUTY:** Listed in 1827 by the Linnean Hill Nursery, Washington, D.C. No description except ripe September.

❦ **RESIDENCE:** A North Carolina apple.

Fruit medium size; skin yellow, shaded and striped with red; flesh subacid. Ripe September/October. Catalog listings: SC, GA, KY (1858–70).

❦ **RETICULE:** Sold from 1824 to 1827 by the Linnean Hill Nursery, Washington, D.C. No description except ripe August.

❦ **REYSER'S GREEN WINTER:** A South Carolina apple listed in 1862 by Pomaria Nurseries of South Carolina: "Small but excellent; ripe December."

❦ **RHEA:** Described to the 1895 meeting of the American Pomological Society. Originated about 1845 on the farm of Captain John P. Walker of Dayton, Rhea County, Tennessee. Brought to attention by J. D. Ellis, who bought the farm in 1885.

Fruit medium, roundish conical (also said to be roundish oblong), sides slightly unequal; skin thin, leathery, smooth, yellow, washed and striped with red; dots few, russet; stem short in a medium-width, deep, irregular, abrupt, dark green cavity with the green extending out over the top of the fruit; calyx open; basin broad, corrugated; flesh white, tender, juicy, mild subacid. Ripe late summer or fall. No catalog listings.

❦ **RHODES ORANGE:** (Rhodes Pearmain?, Rhodes Sweet?) Originated by Colonel Mercer Rhodes of Newton County, Georgia. The tree is susceptible to cedar-apple rust.

Fruit medium to large, roundish oblate, conical; skin yellow or orangish, mottled and striped with red; dots numerous, russet and light gray; stem rather long; calyx closed; flesh whitish, tender, juicy, aromatic, subacid. Ripe July/August. Catalog listings: SC, GA, AL, MS, TX (1857–1906).

❦ **RHYNE:** A North Carolina apple listed from 1860 to 1878 by a South Carolina nursery: "Large, red streaked, beautiful. Ripe November."

❦ **RIABINOUKA** (Berry): A Russian apple sold from 1886 to 1888 by an Alabama and a Louisiana nursery: "Resembles the Alexander but of better flavor. The tree is hardy, of spreading growth and an early bearer. Fruit very large and showy, orange yellow, brilliantly streaked and marked with bright red in the sun. Flesh white, slightly tinged red near the skin, of mild and pleasant flavor, with very little acidity. Though eatable in October, it keeps well."

**RICHARD SWEET:** Apples sent to the USDA in 1908 by Ridder Brothers, Oakland, Garrett County, Maryland.

Fruit medium, roundish, flattened on the ends; skin light yellow, blushed and faintly striped pinkish on the sunny side; dots scattered, dark and russet; stem medium length in a deep, rather narrow, russeted cavity; calyx closed; basin almost narrow; flesh whitish. Ripe December–March. No catalog listings.

**RICHARDSON'S WINTER** (Richardson's Late?): Warder (1867) says this apple originated in Massachusetts, but it was listed from 1857 to 1878 by a Georgia and a South Carolina nursery as a Georgia apple. Fruit large, keeps till spring.

**RIEGEL:** Originated before 1895 with S. D. Riegel of Experiment, Georgia.

Fruit above medium; skin usually yellow, but some apples are nearly covered with light crimson and narrow stripes; flesh yellowish, crisp, subacid. Ripe September. No catalog listings.

**ROANE'S WHITE CRAB** (Rhoan's White Crab): The original tree was a wild seedling on the farm of Colonel John Roane of Virginia. The tree is rather small, similar in growth to the Hewe's Crab and a biennial bearer. A fine cider crab as described by Coxe (1817): "The apple is very small, not larger than the Hewe's Crab, round, the stalk thin, the skin yellow with a small portion of russet above the stem, and spots of red scattered over it. The flesh is rich, dry, of a musky sweetness, rough to the taste from its astringent and fibrous properties. The liquor is remarkably strong and of a syrupy consistency when first made but becoming singularly bright by proper fermentation and racking. It will keep perfectly sweet, in casks well bunged and placed in a cool cellar, through our summer months." Ripe September/October. Catalog listings: DC, NC (1824–53).

**ROBERSON'S WINTER** (Roberson): Originated in Patrick County, Virginia, and said to resemble the York Imperial. A high-quality apple as grown in the piedmont of Virginia.

Fruit large, roundish, often slightly oblate or slightly oblong; skin rich yellow, mostly covered with red blotches and stripes, which are often quite dark red; dots inconspicuous; stem very short in a deep, narrow, russeted cavity; basin wide and deep; flesh yellowish, crisp, juicy, slightly subacid. Ripe November–March, but can be kept later in good storage. Catalog listings: MD, VA, NC (1859–1904).

**ROBERT BRUCE:** Originated before 1860 in Wake County, North Carolina.

Fruit above medium, oblate; skin shaded with crimson; stem short; calyx open; flesh white, coarse, juicy, subacid. Ripe August. No catalog listings.

**ROBERTS RED:** From an 1884 letter written by John Dollins of Albemarle County, Virginia: "Found growing on an old chimney on the farm of H. H. Roberts, Rockfish Township, Nelson County, Virginia." No description. No catalog listings.

**ROBERTSON'S JACOB:** A South Carolina apple listed in 1860 by Pomaria Nurseries of South Carolina: "Large and superior quality. Ripe November and keeps well."

**ROBERTSON'S WHITE** (Roberson White, Robertson White, Robinson's White, White Robinson, Robertson's Pearmain?): Origin possibly Culpepper County, Virginia, where it was once popular. Tree a late bloomer and a regular bearer. As grown in an Illinois agricultural experiment station in 1896, this apple was similar or identical to Winter Sweet Paradise.

Fruit medium, roundish oblate; skin greenish yellow with many dark dots; flesh yellowish, fine-grained, crisp, juicy, subacid. Ripe September/October and may keep until December. Catalog listings: DC, VA, SC, KY (1858–80).

**ROBEY** (Robey's Seedling, Roby's Seedling): Raised before 1852 by Henry R. Robey, a prominent nurseryman of Fredericksburg, Virginia. Sold by two Virginia nurseries from 1859 to 1869 and by a North Carolina nursery in 1872.

Fruit large, round or roundish oblate, conical;

skin mostly red on a yellow background with faint stripes; dots numerous, whitish; flesh yellow, juicy, subacid. Ripe November/December.

❧ **ROCK PIPPIN** (Ridge Pippin?, Lemon, Walnut Stem, Rich Pippin): Sold about 1900 by Faught Branch Nurseries, Rockingham County, Virginia: "One of the most valuable on account of its productiveness and good keeping; during unfavorable seasons it has been uniformly productive; skin yellow sprinkled with cinnamon dots; flesh juicy and crisp with a mild, almost saccharine flavor; in use March and April." This is certainly the Ridge Pippin, which originated in Pennsylvania before 1833.

Fruit rather large, roundish conical (also described as roundish oblong), very ribbed; skin yellow, slightly shaded with red; dots fairly numerous, russet and crimson; stem short in a large cavity; calyx closed; basin abrupt and uneven; flesh yellowish, juicy, crisp, aromatic, almost sweet. Ripe March/April.

❧ **ROCKBRIDGE'S SWEETING:** Listed from 1869 to 1904 by the Franklin Davis Nursery, Richmond, Virginia. No description.

❧ **ROGERS** (Rogers Red?): Rogers originated in Alcorn County, Mississippi, and was described in the 1916 catalog of Corinth Nurseries, Corinth, Mississippi: "This is a fine fall and winter apple. If I was going to pick my best tree I would say Rogers. I am the only one who has this apple for sale. It originated in this county, is blight-proof and the best apple on my list." No description.

In 1915, a Rogers Red was listed by the New Cumberland Nursery Company of Sawyer, Kentucky. No description except a winter apple.

❧ **ROLLIN** (Rolla?, Rolen's Keeper?, Rowland?): Originated in Franklin County, North Carolina, and sold by a Virginia nursery in 1859. This apple is probably identical to Rolen's Keeper as described by Warder (1867) and sold by a Kentucky nursery in 1870.

Fruit medium, roundish oblate; skin yellow stained and striped with dull red, perhaps some russet; stem long in a wide and deep cavity; basin shallow; flesh compact, fine-grained, subacid. Ripe October–January or later in the North.

❧ **ROSE BUD:** Origin supposedly New Castle County, Delaware, before 1900. Tree very productive and the fruit hangs well on the tree.

Fruit medium, roundish oblate; skin yellowish, splashed and striped with light and dark red over almost the entire surface; dots quite large, light-colored; stem medium length and slender in a large cavity that is often russeted; calyx closed; basin broad and deep; flesh yellow, breaking, juicy, moderately fine-grained, mild subacid. Ripe December–March. No catalog listings.

❧ **ROSEMARIN:** A German apple sold by an Alabama and a Louisiana nursery from 1886 to 1888 and probably still grown in Europe.

Fruit large, oblong conical, flattened on the ends; skin bright yellow shaded with red; flesh white, fine-grained, crisp, "sugary acid."

❧ **ROUGH AND READY:** An apple of this name was briefly described in an 1853 North Carolina nursery catalog as small, round, pale red, ripe November–March. A different apple named Rough and Ready was listed in a 1924 Georgia nursery catalog and a 1927 South Carolina catalog: "J. P. Taylor, originator. The best, most prolific, late winter apple; will keep until May."

❧ **ROUND HILL:** Originated in Loudoun County, Virginia, and briefly described in an 1878 Virginia catalog.

Fruit large, round; skin green, flesh subacid. Hangs well on the tree and keeps late. Ripe December–March.

❧ **ROWE'S YELLOW OCTOBER:** A Mississippi apple sold in 1871 by the Fruitland Nursery, Augusta, Georgia: "Medium size, yellow, juicy, vinous, very prolific."

Fruit medium, oblate, regular; skin yellow with numerous dots; stem short in a very shallow cavity; calyx open; basin shallow; flesh white, very juicy, sprightly, vinous. Ripe September/October.

❧ **ROYAL PEARMAIN** (Royal Pearmain of Coxe, Merrit's Pearmain?, Pound Cake?): It is difficult to understand why Warder (1867) attributes the origin of this apple to Ohio when it is so obviously of Virginia origin. Coxe (1817) procured it from planters near Richmond, Virginia, and reported it to be a good table fruit and excellent for cider. In 1829, scions of Royal Pearmain were sent to the noted Long Island nurseryman, William Prince, by a Virginia "connoisseur of fruits."

This apple is almost certainly the same as Merrit's Pearmain, listed by Ragan (1905) as a Virginia apple. It is in all likelihood identical to Pound Cake as described by Downing (1878). *See* Pound Cake.

Fruit large, roundish or oblate; skin rough, yellow, russeted, with a red blush on the sunny side; flesh yellow, firm when picked but becoming tender, sprightly subacid. Ripe October and keeps until January or often later. Catalog listings: DC, NC (1824–60).

❦ **ROYAL RUSSET** (Leathercoat Russet, Old Royal Russet, Passe Pomme de Canada, Leather Coat): An apple called Royal Russet was sold first by Washington, D.C., nurseries (1824–27) and later by a Virginia nursery (1858–1904). There is no description in any of these listings except "ripe winter." These listings are probably for an old Canadian apple named Royal Russet, briefly described by Downing (1878) here.

Fruit medium, roundish oblate, conical; skin yellowish green mostly covered with a brownish russet that is bronzed in the sun; flesh greenish white, firm, acid. Ripe November–February.

❦ **RUBY RED:** Probably originated in the 1920s in Stephenville, Texas, by J. E. Fitzgerald of Fitzgerald's Nursery. Tree a weak grower when young.

Fruit medium size, mostly red. Ripe summer.

❦ **RUCKER'S ORANGE PIPPIN:** Sold from 1901 to 1904 by the Franklin Davis Nursery, Richmond, Virginia. No description.

❦ **RUE'S RELIANCE:** An early autumn apple adapted to the coastal plains that was sold by the J. Van Lindley Nursery of Greensboro, North Carolina, from 1887 to 1895: "This new apple was received from Dr. George N. Ennett of Cedar Point, North Carolina; originated with the Rue family of Carteret County, North Carolina, and is very popular in that section." No description.

❦ **RUTHERFORD:** Originated before 1890 with a Dr. Rutherford near Hot Springs, Arkansas. The tree is slender with long, thin branches, resembling a pear tree in appearance.

Fruit above medium to large, very oblong; skin greenish yellow with a light red blush, but much more red when apples are left on the tree till late in the season; dots few, some areole; stem short in a deep, russeted cavity; basin small, shallow, furrowed; flesh yellowish, fine-grained, mild subacid. Ripe winter and an excellent keeper. No catalog listings.

❦ **RUTLEDGE:** Listed from 1894 to 1910 by two Texas nurseries. An 1894 catalog says: "This variety was obtained from Mr. Frank Rutledge of Travis County, Texas, on whose plantation the original tree now stands. He wrote me in 1891. 'The tree was planted out in 1856. A man named Scott brought some apple seeds from Arkansas in 1854 and planted them. He gave my father, W. P. Rutledge, a seedling tree. The tree is still healthy and entirely free from disease. The body is twenty inches in diameter and the top fifty feet in diameter.' "

Fruit large, roundish but sometimes oblate; skin almost entirely covered with light red with faint darker stripes (also described as "richly striped"); dots numerous, large, russet; stem short and thick in a rather shallow cavity; basin wide, gradually sloped; flesh whitish. Ripe October–December. ❖ **Plate 110.**

❦ **RYESMITH:** Sold in 1921 by Bonham Nurseries, Bonham, Texas: "Special. Large, striped, spreading, upright, good. June to July."

❦ **SACCHARINE** (Zakoritnoe): A Russian apple sold in 1888 by Silver Leaf Nurseries of Boon's Path, Lee County, Virginia: "Received from the Department of Agriculture and has fruited for two years. Resembles the Duchess of Oldenburg in size, color, form and habit of growth but is of much better flavor, being a very mild subacid. Ripens about with Duchess."

❦ **ST. LAURENCE:** A South Carolina apple listed by Pomaria Nurseries of South Carolina in 1860. No description except ripe November.

❦ **SAINT PETERS** (Petrovskoe): A Russian apple imported by the USDA in 1870. Fruit resembles the Early Joe, but the tree is much more cold-hardy.

Sold by an Alabama and a Louisiana nursery from 1886 to 1888. Not a reliable cropper according to Beach (1905).

Fruit medium to rather small, roundish oblate; skin smooth, yellow with numerous short, broken red stripes, but much more red in the sun; dots small, white; stem long in an acute, shallow cavity; calyx closed; basin small and corrugated; flesh white, fine-grained, tender, not very crisp, juicy, spicy subacid. Ripe in August in Vermont.

❦ **SALEM SEEDLING** (Salem?): A Mississippi apple listed by Georgia and Mississippi nurseries from 1861 to 1878.

Fruit large, conical; skin red or red-striped; flesh subacid. Ripe November.

❦ **SANDBROOK:** Sold from 1898 to 1913 by the Eastern Shore Nursery of Denton, Maryland: "An apple of very superior quality, equal to the old American Summer Pearmain; medium size when well grown, prettily striped with lively red; sometimes entirely covered; tree upright and a heavy bearer. Should be in every family orchard." ❖ **Plate 111.**

❦ **SANGAMON REDSTREAK** (Herndon's Seedling): Origin attributed to North Carolina, but trees were being grown in Illinois and Missouri about 1870. No description. No catalog listings.

❦ **SANTOUCHEE** (Panther, Wildcat): A North Carolina apple sold by Georgia and North Carolina nurseries from 1858 to 1877. Tree productive.

Fruit large, roundish to somewhat oblate, conical, oblique; skin waxen white, sometimes faintly flushed pink (also described as smooth, pale yellow); dots few, brown or russet; stem medium length and slender in a large, deep, narrow, furrowed cavity; calyx open in a narrow basin; flesh white, fine-grained, crisp, tender, juicy, subacid to almost sweet (also described as "peculiar but rather pleasant"). Ripe November–February.

❦ **SAP SUCKER:** Listed in 1869 by Richmond Nurseries, Richmond, Virginia. No description.

❦ **SARAH-COOT APPLE:** Originated about 1880 on the farm of Sarah and Coot Holland, Macon County, North Carolina. The tree grows very large, and the fruit is an excellent keeper, often keeping through the winter under leaves beneath the tree.

Fruit medium size; skin yellow. Ripe late. No catalog listings.

❦ **SAUL'S BEAUTY:** Sold in 1880 by John Saul's Nursery, Washington, D.C.: "Small to medium, white with dark spots in the shade but a blush cheek in the sun; flesh white, delicious, of first quality; a vigorous grower, bearing in clusters. October–February."

❦ **SAUL'S SEEDLING:** Sold in 1880 by John Saul's Nursery, Washington, D.C.: "Similar to Newtown Pippin but larger, more tapering toward the blossom end; bright crimson cheek; flesh white, juicy, subacid, delicious. November–February."

❦ **SAUL'S WASHINGTON:** Listed in 1878 by Johns Saul's Nursery, Washington, D.C. No description except ripe winter.

❦ **SAUNDERSON** (Sanderson): Found before 1877 by Colonel D. D. Saunderson growing in an old field belonging to Miss Ella M. Gray near Holly Springs, Mississippi. Tree an annual bearer.

Fruit medium to large, roundish to somewhat oblong; skin whitish, mostly covered with shades and stripes of red, purplish red when exposed to the sun, often with a light bloom; dots numerous, light-colored, a few areole; stem rather short in a deep, sometimes russeted cavity; calyx closed; basin small, slightly corrugated; flesh white, sometimes stained red, tender, juicy, subacid. Ripe late July/August. No catalog listings.

❦ **SAUTA** (Santa): The Georgia pomologist J. Van Buren said he found this apple about 1850 growing on the farm of a Mr. Proctor on the banks of the Sauta or Sautee River or Creek in White County, Georgia, but its origin has also been ascribed to Habersham County, Georgia. The apple is a very late keeper, even when grown in the coastal plains. Popular at one time in Georgia, Mississippi, Alabama, and Tennessee.

Fruit medium to large, roundish oblate to oblate, slightly oblique, sides sometimes unequal; skin smooth, light yellow with some russet; dots few, gray; stem very short in a medium-size, russeted cavity; calyx closed; basin rather large, deep, slightly corrugated; flesh white or whitish yellow, tender, juicy, sprightly subacid. Ripe October–April. Catalog listings: GA, MS, TN (1858–98).

❦ **SAVAGE'S CHEESE** (Savage): Originated in Georgia before 1858.

Fruit medium, oblate; skin yellow, marked and striped with red; flesh white, juicy. Ripe October. No catalog listings.

❦ **SAWYER'S SWEET** (Sawyer Sweeting): Sold in 1870 by the Forest Nursery, Fairview, Kentucky: "Fruit large, greenish with a blush, sweet, good." Ripe summer. Sawyer Sweet has been reported to be a synonym of Golden Sweet, but Golden Sweet is not blushed.

❦ **SCARLET CRANBERRY** (Virginia Star, Robinett): First grown about 1866 by G. W. Robinett of Flag Pond, Virginia, and sold by a Maryland nursery in 1902. Described in the 1891 catalog of Stark Bro's Nursery: "A large winter apple from Virginia and such a remarkable keeper that it will remain in good condition a whole year after being picked. Color light red shaded to deep red and striped with mahogany; flesh yellow, subacid, rich and good. Tree a strong grower and bears heavily annually. Its antiseptic properties are so great that when cut to pieces it will dry perfectly *in the shade* without decaying." The Maryland catalog says the tree is unusually spreading in shape and holds its fruit well. Fruit "markedly conical in shape with bright red stripes over a gray color." ❖ **Plate 112.**

❦ **SCHOOLFIELD:** Originated in Tennessee or Arkansas before 1873. No description except ripe winter. No catalog listings.

❦ **SCOTCH RED:** The original tree grew up in a blackberry patch on the farm of P. P. McRae near Maston, Robeson County, North Carolina. This was an old Scottish settlement in the coastal plains of North Carolina, hence the name. Sold by the J. Van Lindley Nursery of Greensboro, North Carolina, from 1898 to 1915.

Fruit medium, roundish oblong; skin smooth, glossy, nearly entirely dark red with a few russet patches; dots russet; stem short and slender in a deep, abrupt, lightly russeted cavity; calyx closed; basin medium size, gradually sloped, deeply furrowed; flesh white, rather coarse, crisp, sweet. Ripe August–October.

❦ **SCOTTSON** (Scott's Early?): From the 1900 catalog of Bonham Nurseries, Bonham, Texas: "Probably an old sort unidentified. I secured stock from J. W. Scott of Grayson County, Texas; tree large, prolific; fruit most excellent and of great beauty. July 15th–25th." This is probably the same apple as Scott's Early, listed without description by Bonham Nurseries from 1900 to 1904. No description.

❦ **SEAFORD:** Originated in Seaford, Delaware, before 1895.

Fruit medium, roundish; skin smooth, thin, greenish yellow washed with red and indistinctly striped with crimson; dots gray, some indented; stem short in a large, deep, abrupt, russeted cavity; calyx closed; basin small, shallow, russeted; flesh greenish yellow, juicy, subacid. Ripe winter. No catalog listings.

❦ **SECKEL:** Listed by two Virginia nurseries from 1850 to 1869. Probably resembles the Seckel pear, which is small and russeted. No description.

❦ **SEEDLING NO. 1:** An apple sent to the USDA in 1891 by Dr. G. H. Horne of Latham, Arkansas, and described in the 1891 USDA Annual Report: "A large, oblong, cylindrical apple; skin very smooth and of a rich yellow transparent color; flesh yellow, crisp, juicy; flavor pleasant subacid with a delightful aroma; quality best." No catalog listings.

❦ **SEEK-NO-FURTHER:** This is a synonym for at least twelve different apple varieties but is most often applied to Rambo and Westfield Seek-No-Further. The listings in most southern nursery catalogs are obviously for the Westfield Seek-No-Further. Bonham Nurseries, Bonham, Texas, sold a Seek-No-further from 1900 to 1904 that is neither the Rambo nor the Westfield: "Large, flesh and skin yellow, usually striped with red; best quality; prolific; ripens July 15th."

❦ **SELMA:** In 1858, the Fruitland Nursery of Augusta, Georgia, listed an apple named Selma with origin credited to Alabama. In 1861, this same nursery listed an apple named Selma, origin credited to Ohio. An apple named Selma did originate in Ohio before 1854.

Fruit medium or above, roundish; skin yellow with a faint blush and pale russet patches; flesh yellowish white, breaking, subacid. Ripe August/September or later.

❦ **SENECA:** A South Carolina apple sold in 1859 by Hopewell Nurseries, Fredericksburg, Virginia. No description.

❦ **SEPTEMBER APPLE:** A seedling of Buckingham, "resembling its parent but larger." One of the varieties listed in 1920 and named for the months of the year by the Collinsville Nursery, Collinsville, Alabama. No description. *See* August Apple.

❦ **SEPTEMBER RED:** From the 1924 catalog of Newton Nurseries, Newton, Mississippi: "Medium red, yellow flesh, fine quality, thrifty grower and a heavy bearer. This apple has been selected from thirty varieties as being the best of its season."

❦ **SEVIER:** Originated before 1895 with J. M. Bell of Mynatt, Knox County, Tennessee.

Fruit medium to large, roundish, ribbed, sides often unequal; skin tough, smooth except for a few russet knobs, white-washed with red and striped with crimson; dots medium size, russeted; stem short and slender in an irregular, abrupt, deep, large, russeted cavity; basin medium size, abrupt, shallow, furrowed; flesh yellowish, juicy, acid to subacid. Ripe August. No catalog listings.

❦ **SEWELL'S FAVORITE** (Sewall): In 1830, Joel Wallace planted some apple seeds he carried from North Carolina to his new farm near Trinity in Morgan County, Alabama. This tree originated from one of those seeds. It was named and sold by a nurseryman named Sewell in Morgan County about 1870 and was listed by a Tennessee nursery in 1887. Around 1896, Sewell's Favorite was very popular and widely grown in north Alabama where it was considered the best summer apple for that area.

Fruit medium, roundish, flattened on the ends; skin orangish at the stem end, shading to a deeper red at the calyx end with some faint darker red stripes; dots large and small, numerous, gray and russet; stem long in a medium-size, russeted cavity; basin shallow; flesh whitish, fine-grained, melting. Ripe July–September. ❖ **Plate 113.**

❦ **SHACKLEFORD** (Shackle Ford's Best, Shackelford): A Ben Davis type apple, of Ben Davis quality but less highly colored. Originated before 1883 in Clark County, Missouri, near Athens. Tree prolific, hardy, and healthy and said to flourish on poor land. Sold in the South mostly by Maryland nurseries.

Fruit medium to large, roundish or roundish oblong; skin thick, tough, waxy, smooth, pale greenish yellow washed with red and mottled and striped with carmine; dots inconspicuous, small, numerous, sometimes russet or submerged; stem long and slender in a slightly russeted cavity; calyx closed; basin medium to large, rather wide, abrupt, wrinkled; flesh tinged yellow, firm, moderately coarse, crisp, juicy, mild subacid. Ripe December–May. Catalog listings: MD, KY (1897–1904). ❖ **Plate 114.**

❦ **SHANKLIN'S SUMMER:** Sold in 1870 by the Forest Nursery, Fairview, Kentucky: "Fruit large, whitish, tender, juicy, subacid." Ripe summer.

❦ **SHANNON PIPPIN** (Shannon): For years before the turn of the twentieth century, most pomologists thought Shannon, an Arkansas apple, was identical to another old variety called Ohio Pippin. Careful comparison in 1899 by the Arkansas Agricultural Experiment Station proved conclusively that these two varieties, while very similar in appearance, are different apples.

Shannon apples were exhibited at the New Orleans World Exposition in 1884 and were awarded more premiums than any other southern apple. Its eating quality is usually highly praised, but some references rate it as of good quality only. The fruit can be very large; there is a record of a Shannon apple weighing twenty-seven ounces being exhibited in Fayetteville, Arkansas, in 1869.

The early history of the Shannon is not clear. One story is that a man named Granville Shannon bought some apple trees from a tree peddler near Evansville, Arkansas, before the Civil War. By the time the trees fruited, the labels had been lost, so Mr. Shannon named the best variety for himself.

In the nursery, Shannon is hard to propagate and grows very slowly the first year. It then becomes a vigorous tree, but usually is a biennial and often a shy bearer. The fruit ripens on the tree over a period of several weeks. Tom Brown has found an apple that he believes is the Shannon Pippin, but more work is needed to fully identify this apple.

Fruit large to very large, three to four inches in diameter, oblate to roundish oblate, conical; skin smooth, bright yellow, sometimes faintly blushed, with a dull overcast of whitish blotches and streaks; dots small, inconspicuous, whitish or pale green, often submerged, sometimes with russet points; stem short and rather thick in a shallow (Beach says deep), russeted cavity; calyx open; basin moderately shallow, usually furrowed; flesh yellow, rather firm, juicy, tender, breaking, subacid. Ripe September–December. Catalog listings: VA, NC, GA, LA, TN, KY, TX, AR (1870–1925).

❦ **SHARPE'S GREENING** (Sharpe's Winter, Sharp's Winter, Sharp's Apple?): Originated in Alamance County, North Carolina. This is certainly the same as the Sharp's Apple described in an 1896 Illinois agricultural experiment station bulletin that is summarized in the description here. Although Ragan (1905) lists Sharp's Winter as a separate variety, its description is essentially identical to Sharpe's Greening.

Fruit small to medium, rather oblate, ribbed; skin smooth becoming oily, light waxen or greenish yellow, usually blushed and with a thin, white bloom; dots small, inconspicuous, whitish; stem medium length, slender in a medium-size, open, russeted cavity; calyx closed; basin medium size, rather abrupt, corrugated; flesh almost white, very tender, very juicy, mild subacid to almost sweet. Ripe September/October and a good keeper. Catalog listings: VA, NC, SC, GA, KY (1859–1904).

❦ **SHAVER'S SWEET:** Listed in 1896 by the Dayton Nursery, Dayton, Virginia. No description except ripe summer.

❦ **SHAW'S SEEDLING:** Listed in 1860 by a South Carolina nursery.

Fruit large. Ripe December.

❦ **SHEDDAN** (Taylor?): Found about 1882 growing on the farm of John E. Sheddan, Friendsville, Blount County, Tennessee, and thought to be a seedling of Green Cheese × Winesap. Brought to public attention by being exhibited by Mr. Sheddan at the 1894 meeting of the Monroe Horticultural Society. The fruit hangs well on the tree, is rather hard and sour when first picked, but mellows in storage into a very fine eating apple. The tree is slow-growing but very healthy.

Fruit large, roundish oblate; skin smooth, greenish when picked but turning golden yellow in storage with a slight blush on some apples; stem long and curved in an abrupt, large, deep cavity; flesh yellowish, tender, fine-grained, juicy, mild subacid. Ripe January–May. No catalog listings.

❦ **SHELTON'S RED WINTER:** Sold in 1870 by the Forest Nursery, Fairview, Kentucky: "Large, new, handsome and very promising." Ripe winter. No description.

❦ **SHENK:** Originated about 1860 on the west side of Thornton's Gap, Virginia. Tree productive and an annual bearer.

Fruit above medium, roundish conical; skin thick, yellow with some russet patches, washed and striped with mixed red and overspread with gray; dots numerous, yellowish, many with dark centers; cavity medium size, russeted; calyx closed; basin small, shallow, furrowed; flesh yellowish white, fine-grained, tender, very juicy, subacid. Ripe late winter. No catalog listings.

❦ **SHEPHERD'S KEEPER:** Sold from 1898 to 1901 by the Franklin Davis Nursery, Richmond, Virginia: "Origin Carroll County, Maryland. This new seedling apple promises great things. The fruit is medium size, round, deep reddish brown; an annual and heavy bearer. Ready for use January 15 and good until June."

❦ **SHIPLEY GREEN:** From an 1853 issue of the *Western Horticultural Review* magazine: "Origin Frederick County, Maryland. A medium size, oblong, red and rusty winter apple, sour to excess, yet it has its friends. Perhaps when we consider that it will keep as long as wished, and when fully mellow can be eaten with some satisfaction, and that it will bake quite well, and when we consider the perfect growth of the tree and its great bearing qualities, it may still find a place among the long keepers." Listed by the Franklin Davis Nursery, Richmond, Virginia, from 1858 to 1904.

❦ **SHIRLEY** (Shirley's Keeper, York Imperial?, Texas Red?): About 1876, the Texas nurseryman T. V. Munson found several trees of an unknown apple growing near Denison, Texas. Some of the trees were in an old orchard owned by Alexander H. Shirley, and this variety eventually became known as Shirley's Keeper or Shirley. Attempts to trace the apple were unsuccessful. Mr. Munson guessed that the trees had been sold years before by one of the first nurseries in Texas, near Clarksville, which sold an apple called Texas Red, very similar to the Shirley. Fruit of the Shirley was sent to the great pomologist Charles Downing, but he could not identify it. Mr. Munson listed the Shirley apple in his nursery catalogs from 1894 to 1905.

Apples of both Shirley and Texas Red were sent to the USDA in 1894 and were identified by USDA pomologists as the York Imperial. Mr. Munson wrote a detailed letter back to the USDA refuting this identity by carefully comparing the fruit and tree of the Shirley and York Imperial. There the matter stands to this day.

Fruit below to above medium, roundish oblate; skin smooth, greenish yellow mottled and striped with medium red, deeper red on the sunny side; dots inconspicuous, small, light gray; stem long and slender in a rather wide, acute cavity; calyx closed; basin abrupt, medium size, smooth; flesh whitish, firm, rather coarse, briskly subacid. Ripe winter and an excellent keeper. *See also* Texas Red. ❖ **Plate 115.**

❦ **SHOCK:** Originated before 1915 by L. L. Moore of Taylorsville, North Carolina.

Fruit medium, roundish, somewhat flattened; skin yellowish white; flesh subacid. Ripe August. No catalog listings.

❦ **SHRINETOWN PIPPIN:** Listed in 1904 by the Maryland Nursery Company of Baltimore, Maryland: "One of the best winter apples. Succeeds well in Maryland and Pennsylvania." No description.

❦ **SILOAM:** Originated before 1886 near Siloam Springs, Arkansas.

Fruit medium, oblate; skin smooth, yellow, about half covered with dull red stripes and splashes; dots numerous, small, light gray; stem very short in a shallow, russeted cavity; calyx closed; basin shallow; flesh yellow, fine-grained, juicy, subacid. Ripe December to spring. No catalog listings.

❦ **SILVER HILL** (Dougherty): From a letter written in 1896 by G. W. Robinett, Scott County, Virginia: "This apple came from seed of an old tree set out in 1808. William H. Dougherty planted the seed while working in a silver and lead mine near this place. The tree grew up and produces a fine and grand apple. This apple is very large, round, color glossy green with specks, flesh white, quality fine, use table." No catalog listings.

❦ **SIMMONS RED** (Red Everlasting, Simmons, Red Simmons, Simon's Red, Simson's Red?, Everbearing?): About 1840, John W. Davis, who lived near Perry, Houston County, Georgia, planted a seed from a North Carolina apple. The first Simmons Red tree grew up from that seed and bore fruit especially fine for cider and cooking but also good for fresh eating. The tree is vigorous, compact, and heavy-bearing. The fruit ripens on the tree from June until September, hence the name Red Everlasting.

Fruit medium to large, roundish oblate or oblate, slightly conical; skin pale yellow shaded dark crimson in the sun but obscurely striped and splashed with red on the other side; dots numerous, small and large, irregular shaped, yellowish russet; stem short in a broad, deep, uneven, russeted cavity; calyx closed or open; basin deep and nearly smooth; flesh pale yellow, tender, juicy, slightly aromatic, mild subacid. Ripe June–September. Catalog listings: GA, AR (1885–1909). *See* Everbearing Red June.

❦ **SIMS' SEEDLING:** A South Carolina apple listed in 1860 by Pomaria Nurseries of South Carolina. Ripe December.

❦ **SISK:** Originated about 1825 on the farm of Joseph Sisk in Caroline County, Maryland.

Fruit almost large, oblate; skin pale yellow shaded and obscurely striped with two shades of red; dots few, brown; stem short in a broad and deep cavity; calyx open; basin broad, deep, corrugated; flesh whitish yellow, tender, juicy, mild subacid. Ripe October–January. No catalog listings.

❦ **SKELTON** (Skeleton): An Arkansas apple that originated before 1895.

Fruit large, roundish conical; skin smooth, thin, yellow, almost covered with dark red with a few darker stripes and having a thin gray bloom; dots conspicuous, yellow, indented; stem short in a medium-wide, deep, heavily russeted cavity; calyx closed; basin small, abrupt, medium depth, corrugated and cracked; flesh yellowish stained with red, rather fine-grained, tender, juicy, subacid. Ripe late June/July. No catalog listings.

❦ **SKIDMORE:** A Maryland apple, large and red, ripening in August and September. Catalog listings: MD, NC, SC (1836–60).

❦ **SLADKAJA:** A Russian apple sold by Alabama and Louisiana nurseries from 1886 to 1888: "Large, measuring eleven inches around; color clear, waxy white; flesh almost clear white, very tender, pleasant subacid. A good August cooking apple."

❦ **SMITH:** Sold from 1923 to 1925 by the Southern Nursery Company of Winchester, Tennessee: "Originated at Baton Rouge, LA. Large, yellow striped with red; unsurpassed as a cooking apple. A vigorous and productive tree. Especially recommended for planting in south Louisiana and Mississippi and the coast country. Ripens June 1."

❦ **SMITH'S EARLY** (Smith's Large Early?): From the 1880 catalog of Virginia Nurseries, Richmond, Virginia: "Large, round, yellowish, firm, juicy; crisp and pleasant. Tree very vigorous and a remarkable annual bearer. Attains good shipping size a few days later than Early Harvest. Commands the highest price of any apple shipped in July from the Norfolk market."

❦ **SMITH SEEDLING/SMITH'S SEEDLING:** There are five apples named Smith Seedling or Smith's Seedling—three of these are of southern origin, of which two are still available, and the third is described below. *See* Smith Seedling *and* Smith's Seedling of Mississippi *in chapter 5.*

❦ **SMITH'S SEEDLING** of Alabama (Ragsdale): Originated on the farm of Edward Smith in northern Alabama and propagated by a small local nursery in the 1890s.

Fruit large, roundish conical; skin pale green with dark yellow veins, sometimes blushed; flesh yellow, breaking, rather coarse, moderately juicy, subacid. Ripe winter. No catalog listings.

❦ **SMOKYTWIG:** A Kentucky apple that originated before 1867.

Fruit medium or below, oblong conical; skin yellow, mostly covered with red and red stripes (also described as a yellow apple); flesh yellow (also described as white), tender, juicy, almost sweet. Ripe November–January. Catalog listings: VA, KY (1870–1915).

❦ **SNEED** (Sneed Cider): An Alabama cider apple that originated before 1894 with the Sneed brothers of Pronto, Alabama.

Fruit medium, roundish oblate, sides unequal; skin smooth, oily, yellowish green with red stripes and splashes and some russet patches; dots numerous, irregular, sometimes russet; stem short and knobbed in an abrupt, slightly russeted cavity; calyx closed; basin deep, slightly ribbed, with a heavy bloom; flesh white, tough, moderately juicy, sharp acid. Ripe July. No catalog listings.

❦ **SOUTH CAROLINA SUMMER:** From the 1928 catalog of W. T. Hood Nurseries, Richmond, Virginia: "This apple is high colored and as bright as varnished. When other varieties fail, the South Carolina Summer produces fruit. It ripens where it originated, in Spartanburg County, South Carolina, from June 15 to the middle of August. Introduced by us."

Fruit medium, roundish, slightly conical; skin mostly bright red with a few broken darker red stripes; dots tan with black centers; stem medium to long and rather thick in a narrow, deep, russeted cavity; calyx open; basin medium depth, corrugated; flesh whitish, firm, crisp, juicy. Ripe June–August. ❖ **Plate 116.**

❦ **SOUTHERN BEAUTY:** Described in the 1916 catalog of Corinth Nurseries, Corinth, Alcorn County, Mississippi: "Very much like the Yates but twice as large. It has been kept in this county until April 1st. This apple originated in this county, and I am the only one who has it for sale."

❦ **SOUTHERN BELLFLOWER/STRIPED BELLFLOWER:** Both listed as South Carolina apples in the 1860 catalog of Pomaria Nurseries of South Carolina. No descriptions.

❧ **SOUTHERN LADY:** A North Carolina apple sold in 1861 by the Fruitland Nursery, Augusta, Georgia.

Fruit small, oblate; skin whitish, much shaded with crimson; dots numerous, light-colored; stem short and small; calyx closed; flesh yellowish, tender, juicy, aromatic, mild subacid. Ripe September/ October.

❧ **SOUTHERN MAMMOTH:** An apple grown in west Tennessee before 1905.

Fruit large, round; skin red-striped; flesh yellow, fine-grained. Ripe late fall. No catalog listings.

❧ **SOUTHERN PORTER** (Jones, Hogpen, Kidd, Long, Porter, Fall Wylie, Wylie's Favorite): From an 1873 letter to Charles Downing from Dr. A. P. Wylie of Chester, South Carolina: "Rev. William Porter came from Massachusetts about 1770, bringing with him an apple plant or seed which he planted in Chester County, South Carolina. The tree grew and its fruit was fed to hogs. In the hogpen an apple seedling grew up from which this locally famous apple has sprung. It is called Jones more than any other name." Tree very productive and usually a biennial bearer.

Fruit medium, roundish conical; skin bright golden yellow; dots few, gray or brown; stem short in a deep cavity; calyx open; basin large, slightly corrugated; flesh whitish, fine-grained, juicy, mild subacid. Ripe September/October. No catalog listings. ❖ **Plate 117.**

❧ **SOUTHERN QUEEN:** In 1856, Major Samuel Brown of Horry County, South Carolina, planted some apple trees purchased from a North Carolina nursery. One tree, grafted on seedling rootstock, sent up a root sprout that was dug up and planted. The fruit from this sprout was named Southern Queen. There is no description of the fruit except its large size—one apple weighed nineteen ounces and was ripe in October. No catalog listings.

❧ **SOUTHFALL:** A winter apple from Georgia sold in 1859 by Hopewell Nurseries, Fredericksburg, Virginia.

❧ **SPALDING** (Prince George's County Pippin): Described to the 1897 meeting of the American Pomological Society: "Found as a small scrubby tree in a fence row in 1870 in Prince George's County, Virginia. Resembles Virginia Greening somewhat."

Fruit large, roundish, slightly conical, sides often unequal; skin greenish yellow with a reddish or bronze blush on the sunny side; dots scattered, dark brown; stem short to medium length in a rather narrow, abrupt, greenish cavity; calyx open or partially closed; basin wide and shallow, furrowed; flesh yellowish, fine-grained, tender, juicy, subacid. Ripe October. No catalog listings.

❧ **SPANN:** Exhibited in 1853 by William Murray of Whitfield County, Georgia. Originated with the Cherokee Indians.

Fruit green, striped with red; flavor acid. Ripe winter and keeps until February. No catalog listings.

❧ **SPARK'S LATE** (Spark, Celestial Sparks): Originated before 1855 with J. M. Felt of Bayou Sara, Louisiana, and sold by a Georgia nursery in 1890. Grown and admired as far north as Illinois, where one grower said it produced a perfect crop every year. Tree vigorous, productive, and an upright grower.

Fruit above medium to large, roundish to quite oblong, conical; skin smooth, greenish yellow, rarely blushed; dots numerous, rather large, gray or brown; stem long and slender in a deep, acute, green cavity; calyx closed; basin small and shallow; flesh

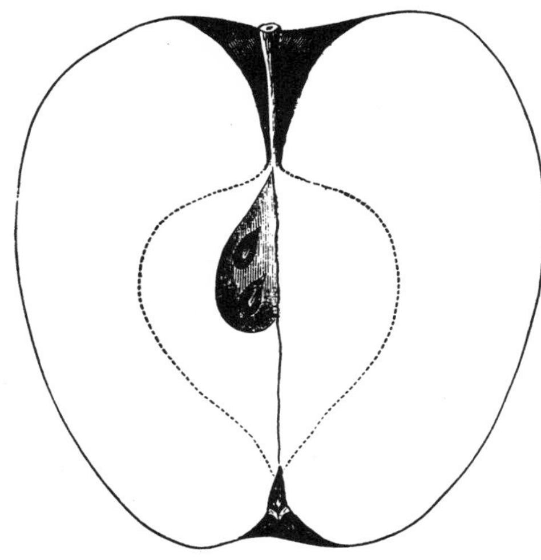

SPARK'S LATE

whitish or yellowish, tender, fine-grained, juicy, mild subacid. Keeps until December when grown in Illinois.

❧ **SPICE APPLES:** This is another apple name where there is total confusion in nomenclature. Ragan (1905) lists twelve apples named Spice plus thirteen synonyms with Spice in the name. Southern nursery catalogs listed many Spice apples such as Virginia Spice, Spice Pippin, Spice Sweet, Winter Spice, Spice Apple, Early Spice, Cumberland Spice, White Spice, and others, often without descriptions. Described here are those Spice apples for which usable information exists. *See also* Virginia Spice.

*Early Spice*: Originated in Chatham County, North Carolina, and sold by North Carolina nurseries from 1853 to 1860. Fruit small, round; skin yellow; flesh yellow, dry, "high flavored." Ripe July/August.

*Winter Spice* (Winter Spicen): A North Carolina apple sold by North Carolina nurseries from 1853 to 1869. Fruit medium, oblong conical; skin pale green; flesh sweet. Ripe October–March.

*Cumberland Spice*: Originated in Cumberland County, New Jersey, and often confused with Ortley, which is a different apple. Fruit above medium, roundish to oblong conical; skin pale, waxy yellow, rarely blushed; dots black or brown; stem short in a shallow cavity; flesh white, tender, juicy, subacid. Ripe December–February. Catalog listings: MD, VA, NC (1836–69).

❧ **SPLENDID:** Originated by Charles Barfield about 1890 or before in Wilkerson County, Georgia. No description. No catalog listing.

❧ **SPRING APPLE/SPRING GREENING:** These two apples were listed in 1853 by the North Carolina Pomological Gardens, a nursery in Greensboro, North Carolina. The Spring Apple is large, round, pale greenish with red. Ripe October–February. The Spring Greening is medium size, round, green. Ripe November–March.

❧ **SPRING GRUB** (Grub?): A North Carolina winter apple sold in 1859 by Hopewell Nurseries, Fredericksburg, Virginia. An apple called Grub was being grown near Charlestown, West Virginia (then Virginia), in 1855, but was said to be a summer apple.

❧ **SPRINGDALE:** An Arkansas apple sold by Stark Bro's Nursery around 1900. According to several old catalogs, it succeeds well all over the South, even in the lower piedmont, and keeps exceptionally well. Freezing does not injure the apples, which develop best flavor when stored until January or later. The tree is resistant to the woolly apple aphid and tends to keep growing until late in the fall, making it susceptible to cold damage in severe winter areas.

Fruit medium, roundish oblate; skin greenish yellow, mostly covered with dull red and indistinct darker red stripes, often has russet streaks and patches; dots numerous, russet; stem short to medium length and thick in a russeted, gradually sloped cavity; basin rather shallow, corrugated, gradually sloped; flesh yellowish green, solid, fairly tender, subacid. Ripe winter. Catalog listings: MD, VA, NC, KY, TX (1894–1919). ❖ **Plate 118.**

❧ **SPRINGFIELD:** Listed in 1855 by Guilford Pomological Nurseries of Greensboro, North Carolina. No description except ripe November–April.

❧ **STAFFORD'S RUSSET/STAFFORD'S PIPPIN /STAFFORD'S SWEETING:** These three apple varieties were listed but not described in 1853 by a North Carolina nursery. An apple named "Spafford Russet" (obviously a mispelling) was tested at an agricultural experiment station in Illinois in the 1880s and described as small, oblate conical, russeted, mild subacid, good in quality. I believe that all of these apples originated with the same Stafford family of Alamance County, North Carolina, which originated the Stafford apple (still available). *See* Stafford.

❧ **STANLEY** (Stanley's Seedling, Stanley's Early): Originated before 1856 in Tuscaloosa County, Alabama.

Fruit large, roundish conical; skin greenish yellow; flesh whitish, tender, moderately juicy, subacid. Ripe August/September. Catalog listings: GA, MS (1871–78).

❧ **STANSILL** (Stansil, Stensill, Stansill's Red): A North Carolina apple discussed at the 1860 meeting of the American Pomological Society. "Endures any amount of heat and remains sound." There is an unusual enlargement of fruit spurs on trees of the Stansill. Trees begin bearing when very young.

Fruit above medium to large, roundish to oblate; skin green with a slight blush on shaded fruit, but more blush on the fruit in the sun; flesh yellow, firm, juicy, subacid. Ripe November–March and best for eating if stored until January. Catalog listings: SC, GA, MS (1858–78).

❦ **STARK'S SEEDLING:** Listed in 1897 by Green River Nurseries, Bowling Green, Kentucky: "A local apple resembling Summer Pearmain in form and general appearance. Has been tested for many years and is very reliable. November."

❦ **STEPP:** Originated on the farm of S. H. Stepp near Dry Creek, Carter County, Tennessee. Eating quality highly praised in an 1896 Tennessee agricultural experiment station bulletin.

Fruit large, roundish oblate; skin yellowish green washed with dull red and striped with crimson; dots conspicuous, brown or russet, some areole; stem short and stout in a large, deep, gradually sloped, slightly russeted cavity; basin large, deep, abrupt, with shallow furrows; flesh yellowish, fine-grained, tender, juicy, mild subacid. Ripe autumn. No catalog listings.

❦ **STETSON'S PEAR APPLE:** Listed without description in 1861 by the Fruitland Nursery, Augusta, Georgia. May be Palmer.

❦ **STEVENSON PIPPIN** (Dwight Apple): From a letter written to Charles Downing in 1880 by Richard Thursto of Van Buren, Arkansas: "Some fifty years ago, by some pursuit of our government, a portion of the Cherokee Indian nation settled in this territory in what is now Pope County. A missionary by the name of Dwight operated the well known Dwight's mission, and the Indians planted and cultivated a number of apple seeds. The trees remained in bearing many years after the mission and the Indians were moved. Only one, the Stevenson Pippin, was considered choice. It was propagated by citizens in the vicinity, including James G. Stevenson of Crawford County, Arkansas."

In 1899, the Stevenson Pippin was "grown in most sections of northwest Arkansas and is considered desirable for family orchards." The tree produces heavy and light crops on alternate years. The description of the fruit is almost identical to the McAfee, which has a synonym of "Stephenson's Pippin."

Fruit medium to large, roundish oblate; skin yellow shaded with light red and striped and splashed with dark red rather thickly over the entire surface; dots large and small, yellow, some areole; stem short in a large, deep, russeted cavity; calyx closed; basin rather large, slightly wrinkled; flesh pale yellow, somewhat coarse, juicy, aromatic, subacid. Ripe October–February. No catalog listings.

❦ **STEVENSON'S WINTER** (Stephenson's Winter, Steven's Winter, Stevens): A hundred years ago, this was a very popular apple that originated in Marshall County, Mississippi, and that was sold by nurseries all over the South. The nurseryman William Summer of South Carolina credited it to Holly Springs, Mississippi, in 1860. Stevenson's Winter was esteemed as a long-keeping apple of excellent eating quality and was considered the finest winter apple in the Memphis, Tennessee, area around 1880, where it sold for premium prices. The tree bears early and heavily. One catalog says the apple has a flavor "much like a pineapple."

Fruit medium or perhaps larger, round or roundish oblate; skin greenish yellow, mostly covered with brown, but some old catalogs say shaded and sometimes striped with dull red; dots medium size, gray; stem long and slender in a rather wide and shallow cavity; calyx open or closed; basin shallow, almost wide; flesh whitish, firm, juicy, tender, fine-grained, aromatic, subacid (some references say sweet). Ripe November–April. Catalog listings: MD, SC, VA, NC, GA, AL, MS, LA, TN, KY, TX (1858–1912).

❦ **STEWARD:** A Texas apple first grown before 1904 by Otto Locke of the Comal Springs Nursery, New Braunfels, Texas.

Fruit medium size, red-striped, ripe late. No catalog listings.

❦ **STEWART:** Described at the 1900 meeting of the Virginia State Horticultural Society as "a promising new variety for late summer and early autumn."

Fruit large, oblate conical; skin yellowish green, prominently washed and streaked with pale red, which shades to dark crimson on fruit in the sun; flesh white, crisp, tender, subacid. Ripe September at Blacksburg, Virginia. No catalog listings.

❦ **STINSON:** First grown before 1895 in Treeville, Tennessee, by a small nursery named Bird, Dew and Hale.

Fruit large, roundish conical; skin greenish yellow washed with pale red and obscurely striped with crimson, overspread with a gray bloom; dots variable in size, russet; stem short in a large, deep, russeted cavity; calyx open; basin medium size, abrupt, furrowed, russeted; flesh yellowish, rather fine-grained, crisp, juicy, subacid. Ripe September. No catalog listings.

❦ **STOKES:** Apples sent to the USDA in 1902 by the prominent Maryland nurseryman, J. W. Kerr.

Fruit below medium, roundish to slightly oblate; skin mostly red with broad, broken, darker red stripes; dots inconspicuous; stem rather long in a gradually sloped, russeted cavity; calyx closed; basin medium size, yellowish; flesh white. Ripe October. No catalog listings.

❦ **STONE'S EXCELSIOR:** Originated about 1874 by Silas M. Stone of Wake County, North Carolina, and listed by a North Carolina nursery in 1886.

Fruit medium to large; skin greenish with red stripes; flesh subacid. Ripe winter and a good keeper.

❦ **STONEWALL** (Stonewall Jackson): There are two southern apples named Stonewall with both having the synonym of Stonewall Jackson. The first originated about 1866 in Monroe County, Alabama, perhaps by a man named Kendall.

Fruit medium, roundish conical, sides unequal; skin whitish yellow, shaded and striped with red; flesh white, firm, not very juicy, brisk subacid. Ripe winter and keeps until May. No catalog listings.

The second Stonewall apple originated before 1872 in Lunenburg County, Virginia, and was listed by a Virginia nursery in 1878.

Fruit medium to large; skin greenish yellow streaked with red; flesh rather mealy, mild subacid. Ripe December–March.

An entirely different apple named Stonewall Jackson originated in Nova Scotia and was not grown in the South.

❦ **STORMPROOF:** Sold in 1923 by the Plainview Nursery of Plainview, Texas. The tree is strong and not easily broken by storms when loaded with fruit.

Fruit medium size, light green in color, sweet, a good keeper.

❦ **STOVER'S BEST** (Stover): Sold from 1869 to 1904 by the Franklin Davis Nursery, Richmond, Virginia. No description.

❦ **STRAWN'S SEEDLING** (Strawn, Straughan's Seedling): Raised by James Strawn of Virginia before 1853. Tree bears heavily. "Fruit always perfect."

Fruit medium to large, roundish; skin greenish yellow with faint red stripes; stem short and fleshy in a small cavity; calyx closed; flesh juicy, crisp, sharply acid when picked, but becomes mild subacid with storage. Ripe December–April. Catalog listings: VA, SC, GA, KY (1858–1904).

❦ **STRIBLING** (Red Harvest): Originated about 1840 with William Stribling of Medon, Madison County, Tennessee. Sold from 1870 to 1897 by Kentucky nurseries and around 1900 by Stark Bro's Nursery, which used the name Red Harvest. Popular in Kentucky before 1900 as an early market apple that "ripens before Early Harvest and Red June are gone." Tree an annual and heavy bearer. An apple thought to be Stribling has been recently found, but further identification is necessary.

Fruit medium or above, oblate, slightly angular; skin greenish white, nearly covered with stripes and splashes of light and dark red, some splashes almost purple; dots conspicuous, yellow; stem short and small in a medium-size cavity; basin rather small and slightly corrugated; flesh white, tender, moderately juicy, mild subacid. Ripe July or early August.

❦ **STRING:** A North Carolina apple listed in 1859 by Hopewell Nurseries, Fredericksburg, Virginia. No description.

❦ **STRINGSTON:** An Australian apple sold from 1913 to 1924 by the Comal Springs Nursery of New Braunfels, Texas: "This new Australian apple has been fruiting here for years; a fine, large, round summer apple, highly colored on the sunny side; the trees bear young, having fruited in the nursery the first year. Ripens end of July."

❦ **STRIPED FALL:** Sold in 1915 by the New Cumberland Nursery, Sawyer, Kentucky. No description.

❦ **STRIPED GREENING:** Listed in 1853 as a good cider apple by the North Carolina Pomological Gardens, Greensboro, North Carolina.

Fruit small, round; skin green with red stripes. Ripe January–March.

❦ **STRIPED JULY** (July, Striped June, Virginia June?): An apple called July or Striped July was grown in Virginia for many years, but its origin was unknown even in 1874. Ragan (1905) believed this apple to be the same as the Virginia June. *See* Virginia June.

In 1893, a Striped July apple was listed by Smith's Nursery of Franklin, Tennessee: "From Wilson County, Tennessee. Tree a fine grower; fruit medium to large, bright red on yellow; flesh yellowish, rich, subacid, very firm and high flavored. An excellent bearer. July 5th to 20th." This also may be the same apple as the Virginia June.

Another apple named Striped July was listed from 1900 to 1904 by Bonham Nurseries, Bonham, Texas: "A local apple. Size above medium, striped with red, subacid, excellent, sure and early bearer; ripens July 10th."

The American pomologist Charles Downing wrote to Dr. Stayman in Kansas in 1877: "I have seen two varieties of Striped July which appear different from the Striped Junes. There is work for someone to get this straightened out."

❦ **STRIPED QUEEN:** An apple grown in Monroe County, Alabama, in 1871. No description. No catalog listings.

❦ **STRIPED ROMANITE:** Listed in 1867 by Westbrook Nurseries, Greensboro, North Carolina. No description except ripe late winter.

❦ **STRIPED SWEETING** (Striped Sweet June?): Origin unknown but sold from 1891 to 1896 by Atlanta Nurseries, Atlanta, Georgia: "Large; yellow, beautifully splashed with red; sweet, sprightly and good. August." An apple of the same name and general description was discussed by the Indiana Horticultural Society in 1872, and an apple named Striped Sweet June was being grown in Kentucky before 1900.

❦ **STROTHER:** A Virginia apple (or perhaps South Carolina). Ripe November. Catalog listings: NC, SC, VA (1860–69).

❦ **STUART'S GOLDEN** (Stewart's Golden, Stump): Originated on the farm of William Stuart, Rush Creek, Ohio, where the tree grew up near a stump. Sold in 1891 by Stark Bro's Nursery and from 1902 to 1904 by Harrison and Sons Nurseries of Berlin, Maryland. Tree a heavy bearer on alternate years. Fruit an excellent keeper of high quality that hangs well on the tree.

Fruit above to below medium, roundish oblate, sometimes oblique; skin clear yellow, but deep orange in the sun, sometimes blushed; dots few, brown; stem short; calyx closed; basin rather large, moderately deep, "saucer shaped"; flesh whitish yellow, breaking, tender, juicy, aromatic, subacid. Ripe December–May. ❖ **Plate 119.**

❦ **SUGAR BALL** (Sugar?, Sugar Apple?): Presumably this is a North Carolina apple, as it was listed by two North Carolina nurseries from 1875 to 1902: "Medium to large size, oblate; yellow; flesh tender, very sweet and good. Middle of August." Another catalog says "ripe September–November."

❦ **SUGAR CANE:** A South Carolina apple sold by Pomaria Nurseries of South Carolina in 1860. No description except ripe August.

❦ **SULLIVAN:** Described at the 1897 meeting of the American Pomological Society as a chance seedling on the farm of Peyton R. Sullivan near Paris, Tennessee.

Fruit medium, oblate, slightly conical, sides unequal; skin smooth, yellow washed with mixed reds and indistinctly striped with crimson, overspread with gray toward the stem end; dots numerous, small, prominent, brown or yellow, many areole; stem short in a wide, deep, russeted cavity; calyx closed or partly open; basin medium size, abrupt, furrowed, cracked; flesh yellowish, fine-grained, tender, juicy, subacid. Ripe winter. No catalog listings.

❦ **SUMMER AMBROSIA:** From the 1915 catalog of the Continental Plant Company, Kittrell, North Carolina: "A medium size, golden flecked red apple of the most excellent flavor. Till you have eaten one of these strains of Ambrosia you can have no idea what a really tip-top apple can be. Ripens in August when apples are scarce."

❦ **SUMMER CHEESE** (Cheese Apple, Maryland Cheese, Prather, Findley, Fall Cheese, Gloucester Cheese): This apple might be confused with the Mangum, which has a synonym of Summer Cheese. The Mangum is a mostly red autumn apple, while Summer Cheese is a mostly yellow summer apple. Downing (1878) rates Summer Cheese as a poor-quality apple, but others give it higher marks.

An 1829 letter to a horticultural magazine states that a Summer Cheese apple was being grown in Old Jamestown, Virginia, about 1750, but no description of this apple is given.

Fruit medium or above, oblate; skin greenish yellow, occasionally slightly blushed; flesh whitish, tender, juicy, subacid. Ripe August/September. Catalog listings (most of these are undoubtedly Mangum): VA, NC, SC, GA, LA, KY (1845–1904).

❦ **SUMMER EXTRA** (Carver's Summer, Carver): First fruited before 1870 on the farm of George Carver near Quincy, Kentucky. A very similar apple named Carver, of Pennsylvania origin, is described by Downing (1878). In spite of their identical names and many similarities, these are probably different apples.

Fruit medium to large, roundish conical; skin light yellow with a pink blush; dots small, scattered, russet; stem rather long and slender in a narrow, almost shallow cavity; calyx closed or half open; basin narrow, deep, abrupt, furrowed; flesh yellowish white, tender, very juicy, subacid. Ripe August. No catalog listings.

❦ **SUMMER GOLDEN PIPPIN:** Probably the old English apple of the same name. Grown in western North Carolina for many years prior to 1900.

Fruit small to medium, ovate, flattened on the calyx end; skin bright yellow, but orangish on the sunny side; flesh yellow, firm, crisp, probably sweet. Ripe July/August. Catalog listings: GA, AL, AR (1898–1906).

❦ **SUMMER GREEN SKIN:** Listed from 1893 to 1902 by the J. Van Lindley Nursery, Greensboro, North Carolina. No description.

❦ **SUMMER HAGLOE** (Hagloe, Russian Hagloe): An old cooking apple of unknown origin, first described in 1817. Tree productive but a slow grower and having new shoots that are thick and blunt.

Fruit large, roundish oblate; skin pale green or whitish yellow striped with red, often with a thin bloom; stem short and thick in a broad, open cavity; calyx closed; basin small and round; flesh white, rather coarse, tender, juicy, subacid. Ripe July/August. Catalog listings: MD, VA, NC (1869–1904).

❦ **SUMMER HAZE:** Listed from 1824 to 1827 by the Linnean Hill Nursery, Washington, D.C. No description except ripe August.

❦ **SUMMER RED:** Briefly mentioned by Warder (1867) as a southern apple and sold in 1870 by the Forest Nursery, Fairview, Kentucky: "Fruit medium, skin white, red cheek, acid." Ripe July/August. This may be the same apple as the Coffman, which has the synonym Summer Red.

❦ **SUMMER RUSSET:** Sold in 1853 by the North Carolina Pomological Gardens, Greensboro, North Carolina.

Fruit medium, round; skin russeted. Ripe August. This may be the old New England apple named Pumpkin Russet, which has the synonym of Summer Russet.

❦ **SUMMER SWEET:** Warder (1867) briefly describes a Georgia apple by this name as large, oblate, yellow skin. There are two other apples called Summer Sweet, and three other apples have Summer Sweet as a synonym. The Cedar Cove Nursery of Yadkin County, North Carolina, sold an apple called Summer Sweet from 1875 to 1902, which was probably identical to the Georgia apple: "Medium size, roundish oblate; pale yellow, sweet, good. August."

❦ **SUMMER SWEET PARADISE** (Summer Paradise, August Pippin, Hare, Hare Pippin, Paradise Summer, Sweet Dumpling, Autumn Paradise?, Paradise Sweet?): An old Pennsylvania apple sold by several southern nurseries. In 1845, A. J. Downing (brother of the famous pomologist Charles Downing) said, "We received it some years ago . . . from Mr. Garber of Columbia, Pennsylvania, and consider it a native fruit." *See also* Winter Sweet Paradise.

Fruit large, round, slightly flattened on the ends; skin rather thick, pale green, sometimes tinged yellow in the sun; dots distinct, large, gray; cavity even, acute, rather deep green; calyx closed; basin shallow and wide; flesh white or yellow, crisp, tender, very juicy, aromatic, sweet. Ripe July/August. Catalog listings: MD, VA, NC, SC, KY (1853–1909).

**SUMMER WAFER:** An Alabama apple that originated before 1898. No description. No catalog listings.

**SUMMER'S LATE GREEN/SUMMER'S LATE STRIPED:** Two apples of South Carolina origin sold from 1856 to 1860 by Pomaria Nurseries, Pomaria, South Carolina. The owner of this nursery was William Summer who probably originated both of these apples. No description except both varieties ripen in November.

**SUMMUM BONUM** (Chief Good): Probably originated with Warwick Miller, who lived three miles west of Louisville, Kentucky. Sold from 1845 to 1870 by two Kentucky nurseries.

Fruit medium to large, roundish, flattened on the stem end; skin light yellow, streaked and mottled with red and with a few splashes of green; stem short and slender in an "open" cavity; basin shallow; flesh white, tender, juicy, aromatic, subacid. Ripe September/October.

**SUNSHINE:** In 1904, the mother of Frank Cathey, Mountain City, Georgia, planted some apple seeds to grow rootstocks. Some of the seedlings were "so straight and pretty" that they were left ungrafted and were planted out to grow. The Sunshine apple resulted from one of those seedlings. The tree bore when three years old and abundantly every year thereafter. Described at the 1914 meeting of the Georgia State Horticultural Society.

Fruit medium, roundish conical, sides unequal; skin tough, waxy, smooth, greenish yellow washed with bright red and streaked with darker red; dots conspicuous, medium to large, rather numerous; stem short and fairly thick in an acute, medium-size cavity; calyx open; basin medium size, ribbed; flesh whitish yellow tinged red near the skin, firm, moderately coarse, juicy, subacid. Ripe August. No catalog listings.

**SUPERB SWEET:** A Massachusetts apple sold by Virginia and Kentucky nurseries from 1845 to 1870. Fruit rather large, roundish conical; skin pale yellow, shaded and mottled with red; flesh white, very tender, sweet. Ripe September/October.

**SUPERB/EARLY SUPERB:** The Superb originated before the Civil War from a seed of the Hall apple in Franklin County, North Carolina. The tree is a "prodigious bearer."

Fruit medium or above, roundish oblate; skin green, sometimes with a blush; stem medium length in a shallow cavity; calyx open; flesh yellow, solid, slightly coarse, subacid. Ripe November–March. Catalog listings: VA, KY (1858–1904).

There is brief mention of another apple named Early Superb that probably originated in Greenup County, Kentucky, before 1840. The tree is a regular bearer but often overbears, resulting in small and imperfect fruit. Ripens with Early Harvest. No description of the fruit. No catalog listings.

**SURECROP:** An Arkansas apple sold by Stark Bro's Nursery before 1905.

Fruit large, conical, red-striped. Ripe June/July.

**SUSANNAH** (Susannah Prize, South Carolina Seedling Apple): The tree originated near Pomaria, South Carolina, and bore its first fruit in 1858. Named for the elderly lady who raised it. Received the premium at the 1859 South Carolina State Fair "contending against twenty-two North Carolina varieties." This apple so impressed the South Carolina pomologist William Summer that he grafted 400 trees in 1860 for sale through his Pomaria Nurseries and priced the trees at fifty cents each (double the normal price).

Fruit large, oblong, oval; skin greenish yellow; stem short and stout in a shallow cavity; calyx closed; flesh yellow, tender, crisp, aromatic. Ripe November and keeps until April. Sold by a North Carolina nursery in 1872.

**SUTOR'S HONEY:** An autumn apple listed in 1875 by the Middletown Nursery of Virginia. No description.

**SUTTON'S SEEDLING:** Described in 1860 by the Georgia pomologist J. Van Buren as "a fine winter apple found growing in a stump in this county." In 1877, Mr. Van Buren wrote, "The Sutton is nothing but the Limbertwig and nothing else as I have fruited both." That same year the noted Georgia nurseryman P. J. Berckmans wrote, "I received Sutton's Seedling from Van Buren about 1858. It is certainly very different from the Limbertwig. I assume things are somewhat mixed up in my good friend's nursery."

Fruit medium size, red. Ripe October. Sold in 1871 by the Fruitland Nursery, Augusta, Georgia.

❧ **SUZY CLARK** (Susy Clarke): A South Carolina apple sold from 1858 to 1878 by South Carolina and Georgia nurseries.

Fruit medium size, striped with red. Ripe May. Listed as a synonym of Carolina Red June by a Mississippi nursery in 1879, probably erroneously.

❧ **SWADLEY** (Red Pippin): First grown by D. C. Swadley of Johnson City, Tennessee, and described at the 1897 meeting of the American Pomological Society.

Fruit medium, roundish oblate; skin thick, tough, rather smooth with some leather cracking, yellow washed with red and striped with dark crimson; dots conspicuous, rough, russet; stem short and stout in a wide, deep, gradually sloped, russeted cavity; calyx open or partly closed; basin large and deep, leather-cracked; flesh yellow, moderately fine-grained, tender, juicy, subacid. Ripe autumn. No catalog listings.

❧ **SWAIN** (Swane, Cellar): Sold by a Maryland and a Washington, D.C., nursery from 1824 to 1857. No description except ripe August.

❧ **SWEET ALICE:** From the 1897 catalog of Green River Nurseries of Bowling Green, Kentucky: "A local apple of Jersey Sweet type, but tree stronger and a better grower. Fruit large; skin yellow mostly covered with light red; flesh tender, juicy and excellent. Introduced by Downer & Bro., Fairview, Kentucky. August."

❧ **SWEET BEN DAVIS** (Sweet Ben): Originated about 1870 on the farm of Garrett Williams in Madison County, Arkansas. Tree closely resembles the Ben Davis tree, but the fruit ripens two weeks earlier and is quite sweet.

Fruit large, roundish, flattened on the ends, slightly oblique, sides slightly unequal; skin smooth except for a few russet knobs, greenish yellow washed with pale red and striped with crimson; dots numerous, brown; cavity large, deep, abrupt, furrowed, russet netted; calyx partly open; flesh whitish, satiny, juicy, sweet. Ripe winter. No catalog listings.

❧ **SWEET BUCKINGHAM:** From an 1884 letter to Charles Downing from the noted North Carolina nurseryman J. Van Lindley: "Sweet Buckingham was planted in my father's orchard about the commencement of the War. Records of that planting were lost. This apple was so fine, looked so much like Buckingham and ripened at the same time, that my father, Joshua Lindley, named it Sweet Buckingham. It may be a known variety as it is an old apple." Sold by the J. Van Lindley Nursery, Greensboro, North Carolina, from 1877 to 1895.

Fruit large, oblate conical; skin mostly covered with red stripes and blotches; flesh fine-grained, sweet. Ripe September/October.

❧ **SWEET CRIMSON:** A Kentucky apple that originated before 1905. No description. No catalog listings.

❧ **SWEET MARY:** Originated with J. W. Dodge of Pomona, Tennessee, who named it for his wife. Sold by Georgia and South Carolina nurseries from 1858 to 1862. Tree has an upright growth habit.

Fruit large to very large, round to slightly oblong, conical; skin smooth, golden yellow; dots few, light brown; stem very short; flesh yellowish to white, crisp, tender, juicy, "rather spicy," sweet. Ripe July or perhaps later.

❧ **SWEET MICHLER:** Listed from 1858 to 1859 by the Fruitland Nursery, Augusta, Georgia. No description.

❧ **SWEET NEVERFAIL:** Listed in 1853 by the North Carolina Pomological Gardens, Greensboro, North Carolina.

Fruit medium size, round; skin pale yellow. Ripe October.

❧ **SWEET ORANGE:** From an 1891 letter to the USDA from G. H. Kennan of Rodgers, Arkansas: "A new winter sweet apple named by me for its color and flavor. I consider it the most perfect sweet apple

I have ever met with, and it seems to me that sugar might be manufactured from it. The original tree is very prolific and bears regularly."

Fruit above medium, oblate; skin lemon yellow with some russet cracking; dots numerous, variable; cavity wide and deep with fine cracks and a light bloom; calyx open; basin has shallow furrows, cracks and a greenish bloom; flesh yellow with darker yellow veins, crisp, moderately juicy, sweet. Ripe winter. No catalog listings.

❦ **SWEET OATS:** An autumn apple listed in 1875 by the Middletown Nursery of Virginia. No description.

❦ **SWEET PIPPIN:** This is a synonym of several apples, but also appears to be a distinct variety sold by Maryland and Virginia nurseries from 1886 to 1904.

Fruit large, oblong; skin golden yellow; flesh white, tender, juicy, "with rich, high saccharine flavor." Ripe November–March.

❦ **SWEET SCENT:** A summer apple mentioned but not described in an 1891 Tennessee agricultural experiment station bulletin. Adapted to the East Tennessee Valley. No catalog listings.

❦ **SWEET VALENTINE:** Mentioned in 1876 as an old tree growing on the farm of John Fulcher near Fairview, Kentucky. No description. No catalog listings.

❦ **SWEET VAN:** A Georgia apple listed in 1859 by Hopewell Nurseries of Fredericksburg, Virginia. No description except ripe winter.

❦ **SWEET VANDEVERE** (Sweet Redstreak, Sweet Harvey, Red Winter Sweet): Origin unknown, but not southern. Sold by several Virginia nurseries from 1858 to 1904. Tree a crooked grower.

Fruit medium, roundish oblate; skin yellow, shaded and striped with dull red; stem short and rather slender in a large, irregular cavity; basin broad, open; flesh tender, juicy, mild, aromatic, sweet. Ripe November–March.

❦ **SWEET WILLIE** (Willie): Originated before 1869 in Todd County, Kentucky. Tree productive.

Fruit large; skin greenish, mostly covered with red stripes; flesh fine-grained, tender, juicy, sweet. Ripe November/December. No catalog listings.

❦ **SWEET WINTER NONSUCH:** Sold from 1869 to 1904 by the Franklin Davis Nursery, Richmond, Virginia. No description.

❦ **SWEETHEART:** From a salesman's brochure of the Georgia Nursery Company, Concord, Georgia, circa 1920: "Fruit very large and handsome, being of a glossy, brilliant red color. Flesh white, blue-grained, tender and melting. Ripening season extends over a period of five or six weeks beginning June 15. Native of Pike County, Georgia."

❦ **SWENSON:** Originated near Siloam Springs, Arkansas, and sold in 1923 by the Swenson Nursery Company of Siloam Springs. Fruit similar to the Delicious in shape and color but larger; flavor subacid. A good shipper and a good cooking apple. Ripe July 10 in Arkansas.

❦ **SWITZER:** A Russian apple imported by the USDA in 1870. Sold from 1886 to 1888 by Alabama and Louisiana nurseries.

Fruit medium, roundish oblate, skin yellow, flesh subacid. Ripe September/October.

❦ **SWITZERLAND APPLE:** Listed from 1908 to 1916 by the Comal Springs Nursery, New Braunfels, Texas: "Introduced from Switzerland to San Antonio, Texas, about 1898. Fruit greenish with red stripes; fine flavor and good keeping qualities. Tree rather dwarf."

❦ **SYLVENTER:** Originated near Roanoke, Chambers County, Alabama, and described to the 1912 meeting of the Alabama State Horticultural Society.

Fruit medium to large, slightly oblate; skin thick, tough, smooth, deep blood red color; dots irregular, yellow, corky, star-shaped; cavity round, medium in depth, slightly russeted; calyx open; basin medium size; flesh whitish yellow, coarse, slightly woody and dry, described both as very subacid and slightly sweet. No catalog listings.

❦ **TALBOT** (Talbot Pippin, Talbert): Said to have originated from seeds planted about 1880 at Georgetown, Texas, and subsequently sold by Texas nurseries from 1895 to 1910. Apples sent to the USDA about 1894 were identified as Limbertwig, a very questionable identification. From the 1898 catalog of the Austin Nursery, Austin, Texas: "The apple for this section. Originated in Williamson County and can be grown anywhere on any kind of soil. The strongest and most vigorous apple tree we have ever seen. Our burning sun seems to have no injurious effect upon it, and it does not lean when young like most other varieties. Does not overcrop, bears regularly. Fruit medium to large, greenish yellow nearly overspread with red; flesh cream color, of fine texture, firm, very juicy and deliciously flavored. Ripens in September and keeps until January."

**TALLULAH:** A Georgia apple exhibited at the 1908 meeting of the Georgia Horticultural Society. No description. No catalog listings.

**TANDY'S SWEETING:** From the 1870 catalog of the Forest Nursery, Fairview, Kentucky: "Fruit below medium, white striped red, sweet." Ripe summer.

**TARQUIN:** Sold in 1845 by a West Virginia (then Virginia) nursery.

Fruit large, roundish; skin yellow. Ripe August/September.

**TATEM'S EARLY:** A summer apple listed from 1872 to 1878 by Pomaria Nurseries of South Carolina. No description.

**TAUNTON:** This fine, high-flavored apple was sold for forty years by Georgia nurseries and by several nurseries in other southern states as well. Its origin is unknown, but is believed to be either Georgia or Alabama. The tree is an open, straggling grower that requires careful pruning, and it bears heavy annual crops.

Fruit large, roundish to oblate, somewhat irregular, conical; skin greenish yellow, striped and splashed with red, especially on the sunny side (some references say a red cheek, others say the fruit is mostly red); dots large, light-colored; stem long and slender (also described as short and thick) in a deep, acute, russeted cavity; calyx closed; basin usually shallow and slightly corrugated; flesh whitish (also described as yellow), tender, juicy, aromatic, acid when grown on rich clay soils but less acid and of higher flavor on sandy loams. Ripe September and keeps until November. Catalog listings: VA, GA, AL, MS, LA, KY, TX (1858–98).

**TAYLOE'S EARLY BELL:** Sold from 1824 to 1827 by the Linnean Hill Nursery, Washington, D.C. No description except ripe June/July.

**TAYLOR'S NO. 1/TAYLOR'S NO. 2/TAYLOR'S NO. 3:** These three apples probably all originated with J. P. Taylor of Greer, South Carolina. Only Taylor's No. 1 is described in the 1927 catalog of the Taylor Nursery, Greenville, South Carolina: "Fruit large, oblong to conical in shape. Flesh rich creamy yellow; color beautiful red with white dots. Very highly flavored; aromatic, crisp, firm, keeps well. Ripens from October 1st to December 1st. Has won lots of prizes. Heavy bearer." Catalog listings: SC, GA (1924–27).

**TENNESSEE RED:** Briefly described by Warder (1867) and sold in 1916 by J. A. Holder and Company of Concord, Tennessee.

Fruit medium, conical; skin red-striped; flesh sweet. Ripe August/September.

**TENNESSEE WILDING:** Briefly described by Warder (1867).

Fruit medium, oblong; skin red-striped; flesh subacid. Ripe winter. No catalog listings.

**TERRAL** (Terral's Late, Terrall's Late, Terrill's Late): Originated about 1857 at Bayou Sara, Louisiana.

Fruit large, oblong; skin whitish with red stripes; flesh white, tender, juicy, subacid. Ripe August/September. No catalog listings.

**TEXAS BEAUTY:** Originated in east Texas. Tree very prolific.

Fruit medium to large, oblong conical; skin light red; flesh yellow, tender. Ripe October. Catalog listings: NC, TX, AR (1906–15).

**TEXAS KING:** Originated by John Steele Kerr and sold by his Texas Nursery Company in 1920: "Large; yellowish splashed and striped red; juicy, crisp, subacid; very vigorous and productive. This has proven a very profitable apple in the Red River Belt. July–August."

**TEXAS RED:** Originated as a seedling on the farm of William Hall, two miles west of Storville, Smith County, Texas, and sold by Texas nurseries from 1898 to 1916. Highly esteemed in east Texas as a valuable, late-keeping apple. The tree tends to bloom late. *See also* Shirley.

Fruit medium or above, roundish oblate; skin "milky red" in the shade, dark red in the sun (also described as striped); dots small, inconspicuous, gray; stem short in a deep, russeted cavity; calyx closed; basin gradually sloped, medium in width and depth; flesh yellowish. Ripe October/November. ❖ **Plate 120.**

**THAETON:** A Virginia apple listed in 1859 by Hopewell Nurseries, Fredericksburg, Virginia. No description.

**THALER** (Charlotten Thaler): A Russian apple sold by Maryland and Virginia nurseries from 1899 to 1928. The fruit is very similar to Yellow Transparent, and Thaler was listed as a synonym of Yellow Transparent by one Virginia nursery.

Fruit medium to large, "sulfur yellow."

**THOMAS APPLE:** A Maryland apple briefly described in an 1853 gardening magazine.

Fruit large, roundish conical; skin greenish yellow; flesh tender, juicy, subacid. Ripe late autumn. No catalog listings.

**THOMAS DUERSON:** Listed in 1870 by the Forest Nursery, Fairview, Kentucky: "Fruit medium size, greenish striped with red." Ripe autumn.

**THOMAS LATE:** A Georgia apple sold from 1858 to 1862 by Georgia and South Carolina nurseries. "Small, red, good keeper, resembles Hall." Ripe January.

**THOMPSON** (Thompson June?): Sold by a nursery in Curve, Tennessee, about 1895: "I am not sure this is a new variety. The original tree stands near Ripley, Tennessee, and has been bearing thirty years. Not being able to identify it, we catalog it under the name Thompson. Season early, a few days earlier than Carolina Red June."

This may well be the same apple as Thompson June, said to have originated on the farm of Harry Thompson near Florence, Kentucky.

Fruit medium to large, oblong; skin red; dots large. Ripe late June through July in Kentucky. "Not as good as Red June."

**THORNTON** (Thornton's Seedling, Thornton's Winter): Originated with S. H. Thornton of Greenville, Alabama, and was exhibited at the Alabama State Fair in 1889. "Prof. J. P. Steele kept them until May and said they were as sound as when received." Fruit large or very large, roundish; skin red with greenish streaks; flesh sweet and juicy. Ripe winter. Catalog listings: NC, GA, LA (1890–98).

**TILLAQUA** (Big Fruit): The original tree was grown by the Cherokee Indians and was found four miles from Franklin, North Carolina, by the early southern pomologist Jarvis Van Buren. The name means "big fruit" in Cherokee. Fruit always described as very large except by Downing (1878) who says it is "above medium." Tree a straggling grower.

Fruit very large, roundish oblate to oblate; skin yellowish, nearly covered with red or dark red; dots large, light-colored; stem short; calyx closed; flesh whitish or yellowish, moderately juicy, brisk subacid. Ripe November–March. Catalog listings: GA, AL, LA (1858–88).

**TIOGA** (Tioga All Summer): From the 1920 catalog of the Texas Nursery Company, Sherman, Texas: "Originated at Tioga, Texas. The fruit is oblong, of a beautiful orange overspread with red and of excellent quality. Has a habit of long, continuous ripening over two months, there being fruit on the tree in different stages of maturity at the same time. June to September. Trade-marked and introduced by us."

**TIPTON'S WINTER:** Listed in the 1916 catalog of J. A. Holder and Company, Concord, Tennessee. No description.

**TITUGA:** An apple exhibited at the 1914 meeting of the Georgia Horticultural Society by D. H. Heskett of Demorest, Georgia. No description. No catalog listings.

**TOCCOA** (Muskmelon): Toccoa originated in the orchard of Jeremiah Taylor near Toccoa Falls, Habersham County, Georgia, and was first propagated by the southern pomologist Jarvis Van Buren. One old catalog says it has a "brisk Spitzenburg flavor" while another says "flavor of banana."

Fruit medium, roundish conical; skin greasy, yellow with a light red cheek in the sun, perhaps with a few darker stripes; dots few, gray; stem slender; calyx closed; basin small and corrugated; flesh yellowish, moderately juicy, tender, aromatic, mild subacid. Ripe August/September. Catalog listings: GA, KY (1861–71).

❦ **TOOLE'S INDIAN RAREPIPE:** Listed in the 1870 catalog of the Forest Nursery, Fairview, Kentucky.

Fruit large, roundish conical; skin greenish yellow with a blush; flesh greenish white, tender, subacid. Ripe summer or perhaps autumn.

❦ **TOPAL:** A Virginia apple sold by two Virginia nurseries from 1858 to 1904.

Fruit oblate, red-striped, subacid.

❦ **TORIAN:** A North Carolina apple sold in 1859 by Hopewell Nurseries, Fredericksburg, Virginia. No description except ripe winter.

❦ **TOWN PIPPIN:** Listed in 1849 and 1851 by a nursery in Stone Mountain, Georgia. Ripe "first of October."

❦ **TOWNSEND** (Hocking?, Seager, Sieger, Towsend): The original tree was found by Stephen Townsend about 1760 in an Indian clearing in Bucks County, Pennsylvania. Sold in the South mostly by Virginia nurseries but also highly recommended by two Texas nurseries from 1885 to 1904. Excellent for fresh eating, cooking, or drying.

Fruit medium to large, roundish to oblate (a Texas catalog says oblong), slightly conical; skin pale yellow striped with dull red, often with a thin bloom; stem rather long and slender in a medium-size, russeted cavity; basin moderately deep; flesh white, tender, juicy, aromatic, subacid. Ripe July–September. Catalog listings: MD, VA, SC, KY, TX (1845–1904).

❦ **TOWSON:** Originated before 1903 with A. L. Towson of Smithburg, Washington County, Maryland.

Fruit medium or above, roundish oblate, slightly conical; skin yellow, mostly covered with two shades of red, well-colored apples are almost purple; dots numerous, white; stem long in a medium-size, russeted cavity; calyx open; basin wide, gradually sloped; flesh whitish tinged with yellow. Ripe late winter. No catalog listings.

❦ **TRACY GREENING:** Apples sent to the USDA in 1917 by a Mr. Dimock of East Corinth, Virginia.

Fruit medium, roundish conical; skin yellowish green with a bright red blush on the sunny side; dots faint gray; stem short in a very small, russeted cavity; basin almost nonexistent; flesh greenish white. Ripe November. No catalog listings.

❦ **TRIPPE'S HORSE:** A Georgia apple listed from 1858 to 1861 by the Fruitland Nursery, Augusta, Georgia: "Resembles the common Horse apple, wood very distinct." Briefly described by Downing (1878) as roundish conical, red-striped. Ripe August.

❦ **TRIPPE'S RAILROAD:** A Georgia apple listed from 1858 to 1869 by the Fruitland Nursery, Augusta, Georgia: "Small, red, very good; found near the Railroad track." Warder (1867) says this apple is round. Ripe fall.

❦ **TRULL:** Originated before 1902 with J. A. May of Canton, North Carolina.

Fruit almost large, roundish conical, distinctly ribbed at the stem end; skin yellow, mostly covered with two shades of red; dots inconspicuous; stem medium length in a deep, narrow, russeted cavity; calyx open; basin medium size, gradually sloped; flesh whitish. Ripe October/November. No catalog listings.

❦ **TRYON:** A South Carolina apple sold in 1860 by Pomaria Nurseries of South Carolina. No description except ripe November.

❦ **TUKOR** (Mirror): Apples sent to the USDA in 1899 by J. S. Breese of Fayetteville, North Carolina.

Fruit medium, roundish oblate; skin light yellow, mostly covered with light red with broken stripes of darker red; dots inconspicuous; stem very short in a small, very shallow, russeted cavity; basin wide; flesh white. Ripe July. No catalog listings.

❦ **TULL:** Originated about 1840 on the farm of Abram Tull, Grant County, Arkansas.

There are two completely different stories concerning the origin of the Tull apple. I give them both here, and you can take your pick.

Sam B. Tull, in a 1930 *Benton Courier* (Arkansas) article, explained the origin of the Tull Apple this way: "One time while hunting, Abraham Tull came into an area that looked to have been a spot of ground that had been used by an Indian family for a home and garden site. It was there he noticed a lone, young apple tree. He dug the tree up and brought it home where he started an apple orchard.

Through the years he shared apple sprouts with neighbors and friends who wanted it in their home orchards. From there it went into a nursery."

Roy L. Wilson wrote a completely different story for the *Sheridan Headlight* newspaper in 1979. "The apple tree has complemented homesteads for years. The distinctive shape of this tree tells those who know that it's a Tull Apple, being a descendant of the seedlings the Tull family brought to Arkansas from Tennessee over 100 years ago. Knowledgeable Grant Countians explain that on the Tull's trek westward their horses and oxen were lazily moving down the trail. The Tull family pulled up several apple seedlings at a fence row for switches to encourage their animals. Eventually these seedlings became trees in Arkansas, occupying territory in the Tull Community."

Root sprouts were dug from the original tree, and several small orchards were established by neighbors of the Tull family. Apples were sold from these orchards for years in Little Rock, Arkansas, before the trees were grafted and sold by nurseries. The Tull tree is healthy, well adapted to southern growing conditions, blooms late and carries its foliage late into the fall. The fruit hangs well on the tree, often into November, and is free from rot.

Fruit medium or above, roundish, flattened on the ends; skin greenish with red stripes, becoming mostly red when ripe, resembling Ralls Janet; dots numerous, white; stem medium length in a greenish cavity; calyx closed; basin gradually sloped; flesh yellow, firm, juicy, crisp, subacid. Ripe October–March. Catalog listings: AL, TN, AR (1898–1920).

❦ **TUNNELL** (Tunnell's Sweet): A seedling that originated about 1885 in the orchard of S. Tunnell, near Cincinnati, Arkansas.

Fruit above medium, roundish oblate; skin thick, tough, greenish yellow, striped and shaded with red with some russet netting; dots numerous, large, yellow with brown centers; stem long and slender in a large, deep, gradually sloped, greenish cavity; calyx partially open; basin large, deep, abrupt, russeted; flesh yellowish, fine-grained, not very juicy, aromatic, sweet. Ripe autumn in Arkansas. No catalog listings.

❦ **TURKEY RED:** A Kentucky apple listed by a Georgia nursery in 1861.

Fruit medium size; skin yellow, nearly covered with red and red stripes; flesh tender, crisp, sweet. Ripe July/August.

❦ **TURN OF THE LANE** (Turn Off Lane, Strawberry, Turn in the Lane, Winter Strawberry): A New Jersey apple sold by North Carolina nurseries from 1853 to 1860.

Fruit medium or below, roundish to oblate, conical; skin yellow, shaded and striped with two shades of red, redder at the stem end; dots small, gray; stem medium length in a medium-size, russeted cavity; basin rather shallow, gradually sloped; flesh white, tender, sprightly subacid. Ripe October–January.

❦ **TURNER'S GREENING:** A Louisiana apple listed in 1862 by Pomaria Nurseries of South Carolina. Ripe November.

❦ **TUSCALOOSA** (Tuscaloosa Seedling): Originated with Andrew Clements of Tuscaloosa County, Alabama, and was awarded the premium at the Montgomery fair in 1858. Considered a superior-quality apple suitable for marketing or home use in the South. Tree a straggling grower but productive.

Fruit medium to large, oblate or roundish oblate, slightly conical; skin yellow with a red cheek (Downing says shaded and striped with red) and some russeting near the stem; dots few, gray; stem slender in a russeted cavity; calyx closed; basin corrugated; flesh yellowish, firm, juicy, crisp, mild subacid. Ripe late September/October and keeps rather well. Catalog listings: SC, GA, AL, MS (1861–95).

❦ **TUSCALOOSA SWEET:** In spite of its name, Downing (1869) says this apple originated in Kentucky.

Fruit large to very large, oblate; skin greenish yellow, becoming deep yellow in the sun; dots small, white surrounded with red; stem medium length in a broad and russeted cavity; calyx closed; flesh yellowish white, crisp, tender, "sparkling sweet." Ripe October–December. No catalog listings.

❦ **TWELVE INCHES:** Sold in 1923 by Lenoir Nurseries of LaGrange, North Carolina. No description. May be the same apple as Foot Around.

❧ **TYLER'S RENNET:** The original tree was discovered prior to 1872 growing in an old seedling orchard in Mount Pleasant, Albemarle County, Virginia. Said to be "good for slaty soils."

Fruit medium, roundish; skin smooth, yellowish white, sometimes with a blush; flesh white, very tender, crisp, juicy, slightly subacid to almost sweet. Ripe early August. No catalog listings.

❧ **TYSON'S RED:** Listed from 1884 to 1898 by Guilford Nurseries, Greensboro, North Carolina. No description.

❧ **UPRIGHT:** Apples sent to the USDA by two Maryland growers in 1904 and 1905.

Fruit medium or above, roundish oblate; skin light green, lightly washed and striped with red, mostly on the calyx end; dots numerous, russet; stem medium length in a moderately deep cavity; calyx almost closed; basin rather shallow to medium depth; flesh greenish white. Ripe December–March. No catalog listings.

❧ **VAN BUREN:** Found about 1868 growing in Habersham County, Georgia, by Elijah Sutton and named for the southern pomologist Jarvis Van Buren. The tree has stout branches "which twist about in all directions" and bears large crops of apples. The fruit is susceptible to bitter rot.

Fruit medium or above, round, slightly conical; skin yellow nearly covered with dark red with specks and patches of russet; stem short and fleshy in a narrow cavity; calyx closed; basin shallow; flesh yellow, juicy, tender, subacid. Ripe October–April. No catalog listings.

❧ **VARIETY:** Listed in 1869 by Richmond Nurseries, Richmond, Virginia. No description.

❧ **VAUGHN'S WINTER** (Vaughan's Winter): Originated in Christian County, Kentucky, and sold in 1870 by the Forest Nursery, Fairview, Kentucky. Tree vigorous, an early bearer and said to succeed best in "elevated situations."

Fruit medium to large, roundish oblate, sides unequal; skin yellowish white, striped and shaded with bright red (Downing says shaded with crimson and lilac, obscurely striped); dots numerous, small, light-colored; stem short in a deep and uneven cavity; calyx closed (Warder says open); basin deep, abrupt, cracked, slightly corrugated; flesh yellowish, tender, fine-grained, juicy, mild subacid. Ripe January–March.

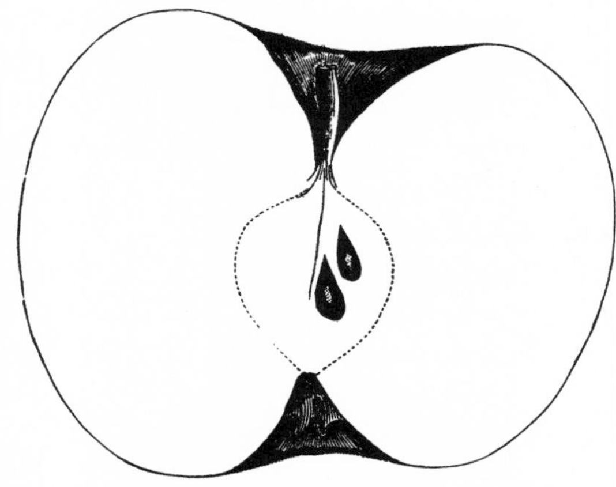

VAUGHN'S WINTER

❧ **VIA'S SEEDLING** (Via): Originated near Richmond, Virginia, and brought to notice by James Via. Considerably grown in Albemarle and Lunenburg counties in Virginia in the 1870s. Described in 1900 as "a very productive variety of fine showy fruit, not susceptible to disease." Sold by Virginia nurseries from 1869 to 1910. *See* Sulser Red.

Fruit medium or above, oblate, sides unequal; skin smooth, greenish yellow washed and striped with pale red and blushed with crimson on the sunny side, sometimes completely red, overspread with a gray bloom; dots numerous, white and russet; stem medium length and thick in a narrow, deep, russeted cavity; calyx closed; basin medium in depth and width, corrugated; flesh yellowish, tinged with red near the calyx, fine-grained, crisp, juicy, mild subacid to almost sweet. Ripe October and keeps until February. ❖ **Plate 121.**

❧ **VICTORIA PIPPIN** (Victoria): The original tree grew before 1877 on the farm of John Benge near Elkton, Cecil County, Maryland. Mr. Benge was an Englishman and named this apple for Queen Victoria. The tree bears heavy and light crops in alternate years, and the fruit is valuable for cooking and marketing.

Fruit medium to large, oblate to roundish oblate; skin yellow, shaded and striped with light and dark red over most of the surface; dots numerous, gray and brown; stem short in a rather large, slightly russeted cavity; calyx closed; basin broad, moderately deep, slightly uneven; flesh yellowish white, rather coarse, juicy, sprightly subacid. Ripe September/October. No catalog listings.

❧ **VICTUALS AND DRINK** (Big Sweet, Pompey, Fall Green Sweet, Green Sweet): An old apple that originated before 1750 near Newark, New Jersey. Sold by two Virginia nurseries from 1858 to 1904.

Fruit varies in size but usually large, oblong (also described as oblate conical), irregular; skin thin, rough, dull yellow, marbled with russet and with a faint blush on the sunny side; stem rather long and slender in an irregular cavity; basin rather shallow; flesh yellowish, tender, breaking, sprightly sweet. Ripe October–January.

❧ **VINELAND** (Reeves Favorite): An old tree found growing near Vineland, Tennessee, and described to the 1895 meeting of the American Pomological Society.

Fruit above medium, roundish oblate, ribbed; skin smooth, oily, greenish yellow blushed dark red on the sunny side, sometimes striped with darker red; dots numerous, yellow or dark green; stem medium length in a large, deep, green cavity; calyx open; basin rather wide and deep, furrowed, some bloom; flesh almost fine-grained, crisp, juicy, mild subacid. Ripe early winter. No catalog listings.

❧ **VIRGIN MARY:** Originated in Boone County, Kentucky, and sold by a Georgia nursery in 1861.

Fruit yellowish white; flesh sweet. Ripe July/August.

❧ **VIRGINIA CHEESE** (Virginia Greening?): Sold from 1875 to 1902 by Cedar Cove Nurseries of Yadkin County, North Carolina: "Large, oblate; skin greenish yellow; flesh tender, juicy, fine flavored; tree upright, vigorous and productive. November to March." This is probably the Virginia Greening under a synonym.

❧ **VIRGINIA JUNE** (June Apple, Herr's June, Striped June, Striped July?, July?): The following is a personal recollection of the great American pomologist W. H. Ragan, written in 1902 while he was with the USDA:

> The Virginia June referred to by Dr. Warder in a note, p. 501, as probably of Indiana origin, was introduced into Putnam County, Indiana, by the late Lewis Shell from Montgomery County, Virginia, by way of Tennessee where he first located. This variety was a very familiar one in my early life. The tree was a stiff, robust grower, and produced its fruit on short spurs on the larger branches. The stem was short and often lipped and thick, the fruit being attached closely to the spurs or branches. The fruit had the clear bright striping of the Summer Rose but was an apple of larger size. Its flesh, until very ripe, was white, dry, and firm but soon became disagreeably mealy and almost flavorless. In its earlier stages of maturity, it was a good market variety on account of its fine showy appearance, and for the kitchen had many admirers among farmer's wives and families. I never knew it outside of our immediate locality and its history and present destiny are alike wrapped in oblivion. Season July and August.

Sold by a Kentucky nursery in 1870.

If it is still grown in the South, Virginia June is probably growing under the catch-all name of Striped June. It appears this apple was called Virginia June in Kentucky, Ohio, and Indiana and perhaps Striped July or July in Tennessee and Virginia. *See* Striped June. An apple named July was considerably grown in Delaware about 1905 to 1915 and generally fits the description of the Virginia June.

Fruit medium or above, nearly round but varying much in shape, often broadly ribbed, with the ribs extending the length of the fruit; skin greenish or yellowish, irregularly striped with bright red; stem short, thick and fleshy, often in a lipped cavity; flesh white, dry, firm, sprightly subacid to acid, becoming quickly mealy when overripe, when the fruit often bursts open. Ripe June/July in the South.

❧ **VIRGINIA QUAKER** (Quaker, May?): Presumably of Virginia origin and sold by Virginia and

Kentucky nurseries from 1845 to 1870. Rather closely fits the description of the May apple and may be identical.

Fruit small, round, slightly conical; skin greenish yellow; dots minute, scattered, black; calyx closed; flesh yellowish white, firm, breaking, subacid. Ripe July.

A different apple named Quaker, a red-striped winter apple, originated in Pennsylvania before 1858. No catalog listings.

**VIRGINIA QUEEN:** Presumably of Virginia origin and said to do well in southwest Virginia. From the name and description, this could be Buckingham.

Fruit large, almost round; skin red-striped; flesh tender, juicy, fine-grained. Ripe October–December. Catalog listings: VA, KY (1845–1900).

**VIRGINIA RED** (Virginia Red Pippin?, Virginia Pippin): Presumably of Virginia origin, but sold by two North Carolina nurseries from 1853 to 1867.

Fruit medium, conical; skin red. Ripe September/October.

**VOLUNTEER:** Originated before 1898 in east Tennessee where the tree was found when some woods were cleared. The tree bears heavily. The apples are large to very large if properly thinned. "Not fit to eat till the New Year. Must be stored in a damp place to obtain perfection, then it becomes mellow with a musky flavor." No description. No catalog listings.

**VOLUNTEER PROLIFIC:** Originated before 1888 on the farm of C. W. Sudy, Myersville, Maryland. No description. No catalog listings.

**VOSS' WINTER:** Probably a North Carolina apple, first described by Warder (1867).

Fruit medium to large, round, sides unequal; skin smooth but with some cracking, white, with a heavy bloom; dots minute, brown; stem long in a deep, russeted cavity; calyx closed; basin deep, abrupt, wavy; flesh whitish yellow, firm, juicy, subacid. Ripe December. No catalog listings.

**WALBRIDGE** (Edgar County Redstreak, Edgar Redstreak): A northern apple sold in the South mainly by Maryland and Virginia nurseries as a late-keeping apple on a productive tree. Beach (1905) rates Walbridge as a fine cooking apple, but not equal in fresh-eating quality to other apples of its season.

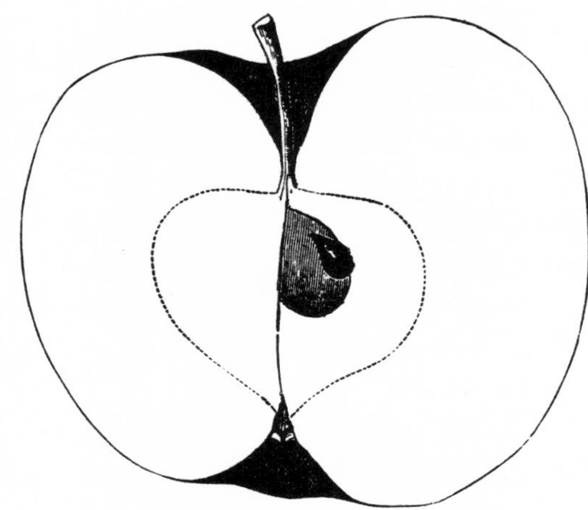

VOSS' WINTER

Originated in 1818 with Joseph Curtis of Paris, Edgar County, Illinois. The first description of this apple was in an 1870 issue of *The Rural New Yorker* magazine.

Fruit medium or below, usually roundish conical but varying in shape; skin smooth, pale yellow washed with red and striped with carmine, often with a thin bloom; stem short to medium length in an acute, deep cavity, sometimes with a fine russet; calyx usually closed; basin small, shallow to almost not depressed at all, furrowed; flesh whitish tinged yellow, firm, crisp, rather tender, juicy, mild subacid. Ripe October–February. Catalog listings: MD, VA, AL, TN, AR (1887–1920).

**WALDON** (Waldona, Waldron, Lady Waldron?): A very large Virginia or West Virginia apple that originated before 1877 and was widely planted at one time in western Virginia. No catalog listings. This is probably the Fallawater, which is often called Waldour in West Virginia.

**WALKER GREENING** (Walker's Greening): A southern apple briefly described by Warder (1867) as oblate, greenish yellow, subacid. Ripe late. No catalog listings.

**WALKER LATE:** Found by William Walker growing in an orchard near Denison, Texas, and sold from 1903 to 1914 by Munson Nurseries of

Denison: "Large, roundish, slightly flattened; more or less bright red striped all over; ripens a month later than Ben Davis and a much better keeper; of extra fine quality; a noble and very valuable market apple."

❧ **WALKER'S YELLOW** (Walker's Winter, Walker Pippin?, Walker Beauty?): Walker's Yellow originated with George Walker of Longstreet, Pulaski County, Georgia, who exhibited it at the Georgia State Fair in 1852.

Beach (1905) describes an apple called Walker Beauty, supposedly a Pennsylvania apple, which closely fits the description of Walker's Yellow. Abbreviated descriptions of an apple called Walker Pippin in several old Georgia and Alabama catalogs also fit Walker's Yellow. An apple called Walker's Pippin is still available, but it ripens in July and is probably a different apple.

Fruit medium to large, roundish or oblong, conical; skin golden yellow, perhaps with a faint blush on the sunny side (an 1869 USDA report says red-striped); stem medium to long in a deep, acute cavity; calyx open; basin small; flesh yellowish white, juicy, firm, rather tart and acid. Ripe October. Catalog listings for Walker's Yellow: SC, KY (1856–70).

❧ **WALKING STICK:** An early-ripening apple listed in 1917 by the J. A. Withrow Nursery of Ellijay, Georgia. No description.

❧ **WALL:** From an 1853 issue of the *Western Horticultural Review* magazine: "This beautiful and valuable apple originated on the farm of Garret Wall, Rabun County, Georgia, and is supposed to be a seedling raised by the Cherokee Indians. The tree is very prolific and the fruit is in season from October to February." Wall was listed by southern nurseries as a distinct variety from 1858 to 1860. From 1861 on, it was usually listed as a synonym of Nickajack. Catalog listings: VA, GA, AL, MS, TX (1858–88).

❧ **WALLACE:** Listed in the 1878 catalog of Pomaria Nurseries of South Carolina. "A seedling from Rev. J. A. Wallace of Alabama. Medium size, of excellent quality, and keeping well until Spring."

❧ **WALLACE'S GREEN PIPPIN:** Said by Warder (1867) to be of Kentucky origin. No description except ripe late. No catalog listings.

❧ **WAR WOMAN:** A Rabun County, Georgia, apple described in a 1905 South Carolina agricultural experiment station bulletin. Tree vigorous, productive.

Fruit medium, oblong; skin yellow, more or less covered with splashes and marblings of bright red; dots large and gray; stem short in a deep, narrow, folded cavity, usually entirely russeted; basin rather shallow and broad; flesh aromatic, mild subacid. Ripe December–April. No catalog listings.

❧ **WARREN** (Waren): Listed in 1920 by the Texas Nursery Company of Sherman, Texas: "A Winesap seedling, origin Texas; a favorite among southern orchardists. Large, deep red, fine flavored. Ripe September."

❧ **WATAUGA:** This apple somewhat resembles the Hoover, which has the synonym of Watauga. There are enough differences, however, to believe that this is a different apple. Said to have originated before 1897 with S. H. Stepp of Dry Creek, Carter County, Tennessee.

Fruit large, roundish oblate; skin thin, tender, smooth, nearly covered with dark crimson; dots numerous, small, light-colored; stem very short and stout in a small, abrupt, green cavity; calyx closed; basin medium size, abrupt; flesh white, fine-grained, tender, melting, juicy. Ripe late summer to early fall. No catalog listings.

❧ **WASHINGTON STRIPE:** Listed from 1869 to 1904 by the Franklin Davis Nursery of Richmond, Virginia. No description.

❧ **WATER MELON:** An apple listed without description from 1858 to 1904 by two Virginia nurseries and different from the apple described in chapter 5 under the name Watermelon. Probably a synonym of Sweet Bough, which is available.

❖ **Plate 122.**

❧ **WATEREE:** A South Carolina apple.

Fruit oblate, red-striped, subacid. Ripe November–January. Catalog listings: VA, NC, SC, GA (1856–69).

❧ **WATTS:** Originated near Palacios, Texas, and sold in 1916 by the Bay City Nursery of Bay City, Texas. "Gives promise of being the finest apple yet for the coast." No description except ripe summer.

**WATWOOD:** Originated on the farm of Nathan Rose, near Blandville, Kentucky, and was once valued in that locality for its quality and keeping ability. Tree bears heavily annually. Listed by a Tennessee nursery in 1889.

Fruit medium, oblate, flattened or depressed on the ends; skin whitish or greenish yellow shaded with pale red over about two-thirds of the surface; dots few, light and gray; stem very short in a broad, deep, slightly russeted cavity; calyx closed; basin rather shallow and slightly corrugated; flesh pale yellow, rather firm and fine-grained, juicy, subacid. Ripe January–March.

**WAUGH'S CRAB:** Probably originated in Culpeper County, Virginia. The fruit is similar to Hewe's Crab, but the tree is less thorny and bears very heavy crops of long-keeping apples, mainly used for winter cider. "The fruit has been left on the tree until Christmas, to freeze and thaw, without much injury. If crushed in January it makes the finest white cider, fully equal to that from Hewe's Crab. From March to June it is a rich table apple, nearly sweet."

Fruit small to below medium, roundish conical; skin greenish white shaded with light red, but splashed and striped with darker red in the sun; stem long and slender; basin abrupt; flesh white, very firm, moderately juicy, rather sweet. Ripe January–April or often later. Catalog listings: VA, NC, GA, KY (1857–95).

**WAVERLY:** Apples sent to the USDA in 1902 by R. M. Givin of Waverly, Humphrey County, Tennessee.

Fruit medium, roundish conical; skin yellow, almost covered with dull red and having grayish blotches; dots small, gray; stem medium length in a rather deep and narrow cavity; calyx open; basin medium size; flesh white, tinged greenish yellow. Ripe October/November. No catalog listings.

**WAYCROSS RED** (Waycross Sweet?): From the 1894 catalog of Cumberland Nurseries, Nashville, Tennessee: "A large red apple that has been growing in Ware County, Georgia, for twenty-five years. The original tree was brought there by an old gentleman from Telfair County, Georgia, where it bore heavy annual crops for more than forty years. The trees are perfectly healthy and vigorous."

Fruit above medium to large, oblate; skin orange-yellow, heavily striped on the sunny side; flesh white, juicy, sweet. Ripe July.

**WEBB'S WINTER:** Originated in Mississippi and sold by Georgia and South Carolina nurseries from 1857 to 1871. Branches are drooping.

Fruit medium, round to slightly oblate; skin greenish yellow, striped and shaded with red or dull red; dots russet; stem long and slender in an acute cavity; calyx closed; basin small and smooth; flesh yellowish (Downing says whitish), fine-grained, very firm or solid, juicy, mild subacid. Ripe November–February.

**WEFONY:** Sold in 1870 by the Forest Nursery, Fairview, Kentucky: "A new apple from North Carolina. Said to be of good size and quality." Ripe winter.

**WELLFORD'S YELLOW** (Wilford's Yellow, C. C. Wellford, Welford's Yellow, Wellford's Seedling): Originated in Essex County, Virginia. Tree very productive.

Fruit rather small, roundish, flattened on the ends; skin pale yellow, sometimes with pale red streaks on one side; flesh yellow, fine-grained, very juicy, aromatic. Ripe November and keeps until June. Catalog listings: MD, DC, VA (1858–80).

**WELTNER:** Sold in 1926 by Mosty Brothers Nurseries of Center Point, Texas: "Bright red, a regular and abundant bearer of fruit of excellent quality. Introduced and highly recommended by Mr. Otto Weltner of the Old Camp Verde Fort, Kerr County, Texas."

**WERT'S MAY:** A summer apple listed from 1872 to 1878 by Pomaria Nurseries of South Carolina. No description.

**WESTBROOK** (Westbrooke): A Virginia apple sold by two Virginia nurseries from 1858 to 1869. No description except ripe October–January.

**WESTERN WEALTH** (Western Wealthy): Originated with Charles Bilger of Callahan County, Texas, from apple seeds brought from Germany. Listed in a 1912 Texas nursery catalog: "Introduced into this country from Germany. Larger than Ben

Davis, which it resembles in color, but very superior in flavor and beyond a doubt the best keeper known. Similar to Winesap in flavor." No description.

**WESTMORELAND** (Westmoreland Rambo): Grown before 1900 from a seed of Rambo by Joseph Kern of Greensburg, Tennessee. Tree vigorous and annually productive.

Fruit large to very large, oblate; skin pale greenish yellow, shaded and striped with light and dark red over almost all the surface; dots few, brown; stem short in a large, deep, slightly greenish cavity; calyx closed or almost closed; basin large, deep, slightly corrugated; flesh whitish, almost coarse, juicy, tender, subacid. Ripe September/October. No catalog listings.

**WETMORE** (Foster): The following is from a letter written to the USDA in 1894 by E. F. Wetmore, Ogden, Rhea County, Tennessee:

> The Foster apple is a native seedling, and the original tree still stands, a monument to be seen in an old field near my home where, about the year 1830, a cabin was built. About that year James Lee purchased some fine apples from a flat boat that floated down the Hiwassee river, his wife saving and planting some of the seeds. The tree, which proved especially valuable, derives its name from Robert Foster who purchased the farm from James Lee. It is well known here and in adjoining counties. The old tree has never failed to bear large crops every year I have known it, as many as forty bushels in some years. The fruit has been kept until the middle of May but is good to use from November on. The roots are very strong. It seems to produce more roots than top, which is a great point in its favor. Apples were a general failure here last year, but this one old tree has supplied my family all the fall and up to the present writing, February 3.

Apparently the USDA changed the name of this apple to Wetmore because another apple was already named Foster.

Fruit medium to large, roundish oblong; skin greenish yellow washed with dull red and indistinctly striped with crimson, some patches of russet; dots conspicuous, medium size, light gray; stem medium length and slender in a medium-size, abrupt, deep, russeted cavity; calyx open; basin large, deep, abrupt, russeted; flesh yellowish white, fine-grained, tender, juicy, subacid. Ripe winter. No catalog listings.

**WETSEL** (Wistal): The original tree was found about 1895 by E. W. Kirkpatrick growing in the orchard of James Wetsel, six miles south of McKinney, Texas. Sold in 1920 by the Texas Nursery Company, Sherman, Texas: "The tree is large and productive and the fruit is an excellent cooking apple which resembles Summer Queen. Large, round, greenish; flesh yellow, firm and good. Originated in the Blackland district of Texas and especially suited to that section. August to September."

**WHIG:** A North Carolina apple sold from 1858 to 1861 by Georgia and South Carolina nurseries. Probably different from the apple named Whig supposedly of Pennsylvania origin.

Fruit medium, oblate conical; skin yellow; flesh subacid. Ripe October.

**WHITE** (White Apple): An apple by this name was described by Warder (1867) as a Kentucky apple.

Fruit small, oblong; skin yellow; flesh sweet. Ripe winter.

An apple named White, from North Carolina, was sold by a Virginia nursery in 1859, without description. This apple may be the same as a White Apple grown in Habersham County, Georgia, in the 1850s, which was considered good for cooking and drying but too acid for dessert. This Georgia apple is medium to large in size and keeps until January. The tree is drooping and a tip bearer. It is quite possible that all of these apples are the same as an apple named Belmont, which has the synonym of White Apple. *See* Belmont.

**WHITE CATLINE** (White Catlin, White Cataline): From an 1853 issue of the *Western Horticultural Review* magazine: "Originated, I believe, in Baltimore County, Maryland. With them it is as fine a late fall or early winter table apple as can possibly be produced. Size small, color pure white, form oblong, flesh tender, breaking and abounding with a rich, pleasant, subacid juice. Tree a fine grower and a great bearer. Fruit always perfect."

Fruit medium, roundish or slightly oblong; skin light yellow to almost white; dots numerous, small, russet; stem very long in a deep, narrow cavity; calyx closed; basin small and shallow; flesh white, tender, juicy, breaking. Ripe November–February. Catalog listings: MD, VA (1836–1901). ❖ **Plate 123.**

❧ **WHITE FALL PIPPIN** (Fall Pippin of Louisville, White Fall, White Pippin?): Warder (1867) says the fruit of White Fall Pippin was sold in large quantities in the markets of Louisville, Kentucky. He could not trace its origin, but was told that it resembles the White Spanish Reinette. Useful for cooking, drying, and fresh eating.

Fruit very large, roundish oblate to roundish; skin smooth, pale yellow with whitish stripes near the stem end, not bronzed or blushed; dots scattered, tiny, dark; stem very short in a wide and wavy cavity; calyx closed; basin narrow, deep, abrupt, folded; flesh yellowish white, breaking, juicy, aromatic, subacid. Ripe October. No catalog listings.

❧ **WHITE MUSK:** Sold from 1824 to 1827 by the Linnean Hill Nursery, Washington, D.C. No description except ripe October/November.

❧ **WHITE PARADISE:** A Kentucky apple sold in 1870 by the Forest Nursery, Fairview, Kentucky.

Fruit small (also described as large), oblong; skin white or yellowish with a blush; flesh compact, subacid. Ripe early winter.

❧ **WHITE RED** (White Red Winter): A southern apple briefly described by Warder (1867). Fruit large, oblong; skin shaded and striped with red; flesh rich and juicy. A good keeper. No catalog listings.

❧ **WHITE SPANISH REINETTE** (Camnesar, Camuesar, Cobbett's Fall Pippin, Elgin Pippin?, Large Fall Pippin, Camenser, White Pippin, Yellow Pippin, York Pippin): An ancient Spanish apple believed to have been introduced into the Gulf states by early Spanish colonists. Called Camnesar in Spain. Well adapted and successfully grown in Natchez, Mississippi. The White Spanish Reinette closely resembles and is often confused with Fall Pippin and is almost certainly identical to Elgin Pippin. *See also* White Fall Pippin.

Fruit very large, oblong to roundish oblate, ribbed; skin yellowish green, perhaps flushed with brown; flesh yellowish white, crisp, tender, subacid to almost sweet. Ripe August/September. Catalog listings: NC, SC (1853–72). Extinct in the United States, but possibly still grown in Europe. *See also* Elgin Pippin.

❧ **WHITE SUGAR** (Autumn Sweet Bough?, Autumn Bough?): Almost certainly the same apple as Autumn Bough. A valuable late summer sweet apple for both cooking and dessert. The tree is healthy, productive, and long-lived. The fruit hangs well on the tree and has been described as having "a sweet, refreshing, vinous flavor."

Fruit medium to large, oblong conical, ribbed; skin smooth, pale yellow or white, sometimes with patches of russet; flesh white, tender, juicy, sweet. Ripe August/September. Catalog listings as White Sugar and Autumn Bough: VA, NC, LA, KY (1853–1904).

❧ **WHITE SUMMER** (Summer Banana?): Sold in 1915 by Crawford and Company of Statesville, North Carolina: "Size medium, color yellow covered with spots of light red and pink; quality fine with a decided banana flavor. The tree is a rather slow grower. August." This is probably the same apple as Summer Banana.

❧ **WHITE WARRINGTON:** Listed by two Virginia nurseries from 1858 to 1869. No description.

❧ **WHITE'S EARLY NONSUCH:** Sold from 1824 to 1827 by the Linnean Hill Nursery of Washington, D.C. No description except ripe August.

❧ **WHITE'S WINTER:** Originated before 1869 in Guilford County, North Carolina.

Fruit medium, roundish oblate; skin yellowish white; flesh juicy. Ripe winter. No catalog listings.

❧ **WHITESCARVER:** Originated before 1871 with R. A. Whitescarver of Laurel Mills, Virginia. Tree bears annually, but heavier on alternate years. Sold by the John Sauls Nursery of Washington, D.C., from 1878 to 1880.

Fruit medium to large, roundish oblate; skin

pale yellowish green; dots scattered, carmine on the sunny side but dark green on the shady side, surrounded by white; stem short in a narrow cavity; calyx closed; basin broad and moderately deep; flesh yellowish white, rather fine-grained, crisp, tender, juicy, subacid. Ripe October–December.

**WHITLEY:** Listed in 1924 by Cureton Nurseries, Austell, Georgia. No description.

**WILFONGS** (Willfong's Red): A North Carolina apple sold from 1858 to 1861 by Georgia and South Carolina nurseries.

Fruit below medium, oblate; skin greenish yellow, shaded with dark purplish red and with indistinct red splashes and stripes; dots light-colored; stem short and stout; calyx closed; flesh whitish, rather firm, moderately juicy, tender, subacid. Ripe December–March.

**WILLIAM J. BRYAN:** From the 1906 catalog of the Yarbrough Brothers Nursery, Stephens, Arkansas: "A seedling of great merit. The original tree is now 40 years old and still bearing heavy crops of large, beautiful fruit that keeps until the following May or June. Originated in Columbia County, Arkansas. Ripens in October." No description.

**WILLSON GOLDEN:** Grown from seed about 1888 by Sandford Willson of Mayville, Banks County, Georgia.

Fruit very large; skin yellow with a golden tinge. A good keeper. No catalog listings.

**WILSON'S JUNE** (Wilson's Red June): The apple named Wilson's June has been traced back to Micajah Wilson, a pioneer who settled in Putnam County, Indiana, in the early 1800s. He brought several southern apple trees with him, probably from North Carolina, including an early-ripening, red-striped apple. This apple became very popular in his vicinity and was called Wilson's June. Downing believed it to be identical to Carolina Red June and listed it as a synonym of this apple in his books. Being red-striped, Wilson's June is not the Carolina Red June, which is a red-blushed apple, but it may be identical to the Virginia June. We do not have a good description of Wilson's June for a comparison with other apples. No catalog listings. *See* Wilson June.

**WILSON'S SUMMER** (Wilson?, Wilson Red?, Mammoth June?, Wilson's Sweet): Wilson's Summer supposedly originated near Salem in Forsyth County, North Carolina, and was sold from 1853 to 1855 by two North Carolina nurseries. An apple named Wilson Red was sold in 1928 by W. T. Hood Nurseries of Richmond, Virginia, and generally fits the description of Wilson's Summer. The Mammoth June also fits the description of Wilson's Summer. Tree medium size and bears abundantly on alternate years.

Fruit below to above medium, roundish to oblate, slightly conical; skin yellowish white, nearly covered with bright red and striped and splashed with crimson (also said to be greenish yellow thickly striped with clear red); dots fairly numerous, light colored; stem short and small in a medium-size, often slightly russeted cavity; calyx closed; basin medium size, almost smooth; flesh white, fine-grained, juicy, mild subacid to almost sweet. Ripe July/August.

**WILSON'S WONDER:** Listed without description on a 1920 order form for the North State Nursery, Julian, North Carolina.

**WINCHESTER APPLE:** Sold from 1827 to 1857 by two Washington, D.C., nurseries. No description except ripe September. There is also a modern apple named Winchester, which was developed at the Virginia Polytechnic Institute about 1960.

**WINSLOW:** A Virginia apple first described in 1854 and sold by a North Carolina nursery in 1898.

Fruit large, round, flattened at the base; skin streaked with dark and light red; dots light brown with "dark flakes;" stem short and slender; calyx open; flesh yellowish white, tender, juicy, subacid. Ripe fall and early winter.

**WINTER ANNET:** Listed from 1824 to 1827 by the Linnean Hill Nursery, Washington, D.C. No description. Probably the same as Annette.

**WINTER BLACK:** Described to the 1877 meeting of the American Pomological Society by Natt Atkinson of Asheville, North Carolina. This is probably the same apple as the Hoover.

Fruit large, oblate, often oblique; skin light yellow, mostly covered with splashes of dark purplish red and carmine; flesh white, tender, moderately juicy, mild subacid. Ripe winter. No catalog listings.

❧ **WINTER BROOK:** A Kentucky apple listed by North Carolina and Georgia nurseries from 1860 to 1861. Fruit oblate, yellow, subacid. Ripe October–March.

❧ **WINTER CLUSTER:** Listed in 1904 by the Franklin Davis Nursery of Richmond, Virginia. No description.

❧ **WINTER EXCELSIOR:** Sold by a North Carolina nursery about 1870.

Fruit large, oblate conical; skin red; flesh yellow, tender, crisp. Ripe winter.

❧ **WINTER GOLDEN PIPPIN:** This apple does not fit the descriptions of the several different apple varieties called Golden Pippin. It was listed in 1845 by the Holly Springs Nursery of Bloomfield, Kentucky.

Fruit large, oblate, yellow. Ripe November–April. "Fine flavor in the spring."

❧ **WINTER GREEN:** Besides being a synonym of Poorhouse, this is also the name of a Kentucky apple described in the 1897 catalog of Green River Nurseries, Bowling Green, Kentucky: "A local name of an old variety introduced by Mr. Campbell. While the tree is a very irregular and straggling grower, this is one of the most desirable apples grown in this section. Color reddish purple, becoming lighter towards the point; quality the very best."

An apple named Winter Green, said to be of South Carolina origin, was listed in 1862 by Pomaria Nurseries of South Carolina without description.

❧ **WINTER HORSE:** First reported in 1853 growing in Habersham County, Georgia, but the 1862 catalog of Pomaria Nurseries of South Carolina states "a seedling of Mr. Rawls of Lexington District, S.C." In Georgia, it ripens about the first of September and keeps for two months. In western North Carolina, it ripens in October and keeps until about March. Sold by North Carolina and South Carolina nurseries from 1855 to 1895.

Fruit medium to large, roundish oblate (also said to be very oblate), sometimes conical, sides often unequal; skin greenish yellow to pale yellowish green when ripe, sometimes with a thin white bloom; cavity deep, russeted; calyx very large and open; basin very deep; flesh yellowish, juicy, subacid. Ripe September–November or later.

A circa 1920 catalog of the Fayette County Nurseries, Fayetteville, Georgia, pictures and briefly describes another apple named Winter Horse: "A new Southern winter Apple of great beauty and excellence. Introduced by J. G. Justice, Marcus, Georgia." The picture of this apple shows it to be mostly red with red stripes. This apple is probably the Nickajack, which has a synonym of Winter Horse.

❧ **WINTER PEACH** (Peach): A Kentucky apple described by Downing (1878). An apple named Peach was sold by two Virginia nurseries from 1858 to 1869, without description.

Fruit below to above medium, oblate conical; skin pale yellow blushed red in the sun; dots numerous, gray; stem short; calyx closed; flesh white, tender, juicy, crisp, subacid. Ripe December–April.

❧ **WINTER SWEET** (Winter Sweeting): Origin unknown.

Fruit medium, round; skin greenish yellow. Ripe October–March. Catalog listings: MD, VA, NC, KY (1845–1915).

A red apple called Winter Sweet was sold in recent years by the late Henry Morton's nursery in Gatlinburg, Tennessee, but it is not this apple.

❧ **WINTER WELLSING:** A cider apple sold from 1824 to 1827 by the Linnean Hill Nursery, Washington, D.C. No description.

❧ **WIREGRASS:** The original tree was a seedling growing on Granberry Farm near Headland, Alabama. In the 1950s, Joseph Norton of Auburn University heard of its quality and collected scions with a graduate student. It was grown in the Auburn University apple collection for a number of years, but no existing trees are now known. Fruit yellow at maturity and similar to the Horse Apple. No catalog listing.

❧ **WOLF'S DEN:** An autumn apple listed but not described in the 1872 catalog of Joshua Lindley near Greensboro, North Carolina.

❧ **WOLF'S FAVORITE:** Sold in 1870 by the Forest Nursery, Fairview, Kentucky: "Fruit. medium, skin greenish, subacid, good." Ripe autumn.

**WOLSEY** (Wolsey Seedling): Originated before 1892 with Henry Wolsey (or Holsey) of Bentonville, Arkansas. Described only as "a fine keeper." No catalog listings.

**WOMACK CHOICE:** The following letter was sent to the USDA in 1917 by Samuel David Elrod (1855–1917), owner of the Pleasant Valley Nursery in McMinnville, Tennessee. I have retained the quaint spelling, but I wish to point out that this letter imparts a lot of clear information. Mr. Elrod used no punctuation so I have added periods between sentences for clarity.

> Gentlemen as to your request I will try to give you a List of our Nursery as Best I can. I am inclsing a cattalogue of our fruit which I am shure you understand Except Too New Varieties Which I Will Describe as Best I can. the *Womack Choice* apple was a New apple in 1861. Mr Monro Womack Brought the apple tree from Comberland mountains and Planted it on his farm in Warren County Tenn. it Grew to be a large tree and a Great Barrer. it Was a Noted tree for its Great Load of Fruit and size. it bore most Ever year. it is a Large Yelow apple gets ripe aBout 10 Dayes Earleyer than the Earley Harvest. the apple is collard Verry much like the Early Harvest But Not quiet So Sour—So in the year 1908 We Started our Nursery and We Got twigs of this tree and Grafted them and have Ben Grafting Ever year since. this apple is a Leader amoung Early apples and Deserves the Leader Ship to. We Gave this apple this name womack Choice in honor of Mr. Womack Because thare was a colney of Womacks Settled at this Plaice and it was there choice apple. as to the Groth of the tree it Beats them all. I find the Roots of this tree allways clean and Strait and Nice. it leades in Groing in the Nursery. So if thare is any thing Els you Want in Regard to this apple I will Give it as Best I can.

**WOOD'S FAVORITE** (Wood): Originated before 1856 with C. B. Wood of Rappahannock County, Virginia. Similar to Maiden's Blush and probably a seedling of it. Tree enormously productive. Sold by Virginia nurseries from 1894 to 1910.

Fruit above medium to large, oblate; skin orange-yellow with a bright red blush; flesh firm, fine-grained, crisp, subacid. Ripe September–December.

**WOOD'S GOLDEN RUSSET:** Sold and probably originated by the Joel Wood Nursery of Wheeling, West Virginia (then in Virginia) in 1845.

Fruit medium, roundish, russeted. Ripe December–March.

**WOOD'S WINTER SWEET** (Wood's Winter): Sold and probably originated by the Joel Wood Nursery of Wheeling, West Virginia (then in Virginia) in 1845.

Fruit medium, conical, red. Ripe February–May. "Excellent for stock."

**WOODBURN'S SPITZENBURG:** Sold from 1858 to 1904 by two Virginia nurseries.

Fruit oblong, red-striped, subacid. Ripe winter.

**WOODHAM'S OCTOBER:** Listed in 1924 by Newton Nurseries of Newton, Mississippi: "Large, dark green, red cheek. Good quality especially for canning. Bears young. Ripens during September and October. Originated in Lauderdale County, Mississippi."

**WOODLAND:** Originated before 1857 in Bayou Sara, Louisiana, and was successfully grown in Illinois in 1874.

Fruit medium or perhaps smaller, oblate; skin smooth, yellowish green, but sometimes red-striped; dots small and scattered; stem medium to long in a deep, lipped, brown cavity; basin deep and abrupt; calyx closed; flesh yellow, rather tough, juicy, subacid. Ripe midwinter. No catalog listings.

**WOODPILE:** First grown by N. R. Keese, Keese, Tennessee, and described to the 1897 meeting of the American Pomological Society.

Fruit large, roundish conical; skin thin, smooth, yellow, washed and indistinctly striped with pale red; dots numerous, brown; stem short in a large, deep, russeted cavity; calyx partly open; basin medium size, abrupt, furrowed, russeted; flesh yellowish, fine-grained, tender, juicy, subacid. Ripe autumn. No catalog listings.

❦ **WOOLFOLKS:** Probably a Kentucky apple, according to Warder (1867).

Fruit medium, oblate; skin very smooth, yellowish green; dots scattered, gray with white bases; stem short and green in a wide, acute, wavy, brown cavity; calyx closed; basin medium, wavy; flesh white, tender, breaking, juicy, subacid. Ripe December–March. No catalog listings.

❦ **WORLD'S WONDER** (Wonder of the World): Probably a synonym of Nickajack. Catalog listings: VA, GA, TN, TX (1857–1905).

❦ **WORLEY'S RED:** Sold from 1869 to 1904 by the Franklin Davis Nursery of Richmond, Virginia. No description.

❦ **WRESTON'S PROLIFIC:** A Kentucky apple, according to Warder (1867). No description. No catalog listings.

❦ **WRIGHT'S SWEETING:** Sold by two Virginia nurseries from 1858 to 1869. No description.

❦ **YADKIN:** A North Carolina apple sold in 1861 by a Georgia nursery. May be the same as Yadkin Beauty, but the descriptions are somewhat different, particularly the time of ripening.

Fruit large, round; skin red-striped with some stripes a darker red; dots large, distinct, scattered, gray; stem medium length in an acute, brown cavity; calyx open; basin abrupt and deep; flesh white, dry, breaking, subacid. Ripe August.

❦ **YADKIN BEAUTY:** Sold from 1886 to 1902 by Cedar Cove Nurseries of Yadkin County, North Carolina: "A fine new apple which originated in Yadkin County a few years back; large size, round, oblate; yellow ground covered with dark red stripes, frequently red all over; flesh yellow, fine-grained, slightly acid. October–January."

❦ **YAHOOLA** (Yahaula): Originated near Yahoola Creek in Lumpkin County, Georgia, where the original tree was found growing on the bank of a gold pit by the southern pomologist Jarvis Van Buren. The tree is productive and bears when young. The fruit hangs well on the tree.

Fruit medium or above, roundish oblate to oblate, conical; skin dull green or yellowish green, specked and streaked with russet (also described as striped with red); stem long and slender; basin medium size; flesh greenish white, juicy, subacid. Ripe September (or perhaps earlier) and keeps until January. Catalog listings: VA, SC, GA, KY (1858–70).

❦ **YANCEY'S PRIZE** (Yancy): Mentioned in 1871 as originating with Charles Yancy of Albemarle County, Virginia. No description. No catalog listings.

❦ **YATES' BONSEEDLING:** Listed in 1916 by the Home Nursery Company of Fayetteville, Arkansas. No description.

❦ **YATES' MAMMOTH:** Sold from 1899 to 1900 by Otto Schwill and Company of Memphis, Tennessee: "A new variety which originated here. Tree vigorous and productive; fruit large, handsome, richly striped and splashed with bright crimson. A showy apple of first quality. November."

❦ **YAZOO** (Brown's Yazoo): Brought to attention by W. H. Cassell of Canton, Mississippi, and discussed at the 1885 meeting of the American Pomological Society. Possibly an old variety for which the original name was lost.

Fruit very large, roundish oblong; skin red-striped. Ripe October and keeps until February in Mississippi. No catalog listings.

❦ **YAZOO SUMMER:** A Mississippi apple sold in 1861 by the Fruitland Nursery, Augusta, Georgia. No description except ripe July.

❦ **YELLOW CHEESE:** Listed but not described by Joshua Lindley's Nursery in North Carolina in 1872. Possibly Green Cheese.

❦ **YELLOW CLUSTER:** Sold from 1920 to 1926 by the Plainview Nursery of Plainview, Texas: "Supposed to be of local origin. Hardy, stocky grower, very resistant against high winds. Fruit large, yellow with a red cheek when exposed to the sun, subacid, of fine flavor, comes into bearing young. One of the very best apples for the Plains country. Ripe August to September."

❦ **YELLOW ENGLISH:** Sold from 1891 to 1894 by Atlanta Nurseries, Atlanta, Georgia: "Medium, yellow covered with pale red; a most excellent winter apple; tree vigorous and a yearly bearer. November to March."

❧ **YELLOW FOREST** (Wild Apple): The original tree was found in 1868 by Captain Joe Winston of Bossier Parish, Louisiana. It was growing wild in some woods and was transplanted by Captain Winston to a site near his house. The tree is an annual bearer of fruit "very clear of rot when even the Shockley rotted badly." The fruit makes a fine cider almost as clear as water and is also useful for drying as it does not turn dark when dried. Sold by Louisiana nurseries from 1887 to 1925.

Fruit medium to large, round to roundish oblate; skin yellow or greenish yellow with a few dark specks and blotches near the stem; flesh tender, juicy, very aromatic, subacid. Ripe September in Louisiana and a good keeper.

❧ **YELLOW MEADOW:** Described by Downing (1867) as a southern apple.

Fruit large, oblate; skin greenish yellow; stem rather slender in a deep, irregular cavity; calyx open; basin shallow; flesh yellow, compact. Ripe November. No catalog listings.

❧ **YELLOW OCTOBER:** Sold in 1857 by the Fruitland Nursery of Augusta, Georgia: "Large and of fine quality."

❧ **YELLOW OZARK PIPPIN:** Grown from a seed of Ben Davis or Winesap planted about 1885 by G. H. Home, Latham, Van Buren County, Arkansas. No description. No catalog listings.

❧ **YELLOW SWEET:** A Texas apple briefly described at the 1899 meeting of the American Pomological Society.

Fruit large, oblate; skin yellow. Ripe August/September. No catalog listings.

❧ **YOPP'S FAVORITE** (Yopp): A Georgia apple from Thomas County, sold for many years by southern nurseries and grown in France about 1900. Tree compact and productive, but susceptible to cedar-apple rust.

Fruit large, roundish to oblate, slightly conical; skin greenish yellow with a faint red cheek in the sun; dots few, russet; stem short and thick in a medium to deep, russeted cavity; calyx open; basin deep; flesh white, fine-grained, juicy, tender, subacid. Ripe September/October. Catalog listings: VA, GA, AL, MS, KY (1857–1904).

❧ **YOUNG AMERICA:** Described as a new variety at the 1875 meeting of the American Pomological Society by Franklin Davis, the noted Virginia nurseryman. Originated in Sussex County, Virginia, and a different apple from the Young America of New York origin. There also is an edible crabapple named Young America. Fruit above medium, skin orange. Ripe late June. No catalog listings.

❧ **ZANE** (Zane Greening): An apple listed in the catalog of a Wheeling, West Virginia (then Virginia) nursery in 1845. A notation in the catalog says: "From N. Zane's orchard."

Fruit large, roundish, dull greenish yellow; flesh greenish white, soft, tender. Ripe February–June.

❧ **ZIEGLER'S SWEETING:** Listed in 1858 by Staunton Nurseries, Staunton, Virginia. No description.

# "Linden Lea"

*W. Barnes*

When leaves that were a-springing,
Now do fade within the copse,
And painted birds do hush their singing
Up upon the timber tops;
And brown-leaved fruits a-turning red
In cloudless sunshine overhead,
With fruit for me, the apple tree
Do lean down low in Linden Lea.

# Bibliography of Important Sources of Information


*Annual Report for 1889 of the North Carolina Agricultural Experiment Station*, pp. 106–7. Raleigh, NC: Edwards & Broughton, 1890.

*The Apple Industry in Delaware*. Delaware Experiment Station Bulletin No. 38, pp 4–20. 1898.

*Apples in North Carolina*. North Carolina State Board of Agriculture Bulletin No. 7, vol. 21, pp. 1–39. Raleigh, NC, 1900.

Ballard, W. R. *Apple Orchard Experiments*. Maryland Agricultural Experiment Station Bulletin No. 178, pp. 1–13, 44–53 College Park, MD, 1913.

Barry, Patrick. *The Fruit Garden*. Auburn and Rochester, NY: Alden & Beardsley, 1857.

Beach, Spencer A. *The Apples of New York*. Vols. 1 & 2. Albany, NY: J. B. Lyon Company, 1905.

*The Best Varieties of Fruits for Tennessee*. Tennessee Agricultural Experiment Station Bulletin, vol. 4, no. 1, pp. 6–11. Knoxville, TN, 1891–92.

Bonner, James C. *A History of Georgia Agriculture 1721–1860*. Athens, GA: University of Georgia Press, 1964.

Brackett, G. B. *The Apple and How to Grow It*. USDA Farmers' Bulletin No. 113. Washington, DC, 1909.

Bridgeman, Thomas. *Fruit Gardening*. Philadelphia, PA: Henry T. Coates & Co., 1844.

Brooks, Reid M. and H. P. Olmo. *Register of New Fruit and Nut Varieties*. 2nd edition. Berkeley, CA: University of California Press, 1972.

Burrill, T. J. and G. W. McCluer. *Varieties of Apples*. Illinois Agricultural Experiment Station Bulletin No. 45, pp. 297–348. Urbana, IL, 1896.

Butz, G. C. *Apples in 1895*. Annual Report of the Pennsylvania State College for the Year 1895, pp. 132–35. Harrisburg, PA: Clarence M. Busch, 1896.

Chambliss C. E. *Some Injurious Insects of the Apple*. Tennessee Agricultural Experiment Station Bulletin, vol. 6, no. 1, pp. 1–27. Knoxville, TN, 1893.

Cole, S. W. *The American Fruit Book*. Boston: John P. Jewett, 1849.

Downing, Andrew Jackson. *The Fruits and Fruit Trees of America*. New York: John Wiley, 1854.

Elliott, Franklin Reuben. *Elliott's Fruit Book*. New York: A. O. Moore, 1858.

*Experiment Orchard*. Virginia Agricultural Experiment Station Bulletin, series of 1889–90, no. 2, pp. 1–9. Lynchburg, VA: J. P. Bell Co., 1889.

*Farmers' Cyclopedia: Abridged Agricultural Records from the USDA and Experiment Stations*. Vol 5. New York: Doubleday, Page & Co., 1916.

Fitz, James. *The Southern Apple and Peach Culturist*. Richmond, VA: J. W. Randolph & English, 1872.

Fraser, Samuel. *American Fruits*. New York: Orange Judd Publishing Co., Inc., 1931.

Funk, J. H. *Fruits for Pennsylvania*. Commonwealth of Pennsylvania, Department of Agriculture, Bulletin No. 152, pp. 148–81. Harrisburg, PA: C. E. Aughinbaugh, 1911.

Fusonie, Alan E. "The Heritage of Original Art and Photo Imaging in USDA: Past, Present and Future." In *Agricultural History* 64, no. 2 (1990).

Geiser, Samuel Ward. *Horticulture and Horticulturists in Early Texas*. Dallas: University Press in Dallas: Southern Methodist University, 1945.

Gould, H. D. *Orchard Fruits in the Piedmont and Blue Ridge Regions of Virginia and the South Atlantic States*. USDA Bulletin No. 135, Washington, DC, 1908.

Hedrick, U. P. *A History of Horticulture in America to 1860*. New York: Oxford University Press, 1950.

*Horticultural Report*. Louisiana Agricultural Experiment Station Bulletin No. 8. Baton Rouge, LA, c. 1890.

Hume, H. H. *Handling the Apple Crop*. North Carolina State Board of Agriculture Bulletin No. 9, vol. 26, pp. 1–22. Raleigh, 1905.

Hutt, W. N. and S. B. Shaw. *Varieties of Fruit for Growing in North Carolina.* North Carolina Department of Agriculture Bulletin No. 9, vol. 29, pp. 1–16, 21–29. Raleigh, NC, 1908.

Kains, M. G. *Home Fruit Grower.* New York: A. T. De La Mare Company, 1918.

Kenrick, William. *The New American Orchardist.* 3rd ed. Boston: Otis, Broaders, and Company, 1841.

Marshall, Roy E. and F. A. Motz. *Establishing the Orchard.* Virginia Agricultural and Mechanical College Bulletin No. 41. Blacksburg, VA, 1919.

Massey, W. F. *The Apple in North Carolina.* North Carolina Agricultural Experiment Station Bulletin No. 149, pp, 307–25. Raleigh, NC, 1898.

Moore, John H. *Agriculture in Antebellum Mississippi.* New York: Octagon Books, 1971.

Morelli, Patricia L. *Index to the United States Department of Agriculture Pomological Watercolor Collection.* Cambridge, England: Chadwyck-Healey Ltd., 1987.

Newman, C. C. *Notes on Varieties of Apples.* South Carolina Agricultural Experiment Station of Clemson Agricultural College, Bulletin 109, pp. 6–38. Columbia, SC: The R. L. Bryan Company, 1905.

*Notes on Apple Culture.* Maryland Agricultural Experiment Station Bulletin No. 92, pp. 76–95. College Park, MD, 1904.

*The Orchard.* Louisiana Agricultural Experiment Station Bulletin No. 9, pp. 428–29. Baton Rouge, LA, 1891.

*Orchard Report.* Louisiana Agricultural Experiment Station Bulletin No. 112, pp 2–9. Baton Rouge, LA, 1908.

Peek, S. W. *The Nursery and the Orchard.* Atlanta, GA: J. P. Harrison & Co., 1885.

Proceedings of Virginia State Horticultural Society. Richmond, VA, 1898–1902.

Proceedings of Georgia State Horticultural Society. Atlanta, GA, 1885–1912

Pryor, Elizabeth B. *Orchard Fruits in the Colonial Chesapeake.* Research Report No. 14, National Colonial Farm, The Accokeek Foundation.

Ragan, William Henry. *Nomenclature of the Apple: A Catalogue of the Known Varieties Referred to in American Publications from 1804–1904.* Bulletin No. 56. Washington, DC: United States Department of Agriculture, 1905.

*Relative Susceptibility of Apples to Rust.* Alabama Agricultural Experiment Station Circular No. 2, Auburn, AL: Department of Botany, 1908.

Report(s) of the (United States) Secretary of Agriculture: Washington, DC, 1891, 1892, 1895.

Report(s) of the (United States) Commissioner of Agriculture: Washington, DC, 1861–75.

Report(s) of the (United States) Commissioner of Patents; Agriculture: Washington, DC, 1855–60.

Reports of Meetings of the American Pomological Society, 1848–97.

Sears, Fred C. *Productive Orcharding.* Philadelphia, PA: J. B. Lippincott Company, 1914.

Shaw, J. K. *Variations in Apples.* Massachusetts Agricultural Experiment Station Bulletin No. 31, pp. 194–213. 1910.

Smith, Muriel W. G. *National Apple Register of the United Kingdom.* London: Ministry of Agriculture, Fisheries and Food, 1971.

Stinson, J. T. *Preliminary Report on Seedling Apples.* Arkansas Agricultural Experiment Station Bulletin No. 49, pp. 1–20. Fayetteville, AR, 1898.

———. *Second Report on Arkansas Seedling Apples.* Arkansas Agricultural Experiment Station Bulletin No. 60, pp. 123–34. Fayetteville, AR, 1899.

Thomas, John Jacobs. *The American Fruit Culturist.* 20th ed. New York: William Wood and Company, 1897.

Thomas, John Jacobs. The American Fruit Culturist. Auburn, NY: Derby, Miller & Company, 1849.

Upshall, W. H., ed. *North American Apples: Varieties, Rootstocks, Outlook.* East Lansing, Michigan: Michigan State University Press, 1970.

Warder, John Ashton. *American Pomology: Apples.* New York: Orange Judd and Company, 1867.

Watts, R. L. *Apples of Tennessee Origin.* Tennessee Agricultural Experiment Station Bulletin, vol. 9, no. 1, pp. 1–34. Knoxville, TN: Bean, Warters & Gaut, 1896.

———. *Apples of Tennessee Origin (Second Report).* Tennessee Agricultural Experiment Station Bulletin, vol. 10, no. 1, pp. 1–18. Knoxville, TN, 1897.

———. *Experiments with Fruit Trees and Vegetables: Orchard Fruits.* Tennessee Agricultural Experiment

Station Bulletin, vol. 4, no. 5. Knoxville, TN, 1891–92.

Waugh, F. A. *The American Apple Orchard*. New York: Orange Judd Company, 1909.

White, William N. *Gardening for the South*. New York: O. Judd Co., 1885.

Wigginton, Brooks Eliot, ed. *The Foxfire Book*. New York: Anchor Press/Doubleday, 1972.

*Work in Horticulture: Best Varieties of Fruits for the Different Sections of Texas*. Texas Agricultural Experiment Station Bulletin No. 5, pp. 22–35. College Station, TX, 1889.

*Yearbook of the United States Department of Agriculture*. Washington, DC, 1871–1925.

**Periodicals:**

*American Gardening*, 1896–99.

*Magazine of Horticulture*, 1844–57.

*The American Agriculturist*, 1850–68.

*The American Garden*, 1888–91.

*The Farmer and Planter*, 1858–60.

*The Gardener's Monthly*, 1873–80.

*The Horticulturist*, 1848–69.

*The Southern Agriculturist, Horticulturist and Register of Rural Affairs*, 1839–44.

*Tilton's Journal of Horticulture*, 1868–71.

*Western Horticultural Review*, 1853.

**Nursery Catalogs:**

A total of 290 old nursery catalogs were used to compile information for this edition of *Old Southern Apples*, as shown below.

Alabama (10): 1886–1928
Arkansas (14): 1903–28
Florida (3): 1896–1915
Georgia (36): 1857–1928
Kentucky (16): 1845–1925
Louisiana (6): 1887–1925
Maryland (20): 1836–1928
Mississippi (4): 1877–1924
North Carolina (64): 1853–1928
South Carolina (6): 1856–1928
Tennessee (18): 1887–1928
Texas (34): 1885–1928
Virginia (41): 1798–1928
Washington, DC (7): 1824–1880

# Sources for Old Southern Apple Trees

In the fifteen years since the first edition of this book was published, the Internet has changed everything. Now, instead of writing to a fruit-tree nursery requesting a catalog, three minutes at the computer will display the catalog, often with color pictures of selected fruit. If you have questions, an e-mail to the nursery will usually get a swift reply. The efficiency of this system still astonishes me.

I have chosen four nurseries that sell antique southern apple trees (although all have modern apples, also). I also list one nursery that sells apple scionwood for those wishing to graft their own trees.

The nurseries selling grafted trees offer them on several different apple rootstocks. Because the rootstock determines the ultimate size of the tree, pay close attention to the description of the rootstocks in the catalogs.

In the South, fruit trees are best planted in late fall and early winter, November and December. New-planted apple trees must be watered during dry periods for at least two years. Loss of young trees is almost always due to lack of water.

**Big Horse Creek Farm**
Ron and Suzanne Joyner, Owners
P. O. Box 70, Lansing, NC 28643 (mailing address)
1610 Old Apples Road, Lansing, NC 28643
Web site: www.bighorsecreekfarm.com
E-mail: oldapples@bighorsecreekfarm.com

About 375 old and new apple varieties (mostly antique southern apples) although not all are listed on the Web site. Nursery stock on four apple rootstocks. No printed catalog. Shipping in fall only. Trees available in fall and spring at the nursery.

**Century Farm Orchards**
David Vernon, Owner
P. O. Box 271, Altamahaw, NC 27270 (mailing address)
1614 Rice Road, Reidsville, NC 27320
Web site: www.centuryfarmorchards.com
E-mail: david@centuryfarmorchards.com
Telephone: (336) 349-5709

About 400 varieties (mostly antique southern apples). Two apple rootstocks for nursery stock. Printed catalog available. Shipping November to April. Open house at the nursery every Saturday in November with cider, apple tastings, sales. Rootstocks for sale.

**Kelly's Old Timey Apple Trees**
Steve Kelly, Owner
263 Hen Reasor Road, Big Stone Gap, VA 24219
E-mail: kellysoldtimeyappletrees@comcast.net
Telephone: (276) 523-4038

Sells and ships scionwood (not bud wood) of old and new apple varieties, including most antique southern apples. List by mail or e-mail. Some grafted trees available at the nursery.

**Urban Homestead**
Tim and Donna Hensley, Owners
818 Cumberland Street, Bristol, VA 24201-4172
Web site: www.oldvaapples.com
E-mail: urbanhomestead@aol.com
Telephone: (276) 466-2931

Two hundred varieties listed in current catalog (about 120 antique southern apples). Most on MM111 rootstock (large semi-dwarf) with a few on other rootstocks. Printed catalog available for $3.00. Rootstocks for sale. Shipping November–December and March–April as weather permits. Nursery open by appointment only.

**Vintage Virginia Apples**
The Shelton Family, Owners
P. O. Box 210, North Garden, VA 22959 (mailing address)
2545 Rural Ridge Lane, North Garden, VA 22959
Web site: www.vintagevirginiaapples.com
E-mail: Fruit@vintagevirginiaapples.com
Telephone: (434) 297-2326

About 200 varieties listed in the online catalog (62 antique southern apples). Two apple rootstocks for nursery stock but others occasionally available. Shipping December to March as weather permits. A cidery is located at the nursery. Rootstocks and a full line of tools and supplies are sold through the catalog.

# Index of Apple Names and Synonyms

*Note*: Apple names are capitalized, synonyms are uppercase and lowercase.

Chelsea Green Publishing is committed to preserving ancient forests and natural resources. We elected to print this title on 30% postconsumer recycled paper, processed chlorine-free. As a result, for this printing, we have saved:

**14 Trees (40' tall and 6-8" diameter)**
**6,546 Gallons of Wastewater**
**6 million BTUs Total Energy**
**438 Pounds of Solid Waste**
**1,207 Pounds of Greenhouse Gases**

Chelsea Green Publishing made this paper choice because we are a member of the Green Press Initiative, a nonprofit program dedicated to supporting authors, publishers, and suppliers in their efforts to reduce their use of fiber obtained from endangered forests. For more information, visit www.greenpressinitiative.org.

Environmental impact estimates were made using the Environmental Defense Paper Calculator. For more information visit: www.papercalculator.org.